The Cambridge History of
Latin American Literature

VOLUME I

The Cambridge History of Latin American Literature

Edited by

Roberto González Echevarría and Enrique Pupo-Walker

The Cambridge History of Latin American Literature is by far the most comprehensive and authoritative work of its kind ever written. Its three volumes cover the whole sweep of Latin American literature (including Brazilian) from pre-Columbian times to the present, and contain chapters on Spanish American writing in the US. Over forty specialists in North America, Latin America, and Britain have contributed to what is not only the most reliable, up-to-date, and convenient reference work on its subject, but also a set of books containing innovative approaches and fresh research that will expand and animate the field for years to come. The *History* is unique in its thorough coverage of previously neglected areas, in its detailed discussion of countless writers in various genres, and in its inclusion of extensive annotated bibliographies.

Volume 1 begins with pre-Columbian traditions and their first contact with European culture, continuing through to the end of the nineteenth century. New World historiography, epic poetry, theatre, the novel, and the essay form are among the areas covered in this comprehensive and authoritative treatment.

Volume 2 provides coverage of all genres from the end of the nineteenth century up to García Márquez's *One Hundred Years of Solitude* and beyond to 1990, thus including discussion of Spanish American literature's best-known works. The novel, poetry, autobiographical narrative, the short story, Afro-Hispanic American literature, theatre, and Chicano literature are among the areas treated in this wide-ranging volume.

Volume 3 is devoted partly to the history of Brazilian literature, from the earliest writing through the colonial period and the Portuguese-language traditions of the nineteenth and twentieth centuries; and partly also to an extensive bibliographical section in which annotated reading lists relating to the chapters in all three volumes of *The Cambridge History of Latin American Literature* are presented. These bibliographies are a unique feature of the *History*, further enhancing its immense value as a reference work.

Contents of the other two volumes

The Cambridge History of Latin American Literature

VOLUME I

Discovery to Modernism

Edited by

Roberto González Echevarría

Yale University

and

Enrique Pupo-Walker

Vanderbilt University

 CAMBRIDGE
UNIVERSITY PRESS

Published by the Press Syndicate of the University of Cambridge
The Pitt Building, Trumpington Street, Cambridge CB2 1RP
40 West 20th Street, New York, NY 10011-4211, USA
10 Stamford Road, Oakleigh, Melbourne 3166, Australia

First published 1996

Printed in Great Britain at the University Press, Cambridge

A catalogue record for this book is available from the British Library

Library of Congress cataloguing in publication data

The Cambridge history of Latin American literature / edited by Roberto
González Echevarría and Enrique Pupo-Walker.
p. cm.
Contents: v. 1. Discovery to Modernism – v. 2. The twentieth
century – v. 3. Brazilian literature; bibliographies.
ISBN 0 521 34069 1 (v. 1). – ISBN 0 521 34070 5 (v. 2). – ISBN
0 521 41035 5 (v. 3) (hardback)
1. Latin American literature – History and criticism. I. González
Echevarría, Roberto. II. Pupo-Walker, Enrique.
PQ7081.A1C35 1995
860.9'8 – dc20   93-37750 CIP

ISBN 0 521 34069 1 hardback

Contents

Contributors

Rolena Adorno, *Princeton University*
Antonio Benítez-Rojo, *Amherst College*
David H. Bost, *Furman University*
Andrew Bush, *Vassar College*
Frank Dauster, *Rutgers University*
Roberto González Echevarría, *Yale University*
Asunción Lavrin, *Arizona State University*
Frederick Luciani, *Colgate University*
Josefina Ludmer, *Yale University*
Stephanie Merrim, *Brown University*
Margarita Peña, *Colegio de México*
Enrique Pupo-Walker, *Vanderbilt University*
Kathleen Ross, *New York University*
Nicolas Shumway, *University of Texas*
Martin S. Stabb, *Pennsylvania State University*
Karen Stolley, *Emory University*

General preface

In 1893, the renowned Spanish critic and historian Marcelino Menéndez y Pelayo published his vastly influential *Antología de la poesía hispano-americana*, not only the first history of Spanish American poetry, but truly the first history of Spanish American literature. The *Antología* appeared just as *Modernismo* [Modernism], the first poetic movement developed in Spanish America, was achieving its greatest acclaim throughout the Hispanic world. With *Modernismo* Spanish American literature came of age, while the *Antología*, compiled and prefaced by the most authoritative critic of the language, gave it institutional substance and academic respectability. The present *History* appears in the wake of the most remarkable period of expansion and international recognition ever enjoyed by Latin American literature. The consolidation of Latin American literature as an academic discipline and a recognized category in the world book market was made possible by the achievements of writers as diverse as Jorge Luis Borges, Alejo Carpentier, Julio Cortázar, João Guimarães Rosa, José Lezama Lima, Gabriel García Márquez, Octavio Paz, Mario Vargas Llosa, and many others. García Márquez and Paz attained the ultimate recognition, the Nobel Prize. Without the distinction and accomplishments of these writers, the public at large, not to mention publishing houses and universities throughout the world, would have continued to treat Latin American literary production as an appendix to Spanish literature, dependent on someone like Menéndez y Pelayo for legitimation. It is to them too that this *History* owes its existence. *Modernismo* gave Latin America a place in the Spanish-language literary world; writers like the ones mentioned above placed it at the center of world literature.

Latin American literature today enjoys a truly international currency. Latin American novelists in particular are read and imitated not only in the West but throughout the world. For instance, Leo Ou-fan-Lee, a professor of Chinese literature at the University of Chicago, has written recently that Latin American writers "now exert a powerful impact on many young Chinese writers". As recently as thirty years ago such a statement would have been unthinkable. Given its universal reach and appeal, it is perhaps appropriate that this *History* should be the effort of a group of scholars working in the United States, England, and continental Europe, as well as in Latin America. Latin American literature is today at the pinnacle of the international literary movements that began with the Avant-Garde in the 1920s. Those movements, as well as their aftermath, are cosmopolitan in essence.

The *History* attempts to take full advantage of its collective and international cast, while at the same time aiming to be a coherent statement, conceived within a common set of scholarly guidelines and academic values. As an academic history, ours is concerned with historical fact and accuracy, with sources and influences, and with the relationship of literature to history in general. Our work, in other words, takes full account of the past, not only in the object of our study, but in the previous studies of that object. We build on what has been done before, and if and when we do not, we give our reasons. We aim not just to tell a story, but also to tell how that story has been told before. Aside from those givens, issuing no doubt from large ideological investments, ours is a work that is not dominated by narrow philosophical or methodological constraints. In contrast to most others, the *History* is not limited by the ideological or aesthetic values of a single author. In the invitations to participate in the project, the editors asked each contributor to be innovative in his or her approach to the field. Each was consulted about the limits of his or her area of study and about the very assumptions that make it a coherent subset within Latin American literary history. Everyone was asked, in short, to be self-conscious in her or his choices, not merely to review a field and to furnish an *état présent*. In this sense the *History* is not only a history of Latin American literature, but equally a statement on the current status of Latin American historiography. While the latitude given to each contributor has resulted in some unevenness, the editors believe that eclecticism enhances the value of the *History*, both as a reference tool and as an intellectual venture. Some literary works that previously had not been given much attention (in some cases none at all) have been examined by our contributors, thus effectively incorporating them into the canon. For instance, this is the first history of Latin American literature to provide detailed coverage of the colonial period, the works of women writers, and the literature written in Spanish by Chicano and other Hispanic authors in various regions of North America. Similarly, this is the first history of Latin American literature to link meaningfully the works of Afro-Hispanic and Afro-American authors. The *History* also brings together Brazilian and Spanish-American literatures, giving the former the full individual attention it naturally deserves, but also underscoring their contiguities, continuities, and discontinuities. In short, the editors feel that our *History* is a reassessment and expansion of the canon of Latin American literature, seen in a broad, new-world context.

We are fully aware, of course, that large ideological presuppositions underlie our enterprise. The first concerns the very existence of Latin American literature as such. Since its deliberate creation as a concept and field of endeavor in the 1830s, Latin American literature has debated whether it is a literature at all or in fact a series of national literatures that share a common language. The most prominent writers, from Andrés Bello to Paz, have argued in favor of the existence of a Latin American literature that transcends national boundaries; and if one thinks of tradition as being made up by the major works, as we do here, then one can assume the existence of a Latin American literature. But not everyone has always been convinced, and we do not question that there are peculiarities that distinguish some national literatures within Latin America. The case of Brazil is a special one, of course: there is no doubt that Brazilian literature is a national literature as original and self-contained as French, Italian, or Spanish literature; its ties to a broader Latin American literature, however, are strong, if fluid and ever-changing over time. But Cuban, Mexican, Argentinian, Chilean, and Colombian literatures are also marked by national characteristics that are undeniable. These national inflections are for the most part thematic. For instance, the lives of Blacks and their African retentions play a very significant role in Caribbean literature, whereas in the Southern Cone it is the gaucho and his mores that provide a strong thematic strain. There is, however, a certain homology in the way these figures appear in their respective national or regional literatures, one that extends to how the Indian is portrayed in areas such as Peru and Mexico. National traditions stress the differences and remain local. But the stronger authors and works cross frontiers or dwell on the homology. They constitute a kind of overarching literature to which all aspire. Our assumption here has been that the most significant and influential part of Latin American literature is the one engaged in a transnational intertextual exchange. The recuperation of the colonial period, when Spanish America was one, is part of this struggle to constitute a continental literature with a common origin and discourse. This is one of the strongest forces behind the recent increase in scholarship on the colonial period.

The breadth of this undertaking is particularly evident in the chapters on colonial literature, both Brazilian and Spanish American. Until a few years ago, colonial literature was chiefly the object of antiquarian interest, but in recent years this has changed drastically in fundamental and irreversible ways. The editors and contributors have sought to reflect that change. Before the 1960s, few universities (in Latin America or elsewhere) offered courses on Latin American writers of the colonial period, but now many include in their programs of study Sor Juana Inés de la Cruz, Bernal Díaz del Castillo, Garcilaso de la Vega, el Inca, and many others. At the post-graduate level there are now monographic courses dealing with those figures, as well as with Columbus, Gonzalo Fernández de Oviedo, and many other historians of the discovery and conquest of America. Scholarship on these authors has increased significantly in scope and sophistication. There are now international symposia devoted solely to colonial literature, as well as sessions within established, periodical meetings, such as the yearly conventions of the Modern Language Association of America.

Appropriately, given the nature of the chronicles, this *History* incorporates scholarly materials and methodological tools that are not common to literary scholarship. The interdisciplinary bent of this part of our venture is enhanced by the contributions of Asunción Lavrin (in Volume 1) and Thomas Skidmore (in Volume 3), well-known historians of Spanish and Portuguese America respectively. This productive linkage of disciplines is the natural byproduct of recent scholarship. In the past two decades, the study of colonial Spanish American literature has been enriched by its broad interdisciplinary scope. The reassessment of early historiography of the Americas combines quite freely the findings of rhetorical analyses, historical scholarship, anthropology and archaeology. This unprecedented and expanding convergence of disciplines has made possible forms of scholarly cooperation that are exceptional in Hispanic studies, and that certainly point to the research agendas of the future.

The incorporation of the colonial period into the study of Latin American literature has improved the overall quality of the criticism devoted to this literature by showing the inadequacy of journalistic approaches that are based exclusively on the most recent literary production. This development is intimately tied to the academic legitimation of Latin American literature as an academic discipline, a fairly recent phenomenon. Curiously, this movement also brings out the strong ties Latin American literature still has with Spanish and Portuguese literature, both in the colonial period and in the present. If the Iberian Middle Ages, Renaissance, and Baroque are such a powerful presence in Latin American literature, then this literature shares a living past with its metropolitan counterparts. From a scholarly perspective what this means is that scholars of colonial literature (and one hopes, also of modern literature) must now have a strong background in medieval, renaissance, and Golden Age literatures. A full sixth of the *History* is devoted to the colonial period, and the chapters devoted to the modern periods reflect the weight of that living past.

One reason for this increase in colonial studies is that modern Latin American authors have discovered in the works of the colonial Baroque, or in the chronicles of the discovery and conquest, the starting point of the literary tradition to which they belong. Octavio Paz's voluminous study of Sor Juana is but the latest evidence of this phenomenon. Carpentier, García Márquez, Neruda, and many other contemporary writers have either written about colonial figures or declared their debt to them in interviews and other pronouncements. Haroldo de Campos has developed theories of Brazilian literature based on the continued presence of the colonial Baroque, or the self-conscious return to it. Many contemporary works, both in Spanish and Portuguese, include topics, characters, and stories drawn from colonial texts. This return to the colonial past, highlighting its pertinence in the present, rounds out the Latin American literary tradition and endows it for the first time with a density of five centuries. It does not matter that, if examined closely, this is nothing more than an enabling pretext, or a fable about origins. Literature creates its own historical fictions, its own history being one of them. Our *History*, while being as concrete and factual as possible, reflects the fullness and influence of that fiction. In this sense, too, ours is a history of the history of Latin American literature.

The editors feel that the *History* is the first to recognize the richness and diversity of Latin American literature in the nineteenth century (preceding *Modernismo*). This field, which has yet to acquire the institutional recognition accorded to the colonial period, has of late begun to draw attention from scholars as well as writers. The chapters devoted to both Spanish American and Brazilian literature of the nineteenth century are among the most innovative, and constitute the area where the freshest research is offered by our contributors. More than a history bringing to closure the study of this promising field, work on the nineteenth century in the *History* may very well constitute the founding of a new area of specialization.

The richness and depth of Latin American literature in the colonial period and during the past century is one of the features, perhaps the strongest, that distinguishes it from other literatures of the so-called Third World. In the 1960s, in the wake of the Cuban Revolution and other political movements aimed at breaking the grip of colonialism, many Latin American authors allied themselves with authors whose plight seemed similar to theirs. Regardless of the outcome of those political alliances the fact is that if by Third World one refers to countries that emerged from the debacle of nineteenth-century colonialism, then Latin America, being the product of a much older and different colonialism, had to have a very different literary tradition. The literatures of the Third World emerged, for the most part, in our own century, whereas those of Latin America reach back really to, at least, the sixteenth. The burden of Latin American culture is a Western culture that extends back to the Middle Ages, when the foundations of the Spanish Empire in the New World were set. Latin American culture, particularly Spanish, was, from the beginning, one of ostentatious viceregal capitals, surpassing in splendor cities of the Old World, often because they had to compete with magnificent urban centers constructed by the Aztecs, Mayas, or Incas. This urban quality of Latin American culture also obeyed Spanish Neo-Scholasticism, grounded on the Aristotelian notion that civilization was, as the etymology indicates, something proper to cities. Latin American colonial culture, in many ways medieval, is so distant from that of North America, or countries of the Third World, that gross distortions and misreadings are bound to occur in comparing them. Desire for solidarity with the Third World is a significant element of recent Latin American literature perhaps even as a movement, but it does not make of Latin American literature a Third-World literature. Latin American literature is not a new literature, even if one of its enabling pretexts or founding fables is its newness. Our *History*, we hope, makes this very clear, with abundant supporting evidence.

The question of the new is so poignant in Latin American literature precisely because it is such an old culture, both back through its European roots, and through those of the native and African cultures. The entire history of Macondo, the fictional town in García Márquez's *One Hundred Years of Solitude* which is a microcosmic representation of Latin America, has been written in advance, in Sanskrit, by a wizard; it is a story that emerges from the very origins of history and writing. In those origins writing precedes history. The literatures of the Third World are recent; some came into being in the twentieth century. Latin American writers find predecessors, within what they consider as their own literature, in the sixteenth and seventeenth centuries. Paz's passionate and polemical literary biography of Sor Juana Inés de la Cruz is a case in point. There were renaissance-style literary academies in Lima at the turn of the sixteenth to the seventeenth century, and hundreds of Petrarchan poets in seventeenth-century Mexico. If anyone should doubt this he or she ought to read Alicia de Colombí-Monguió's superb *Petrarquismo peruano*, and Irving A. Leonard's classic *Books of the Brave* and *Baroque Times in Old Mexico*.

The editors and contributors have spared no effort in making the *History* a reliable, informative, and useful reference work and research tool. Hence, we have been careful to be thorough in providing dates and bibliographic information in general. In fact, we feel that the selective, annotated bibliographies relating to each chapter (and reproduced in Volume 3) constitute in and of themselves a significant contribution to the field, as does the general bibliography at the end, which was compiled by a professional bibliographer. In some instances (Carlos Alonso's comprehensive list of regionalist novels is a good example) the bibliographies are the result of ground-breaking research. All secondary bibliographies are selective and the annotations are meant to guide future scholars to the latest, the newest, and the most promising work. Read in conjunction with their respective chapters, these bibliographies should bring a critic to the point where he or she can begin to make the next original contribution. The editors sincerely hope that this will very often be the case and that the *History* will help to provide an auspicious opening to the second one hundred years of Latin American literary historiography.

The *Cambridge History of Latin American Literature* draws upon a long tradition of collaborative scholarship that began with the *Cambridge Modern History* (1902–1912) and includes the eight-volume *Cambridge History of Latin America*. In its format, general guidelines and scholarly values, the *Cambridge History of Latin American Literature* aspires to the rigor and accessibility for which these predecessors are known.

RGE and EPW

Acknowledgments

A collaborative work such as this is by its very nature the product of many people, some whose names appear as contributors or editors, and others whose contributions are not so obvious. We should like to thank here as many of those as possible, painfully aware that we are bound to make errors of omission. We apologize for them in advance.

First of all, we must thank those contributors who have also helped us in many ways other than writing their chapters. First and foremost we thank Professor David Haberly, who was our consultant for the volume on Brazilian literature. Professor Haberly discussed possible contributors with us, read the chapters for volume 3 and offered many valuable suggestions about how to shape the material. He also completed the chapter written by José Guilherme Merquior, whose premature death occurred in February 1991. In editing that volume, we were also aided by Professor K. David Jackson, whose expertise in all matters Brazilian, and abilities as a translator were both crucial. Other contributors also assisted us in similar ways in editing volumes 1 and 2. Professor Cathy L. Jrade read several manuscripts, offered detailed suggestions about various matters, helped us with the prologues, and participated with the two editors in meetings at which critical decisions were made. We acknowledge our great debt to Professor Jrade, who also served as a sounding board for ideas, several of which she helped sharpen or discard. Professor Sylvia Molloy gave us important advice concerning the selection of contributors, and also in how best to incorporate the work of women writers into the *History*. Professors Aníbal González Pérez, Gustavo Pérez Firmat and Kathleen Ross also aided us with their counsel, friendship, and erudition. We are especially grateful to Andrew Bush and José Quiroga. We asked them for important contributions which they had to write in a very limited period of time.

The library staffs at both Yale and Vanderbilt helped with bibliographical matters, and the staffs at the respective offices of grants and contracts were our link to the foundations that made the *History* possible. We should like to single out here Steven H. Smartt at Vanderbilt, and Alice

Oliver at Yale. We have, of course, an enormous debt of gratitude to the National Endowment for the Humanities, which provided a three-year grant that allowed us to continue work during the summers, and to the Rockefeller Foundation for a grant to round out the sum provided by the Endowment. At the Endowment we were graciously assisted by David Wise, who was always patient with our queries and requests. Completion of a project as complex and time-consuming as this would have been impossible without the financial backing of these institutions, and we wish to make public our heartfelt appreciation.

During the five-year period that we have spent in this project, the office for the *Cambridge History of Latin American Literature* has been the Center for Latin American and Iberian Studies at Vanderbilt. We have profited from all the facilities available at the Center, and want to thank Vanderbilt for its generosity in putting them at our disposal. The most invaluable resource at the Center, and the person to whom we owe the greatest debt of gratitude, is Mrs. Norma Antillón, Secretary Technical to the Director. Given the demands of our many other academic responsibilities, which often took us far from the *History*, Mrs. Antillón was the one continuous presence; at times she seemed to *be* the *History*, as the many contributors who dealt with her in our absence know well. It would be impossible even to attempt to enumerate her many contributions and we would rather simply express to her our profound gratitude for her loyalty, devotion, attentiveness, and unswerving commitment to the successful completion of this work. We also wish to convey our appreciation to Mrs. Sandra Guardo, secretary to the Department of Spanish and Portuguese at Yale University. She was a valuable resource on many occasions. In addition, Mrs. Suzan McIntire, secretary to the Center for International Programs at Vanderbilt, was helpful to us in administrative aspects of this project.

We would also like to recognize Mr. Kevin Taylor at Cambridge University Press (England) for his exemplary attention to all matters pertaining to this *History*. We are also grateful to Mrs. Jay Williams, who provided valuable advice about contractual matters and helped improve the style of several chapters. We also wish to thank the translators, who labored hard to transform Spanish and Portuguese prose into academic English; they are Susan Griswold, Georgina Dopico Black, David Jackson and Cindy Najmulski.

Finally, we gratefully thank our wives Betty and Isabel for their patience and encouragement, and for making our meetings not only possible, but enjoyable.

ROBERTO GONZÁLEZ ECHEVARRÍA
ENRIQUE PUPO-WALKER

Introduction to Volume 1

The conception of Spanish American literature as a distinct category emerged from romantic scholarship and was loosely based on deterministic and transcendental notions of history, tradition, and cultural milieu. Indeed, romantic literature represented with singular ease factual and legendary events that were often drawn from a broad legacy of texts. Yet, in the nationalistic context of nineteenth-century Spanish America, European *belles lettres* could not be assumed to be the sole precursor of an American literary tradition. Instead, influential authors of that period chose to look upon the early chronicles of discovery and exploration of the New World as fundamental components of Spanish American literary historiography and prose fiction. Such a foundational notion is suggested in the *Infortunios de Alonso Ramírez* (1680) and other writings by the Mexican savant Carlos de Sigüenza y Góngora (1645–1700). Much the same can be said of the *Lazarillo de ciegos caminantes* (1773), by the Spaniard Alonso Carrió de la Vandera (1715–1778). Predictably, the references to historiographic models represented by the narratives of Gonzalo Fernández de Oviedo (1478–1557), Francisco López de Gómara (1512–1572) and Alvar Núñez Cabeza de Vaca (?1490–1557?), become more assertive in the essays and fictions written by the Argentinians Esteban Echeverría (1805–1851), Juan Bautista Alberdi (1810–1884), and by the Colombian José Caicedo Rojas (1816–1897), among others. Without intending to do so, the early chronicles of the Indies had consolidated, for readers of many nations, an American iconography and typology that was further codified in major poetic texts. *La araucana* (1569–1589) by Alonso de Ercilla (1533–1594), *Grandeza mexicana* (1602) by Bernardo de Balbuena (1562–1627), and Lope de Vega's play *El nuevo mundo descubierto por Cristóbal Colón* (1611) stand as salient examples of this process of recodification of Spanish American realities. Moreover, the iconographic material contained in the narratives of discovery and

exploration reappeared in numerous historical accounts, fictions, paintings, and graphic illustrations produced in the nineteenth and twentieth
centuries. The splendid illustrations contained in Ramón de la Sagra's
Atlas physique, politique et naturelle de Cuba, or the vast landscapes
painted by the German Johann M. Rugendas and the Mexican José María
Velasco are landmarks of that rich American iconography.

Nevertheless, adopting the chronicles of the discovery and conquest of
America as founding texts required a considerable stretching of the
boundaries of literary history. One must remember that the early
narratives of discovery are hybrid texts that the modern reader associates
with the discourses of history, theology, anthropology, geography, and
the natural sciences. Yet the appeal of those books is not determined
exclusively by the wealth of their diverse and often contradictory data. We
are also drawn to the more imaginative and individualized aspects of these
narratives. The reader will find especially attractive numerous episodes of
delusion, self-discovery, and failure, as well as instances when writing
evokes concealed imaginings or simply becomes an act of personal
legitimation. Such timeless matters are akin to literary concerns and also
require an eclectic reading that does not differ greatly from the kind that
must be applied to many literary texts produced in Spanish America since
the nineteenth century. Thus the process of reading history tells us,
obliquely, a great deal about the formative process of literary activity in
Spanish America. Indeed, non-literary discourses have been central
components of much of the fiction written since the sixteenth century, but
only in recent times have we begun to understand the peculiarly syncretic
make-up of literary discourses in Spanish America. If nothing else, observations outlined above point toward the extraordinary relevance of
colonial letters in the cultural history of Spanish America. The pioneering
scholarship produced in the first half of this century by Irving A. Leonard,
Edmundo O'Gorman, and José J. Arrom, among others, suggested the
need for a thorough examination of the textual practices of the past.
Luckily, a growing contingent of scholars is now conducting a systematic
reappraisal of the literary historiography of the Americas. Their work is
enhanced by a broad theoretical base and a firm philological and
historical grounding. In addition, many recent studies have produced
detailed readings which illuminate the singularity of the texts considered.
Fortunately many of the individuals responsible for the renovation of
Colonial Studies have contributed generously to this *History.*

This volume is framed by an innovative chapter in which Roberto
González Echevarría elucidates the controversial and hesitant origins of
literary historiography of Spanish America. Subsequently, Rolena
Adorno discusses verbal creation amongst indigenous peoples of the New
World. She correctly states that without the presence of native voices

(including *mestizo* writers) "there can be no full history of Colonial Spanish American culture". The works glossed in that chapter correspond mainly to the interpretive responses made by native American cultures to life under colonial rule. In the next eight chapters coverage given to the colonial period goes well beyond the information contained in previous histories of Latin American literature. In her examination of "The first fifty years of Hispanic New World historiography," Stephanie Merrim not only comments on the relevant texts, she also reveals, through close readings, the kinds of infra-history which often resulted from instances of disobedience, cruelty, and self-interest, or from failed attempts to colonize or to obtain religious conversions. Professor Merrim makes it clear that many of the earliest narratives about the New World derived from personal ambitions or from a need to seek pardon and legitimation. At times, those early chronicles framed their descriptions of American realities with legendary topics and utopian notions that would eventually resonate in modern Latin American fiction. No less revealing are the questions raised by Kathleen Ross when discussing historiographic narratives written from 1550 to 1620. She explains the criteria which allow the inclusion of historical discourse into the literary canon of Latin America and goes on to describe how traditional historians and literary scholars have read Spanish American colonial texts. This thoughtful analysis of current modes of inquiry reveals the interdisciplinary and theoretical considerations that are at the root of recent studies of colonial letters.

In his appraisal of historical writing in the late colonial period David Bost demonstrates, as do Merrim and Ross, how imaginative readings of historical discourse can enhance our understanding of the past and of the texts in question. Bost also makes us aware of a large *corpus* of texts that have been neglected by both historical and literary scholarship. The extraordinary output of lyrical and epic poetry written during the colonial period is assessed by Roberto González Echevarría and Margarita Peña. In both essays textual commentary on distinctive features of the texts is supplemented by the identification of relevant works that are little known even among specialists in colonial literature. That broad sweep of literary creativity is complemented by three chapters describing theatrical activities during the first three centuries of colonial rule. In them Frederick Luciani brings to our attention a broad range of works written and performed during that period. With much fresh evidence, Luciani analyzes the syncretic content of many plays and their artistic and ritual functions. The spectrum of cultural life in the main viceroyalties is the responsibility of Asunción Lavrin. With the tools of the historian, Professor Lavrin leads us to evidence obtained from archival materials and other primary sources. She makes explicit the processes of the cultural interaction that took place among European and indigenous peoples. Native cultures, she tells us, were a formidable deterrent to the Spanish ambition of self-replication. Contrary to popular notions, the physical defeat of the Amerindians did not bring about a total distortion of their cultural legacies nor did it blur all forms of artistic creativity. As Lavrin discusses the early formation of Spanish American society in New Spain, we also learn how the Spanish imperial bureaucracy became firmly established in the viceroyalties. Lavrin's essay is complemented by Karen Stolley's characterization of cultural life mainly in the viceroyalties of Peru and the River Plate area. Her essay focuses primarily on literary output, but also focuses on the relevance of popular culture in the final stages of the Spanish Empire.

The struggles for political independence and the unrest that prevailed in the early republican period are reflected vividly in the neoclassical and romantic poetry written toward the beginning of the nineteenth century. Andrew Bush offers a keen and original reading of those texts in a substantial chapter where a great deal of fresh material is unveiled. The controversial imprint of modernity on Spanish America and the critical discourses that emerged from that uneven process are the concern of Nicolas Shumway and Martin Stabb. They discuss a large *corpus* of essays and underscore the centrality of that genre in political and literary texts produced in the nineteenth century.

In a crucial but forgotten essay, Andrés Bello (1781–1865) emphasized the role of historical and fictional narratives in the consolidation of national identity. That discursive enterprise is the cornerstone of Antonio Benítez-Rojo's essay on nineteenth-century fiction. He focuses on the novel and particularly on the role that fiction plays as an imaginative infrastructure of the nation. The extensive interdisciplinary assessment of the novel offered by Benítez-Rojo is complemented by chapters that Enrique Pupo-Walker and Josefina Ludmer devote to the brief narrative in the nineteenth century and to the gaucho genre. Professor Ludmer's perceptive reading of that particular modality of literary creation considers a broad pattern of traditional and non-literary sources and also the texts of literate authors who appropriated the rustic language and themes used by gauchos and *payadores*. This volume is rounded out by Frank Dauster's thorough description of theatrical activities in the nineteenth century. He chronicles the dominant forms of theatrical representation and the uneven achievements of that genre during the early phases of the republican period. Like many other contributors to this *History*, Dauster underlines the difficulties involved in treating a number of national literatures jointly. Such an effort, he says, turns the historiography of Spanish American letters into a polemical undertaking. Thus, in the eighteen chapters contained in this volume the literary historiography of Spanish America is enriched by both new data and analytical content. We believe that much of what is offered here is likely to affect the way we read many important, as well as lesser-known, texts. Those results are consistent with our goals: more than disseminating knowledge, we have sought to amplify it.

ENRIQUE PUPO-WALKER

1

A brief history of the history of Spanish American Literature[1]

Roberto González Echevarría

It was not until the late eighteenth and early nineteenth centuries, when the idea of literature as an independent category emerged, that it became possible to conceive of a Spanish American literature, one, moreover, worthy of a history. From the early Renaissance on, arts and letters were thought to be derived from the classics, the immanent and ideal model of all aesthetic expression, either as copy or corruption. The fundamental change that allowed for the possibility of a Spanish American literature was the gradual abandonment of the formalist abstraction of Neoclassicism, and the adoption of a psychological, empirical, and contingent concept of artistic creation. If the milieu, in all its concrete details, and the individual psychology of the creator are determining factors in artistic creation, then the work will reflect the conditions that define that individual and the particular nature that surrounds him and which he expresses. The issue of the difference of American nature could not be thought of in terms of its influence on the creation of literature until the emergence of what can be broadly termed the romantic spirit.

This does not mean, however, that some writers of the colonial Baroque did not write as if there were already an American literary tradition. Tradition is not synonymous with literary history. Tradition is the sum of works that a writer or group of writers conceive as antecedent, as origin, as the connection with a literary past from which they issue. Tradition is a binding, living, and dynamic past. Its existence may or may not be explicit, but it is necessarily and always implicit. Literary history, on the other hand, is the conscious and deliberate activity of recounting how certain works determine each other in time and among people who share a language and sometimes a geographic space. It is an activity that is metadiscursive in intention, and that manifests itself not only in the actual

---

[1] Whenever I write Latin American I mean to include Brazilian literature. For the history of Brazilian literary historiography see Chapter 1 of volume 3, by Benedito Nunes.

writing of literary histories, but also in essays, didactic works destined to shape a curriculum, and, quite often, in the edition of anthologies. Histories, manuals, critical essays, and anthologies are the narrative forms through which literary history is expressed. Yet, in their historiographical dimension, these books are also the product of the stories they tell, inasmuch as they often share a common ideology with the literary works whose history they narrate. For this reason it is possible to argue that literary histories are not really metadiscursive, but rather that they belong to the textual economy of the period in which they are written. Literary history, then, is a narrative form, perhaps even a minor genre, born in the period between the Enlightenment and Romanticism, in the transition from a conception of literature as one and eternal to another of literature as the creation of a given time and place which determine its characteristics. Herder, Schlegel, Villemain, La Harpe, Sismondi, Madame de Staël, Sainte-Beuve, are the all too familiar names at the head of the history of literary history.

Paradoxically, because it was produced in regions so distant and so different from Europe, both in terms of its geography and its culture, Spanish American literature and its history could only be conceived of in the context of these European ideas. The more distinct, the more peculiar and different, the more likely literature was to be thought through notions created to promote the expression of the new. The individuality, the difference at the origin postulated by Romanticism, transforms the distance that separates Europe from America into an enabling factor in Spanish American literary creation, one that serves as its pre-text or as its foundational myth. Without this prerequisite originality, Spanish American literature would have always had to think of itself as a belated, distant, and inauthentic manifestation of European literature. However, it can also be argued, if one were to adhere to neoclassic doctrine, that all literature, wherever it is created, will follow classical forms, which are neither diminished nor made inauthentic by their distance from the place of origin. In this line of argument, Spanish American literary works really differ little from European ones. This position has been intermittently defended, consciously or unconsciously, by various Spanish American writers, among them some of the most prominent, like Octavio Paz and Jorge Luis Borges. Yet the position that has prevailed has been the other, more polemical one, which assigns Spanish American literature an individuality sometimes linked with the struggle for political and cultural independence.

If the idea of Spanish American literature has existed since the beginning of the nineteenth century, and if the very idea of literature has also existed only since that period, then Spanish American literature has existed since there has been literature. In this sense, it is not a recent literature, as some would suggest, but rather a literature whose foundational peculiarities are more concrete and intense than those of European literatures, but not necessarily different. This is my own position as I reconstruct somewhat schematically the story of the multifaceted social, political, and textual activities that first defined the boundaries of Spanish American literature and its history. This reconstruction is the opposite of what Enrique Anderson Imbert set out to do in his valuable and canonical *Historia de la literatura hispanoamericana* [*Spanish-American Literature. A History*]. For Anderson Imbert, what mattered was what he conceived as the history of literature itself, not the activity that produced it and defined it: "In Spanish America there are often extraordinary personalities in literary life who study and promote literature, but who do not produce it. Furthermore, at times the men who most influence literary groups are precisely the ones who write neither poetry, nor novels, nor dramas. It may be lamentable, but it is obvious that they do not belong to a history of poetry, novels, and dramas" (*A History*, 16). I, on the contrary, attempt to focus precisely on those figures that make literary production possible, defining it and inventing it in the process.

The inherent difficulties of this task, beyond the most tangible ones involving the actual research itself, arise from the possibility of fragmentation already implicit in the romantic concept of national literatures and literary historiography. Because, inasmuch as it is possible to think in terms of a Spanish American literature that exists by virtue of its temporal and spatial distance from European literatures, it is also possible to think in terms of an Argentinian literature, a Mexican literature, a Cuban literature, and so forth. This dilemma has been the source of many polemics that extend to the present, as well as of the most varied solutions, none entirely satisfactory. If diversity is renounced, then Spanish American literature is a mere projection of European literature; if diversity is embraced, then the existence of a Costa Rican, a Colombian, or a Bolivian literature cannot be denied. For some, the defense of one position or the other has become a kind of crusade, appealing either to a national or a cultural loyalty whose source would be a love of language or of certain local traditions. In the final analysis, the polemic itself cannot be ignored; it is part and parcel of the continuous effort of Spanish American literature to define itself. However, it is a process of formation that does not lead to a satisfactory solution, and whose function is only part of the whole, not that which defines the whole.

This inquiry into the origins of Spanish American literary historiography has as its inevitable point of departure a reading and gloss of the first major narrative enterprise taking Spanish American literature as its object: Marcelino Menéndez y Pelayo's *Antología de poetas hispanoamericanos*. Although the *Antología* only includes poetry, as a history it takes poetry really to mean literature. As such, Menéndez y Pelayo's influential work, reissued as an *Historia de la poesía hispanoamericana*, played a vital role in the elaboration of Spanish American literary historiography, both at a continental level, and on that of each individual Spanish American country. The first question asked of the venerable and often quite irritating *Antología* was the following: what were Menéndez y Pelayo's sources, what books were at his disposal as he labored to produce his vast and influential panorama? An inquiry into Menéndez y Pelayo's library unveils a good portion of the map outlining the diffusion of Spanish American literature in the nineteenth century. It also brings to the surface the names of the founders and promoters of Spanish American literature, making it possible, by going directly to their works, to step beyond the confines of Menéndez y Pelayo's library, even while recognizing its impressive range.

As in nearly everything concerning the origins of Spanish American literature, the founding figure is that of Venezuelan Andrés Bello (1781–1865). Bello, of course, cuts across fields and disciplines: he was a poet, a grammarian, a classicist, an educator, a botanist, and the drafter of Chile's civil code. For our purposes, however, Bello is fundamental for two reasons. First, though a Neoclassicist by training, his interest in the various possibilities inherent in American nature, one of them being as source of poetic inspiration, marks him as a Romantic. He neatly straddles the two tendencies at whose juncture the idea of a Spanish American literature developed. Second, during his prolonged exile in London (1810–1829), Bello's activities as cultural promoter and editor foreshadows the work that other Spanish American writers will carry out, about thirty years later, in Paris. In those years Bello publishes two journals, *Biblioteca Americana* and *Repertorio Americano* which are the forebears of many influential Spanish American journals published in Europe, from *Correo Americano* in the mid nineteenth century to *Mundo Nuevo* in the 1960s. It is through these journals, and the activities surrounding them, which involved Spanish Americans from several countries, that Bello gave impetus to the possibility of a Spanish American literature, independent from that of Europe because it reflects a peculiar American nature. This is the theme of his great poems of the period, particularly the "Alocución a la poesía," published in *Repertorio*. Bello's was a romantic spirit, who had experienced the culmination of Romanticism in London, arguably its most important center, but who expressed himself in neoclassic form. His followers, the founders of the Spanish American literary tradition, would be romantic in both spirit and form, but none would surpass the master as poet, editor, or thinker. These founders are the ones on whose work Menéndez y Pelayo based his famous *Antología*.

The general profile of these founders is as follows. They were, naturally, Romantics, many of them Argentinian, but also Peruvian, Chilean, Venezuelan, and Colombian. They acquire or reaffirm their sense of continental citizenship in their travels to other Spanish American countries, either as political exiles or in the diplomatic service of their respective governments. More likely, however, they will discover each other in Paris, where they also wind up as exiles or diplomats, and where they publish some of their anthologies and other works of criticism. Paris became then, and continues to be today, the cultural supracapital of Latin America. These founders, who meet in the inevitable cafés and created the now familiar artistic and political allegiances, are for the most part politically active and concerned with education in their respective countries of origin, which are in the turbulent process of organizing themselves into republics. Literature, needless to say, plays an important part in the curricula being devised for the nascent school systems and universities.

This sense of being part of a continental cultural and even political domain is revealed in collections of essays compiled by a given author, containing writers from Latin American countries other than his, and in anthologies, where, for instance, an Argentinian editor included Cuban poets like José María Heredia or Plácido (José de la Concepción Valdés). There is even one anthology that includes Brazilian poets in the original Portuguese; its editor was the Argentinian Francisco Lagomaggiore, and the collection was titled *América literaria; producciones selectas en prosa y verso*. Yet another, edited also in Argentina by Carlos Romagosa, included North American poets (Poe, Longfellow, and Whitman) in Spanish translation: *Joyas poéticas americanas. Colección de poesías escogidas. Originales de autores nacidos en América*.

A representative example of this group of founders is the Colombian José María Torres Caicedo (1830–1889), a diplomat, essayist and critic who lived in Paris toward the middle of the century, where he came to know many other Latin Americans like him, about whom he wrote in a series of volumes that he called *Ensayos biográficos y de crítica literaria sobre los principales publicistas, historiadores, poetas y literatos de América Latina*. Torres Caicedo was one of the first and most assiduous promoters of the term *Latin America*, and had planned to write what would have been the first history of Latin American literature. He died in an insane asylum in Auteuil, near Paris, as the Argentinian scholar Emilio Carilla reports in the most complete study devoted to Torres Caicedo, whom he considers the "discoverer" of Argentinian literature, because of the studies that the Colombian devoted to the likes of Juan Bautista Alberdi (Carilla, "José María Torres Caicedo, 'descubridor' de la literatura argentina"). The founders of Spanish American literary history were not exclusively editors of anthologies; some were critics, chroniclers, journalists, and scholars. They also had their predecessors.

Before these founders formulated the concepts that were to give rise to

Spanish American literary historiography, and also as they did so, there existed a group of individuals, scattered in time and space and without a common sense of purpose, who constituted a kind of tradition of their own, and who preserved the memory of works written in Spanish America during the fifteenth, sixteenth, and seventeenth centuries. This formidable if forgotten lineage is composed of antiquarians, bibliophiles, and bibliographers and continues to the present day. Its genealogy extends from Antonio de León Pinelo (Peru, late sixteenth century–1600), to Nicolás Antonio (Spain, 1617–1684), to Juan José Eguiara y Eguren (Mexico, 1695–1763), and more recently from Alejandro Tapia y Rivera (Puerto Rico, 1826–1882), to Joaquín Icazbalceta (Mexico, 1825–1894) and José Toribio Medina (Chile, 1852–1930). While some of them, like Tapia y Rivera, were also poets, they were above all collectors and bibliographers. But the word "collector" is not meant to suggest a passive hoarder of old books and papers. In some cases, like that of José Mariano Beristáin y Souza (Mexico, 1756–1817), these antiquarians wrote true books of literary criticism. His *Bibliotheca Hispano-Americana Septentrional*, for example, published in 1816, contains incisive essays under the entries for Columbus, Sor Juana, Hernán Cortés, and others. To be sure, this group did not promote the idea that the works they listed and discussed constituted an autochtonous body of literature (with the exception of Medina and García Icazbalceta), but rather a prolix example of American genius applied to the task of composing literature in the universal and ahistorical sense that prevails until Romanticism. This notwithstanding, the work of these collectors made available to the founders knowledge that was indispensable for the elaboration of a historical beginning, an origin for their narrative scheme.

The founders did have a common sense of purpose and did establish a strong connection between their activities and the independence of the continent. They were a prolific group that has been the object of excellent studies by Rosalba Campra and Beatriz González Stephan. What stands out among the considerable assortment of books either written or edited by them is the prodigious number of anthologies. The most important among these is undoubtedly the first: *América poética*, compiled by the Argentinian Juan María Gutiérrez, and published, significantly, in Valparaíso, Chile, not in Buenos Aires, during the author's exile there. In a gesture that proclaims his desire to found an American poetic tradition, Gutiérrez opens *América poética* with Bello's "Alocución" as a kind of epigraph. His anthology would be the answer to the Venezuelan's call to the Muses, a truly foundational act of continental dimensions. Many others followed, including a new *América poética* (Paris, 1875), edited by the Chilean José Domingo Cortés. Cortés was also the author of a *Parnaso peruano*, as well as of a *Parnaso arjentino* [sic]. Cortés was, obviously, the most assiduous of these founding anthologists, whose collections were not only called "parnasos," but also "galerías," "albums," "coronas," "ramilletes," "guirnaldas," and "mixturas." The picturesque titles of these venerable volumes, many of which served as Menéndez y Pelayo's sources, give us the tenor of the times, a glimpse of the beginnings of the Spanish American literary tradition, as well as of the earliest manifestations of a kind of Spanish American literary historiography. That tradition and early history is, of course, not only textual, but also human, in that it is constituted as much by the traffic of individuals as by that of books. It is a transcontinental traffic that naturally continues until the present. It affects the concept of a Spanish American literature, as opposed to national literatures, in a very powerful way.

In chronological order the appearance of anthologies begins with the anonymous but fundamental *La lira argentina, o colección de las piezas poéticas, dadas a luz en Buenos Ayres durante la guerra de su independencia* and ends, after that all-important peak in *América poética*, with Pedro Pablo Figueroa's *Prosistas y poetas de América moderna*. By this time *Modernismo* was already in full swing. The tendency culminates with the publication of "parnasos" of nearly all Spanish American countries by Barcelona's Editorial Maucci, between approximately 1910 and 1925. These are uneven collections of a chiefly commercial nature, sometimes without even a prologue or biographical notes. These modest books still reveal, however, the extent to which American poetry was prized after *Modernismo* [Modernism], and the longevity of the poetic movement that the founders initiated and promoted with their anthologies.

In addition to these anthologies, there also began to appear, after the midpoint of the nineteenth century, books of criticism or literary journalism about Spanish American writers, written by other Spanish Americans, attesting to the depth and breadth of the tradition. For example, as already mentioned, in 1863 the Colombian José María Torres Caicedo published a biographical essay about the Argentinian Juan Bautista Alberdi, and in 1882 the Chilean Miguel Luis Amunátegui published a biography of the Venezuelan Andrés Bello, entitled *Vida de Don Andrés Bello*. Torres Caicedo, as we saw, was a promoter of Latin American cultural unity, and published in Paris a journal called *El Correo de Ultramar*, where his articles on fellow writers appeared (Carilla, "El primer biógrafo de Alberdi [José María Torres Caicedo]"). Among other volumes of this kind one should mention the Venezuelan Rufino Blanco-Fombona's *Autores americanos juzgados por los españoles*; the Chilean José Victoriano Lastarria's *Recuerdos literarios: datos para la historia literaria de América española i el progreso intelectual en Chile*; the Mexican Francisco Sosa's collection of essays *Escritores y poetas sud-americanos*, which already argues against some of its predecessors, and the Argentinian Martín García Merou's entertaining and indiscreet *Confidencias literarias*.

Works of a more academic nature were also published, such as those by the Chilean Diego Barros Arana, whose projected *Bibliotheca Americana. Collection d'ouvrages inédits ou rares sur l'Amérique* attempted to publish in Paris editions of sixteenth- and seventeenth-century works. There are also the many studies by the Mexican Joaquín García Icazbalceta, as well as his translations of Francisco Cervantes de Salazar's Latin dialogues, and his treatise entitled *Francisco de Terrazas y otros poetas del siglo XVI*. In Chile, Gregorio Víctor Amunátegui and B. Vicuña Mackenna published their *Informes presentados al decano de la Facultad de Humanidades sobre la Historia de la literatura colonial de Chile (1541–1810)*, a critical response to José Toribio Medina's *Historia de la literatura colonial de Chile*, which had been entered in a contest and published in 1878. Meanwhile, the Colombian José María Vergara y Vergara published his *Historia de la literatura en Nueva Granada*, the first part of which was subtitled *Desde la conquista hasta la independencia (1538–1820)* and the Equatorian Juan León Mera his *Ojeada histórico-crítica sobre la poesía ecuatoriana desde su época más remota hasta nuestros días*, the second edition of which appeared in 1893.

The historical orientation of these academic books stands in contrast to the more journalistic, present-day bias of many, though certainly not all, anthologies. Many of the latter, as well as some of the early literary journalism, constitute American poetic manifestoes, not only because they gather poems by poets from a variety of Spanish American countries, but also because they incorporate, almost exclusively, works from the period immediately following Independence. It seems clear that one of the ideas implicit in these books is that Spanish American literature begins with political freedom from the metropolis and the birth of the new nations. But naturally, from the historical spirit that prevailed among these Romantics, thinking about the existence of Spanish American literature and writing its history meant elaborating a narrative which should have a beginning, a middle, and, if not an end, at least ties to their present. The romantic imagination in which the idea of a Spanish American literature takes place is eminently narrative, as is the science of philology, which expresses the concept of the birth and development of national languages and literatures as an evolution, understandable in much the same way as that of the fossils discovered and studied by the naturalists. What could constitute the beginning of that literature?

In the philological tradition, literary history originated with an epic song, which expressed the birth of a language and a literature that began in the popular, oral tradition. This gave rise to foundational studies of the *Chanson de Roland*, the *Nibelungenlied*, and the *Poema de Mío Cid*. It should be remembered here that Bello was the first critic to devote important studies to the *Poema*, which culminated in an edition. Quite clearly, the origin of a Spanish American literary tradition, the beginning of the narrative of this history, could well have been medieval or renaissance Spanish literature. Yet this would not have made it distinct and autochthonous in its development, but rather a mere appendix, branch or deviation. The origin had to be a literature written in the colony, with all the delicate and complicated issues such an idea would inevitably generate. Juan María Gutiérrez, José Antonio Echeverría, José Toribio Medina, and other founders of Spanish American literary historiography would formulate a narrative beginning that originates in the colony and that often places a renaissance epic such as *La araucana*, *Espejo de paciencia*, or *Arauco domado*, at its roots.

Works of the colonial period were problematic because the era in which they emerged belonged to the Spanish past that Independence had attempted to eradicate. How could works conceived under the aegis of *coloniaje*, the negative term used to refer to the colonial era, be privileged as being the origin? There was also an aesthetic difficulty. Many of the colonial works were explicitly baroque, a style the Romantics detested and associated with Spanish domination. Creating an origin out of these elements was not at all an easy task. The way in which Juan María Gutiérrez and José Toribio Medina dealt with these issues is exemplary in the way Spanish American literary historiography attempted to become a narrative. In spite of the nearly fifty years separating them, Gutiérrez and Medina start their narrative projects from a common beginning, based on identical foundational ideas. What these founders effectively accomplish is a monumentalization of the colonial epic based on the romantic-philological model of the origin and evolution of European languages.

By monumentalization I mean granting something a privileged position, forcing it to embody, in its purest state, the core of metaphors constituting an ideology. These metaphors are intensified in an inverse proportion to the inadequacy of the object being monumentalized. The monument, in this sense, is erected according to patterns analogous to those that operate within fiction, but is characterized as the kind of discourse that claims to reveal or contain the truth about its own origin. The truth, what is authentic or appropriate, is the obsessive theme of monumentalization as discourse. This is, then, the projection or hypostasis of the conceptual-metaphoric nucleus that constitutes an ideology and within which is frequently housed a discipline, such as literary history or criticism. The romantic philological model was based on the kind of evolutionary scheme that progressed from the simple to the complex, from the primitive to the decadent, from the singular to the plural and prolix, from clarity to ambiguity and confusion. Hence the epic's allure for a romantic project of literary historiography, given its one-piece heroes and its Manichean world divided neatly between good and evil. The epic thus becomes the sought-for origin, whose world of violence (killings, revenge, bloody battles) echoes the rupture, the break of a birth. There is an exaltation of national values associated with this aesthetic; a linguistic, ethical, and political simplicity that is a projection of the general primitivism of romantic ideology, which explains its rejection of the Baroque. Yet the colonial epic was a typical renaissance product, derived from Ariosto and Tasso, and with characteristics diametrically opposed to the romantic conception of a national epic. This is a challenge that provokes one of the most characteristic philological fictions composed by the founders.

During his exile in Chile, Juan María Gutiérrez took on the daunting task of composing a scholarly edition of the *Arauco domado*, which was eventually published in Valparaiso in 1848. His project has much in common with that of the Cuban José Antonio Echeverría, who "discovered" the *Espejo de paciencia*, an epic he too situates at the foundation of the Cuban literary tradition, and which he culls out of the first history of the island ever published (González Echevarría, "Reflections on *Espejo de paciencia*"). Gutiérrez's interest in the epic also parallels that of the Chilean Diego Barros Arana, whose edition of Captain Fernando Alvarez de Toledo's *Purén indómito* inaugurated his series of colonial American works published in Paris. No matter how modest Gutiérrez's edition of Oña's poem may seem today, its elaboration was an act fraught with ideological choices that the Argentinian made with consummate care and deliberation. In an essay contemporaneous with the edition and collected in a volume entitled *Escritores coloniales americanos*, Gutiérrez lays out the criteria, beyond that of his collector's vocation, that led him to study Oña's poem and make it available to the American public. It may seem surprising to us, but Gutiérrez had no illusions about the literary value of *Arauco domado*: "Two centuries have passed over the poem we are speaking about, and taking its age into account it has the right to have its inflections of bad taste forgiven, its sententious affectation, the flagging intonation, the unkept and uncultured tone that stain its stanzas" (p. 360). What matters to Gutiérrez, in his effort to monumentalize the poem, is the historic truth that it supposedly contains, and, as a result, its value in attesting to Chile's and America's singularity as a territory capable of producing its own original artistic expression. America's fundamental and foundational differences are not a function of the renaissance packaging of Oña's poem (which, on the contrary, would constitute an impediment to the expression of its genuineness and authenticity) but rather the contents, which forthrightly reflect verifiable episodes that mark a true origin in a given time and space: "Oña's book is not precious because it has become so rare to find in the world, but because it is one of the sources to which one must go to soak oneself in the truth when writing about certain episodes about the primitive history of Chile" (p. 357). The key terms here are "to soak oneself in the truth" and "primitive history," which go back to the romantic formulation of the national epic. The artistic defects, the coarseness, lend the poem greater authenticity. Reading *Arauco domado* is equivalent to "reliving" that "primitive" history, to letting oneself be penetrated by history itself in its pristine form, to being "soaked in truth." Primitivism, in this context, transports one to that shapeless origin wherein truth shines amidst the violence of birth. Oña's motives, according to Gutiérrez, can be summarized as follows: "He was duty-bound to sing the glories of the fatherland, the soil where he was born that he had to describe" (p. 356). The compiler of *América poética* concludes his essay with a resonant manifesto of poetic Americanism and a defense of colonial literature. He first explains that by virtue of America having been inseparable from the metropolis, American men and their deeds were indistinguishable from those of Spain, hence their difference was not properly credited ("American men and their works were taken to be Spanish"), and he proclaims that "the glories of the American Continent have only begun to be ours since the beginning of this century" (p. 372). He ends with a declaration that is itself the gloss of a line from Bernardo de Balbuena's *Grandeza mexicana*:

> Those who served as inspiration to portentous European masters were destined to be born *Where there was thought to be no world*. If the Mexican Ruiz de Alarcón had not written *La verdad sospechosa*, the French theater would not have, among its classical beauties, Corneille's *Le Menteur*. If Pedro de Oña had not written *Arauco domado*, it is quite probable that Lope de Vega would not have written either the play by the same title, nor the love song and the scene on the banks of the lake between Caupolicán and his mistress that embellish the first act.
>
> (p. 372)

Colonial writers appear here not as the followers of the European ones, but, on the contrary, as their precursors, dwellers in that primeval moment of history that can only be adequately expressed in an epic poem. The monumentalization is completed with this final gesture.

Gutiérrez was prudent enough to erect as the monument in the origin a work written by a native of the New World. José Toribio Medina, on the other hand, imposed upon himself the more arduous task of making of *La araucana* the necessary foundation, in spite of Ercilla's irreducible Spanishness, which Medina never downplays or denies. How, then, can the poem be considered Chilean? Medina's argument is presented as follows: the only literary works from colonial Chile worthy of attention are those that depict the wars with the Araucanian Indians. Medina says in the introduction to his *Historia de la literatura colonial de Chile*: "Who would read today about the lives of mystical characters, the bloated volumes of sermons, the compilations of extravagant verse that were written at that time in the capital of the viceroyalty? On the other hand, are none of the numerous books written about the wars in Arauco monuments deserving of consultation?" (p. xii). The subject of wars is, as we have seen, an important component of the epic, one of those that define it and make it distinctive. A second crucial fact can be added to this, namely, that the poets who sang of the Araucan wars were all participants in those actions, and as a result their testimony is trustworthy, the product of direct experience, not of literature. As such, that literature is already Chilean because it emerges from episodes that occurred in Chilean territory, episodes that determine the character of all texts born of them, regardless of a writer's nationality: "The deeds carried out on that narrow stretch of land [Arauco], were the ones that awakened Ercilla's poetic genius and unquestionably influenced the inclination of his work [...] This is why *La Araucana* is eminently Chilean, and should have a place in our literature..." (p. 4). Medina attributes to the wars of Arauco the initial spark of Ercilla's poetic gift: not merely the poem, but the very possibility of writing originates at the moment when the poet confronts his new surroundings, a meeting that marks him indelibly and enables him to produce the foundational text. This is the reason Medina opens his *Historia de la literatura colonial de Chile* with three chapters about Ercilla, the pedestal upon which he will erect his entire narrative project.

That project was, of course, a history of Chilean literature in the colonial period, not of Spanish American literature as a whole, although in other countries (as in the case of Cuba mentioned above), a parallel process was under way. Yet, despite all the activity summarized above, no history of Spanish American literature was written during the nineteenth century. The first work that can be considered a history of Spanish American literature was Menéndez y Pelayo's *Antología de poetas hispano-americanos*, the first volume of which appeared in 1893. The project of a full-fledged history, which some like Torres Caicedo had envisioned, was probably postponed by the more pressing need to write the histories of each national literature, which did begin to appear during the nineteenth century. This was a task that was incited by the prevalent nationalisms and was often tied to the elaboration of school programs, university curricula, and the like. Torres Caicedo's unfinished project and Menéndez y Pelayo's successful one share one quality with nearly all the comprehensive histories of Spanish American literature written since then. They are written outside Spanish America, either by Spanish Americans or by foreigners. It is as if the broad view could only be focused with distance, and without the nationalistic pressures of each fatherland.

Yet the mere existence of these founders, and particularly of their books and magazines, changes the conceptions generally held about when the idea of Spanish American literature began to emerge. Emir Rodríguez Monegal, for instance, wrote in his *Borzoi Anthology of Latin American Literature* that "Only with the advent of modernism did a general Spanish American literature begin to emerge out of separate strands of development. Writers began to circulate all over the continent; for the first time their works were published and discussed outside their native countries, and achieved fame even in Spain and France" (1, 337). The anthologies, critical works, and even scholarly treatises discussed here demonstrate that the process had begun at least forty years before. Menéndez y Pelayo's *Antología* stops precisely when *Modernismo* is beginning to loom on his horizon (the early 1890s), and he had already had access to quite a few books that had either crossed the Atlantic to reach his voracious library, or been published in neighboring France, or in Spain itself.

Menéndez y Pelayo's *Antología* remains the first and most influential statement on the topic. Evidence of this enduring influence is not only the widespread presence of the Spaniard's judgments in histories of national literatures throughout Spanish America, but also how histories written years later by Spanish Americans (for instance, José J. Arrom's) are conceived *against* the Spaniard's principles and opinions. Whether positive or negative, Menéndez y Pelayo's *Antología* is the point of departure for most of the historiography of Spanish American literature in the twentieth century. Because he was so opinionated, self-assured, and paternalistic, it is often difficult to come to terms with the fact that Menéndez y Pelayo's *Antología* was a major accomplishment; that the weighty tomes are still replete with valuable information and analyses, not to mention carefully reproduced texts. Menéndez y Pelayo was able to gather a prodigious amount of information from all corners of Spanish America at a time when communications were slow and unreliable, and when very few scholars, if any, had a comprehensive knowledge of the poetry being produced in the New World. Because of the dramatic progress in communications, as well as many other improvements, his feat will never be equalled.

The foregoing must be kept in mind earnestly when one considers Menéndez y Pelayo's motives for bringing about such an impressive compilation. As should be evident from the date of publication of the first volume, the *Antología* was conceived to commemorate the four-hundredth anniversary of the discovery of America, or as Menéndez y Pelayo puts it with his customary bombast: "that marvelous and superhuman deed, thanks to which our language was allowed to resonate mightily from the banks of the Rio Bravo to the lands of Tierra del Fuego"

(*Antología*, iv). The Royal Spanish Academy, of which Menéndez y Pelayo humbly considers himself a mere scribe, wishes to compensate for the sorrowful state of Spain as a world power with this proud display of its enduring influence and survival – he has earlier discussed how Greece and Rome live on through their colonies. The *Antología*, this "modest monument erected to the glory of our common language" (p. iv), will, furthermore, grant "Spanish American poetry official entry to the treasure of Spanish literature, where it should have been incorporated a long time ago" (p. v). The inclusiveness of the *Antología*, it is clear, reproduces the lost unity of the Spanish Empire, a transnational identity could not lead the new Spanish American nations to any other common origin than Spain itself. Another motive, and again the date of the *Antología* is crucial, is to ward off what Menéndez y Pelayo sees as the pernicious influence of French poetry on Spanish American poetry, which is leading it away from its true Hispanic sources. *Modernismo* is exploding around him, and anything modern alarmed the Spanish sage, who saw plainly that it would imply a rejection of the retrograde Mother Country, and play havoc with his system of values.

Menéndez y Pelayo's unrestrained colonialism is also shockingly manifest in his conception of the character of Spanish American poetry. He claims that Spanish American poetry has undergone all the changes brought about by artistic movements in Europe, with no visible differ- ence, except that brought about by the description of the peculiar landscape of the continent and the political ardor created by the Wars of Independence. Hence for him the most original Spanish American poetry is the descriptive or political: Andrés Bello, Joaquín Olmedo, and José María Heredia are the best Spanish American poets (though he regrets the latter's anti-Spanish stance). Of course, what Menéndez y Pelayo is attempting, quite explicitly, is to deny the influence of the indigenous peoples of the New World on Spanish American poetry, thereby underlin- ing the purity of its Spanish lineage: "about the few and obscure literary fragments remaining of those primitive languages. . .their influence on Spanish poetry in America has been so slight, or better, so non-existent (outside of the passing whims of this or that poet), that the history of that poetry can be told in its entirety omitting altogether those alleged origins and leaving them to the philologian's study and analysis" (p. viii). This idea is repeated with annoying insistence throughout the *Antología*, and as a result much Spanish American literature and criticism is written to counter it, projecting the *Antología*'s influence to the present.

Menéndez y Pelayo divided his *Antología* according to region or nation. He devotes most of the space to Mexico, Chile, Peru, and Argentina, providing in passing the most complete history of colonial Spanish American poetry available then and now. He then studies national literatures until more or less his day, but leaving out living writers for fear of making hasty judgments. This limits his range considerably, but what is left of his study of eighteenth- and nineteenth-century Spanish American poetry is quite remarkable. The Spaniard was a Neoclassicist at heart, hence he was enthralled by odes written by the likes of Bello, Heredia, and Olmedo. He was also quite taken with nationalistic poetry, inspired by military feats like those of Simón Bolívar. Menéndez y Pelayo was not far off the mark in these predilections, and there can be little doubt that his *Antología* helped to canonize those worthy writers. One is less sanguine about his judgments, however, when noting that one of the models with which he compares these Spanish Americans is the shallow and bombastic Quintana, a Spanish poet mercifully forgotten today. One is also irritated, of course, by his dismissal of poets like Plácido, less academic in their classicism, hence more romantic, about whom the Spaniard says, with intolerable condescension, that he "writes nonsense, although sonorous nonsense" (II, xxxvi). The list of extremely orthodox as well as rhetorically and grammatically correct poets whom Menéndez y Pelayo lauds, but who have, quite rightly, been relegated to footnotes in national histories of literature, is very long. However, the value of the *Antología* as a reminder of the existence of a unity worth preserving and cherishing is undeniable, and would be reasserted, ironically, by the *modernista* [modernist] movement he so abhorred, and by its most influential figure, Rubén Darío. The peripatetic Nicaraguan would rekindle the unity of all Spanish poetry, including most energetically that of Spain, at the same time as the volumes of the *Antología* were circulating throughout Spanish America. It would be short-sighted to view these two as antithetic phenomena.

According to Carlos Hamilton, the first chair in the United States exclusively devoted to Spanish American literature was inaugurated at Columbia University by Federico de Onís in 1916 (Hamilton, *História de la literatura hispanoamericana*, 7). In that same year, another member of the Columbia faculty, Alfred Coester, published his *The Literary History of Spanish America*, which was, strictly speaking, the first history of Spanish American literature, given that Menéndez y Pelayo's was a history of poetry. Coester's work owes much to Menéndez y Pelayo's *Antología*, and like it, has much to offer still, in spite of very questionable premises. His intention in writing the book is to make Spanish Americans known to his fellow countrymen, for "The main characteristics and trends of the Spanish-American mind are revealed in his literature" (p. vii). However, Coester is not even sure that what Spanish Americans write is literature: "But shall we call Spanish-American writings literature?" (p. vii). He answers with a very revealing anecdote worth citing:

> A professor in Argentina wished a few years ago to establish a course for students in Spanish-American literature. The plan was opposed by Bartolomé Mitre, ex-President of the republic and himself a poet and

historian of the first rank, on the ground that such a thing did not exist. He held the view that mere numbers of books did not form a literature; though united by the bond of a common language, the printed productions of Spanish Americans had no logical union nor gave evidence of an evolution toward a definite goal. On the other hand, he admitted that their "literary productions might be considered, not as models but as facts, classified as the expression of their social life during three periods, the colonial epoch, the struggle for freedom, and the independent existence of the several republics."   (p. viii)

Coester adopts this division suggested by Mitre. His history covers the colonial period as a whole, divides the Revolutionary Period into two, south and north (Mexico and the Antilles), then devotes chapters to the literatures of individual countries, except for Bolivia, which is paired with Peru (respecting colonial boundaries), and the central American countries, which he subsumes in a chapter covering the Dominican Republic and Puerto Rico. He closes with a chapter on the *modernista* movement that again restores the unity.

Coester warns, however, that "the originality of Spanish-American literature lies chiefly in the subject-matter, in its pictures of natural scenery and social life" (p. ix). He adds, echoing Menéndez y Pelayo, that the "form of Latin American literature has been imitative while the matter original" (p. x). He wishes the reader to have these qualifications in mind: "The reader, aware at the outset that he has before him an extremely provincial type of literature, will not expect great masterpieces" (p. x). Having said this, however, Coester produces a quite remarkable volume, with detailed information that shows that his research was extensive, serious, and little affected by his prejudiced view of the subject matter. Coester's knowledge of nineteenth-century Spanish American journals is outstanding, made possible by the extensive collections he had at his disposal at Harvard, Columbia, and the Hispanic Society of America. He also had the help of Pedro and Max Henríquez Ureña, and his mentor J. D. M. Ford. His overview of the colonial period is also quite complete, as is his concluding chapter on *Modernismo*.

Coester is followed by one of the few exceptions to the rule that comprehensive histories of Spanish American literature are written abroad, Luis Alberto Sánchez's *Nueva historia de la literatura americana*, which was written at home by the Peruvian. This was, as far as I know, the first history of Spanish American literature written by a Spanish American. Sánchez is cautious in his approach to the polemical issues, and relies on Menéndez y Pelayo's *Antología* as authority to back up his opinions. He speaks of the existence already of a "sensibility, a direction, and culture" (p. 23) that are properly Spanish American. Sánchez writes in a completely different climate from Menéndez y Pelayo, however, one in which the self-assurance in European culture shown by the Spaniard has been lost with the catastrophes of the First World War. A general climate of repudiation of the West and exaltation of the "primitive" as well as powerful political movements against the rule of the classes that had guided Europe in the nineteenth century turned artists to a search for radically new modes of expression. In Spanish America the Mexican Revolution had brought attention to the decisive Indian component of Mexican culture, and in the Caribbean the Afro-Antillean movement had exalted the African component in the culture of the islands. In Sánchez's case it is clear that his orientation is influenced by APRISMO, the political movement led by Raúl Haya de la Torre that sought to do for Peruvian society what the Mexican Revolution had done for Mexico: to make the impact of the Indian population visible and to turn it into a political program. For him, too, it is the novel, rather than poetry, that has brought out the true character of Spanish America. Sánchez sees in the *novela de la tierra* the epic that Spanish America was looking for (p. 35). The *Nueva historia de la literatura americana* is far less reliable than Menéndez y Pelayo's *Antología* and far from Coester's *History* in terms of its overall quality. However, it is a harbinger of things to come and a true reflection of the ideology underlying Spanish American literature in the wake of the artistic and political avant-garde movements of the 1920s.

The next history of Spanish American literature, strictly in terms of publication date, was Arturo Torres Ríoseco's *The Epic of Latin American Literature*, written by the Chilean while a professor in the Department of Spanish at the University of California. It is truly a history of *Latin American* literature, because it includes Brazil. Torres Ríoseco was already the author of an *Antología de la literatura hispanoamericana* (New York, F. S. Crofts & Co., 1939), which anticipates his *Epic*. Both books were written with the US public in mind, particularly university students (the preface to the *Antología* has an interesting account of Latin American literary studies in the US up to that point). His aim is to show that Latin American literature has reached a golden age because its authors have realized that an "earthbound" conscience can lead them away from imitation. He extols, as did Sánchez, the *novela de la tierra*, which is really his point of departure. In spite of its unfortunate title and somewhat proselytizing tone, the *Epic* is a well-researched, broad-ranging book with much useful information. It was a popular book in its time, being issued in a second, augmented edition, by the California Press (1961), and having enjoyed the rare privilege of being translated into Chinese (Beijing, 1972).

Torres Ríoseco is closely followed by the Dominican Pedro Henríquez Ureña's *Literary Currents in Hispanic America*, the first really significant history of Spanish American literature, which originated as the Charles

Eliot Norton Lectures at Harvard for 1940–1941. As well as the distance apparently needed to capture the broad view of Spanish American literary history, an additional element appears in Henríquez Ureña: his book was originally written in English and translated into Spanish, after his premature death, by Joaquín Díez-Canedo. (It appears that Torres Ríoseco wrote his *Epic* in Spanish and either he or someone else translated it into English.) *Literary Currents* is a superb book, the product of a man of letters as well as a scholar, whose prodigious cultural background is evident on every page. It seems as if Henríquez Ureña had read everything in every European language. His book is still persuasive because of his ability to see Spanish American literature in such a rich context with such naturalness, and also because of his minute knowledge of the literature and art of each Spanish American country. Hence when he speaks of Spanish America's search for individual artistic expression, the main theme of the book, he does not sound provincial, as is often the case with his many disciples and imitators. A true heir of Bello, with whom he begins his history, only to go back to the colonial period, Henríquez Ureña was a humanist in the very best tradition and in every sense of the term.

Although Henríquez Ureña claims that his book is not a complete history of Spanish American literature, but only of that literature in search of Spanish American expression, the truth is that *Literary Currents* is not only a history of Spanish American literature, but perhaps still the best. Henríquez Ureña's most felicitous strategy concerns the colonial period, that is to say, the beginning of Spanish American literary historiography, which, as seen before, was a major source of concern for the founders. In a fascinating first chapter, where he displays his vast knowledge of medieval and renaissance letters, Henríquez Ureña maps out the founding topics of Spanish American literature. Some of these, like the depiction of "natural man" were to have a lasting impact on European thought. The recurrence of utopias placed in America (More), the Edenic description of nature, the disputes about how to deal with indigenous populations, become a treasure of topics and tropes that will become the core of Spanish American literature. The origin of Spanish American history is to be found in that trove of topics, in that thematic, a kind of literary mythology that weaves itself in and out of poems, novels, essays, and plays throughout time. In this way, Henríquez Ureña cuts through the problems of nationality. By founding literary tradition in tropes, in literary discourse, as it were, Henríquez Ureña successfully binds Spanish American literary history, allowing one to see the continuity between Columbus and Carpentier, or between Balbuena and Neruda.

Henríquez Ureña's is a holistic view of culture. *Literary Currents* is also a history of Spanish American culture, and even just a history of Spanish America (including, by the way, Brazil). His chronological subdivisions fall naturally within this broad scheme, with three periods parcelling out the nineteenth century, and two leading up to his day. The Spanish version, published in Mexico, has incorporated a more complete scholarly apparatus involving notes and bibliography taken from Henríquez Ureña's other comprehensive volume, his *Historia de la cultura en la América Hispánica* (1947). *Las corrientes literarias en la América hispánica* is as detailed a history of Spanish American literature as there is, with the exception of Enrique Anderson Imbert's (to which more space will be devoted below), and a book that is the culmination of the tradition whose history it aims to relate: that of the search for American expression. Other books will follow it, such as José Lezama Lima's brilliant *La expresión americana* (1958), making contributions of their own, but none will surpass it in richness, elegance of thought and style, and intellectual rigor.

Henríquez Ureña was followed by another exception, Julio A. Leguizamón's, *Historia de la literatura hispanoamericana*, written and published by the Argentinian in his native Buenos Aires. The massive, two-volume history grew out of a bibliography of Spanish American literature which the Argentinian set out to compile. The *Historia* retains much of the bibliographical cast of the original project, particularly in the chapters dealing with contemporary literature. In this sense, Leguizamón is more the heir of the antiquarians, bibliophiles, and bibliographers discussed above. Leguizamón's dependence on Menéndez y Pelayo is extensive, and his criteria for chronological and geographical divisions are vaguely derived from the Spaniard. The *Historia* is a handsomely printed and bound set that was intended more as a reference work than as a work of literary historiography. It is significant that a publishing house such as Emecé in Buenos Aires would have been willing to risk such an expensive book dealing with Spanish American literary history. It seems to indicate that by the mid 1940s the existence of the field is a given. The appearance of histories of Spanish American literature in languages other than Spanish or Portuguese seems to indicate the same.

Two French professors published histories of Spanish American literature in the early 1950s: Robert Bazin's *Histoire de la littérature américaine de langue espagnole* and Charles V. Aubrun, *Histoire des lettres hispano-américaines*. Bazin's is a manual for French schools whose principal merit, according to its authors, is "merely to exist" Aubrun's is more ambitious, though its author also calls it a "manual." He opines that great works are rare in Spanish America, where the quality of life "has not allowed its strong personalities to realize themselves in works of eternal value" (p. 5). For Aubrun, whose criteria are avowedly aesthetic, Spanish American literature does not begin to have an independent life until the 1890s, claiming that until then there was a strong, lingering Spanish influence. None of these works come close to Henríquez Ureña's, and were soon superseded by the publication of Anderson Imbert's monumental history.

Argentinian scholar, critic, and writer Enrique Anderson Imbert published his *Historia de la literatura hispanoamericana* while a professor at the University of Michigan. It remains to this day the most authoritative of all the histories, by far the most inclusive and detailed, and the one written by the best literary critic. A man of exquisite taste and sensibility, the author of fine essays and short stories, Anderson Imbert also proved to be a relentless researcher, with a powerful capacity to process enormous amounts of information. His *Historia* covers the range of Spanish American literature from Columbus to the latest novels and poems. Anderson Imbert is careful to include writers from all Spanish American countries and to mention works of all genres, providing the basic facts, such as dates, as well as an overall appraisal of each significant period. He parcels his history, approximately by generations, but is not wedded to the strictures of method. Anderson Imbert is not interested, as was Henríquez Ureña, in Spanish American literature as a search for or expression of cultural identity. He is interested in Spanish American literature as literature, as the expression or creation of aesthetic values.

Anderson Imbert is, above all, a formalist critic, with an idealistic conception of historical development, in the sense that he chronicles, precisely, the history of ideas and artistic movements. History in the stricter sense serves as a background, ably integrated into the picture when necessary, but never obtrusively. Anderson Imbert voices his ambitions and frustrations in this revealing opening paragraph of the "Prolog" to the *Historia*:

> Of the many dangers an historian of literature risks, two are quite serious: that of specializing in the study of isolated great books, and that of specializing in the study of the circumstances under which those books were written. If the historian elects the first, he produces a collection of unconnected critical essays, that is, a history of literature containing very little history. If he chooses the second, the result will be a series of external references to the process of civilization, that is, a history of literature containing very little literature. Is it possible to achieve a history of literature that fulfills both the true historical and the true literary function? At least, is it possible to attempt one? It would be a history that gave meaning to the expressive moments of certain men who, through the passing of the centuries, set themselves to write. Instead of isolating the literature produced, on the one hand, and the circumstances under which it was produced, on the other, this history would integrate the two within the concrete existence of the writers. Each writer asserts those esthetic values that he has formed while contemplating the possibilities of his historical environment, and these are the values that should constitute the real subject matter of any history of literature.   (*A History*, 15)

In his best moments, which are many, Anderson Imbert realizes this desired synthesis of text and context, given the elegant seamlessness of his discourse. The *Historia* is rich in insightful readings mainly of the major works, and with quite useful overviews of a history that is really never truly historical, but more ideological.

In any case, Anderson Imbert is not only vexed by the difficulty of this task in the abstract, but more by the prospect of its application to Spanish American literary history. Echoing sentiments found earlier in Coester, and repeated in Aubrun, Anderson Imbert deplores the overall quality of Spanish American literature, particularly the absence of truly great works: "The effective contributions of Spanish-American literature to international literature are minimal," he asserts, and after citing a dozen or so writers "who would do honor to any literature," laments that "In general, we are afflicted by improvisation, disorder, fragmentation, and impurity" (pp. 15–16). This condition of Spanish American literature forces him to include "many unaccomplished writers," while "we anxiously look for the few who have expressed aesthetic values that can be assigned to the category of beauty" (p. 16). This aggravation does not stop Anderson Imbert from writing memorable pages about the chroniclers of the discovery and conquest of the New World, though he knows that they did not write with the purpose of reaching that elusive category of beauty. In other cases he is not so kind, but on the whole, he is generous in his judgments and, more often than not, not far off the mark in his assessments. In this practice of passing aesthetic judgments he follows Menéndez y Pelayo's *Antología*, to which his *Historia* is a worthy heir. The main difference, however, between the Spaniard and the Argentinian is that Anderson Imbert is also an heir to *Modernismo* and the Avant-Garde, and therefore his aestheticism is based on more cosmopolitan values. Yet in terms of inclusiveness, Anderson Imbert's *Historia de la literatura hispanoamericana* is the first successful historical enterprise to best Menéndez y Pelayo's *Antología*.

Anderson Imbert's *Historia*, re-issued several times in the 1950s, was followed by Angel Valbuena Briones's, *Literatura hispanoamericana*, published as the fourth volume of Angel Valbuena Pratt's popular *Historia de la literatura española*. Not too concerned with issues of historiography, Valbuena Briones begins his volume with Bernal Díaz del Castillo, whose *Historia verdadera* he terms a great Spanish American book written by a Spaniard. As in Menéndez y Pelayo, Valbuena Briones emphasizes the links between Spanish American literature and Spain, thus closing his volume with a paean to Alfonso Reyes, whose links to the fatherland and devotion to Spanish literature are well-known.

José J. Arrom, a Cuban, wrote his *Esquema generacional de las letras hispanoamericanas* at Yale, where he was professor of Spanish American literature for over thirty years. It is the most explicit of the histories concerning its historiographic point of departure. Arrom, a disciple of Henríquez Ureña not only in the details of his methodology, but in the overall objective of his book, which is to discover the peculiarities of Spanish American expression, follows a generational method, as his title proclaims. He claims that he follows in this Henríquez Ureña, who had divided his history in generations lasting thirty years, without explicitly saying so. Arrom, a critic of Anderson Imbert (and Menéndez y Pelayo), takes for granted much of what had been polemical in the origins of Spanish American historiography, mainly the overall unity of Spanish American literature, stating that the only problem is to find a chronological unit to organize the mass of literature that has accumulated during four centuries of creation. As is obvious, he also assumes that the colonial period is part of Spanish American literature. It is clear that Arrom's application of the generation method is far too mechanical, and seeks precision sometimes by invoking different categories of events: for instance, the publication of a book and the moment when it was written. The method also assumes that all of Spanish American history, not just literature, moves at the same thirty-year pace. Arrom falls into the trap that Anderson Imbert had warned against in his prologue, when he says that "excessive regularity [in periodization] would indicate that the historian, through his great desire to embellish his vision, is allowing himself to be carried along by symmetries and metaphors" (*A History*, 17). The failings of the *Esquema* are most obvious in periods of either very little or too much production, where Arrom either has to give undue relevance to very obscure works, or force the material into a strait-jacket. Furthermore, as opposed to Henríquez Ureña, whose familiarity with European literatures allowed him to place Spanish American literature in a vast context, Arrom's generational method makes Spanish American literature seem autarchic and self-generated, a quality that it most certainly does not have. There is a stifling academicism in the *Esquema*, as if books had been piled on separate tables in a library and organized according to their author's dates. In addition, Arrom is weakest as a critic when it comes to the modern period, particularly after *Modernismo*, when Spanish American literature is at its most cosmopolitan. The *Esquema* is, in fact, inimical to modern Spanish American literature; its ideological underpinning is to be found, ultimately, in a kind of nineteenth-century biologism.

Having said this, however, one must add that Arrom's *Esquema* is the best introduction to colonial letters available, and a major contribution to the study of the *Barroco de Indias*. There are many insights scattered also throughout other periods, but the chapters on colonial literature, which is the foundation of Arrom's project, are by far the best in the book. Although he follows Henríquez Ureña in the discussion of topics of

Spanish American letters that emerge in the sixteenth century, Arrom gives a fuller treatment to how Spaniards became Creoles, claiming explicitly that by the sixteenth century American literature was being written by people with an American perspective. This is really Arrom's boldest, and perhaps most productive argument in the *Esquema*: locating the origin of an American creative consciousness further back in history. This insight is most useful in its application to works of the *Barroco de Indias*, many of which are rescued from oblivion by Arrom's perspective: the excesses of American baroque aesthetics issue from the effort to incorporate American reality into European molds of expression. Arrom's discussion of poets like Bernardo de Balbuena and Hernando Domínguez Camargo are exemplary in this respect. Arrom's contribution to the study of what I call the colonial Baroque (see chapter 6 of this *History*) is substantial, and has been bolstered in the second edition of the *Esquema*. It is the most modern element of the book, the part that best links it to contemporary Spanish American literature.

No truly significant overall history of Spanish American literature has been published since Arrom's, by which I mean a work conceived from an explicit historiographic point of view that attempts to cover the sweep of Spanish American literature. This does not mean, of course, that the many partial attempts, or projects of such a history, published since the 1960s are of no value. The very existence of these books is, in and of itself, a historical fact of particular relevance. They reveal the increasing interest in Latin American literature both in Latin America and abroad. Recent developments, such as the so-called Boom of the Latin American novel and the Cuban Revolution, focused world attention on Latin American literature, drastically changing its own self-perception and that of those who write about it.

Although very insightful in its assessment of individual authors, Giuseppe Bellini's *Historia de la literatura hispanoamericana* is in part a re-write of a work published in the 1950s. Emiliano Díez-Echarri and José María Roca Franquesa's *Historia de la literatura española e hispanoamericana*, lavish in historical detail and bibliographic information, as well as beautifully written, provides the best integration of peninsular and American literatures. It is, unfortunately, often overlooked. Raimundo Lazo's *Historia de la literatura hispanoamericana* sees the colonial period of each region as precursor of national literatures and mixes history and literary history convincingly. It is also often ignored. Jean Franco's *An Introduction to Spanish American Literature* and her *Spanish American Literature Since Independence* (1973) circulated in the English-speaking world, where they profited from the sudden popularity of Latin American literature in the academic world. Luis Leal's *Breve historia de la literatura hispanoamericana* is a fine manual. Luis Iñigo Madrigal edited the collective *Historia de la literatura hispanoamericana,* a very uneven project beset by very poor copy-editing, while Cedomil Goic gathered critical fragments on significant authors and movements in his *Historia y crítica de la literatura hispanoamericana.* Both of these books give proof of the prominence achieved by Spanish American literature in Spain, where several chairs on the subject have been created in the past twenty-five years.

Paramount among the more ambitious historiographic projects are Octavio Paz's *Los hijos del limo: Del romanticismo a la vanguardia* [*Children of the Mire*] which, like Henríquez Ureña's *Literary Currents* was the product of the Charles Eliot Norton lectures at Harvard, this time in 1972, and Emir Rodríguez Monegal's *Borzoi Anthology of Latin America Literature: From the time of Columbus to the twentieth century,* compiled by the Uruguayan critic while he was a professor at Yale. Like Franco's, the *Anthology* is fundamentally a pedagogical tool conceived to take advantage of the sudden popularity of Latin American literature in the English-speaking world. It does cover the full range of Latin American literature, including Brazil. Director of the influential magazine *Mundo Nuevo,* published in Paris during late 1960s, Rodríguez Monegal played a role similar to that of the compilers of anthologies in the nineteenth century. Like his predecessors, Rodríguez Monegal's center of operations was Paris, from which his magazine helped bring about the Boom of the Latin American novel, a movement of continental dimensions and aspirations that had a tremendous impact on the criticism of Latin American literature as a whole. The most important was to endow Latin American writers, as well as those who write about Latin American literature, with a sense of the prominence and relevance of that literature. Latin American literature is no longer seen as the poor cousin of Spanish literature, or as a mere reflection of European literatures, hopelessly out of pace with developments in the centers of culture. There is no need, in other words, to apologize for the quality of Spanish American literary works, as Anderson Imbert had done. Latin Americans now feel that their literature is one of the leading world literatures, perhaps the only one to enjoy a truly international currency. While this attitude prevails mostly among writers of narrative prose, there is a chain reaction that affects poetry, the essay, and even drama, in decreasing proportion. The last thirty years have seen four Nobel Prizes from Spanish America: Miguel Angel Asturias (Guatemala), Pablo Neruda (Chile), Gabriel García Márquez (Colombia), and Octavio Paz (Mexico). Two poets and two novelists have attained that ultimate recognition, but many felt that Alejo Carpentier (Cuba), and above all Jorge Luis Borges (Argentina), deserved the prize, and today many clamor for Carlos Fuentes (Mexico), and Mario Vargas Llosa (Peru). Yet this is only the tip of the iceberg. Latin American writers have won numerous prizes in the past thirty years, and their books, both in the original and in translation, have sold as never before. In addition, important literary journals have devoted countless special issues to Latin American literature or to individual Latin American writers, chairs have been founded at prestigious universities to study it. In short, because of the international character of the Boom, the history of Latin American literature could no longer be conceived as a self-enclosed development, a genealogy leading from Rómulo Gallegos to Gabriel García Márquez, or from Rubén Darío to Octavio Paz. It became evident that Latin American literature was produced at the crossroads of all the major modern literary traditions. This is reflected in the construction as well as the tone of Rodríguez Monegal's *Anthology*.

Paz's *Children of the Mire* deals only with poetry, but his formulation is capacious enough to encompass the whole of Spanish American literature. His point of departure is that modern poetry is created against modernity, meaning against the rationalist claims that issue from the Enlightenment. Yet, since, as he believes, there was no Enlightenment in the Hispanic world, romantic poetry, the foundation of modern literature, was necessarily hollow. The Romantics, Paz claims, had nothing to oppose. There is no significant Romanticism in Spanish, hence modern poetry does not really begin until *Modernismo* and the Avant-Garde. Paz's premises are refuted in this *History* in Andrew Bush's chapter on eighteenth- and nineteenth-century Spanish American poetry, and books such as Flitter's furnish evidence that also raises questions about them. Be that as it may, what is indisputable is that, by denying the Romantics as precursors, Paz and other current Spanish American writers then reach further back to the Baroque as their origin. If this is an enabling fiction, a literary myth, so be it, the important matter is that at this point in Spanish American literary history, the Baroque is perceived as a more current, vibrant, and present origin than Romanticism. Work by Bush and others on the eighteenth and nineteenth centuries – a field in dire need of a reassessment that Paz really did not carry out – is likely to change that perception in the near future. Yet as a historiographic project, Paz's, like Rodríguez Monegal's, reflects the yearning of Spanish American writers for an origin as close to the beginning as possible, to recover the works of colonial writers and rewrite them from a modern perspective. Ironically, this is a very romantic kind of project, very much akin to what the European Romantics did with the Middle Ages.

A different sort of project emerged during the past thirty years, given impetus above all by the Cuban Revolution; first by its triumphs, later by the propaganda efforts of the regime in the cultural realm on a continent-wide scale. This venture was to write a social history of Spanish American literature, one that, from a Marxist perspective, would see that history as the result of the social praxis of the elites, that is, of the groups that produced that literature. Alejandro Losada, Ana Pizarro, and others, published interesting prolegomena to this endeavor, but no history has emerged, except for scattered, and very partial efforts. The most successful among these was Angel Rama's *La ciudad letrada*, which, particularly in the modern period, establishes interesting connections between the "lettered" (enlightened) elites and the production of literature. But Rama, who did not even live to see this essay into print, had no time to develop fully what would have needed years of research. One wonders about the fate of all these projects in the wake of the collapse of Communism in eastern Europe and the Soviet Union, and the general discredit of Marxism.

Perhaps, given the enormous growth of the field, it is impossible to write a history of Spanish American literature as a continuous narrative from a single methodological point of view. The embarrassment of riches brought about by extensive and intensive study of Spanish American literature has, paradoxically, made such a project impossible. It could very well also be that literary history as a narrative form is already obsolete, particularly when dealing with such a variegated phenomenon as Spanish American literature. Current methodological fashions make it seem unlikely that a history such as Arrom's or Anderson Imbert's will again be written. I, for one, do not believe that prose and poetry are chronologically compatible, and have tried a different approach when attempting a history of the Latin American narrative (*Myth and Archive*). What I observe around me as I write these pages seems to indicate that others feel the same.

In the case of the present history, our aim has been to produce, by using a patchwork of differing approaches, a kind of present-state of Latin American literary historiography.

2

Cultures in contact: Mesoamerica, the Andes, and the European written tradition
Rolena Adorno

The range of texts and traditions to be considered here corresponds ultimately to the interpretive responses made by native American cultures to life under colonialism. Without colonialism from Europe, there would not exist this *corpus* of cultural productions, "written down" in alphabetic script in various languages. Without the inclusion of native American voices and related subject positions (such as those taken by *mestizo* writers), there can be no full history of colonial Spanish American culture as manifest in the spoken and written word. "Cultures in contact" is thus the point of departure from which we begin this essay on indigenous American cultural expression after 1492.

Introduction: Cultures in contact

> But, we,
> what now, immediately, will we say?
> Supposing that we, we are those who
> shelter the people,
> we are mothers to the people, we are
> fathers to the people,
> perchance, then, are we, here before you,
> to destroy it, the ancient law;
> the one which was greatly esteemed
> by our grandparents, our women;
> the one which they would go speaking of
> favorably,
> the one which they would go admiring,
> the lords, the speakers?
> (Klor de Alva, "The Aztec–Spanish
> dialogues [1524]," 107–8)

These words represent one of the earliest examples of the cultural traditions to be considered here. Like most of those to be studied, this passage reconstructs an earlier formulation. Set down in 1564 by Fray Bernardino de Sahagún and his four Nahua collaborators, Antonio Valeriano, Antonio Vegerano, Martín Iacobita, and Andrés Leonardo, these words recalled a dialogue which was to have taken place in 1524 between the first twelve Franciscan friars in New Spain and the elders and priests of the Mexica (Aztec) people. Like many of such reformulations, the historicity of this one is coming to be accepted (León-Portilla, *Coloquios y doctrina del México antiguo*, 23–5). Let us return to the account as the Aztec lords and elders convene to prepare a response:

> Then, immediately, thus, they held a dialogue with
> one another,
> for a very long time, the discourse itself was made with
> great care,
> two times, three times, the words were made to be heard
> by the ones who offer incense,
> just as the divine guardians say them.
> And those who heard this were
> greatly disturbed,
> greatly saddened,
> as if they had fallen and were scared,
> frightened.
> However, then when the word had been born,
> and after the discourse was unified,
> it was resolved that the next day
> all the men would go together,
> would go assembled before the face
> of the twelve divine guardians.
> (Klor de Alva, "The Aztec–Spanish
> dialogues," 112–13)

The scene sums up the pertinent aspects of the present essay: the keepers of the ancient word of European and Amerindian cultural traditions come together. Military and political power is on the side of one, but it cannot overcome the cultural and spiritual authority of the other. The anguish produced by the confrontation between the old gods and the new Christian deity results first in a private discussion among the Aztec learned men (*tlamatinime*) and then a public response offered to the Franciscan friars. Having conferred until "the word had been born" and "the discourse unified," the "knowers of the word" went "before the face of the twelve divine guardians" (Klor de Alva, 'The Aztec–Spanish dialogues," 108, 112–13). In this idealized setting, we hear the learned voices of pre-Columbian native tradition, of those who "cause the book to cackle; the black, the color is in the paintings they continually carry" (pp. 109–10).

While Sahagún and his collaborators succeeded in recreating that initial moment when the native lords came into contact with foreign ideas and ideologies, most of the cultural productions that occupy us here reflect subsequent moments during the long colonial period of cultural coexistence. This situation was perhaps first best described by a native Mexican lord in a conversation with Fray Diego Durán. Durán recalls how he had reprimanded the presumably Christian gentleman for sponsoring a native wedding feast that was both expensive and pagan. The native quickly replied, "Father, do not be astonished! We are still *nepantla*!" (*Historia de las Indias de Nueva España*, II, 268). On inquiring of his interlocutor to which "in the middle" he referred by the use of that particular "word and metaphor," the latter replied to Durán that he meant that the post-Conquest Mexica were still "neutral," neither fully devoted to one religion nor the other, and, in effect, participating in both.

This image of *nepantlism*, defined by León-Portilla as the "situation in which a person remains suspended in the middle between a lost or disfigured past and a present that has not been assimilated or understood" (Klor de Alva, "Spiritual conflict and accommodation in New Spain," 353), should be kept in mind in the discussion that follows. As recent scholarship has shown (see León-Portilla, "Testimonios nahuas sobre la conquista espiritual"; Klor de Alva, "Spiritual conflict"; Adorno, *Guaman Poma*; MacCormack, "Pachacuti"), characterizing these polycultural works as evidence of cultural syncretism (the production of a harmonious whole which is quite different from *nepantlism*) is often misleading. Thus, our own summary of the cultural domain to be studied is as follows:

Produced in the colonial period, most often with reference to the pre-Columbian, and created by individuals who preserved and communicated their native traditions through recourse to the foreign, the traditions under consideration here bring together diverse cultural formulations and symbolizing activities both oral and written. Diverse systems of thought and expression come together in these cultural productions yet the resultant reformulations of native experience tend not so much to resolve tension or conflict between the donor cultures as to create new cultural syntheses whose hallmark is the uneasy coexistence of their diverse and sometimes contradictory components.

What kind of cultural production? What kind of history?

In the 1880s, Daniel G. Brinton was among the first to pioneer the consideration of indigenous American cultural expression as literature. Under the title, "The Library of Aboriginal American Literatures," he published a series of Amerindian texts and studies which he anticipated with a monograph entitled *Aboriginal American Authors and their*

productions. . . .a chapter in the history of literature. A century later, we
are still concerned with the issues raised by Brinton, and the current
interest in treating colonial native American cultural productions as
literature has stemmed, for Mesoamerica, from the monumental work of
Garibay (*Historia de la literatura nahuatl*) and León-Portilla (*Literaturas
precolombinas de México; Literatura del México antiguo*), and, for Peru
(used here in its colonial sense, meaning most of Spanish South America),
by Arguedas (*Tupac Amaru; Dioses y hombres*), Farfán (*Poesía folklórica
quechua; El drama quechua Apu Ollantay*), and Lara (*La tragedia del fin
de Atawallpa; La literatura de los quechuas*). The literary conceptualization of verbal cultural productions has constituted an essential step in
their valorization by our own Euroamerican post-industrial culture. (This
kind of appreciation stands quite apart from the privilege that colonial
native documents have enjoyed for their contributions to historical and
anthropological studies.)

By this date, however, these cultural productions have been validated as
worthy of appreciation within a wider, interdisciplinary purview which
construes cultural studies and the reconstruction of colonial cultural
history in a more comprehensive, more complex light. As a rubric under
which to work, "literature" lately has left investigators uncomfortable,
for it tends to limit study to a set of criteria and questions best suited to the
belletristic production of classical and biblical Western traditions. Thus,
"literature" as a descriptive or analytical designation has paled in its
usefulness and we can acknowledge that "literature," as an eighteenth-
century concept, regionally localized to the Mediterranean world of
Greco-Roman and Judeo-Christian traditions (see Mignolo, "La lengua,
la letra, el territorio,"), accommodates a field of creative activity and
critical reflection different from, and only loosely related to, the ones
considered here.

If, however, we set aside the content of the specific Western *corpus* to
which the term "literature" has been applied definitively, and consider
instead the principles of reflection and interpretation by which a culture
comes to understand itself through verbalizing, symbolizing activities,
then we see that the traditions examined here do have something in
common with the literary. A pertinent qualification regarding such an
assessment concerns the fact that that which is defined as "literary" is so
determined by the participants of a culture from within its own confines.
From within the cultural system of post-industrial Western societies, we
can recognize the great historical, dramatic, novelistic, and lyrical
interpretations of our own culture. It is difficult if not impossible to
recognize such understandings by cultures vastly different from our own,
such as those native to the Americas. Thus, when we say "this is not
literature" about the *Popol Vuh*, we need to be very clear that we are
rejecting it for membership within a specific historical–cultural *corpus*

constituted by the Greco-Roman and Judeo-Christian traditions, and not that we are excluding it from the great achievements of humanity's collective interpretations of diverse and regional cultural experience. It is in this latter sense that the present essay is pertinent to a "history of Latin American literature."

In this discussion, the native American cultural traditions, known only through being preserved in writing in colonial times, are seen as complementary, not as antecedent, to the development of Latin American literature. In the past, the legacy of pre-Columbian Amerindian expression has been emblematized (but not established) as a precursor to the foundational literature of Spanish America. In contrast, the position taken here is that the preservation of the legacy of ancient native culture is of necessity a polycultural and colonial phenomenon. Therefore, it reveals not the pre-Columbian past but rather the processes of cultural exchange in colonial times. The present account does not portray indigenous American culture as being absorbed into the European, but rather as one of native adaptation, survival, and innovation in a complex polycultural environment.

The problem of terminology is immediate, and the familiar designation "text" for these complex cultural productions seems appropriate. Because of its root meaning "to weave," it is perhaps etymologically more compatible with the oral utterance (Ong, *Orality and literacy*, 13) at the same time as it suggests the integration of diverse cultural formulations and various types of symbolizing activities.

What kinds of questions are being asked of these texts? These verbal "weavings" submit themselves to only some of the questions posed to the *belles lettres* tradition. Certain philological and textual concerns are pertinent, such as the establishment of texts, questions of sources and influences, the internal relations of a text in its parts. Depending on the particular textual types analyzed, the application of Western literary models has only occasionally helped in the comprehension of the internal mechanisms of hybrid cultural production. Instead, an emphasis on the production of these texts is reorienting our pursuits. By reconstructing the circumstances of the creation of these cultural expressions, and by examining the purposes for which they were written, we can evaluate more effectively the evidence of the intersection of native American cultures and the European written tradition. Insofar as we consider text-based activities as constitutive (rather than merely reflective) of social practices, the written and transcribed texts of collective or individual authorship can teach us a great deal about the interpenetration of European and Amerindian culture in the colonial period. It is cultural history in this fuller sense to which this complement to literary history, and literary history itself, can contribute.

Authorship and its agendas

All of the cultural productions examined here are elite when not sacred in content and the individuals who produced them likewise were elite in perspective and/or training. In the latter instance, "elite" need not refer to the social status of the individual within the traditional native hierarchy but rather the access to the institutions (such as written culture) of colonial society. From the point of view of their reception, therefore, these texts studied in their own right pertain more to intellectual and cultural than to social history.

As noted at the outset, it is impossible to consider native traditions in colonial times without taking into account the interaction of indigenous American elites with the European clergy. Alphabetic writing and native tradition came together as writing was used as an institution of colonialism to account for and manage native societies, eradicate their traditional spiritual practices, and evangelize the native peoples. Paradoxically, this implementation of written culture to suppress the native heritage also worked to preserve its noblest fruits. In Mexico, Fray Bernardino de Sahagún's lifelong efforts produced one of the world's most monumental studies of a sixteenth-century society; in Peru, the *criollo* priest Francisco de Avila's compilation of native traditions, written for the purpose of eradicating them, produced the magnificent account of Andean spiritual life and belief contained in the *Runa yndio ñiscap machoncuna*, better known as the manuscript from Huarochirí. The very preservation (and destruction) of native Amerindian cultural expression was made possible from the first by the European clergy. Any full consideration of our topic requires the study of the missionary writers. See Cline (*Guide to Ethnohistorical Sources*) for a summary and annotated bibliography of religious chroniclers and historians writing on the native cultures of Mesoamerica and the 1986 Pease edition of Porras Barrenechea (*Los cronistas del Perú, 1528–1650*) for the same on colonial Peru.

For missionary inquiries into native tradition, the collaboration of native informants was essential. Quite often, it was the ethnic lords and their heirs who became bilingual informants. In Mexico, many were trained by friars in institutions such as the Colegio de la Santa Cruz de Santiago Tlaltelolco, founded by the Franciscans (see Garibay, *Historia*); in Peru, *colegios* for the sons of native lords were organized by the Jesuits (see Albó, "Jesuitas y culturas indígenas"). There were many routes by which natives became competent in the language of the conquerors and therefore became known as *indios ladinos*. In 1611, Covarrubias (*Tesoro de la lengua*, 747) defined as being *ladino* the outsider ("*al morisco y al estrangero*") who was so competent in Castilian that he would not be taken for a foreigner and who was remarkably prudent and shrewd in all his dealings. *Indio ladino* became the term used for all natives – whether ethnic lord or highway vagabond – who mastered the colonial language; the social types and individuals who came to be called *indio ladino* are many and varied and have not been systematically studied.

On learning reading and writing, native individuals became scribes as well as oral interpreters (see Solano "El intérprete"). In such circumstances, the independent native use of writing came into existence and yielded two variant types of written expression which were sometimes mutually exclusive, and occasionally overlapped. On the one hand, there were efforts to communicate the interests of native society to its foreign overlords (*relaciones* and chronicles written in Spanish) and, on the other, initiatives were taken to preserve the native heritage from foreign intrusion (the Maya language texts set down in Roman alphabet, such as the *Popol Vuh* and the *Books of Chilam Balam* of the Quiché and Yucatec Maya, respectively).

How oral and hieroglyphic (pictogram, ideogram) written traditions were transformed when recorded in alphabetic writing is one of the major areas of investigation pertinent to the types of cultural interaction of interest here. See Gruzinski (*La Colonisation de l'imaginaire*) for a study of the impact of written culture on the traditional arts of record-keeping and remembrance in colonial Mexico; Mignolo ("Anahuac y sus otros") for a theoretical formulation of the study of early colonial, mixed oral/written traditions; Scharlau and Münzel (*Qellgay*), Scharlau ("Mündliche überlieferung-Schriftlich gefasst"; "Escrituras en contacto"), and Scharlau (ed.) (*Bild-Wort-Schrift*) for these processes of cultural transformation in colonial Peru as well as Mexico.

With the exception of those texts which do not take native American experience and culture as their object (see Garibay, *Historia*, II, 222–33), the surviving texts of the Spanish/American encounter include these characteristics: (1) the imperative to preserve the knowledge of the native culture, marginalized, denigrated, or forced into a clandestine existence, (2) the expression of bitterness over the destruction of native cultural monuments, (3) the elaboration of prophecy, both to explain present historical circumstances and to anticipate an uncertain future, (4) the rise of messianic movements, preserved as prophecies promising the overthrow of foreign domination and restoration of the traditional order, (5) the reformulation of ethnic history in the attempt to recover it, and (6) the effort to make sense of conflicting spiritual beliefs and ideologies, usually leaving the contradictions unresolved. See Luce López-Baralt ("Crónica de la destrucción de un mundo"), Salomon ("Chronicles of the impossible"), Adorno ("La *ciudad letrada*") for more detailed accounts and a comparison of native American and Spanish *morisco* literary responses to efforts to suppress their cultures.

The question of orality

A prominent consideration in the study of these Spanish American cultural traditions is the coexistence of the oral and the written. The current debates on the nature and development of literacy (Jack Goody, Brian V. Street), underscore the scholarly difficulty of apprehending the truly oral culture as well as that of evaluating the oral residue in written documents.

From our own perspective as members of written cultures, it is easy to underestimate the power of human speech in its ritual and formal uses. Testimony pertaining to the pre-Columbian era in the writings of early colonial times allows us to reorient our understanding. For example, the *Códice Matritense* describes the ideal Nahuatl narrator or *tlaquetzqui* as one who "says things with the spirit, the lips and the mouth of an artist": "The good narrator...has flowers on his lips. His speech overflows with advice, flowers come from his mouth." The bad narrator, meanwhile, "says useless words, he is without dignity" (León-Portilla, *Precolumbian Literatures*, 27–8). The *huehuehtlahtolli* discourses ("speeches of the elders") preserved in written form attest to the role that formal, oral speech played as the source of learning and training for life in Nahua society. The transcriptions of Yucatec Maya *katun* prophecies reveal that wanton, irresponsible speech was considered one of the primary constituents of a society in the process of degeneration and disintegration (Roys, "The Maya Katun prophecies," 24). The *Popol Vuh* tells us that, among the Quiché Maya, the ancient word (sacred speech) was the potential and source for everything done in their land (D. Tedlock, *Popol Vuh*, 71). In the Andes, native chroniclers ascribed the obedience of the ancient Andeans to the first Inca to the remarkable powers of speech of Manco Capac and Mama Ocllo (El Inca Garcilaso de la Vega, *Obras completas*, II, 27–8; Guaman Poma, *Nueva crónica*, 81).

One of the issues concerning the relationship of orality to the written tradition, and orality as the mediator between the hieroglyphic and alphabetic traditions of writing, is that of the presumed transition from oral to written expression. Although it is often assumed that the written tradition supplanted learned oral traditions and hieroglyphic writing, the evidence shows that well into the seventeenth century (Roys, *The Book of Chilam Balam*, 3–5) and in some cases to the nineteenth, traditional modes of preserving and creating knowledge endured.

The preservation in writing of single recitations of hieroglyphic texts or performances of oral discourses is one of the fundamental accomplishments of Spanish missionary, native American, and *mestizo* writers. The manner of transcribing and translating these texts varied. Among the lowland Yucatec Maya, for example, literal renderings of the content of glyphs were common; in existing books of *Chilam Balam*, sections of prose are literal glyphic translations (Roys, *The Book of Chilam Balam*, 5). Among the highland Maya, however, narrative glosses were more frequent. As Dennis Tedlock (*Popol Vuh*, 32) pointed out in his discussion of how the representatives of the three lordly lineages of Q'umaraqaj (Utatlán) created a written text of the *Popol Vuh*, a glyph-by-glyph translation would have resulted in "a text that would have made little sense to anyone but a fully trained diviner and performer." Instead, the writers quoted what a reader of the ancient text would have said when giving a "long performance," narrating the story that lay behind the signs of the hieroglyphic text (D. Tedlock, *Popol Vuh*, 32). The preservation of such performances, frozen in time and set in writing, often conceal rather than reveal the fundamental features of oral traditions. On this point, Dennis Tedlock (*The Spoken Word*, 13, 19) has offered the crucial insight that oral traditions are not to be characterized by the apparently monologic quality of the single performance but rather by the situation of their utterance within a much larger dialogue.

A further problem of "writing down" oral transcriptions concerns metrical form. More recent views argue that maximum fidelity to compositions from non-European cultures is best achieved by trying to reproduce the units of the original composition rather than imposing versification criteria from the European tradition. This stance acknowledges the limitations of European literary paradigms for analyzing native American verbal productions (see León-Portilla in Edmonson [ed.], *Supplement*).

The relative value to be assigned to written and orally transcribed sources is an important issue in the works under consideration here. A common bias in scholarship has been to consider the unwritten to be mythical when the mythic is taken to be the fictional and false ("not literally true"). For example, native chronicle accounts have previously been judged as fanciful because they contradicted, or were not corroborated by, European sources. Today scholars are finding that these accounts describe events and perceptions that were simply unnoticed or unshared by European participants or their eventual historians (Recinos, *Crónicas indígenas*; MacCormack, "Atahualpa y el libro"). This is but one area in which assumptions about the status of the oral versus the written are under serious reconsideration.

Time: past in the present

The theme of "Time: past in the present" has two manifestations: one concerns the fact that early colonial writings about past native traditions and history were intimately involved with the interests of the present. The other implies the conceptualization of time itself in these writings, and these problems include: the relationship of the temporal to the atemporal, that of different concepts of time (the linear versus the cyclical), and, finally, the relationship of the concept of time to that of space.

Although many of these cultural productions are retrospective in content, the concern for the present – for explaining the present on the basis of the past – is an abiding preoccupation in all of them. Often these works have been characterized as nostalgic recollections for a past irretrievably lost. Although such observations and characterizations may also be true, they tend to distort rather than elucidate the evidence at hand. Ethnographic and historical research as well as textual studies have revealed that native writings such as dynastic histories and genealogies had immediate practical objectives (see González Echevarría "José Arrom"; Farriss, *Maya Society under Colonial Rule*, 246–7; Adorno, *Guaman Poma*). Overall, the Meso- and Andean American chronicles, *títulos* and *relaciones* can be seen within the larger purview of the Spanish legal system and the *probanzas de méritos y servicios* that absorbed the attention of all claimants to property and prerogatives.

As the basic coordinates of human experience, the concepts of time and space are the most difficult to understand cross-culturally. In colonial texts of pre-Hispanic heritage, the question is not simply one of isolating or identifying the autochthonous American concepts but also determining the degree to which they are adapted to European chronology. As Frank Salomon has pointed out in his study of native Peruvian chroniclers ("Chronicles," 9), "the root of the conflict. . .within indigenous chronicles is the difference between Andean and European assumptions about the relation of the historical and the atemporal."

The study of the texts discussed here requires that we cease to separate myth and history into discrete categories and instead entertain the possibility of their convergence. As we see them, there exist the atemporal world of the gods and the temporal world of humanity. Nevertheless, the *Popol Vuh* and the Huarochirí traditions teach us that Maya and Andean conceptualizations of the two spheres were, as Dennis Tedlock (*Popol Vuh*, 63) put it for the *Popol Vuh*, "complementary rather than opposed, interpenetrating rather than mutually exclusive."

On the common dichotomy of linear versus cyclical time, we cannot assume that a pure concept of cyclical time overwhelmed any notion of linearity, as studies of both the highland Maya and the Quechua traditions show (D. Tedlock, *Popol Vuh*; Salomon, "Chronicles"). As a way of conceiving Amerindian notions of time in general, it is best to think of the geometric figures of neither the circle nor the straight line, but rather of that of the helix: a curving, spiraling line that never runs over its previous path but reiterates its basic movement. That is, time and experience were not expected to repeat themselves precisely; meanwhile, the burdens of time were accumulated rather than replaced (B. Tedlock, *Time and the Highland Maya*, 176–7; D. Tedlock, *Popol Vuh*, 64; Salomon, "Chronicles," 10–11). "One cannot erase time," her Quiché teacher announced to Barbara Tedlock (*Time*, 177), who notes that even successive creations and cataclysmic destructions of the world described in the *Popol Vuh* were not analytically compartmentalized, but that, rather, each age retained heritages from all previous ages. In this way, the investigation of events from another time involved a dialectic between the unique or the linear and the cyclical or the repeated (B. Tedlock, *Time*, 177).

We see from the Quiché example that the search for pattern and meaning did not deny but in fact made possible the assimilation of information that extended beyond the confines of the particular autochthonous world and its historical and cultural experience (D. Tedlock, *Popol Vuh*, 64; Roys, *Book of Chilam Balam*, 3–4; Szemiński, "Las generaciones," 105–6). The prophecies of the arrival of far-away peoples found in indigenous and missionary accounts of post-Conquest tradition are an appropriate example of this phenomenon. Taken, even recently, as proof of the rigidity of autochthonous American cultural tradition (Todorov, *The Conquest of America*), these post-Conquest testimonies, apart from their emphasis and exaggeration by Europeans, may be interpreted as an indication of the ability to incorporate and integrate that which was new and foreign. Early colonial writings – from Mayan codices to Peruvian chronicles – evidence this accumulative, improvisational, and adaptive quality.

Another fundamental consideration is the relatedness of concepts of time and space in Mesoamerican and Andean traditions. As Burkhart (*The Slippery Earth*, 72) observes for Mesoamerica, "time cannot be divorced from space. Spatial distance correlated with distance in time." Again, there are significant differences in European and Amerindian assumptions about these relationships. These differences lead us in general to simplify and make rigid the extraordinarily complex aspects of Amerindian time–space relationships. Yet the homology between time and space occurs not at the level of isolated units but at those of general principles of organization (Wachtel, *Sociedad e ideología*, 182). All in all, time–space and history–myth relationships for the pre-Columbian and post-Conquest Amerindian tended, as the Tedlocks (B. Tedlock, *Time*; D. Tedlock, *Popol Vuh*) have concluded, more toward integration rather than separation, accumulation rather than substitution, and interpenetration rather than exclusivity. For Mesoamerica, see Caso, *El pueblo del sol*; León-Portilla, *Aztec Thought and Culture*; B. Tedlock, *Time*; D. Tedlock, *Popol Vuh*; Burkhart, *The Slippery Earth*. For the Andes: Ossio,

Ideología mesiánica; Wachtel, *Sociedad e ideología*; Salomon, "Chronicles"; Szemiński, "De la imagen de Wiraqucan"; *Un Kuraca*.

The four major culture areas

For the purposes of this essay, the colonial native cultural traditions of four geographical–cultural areas will be studied: the Nahua of Central Mexico, the Yucatec Maya of the lowland Maya area, the Quiché Maya of the Maya highlands, and the Quechua of the South American Andes. For Mesoamerica, the areas to be considered follow the divisions made in the *Handbook of Middle American Indians* in its census of Middle American prose manuscripts in the native historical tradition (Gibson and Glass in Cline *et al* [eds.] *Guide...Part Four*). The reader should consult the *Handbook* for Northern and Western Mexico (the Tarascan tradition of Michoacán), Oaxaca, and Central America. Brinton's 1883 study of the dance-drama *The Güegüense* is an appropriate point of departure for the study of that Nahuatl-Mangue tradition of Nicaragua. For the Andes, we consider the major Quechua traditions. For the Circum-Caribbean region, the voices of the native peoples are best heard in the *Relación acerca de las antigüedades de los indios* of Fray Ramón Pané (see Arrom, *Mitología*, Pané, *Relación*, and M. López-Baralt, *El mito taíno*). Colonial/native traditions for Brazil are studied in another volume of this *History*.

The differences among the colonial traditions of the Nahuas, the highland and lowland Mayas, and the Quechua-speaking Andeans are striking. In the two great colonial centers of Mexico and Peru, seats of the Aztec and Inca imperial cultures that flourished at the time of the Spanish invasion, we find an abundance of native and native-inspired texts designed precisely to communicate with the dominant society. Occupying a position outside the two great centers of colonial power, both the highland Quiché and lowland Yucatec Mayas developed written colonial traditions apart from and in defiance to the foreign society of the colonizers.

Between the Nahua and the Andean peoples, there is still another significant contrast. In the central valley of Mexico, the Nahuas produced, thanks to the impetus of Franciscan schooling, an impressive *corpus* of intellectual work, mostly concerned with the preservation of pre-Columbian history and culture. In Peru, on the other hand, we find a mere handful of attributed and anonymous works, yet among them are texts of extraordinary complexity and richness.

Accounting for all the differences mentioned above is beyond the scope of the present essay. Taking note of the differences serves to remind us, however, of the diversity of colonial cultures produced out of the interaction over time of a single European power with the vastly different cultural areas of Mesoamerica and the Andes, within each of which there existed considerable regional differences.

Although cultural production of the early colonial period, roughly 1525–1650, will be emphasized, some of the traditions to be considered only became known to Europeans in subsequent centuries (such as the eighteenth-century discovery and copy of the *Popol Vuh* made by the Spanish priest Francisco Ximénez), and the practice and performance of some traditions (such as Guatemalan dance-dramas) continue to the present day.

Since it is impossible here to give each area of cultural production its due, the liberally given bibliographic recommendations should be taken as an essential feature of each brief account.

The Nahua tradition

After a two-year war waged by Spanish and native allied forces under Hernán Cortés ended in the defeat of the Aztec confederation (the Triple Alliance), Spanish sovereignty was asserted in the Central Valley of Mexico in 1521. Shortly thereafter, the Mendicant orders, that is, the Franciscans (1523–1524), the Dominicans (1526), and the Augustinians (1533), established themselves to evangelize the native peoples (Ricard, *The Spiritual Conquest of Mexico*, 2–3). Religious schools were founded early, starting with that of the Flemish friar Pedro de Gante in 1523. Of singular importance was the foundation of the Colegio de la Santa Cruz de Santiago Tlaltelolco, opened on January 6, 1536.

The richest and most varied of the written traditions under consideration here is that of the Nahuatl-speaking peoples of Central Mexico. The introduction of alphabetic writing fomented the conservation of Nahuatl culture and the development of an extraordinary written tradition in Nahuatl that extended through the entire colonial period. In the sixteenth century, the activity of the friars helped to produce a bi- or trilingual class of learned Nahuatl-speakers whose literary and historiographic pursuits, in Spanish, Nahuatl, and sometimes Latin, have come to constitute a considerable written tradition. Garibay (*Historia*) offers the most comprehensive account of the written cultural productions of authors of Nahua background and an important survey of primary texts and translations. Part 2 of his work, covering the period 1521–1750, is relevant for the work of the missionary friars and native scholars, covering genres from the religious–didactic to the historical and taking into account the immense linguistic and cultural labors of translation.

Established by the Franciscans for the sons of the Nahua elites, the goal of the Colegio de Tlaltelolco was to educate the lordly classes in the European manner. Without access to the Roman Catholic priesthood, however, these well-educated nobles had few outlets for their learning. With its European teachers and Mexican students (eventual teachers), the Colegio was central to colonial intellectual life based on the interpenetration of Spanish and Nahua culture. The full history of the Colegio's work, its teachers and students, development and decline (by mid-century), remains to be written. The reader is invited to consult, however, Baudot, *Utopía*; Borgia Steck, *El primer colegio*; Duverger, *La conversion des Indiens*; Garibay, *Historia*, II, 215–20; Ocaranza, *El imperial colegio*; Ricard, *Spiritual Conquest*. See León-Portilla, *Los franciscanos*, for sixteenth-century Nahua views of Franciscan activity.

Of the cultural productions in Nahuatl and Spanish surveyed by Garibay, the portion best documented and studied to date is that of the historical tradition (Gibson, and Glass in Cline *et al.*, *Guide...Part Four*). In Mexico there were a number of historical writers in the native tradition. Most notable are Hernando Alvarado Tezozomoc (active 1598–early seventeenth century), Fernando de Alva Ixtlilxóchitl (*c.* 1578–1648), Domingo Francisco de San Antón Muñón Chimalpain Quauhtle-huanitzin (b. 1579), Diego Muñoz Camargo (*c.* 1529–1599), and Juan Bautista de Pomar (active 1582). Each of these individuals related native history according to the perspective of his particular dynastic heritage, thus representing several of the basic ethnic divisions identified by Gibson (*The Aztecs*, 9, 21) for the Central Valley of Mexico at the time of the Spaniards' arrival.

Alvarado Tezozomoc was of Mexica (Aztec) descent; as the son of one of the *tlatoani* or lords of Tenochtitlán under the Spaniards and Francisca de Montezuma, he was a grandson of Montezuma II (Garibay, *Historia*, II, 299; Keen, *The Aztec Image*, 132). Tezozomoc left a major narrative account of the Mexica rise to power in the late fourteenth century to the Spanish conquest in his *Crónica mexicana* (1598); he wrote in Nahuatl the *Crónica Mexicayotl* in 1609 (Gibson and Glass in Cline *et al.*, *Guide ...Part Four*, 326). Juan Bautista de Pomar was a *mestizo* descendant of the pre-Conquest Acolhua rulers of Texcoco. His *Relación de Texcoco*, which was later known by Alva Ixtlilxóchitl, was written in response to the *relación geográfica* questionnaire of 1577 and is considered a major source on native deities and other aspects of pre-Columbian and colonial culture (Gibson and Glass in Cline *et al.*, *Guide...Part Four*, 355). Alva Ixtlilxóchitl was a descendant of the Acolhuaque, the lords of Texcoco, and left abundant accounts of Acolhua history in his *Historia chichimeca* and various *relaciones* in Spanish. Chimalpáin descended from the Chalcas and left detailed accounts of their history in his *relaciones*, written in Nahuatl (Gibson, *The Aztecs*, 15). Diego Muñoz Camargo's work represents the perspective of the Tlascalans, who inhabited an area northeast of the Central Valley of Mexico and were unconquered enemies of the Mexica. Muñoz Camargo was the son of the *conquistador* Diego Muñoz and a native woman; he married a noblewoman of Tlaxcala (Keen, *The Aztec Image*, 127) and wrote the *Historia de Tlaxcala* (late sixteenth century) which covers migration, dynastic history, and the Spanish conquest of Mexico with the help of Tlaxcalan allies (Gibson and Glass in Cline *et al.*, *Guide. . .Part Four*, 350–1).

Each of these authors, like their counterparts in Peru after the tenure of the Viceroy Francisco de Toledo (1569–1581), saw native history in the broad sweep, from the origins of the dynasty through Spanish domination. In every case, the retrieval of the past was undertaken to influence the present. These writers are currently the object of new and comprehensive study; for basic references now available see Garibay (*Historia*), Gibson and Glass (in Cline *et al.*, *Guide. . .Part Four*); for a summary of the dynastic histories contained in colonial texts, see Jiménez Moreno ("Síntesis").

Apart from the texts of native authorship, we find indirect but remarkable evidence of native attitudes and patterns of meaning in the writings of Spanish missionaries. In order of magnitude and for the conservation of Nahua cultural traditions, the lifelong work of the Franciscan friar Bernardino de Sahagún and his Nahua collaborators and informants is without peer. The works of Fray Andrés de Olmos, Fray Toribio de Benavente Motolinía, Fray Francisco de las Navas, Fray Diego Durán, Fray Jerónimo de Mendieta, and Fray Juan de Torquemada are also crucial. See Cline (ed.) *Guide. . .Part Two*, and Gibson (in Cline *et al.*, *Guide. . .Part Four*) for guides to this most important *corpus* and Baudot, *Utopía*, Edmonson (ed.) *Sixteenth-century Mexico*, Horcasitas, *El teatro nahuatl*, Klor de Alva *et al.* (eds.) *The Work of Bernardino de Sahagún* for relevant studies. Garibay (*Historia*), Jiménez Moreno ("La historiografía tetzcocana"), and Gibson and Glass (in Cline *et al.*, *Guide. . .Part Four*) classify by stages these sixteenth-century works of Spanish/Nahua collaboration. Works such as the *Anónimo franciscano de Culhuacán*, the *Relación de Michoacán*, the *Historia de los mexicanos por sus pinturas* should also be taken into account; see Gibson (in Cline *et al.*, *Guide. . .Part Four*).

Among the oral traditions of pre-Hispanic heritage preserved in written form, León-Portilla (in Edmonson [ed.] *Supplement*, 12, 20) identifies two major groupings which he significantly declines to equate with the European structures of prose and poetry: the *tlahtolli* ("word, discourse, narrative") and the *cuicatl* ("songs, hymns, words"). Within the *tlahtolli* class, which would include what we call "myths, legends, annals, chronicles, histories, and tales" (León-Portilla in Edmonson [ed.] *Supplement*, 20) are the *huehuehtlahtolli*, which consisted of exchanges between superior and subordinate (father and son, husband and wife, host and guest). Designed to teach Aztec values and good conduct, the *huehueht-lahtolli* were adapted to the teaching of Christian beliefs and remained an important native tradition throughout colonial times (see Gibson and Glass in Cline *et al.*, *Guide. . .Part Four*; Baudot, *Utopía*; Karttunen and Lockhart, *The Art of Nahuatl Speech*).

The other verbal art of pre-Columbian origin mentioned above was the *cuicatl*, "songs, hymns, poems," many of which were of sacred tradition, produced by the *cuicapicqui* or "songmakers" (León-Portilla in Edmonson, *Supplement*, 8). León-Portilla (in Edmonson, *Supplement*, 12–20) resolves the particular problems of paleographic transcription and translation of the *cuicatl* by resisting the temptation to divide the text into lines or verses based on parallelism or complementarity of meaning. He relies instead on the units of expression as the manuscripts present them; his approach is typical of more recent attempts to handle questions of cadence, rhythm, and measure in the recovery of native traditions. See Gibson and Glass (in Cline *et al.*, *Guide. . .Part Four*) for main compilations of the *cuicatl*, Garibay (*Poesía náhuatl*) for editions of the two major collections, and Bierhorst (*Cantares mexicanos*) for an English translation.

Other types of work, considered by Garibay to be the most original of the colonial Nahuatl traditions, are the cross-cultural dialogue (such as the one that begins this essay) and the historical narration which feature the veiled defense or apology. Garibay (*Historia*, II, 235–6) considered the *Libro de los coloquios*, Book XII of the Florentine Codex, and the *Relación de las apariciones guadalupanas* to be the outstanding representatives of this group. They reveal, at the level of greatest cultural complexity, the significance of the Spanish/American encounter from the native viewpoint. The *Coloquios* constitute one of the few great moments of dialogue between European and native American traditions; see Klor de Alva ("Aztec-Spanish dialogues"), León-Portilla (*Coloquios y doctrina*), and Duverger (*La conversión*) for recent translations and commentary.

For the history and culture of colonial Mexico, especially pertaining to European/native interaction, see Gibson (*The Aztecs*), Liss (*Mexico under Spain*), Gibson and Wachtel in Bethell, *Cambridge History*, vols. I and II; Lafaye in Bethell (*The Cambridge History of Latin America*, vol. II), and Keen (*The Aztec Image*).

The highland Maya: Quiché and Cakchiquel traditions

Spanish intervention in the Quiché kingdom in the highlands of present-day Guatemala began in December 1523, when the Spanish invaded under the leadership of Pedro de Alvarado. Seven months later, in July 1524, the Quiché capital of Q'umaraqaj (Utatlán) surrendered and Alvarado founded the Spanish city of Guatemala. Another principal highland nation, that of the Cakchiquels, which had offered friendship to Cortés in 1520, now provided the warriors who helped the Spanish subdue the greater Quiché community. Quiché resistance to the invasion, however, lasted several more years.

Although not as voluminous as Nahuatl written traditions, those of the Quiché Maya, according to Edmonson (in Edmonson, *Supplement* 107), are more continuously documentable. The most extraordinary cultural legacy of the Quichés is the *Popol Vuh*. Between 1554 and 1558, in the town of Quiché northwest of present-day Guatemala City, the writers of the alphabetic version wrote down what they remembered or saw of the hieroglyphic text known as the "Council Book," "a place to see 'The Light that Came from Across the Sea,' the account of 'Our Place in the Shadows,' a place to see 'The Dawn of Life'," (D. Tedlock, *Popol Vuh*, 71). On seeing the sacred text or a subsequent version of it in the neighboring town of Chichicastenango between 1701 and 1703, the Dominican friar Francisco Ximénez made what is known today as the only surviving copy of the Quiché text of the *Popol Vuh*; to it he added a Spanish translation (D. Tedlock, *Popol Vuh*, 28–31).

Beginning with the creation of man and extending through the Spanish conquest, the *Popol Vuh* constitutes a claim to supremacy of three branches of the lordly Quichés and includes accounts of the conquests and tribute rights of the Quiché state. As a repository of much earlier traditions, the colonial character of the sixteenth-century *Popol Vuh* is evident in the confrontation of ancient and Christian teaching and the clandestinity regarding the preservation of the sacred Maya traditions (D. Tedlock, *Popol Vuh*, 33, 60, 71).

Another significant historical tradition of the colonial Quiché is found in the *títulos* of oral tradition which were preserved in the Maya language and Roman alphabet by indigenous writers. Often written to support claims to land, office and title by appealing to the antiquity of the nobility of the authors (Edmonson in Edmonson, *Supplement*, 116–21) and sometimes unrelated to claims to land (Carmack, *Quichean Civilization*, 19), *títulos* often began with accounts of the Fourth Creation and documented the descent of their authors from the First Four Fathers of Mayan tradition (Carmack, *Quichean Civilization*, 117–19; D. Tedlock, *Popol Vuh*, 60). Recinos (*Crónicas indígenas*) translated into Spanish an important, small collection of such *títulos* and histories, which complements those of the two major surviving traditions (the *Popol Vuh*, the *Anales de los Cakchiqueles*) of the highland area.

The dance-drama is another important category of cultural production among the colonial Quiché. About this type of cultural production in general, Mace (*Two Spanish-Quiché Dance-Dramas*, 9) declares: "The ritual dances and dance-dramas which the Spaniards called *bailes* were among the most important forms of worship practiced by the Indians of Middle America." The most well-known example is the *Rabinal Achi* or *The Dance of the Trumpet* which celebrates the military valor and commemorates the sacrifice of a lord of Quiché. The *Rabinal Achi*, collected in Rabinal in 1850 and written in Quiché with no Spanish words, reflects an extraordinary, long-term resistance to European influence. It has been more recently translated into Spanish (Monterde, *Teatro indígena*). See Mace (*Two...Dance-Dramas*) for a general introduction to the subject and an extensive study of two Spanish-Quiché dance-dramas of Rabinal; Bode ("Dance") offers an extensive study of the Quiché *Danza de la conquista*.

The Cakchiquels were another important highland Maya group. Earlier forming a single nation with the Quichés, the Cakchiquels became a well-organized and aggressive nation devoted to military and economic expansion. Along with the *Popol Vuh* of the Quichés, the *Anales de los Cakchiqueles* constitutes the most important accounts of native traditions among the highland Maya. The *Anales* provide the most complete single account of Cakchiquel society and culture over time, beginning with the creation, the migration of the Cakchiquel ancestors from Tulán to the Lake Atitlán region, the founding of Iximche, their capital, and continuing with accounts of military history through their relations with the first Spaniards in 1524 and ending in the year 1601.

For a complete bibliography of manuscript and published prose sources of the highland Maya, see Gibson (in Cline *et al.*, *Guide...Part Four*, 391–8); Carmack (*Quichean Civilization*) provides a detailed inventory and descriptions of Quiché and Quiché-related sources and texts. Edmonson (in Edmonson, *Supplement*) surveys colonial Quiché prose and verse traditions. For Quiché texts in Spanish or English translation and commentaries, see Brinton (*Annals*), Recinos, (*Popol Vuh*, *Memorial*, *Crónicas*), Recinos and Goetz, (*Annals of the Cakchiquels*), Bode ("The Dance of the conquest of Guatemala"), Mace, (*Spanish-Quiché Dance-dramas*), D. Tedlock (*The Spoken Word; Popol Vuh*). For Quiché society and culture, see Carmack (*Quiché Mayas*) and B. Tedlock (*Time*).

The lowland Maya of Yucatan

The first Spanish notice of the existence of Yucatan occurred in 1517 during Francisco Hernández de Córdoba's voyage of exploration from Cuba. After campaigns into the Mesoamerican highlands and Honduras, Spanish efforts to subdue Yucatan began in 1527 under the leadership of one of Cortés's lieutenants, Francisco de Montejo. With the suppression in 1547 of the Great Revolt (the Maya uprising of the central and eastern regions), the Spanish hold on the peninsula was assured. Yet, as the territory of Yucatan was divided into at least sixteen autonomous principalities, each had to be dealt with separately. The stout resistance of the Yucatecan Mayas proved an ongoing problem (Farriss, *Maya Society*, 12–14).

The most significant surviving body of pre-Columbian Maya cultural traditions – the *Books of Chilam Balam* – is a measure of that cultural resistance. Named overall for the fifteenth-century Maya priest Balam who prophetically announced the arrival of a new religion, the various *Books of Chilam Balam* are also identified by the names of the towns in which they were found. Gibson's (in Cline *et al.*, *Guide...Part Four*, 380) census records fourteen such known examples, most of which date from the eighteenth and nineteenth centuries but contain material from much earlier times. Transcribed from native hieroglyphic texts, these colonial documents were kept from the eyes of the colonizers.

Writing about the survival of Maya religious and ritual practices in his *Informe contra idolorum cultores del obispado de Yucatán* (1613), the missionary priest Pedro Sánchez de Aguilar described how the Yucatec Maya read from their books in their assemblies, recited historical accounts, chanted others to drum accompaniment, sang still others, and enacted the dramatic presentations contained therein (cited in Roys, *Book of Chilam Balam*, 5). Although the colonial clergy condemned the *Books of Chilam Balam*, they were not used as prima facie evidence of the crime of idolatry as were texts written in hieroglyphics (Roys, *Book of Chilam Balam*, 5). The likelihood that every community preserved, used, and updated its own copy is a testimony to the centrality of the Chilam Balam traditions. Cumulative in chronology and encyclopedic in scope, the surviving Chilam Balam texts preserve ancient traditions as well as historical accounts from colonial times; religion, history, chronology, medicine and prophecy are represented.

The Maya prophecies pertained to the day, the year (*tun*), the twenty-year cycle (*katun*), or to named prophets (the return of Kukulcan-Quetzalcoatl) (Roys, *Book of Chilam Balam*, 182). *Katun* prophecies with historical allusions were of particular importance; an event occurring in one *katun* could be expected to occur in another, some *katuns* later. History and prophecy were thus closely linked and books of prophecy were also considered historical (see Edmonson, *The Ancient Future of the Itza*).

Most extraordinary is the synthetic character of the *Books of Chilam Balam*, and their exclusive Maya use. Integrating traditional Maya beliefs with European Christian influences in matters of religion, Maya religious texts were interpolated with Christian concepts, and materials in the vulgate Latin and Maya translations of Spanish religious tracts were introduced. In the field of chronology, European almanacs containing astrological predictions were copied and translated and interspersed among elements of the native calendar. In medical texts, European and Maya remedies were intermingled and fused. Although the best known of the *Books of Chilam Balam*, that of Chumayel, is considered to have little European influence, it is one of the few in which the prophet Balam's announcement of a new religion was taken to signify (no doubt thanks to the influence of Franciscan friars) the arrival of the Europeans and the Spanish conquest. The *Chumayel* also reveals the extent to which Maya traditions survived successive invasions of foreigners; see Brotherston ("Continuity"). Overall, the *Books of Chilam Balam* represent a most remarkable tradition of continuity and change within the history of colonial cultural production.

In addition to the Chilam Balam traditions, the colonial Yucatec Maya produced chronicles of Maya history, works of dramatic and lyrical character, medical texts, and divinatory almanacs. One type of lyrical composition is represented by the fifteen songs of the *Cantares de Dzitbalché*, which is the only known example of its type. See Barrera Vázquez (*El libro de los Cantares*).

Created in the sixteenth century, chronicles and *títulos* (land and boundary claims) with historical narration were important, including the *Chronicle of Calkini* (1577–1813), the *Chronicle of Yaxkukul* (1511–1553) by Macan Pech, and the *Chronicle of Chac Xulub Chen* (1511–1562) by Nakuk Pech, as well as numerous collections of land documents (Edmonson and Bricker, "Yucatecan Mayan literature," 50). Commemorative and historical drama with ritual and prophetic values are quite documentable for the sixteenth and seventeenth centuries. Edmonson and Bricker (pp. 49–51) cite the *Ceremonials of the Katun*, the *May*, and the *Baktun* as ritual dramas performed to inaugurate new cycles, noting that the Maya "maintained their traditional calendric ritual, which eventually outlasted the Spanish empire itself."

Gibson (in Cline *et al.*, *Guide…Part Four*, 379–91) surveys the lowland Maya prose texts which he assigns to the native historical tradition; see also Glass (in Cline *et al.*, *Guide…Part Four*) for annotated references and Edmonson and Bricker for an analysis, century by century, of Yucatec Maya cultural productions. Together, the three bibliographic essays provide access to the full range of published texts and translations of the native language production of the colonial Yucatec Maya. For major texts, translations, and commentary, see Barrera Vázquez and Morley ("Maya chronicles"), Mediz Bollo (*Libro de Chilam Balam de Chumayel*), Roys (*Book of Chilam Balam*, "The Prophecies of the Maya Tuns," "The Maya Katun prophecies") Craine and Reindorp (*The Códex Pérez*), Brotherston, ("Continuity"), Edmonson (*Ancient Future, Heaven-born Mérida*).

The Quechua-speaking peoples of the Andes

The Spanish penetration of Peru began on Pizarro's third voyage from Panama, commencing on November 16, 1532 with the surprise attack and capture of the Inca prince Atahualpa, who was fighting a war of dynastic succession against his half-brother Huáscar. The conquest was not easily achieved, however, because of the forty-year resistance organized from Vilcabamba by Inca successors. This resistance, of which Manco Inca's siege of Cuzco during 1536–1537 is a notable example, ended with Toledo's declaration of war on Vilcabamba, and the capture and execution of Tupac Amaru in 1572.

Titu Cusi Yupanqui, who had ruled the dissident state of Vilcabamba from 1557 to 1570 as a tutor to his brother Tupac Amaru, dictated an account of Manco Inca's complaints against the Spanish in Cuzco. His Quechua testimony was transcribed by the Augustinian Fray Marcos de García in 1570; only the Spanish translation survives (see Titu Cusi Yupanqui, *Ynstrucción del Ynga don Diego de Castro Titu Cussi Yupanqui...*). Other Inca testimonial accounts of the Spanish conquest are found in Guillén Guillén (*Versión Inca de la conquista*).

The colonial Quechua-language tradition of the Andes stands in apparent contrast to the Nahua and Maya traditions of Mesoamerica, insofar as the existence of a Quechua notarial or scribal tradition and written texts produced by monolingual Quechua speakers is concerned. The extent of colonial record-keeping in Quechua remains to be ascertained. In any case, to date we know only a handful of texts (in Spanish and Quechua) that were written by bilingual native Quechua-speakers. Missionary writers have been important in giving indirect access to others (see Lara, *La literatura de los quechuas*).

The known writings in the European-style chronicle tradition are three: Juan de Santacruz Pachacuti Yamqui, *Relación de antigüedades deste reyno del Pirú* (1613?); Felipe Guaman Poma de Ayala, *El primer nueva corónica y buen gobierno* (1612–1615); and the Inca Garcilaso de la Vega, *Primera y segunda partes de los Comentarios reales de los Incas* (1609, 1617). Of the three chroniclers writing the history of the Incas, only the Inca Garcilaso, the son of the Spanish captain Sebastián Garcilaso de la Vega and the Inca *palla* (noblewoman) Isabel Chimpu Ocllo, reconstructed the dynastic history of the Incas from the Inca perspective. Guaman Poma identified himself primarily with the pre-Incaic dynasty of the Yarovilca of the Huánuco region of Chinchaysuyo, even though he claimed matrilineal descent from the Incas. Santacruz Pachacuti Yamqui was also an outsider to the Cuzco royalty, being a *kuraka* (ethnic lord) of the Collahuas, midway between Cuzco and Lake Titicaca, in Collasuyo.

El Inca Garcilaso elucidated Quechua concepts as part of his effort to know Inca history and culture; Guaman Poma and Pachacuti Yamqui included significant Quechua interpolations in their Spanish language texts. Like the colonial Mesoamerican writings of historical tradition, the authors of these texts painted theirs in broad strokes, elaborating a grand cosmological design written from a strong sense of the need to redeem the present. Only one of them (Felipe Guaman Poma de Ayala) commented in depth on colonial society; in this respect his *Nueva corónica y buen gobierno* stands out from its peers in both the viceroyalties of New Spain and Peru and makes explicit the native historian's need to relate traditional, historical prerogatives to contemporary colonial claims. For commentaries on these works and authors, see Adorno (*Guaman Poma*), Chang-Rodríguez (*La apropiación del signo*), Jákfalvi-Leiva (*Traducción, escritura y violencia colonizadora*), M. López-Baralt (*Icono y conquista*), MacCormack ("Pachacuti," "Atahualpa y el libro"), Pease ("Introducción"), Pupo-Walker (*Historia, creación y profecía*), Scharlau ("Abhangigkeit und Autonomie"), Szemiński ("De la imagen de Wiraqucan"), and Zamora (*Language, Authority and Indigenous History*).

The greatest Quechua-language text from the early colonial period is the manuscript from Huarochirí, *Runa yndio ñiscap machoncuna*. The oral traditions set down in alphabetic writing at the turn of the seventeenth century in the colonial resettlement at San Damián de Checa in the province of Huarochirí were gathered at the direction of the local parish priest Francisco de Avila. The account no doubt served him in his efforts to locate and identify the traditional ritual sites and practices whose eradication he undertook in 1608 (Acosta, "Estudio biográfico sobre Francisco de Avila," 596).

In the first Spanish translation of this Quechua document, José María Arguedas called it appropriately *Dioses y hombres de Huarochirí* (p. 9) and described it as "the total conception that ancient humanity had about its origin, the world, the relations of man to the universe and the relations of human beings among themselves" as well as the perturbations occasioned by the Hispanic domination. Utilizing the testimony of individuals who were not external observers but rather active participants in the traditions they described, the narrators tell of the genealogy of the deities, the conflicts between them, and their conflict against the Spanish Christians who would destroy them. From the colonial native perspective, the epic struggle was between the old gods and the new; the Huarochirí manuscript contains accounts (chapters 20, 21) which reveal the spiritual anguish of the new convert pursued by the ancient deities.

The traditions gathered in Huarochirí represent neither a local nor a parochial tradition. Since San Damián was a forced resettlement, the deities, people, and rituals described were displaced from other areas. Like the great monuments of the highland and lowland Maya, the accounts include ritual ceremonies and sacred songs transcribed and transformed from the oral traditions. For translations of the text and commentaries, see Acosta ("Estudio biográfico"), Salomon ("Chronicles"), Salomon and Urioste (*The Huarochirí Manuscript*), Taylor (*Ritos y tradiciones*), and Urioste (*Hijos de Pariya Qaga*).

Apart from the investigations undertaken at the direction of Francisco de Avila, several other Spanish and *criollo* ecclesiastical authors on native colonial culture should be referenced. They include: Cristóbal de Albornoz, the church inspector and castigator of the revitalist movement of *Taki Unguy* in Lucanas in the 1560s, the *mestizo* priest from Cuzco Cristóbal de Molina, the priest Miguel Cabello Balboa, the Jesuit priest José de Acosta, the Mercedarian friar Martín de Murúa, and the Jesuit priest Bernabé de Cobo. See Rowe ("Inca culture," 192–7) and Porras Barrenechea (*Los cronistas del Perú*) for a review of these and other important sixteenth-century European interpretations of Andean culture.

Although the missionary/native collaboration in the Andes has not been documented as systematically as that between the Franciscans and the Nahuas in colonial Mexico, the relationship between the intellectual work and writings of Europeans and native Andeans needs further exploration. The conceptual coincidences, for example, between a native writer such as Guaman Poma de Ayala and the accounts of Fernando de Montesinos, Fray Buenaventura de Salinas y Córdoba, and Fray Martín de Murúa, suggest that much more might be learned about this type of colonial cultural production in Peru. See Imbelloni ("La tradición peruana") and Ballesteros Gaibrois ("Relación entre Fray Martín"; "Dos cronistas paralelos") on this example, and Quiroga (*Coloquios de la verdad*) for a series of dialogues revealing a pro-Andean missionary outlook on colonial/native relations.

The colonial dramas, of which the *Apu Ollantay* and the *Tragedia del fin de Atahualpa* are the best-known examples, reveal another constellation within the Andean imaginative universe which serves to interpret Andean experience. These dramatic compositions in verse, as well as two other known examples, probably originated in the eighteenth century (Mannheim, "On the sibilants of colonial southern Peruvian Quechua," 182). The origin, authorship and cultural provenance of the *Apu Ollantay* have been the object of much debate; the work exists in at least nine manuscript versions (Mannheim, "On. . .sibilants," 184). Lara (*La literatura*, 89) describes the *Apu Ollantay* as well as the *Tragedia del fin de Atahualpa* as works in the tradition of the *wanka*, dramatic compositions enacting historical deeds in which solemnity and sorrow are tempered by humor. See Lara (*La tragedia*, *La literatura*) and Meneses (*Teatro quechua colonial*) on colonial Quechua drama.

For a survey of colonial Quechua traditions identified as poetic, dramatic, and narrative (excluding the chronicles), see Lara (*La litera-tura*). The Pease edition of Porras Barrenechea (*Los cronistas del Perú*) is the best source for the indigenous chroniclers and the entire colonial Peruvian tradition of historiography. The fundamental inventory of Quechua-language writings of the colonial period is Rivet and Créqui-Monfort (*Bibliographie des langues aymará et kicua*); see also Mannheim ("On. . .sibilants"). For the political, social, and economic background of pre-Columbian and colonial Quechua culture, see Hemming (*The Con-quest of the Incas*), Rowe ("The Incas under Spanish Colonial institu-tions," "Inca culture at the time of the Spanish Conquest"), Kubler ("The Quechua in the colonial world"), Murra (in Bethell, *Cambridge History*), Stern (*Peru's Indian Peoples*), Spalding (*Huarochiri*), Duviols (*La destruc-ción de las religiones andinas*) and Wachtel (*Sociedad e ideología, The Vision of the Vanquished*). On the history of Spanish colonial linguistic policy toward Quechua, see Mannheim ("Una nación acorralada"). On native colonial spiritual beliefs and ideology, see Pease (*El Dios creador andino*) and Ossio (*Ideología mesiánica*).

Conclusion

We return to the Spanish/Aztec dialogues of 1524. The friars speak to the Mexica lords, referring to the Holy Scriptures:

> This one is, indeed, the very straight word,
> by which it appears how we were made,
> we, we men on the earth.
> Indeed, all are divine words,
> and verily, we know it,
> indeed, many are your careless mistakes,
> these they caused to be left with you,
> the ones who already left, your fathers.
> In what concerns these,
> nothing is straight,
> nothing is real,
> nothing is a following of truth,
> all that is only frivolous words.
> But all this we tell you,
> it is all in the divine book,
> there it lies painted.
>
> (Klor de Alva, "The Aztec–Spanish
> dialogues," 175–6)

With these words, the "divine guardians," the missionaries in the dialogue recreated by Sahagún, Valeriano, Vegerano, Iacobita, and Leonardo, proclaim the victory of the ancient word of the Christians, describing it in terms reminiscent of the Aztec writing tradition ("there it lies painted"). The triumph of the Europeans' "very straight words" over the Mexica's "frivolous words" is announced but this prophecy was not to be so easily fulfilled. As we have seen, the survival of autochthonous cultural traditions and their adaptation to the needs of life under colonialism endured to the end of colonial times and beyond.

On this theme, we close with a contemporary Andean example. In the early 1970s, Alejandro Ortiz Rescaniere collected current versions of the myth of Inkarrí which prophesy the return of Andean gods and Inca rule. Among Ayacuchan versions of the myth of Inkarrí, a Quechua-speaking shepherd from Chacaray tells how Inkarrí, the son of the Mother Moon and Father Sun, was beheaded; his body remained in Peru, but his head was taken to Spain. Whether or not the shepherd who narrates this Quechua tale believes that the Inca will return, it is clear that he perceives Western sacred and written tradition to be located far from him. The shepherd relates:

> When he died, Jesus Christ, the powerful one from heaven appeared. But Jesus Christ remains apart; he does not mingle with us. He holds the world in his hand, like an orange.
>
> (Ortiz Rescaniere, *De Adaneva a Inkarrí*, 132)

For this modern Quechua speaker, the two worlds – his own and that of the Europeans' god – are separate (pp. 59, 86, 161). The shepherd evinces no expectation, and expresses no lost hope, that they should become one.

This account emblematizes one of the cultural legacies of the European adventure to Hispanicize the New World that began 500 years ago. The narration is traditional, oral, and in an Amerindian language. Its notions about to whom the "very straight" and the "frivolous" words belong, is clear. The Amerindian narrator has come to terms with *nepantlism* and seems to have made a home of it. The figure now occupying the uneasy intermediate position is the source of legitimatized European ideology itself. The texts and traditions examined here form a significant part of the long history of Spanish colonization in the Americas. Less integrated into that history than complementary to it, the stories they tell (and sometimes conceal) narrate in an infinity of ways the drama of cultures in contact and the risks and challenges inherent in the pursuit of cultural survival.

3

The first fifty years of Hispanic New World historiography: the Caribbean, Mexico, and Central America

Stephanie Merrim

Within fifty years of Columbus's landing, the sedentary areas of Latin America had been conquered by Spain, inaugurating its Golden Age. Sieges of the new-found lands took on epic dimensions and reaped victories of monumental importance for the Spanish church and state. The Spanish soldiers themselves were said to rival the ancient Romans for their loyalty and heroism in conquest as time and again the few vanquished the many.

Focusing our sights on the first wave of conquests in the Caribbean, Mexico, and Central America, however, we are struck by an ironic if perhaps inevitable fact: that this larger tissue of Spanish victories, heroism and loyalty was woven in significant ways of failures and transgressions. Less than heroic actions underlie and even enable the eventual victories. Of course, the whole Discovery and Conquest rests on Columbus's original miscalculations. However, let us not forget, to mention but a few egregious examples, that Columbus was later sent back to Spain in chains; that the conquest of Mexico issued from Hernán Cortés's disobedience of Diego Velázquez; that Alvar Núñez Cabeza de Vaca's peregrinations of discovery across the North American southwest to Mexico were occasioned by the shipwreck and deaths of his companions. Disobedience of superiors, cruelty to the native populations, self-interest, failed attempts at religious conversion, incomprehension of the New World, and so on, form the landmarks in a 'thick' description of the Conquest, as seen from within.

It is particularly this infra-history which would compel the explorers and conquerors to provide their contemporaries, and posterity, with the first European historical records of the New World. Failures required justification, trespasses reparation, errors and confusions explanation, inequities redressing. Many of the earliest historiographical writings from the New World were motivated not only by the desire to recount victories but to an important degree by the need to seek pardon, legitimation, power, and reward, which needs would lend special urgency to their writings. Special urgency *and* narrative interest – for out of necessity the actor–chroniclers of the New World contrived complex verbal strategies in mounting their self-defenses and petitions. Rather than being ancillary to action, writing was an essential form of action, and a sense of what their words would *do* weighed heavily upon these early writers. So it was that men of arms, at times ill-prepared for the task, became men of letters, who could create texts as nuanced and strategically crafted as many works of literature. Carefully couched in the languages of success, they would proffer their failures. So it was, too, that their texts would often acquire a complexity proportionate to those of the malfeasances of which the authors seek to render accounts.[1]

The fact that they recorded a new reality also endows these writings with an enormous intrinsic interest. As they "invented" the New World, to use Edmundo O'Gorman's famous phrase, the early writers framed the founding images and topics – of utopia, civilization and barbarism – which would resonate in European and Latin American writings, as well as influence colonialist policies, for centuries to come. At the same time, for the players of the Conquest writing to the Crown was more a routine than a reflective act, an act of obligation, service and reporting. In the preamble to the *Quinta carta-relación* [*Fifth Letter*], for example, Cortés promised to provide Charles V with all the details, even of the disastrous expedition to Honduras, "so as not to change my habit of disclosing everything to your majesty" (p. 337). Thousands upon thousands of pages were spent by Cortés and the others in this effort: a recent edition of Columbus's public writings contains about 400 pages, official chronicler Fernández de Oviedo's *Historia general y natural de las Indias* alone runs into the thousands. We witness here not only the inception of the representation of America, but also of the scaffolding of paperwork which engorged and fueled the legal machinery of the colonies.

It is the desire of our essay both to discern the shape of this unwieldy *corpus* of writings, and to analyze the complex shapes of its key individual

---

[1] Here, and in subsequent arguments, I naturally draw upon my other writings on this period. These include: "The *Sumario de la natural historia de las Indias*: Fernández de Oviedo's apprehension of the new in nature and culture" in René Jara and Nicholas Spadaccini (eds.), *1492–1992: Re/Discovering colonial writing*, Hispanic Issues, Minneapolis, The Prisma Institute, 1989; "Civilización y barbarie: Prescott como lector de Cortés," *La historia en la literatura iberoamericana. Memorias del XXVI Congreso del Instituto Internacional de Literatura Iberoamericana*, 1989; "Ariadne's thread: auto-bio-graphy, history and Cortés's *Segunda carta-relación*," *Dispositio*, 11, 28–9 (1986), 57–83; "'Un *mare magno e oculto*': anatomy of Fernández de Oviedo's *Historia general y natural de las Indias*," *Revista de Estudios Hispánicos*, 11 (1984), 101–20; "The castle of discourse: Fernández de Oviedo's *Don Claribalte* (1519)," *Modern Language Notes*, 97 (1982), 329–46; "Historia y escritura en las crónicas de Indias: ensayo de un método," *Explicación de Textos Literarios*, 9: 2 (1981), 193–200.

texts. Such intentions, together with the unconventional nature of our subject, have led us to write a "literary history" of a somewhat unusual sort. Since, as the reader is well aware, the study of historiography from a literary point of view is a relatively new field, there are few givens. To write a literary history of historiography thus entails developing a set of criteria in accordance with which one establishes a canon, a presumptuous but unavoidable exercise. Consequently, even necessarily, we have chosen not simply to survey all the writings of this period (for their literary value is uneven), nor to follow the more obvious path of focusing on founding impressions of America (which would hardly do justice to the complexity of the texts). Instead, we will analyze in some detail "the invention of America" and other issues in the context of representative works which, in our estimation, hold the greatest cultural *and* textual interest – the latter particularly as a result of the dynamics of petition and persuasion discussed above. These include the works of Christopher Columbus, Fray Ramón Pané, Hernán Cortés, Gonzalo Fernández de Oviedo, and Bartolomé de las Casas.

Here we have authors of the most varying educations and ideologies, texts of the most diverse natures. Yet, Europeans all, the writers share a larger cultural heritage – medieval in its religious fervor, renaissance in its spirit of commercial and scientific initiative, Spanish in its sense of honor. Each writer, to a greater or lesser degree, has been party to the Conquest and subscribes in his own way to the goal of religious conversion of the native peoples. Each writes both of and from the New World, describing his subject to the Old World for the first time and contributing yet another piece to the collective enterprise of conquest and conversion. Hence, *every one* of these works tells a tale of gold and souls and provides its own portrait of the Amerindians. For these reasons, and for the purposes of analysis, we might therefore understand the historiography of the first fifty years of the Hispanic New World as a textual "family" and series. As in any family, its members at once share certain defining traits and retain their individuality. In order to showcase both familial aspects, of communality and uniqueness, we shall treat the works as a textual series, drawing comparisons between them and showing how they echo and fold back on each other.

The general task of registering both the events and the multiform reality of the New World, and their more particular concerns with apology, would give rise to the defining features of the textual "family." Let us, in a schematic way to be fleshed out by the discussions of individual works, set forth the features that we shall encounter in each text.

1. *Autobiography and historiography.* Participants turned historians by default, the writers are concerned not only with the historical events but also with their role in them. Thus does the author's "I" enter

historiography, endowing it with an autobiographical dimension. Caught up in their individual plights, they wrote "history" in terms of their own personal circumstances, creating what we might call an "auto-historical" discourse. The molding of a literary *persona* for one's self in accordance with the lines established by literature and hagiography, and, importantly, an emerging consciousness of their role as writers, would result from the personalizing of historiography.

2. *The writer's sense of his reader: pragmatics.* As the writer's "I" enters historiography so, as we have noted, do his self-interests. By writing, the author seeks to obtain any of a number of rewards, tangible and intangible, from power to fame. Such rewards could evolve only from the vital conjunction of the text with the reader who could bestow them, the Crown. The strategies, form, and content of these works will therefore profoundly reflect and be conditioned by the writer's relationship to his audience, that is, by the *pragmatic context*. To understand the dynamics, literary and otherwise, of the texts we must reconstruct this context: to whom were they written, under what circumstances, and to what ends – which takes us to the genre of the *relación*.

3. *Making a case: the relación.* Columbus composed a diary, Cortés letters, Oviedo a "summary" of New World natural and cultural phenomena. Yet beneath these varied formats lie the dynamics of petition which characterize a certain kind of *relación*, a genre in which Pané, Cortés, Cabeza de Vaca, and Las Casas would explicitly inscribe their works. The *relación de hechos* (report of acts) was a humble forensic genre rooted in feudalism, the genre of which ordinary people would avail themselves to present their own life-stories and legal cases in petitioning for reward for services rendered. Addressed to superiors who sat in judgment, a forum for autobiographical information, familiar even to the less-educated, the earthy *relación* well suited the particular needs of New World writers.

4. *Hybrid texts.* Accommodating an extraordinary range of information, early New World writings would overflow even the amorphous bounds of the *relación*. These texts were hybrids, baggy monsters encompassing many nascent fields of knowledge which would later become disciplines in their own right. As Francisco Esteve-Barba has written, each historian became "a new Herodotus: triple father of History, Ethnography, and Geography [and, we might add, Autobiography], all in one" (*Historia de la historiografía indiana*, 12). Another essential factor contributing to the hybrid nature of these works is the wide use that their authors would make of other texts and textual models: philosophical and legal writings as well as the novel of chivalry, the epic, the classics, hagiography, myth, early travel accounts, and so on. Such models would play several crucial roles for the authors, channeling their

confused perceptions, allowing them to couch the new in familiar terms, and serving as the cornerstones of textual strategies. We shall greatly develop this theme in the course of our analyses.

By the end of the first fifty years of the New World's existence for the Old, a full cycle had been completed. The new lands of a particular region had been discovered, appropriated, and settled by Spain. Similarly, a whole cycle of stories had been told, stories both vastly different and interrelated. The textual family's protean story of gold and souls and the shared features just outlined accommodate the cross-currents of an always evolving tale. From the pastoral "barbarism" of the West Indies to the refined civilization of the Aztecs, from resistance to assimilation to defense of the Indians' "otherness," from the discovery to the destruction of the New World and, figuratively from the Creation to the Fall – we shall follow the twisting course of this story.

Christopher Columbus: the Diario de a bordo *(1492)* and the Relación del tercer viaje *(1498)*

The story begins, naturally, with the extraordinarily rich and often lyrical *Diario de a bordo* [*Diary of Christopher Columbus's First Voyage to America*, 1492–1493] of Christopher Columbus (1451–1506). His *Diario* details, generally day by day, the explorer's first travels to the New World – principally, to Cuba and Hispaniola – in search of the Orient. The original now lost, the *Diario* is available to us only in Bartolomé de las Casas's selective yet copious transcription, which alternates Columbus's own words with the transcriber's summaries (a matter to which we shall eventually return).

Las Casas, advocate of the Indies as well as the Indians, gives full vent to the expressions of "marvel" with which Columbus imparts his first impressions of the New World, and for which the *Diario* has become famous. Hyperbole abounds as Columbus praises the beauty of the peoples, the diversity of the landscape, so different from Spain's. With a repetitive vocabulary and formulaically conjugating a few elements (a landscape of blue and green, soft breezes, high mountains, fertile lands, songs of imaginary nightingales, beautiful and gentle people), the entranced Columbus breathes life into the West Indies for his readers. Though relatively limited in its resources, his portrait effectively invoked the pastoral and utopian landscape previously known only to literature and founded an Edenic image of America which captured Europe's imagination.

It is a commonplace among scholars to mention the poverty of Columbus's Spanish, believed to be his first written language. Yet clearly

Columbus's writings are not lacking in artfulness. The *Diario* itself represents a generic innovation, being a personal journal explicitly addressed to the Catholic Kings. In it, mindful of the Crown's expectations, Columbus must perform the delicate task of adjusting what he indeed found to what he needed to find – the Orient, gold, spices, and souls for religious conversion. To cover his failures, Columbus marshalls a "language" of success, in the sense of a strategy, thematics, stylistics. Truly, as we shall see, does his mercurial word invent rather than name America.

Throughout the *Diario* Columbus maintains the double optics, mercantile and religious, which accorded with both his and the Crown's needs. Thus these, the first European portraits of the natives of the New World, are framed in terms of the Indians' receptivity to trade and conversion. For the most part, Columbus lumps all the Indians into one group, which he consistently characterizes as innocent, childlike and peaceful: generous to a fault (they "give away all they have"; "give like brutes"), thrilled with the trinkets the Spanish try to exchange for gold, neither needing nor possessing arms. To Columbus's eye having no religious "sects" nor developed culture, the Indians are a *tabula rasa* upon which Spanish culture can easily be inscribed (he intones, "and I believe that they will very easily become Christians"). As the following example, from the very day of the landfall, illustrates, mercantile and religious interests flow seamlessly together in Columbus's depiction of the Indians:

> And I, to gain their friendship, since I knew that these people would best be freed and converted to Our Holy Faith by Love rather than force, gave a few of them some colored caps and glass beads that they placed around their necks, and many other things of little value, which gave them much pleasure and so won them over that it was a marvel. They then came out to the launches of the boats where we were, swimming and bringing us parrots and skeins of cotton thread and javelins and many other things and they traded them for the things we gave them, like little glass beads and bells (October 11, pp. 90–1)[2]

The major exception to this homogeneous portrait of receptive natives comes with the Caribs, and can be attributed in part to the readings which shaped Columbus's expectations for his journey. From the more than 2,000 marginal comments in Columbus's copies of early travel works by Marco Polo, Pierre D'Ailly, Anaes Silvius, and Pliny, scholars have pieced together a picture of the oriental world of mythical riches, high civilization, and temperate climate which motivated Columbus's voyage. Whether or not, as has been hotly debated for centuries, Columbus had

---

[2] Citations from the *Diario* are taken from Arranz's modernized edition (1985); citations from all other works by Columbus are from Varela's 1984 edition.

prior knowledge of the existence of the New World *per se*, is almost immaterial in terms of his writings. For, to the very end, Columbus would equate the new reality to his *a priori* models: even after three journeys he states unequivocally in a report to the Pope in 1502: "This island is Tharsis, it is Cethia, it is Ophir and Ophaz and Cipanga [Japan]" (p. 311). Further, as Beatriz Pastor has amply detailed (*Discurso narrativo de la conquista de América*, Ch. 1), in the writings of the first and subsequent voyages Columbus would adjust his depictions to the set expectations he never abandoned, no matter how little the actual reality conformed to them. Formulaic references to the mild climate, lush landscape, ever lighter-skinned peoples, traces of gold, all respond to this process, which Pastor terms "descriptive verification." Such a process would lead Columbus to a curious understanding of the more aggressive Caribs, who threatened the "gentle" Arawaks and were rumored to be "cannibals" [caníbales]. Though the Caribs ill-suited his other interests, Columbus would establish in the *Diario* the etymology Carib > Caniba > caníbal > people of the Great Kan ("the Caniba are no less than the peoples of the Great Kan," December 11, p. 146), and for this reason defend the arms-bearing Caribs as "beings of reason" (November 23, p. 128).

The new lands, we see, were not what Columbus or the Crown had hoped they would be. However, through a series of transparent maneuvers Columbus would portray their *potential* to become so, or at least to serve the Crown. A sense of futureness dominates the text: noting that each land discovered is better than the previous one, Columbus establishes an inexorable rhythm of improvement and promise. At the same time, he insistently notes the presence of rivers, possible sources of gold or potential commercial ports, and the fertility of the lands, ripe for development: "It was a marvel to see those valleys and the good rivers and good waters and the lands made for bread, for livestock of all types, of which they have none [!], for orchards and for everything in the world that a man could ask" (December 16, p. 152). The word "señal" (signal, sign) echoes throughout the *Diario* as what Columbus sees becomes an index of what he hopes to find, particularly of gold and other valuable booty: "the Admiral says that he saw one of them with a piece of wrought silver fastened to his nose, which he took as a sign that there was silver in those lands" (November 1, p. 112). The signs are not always so clear. Columbus repeatedly admits to being stymied by his inability to discern the potential which inheres in the new natural phenomena: "and then there are thousands of kinds of trees and all of them bear their own fruits, and they all have a marvellous scent, and it grieves me more than anything in the world not to know what they are, because I am entirely sure that they are valuable" (October 21, p. 104). It is this, practical, aspect of the "otherness" of the New World which gives Columbus greatest pause in the *Diario*.

In the New World of Columbus's *Diario*, pulsating with immanence, trees are always about to reveal their true precious nature, crops about to yield their treasure, Columbus about to reach the lands of gold but impeded by a storm. A crucial change, however, occurs when the Admiral writes about Hispaniola, which he deftly portrays as that place in which what was sought becomes one with what was found. Here, finally, Columbus finds a more complex society approaching the oriental civilization he expected. Its chief he calls a "King;" its people, he says, "would be almost as white as in Spain" (December 16, p. 152) if they protected themselves from the sun; its ceremonial he endows with a curious pomp: "Your Majesties would undoubtedly be impressed with the status and reverence that all accord him [the "King"], since they are all naked" (December 18, p. 155). The natives of this new land, which evokes both Spain and the East, accord Columbus a magnificent reception. He is thronged by crowds, the "King" cedes his lands to him (December 18, p. 156), and best yet, Hispaniola seems to be the long-sought source of gold. Though little more than nuggets ever appear, the *tales* of gold escalate – tales of nearby islands "with more gold than land" (December 22, p. 162), of the King who promises to cover Columbus with gold (December 27, p. 172), to build him a life-size statue all of gold (January 2, p. 177). Cibao, in the interior of Hispaniola, Columbus concludes, *is* Cipango (December 24, p. 166; January 4, p. 179), and in an emblematic moment, he dresses the "King" in Spanish clothes (December 26, p. 170), symbolically cementing the two worlds. Shortly afterwards, on the strength of these reported tales of gold, Columbus decides to return to Spain, because, as he says, "he had found what he was looking for" (January 9, p. 184).

Indeed, this may not be untrue; he may have found what *he* sought. Throughout the *Diario*, as the reader can deduce, Columbus has managed to skirt outright lies. This effort is bolstered by certain persistent stylistic constructions. Columbus's language in the *Diario* tends to imprecision in its use of hyperbolic expressions ("most marvellously wrought", p. 92); dramatic but imprecise adjectives (much, so, all, many, good); nebulous statistics (infinite islands, a thousand ways). Verbs of thought and perception render statements equivocal (he didn't doubt, he understood, it seemed, he thought). Extensive use of the subjunctive and of conditional clauses ("and they give of what they have for whatever is given them, without complaining that it is little, and I believe that they would do the same with spices and gold if they had them", p. 138) can also impart a wonderful slipperiness to a statement. Taking his style together with the devices of description and potentiality already discussed, we see that

Columbus may have had little to lose in inviting "wise men" to come to the New World, to "see the truth of all he says" (November 27, p. 134) – for he has negotiated a language beyond truth and falsehood.

Columbus displays the greatest variety of strategies and invention of any single author in our period. Given the disappointing yield of gold and souls from the second voyage, in the "Memorial a A. Torres" (1494) ["Memoir to A. Torres"] he would outline a plan for the cannibals to be sent to Spain as slaves. In the *Relación del cuarto viaje* (1503) [*Relation of the Fourth Voyage*], broken in spirit and perhaps in mind, the Columbus who had been signing himself "Christo ferens" ["bearer for Christ"] would renew hallucinated promises of gold, now backed by the divine voice he claims to have heard. His once conventionally heroic textual *persona* becomes pathetic and emotive. The Admiral, as Alejo Carpentier's acute reading of Columbus in his novel *El arpa y la sombra* [*The Harp and the Shadow*] dramatizes, reinvents himself, his mission, and his argumentation with each stage.

Of the *Relación del tercer viaje* [*Relation of the Third Voyage*] Carpentier has his character Columbus state: "And, as had I tried to substitute the Flesh of the Indies for the Gold of the Indies, upon seeing that gold was not to be found nor flesh to be sold, prodigious wizard that I am, I began to substitute words for gold and flesh" (p. 154). Cynicism tinges Carpentier's reading; nevertheless, in various aspects of the *Relación* we can see the displacement from world to word which gives this text such particular interest. During his third voyage, Columbus had stopped briefly in the gulf of Paria off the coast of Venezuela, unknowingly "discovering" South America. Having found sorely needed fresh water there, he sailed to Hispaniola to learn that in the wake of a rebellion led by Francisco Roldán, the Crown's envoy Francisco de Bobadilla had taken power, and possession of Columbus's holdings. None of these adverse occurrences, however, appear in the *Relación*, written shortly after Columbus's arrival in Santo Domingo. Instead, Columbus devotes most of the report to matters intangible and theoretical, culminating in the startling theory of Earthly Paradise.

Adhering to epistolary rhetoric, the *Relación* begins with prefatory remarks (the *exordium*) and ends with a persuasive conclusion (the *peroratio*). For emphasis, these two sections echo each other's themes and argumentation. Columbus bitterly acknowledges that he has been cruelly discredited for not sending back "ships laden with gold" (pp. 204 and 218). In lieu of material goods, Columbus will now turn the Crown's thoughts to the intangible benefits to be gained from his discovery. Certainly the spreading of "our holy faith" (p. 218) is of no small consequence. Yet Columbus also impresses upon the Crown the intangibles of fame and glory that the discovery of this, now termed an "*other world*" (pp. 205 and 218; our emphasis), will bring. He lists examples of rulers who, considering it to be their duty, "devoted their efforts to gaining knowledge, to conquering and keeping new lands" (p. 219), regardless of financial losses. Masterfully, the author reminds King Ferdinand of his promise that the Crown's "intention was to pursue and sustain this enterprise, even if nothing was gained from it but stones and sand, and that he held the expense incurred to be of little consequence" (p. 219, similarly p. 205), thus fitting the King's words to his own purposes.

In the *narratio* or body of the *Relación*, while recounting the voyage itself Columbus turns his sights for the first time to larger speculations about this "other world" he has found. The discovery of fresh water in Paria demanded such theorizing, for if Paria is an island, how could the water be fresh? And (as several scholars have explained),[3] if Paria is not an island, could it possibly comprise another body of land outside the known continuous land mass, the Orbis Terrarum charted by medieval Christian cosmography? The world-picture that Columbus had inherited disallowed as heretical the existence below the Equator of habitable lands, of an Orbis Alterius alien to Christianity.

The theory of an Earthly Paradise entailed an ideal solution to this and other of Columbus's dilemmas. Presenting himself now as a scholar, with a dense show of erudition Columbus refutes Ptolemy and others to claim that the world is not a sphere but rather a ball with a pear-shaped projection. Conflating cosmography, empiricism and biblical legend, as well as the sacred and the erotic, he argues that at the tip of the pear – as if, he says, at the nipple of a woman's breast – lies Earthly Paradise. Therein is to be found the source of the "gentle climate" (p. 216) Columbus had described in the *Diario*; there "are born precious objects" (p. 216); thence flow the four principal rivers of the world (p. 215), the fresh water which had so baffled Columbus. Since, as Columbus had stated at the end of the *Diario*, sacred theologians and wise philosophers have situated Earthly Paradise "at the end of the East" (p. 208), Columbus's new theory leaves his oriental model intact. Moreover, it fully sanctions the incompleteness which has characterized his discoveries, for Earthly Paradise, the greatest reward of Columbus's efforts, cannot and should not be penetrated. It must remain intangible and untouched: "I believe that there is to be found Earthly Paradise, which can only be reached by divine sanction" (p. 216).

Even if not conceived in or as madness, Columbus's theory appears to have been received as folly. There is no evidence that the Crown was impressed by their extraordinary new possession; Columbus was to wait a full six weeks to be received in court after his return, having been sent to Spain in chains by Bobadilla. Uneven exchanges had pushed language too far in the service of self-apology, without coming up with the reality to match it.

[3] See O'Gorman, *The Invention of America*, 94–104, and Boorstin, *The Discoverers*, Ch. 32.

Fray Ramón Pané: Relación acerca de las antigüedades de los Indios
(1498)

The *Diario*'s portrayal of Columbus's understanding of the Amerindians' languages betrays his vexed relationship with the Indians. At certain crucial points Columbus attributes words to the natives which he could not possibly have understood (as when quoting their cry that the Spaniards had descended from Heaven); at others, he admits to complete mutual incomprehension. To remedy the latter situation, in 1495 Columbus sent the Hieronymite friar Ramón Pané (dates unknown) to Hispaniola to learn the languages of the Taínos and with orders to investigate their "idolatries and beliefs" (p. 21). Pané presents the results of his efforts in a simply written *relación* which falls into three parts: a transcription of Taíno myths, as recounted to Pané by native informants; a description of their religious practices; Pané's account of his successes and failures in baptizing the natives. Taken together, thanks to the diligence of this self-stated "poor hermit," Columbus's orders produced the first ethnographic study of the New World, the closest we possess to a first-hand account of Taíno culture. Let us therefore begin by surveying the cultural content of this founding text, and then turn to the manner in which Pané "processes" his experience of the native worlds.

To the untutored, the Taíno myths faithfully transcribed by Pané in the first eleven chapters appear as confounding tales of sexual mischief, tricksters, transformations, and transgressions: Mácocael emerges from a cave to be transformed by the Sun into a stone. Guahayona spirits away the women of Hispaniola to the island of Matininó. The *inriri* bird creates a new supply of women by pecking a sex into unsexed creatures which fall from trees. Four twin brothers steal cassava bread and are rewarded with the hallucinogenic *cohoba* powder. From the shoulder of Deminán Caracaracol springs a tortoise-woman, which the brothers settle down to raise. Modern exegetes, however, have ferreted out the profound significance of the Taíno myths. Linking them to the Arawak archetypes to which they have been traced, anthropologists (see Arrom, *Mitología y artes prehispánicas de las Antillas*, Alegría, *Apuntes en torno a la mitología de los indios taínos*, López-Baralt, *El mito taíno*) have understood these tales respectively to represent among other things, a creation myth, the origins of exogamy, puberty rituals, the bestowing of the culture's bases, and the transition from a hunting–gathering to a sedentary agricultural society.

The second section of Pané's text moves from hearing to seeing, from myth to ritual and legend, and from mythic time–space to a historical present. In Chapters 12–25, Pané discusses Taíno religious practices, many of which he personally witnessed, focusing on conceptions of the after-life, the practices of the *behiques* or priest-shamans, the effects of *cohoba*, and the *cemís* or household gods. From the chapters devoted to particular *cemí*-gods (20–24) the reader, though not Pané, unearths important cultural information: an explanation of hurricanes (23), of the building of temples (24), and the legend of a *cemí* who rebelled against the Spaniards (22). Pulling this latter thread of Spanish domination into the present, and future, the section ends by imparting a dramatic prophecy of destruction transmitted to Pané by two Taíno chiefs. Similar to the prophecy to which Cortés's Moctezuma would allegedly take recourse, it predicts that "a clothed people would come to their lands who would dominate and kill them, and that they would die of hunger" (p. 48).

From what can be gathered from his *relación*, the significance of the information we have detailed was largely lost on Pané. Although it was inevitable that he be unable to think in modern anthropological terms, much depends on Pané's world-view. Of Pané's background we know little, beyond the fact that he was Catalan by birth. Las Casas, who met him, describes Pané as a "simple-minded person...who didn't speak Spanish all that well" (Arrom edition of Pané, p. 117), capable of preaching only the rudiments of the faith "in a very defective and confused way" (Arrom edition of Pané, p. 105). The rest we must deduce from his *relación* – which assumes the cast of a fifteenth-century "everyman's" reading of the other, bespeaking a person of a narrow cultural frame of reference.

How does Pané tell the often bawdy, certainly baffling, Taíno tales? To his great credit and our benefit, he clearly considers himself to be bound by the task of providing an informative *relación* ("*on the orders* of the illustrious Admiral...I write what I have been able to learn and find out about the beliefs and idolatries of the Indians..." p. 21, our emphasis). "What I saw was what you get" (roughly translated, p. 45), he says: for the most part Pané remains a faithful scribe, impartially and unobtrusively transcribing what he was told just as it was told to him. Nevertheless, at times Pané cannot refrain from commenting on what he perceives as the illogic of the myths, their disorder. On these occasions, the friar apologizes for his text, attributing its defects to the Taíno's lack of a system of writing. For example: "And as they have neither a system of writing nor written documents, they don't know how to tell such stories well, nor can I write them down well. For this reason I believe that what I'm putting first should go last. . . . But everything I write down I say just as they tell me, that's how I write it; I put things as I have heard them from the natives of the country" (p. 26). Pané's encounter with the discourse of the other, we see, is marked by his incomprehension of oral modes of transmission.

In Pané the religious practices of the natives strike a central nerve. Though still largely objective, Pané interjects his biases here in subtle and not so subtle ways. He repeatedly remarks upon the drunken unreason produced by the ceremonial ingesting of *cohoba* as well as on the hoaxes of the *behiques*, whom he terms "sorcerers" and "witch doctors" (p. 41). Of the *cemís* and their worshippers he pointedly remarks: "These simple ignorant people, having no knowledge of our holy faith, believe that their idols, or more correctly, their demons, actually do these things" (p. 35). The friar's lack of a larger perspective emerges all the more clearly when contrasted with the comments on Pané's text of Pedro Mártir de Anglería and Bartolomé de las Casas, both of whom were influenced by renaissance humanism. Mártir compares the *cemís* to the dryads, satyrs, and fauns of classical myths (Arrom edition of Pané, p. 98). Las Casas attempts to discern in the fictions of the *behiques* an allegory or moral similar to those of classical poets (Arrom edition of Pané, p. 114). A sense of cultural relativism, a knowledge of "other stories," allows Pané's commentators to transcend a narrowly religious reaction against these novelties.

Perhaps countering the "other stories" to which *he* had earlier yielded his text, when in the brief third section of the *relación* (Chs. 25–6) Pané finally tells his own story of efforts to proselytize, he reclaims a more conventional approach to writing history. "Now I want to tell what I have seen and experienced..." (p. 48), he begins, for the first time foregrounding his "I" and actions, and thus moving into the autobiographical mode of the *relación de hechos*. Whereas before Pané was obliged to tell alien tales, he will now tell an almost exemplary one with hagiographic undertones – of conversions, martyrdom and miracles. And whereas before he suspected that his faithful transcription was putting first what should go last, now Pané will chronologically recount his encounters with chiefs Guarionex and Mabiatué, making precise note of dates and places. This counterpoint between the first and third sections in effect produces a *mestizo* text, first Taíno then Spanish in its logic.

The third section falls short of being an entirely exemplary Christian tale in that it must communicate both dramatic successes and failures at conversion. Pané seems to have sensed the larger import at least of the Taíno's dire prophecy, i.e., that it might well relate to the arrival of the Spaniards. The autobiographical third section begins in mid-chapter, immediately after the recounting of the prophecy, and in it Pané is at pains to show that the Spaniards have come not to obliterate but to enlighten the Indians. Textually, he devotes the most space to the baptism of the first Indian, Juan Mateo. In reality, however, the failures outweighed the successes, and Pané must describe the murder of several christianized Taínos, his exasperating failure to convert Guarionex, and the desecration of the Catholic images. Mitigating these failures for Pané, on the site where the images were buried there sprouted "two or three yams...in the shape of a cross" (p. 54), an intervention which he construes as a "miracle."

His evangelical attempts divinely sanctioned yet thwarted, the friar takes a strong stand in the last chapter, exhorting that when necessary the Indians be converted by force. He states, turning to new purpose Columbus's notion of the natives' tractability, "And truly the island has a great need for people who will punish the rulers when they deserve it [and] make known to these peoples the ways of the holy Catholic faith and indoctrinate them in it; because they cannot and will not resist" (pp. 54–5). In formulating a policy statement as his petition, Pané has exceeded the role of a faithful "relator" (writer of a *relación*). And indeed, there are indications that the friar considered his work to be something more than a *relación*. In Chapter 25, for example, he calls it a "book" and a comment by Mártir suggests that the work may have been published.[4] Pané's experience (unlike that of later writers), has failed to produce greater sympathy in him for the natives; frustration, incomprehension, and the staunch defense of his world-view have launched this "poor hermit" from relator to author.

Hernán Cortés: Segunda carta-relación *(1520) and other writings from Mexico*

Though Pané may have pretended to authorship, he remains a relatively straightforward informer, who portrays his circumstances without notable guile or self-interest. Hernán Cortés (1485–1547), on the other hand, was a brilliant politician and tactician in life and in art. All of Cortés's major writings are feats of engineering; we shall illustrate his craft through an analysis of perhaps the most noteworthy in words and deeds, the *Segunda carta-relación* [*Second Letter*].

The dazzling victories which Cortés depicts in the text are the accomplishments of a military mastermind, one who quickly perceived and capitalized upon the antagonism between the Aztecs and surrounding tribes, and without violence finessed the surrender of Tenochtitlán by Moctezuma. His most triumphant early actions in the Mexican arena thus result more from cunning or *froda* than from *forza*, and at every step Cortés discloses the acute workings of his mind. We are made party to his strategizing through an omnipresent cognitive pattern that structures this and other texts, in which Cortés typically SEES what is going on or receives information, REFLECTS on what he has perceived or learned, DECIDES his course of action, and ACTS, generally successfully. For example: (deciding to leave Tenochtitlán to confront Pánfilo de Narváez) "And as *I saw* the great harm that was beginning to be stirred up and how the country was in revolt because of Narváez, it *seemed to me* that if I went to where he was, it would be calmed down...and also because *I intended* to come to terms

---

[4] As Alegría (*Apuntes*) notes on p. 41, Pedro Mártir states that Pané was the "author of a little book."

with Narváez to put an end to the great evil which had begun. And so *I departed* that very same day..." (p. 147, our emphasis).

The departure whose inception Cortés describes here and which would lead to the loss of the Mexican empire, betokens the equally stunning debacles and trespasses which the *relación* must address. It is well known that Cortés departed hastily for Mexico from Cuba, in defiance of its governor Diego Velázquez. Arriving in Veracruz, Cortés dissociated himself from Velázquez's authority and constituted a municipal council which named him its leader and captain. Cortés and, purportedly, his men drafted a letter (to which we will return) informing the throne of these events, and then proceeded towards the Aztec capital. There, soon after Moctezuma "surrendered" his empire to Spain, Cortés took this emperor prisoner – a presumptuous move for a commoner. Within a short time of his victory, however, Cortés received word that Velázquez's envoy, Pánfilo de Narváez, had come to arrest the rebel and appropriate his gains. Departing for the coast to do battle with Narváez, Cortés left Tenochtit-lán in the hands of Pedro de Alvarado – who had multitudes of Aztecs massacred during a religious ceremony. When Cortés returned, the Spaniards were under siege, and he and his men were forced to take flight. With this, known as the "Night of Sorrows," Cortés effectively lost the Empire he had so swiftly won.

In the *Segunda carta-relación* Cortés obviously had a second battle to be fought, a verbal battle, and one for which he was eminently suited. In fact, with his two years of study in Salamanca, notarial training, and several years of experience as Diego Velázquez's secretary, Cortés had acquired a skill in drafting and interpreting legal documents that perhaps better prepared him for the verbal than the physical battle. Writing, then, in the throes of the reconquest of Mexico, Cortés must vindicate the above acts; secure Charles V's sanction (which he had not yet received) of his official disobedience; enlist the throne's aid for the new battles. To accomplish these goals, Cortés engages in a Machiavellian verbal war whose strategies and maneuvers rival those which characterize his leadership. In service of his own needs the conqueror conflates his personal interests with those of the Crown, and produces an intricate text which features the following tactics and their consequences.

In fashioning his self-image, Cortés re-establishes his loyalty to the Crown and exalts his own person

At the heart of the *Segunda carta-relación* lies the transformation of rebel into model leader (see Pastor, *Discurso*, Ch. 2). Throughout this and his other *relaciones*, Cortés depicts himself in accordance with the late medieval topic of the selfless vassal whose only desire is to serve his monarch. As his self-portrayal would have it, Cortés's own interests are completely subordinated to those of the Crown. The Captain underscores the absolute continuum between himself and the Emperor, both as reflected in his own actions ("In my last *relación*, very excellent Prince, I informed your majesty of the cities and towns which to that date had offered themselves unto your royal service, and which I had subjected and conquered for you," p. 81) and as perceived by others (Cortés's Moctezuma vows, "we will obey you and take you for sovereign in place of the great sovereign of whom you speak," p.117). Similarly, Cortés's comportment presents Charles V with the image of an ideal Catholic monarch, for he shows himself routinely and benevolently pardoning the Indians who offer themselves as vassals.

Though Cortés's text may incite the modern reader to lament the villainy of conquest, it attained to the heroic narrative of its time. Overlying the implicit image of himself as political mastermind, Cortés constructs a *persona* more akin to that of the epic hero. He endows himself with extraordinary personal valor, a certain religious zeal, and unerring foresight. He places himself at the helm of the Conquest – no other heroic individual emerges, all other power-wielding figures are denigrated. Cortés's "I" dominates the text and rules its verbs, for he uses the first person singular even when narrating the actions of the group. Infantry soldier Bernal Díaz del Castillo's famed "democratic" version of the conquest of Mexico in his *Historia verdadera de la conquista de la Nueva España, c.* 1568 [*The Discovery and Conquest of Mexico*] has Cortés receiving apt counsel from his men at crucial junctures. In Cortés's version, the hero acts independently; only when a questionable decision has been taken, as in the resolve to flee Tenochtitlán (p. 162), does he attribute it to the group.

Cortés exalts his discoveries, suiting them to the Crown's needs

Equally glorious is the image of Mexico which Cortés offers to Charles V. Columbus's *Españ*ola was a Spain *in potentia*, still tropically paradisiacal. In Mexico Cortés appears to have found the world that Columbus sought, that is, a great civilization boasting unlimited riches. He baptizes it "New Spain" (p. 137) and informs Charles V that the sovereign can consider himself "new emperor" (p. 80) of these lands which, as Cortés's description of Mexico will imply, should provide for the economic needs of the Spanish empire. "New Spain" will complement and sustain imperial Spain. Accordingly, the grandeur of Mexico, its "barbarous" civilization, becomes the ruling theme of Cortés's depiction. A cluster of sentences contains the key to his Mexico:

> And, so as not to be too long-winded in the description of the things of this great city (though to be brief does not do them justice), I will only say that in their commerce and ways these people live almost as in

Spain, and with the same harmony and order as in Spain, and considering that they are a barbarous people and so cut off from the knowledge of God and from other peoples of reason, it is truly remarkable what they have achieved.

Regarding the service of Muteczuma and all that is remarkable in his magnificence and power, there is so much to write that I swear to your highness I don't know where to begin even to recount some part of it; for, as I have already said, how can there be anything more magnificent than that this barbarian lord should have had fashioned into gold and silver and precious stones and feathers all the things to be found under the heavens in his lands...   (p. 137)

This passage forms part of the exhaustive "inventory" in which, after taking Moctezuma prisoner, Cortés lists the Crown's new possessions with an eye to the pecuniary. Mexico, we see here, appears as a counterpart of Spain, but featuring an almost oriental splendor. And Cortés, overcome with awe, marvels at the unnatural conjunction of barbarism and civilization in Moctezuma's court. Barbarism, in six-teenth-century Castilian, at once meant foreign, savage, and pagan. Clearly for Cortés paganism does not impede the creation of a civilization, of "harmony and order," or of magnificent artifacts of gold. In fact, proselytizing against paganism plays a very secondary role in the *Segunda carta-relación*. Only once does Cortés show himself preaching to the Aztecs (p. 89). While other chroniclers were repelled by Aztec religious practices, Cortés admires the height of the temples and the size of the idols. The material splendor of Mexico's civilization eclipses its barbarism.

Cortés justifies his transgressions

Beyond this brief discussion of religion, and of the goods and "harmony and order" of their marketplaces, Cortés provides relatively little infor-mation about the Indian worlds he encountered. His "letter–relation–autobiography" is hardly an ethnography, but rather a military memoir in which the Indian peoples served purely strategic functions, real and textual. Cortés dismisses the massacre of thousands of Cholulans, a key maneuver in his military plan, saying: "the next day the whole city was full of people...as if what had happened had never taken place" (p. 105). After each siege, Cortés shows the Indians formulaically begging his pardon and swearing loyalty to the Spanish King, which thus serves as well what J. H. Elliott ("Cortés, Velázquez and Charles V", xxvii) has called the "imperial theme" of this letter designed to flatter the new Emperor Charles V.

The portrait in the *Segunda carta-relación* of one Aztec, Moctezuma, remains so extraordinary and suspect that it has given rise to questions which persist to this day. Did Moctezuma, as the two speeches which Cortés places in his mouth would have it, really cede his empire, believing the Spanish King to be a long-awaited Aztec forefather come to reclaim his birthright? Did Moctezuma go willingly into captivity? Was he indeed stoned to death by his own peoples? At least one aspect of these uncanny scenarios admits no question: that Cortés, mindful of the threat to sovereignty that his deposing of an emperor might entail, was at pains to represent Moctezuma's surrender as voluntary.

Moreover, in subtle ways Moctezuma is shown to merit his fate. The American historian W. H. Prescott well read the mixed signals planted by Cortés when he stated: "It is not easy to depict the portrait of Montezuma in its true colors, since it has been exhibited to us under two aspects, of the most opposite and contradictory character" (*History of the Conquest of Mexico*, 437). On the one hand, in the inventory sections Moctezuma appears as a sovereign of boundless wealth and power. As such, however, he abuses his power, being a tyrant hated by the peoples he subjugates and a traitor who double-deals the Spanish King even after swearing loyalty to him. On the other hand, the fearsome Moctezuma displays a love of frivolity and luxury, his tragic flaw. Puerile, as were Columbus's Indians, and self-indulgent, Cortés's Moctezuma amuses himself during his confinement ("And many times he went [to his country residences] to entertain himself, and he always returned very happy and content," p. 122). Seemingly oblivious of the events taking place around him, this Moctezuma lets himself be ruined by his excessive refinement, or civilization.

Complex as his treatment of Moctezuma may be, the central rallying point of Cortés's contrivances undoubtedly lies in the textual campaign he mounts against Diego Velázquez and Pánfilo de Narváez. Several scholars (see Elliott, "Cortés", Frankl, "Hernán Cortés", Pastor, *Discurso*) have traced the bold lines of Cortés's argumentation against his arch-enemies in the first and second letters. To wit: greed for material gain motivated them to seize Mexico for themselves and not for the Crown. Where Cortés allegedly acts as a loyal vassal in the interests of the Crown, they act out of *self*-interest. Traitors, Velázquez and Narváez incite the Indians and Moctezuma to rebel against Cortés and thus against the throne. Obedience to Velázquez, himself disloyal, thus comprises complicity with a traitor and – the final twist – rebellion against Velázquez, loyal service to the King. In framing this defense, Cortés draws upon other techniques that would come to characterize his writings. First, though there are strong indications that his *relaciones* are drafted after the fact from notes taken as the events ensued, Cortés adheres to a chronological development which eschews any over-viewing remarks or overt chronological re-ordering. Crafting them from within, he allows events to unfold in their own, seemingly ineluctable, way. Second, Cortés characterizes his allies and enemies in Manichean terms. As his ire against the interlopers swells, Cortés's invective reaches a dark fever pitch: "and should they not comply I would proceed against them as against traitors and perfidious and evil vassals who had rebelled against their king and who would usurp his realms and dominions..." (p. 150).

Cortés vindicates his failures and pleads for aid

Cortés may not re-order, but he does suppress events. To cite the most blatant example, at no point in the *relación* does he mention Alvarado's temporary leadership from which evolved the loss of Mexico. Instead, once again, the blame is imputed to Narváez. Cortés foresees that were he to leave Tenochtitlán for the coast to attend to Narváez, "the people would revolt and I would lose all the gold and jewels and the city itself" (p. 146). As a product of this self-fulfilling prophecy, whereas in the world of historical events Narváez and Velázquez almost destroy Cortés, in the textual world they ostensibly redeem him.

To narrate his only admitted failure, the events of the "Night of Sorrows" and their aftermath, the author convenes a dramatic set of techniques. Assuming an unusually emotional tone, Cortés enhances his plea for aid by giving full bathetic vent to his men's suffering, his own heroism, and the insuperable odds against them. Cortés passes as well into a mode reminiscent of the epic and the novel of chivalry in repeatedly attributing to God his small victories within the larger defeat: "had God not mysteriously desired to save us, it would have been impossible to escape from there, and already those remaining in the city had spread the news that I was dead" (p. 161). If God, as it seems, is on Cortés's side, how can the Crown deny him? After the escape from Tenochtitlán, however, the narrative returns to its formulaic rhythm, and to a triumphal mode: Cortés circles the Anáhuac Valley gaining new allies who, as ever, swear loyalty to the King. The *relación* ends with a plea for aid, having implied that the "Night of Sorrows" was less a failure than a gateway to further victories.

Even after achieving the reconquest of Mexico, mixed in with his victories Cortés would find himself having to relate failures tantamount to that of the "Night of Sorrows" and having to contrive the means to do so. In the *Tercera carta-relación* (1522) [*Third Letter*], for example, still lacking a reply from Charles V to his earlier missives, Cortés must address the fact that he razed the magnificent Tenochtitlán in reconquering it. He presents himself as a peace-loving conqueror, forced to become a warmonger by the suicidal Aztecs bent on self-destruction. While the designs, such as this, of his works respond to the ever-varying circumstances, in large part Cortés executes them through stock devices – many of which we have seen deployed in the *Segunda relación*. The Cortés of the

Cuarta carta-relación (1524) [*Fourth Letter*], now legitimated by the Spanish Emperor, feels more confident to disclose the "unrest" and mutinous "tumults" which rock the lands. Petitioning for further honors, he again vilifies his enemies for their disservice and makes great show of his own services to the Crown. Cortés emerges from the disastrous expedition to Honduras, subject of the *Quinta carta-relación* (1526) [*Fifth Letter*], a shaken and beleaguered man. His writings abandon their characteristic heroic posture, reverting to the pathos-laden emotional tone found at the end of the *Segunda relación* and carrying expressions of religious zeal to greater, and more genuine, heights. Cortés's spirit and world-view have suffered significant changes; his "language" stretches to accommodate them.

Unlike the protean writings of Columbus, then, those of Cortés draw on a limited but adaptable repertory of techniques. The presence of these characteristics in the 1519 letter, allegedly authored by the collective "Justiciary and Municipal Council of the Rica Villa de la Vera Cruz," has helped scholars identify Cortés as its architect and the legal code of Alfonso X as his pervasive political model. As Víctor Frankl argues in his pioneering article ("Hernán Cortés" 58), "The author of the *First Letter of Relation* is undoubtedly Cortés himself. Both the formal structure of the letter – analogous forms of which we find in subsequent letters – and its predominant ideological motifs, also reflected in later letters, serve as proof." The Alfonsine *Siete partidas* (dating from 1256 to 1263) provided Cortés with the ideological model of vassals and their monarch united in the common enterprise of defending the state against selfish private interest which would resonate throughout his works.[5] In the 1519 letter Cortés embroiders this paradigm using the Manichean rhetorical mode characteristic of his later writings. He zestfully depicts Velázquez as motivated by sheer greed and himself by the "zeal to serve your Majesties" (p. 48). This polarization, in turn, entitles Cortés to flout Velázquez's authority and to constitute the council of Vera Cruz in protection of the Crown's interests, actions which lay the foundations for the conqueror's subsequent maneuvers.

Given the unmistakable continuity in style, thought and actions between the first and later letters, why does Cortés here disguise his "I"? The *Siete partidas* submits that only by a consensus of all citizens can laws be set aside for the common good. Accordingly, in its key legal portion the letter switches from a third person singular to a first person plural narration. In the name of the people this "we," the body of soldiers, unanimously urges Cortés to found a town, to assume its leadership and, ultimately, that Velázquez be stripped of his powers. Cortés, in the third person, presents himself as reluctantly acceding to their requests. It is a

---

[5] Our summary of the *Siete partidas* echoes Elliott's ("Cortés") at this and other points.

masterful move, a fitting emblem of Cortés's virtuoso performances on the political, legal and literary fronts.

Gonzalo Fernández de Oviedo: Sumario de la natural historia de las Indias *(1526) and* Historia general y natural de las Indias *(1535);* Pedro Mártir de Anglería, Décadas del Nuevo Mundo *(1493–1525)*

Did anyone, we might ask as has been asked before, see the New World as if entirely for the first time? We have already formed an idea of how that question might be answered with respect to Columbus. Gonzalo Fernández de Oviedo (1478–1557), on the other hand, has been credited with being one of the first explorers capable of perceiving a new meaning in America (O'Gorman, *Cuatro historiadores de Indias*, 55). This judgment offers a provocative point of entry into Oviedo's life, thinking, and writing, particularly in terms of his *Sumario* [*Natural History of the West Indies*]. For Oviedo was raised in the Spanish court, versed in Italian renaissance culture, and a passionate devotee of things aristocratic. At the same time, he became something of a soldier of fortune who arrived in the New World early on (1514) with the post of Overseer of the Gold Foundries, spent most of his life in the Indies, and became their official chronicler (1532) as well as councilman in perpetuity of Santo Domingo and governor of its fortress. Voracious chronicler, Erasmist, staunch imperialist and Christian, Oviedo was at once *the purveyor of the new and the guardian of the old*. Let us examine in the context of the *Sumario* how this unusual conjunction shapes his attitudes towards and writings on the Indies.

The *Sumario*, the first natural history of the New World and first ethnography of Central America, was written at the request of Charles V to satisfy his curiosity about his new holdings. Oviedo composed it in Spain, from memory, reconstructing notes he had already taken for the *Historia general* (the material of the *Sumario* reappears, augmented, in the longer work). The *Sumario* follows a geographical path and the scientific taxonomy from Pliny's *Natural History*, proceeding from Hispaniola to Tierra Firme and detailing each body's fauna, flora, peoples, and "certain rites and ceremonies of these savage peoples" (p. 49).

The larger design notwithstanding, as its title indicates Oviedo's *Sumario* remains an associative miscellanea, of the peculiar and unusual facts pertaining to his subjects. In the *Sumario*'s preface Oviedo elucidates the work's purpose and the criterion of its material – to proffer novel information. "If what is contained herein lacks order," he writes, "I beg Your Majesty not to mind, but rather to consider the new things in it, which is the goal that has moved me…" (p. 49). Interestingly enough,

Oviedo's first experiences in the New World had produced a different kind of text, an aristocratic novel of chivalry set in Spain (and perhaps written in the Indies) and entitled *Don Claribalte* (1519), which contained not a word about the New World. Nonetheless, Oviedo's initial retreat into the chivalric romance, shot through as the genre is with the miraculous and awesome, could easily have sowed in him the propensity to seek out and acknowledge the new and the marvellous which now comes to the fore in the *Sumario*.

Brought to bear on nature, the criterion of novelty produced dramatically different effects than when applied to culture. Oviedo's portraits of the new flora and fauna display hyperbolic enthusiasm or balanced appreciation. He describes his subjects according to two basic parameters, the aesthetic and the practical, analytically proceeding part by part over the sensuous surface of the phenomena in a non-technical, non-theoretical, and often lyrical language. Almost romantic in his depictions, Oviedo creates and animates striking vignettes through recourse to anecdote and appeal to the senses of sight, smell, hearing, taste and touch. Typically, as in this thumbnail sketch of the "Leopards" (which are actually jaguars!) he departs from comparisons with the known to end up with the unknown and surprising: "There are also leopards in Tierra Firme, of the same shape and appearance to those seen here and in Africa, and they are swift and fierce; but neither these nor the lions up to now have harmed Christians, nor do they eat the Indians, as do the tigers" (p. 98). As we see here, captivated by the new phenomena, Oviedo often incurs in acts of benign credulousness. Novelty ignites in him a fascination not only with the beautiful but also with the dangerous and grotesque: he glories in the diversity of nature and its hidden secrets.

Oviedo's writing of the novelties of the New World natural phenomena is, to an important degree, a re-writing, which balances erudition and empiricism. Perhaps, as the acknowledgment to the classical author in the preface suggests, Oviedo set out to be the Pliny of the New World, for the *Natural History* (1st c. AD) conceivably inspired not only the *Sumario*'s taxonomy of animals, but also its utilitarian view of science, its sensuousness, and exuberant appreciation of nature. Something of a Book of World Records, the *Natural History* both revels in the superlative and the curious and gravitates towards the extremes of human and natural phenomena, as does the *Sumario*. At the same time, Oviedo attaches much importance in the preface to his own extensive firsthand knowledge of the *Sumario*'s material, to which he attributes the truth and uniqueness of his text. This experience and experimentation echo insistently throughout the *Sumario*'s natural descriptions as Oviedo backs them with references to his "I" that has tasted, witnessed, touched, heard, and so on, the various phenomena – which makes the *Sumario* a *de facto* autobiography.

Throwing into relief his own contribution, he also counters the ancients, correcting and modifying their observations as well as noting those phenomena which are entirely new. The interplay of empiricism and erudition allows Oviedo to see beyond the classics, a grid which in the Renaissance both enabled and impeded new scientific perceptions.[6]

Comprehension of the new by Oviedo and other chroniclers, to use J. H. Elliott's words, did not progress in a linear fashion, but rather entailed "a series of advances and retreats" (*The Old World*, 14). The practical or extrinsic aspects of Amerindian culture – their food, food-gathering, and living arrangements – occasion the same appreciative equanimity and descriptive techniques found in Oviedo's characterizations of nature. The author's aristocratic eye conditions him to admire, as well, manifestations of Indian nobility and pageantry. When, however, in the long Chapter 10, "The Indians of Tierra Firme: their customs, rites and ceremonies," he turns his attention to these intrinsic features of the native world, Oviedo's apprehension of the new becomes one of ill-will and sensationalism. Though he generally maintains a factual stance and his language only rarely curdles into invective (as in describing the Indians of Urabá: "and they eat human flesh, and they are abominable, sodomites, and cruel. . .," p. 73), Oviedo's selection of "novel" material betrays his judgmental attitude toward the Indians whom he sees as "laced" in the devil's clutches (p. 84). In Chapter 10 and other parts of the *Sumario* Oviedo treats, with a certain credulousness and sometimes overt condemnation: cannibalism, devil worship, shamanic practices, sacrifices, homosexuality, sodomy, polygamy, rape, nudity, abortions, burial rituals, war practices, and so on. To him, in this unfortunate vein, we owe the first portrait of the real indigenous women (as opposed to the mythic Amazons described by Columbus and Pané), whom he grotesquely represents as creatures of unbridled sensuality. Bearer of the Spanish moral code, Oviedo codifies New World culture according to his world's parameters.

Though in large measure for Oviedo and Pané the differences between the Old World and the New are the same, Oviedo's familiarity with other contexts tempers – but not undoes – his harsh portrait of the Indians. At one point he states that far from being unique to the Indians such practices as sacrifices, superstitions, and devil worship were common to the Greek, Roman, and Trojan pagan worlds (p. 82). Furthermore, unlike other chroniclers, Oviedo perceived the Indians as forming part of the human race: "in some places they are black, in other provinces very white, but they are all men" (p. 94). In Book Two of the *Historia* Oviedo would claim that the Indies were in fact the legendary Hesperides, which he argues were formerly possessed by Spain. The Indians' condition as lapsed

[6] See chapter 1 of Elliott's *The Old World and the New* and Alvarez López ("La historia natural en Fernández de Oviedo") for a discussion of this important theme.

Spaniards and Catholics, then, both qualifies them as human beings and justifies Oviedo's moralistic stance.

Neither this nor Oviedo's criterion of novelty, however, fully explains his readiness to tell transgressive tales. The author's unabashed prurience, suspension of decorum (this is, after all, a *relación* addressed to the King), and scandal sheet sensationalism are unmatched in contemporaneous works and certainly run counter to Pané's discomfort with his exotic material. On the one hand, we can trace Oviedo's attitude to the early "ethnographies" with which he was familiar. In the *Historia* Oviedo cites not only Pliny but also St Isidore and Pedro Mejía. These Spanish authors, like Pliny, wrote works of a popular cast propagating tales of the curiosities, marvels, monsters, and bizarre practices of little-known places and peoples (see Hogden, *Early Anthropology in the Sixteenth and Seventeenth Centuries*, Chs. 1 and 2) Once again, in presenting his new material Oviedo is still in a sense telling old tales.

On the other hand, a rather more comprehensive explanation of Oviedo's delight in shocking information and his criterion of novelty is to be found in the dynamics of the *relación* (he variously terms his work a "summary," a "repertory" and a "*relación*"). We know what Oviedo thinks about the state of the Indians' souls; what has this Overseer of the Foundries to say of gold? The author devotes the last three chapters of the *Sumario* to the precious commodities of gold and pearls. Though he has not before, here Oviedo directly addresses the Crown's material concerns, with hyperbolic praise for the innumerable riches contained in the Indies. At the same time, the author ostentatiously displays his *knowledge* regarding mining, navigation, and pearl-fishing, noting that he has often been paid as a consultant (pp. 161–2). Oviedo, not a conqueror who can deliver to the Crown the actual booty of his labors, makes his writing and unique information of all sorts something of a material commodity – his "gold" and his service. In the last sentence of the *Sumario*, he concludes: "since this material is without comparison, and so bizarre, I regard my vigils, and the time and efforts that it has cost me to see and register these things as well spent, and particularly so if your majesty should consider himself well served by this small service..." (p. 178). With Oviedo, knowledge becomes a valuable unit of exchange in the conquest of America, and his conquest an intellectual one.

The new and the classical, erudition and empiricism, word and wealth, all join forces in the *Sumario* to "authorize" Oviedo, that is, to give authority to his efforts and to showcase him as an author. Oviedo would take this dual "authorizing" to new heights and effects in the *Historia general y natural de las Indias*. In 1532, the same year that he lost the governership of Cartagena to which he had aspired, Oviedo was appointed Official Chronicler by Charles V. One might surmise that, having failed to achieve political position, Oviedo would aim for recognition and even a certain kind of power as a writer. Indeed, in the Prologue to the *Historia*, he emphasizes his "natural inclination" (Tudela Bueso edition, vol. 1, 4) to writing, swears to "dedicate the rest of his life" (1, 9) to chronicling every corner of the world under his charge as a writer, and underscores the physical travails and dangers that acquiring knowledge has cost him. Oviedo's biographers maintain that he never ceased to press for political position (see Otté, "Aspiraciones y actividades heterogéneas de Gonzalo Fernández de Oviedo, cronista"). Be there or not a hidden agenda in his disclaiming of material rewards, here he speaks as a writer and intellectual who makes it clear that the only rewards he desires are intangible: the salvation of his soul, the "grace" of the King, and "my honor" (1, 12). For Cortés and other actors *cum* chroniclers the abstract "fama" (fame and good reputation) so prized in Golden Age Spain were secondary products of their writings. For Oviedo the writer, "fama" was ostensibly the primary goal. The magnified sense of authorship and writing that we have found in Oviedo, a new development in the historiography of the New World reflecting a new relationship with the Crown, would shape the most characteristic features of the *Historia* – to which we now turn.

In the Prologue and elsewhere Oviedo declares himself to be overwhelmed by the enormity of his material. And well he might be, for in the omnivorous *Historia* Oviedo sets himself the task of chronicling the discovery, conquest, settlement, nature, and culture of the Caribbean, Mexico, Central *and* South America, from the inception of their existence for the Old World to the present. A compulsive writer, Oviedo conceivably began constructing the *Historia* in 1514 and continued to compose it, in tandem with other weighty projects, to his death in 1557. As a result, the five-volume Tudela Bueso edition of the fifty-book *Historia* contains more than 2,000 pages. Perhaps due to its forbidding bulk, only about one-quarter of the work saw print in Oviedo's lifetime (the *Historia* was published in its entirety for the first time in 1851): in 1535, the prologue, first nineteen and part of what would become the fiftieth books, were published in Seville, while a second edition of the material came out in 1547. The 1535 version (volumes I and II of the Tudela Bueso edition from which we quote) contains, in expanded form, all the material of the *Sumario*, and also the navigation routes and the Spanish history to that date of Hispaniola, Puerto Rico, Cuba, Tierra Firme, and Jamaica; it ends, as would the final *Historia*, with tales of shipwrecks. In the 1535 version we find, as well, almost all the defining features of the definitive *Historia*. We shall focus on these features while bringing in pertinent material from the full work.

In view of his attitudes towards authorship, it is curious that both the manner in which Oviedo compiled the *Historia* and the work's resulting structure appear to entail a *lack* of authorial direction on his part. In Santo Domingo, Oviedo received from all principal actors and political figures in the Conquest the reports that the Crown had ordered be sent to him. Its sources make the *Historia* the greatest single repository of information on the early years of the Spanish New World. As reports arrived, Oviedo would incorporate them into the *Historia*. Overall, the *Historia* attempts to follow a dual design, geographical and chronological. As if drawing a supreme map, the work focuses on an area, outlines its geographic contours, and then fills in the map with the cultural and natural phenomena as well as historical events in chronological order pertaining to that region. Yet Oviedo, so entranced with his sources, would vitiate that design by presenting multiple, even contradictory, accounts of the same events and by disrupting the chronological development to incorporate information as it arrived. Chapter headings such as the following give an idea of Oviedo's predilections and of the incoherencies which have tarnished the *Historia*'s reputation as a well-crafted history: "Of a case recently come to the attention of the author of these histories, with new material, recently occurred, remarkable to all who have heard and learned of it..." (I, 221).

Irrespective of his personal predilections, Oviedo's *modus operandi* recalls that of medieval chroniclers whose task it was essentially to transcribe historical sources. In fact, Oviedo describes himself as one who accumulates and compiles material. Yet, working within this mode, he creates special roles for the chronicler, and despite the appearance of textual disorder controls his material in the following ways. First, he rarely limits himself to the mere transcription of his sources. Rather, he generally edits, synthesizes and rewrites them: adding personal judgments and correcting their information, weaving them into a third-person narrative, and often enlivening their utilitarian prose with invented speeches, characterization, and psychological nuance. With Oviedo, Gerbi observes, the chronicle genre "which was on its last legs in Europe, takes on a new lease on life in the Indies and rises to 'real literary heights'" (*Nature in the New World*, 245). Second, he assumes personal responsibility for the veracity of his sources, claiming the space between events and their depiction as his own territory (hence the editorial interventions we have mentioned). Third, he transforms his *Historia* into a kind of encyclopedia by elaborately cross-referencing its material. And finally, aware of the peculiarities of his text, he puts forth a notion of truth that justifies the multiple versions of particular events that he frequently offers. In Book 33 the author presents truth to be the sum of diverse perspectives. Since no one but God holds the key to absolute truth, Oviedo suggests with an interesting metaphor that mortals, and the *Historia*, can only function like a courtroom which admits a gamut of testimonies (IV, 224).

Other of our historians had paused to reflect on their task as writers.

Both Columbus and Cortés have literarily self-conscious moments in which they claim themselves to be incapable of registering the abundance and extraordinary nature of the material of the New World. Oviedo takes literary self-consciousness much further and offers a theoretical justification for the material and structure of his text. In book after book of the *Historia* he reiterates the typically renaissance notion that in nature, which is God's handiwork, we can read His signature; the contemplation of nature leads to the contemplation of God. Oviedo transplants this Spanish renaissance attitude, adapting it to the challenges of the New World. For him, the vast unexplored reality of the Indies comprises a *"mare magno"* fraught with "secrets," that is, with new examples of God's infinite powers: "The secrets of this great world of our Indies will always teach new things, both to us and to those who follow us in this contemplation and delightful reading of the works of God" (I, 224). It is the purpose, Oviedo indicates in Book 32, of both the general (the properly historical) and natural poles of the *Historia* to reveal such virgin secrets. Even the autobiographical information which Oviedo presents, much more substantial than in the *Sumario*, accords with the notion of secrets. For example, he introduces his wife in Book 6 by noting that she never spat and that overnight her hair turned white. In his theological explanation, then, we find the ultimate rationalization of the criterion of novelty. Further, that the secrets unfold at their own unpredictable pace vindicates the extremely random manner in which information is inserted in the *Historia*, the writing of Oviedo's reading of the world's secrets. For this reason, Oviedo compares his *Historia* to a banquet of savory and varied dishes (I, 218 *et passim*).

So delicious is the banquet, so captivating the text's "secrets," that Oviedo intends his work to tempt readers away from more pernicious readings. Though himself the author of a novel of chivalry, later in life Oviedo evinces an Erasmian's dislike for this frivolous pastime, denouncing the novels as "depraved treatises," "completely lacking in truth" (II, 312). Harboring considerable literary ambitions for the *Historia*, Oviedo repeatedly offers it as substitute for and corrective counterpart of the novel of chivalry. His *Historia* replaces the "fabulous vanities" of the novel of chivalry with the real marvels of the New World that turn one's thoughts to God: "So foreign and new are these things in themselves that there is no need for fictions to win the reader's admiration or to justify our infinite thanks to the Master of Nature" (II, 7).

The didactic and moralistic tendencies of Erasmianism, in combination with Oviedo's own judgmental character, determine the last and the major of the *Historia*'s new roles. We have seen that Oviedo, Official Chronicler, ostensibly aspires to no material reward. His post requires him, as Oviedo himself notes, to remain faithful only to the "purity and value of the truth" (I, clxvi). Free to speak the truth, in fact morally and professionally obligated to do so, Oviedo styles himself as a severe critic of the Conquest, making the *Historia* a huge forum for the verbal punishment of immorality of all sorts.

It is important to note that in the *Historia* Oviedo prominently displays the sins of the Spaniards as well as what he considers to be those of the pagan Indians, making his work something of a universal history of infamy. (Praise, we should note, is given where Oviedo deems it due, but this is not generally the case.) In fact, much of the general part of the history revolves almost unrelievedly around the topics which Oviedo at one point defines as "uprisings and evils and ugly deeds, combined with the betrayals and treacheries and lack of loyalty in certain men who have come here..." (II, 40). For Oviedo, the New World is a 'House of Discord" (II, 408), and his *Historia* teems with stories of overweening ambition, power abused, and honor forsaken. Neither conquerors nor priests escape his condemnation. Gold and souls are placed on the same plane as Oviedo deplores their loss – he exposes the greedy priests who neglect their religious obligations to garner wealth. Oviedo's position as Overseer of the Gold Foundries gave him a window onto the world of Spanish avarice, against which he repeatedly inveighs, for example: "men's wicked greed disposes them to all kinds of travails, revulsions and dangers" (II, 144). Curiously enough, at these points his vehement tone, moral stance and unflagging criticisms of the Spaniards render Oviedo's voice virtually indistinguishable from that of his pro-Indian adversary, Bartolomé de las Casas.

Probably the more telling comparison, throwing into relief fundamental characteristics of both works, is the one to be drawn between Oviedo's *Historia* and the *Décadas del Nuevo Mundo* [*De orbe novo. The Eight Decades of Peter Marty d'Anghera*] by Pedro Mártir de Anglería (1457–1526). Their circumstances and methodology bear interesting resemblances. A Milanese steeped in Italian Humanism, Mártir spent many years in the Spanish court of Ferdinand and Isabel as confessor to the Queen, and as *de facto* Chronicler of the Indies. Though he never set foot in the New World (for which reason we accord his work less prominence in this essay), Mártir zealously gathered what information he could about the New World, reading reports and interviewing participants in the events. Writing in Latin between 1493 and 1525, he circulated this information in letters to his correspondents that were published in piecemeal fashion as the *Décadas* and eventually as the volume *De orbe novo*. Like Oviedo and with equal disorder, he would impart information as it reached him, thrilled with each new morsel ("What plate could be more delicious to an intelligent mind than this news...?", p. x) and with particular relish for the novelties of the New World.

Oviedo, writing to the Crown from Santo Domingo, makes knowledge his currency, moral weapon, and power in the conquest of the New World. Mártir, largely outside of the fray, writes history as a detached intellectual, achieving recognition for his cultural sophistication. The *Décadas* therefore lack the very aggressive self-consciousness that characterizes the *Historia* on several fronts. Trenchant judgments, vendettas, autobiography, and theorizing about history, all take a back seat for the serene Mártir to the casting of his information in humanist terms. For, as we glimpsed in his interpretation of Pané's *relación*, Mártir sees the New World as the reincarnation of the golden age of classical myths, as the pastoral and utopian mythical world come to life. With this perspective he circumvents the thorny issues of New World events, preferring to concentrate with Olympian transcendence on the "delightful and genial" (p. 319) subjects that, as we shall see, he embroiders to great literary effect. Catering to his readers' enjoyment, which depends on both his polished style and the novelty of the material, Mártir writes with the sole aim of giving pleasure: "I could hardly adorn a thing with more elegant trappings...because I never took pen in hand to write as a historian, but only to give pleasure" (p. 7). Thus, where Oviedo uses his information to a variety of ends, Mártir considers the humanist's sensibility and zeal for knowledge to be sufficient ends in themselves.

The *Décadas* are a magnificent example of the humanist literary aesthetic of the Old World. Mártir rallies a wide variety of rhetorical devices, vivid verbs, adjectives, images, and superlatives, as well as examples from classical history and myth, in the effort to give history the flavor of a story. With admirable flair and balanced sentences, he dramatizes his accounts – extrapolating details, rounding out the characters and presenting idealized portraits of the lush New World landscape somewhat reminiscent of Columbus's. His is an elegantly controlled yet emotive, colorful, and lively writing.

Despite the humanist tendencies which we saw deployed in the *Sumario*, and perhaps betraying a certain "anxiety of influence," Oviedo took exception to the writings of his fellow chronicler. He railed at Mártir and similar historians who write in an ornate and artificial style, with no direct knowledge of their subjects. The New World, and especially the "House of Discord" would require another aesthetic. As Oviedo tells us with reference to the *Historia*, it would be a simple style with a moralistic bent: the common and uneducated will find in his lines "sufficient examples for the punishment and correction of their lives" (III, 364). When Oviedo shapes the raw historical material into a story, unlike Mártir's they are likely to be exemplary tales, often capped with moralizing aphorisms. Moreover, as one deduces from the *Historia*, the narrative of the New World from within would feature local anecdotes and detail, and even a measure of sarcasm and black humor. Thoroughly engaged with its material and lacking a transcendent perspective, New World historiography such as the *Historia* would show what really happens when the stuff of the novels of chivalry meets reality. Indeed, the delight in the "baroque, anecdotal and minute" (Salas, *Tres cronistas de Indias*, 103) for which the *Historia* has been roundly criticized, would endure in works such as Bernal Díaz del Castillo's, *Historia verdadera de la conquista de la Nueva España (c.* 1568) and Juan Rodríguez Freyle's *El carnero* (1636–1638) [*The Conquest of New Granada*], to become a defining characteristic of colonial narrative.

Alvar Núñez Cabeza de Vaca: Naufragios *(1542)*

In 1527 Alvar Núñez (1490?–1559?) set sail as deputy and treasurer of the 600-man expedition led by Pánfilo de Narváez, under orders to explore and conquer Florida. A series of catastrophic shipwrecks left Núñez on land as captain of vastly reduced forces, and condemned to eight years of wanderings across southwestern North America from Texas to California and finally to Mexico, where his company rejoined other Spaniards. Only four of the men emerged alive from the travails of this shipwrecked life in Indian territories. Alvar Núñez would tell their tale and his own in a *relación* to the Crown written sometime after 1537, published in 1542, and later aptly titled *Naufragios* [*Relation of Núñez Cabeza de Vaca*]. Now, from Homer to the Byzantine novel and beyond, shipwrecks possess a rich literary history and are charged with symbolic possibilities, of rebirth of the individual and recreation of society. New World historiography would not fail to capitalize on the special resonances of shipwrecks. When Oviedo presents Núñez's *relación* in Book XXXIII of the *Historia*, he frames it as a moral tale. In his version the Spaniards are cast into wandering in atonement for the greed exemplified by their leader Narváez, from which journey the "pilgrims" are rescued by God, who endows them with miraculous healing powers. (We find a similar allegorical thrust in the tales of shipwrecks presented in the fiftieth book of the *Historia*, mentioned above). When Núñez tells his own shipwreck tale of rebirth into Indian life, he endows it not only with moral but also with exalted human and literary dimensions. Núñez's *Naufragios* is one of the richest works in early colonial narrative, and the one which has received the most worthy critical treatment.[7] For here the shipwreck tale

The considerable ethnographic, ideological and literary interest of *Naufragios* has merited it much, and sophisticated, critical attention. Since the text so exemplifies the premises of this study, it has often been discussed in terms similar to ours. Our discussion thus relies heavily, and gratefully, on the studies by Lagmanovich ("Los *Naufragios*...como construcción narrativa"), Lewis ("Los *Naufragios* de Alvar Núñez"), Molloy ("Alteridad y reconocimiento en los *Naufragios*"), and Pupo-Walker (*La vocación literaria*, "Pesquisas," and "Notas"), as joins forces with an authentic portrait of Indian life of the New World and with the *relación*, of a failed expedition, resulting in a multi-faceted work each of whose aspects we shall treat in turn.

In the characteristic heroic tale of the Spanish Conquest, such as we have found in Cortés or to a degree in Columbus (and later in Bernal Díaz and Francisco López de Gómara), the conqueror arrives at a new place, conquers it, and imposes his society's culture on the subjugated territory. With Núñez we witness the shipwreck not only of the conquerors but also of the colonialist enterprise. As this conqueror is conquered by the Indians – both overpowered by them and enticed to greater understanding of their world – he undergoes a spiritual transformation and the heroic tale perforce suffers significant reversals. The first stage of this unfolding drama, after their early shipwrecks, finds the Spaniards trying desperately to survive in Florida by the familiar means of capturing Indians and bribing them with small trinkets. Their definitive shipwreck on the peninsula which they name the Isla de Mal Hado (the Isle of Bad Fortune, near Galveston, Texas), however, entails a symbolic death and rebirth. "[A]s naked as when we were born and having lost all we had with us," Núñez writes, "we were the very figure of death" (p. 72). Like the figuratively and literally naked Indians portrayed by Columbus, they are now apt subjects for the apprenticeship to a new culture which begins shortly thereafter. The Indians who encounter them in this piteous state allegedly weep to see the Spaniards so transfigured, yet they assign their captives brutal tasks. Similar to Cortés but to different purpose, Núñez soon realizes that the tribes are at war and makes himself a merchant who circulates between the hostile groups, thus securing for himself freedom of movement and from slavery. Yet the next step in this picaresque battle against hunger finds him a slave once again, of the one-eyed Indian and his family who hold another Spaniard captive. Here Núñez learns to eat the *tunas* (prickly pears) which are the sustenance and center of the Indians' existence.

The goal of Núñez's expedition is neither conquest nor discovery, but rather sheer survival and return. To this end, he and his companions effect their escape from the Isla de Mal Hado and its *tuna*-gathering Indians, who have displayed a sadism towards the foreigners tantamount to that of certain Spaniards towards the Indians. At this crucial point six years after their shipwreck, when the Spaniards are left to their own devices, they resort to a hybrid form of faith-healing. The Indians of the Isla de Mal

well as on Carreño ("*Naufragios*"), Invernizzi ("Naufragios e infortunios"), Lafaye ("Les miracles"), and my own writings on the subject ("Historia y escritura," *Ariadne's Thread*). Such recent critical works overlap and build upon each other, in a productive dialogue. For this reason, and to avoid over-burdening our essay, we have not cited the source(s) of several points – and ask the authors' indulgence for these omissions.

Hado had earlier forced them to heal by threatening to take away their food; reluctantly the Spaniards agreed, and performed a ceremony which merged elements of the Indian ritual they had witnessed with practices taken from the Catholic mass. Núñez writes that from this event they had acquired the fame as healers which they would now turn into their passport out of penury and slavery. As the small group of Spaniards passes from tribe to tribe, "with the help of God" they effect ever more miraculous cures on ever growing numbers of Indians. From their adaptation of an Indian ceremony, curiously enough, they are successful in obtaining the hallmarks of their own civilization: cooked meat and houses. Their reputation and the divine powers attributed to them grow, causing the Spaniards to acquire a following of 3–4,000 Indians. Having found a place in the Indian world, no longer having to struggle for survival, Núñez makes a place for it in his mind. The increasingly detailed ethnographic information about each tribe that he registers in *Naufragios* reflects his sharpened perceptions.

At the height of their triumphs, the Spaniards come upon indications of the presence of other "Christians" – a copper bell fashioned in a manner unusual to the Indians. In the beginning Núñez had described gold as "all that we value" (p. 48); now they prize metals for their less material value as signs of civilization. As he undertakes his return to the Spanish world, it is not gold but souls upon which Núñez places the most premium. Healing, in the last five chapters, cedes to explicit preaching to the Indians who have been terrified by the violence of other Spaniards (Núñez has now mastered six Indian languages). And, as opposed to the efforts at conversion seen in most of our texts, Núñez's bear fruit – for the Indians readily obey these Spaniards whose beneficial actions have gained them such "authority" in the New World. The greatest fruits of Núñez's experiences, however, emerge in his dramatic return to the Spanish world. While the first Spaniards Núñez encounters are amazed at his Indian appearance ("they were greatly disturbed to see me so strangely dressed and in the company of Indians," p. 130) Núñez himself has been appalled at the cruel treatment the Spanish have accorded the Indians. The "conquered" conqueror now preaches to his *own kind* in benefit of the Indians, using his achievements to argue, as did Bartolomé de las Casas, for the fair treatment and non-violent conversion of the indigenous peoples.

Other, more pointed, ironies underscore the distinctive character of Núñez's tale and experiences *vis-à-vis* those in our purview. In *Naufragios* there is no mention of Indian cannibalism. Only Spaniards (other than Núñez and his men) resort to cannibalism in the effort to survive. The Indians are reportedly scandalized at their behavior. Nor are Indian religious practices seen by Núñez as diabolical. The only "devil" to

appear in the text is "Mala Cosa" ["Bad thing"]. A demonic double of
Núñez and his men, this legendary bearded healer cured the Indians
through terrifyingly violent techniques. In *Naufragios*, another legend, of
the Spaniards as "Children of the Sun," reemerges in an unexpected
context. As the Spaniards perform their cures, the natives who accompany
them begin to charge their fellow Indians for the foreigners' services and
indeed to rob and pillage them. "[A]nd to console them," writes Núñez,
"the thieves told them that we were the children of the Sun" (p. 114). For
once, the Spaniards deny their own divinity, denouncing the title as a lie
which their fellow-travellers have fabricated to suit their own gain. We
can intuit from this that a second unwonted development is involved in
the cures as portrayed by Núñez. When, fulfilling Columbus's description,
the cured Indians give all too generously of their possessions, the
Spaniards refuse material gain beyond that necessary for sustenance. It is
the entrepreneurial Indians, re-enacting certain of the worst aspects of the
Spanish Conquest, who terrorize and plunder.

Finally we note the irony that, having left their own civilization behind,
the Spaniards are purportedly able to realize its purest values, untainted
by the greed and immorality endemic in the Conquest. In one of the last
chapters Núñez has the Indians offer an extraordinary panegyric to the
"difference" of the friendly Spaniards, as his native followers draw a
comparison between the Spaniards they know and those whom they fear.
(The Indians whom Núñez overhears maintain) "that we cured the sick,
and they killed the healthy; and that we were naked and barefoot while
they were clothed and on horses and with lances; and that we coveted
nothing...while the others desired only to steal everything they found..."
(p. 132). What the "we," in their purity, have achieved is something
approaching the millenary state envisioned by the Franciscans for the
New World. Núñez leaves the Indians setting up churches, and transformed, one might conclude, into better Christians than the Spaniards
who would enslave them.

In thus emphasizing his fame and success in the Indian world, Núñez
clearly has in mind his fame and success in the world of the Spanish court.
Núñez's remarks in the prologue reveal that the author expects his
relación to redress the failures of the shipwrecked expedition. Either
fortune or God, he explains in the apologetic vein characteristic of the
prologue, can foil an individual's "desire and will" to serve. In setting out
on this expedition, Núñez had believed that his "works and services"
would speak for him in such a manner that "I would have no need to speak
in order to be counted"[8] among those who render Charles V service.

---

[8] The prologue to *Naufragios*, though much studied recently, has not been reproduced in most
readily available editions; it can be found in Billy Thurman Mart's "A critical edition with a
study of the style of *La Relación* by Alvar Núñez Cabeza de Vaca" (unpublished dissertation,
University of Southern California, 1974). Regretfully, we have only been able to consult the

Instead, he can only offer this report of his misadventures, "which I beg be received in name of service, for only this could a man who emerged naked take away with him" (cited in Pastor, *Discurso*, 292). As was the case with Oviedo, but now under more dire circumstances, in lieu of heroic actions and material booty the *relación* becomes the primary form of service.

This *relación*, an act of service in itself, also makes a case for the various services Núñez rendered the Crown in the New World. The careful reader can discern in *Naufragios* three distinct registers – units of style and content – each of which bespeaks a different kind of meritorious service. The first register corresponds to the tragic phase, that of the actual shipwrecks and the miseries they occasioned. Here we find Núñez assuming a patently non-heroic voice which emotively dramatizes the hostile environment, sufferings and misfortunes of which they were victims. A climate of bad omens (in Florida they find the coffins of several Castilian merchants) and optics of fear ("within a half hour there came another hundred arrow-shooting Indians, and no matter what their size, our fear made them out to be giants," p. 71) mark this section. Núñez repeatedly enumerates long lists of the obstacles they faced. In a similar vein, he makes notable use in this first section of the *brevitatis formula*, a rhetorical device of understatement which here serves to intensify that which it cuts short: "I'll leave off telling this at length since anyone can imagine what might happen in so strange and evil a land, so lacking in any kind of relief..." (p. 32). Further, as we saw earlier, at crucial moments and to great effect Núñez switches narrative perspective to detail the *Indians'* reactions to the Spaniards' reduced state. All of these devices, in accentuating the hardships they have endured, make a compelling case for suffering as a service in itself, worthy of reward.

In the prologue Núñez promises to "bring Your Majesty the *relación* of that which in ten years, and in the many and strange lands through which I wandered lost and naked, I was able to learn and see" (cited in Lewis, "Los *Naufragios* de Alvar Núñez," 684). His experiences in the New World have turned our author from a man of arms into a man of letters whose report can serve as a guide for future travellers: "I have desired to tell this so that...those who might come here are advised of their [the Indians'] customs" (pp. 106–7). The second register, then, are the extensive sections of ethnographic observations interspersed in the narrative of his life among the Indians after the shipwrecks. Like Oviedo, Núñez concentrates on the "strange customs" (p. 80) of the Indian world, but his accounts are largely lacking in the eurocentric biases found in most early New World ethnography. Unlike Pané and Oviedo, Núñez draws

prologue in its entirety in the English translation by Buckingham Smith; we translate from those substantial portions quoted in Spanish by Lewis ("Los *Naufragios*") and Pastor (*Discurso*). Enrique Pupo-Walker prepared the first critical edition of *Naufragios* (Madrid, Castalia, 1992). Unfortunately, it was not available when I wrote this essay.

few comparisons, implicit or explicit, with his own world or other cultures. This is not a narrow perspective: he sees the Indian world not as barbaric, but as a civilization in its own right whose customs it is his duty to report.

Critics have not failed to note that whereas the first nineteen chapters of *Naufragios* cover six years of his experiences, the second nineteen (beginning when the Spaniards become full-time healers) cover only two. This triumphant and privileged phase of Núñez's experiences, our third register, contains the most enigmatic features of the text. In the elaborately wrought final section we find a landscape of miraculous and portentous events endowed with hagiographic and literary overtones. From Núñez's resuscitations of the dead to the prophecy by the "Mooress from Hornachos" that the expedition would fail and that God would work miracles for, and indeed make wealthy, anyone who managed to survive it, here the author creates an imaginative climate which renders the supernatural natural and expectable. As Núñez writes in the prologue: the reader will find in his text "certain very new things which although they are difficult for some to believe, can be believed with no doubt, and believed to be true" (cited in Lewis "Los *Naufragios*," 685). Despite his assurances, the reality of the incredible events remains in question; however, the *function* of these elements in the text is unquestionable. For, as it did for Cortés, the portrayal of his misfortunes as determined by a God who performs miracles on the Spaniards' behalf directly serves Núñez's apologetic interests. Culminating in the sermons which Núñez transcribes through indirect discourse in the text's final chapters, and in his evangelical achievements, the third register transforms the failed expedition into a spiritual success, another kind of heroic tale.

Núñez's use of biblical allusions and hagiographic resonances in this phase merits special attention. In narrating the miraculous cures he has effected, the author observes a certain delicacy, taking care to attribute them to God. A symbolic incident at the outset of his career as a faith-healer (in chapter 21) can be construed as divinely sanctioning Núñez: naked and lost in the wilderness, he comes upon a burning bush whose heat keeps him alive for five days. In the next chapter we find Núñez reviving the dead and placed in the position of principal healer. During his five days in the wilderness, Núñez allegedly ate nothing, and his unshod feet streamed with blood. Similar moments of martyrdom are thrust upon him by the circumstances, and the emotive tone of the earlier tragic phase takes on heroic saintly echoes: "Finding myself in these trying circumstances I had no choice or consolation but to think of the Passion of our redeemer Jesus Christ and of the blood he spilt for me..." (pp. 101–2). Later, accompanied by their vast cult of Indians who believed that "we had come from Heaven" (p. 124) and *en route* back to the Spanish world, the Spaniards hardly eat or sleep, propelled by an asceticism that they seem to have taken upon themselves to set an example for their followers. Much as the Spaniards might appear to determine their own fate, at the very end of the text Núñez presents the entire adventure as preordained. As we mentioned above, the author draws upon the prophecy – a device found in hagiography, the Byzantine novel, and in other shipwreck tales – to set his enterprise in a circular and providential framework: "[A]nd everything in the trip had happened to us just as she predicted" (p. 141).

Martyrdom is but one of the guises in which Núñez casts himself. The author carves out a positive role for himself in each phase of this three-act drama. Hoping to be awarded the Governorship of Florida (which, unbeknownst to him, had already been given to Hernando de Soto), Núñez wastes no opportunity to present his own actions in a favorable light. At first, he insistently contrasts himself with Narváez, criticizing the leader's cowardly ineptitude and taking the helm of the ship, and expedition, when Narváez bails out. In the second mode he highlights his role as writer, chosen imparter of ethnographic information. Throughout, and increasingly in the third mode, Núñez focuses the narration on himself and his heroic achievements as the most outstanding healer, leader of the expedition back to the Spanish world, and intermediary on the Indian's behalf. It is this heroic image of Núñez (rather than that of the picaresque anti-hero, another possible reading of the work) which has been consecrated over the years by the readers of *Naufragios* – proof of the efficacy of Núñez's self-portrayal (Lewis, "Los *Naufragios*," 688–9). And, we might surmise, it was to a degree his effective transformation of anti-hero into hero of many dimensions and of shipwreck into heroic tale, which won him the Governorship of Río de la Plata from Charles V shortly after he presented this *relación*.

Bartolomé de las Casas, Brevísima relación de la destrucción de las Indias *(1542)*

We have seen that Oviedo and Núñez, writing from personal experience, carry the writings of the Indies onto a new plane critical of the Conquest. In Spain, too, the question of the Indies and particularly of the rights of the Indians had become more pressing on several fronts. By the time Oviedo and Núñez wrote, early laws regarding the Indians (the Laws of Burgos, 1512) had been enacted to little effect, the overseeing Council of the Indies had been formed (1524), and royal and papal edicts had been issued to protect the Indians' rights. Further, with the advent in the 1520s of Spain's juridical–theological renaissance through the efforts of the so-called School of Salamanca, the debate on the Indians had taken on philosophical dimensions. In his famous lectures at the University of Salamanca from

1529 to 1546, Francisco de Vitoria argued that the Indians should be considered rational beings with rights of dominion to their lands (see Pagden, *The Fall of Natural Man*, Ch. 4). In 1542, exactly fifty years and one month after Columbus's landfall, the debate came to a head as the Crown promulgated the New Laws abolishing the *encomienda* – the most sweeping reforms of Spanish Indianist policy to be proposed during the entire colonial period.

The Dominican friar, Bartolomé de las Casas (1474–1557) played a key role in this drama. Since 1514 he had single-mindedly devoted himself to defending the Indians' rights to their lands and peaceful measures of conversion. In the New World he had tried, if unsuccessfully, to put his theories into effect; when these efforts failed he turned to writing and drafted several treatises to the Council of the Indies advocating the rights of the native populations along the lines proposed by the School of Salamanca. After having been summoned to address the Council of the Indies then considering the New Laws, Las Casas was asked by Charles V to present in writing a summary of his position. The result was the *Brevísima* [*The Spanish Colonie*], composed for the Crown in 1542 to promote the New Laws which his ideas had helped to shape, and updated and published ten years later.

This monolithic denunciation of the Spanish destruction of the Indies speaks in many tongues to promote its cause. An unrelenting *memorial de agravios* [memoir of offenses], the *Brevísima* presents evidence, general and particular, of the damage wrought by the Spanish. It adheres to the outward scaffolding of a *history* in chronologically and systematically examining the decimation of each known territory of the New World. Something of an anti-history as well, the *Brevísima* details from a global point of view the story that Núñez – filtered through the prism of his own experiences and objectives – had begun to tell, that is, the history not of the Indies but of the Indians under fifty years of Spanish domination. As such, the *Brevísima* *re*tells, among others, the stories told by Columbus, Pané, and Cortés, filling in the spaces they often strategically left blank. (When, for example, Las Casas recounts the first stages of the conquest of Mexico, he focuses exclusively on the slaughter of the Cholulans, the imprisonment of Moctezuma, and Alvarado's massacre of the Aztecs.) The *Brevísima* argues the Indians' case from a *philosophical* position and demonstrates that the Spanish actions have violated divine, human, and natural laws. Las Casas adduces *autobiographical* information, personal testimony backed by the integrity of his "I," in support of the *Brevísima*'s claims. Finally, as its title indicates, the *Brevísima* is a *relación*, urging the Crown to support the reforms or risk Spain's moral perdition. This petition had taken on even greater urgency by 1552 in that the violent opposition the colonists mounted to the New Laws had caused the reforms to be largely revoked in 1545.

From our "very brief" summary, the reader can deduce the distinguishing features of the *Brevísima*, as over/against the texts of its period. To
wit: that with the most urgent petition and persuasion, and speaking from
a retrospective point of view, Las Casas evolves a new, highly effective
way of writing history. Indeed, he explicitly takes issue with those who
"think and say and *write* that the victories they have achieved by ravaging
the Indians have all been God-given because their iniquitous wars are
just" (p. 125, our emphasis). To give lie to such writings, Las Casas's
argumentation categorically and ironically subverts the premises of this
putative evangelical conquest, demythifying the Spanish enterprise.
According to Las Casas: the Spanish conquerors, supposed bearers of the
Word, have turned the paradisiacal Indies into an inferno; the Spanish
haven't performed a single redeeming act nor the Indians committed a
single offense; if there is a just war, it is of the inherently saintly Indians
against the "civilized" Spaniards, whose actions reveal them to be totally
devoid of reason; service to the Crown, under these circumstances,
constitutes disservice to God; and so on. Unlike those of Núñez, the
ironies of Las Casas's argument consciously – rather than by default –
invert the premises of the heroic tale. Moreover, having read Columbus's
early writings (cf. p. 85), Las Casas exposes what has happened to certain
of their key assertions. Columbus's idealized innocent and tractable
Indians, portrayed by Las Casas in exactly the same terms, are forced to
become tragic heroes who vainly resist the brutality of the diabolical
Spanish. And God, once on the side of the pious conquerors, now aids the
Indians in their resistance. The Indians of the *Diario* "give like brutes,"
those of the *Brevísima*, in a realized metaphor, are treated as if they were
beasts. The disillusioned natives now clearly understand that the Spanish
haven't "come from Heaven" – except if it is gold that sits on the heavenly
throne. Where Columbus insists on his inability to put the new reality into
words, reiterating that "this must be seen to be believed," Las Casas can
only repeat that to see is to *dis*believe the atrocities that have been
committed: "no human tongue nor news nor effort could suffice to
recount these shocking actions..." (p. 105). Las Casas, we see, uses the
language of the Discovery to express the destruction of the Indies.

Oviedo and Núñez make writing their form of service and substitute for
goods; with Las Casas writing is necessarily a form of action in itself. And
when words act in the *Brevísima*, they act forcefully, for once with no
subtle strategy or hidden agenda. His vitriolic style, a full-blown rhetoric
of denunciation, stops at nothing in the efforts to persuade. A couple of
excerpts from the prologue illustrate the consistent features of Las Casas's
stylistic system: "All of these universal and infinite peoples *a toto genero*
were created by God to be the simplest of beings, with no evil or duplicity,
the most obedient, the most faithful to their natural sovereigns and to the
Christians whom they serve..." (p. 76); "Shortly after meeting them, like

wolves and tigers and the cruellest lions who hadn't eaten for days, the Spanish attacked these docile lambs endowed by their Maker and Creator with the aforementioned qualities. And for forty years now, to the present day, they have done nothing but rend, kill, distress, cause pain, torment, and destroy these lambs" (p. 77). Las Casas argues through totalizing extremes (*all* these innocent Indians, the Spanish have *only* wrought destruction) and Manichean antitheses (innocent Indians, cruel Spaniards), enhanced by the biblical image, repeated over twenty times in the text, of docile sheep versus cruel wolves and tigers. The use of anaphoric constructions, chains of synonymous adjectives or verbs, superlatives, hyperboles, and, at other points, intensely emotional exclamations, render Las Casas's style overwhelmingly emphatic. The same insistent quality characterizes the structure of the work. Las Casas's exposition formulaically demonstrates how in place after place exactly the same events have occurred. Each section devoted to each territory displays an identical overall pattern (whose first part is again reminiscent of Columbus's *Diario*): the land is a paradisiacal *locus amoenus* teeming with people, the Spanish arrive and are received generously by the Indians, they proceed to betray that confidence by brutalizing the natives and sacking their lands. Above and beyond the content of the *Brevísima*, then, it is perhaps the work's emphatic style and structure that have caused it to be taken as the definitive statement of the "black legend" of the Spanish Conquest.

As its association with the "black legend" suggests, the *Brevísima*'s telescopic and persuasive aims occasioned a mode of writing history that has proved both effective and highly problematical. In composing from Spain a "most brief summary of a very diffuse history" (p. 73), Las Casas distances himself from the particularized tangles of a history of the New World from within such as Oviedo's, to bring to light what he views as the general principles of events in the Indies. Flatly, tendentiously, simplistically, he reduces all spaces and events to a single matrix of Indian innocence abused by Spanish greed and brutality, observing a self-stated "rule" as the governing principle of his writing: "And they [the cruelties] are so great, that they confirm the rule that we stated at the outset: that the more they proceeded to discover and lose people and lands, the more remarkable were the cruelties and iniquities against God and his children that they perpetrated" (p. 154). When, as he does in many instances, Las Casas cites a particular event, it is to illustrate and dramatically punctuate the general principle. The lack of specificity implicates other levels of the text in notorious ways. Las Casas takes egregious liberties with facts and statistics, inflating them and using them as mere stylistic weapons in his verbal battle (one example among the legions: in the Lucayos, "where there were more than five hundred thousand souls, today there remains not a single creature," p. 77). As he reduces all the "tyrants" to a single paradigm, he fails to name those whom he accuses. Las Casas also fails to mention the waves of disease that decimated the native populations; the only "pestilence" (p. 102) he identifies as such are the Spaniards.

All of the factors discussed in the preceding paragraph have provided ample fodder for those who would deny the *Brevísima*, and thus the "black legend," any truth or merit. While it would be inappropriate for a study such as ours to take a position in this debate, it does befit us to offer certain insights to be gained from setting the work in its context. First, one should note that in the context of Las Casas's own works, the *Brevísima* is but a synoptic and overtly tendentious summary of the massive *Historia de las Indias* which the friar had begun in 1527. There are to be found many of the missing particulars, proof of assertions, the naming of names. Of equal import is the political and philosophical context detailed at the outset of our analysis of the *Brevísima*, and the many tongues in which the text speaks. The real problem regarding the *Brevísima*'s factual license would seem to revolve around the issue of whether the text is a history, for histories involve a commitment to a particular kind of truth. Monolithic as it may appear, the *Brevísima* is clearly more than a history: it should be viewed as a product of its times, as a transitional and *multi-dimensional* text which accommodates the retrospective historical, as well as new moral, philosophical, and political concerns that had come to the fore and were demanding expression. Further, given the nature and bent of Las Casas's quest, we might conclude that it is the moralist's voice which overrides and subsumes all the voices – as a history, *memorial de agravios*, *relación*, philosophical treatise, autobiography – in which the text speaks. Avalle Arce contends in his brilliant analysis of the *Brevísima* ("Las hipérboles del padre Las Casas"), that writing more as an outraged moralist than as an historian, Las Casas moves within the realm of absolutes; he serves a higher truth, the Truth; such a truth holds no truck with relativism or nuance. Thus perhaps can be understood, if not wholly justified, Las Casas's idiosyncratic treatment of historical fact and the *Brevísima*'s writing of history.

Christopher Columbus, Diario de a bordo, redux, *and conclusions*

Our study of the textual family of the first fifty years would leave an important stone unturned should we fail to examine its inaugural text, Columbus's *Diario*, within the framework of the writings of its transcriber. For, to fully understand the crucial issue of Columbus's representation of the New World, we must understand the *Diario* at least to a degree as Las Casas's text. Before doing so, however, we must address a couple of the mysteries surrounding Las Casas's transcription, actually an abstract, of Columbus's work. Why did Las Casas compose an abstract of the *Diario*? A comparison of the *Diario* and Las Casas's *Historia de las Indias* finds that those issues which figure most prominently in the *Diario* comprise the bases of Las Casas's arguments in the historical work. From this we and others have concluded, as is logical, that Las Casas transcribed and abstracted the *Diario* with a clear eye to his own arguments, much in the way that scholars take notes on works for personal use. The matter of exactly when Las Casas executed the undated transcription remains the subject of informed conjecture; at least for the purposes of our argument, it is almost immaterial.

The question of precisely how Las Casas transcribed the *Diario*, on the other hand, is of great consequence, and affords the gateway to another reading of the work. We noted earlier that Las Casas's abstract alternates clearly demarcated direct quotations of Columbus's words with third person summaries of the *Diario*'s entries (see Zamora, "Todas son palabras formales del Almirante" for a discussion of Las Casas's editorial interventions). As could be expected given the friar's purpose in transcribing the *Diario*, the passages exactly reproduced from Columbus's work are a blueprint of Las Casas's own concerns. They insistently focus on a select cluster of issues: the Indies as a *locus amoenus*; the natural generosity, meekness, goodness, and physical perfection of the Indians; how easily they will become Christians; the greed of the Spaniards in their search for gold; the providentialism of the Discovery, and so on. In these formulae of the Discovery, we easily recognize the seeds of the arguments against the destruction found in the *Brevísima* and the *Historia de las Indias*. By the same token, what we are allowed to hear of Columbus's own voice in fact echoes the voice of Las Casas. As the reader will have noted, in both the style and ideology of their portrayal of the Indians, the voices of Las Casas and Columbus bear an uncanny resemblance to each other.

Much as the two voices may produce almost identical utterances, the *meaning* of these statements in the *Diario* varies tremendously according to each author's intentions. The *Diario*, read within the context of Las Casas's works is, naturally, a very different text from the *Diario* read from the point of view of Columbus. Though it would be interesting indeed to analyze all of the direct quotations in the *Diario* from this perspective, here we must limit ourselves to a couple of pointed examples. "Your Majesties would undoubtedly be impressed with the status and reverence that all accord him [the "King"], since they are all naked" (*Diario*, p. 155). Columbus uses this quotation referring to the ceremonial tendencies of the natives of Hispaniola as proof that he has reached Cipango/Japan; Las Casas conceivably makes note of it to bolster his Aristotelian argument that the Indians are rational beings by virtue of their proven ability to form a polity. "They are peoples like the others that I have found and with the same beliefs, and they believed that we came from Heaven, and they give of what they have for whatever is given them…and I believe that they would do the same with spices and gold if they had them" (*Diario*, p. 138). Placed in the context of Las Casas's works, the accent falls on the Indians' intrinsic generosity and naïve adulation of the Spaniards; in Columbus's world the word GOLD leaps from the page. Truly it is intriguing to see a very different text – Las Casas's – emerge from Columbus's words. What in Columbus may be strategizing and self-interest, in Las Casas's system becomes the more direct expression of larger philosophical and moral interests. And what some would see as the origins of the New World discourse of colonialism in Columbus thus shares the same space as the seminal elements of Las Casas's discourse of anti-colonialism.

The intimate connections between the *Diario* and the *Brevísima* provide food for much thought, as well as for the brief conclusions to this essay. First, it is clear that with Columbus and Las Casas our cycle of texts has come full circle. Not only do its beginnings contain its end, but, as we stated at the outset, a trajectory has been completed: from the Discovery to the destruction, the Creation to the Fall, the exploitation to the defense of the Indians. A whole complement of stories has been told, and in fact, in 1552 with the *Historia de las Indias y la conquista de México* [*Cortés: The life of the Conqueror by his secretary*] by Cortés's chaplain Francisco López de Gómara, they would begin to be *retold*. Gómara's adulatory and rhetorically elegant secondhand perspective idealizes, weaves together, and polishes the *cartas de relación* of Cortés.

Second, though we have noted considerable progress in the writers' attitudes toward the native peoples, an independent image of the Indians has yet to emerge. Both Columbus and Las Casas idealize the Indians in identical terms, to different but obvious purposes. Pané and Oviedo's visions are circumscribed by their own cultural perspective. Cortés and even, to a degree, Núñez, characterize the Indians in ways that suit their apologetic textual designs. All of the writers in some way "use" the Indians in their narrative stratagems. We will have to wait for the next generation, of the missionary-historians such as Bernardino de Sahagún and Motolinía who collected the Indians' versions of their history, to hear the natives tell their tales in something approaching their own words.

Finally, the two different voices – of Columbus and of Las Casas – that we have distinguished in the *Diario*, bear an important message *vis-à-vis* the approach that we have proposed for the reading of the historiographical texts of the first fifty years of New World writings and, perhaps, beyond. An understanding of the context, pragmatic and intellectual, in which Columbus and Las Casas wrote allowed us to discern the divergent meanings enclosed in a single statement. So, too, have we found it essential to situate all of our texts within their larger context in order to discern their narrative strategies and literary dimensions. For to a significant degree it has been the non-literary external factors that give rise to apology and petition which have engendered the narrative interest of these texts. From this we can conclude that when aiming to unlock the literary chambers of historiographical texts, literary analysis may profitably venture beyond its own terrain and, to invoke J. L. Austin, explore the world of "doing things with words."

[4]

Historians of the conquest and colonization of the New World: 1550–1620

Kathleen Ross

Introduction

Who were the historians writing about the conquest and colonization of Spanish America after the mid sixteenth century? What is their importance to a history of Spanish American literature? How may a history of historiography go about portraying the literary currents of an era? This essay will address these questions, with the goals of making new voices heard and of listening to old ones in new ways. Any study that attempts to sum up seventy years of written history must pick and choose from among many sources, and will of necessity be informed by the critical thought of its own time. As we approach the period 1550–1620, however, some problems specific to this era and its literature come into play. Their definition is in and of itself an important part of this literary history, and is thus the initial matter to which we turn our attention.

The first of these problems has to do with the relationship between text and culture. The discussion of texts here will be complemented with a description of their extra-textual surroundings during the years in question; this is done with the conviction that the writing of the period was not a mere reflection of its milieu, but rather that it engaged the outside culture and indeed was instrumental in its creation. Matters are complicated for the years 1550–1620, however, by the fact that while some texts were published upon completion or shortly thereafter, others were not in print until hundreds of years later, principally the nineteenth century. We are thus dealing with a dual process of historical formation: the texts that affected their own era on the one hand, and on the other, those that define literary history as we see it today. It is necessary to carry out a dual reading of both traditions if we wish to portray with clarity the writing of these seventy years, recognizing which works interacted with their contemporary culture and which ones entered Spanish American literary history after Independence.

This process is entirely different – and indeed, contrary – to that of rediscovering works widely read in their own day but now forgotten. Such a resurrection of texts, a labor of literary history that has become particularly important to the fields of women's studies and ethnic studies in North America, is appropriate to the modern period, but not to 1550–1620. For, as we know, opportunities for publication were extremely limited in Spanish America at that time, owing to the newness of the printing press (established in 1535 in Mexico City; 1583 in Lima) and the censorship of church and state. Few people were literate in Spanish and there were fewer still with time and space to write. Many of the works to be discussed here were written with the European audience in mind, and some were written by Spaniards.

This brings us to a second consideration, that of the nature of colonial literature during this period, and the meaning of the term "colonial." Most of the population in Spanish America in the late sixteenth and early seventeenth centuries lived under the domination of a European minority; this included both Spanish and creole (American-born Spanish) groups. European control was cultural as well as political and economic. While native Amerindian culture survived, and even resisted such control, it was subject to suppression at the hands of the conquerors. Yet the story of missionaries who tried to preserve such a disappearing culture is also part of the history of this era, and is an important part of the picture of a society in formation.

The most challenging aspect of the writing of these years, though, is accounting for the emergence of writers whose very existence was owned to the Conquest. Creole, *mestizo*, and mulatto historians, Christianized Indian nobility composing their words in Latin and Spanish: this is the story of a new literature born of the rich cultural mixture that was colonial Spanish America. Among these voices were those who were ignored or silenced by the powers of church and state. As we hear them now, four centuries later, we should recognize not only resistance or compliance with European rule, but also an active participation in the definition of New World history for that era and for our own, in a difference that would come to be called American.

To describe the histories of 1550–1620 and their cultural context fully, then, implies another dual awareness, that of the metropolis alongside the colony. Spain's experience during those years was in some ways decisive for America, and in other ways determined largely by the activity taking place in its Western empire. The context of the period, the factors outside of historical writing that become a part of it and are indeed shaped by it, is trans-Atlantic. As Spanish cultural institutions were transferred to American soil, they evolved into American customs that variously imitated, changed, or exaggerated the European model. The writing of history was no exception, and in order to understand that of these seventy years in Spanish America, we must have an idea of the model as well as its variation.

What a literary history of the historians of 1550–1620 demands, then, is really a triple vision: of the period itself, of contemporary Spain, and of the way these histories were read in the nineteenth century, which to a great degree influences the way we read them today. All three ways of seeing play important roles in the creation of a literary identity that makes up a crucial chapter of the history of the literature of Spanish America.

A final important concept has to do with categories of discourse. "History" takes many guises during 1550–1620. As we shall see in the course of our discussion, the category of *historia* was only one of several forms employed by writers attempting to record the events of their own time or those of the past. This loosening of traditional definitions was another change resulting from the expansion of the world to include the American continent.

The inclusion of a history of historiography in a volume of literary history raises the question of boundaries between the imaginary and the veridical. Here again, we must stretch the sometimes rigid categories of our own present in order to appreciate the writing of another era. Using the terminology of modern literary genres to characterize complex, hybrid narrative forms does little to further our understanding of such works. Likewise, placing modern demands for objectivity on pre-modern history shortchanges works written with other goals in mind. Certainly this is true for the histories of 1550–1620, written in an era when history was part of rhetoric, and the meanings of words such as truth and fiction were quite different from today's definitions. Our literary history of historical writing will proceed from these assumptions.

Historical background of the era: Spain and America

What defines the time span of 1550–1620 in Spain? The reigns of two kings, the end of the Renaissance and the beginning of the baroque age in art and literature, and the closing of the country to the rest of Europe are among the era's best-known episodes. A bankrupt metropolitan treasury and a falling off of trade with America are others, perhaps less immediately recalled. In the trans-Atlantic American colonies, equally significant events were taking place: the settling of the "Indian question" with an uneasy truce between *encomenderos* (colonizers who received Indians along with land) and the Crown; the expansion of industry and production; luxury for the elite classes who relied on native and slave labor. Women began to emigrate from Spain in greater numbers. New generations born after the earlier period of violence reached maturity during these years, which marked the end of the age of conquest and the beginning of a new, heterogeneous society.

When King Philip II ascended the thrones of Spain, Italy, and the Netherlands in 1556, he inherited power over an America vastly different from that of the beginning decades of the century. The drama of encounter between Old and New Worlds, the thrill of discovery and the terror of conquest, were now taking place only at the remotest of frontiers, and the basic structures of governance were in place. There remained the tasks of internal expansion, both material and symbolic, that would consolidate and build upon the work of the Conquest.

Sugar cane was first planted in Cuba in 1550; tobacco was introduced into Europe five years later. This exchange of natural products is emblematic of the changes wrought by the presence of Europe in America, and of the relationship between colony and colonizer at mid century. For alongside the exploitation of the riches of the New World by the Old, a heterogeneous culture was beginning to form in the Indies. Against a background of indigenous culture which never entirely disappeared despite great modification, creoles, *mestizos*, and mulattos began their own production – written and otherwise – as the first generations born in America came to maturity. The sugar cane planted in Cuba, and more crucially the silver mines of Mexico and Peru, would play an important role in the creation of a more self-sufficient economy that would gradually separate America from Spain.

The seventy-year span of 1550–1620 can be divided roughly into two segments: the reign of Philip II (1556–1598) and that of his son Philip III (1598–1621). While the history of monarchs and aristocrats is certainly not definitive of an era's character, in the case of historical writing we may begin here to understand who wrote what, and why. The kind of government enforced by the King and the limitations placed on publication of materials were key factors in determining the texts that went to press. The fate of the narratives that were not printed until several hundred years later rested, as well, with directives from the Crown.

Philip II's obsession with bureaucracy and documentation left a legacy of paper that had crossed the ocean in both directions, and his preoccupation with heresy brought the Inquisition to America in 1571. Thus, both the quantity and quality of writing were affected by the King's mode of governance. Legal forms of discourse in particular defined as never before the narratives of the Indies, and these were still largely composed by Spaniards. Another kind of story was being told by native Indian narrators to Spanish missionaries and recorded, but it would only be towards the end of Philip's reign that the first American-born writers of

Spanish (of both indigenous and European descent) would compose their own histories.

With the ascendence of Philip III there began a century of decline and decadence that rotted from the top down, as the monarch abdicated moral leadership and embraced the interests of competing sectors of the ruling elite. By this time, that elite intertwined metropolitan and colonial branches, as colonization continued and American society grew more complex. In this climate of dwindling resources and sharper racial divisions, the first generations of *mestizo* historians began the work of re-writing the chronicles of conquest to include their vision of the events since 1492. It was a revisionist and interpretive task, carried out by a new kind of historian.

A literature that reflected all of these developments also participated in their evolution. Historians such as Bartolomé de Las Casas, Francisco López de Gómara, Bernardino de Sahagún, and José de Acosta continued the work of "naming" America and its inhabitants for European readers. Pedro Cieza de León, Agustín de Zárate and Ruy Díaz de Guzmán chronicled the expansion of the empire into Peru, Chile, and Argentina. In Pedro de Valdivia, we have the voice of a conqueror from the earlier half of the sixteenth century, not published until later decades. From Juan Suárez de Peralta, Fernando Alvarado Tezozomoc, and Fernando de Alva Ixtlilxóchitl come other voices, those of the descendants of both Spanish and Aztec nobility; their work saw print only in the nineteenth century. Garcilaso Inca de la Vega and Guaman Poma de Ayala give us two very different texts of Andean colonization. In Bernal Díaz del Castillo, we see the conqueror made colonizer, a life spanning most of the sixteenth century.

Women writers, living almost exclusively in cloistered convents, formed a significant group of historians in the colonies. Narratives by *cronistas* such as Mariana de la Encarnación and Inés de la Cruz are just beginning to be studied by scholars, and still exist mostly in manuscript. Since the first American convents for women were founded in Mexico during the reign of Philip II, it is really during this time that women's literature in Spanish America has its roots. Women began to emigrate from Spain in greater numbers after mid-century; both Spanish writers and their creole sisters participated in the establishment of large female communities in the convents, which played an important role in urban culture.

Thus a survey of these seventy years recounts a turning point in the literary history of Spanish America: the place where American-born writers join Spanish soldiers and clerics as narrators of the New World. The modification of European models for chronicles and histories, the importance of the eyewitness that marked the narrative of America from its beginnings, take on a different cast during this period. The narrators of the second half of the sixteenth century, and those of the first two decades of the seventeenth, are in large part witnesses to the phenomena of a rapidly changing society, which they themselves help to create through language and memory.

1550–1599: intellectual and rhetorical currents

The second half of the sixteenth century saw the end of the significant influence of renaissance Humanism in Spanish intellectual circles, as the rigid methods of scholasticism gained a stranglehold on education and learning. This scholastic trend, begun earlier, became increasingly hardened as the century progressed; as J. H. Elliott has observed, the events of the years 1556–1563 irreversibly transformed renaissance Spain into counter-Reformation Spain, as a society open to the rest of Europe effectively became closed to the outside (Elliott, *Imperial Spain 1469–1716*, 221). It was a change that would define Spain, and in turn its American colonies, for centuries to come. In a society defined by counter-Reformation orthodoxy, there was no room for the thought of Erasmus or others who did not adhere to the strictest Catholicism. Many humanist scholars left Spain for more congenial nations, principally Italy.

The division of Spain and its American possessions from the German Empire upon the ascent of Philip II further deepened Iberian isolation. As the protestant Reformation spread, Spain locked its intellectual door ever tighter, and the Inquisition ensured the intimidation or repression of those who strayed. Although the anti-Spanish ideology of the Black Legend – the portrayal of Spain as a ruthless, barbaric conquering power – may tend to exaggerate the sheer bloodiness of the church's control, the threat of violence cast a pall over intellectual activity that was constant and ominous. There is much as yet unknown in this area; research into the literature confiscated by the Inquisition is a brand-new enterprise. Efforts are underway in Mexico to catalogue such texts, located in the National Archive. When they are so documented, the picture we will have of colonial literature may be very different, especially for the seventeenth and eighteenth centuries.

What these changes meant for the American colonies, entering a crucial phase of commercial and cultural expansion, was the implantation of a colonial regime that attempted the strictest of control over the life of the mind as well as the spirit. The institutions of church and state introduced to the Indies during the time of conquest – the most important for literature being the universities, monasteries and convents – took permanent root during this era of philosophical stagnation. Their apparatus was designed and determined to maintain the religious purity of America.

Within these limitations, the historians of the latter half of the sixteenth century created heterogeneous narrative forms to tell the story of the end of conquest and the beginning of colonization. Though European rhetorical models had been adapted to narrate American reality since Columbus's first Caribbean encounter, it is at this time that entirely new forms emerge, unclassifiable according to Old World standards. This was also the period when the "Golden Age" of Spanish literature began, with a wealth of novels, theatre, and poetry issuing forth and rapidly reaching the Indies, where their influence was great.

Royal laws and decrees came across the sea in mounting numbers after Philip II took the throne, and many were meant to control the activities of reading, writing, and publishing. The novel, to take one well-known example, had already been prohibited as too dangerously imaginative for the newly converted, although we know from Irving Leonard's studies that Spanish novels such as *Lazarillo de Tormes* (1554) and *Don Quijote* (Part 1, 1605; Part 2, 1615) did make their way to the private libraries of colonial readers (Leonard, *Book of the Brave*; *Baroque Times in Old Mexico*). Whether or not novels were written in Spanish America before the nineteenth century is a much-debated topic for literary criticism that will be touched on later in this essay.

The rubric of *crónica*, *corónica*, or *chrónica* – all of which are translated as "chronicle" – was, through the Middle Ages, applied to writing that dealt with past or present events in a straightforward, unembellished chronological manner. *Historia* or history, by contrast, implied authorship by someone who possessed the tools and learning needed in order to make inquiry into a subject, then place it within a universal context. Familiarity with rhetoric, the rules for moving and persuading an audience, was thus a prerequisite for the historian, who was expected to please the reader with writing of a high caliber. Personal experience, however, had nothing to do with the fitness of the historian to interpret his subject.

By 1550, the word *crónica* was being used interchangably with *historia* by those writing about events in the New World (Mignolo, "Cartas, crónicas y relaciones," 75–8), as experience became as important as learning for the historian. Metropolitan histories continued to be written during these years, authored by official court historians such as Francisco López de Gómara who had never set foot in America. Alongside them, histories written in the New World by eyewitnesses such as Bernal Díaz del Castillo took on a revisionist cast as they reacted to the court historians' lack of firsthand knowledge. The privileging of the participant who can state from experience what he or she has seen, despite a lack of education, is a phenomenon of New World expansion. Indeed, a recurrent theme of the histories of the seventy years concerning us here could be characterized as the re-interpretation of the histories of conquest from the vantage point of a society becoming involved in the process of colonization.

The legal report, or *relación*, written from obligation on the part of the narrator to inform the Crown of new developments, had been a standard vehicle for describing the New World since the period of discovery. It became institutionalized in the 1570s with the creation of the title *cronista mayor de Indias* [Chief Chronicler of the Indies]. The *cronista mayor* established a code, really a questionnaire, which the informant would follow while writing. Some works, too, were still written after 1550 under the title of *carta* [letter], as had been true during the earlier half of the century. The *carta* was, like the *relación*, a legal form that was written in order to apprise the Crown of new developments. Written close to the time of action, it is especially identified with conquerors such as Hernán Cortés. During the time of Philip II, actual conquests were only occurring at the farthest frontiers. However, Pedro de Valdivia, who had arrived in Chile to found Santiago in 1541, did write *cartas* some years later before his death in 1554.

The writing of religious figures, and in particular that of the regular clergy who were engaged in the conversion of indigenous peoples to Catholicism, had been a key element in the great debates of the first half of the 1500s. We may think of these texts, by authors such as Bartolomé de Las Casas and Fray Toribio de Motolinía (*Historia de los indios de la Nueva España c.* 1541; published Mexico, 1858) [*Motolinía's History of the Indians of New Spain*] as part of the literature of conquest, for they attempted to record the devastation wrought on the conquered by Europe. Moreover, much of what they wrote was part of an intense dialogue between the church, the Crown, and the conquerors of America regarding the rationality of indigenous people and their potential for enslavement. The debate had raged during the reigns of the Catholic Kings and of Emperor Charles V and had brought about the promulgation of the New Laws of 1542; these were designed to abolish the system of personal service embodied in the *encomienda*. The resultant furor culminated in the great debate of 1550 between Las Casas and Juan Ginés de Sepúlveda at Valladolid and the publication in Spain, in 1552, of Las Casas's famous *Brevísima relación de la destrucción de las Indias* [*Brief Account of the Destruction of the Indies*].

During the monarchy of Philip II, religious writers continued to be important historiographers, but now their task was one of recording a rapidly disappearing indigenous culture and history before it was entirely lost. The epidemics of smallpox and other European diseases that ravaged the native population from the Conquest onward had taken a huge toll by the middle of the sixteenth century. As Indian civilization became but a shadow of its former self, the pace of European immigration was stepped up, and the resultant demographic changes were dramatic up and down the continent. The religious historiographers of this era, such as Fray Bernardino de Sahagún, drew on information culled from Latinized Indians (among others) and documented the natives' reactions to the Conquest itself. Thus, a fundamental shift was made as histories began to concentrate on indigenous cultures as part of the past, rather than the present.

The second half of the sixteenth century in Spain witnessed the phenomenon of religious mysticism at its height, expressed in the writings of St. Teresa of Avila, St. John of the Cross and Fray Luis de León. St. Teresa, in particular, would greatly influence the Spanish and creole nuns of America who would follow her example as both mystic and writer in the early part of the next century. Her inspiration would lead these women to found convents following the Reformed Carmelite rule, and to write about their experience in doing so.

Some of the works written by the many historians of these years will be examined in greater detail in the second part of our study. It is appropriate to end this brief overview of 1550–1599 by mentioning Fernando Alvarado Tezozomoc's *Crónica mexicana* [*Chronicle of the Mexicans*] written near the end of the century before the author's death, about 1598. The work of Tezozomoc, descended from the Aztec nobility, attacks Aztec religious beliefs and gods, while providing a thoroughly indigenous point of view on the events described. Such were the texts being composed by the end of the sixteenth century in America.

1600–1620: years of crisis and change

The seventeenth century was a time of crisis for Spain and for Europe. Wars fought for political and religious motives sapped royal treasuries, while disease wiped out many lives and economies plummeted. In Spain, Philip III was the ineffectual ruler of a corruption-riddled court. The glories of the age of conquest gave way to decadence. In Hispanic America, and especially in New Spain, this was the century that has been dubbed "forgotten" by historians such as Lesley Byrd Simpson. Indeed, until recently little attention was devoted to these years in Spanish America by present-day historians, who preferred to focus on the sixteenth century's explorations, or on conditions leading to revolution in the eighteenth. Certainly it is true that the seventeenth century in America lacked the exciting new conquests that preceded it, or the spirit of enlightened reform that followed. This was an era of repression, orthodoxy, and fear. But in all the arts and especially in literature, the seventeenth century represents a richness not seen again in the Hispanic world on either side of the Atlantic for another 300 years.

This paradox of artistic wealth and economic penury has not, of course, gone unnoticed. Historians and critics of Spain and its literature have had much say on the subject, and the bibliography on such giants of Spanish literature as Miguel de Cervantes, Lope de Vega, and Luis de Góngora – all publishing during the monarchy of Philip III – is immense. The decades of transition between the centuries, which concern us here, were particularly productive ones in Spain. The works of the great writers mentioned above, plus others such as Francisco de Quevedo, saw print during these years.

As historians have begun to delve deeper into Spanish America's seventeenth century, a crucial question has been asked: did Spain's crisis simply cross the ocean as one more legacy of colonialism? Years ago this assumption was made, and is still adhered to by some, but important historical scholarship through the 1970s and 1980s has shown a greater degree of self-sufficiency in the American economy than previously thought. Such assertions are based on different types of evidence, including mining records and treasury accounts. Thus arguments are being made that, throughout the seventeenth century, rather than a generalized level of crisis, the American colonies experienced fluctuating periods of expansion and contraction. Moreover, these differed from one part of the empire to another.

Debate on this issue remains heated in the field of history. In literature, a similar polemic currently rages regarding the writing of the period in America, which is often referred to as the *Barroco de Indias*, or Spanish American Baroque. Though the Baroque Age between 1600 and 1620 is more directly concerned with poetry than with history, it is useful to review the ideas behind these arguments, for they ultimately have to do with the definition of the society surrounding historical writing as well. The question about Spanish American baroque literature mirrors the historians' debate: did the European Baroque implant itself in America as an imposed style? Was it imported to the colonies along with economic crisis and religious orthodoxy, one more example of colonial domination? Was there anything especially American about Spanish American Baroque?

As we have learned more about the seventeenth century, the scholarship dealing with this controversy has become more sophisticated. In part this also has to do with a refinement of the definition of "Baroque," a critical term that literature borrowed from art history. Baroque has been increasingly understood as a complex phenomenon involving more than style; it encompasses the culture of Absolutism, orthodoxy, and crisis that swept through Europe during this period. Some argue that this state of affairs was at the base of the explosion of baroque literature in America evident from the early seventeenth to the mid eighteenth centuries; that the *Barroco de Indias* involved only a tiny minority of privileged creole writers, laboring under the influence of the Spanish state. Others see in the very excesses and exaggerations of baroque style the beginnings of an American idiom, a liberation from classical form that reflected the heterogeneity of colonial life.

We will ask another question which is relevant to the histories written between 1600 and 1620: where is a difference between Spain and America to be found in the writing of the Spanish American Baroque if not in details of style? Here, the consciousness of the creole or American-born Spaniard enters the equation, for creole writers such as Carlos de Sigüenza y Góngora (Mexico, 1645–1700) and Sor Juana Inés de la Cruz (Mexico, 1651–1695) are the names immediately associated with the *Barroco de Indias*. They belong to the late seventeenth century rather than the early decades and so lie outside the scope of this essay. But the identity of the creole, located somewhere between Europe and America, is crucial to our understanding of just what happened in this first full century of colonial life, as we will see in the work of Juan Suárez de Peralta.

The histories written in the early decades of the seventeenth century, for the most part, do not show the stylistic detail recognizable as Baroque, for they were written by authors schooled in sixteenth-century philosophy and rhetoric. Baroque historiography in the Indies would be a post-1650 phenomenon. However, it is possible to discern in a work such as that of Guaman Poma de Ayala the influence of the era of Absolutism that began in Spain in the later decades of the sixteenth century (Adorno, *Guaman Poma*).

The concentration of historical writing in and around the Caribbean, a characteristic of the first half-century of conquest, had changed by 1620 to include the entire continent. In the work of Ruy Díaz de Guzmán, history extends into the Argentinian region, the southern limits of the Empire. In the north, Fernando Alva Ixtlilxóchitl writes the history of the Chichimeca tribe of upper Mexico, which had migrated to the Anahuac Valley of central Mexico.

New voices from new sectors of society, in far-reaching parts of an extensive empire: this is the legacy of history in early seventeenth-century Spanish America. With this introduction we may proceed to a reading of the texts themselves.

Histories and historians of the sixteenth century: 1550–1599

To consider individual texts in greater detail, we will trace arcs through time connecting groups of works, rather than proceed according to a strictly linear chronology. For texts written by official or approved historians – all Spanish during these fifty years – these arcs approximate the manner in which the texts themselves interacted with each other in the formation of a historiographical canon of authorities. Interspersed with such "authorized" histories are those which offer alternative accounts, narrated by creole and indigenous writers. Some of the latter entered modern literary history after Independence during the nineteenth century, some at later dates. As we examine these works and their significance to Spanish American literature, that differential between the newer and older traditions will be teased out in our analysis.

The starting point for this section is the most classical of historical forms, the *historia* written by a learned author. Two very different examples, those of Las Casas and López de Gómara, show how the pedigree of the form did not prevent its utilization as a vehicle for ideology. By following the interaction of these two texts and the decidedly non-classical history of Bernal Díaz that succeeded them, we observe the changes wrought on history by the ascendence of the eyewitness as a reliable narrator.

While these histories dealt largely, or totally, with the Caribbean and New Spain, the first histories about Peru were being published during the same period. The extensive writing of Pedro de Cieza de León is of principal interest here, though we will refer to the work of Agustín de Zárate as well. The writings of the last conquerors of a far-flung empire, exemplified by the letters of Pedro de Valdivia, fill out the panorama of the expansion of Spanish power at mid-century. Diego de Landa's anthropological discussion of Mayan civilization, written in the 1560s, provides an epilogue to the story of conquest along the margins of America.

These histories relate only one part of that story, however. Through the work of Bernardino de Sahagún and other missionaries, what Miguel León-Portilla has named the "vision of the vanquished" began to be told, as Sahagún's history frames the accounts of his native informants. With this we return to New Spain, for the perspective from native Andean writers would only be written down in the early part of the next century.

In the last decades of the 1500s, three historians sum up the impact of one hundred years of European presence in the New World: José de Acosta, a Jesuit historian writing from experience in both the Mexican and Peruvian centers of colonization; Hernando Alvarado Tezozomoc, narrating his chronicle as a colonized, Latinized member of the native Mexican nobility; and Juan Suárez de Peralta, of the first generation of creole authors, lamenting what has already become a deep rift between peninsular and American-born Spaniards. These are the voices of a new history and a new culture in formation.

Three histories of conquest: Las Casas, López de Gómara, and Bernal Díaz del Castillo

The "natural" or "general" history was the form closest to classical history, and indeed derived its models from ancient authors such as Pliny (Mignolo, "Cartas", 75–89). "History," in these titles, indicated the placing of the text within a tradition of rhetoric and learning; by extension, the historian places himself within that group of educated writers qualified to continue the tradition. We have already mentioned how the histories of Spanish America forced a broadening of such categories, as firsthand knowledge became more and more valued. Two of the three texts we will examine here were inscribed within the learned form: Las Casas's *Historia general de las Indias* (written 1527–1562, published Madrid, 1875) [*History of the Indies*] and López de Gómara's *Historia de las Indias y la conquista de México* (Madrid, 1552) [*Cortés: The life of the Conqueror by his secretary*]. The third, Bernal Díaz del Castillo's *Historia verdadera de la conquista de la Nueva España* (written 1555?–1584, published Madrid, 1632) [*The Discovery and Conquest of Mexico*], demonstrates how New World historiography expanded the classical form, and exists in intimate dialogue with the other two.

These three Spanish historians approached the task of narrating New World events in very divergent ways and with very different agendas. Las Casas, the great defender of the rights of the Indians, used his multi-volume work to argue against the injustice of violent conquest. The *Historia general* invokes the same beliefs present in the *Brevísima relación*, but within an armature of historical research that takes a less polemicized, while equally passionate tone. Divided into three volumes, the *Historia* begins by establishing the work's authority in a prologue that at once both continues a tradition, and strives to correct the prior errors of biased historians who have contributed to ignorant attitudes toward indigenous peoples.

In his extensive and valuable introductory study to the 1951 Mexican edition of the *Historia*, the historian Lewis Hanke examines the reluctance of past or present critics to accept the friar's work as that of an historian. The principal weapon wielded by these critics is Las Casas's use of inflated numbers when recounting the death and destruction caused by the Conquest and its aftermath. Hanke, however, argues that this was common to other writers of the time as well, and situates Las Casas squarely in the center of the principal controversy swirling around the practice of New World historiography: that of the privileging of the eyewitness to revolutionary events.

Las Casas, who had participated in the early colonization of Cuba and had lived in other Caribbean and Mexican locations, and who after 1547 maintained from his Spanish monastery a voluminous correspondence with others still in America, was an activist friar arguing for the rights of the Indians. With his *Historia*, he chose a learned medium to tell the story of the years 1492–1520, years he had lived in intense association with things American. As Hanke notes (pp. xxxviii–ix), Las Casas in 1559 expressly forbade publication of his long work for a period of forty years, perhaps in order to allow an interval for the cooling of passions inspired by the *Brevísima relación*. In this way the *Historia* would survive intact to move and inspire future generations. Though in fact the entire text was not published until 1875, the work was copied in several manuscripts and circulated among historians (one notable case being that of Antonio de Herrera, who became the official court historian or *cronista mayor* in 1597 and used Las Casas's text extensively as a source for his own work).

The *Historia*, then, does not attempt to be passionless or objective in relating its story of the first three decades of European presence in America. Las Casas felt that being a witness to the events, even more than an educated man of God, authorized him to write the definitive, true history of the conquest and colonization carried out during those years. While his work is peppered with erudite references to classical and church authorities, its arguments are clearly tendentious and ideological in design. The basic messages of the brutality of violent conquest and the need for peaceful conversion, the inherent goodness and rationality of the Indians, and the wickedness of money-hungry Spaniards emerge in different rhetorical guises all throughout this long work.

It is important to see this scaffolding of passionate argument, then, as essential to New World historiography as Las Casas defined it, not as a methodological flaw. The sixteenth-century historian did not care to be objective in the modern sense, although he did want to tell the truth; that one could get to such truth through the power of personal experience was the challenge presented to the *status quo* by historians who had been to the New World. Gonzalo Fernández de Oviedo was the first to publish a learned history informed by eyewitness testimony in his *Sumario* (1526); Las Casas began his own *Historia* immediately afterwards in order to tell the story from another point of view, which he considered to be the only truth. This truth, for Las Casas, was religiously inspired and had to do with saving the soul of Spain, a country he saw as engaged in grievously sinful conduct, as well as saving the lives of innocent Indians.

The three volumes of the *Historia* make for difficult reading. Las Casas's prose is dense, with long sentences and numerous classical and biblical references. It shows no influence of renaissance Humanism in its style, betraying instead the friar's roots in scholastic theology and medieval Latin. Moreover, though a chronology is followed, different periods of time are afforded unequal emphasis. Thus, though the first volume treats the years 1492–1500, the second 1501–1510, and the third 1511–1520, a disproportionately large number of pages are devoted to the initial time span and to the actions of Columbus. Clearly, Las Casas wrote most about what interested him most, with no particular concern for balance.

The most widely anthologized excerpt from the *Historia* is undoubtedly the story of the Indian leader Enrique or Enriquillo of the island Hispaniola. It is included in Chapters 125–7 of the third volume (pp. 259–70). Here Las Casas makes an impassioned argument for the abolition of the *encomienda* system, which condemned indigenous laborers to *de facto* slavery. By showing the suffering endured by the Christianized Enrique at the hands of the *encomendero* Valenzuela, what is depicted with broad, general strokes in the *Brevísima* now becomes intensely specific and vivid. Enrique first tries to work for change through the channels of Spanish government and rebels only when no other recourse is left open to him. He embodies all that is good in humankind: piety, intelligence, reason, and leadership. Valenzuela, in contrast, is a greedy, cruel, and base man, the portrait of evil and sin.

Enrique is the "good" voice of moderation who controls other, more dangerous rebellions led by the "bad" Indians Ciguayo and Tamayo, and who ultimately foments peace between conqueror and conquered. He represents true Christian values, while Valenzuela makes a mockery of them. Las Casas here manipulates the reader's sympathies through the rhetoric of hyperbole, purposely setting out to persuade through the emotions. By making Enrique so ideal, so noble despite his pagan origins, the historian creates a character difficult for European readers to dismiss.

The dramatic, narrative quality of these three chapters of the *Historia* was the inspiration for the nineteenth-century novel *Enriquillo* (1878 and 1882) by the Dominican writer Manuel de Jesús Galván, a work destined to become a national classic of the Dominican Republic. Certainly this post-Independence reincarnation explains the frequent inclusion of Las Casas's story of Enrique in modern-day anthologies, showing how romantic taste in literature still determines, to a great extent, the way we read colonial writing.

Las Casas profiled Columbus as a great though tragic man, with the conviction that God had guided the Admiral (and Spain) to the New World. Francisco López de Gómara placed another hero at the center of his *Historia de las Indias y la conquista de México*: Hernán Cortés. With this change the emphasis shifts from discovery to conquest, from navigational to strategic skill, and from personal vision to personal power. It is a renaissance history, built around the biography of a hero of legendary proportion.

Gómara, Cortés's confessor, lived at Cortés's home in Spain between

1540 and 1547. He thus had the conqueror's personal testimony as a source for his work, as well as the already published *Cartas de relación* written during Cortés's campaigns. By this time the works of Pedro Mártir de Anglería and Fernández de Oviedo, among other works, were also at his disposal. Indeed, we may see in Gómara's text the beginnings of a constant, explicit system of references as each history re-tells the original story of Spain's presence in the New World. Though Las Casas's *Historia*, written over a period spanning the three middle decades of the sixteenth century, participates somewhat in this endeavour – notably as a critical response to both Oviedo and Gómara – the friar still relied on original documentation and personal observation as his primary sources. But as the chronicles of the initial encounter of Old with New began to form what we might call the historical "canon" of published and officially approved accounts, they themselves became authorities to be cited and consulted. This was the process by which López de Gómara wrote the history of a continent he had never seen with his own eyes, looking instead through those of others.

The work is divided into two parts, the first being a general history of place, people and things which situates the New World into a universal context. Here we find chapters comparing indigenous peoples to animals, and worse: "they are great sodomizers, good-for-nothings, liars, ingrates, unreliable, and despicable" (Chapter 28). This is the expression of the metropolitan viewpoint against which Las Casas struggled, a voice heard as well in the work of Oviedo and Sepúlveda, important references for Gómara. Reading passages like these, it is clear why Las Casas would, in 1553, influence Philip II to issue a royal prohibition against the reprinting or sale of Gómara's work.

However, it is the second part of the work, the *Historia de la conquista*, that interests us more in thinking through the literary history of these years. This is where Gómara's version of events, culled mostly from Cortés's letters and personal testimony, takes a more idiosyncratic turn, choosing as it does to tell the story of the conquest of Mexico as a biography of its conqueror. The *Historia de la conquista* begins with Cortés's birth and ends with his death; it is dedicated to Martín Cortés, Hernán's son and heir to the title of Marqués del Valle. This dedication, praising as it does the system of inherited titles and estates that the colonizers of the New World struggled to set up against the will of the Crown, is a blatantly political statement expressed in the most elegant of prose. If the underlying agenda of Las Casas's history was the defense of the Indians, that of López de Gómara's was the perpetuation of a new aristocracy, ennobled for its service to God and King.

Thus it is that this history aggrandizes Cortés, portraying him as a noble hero of the renaissance type, though a providential explanation for his actions at the same time sets Gómara's religious ideology closer to the Middle Ages. By rewriting Cortés's letters with a historian's erudition and style, Gómara initiates a new period in New World historiography: a second wave that defines foundational texts, even as it tailors them to fit current political realities.

With Bernal's *Historia verdadera*, this evolution goes one step further, adding another layer of rewriting onto Gómara's revision of the story of the conquest of New Spain. Bernal Díaz, the old soldier who accompanied Cortés on his campaign through Mexico and thirty years later began recording his recollections in a vivid, personal narrative packed with detail, is the stuff that literary legends are made of. His text has been the object of extensive anthologizing and speculation, as historians and critics have asked again and again why Bernal wrote. Miguel León-Portilla's lucid introduction to the most recent edition of the work examines this question, setting out all the answers that have been generated since the nineteenth century. It was then that the *Historia verdadera* really began to be read as literature, and thus when myths began to be formed. In brief, we will attempt an unraveling of those myths in our summary of Bernal and his memoir.

The *Historia verdadera* exists somewhere in the interstices of history, autobiography, and the legal form of the *relación*. Narrated in over 200 short chapters, like the histories of Las Casas and Gómara it has at its center the life of an exceptional man – but here that man and the author are one and the same. Bernal begins the story with his voyage to the New World in 1514, and some 900 pages later has covered the years to 1550. León-Portilla makes a convincing case for believing that Bernal had begun his *Historia* shortly after the latter date ("Introducción," 9–10) and had continued writing until his death in 1584. According to this scheme, the 1552 publication of Gómara's history/biography of Cortés, which Bernal read some years later in Guatemala, served as a motivation to move ahead with the composition of a work already conceived and begun, not as the inspiration for the writing itself. Be that as it may, Gómara is a main player in the drama Bernal relates, for he serves as a foil for the soldier-*cum*-historian who claims authority through experience rather than education or position. Bernal's desire is to tell the story with a different voice, that of an eyewitness to history, and his frequent criticisms of Gómara's version of events are a constant thread running through these pages.

It is no wonder, then, that Bernal Díaz has most often been read by modern readers as a representative of the little man, the voice of the collective "we" of the soldiers rather than the "I" of the general, the forgotten voice of the people. Recent critical studies have embarked on a demythification of this reading. They have focused instead, for instance, on Bernal's use of legal rhetoric as a model for his chronicle (González Echevarría, "Humanismo, retórica y las crónicas de la conquista," 9–25) or on his position as an *encomendero* seeking to justify the continuation of that system (Adorno, "Discourses on colonialism"). The latter article points out as well Bernal's dialogue with a powerful historical voice not as readily apparent as Gómara's: that of Las Casas, bishop of Chiapas, living close by Bernal's lands in Guatemala. Once again, the presence of prior histories in every new narration, the constant references made by each to the other that increase with the years like so many coatings of paint, form a richness of text that can really only be appreciated by suspending our modern inclination to read for plot and character, to see history as novel.

A commonplace of that modern perspective has been to read the *Historia verdadera* with the influence of the novels of chivalry in mind. These fictional adventures, the popular romances of Spain's fifteenth and sixteenth centuries, were made the butt of Cervantes's parodic humor in *Don Quixote* for their fanciful plots filled with dragons and damsels, princes and exotic lands. The best-known, of course, is *Amadís de Gaula* (1508) which served as a model for many sequels and imitators. Bernal himself confesses a fondness for this type of literature, and Irving Leonard in his 1949 study *Books of the Brave* speculated that the fantastic prose of chivalric novels offered a ready model for Spaniards encountering the wonders of America for the first time. Similar to the case of Las Casas's Enriquillo, the *Historia verdadera* has been admired for its "literary" or imaginative quality.

Undoubtedly, the power of imagination is at work in Bernal's process of reminiscence, and the fantasies of chivalry served as one point of comparison. But there were other reasons for the writing of the *Historia verdadera*: Bernal's wish for just remuneration for the original soldiers participating in the Conquest and his desire to show his own role in the conflict. These were matters that bore directly on legal status and material loss or gain, and were in turn interwoven with the histories of other writers such as Las Casas and Gómara. It is clear that colonial historiography was taking part in the formation of policy and ideology, even while it strove to please the reader while doing so.

Andean empires: the Spanish histories of Peru

The three accounts of events in New Spain and the Caribbean we have examined, then, demonstrate how the definition of history was made elastic by the expansion of the world map to include the American continents. This trans-Atlantic expansion was, after 1530, complemented by the southern march into the Incan empire, soon to be named Peru. By mid-century, Spanish historians had turned their attention to these dramatic events.

As military campaigns pushed further into South America, official reports from the field, or *relaciones*, were written to apprise the Crown of new developments. During this period Fernández de Oviedo continued to prepare his *Historia general y natural de las Indias* [*General and Natural History of the Indies*], the first volume of which appeared in 1535 and 1547. Oviedo had been named *cronista general*, or official historian, by the Crown in 1532. Thus, as reports were compiled from the scenes of battle they were sent on to him, and some were included in part in the *Historia general*, such as Francisco de Jerez's *Verdadera relación de la conquista del Perú* (Seville, 1534) [*True Report of the Conquest of Peru*]. Jerez served in Francisco Pizarro's company, and the account gives a favorable portrait of his captain.

Other reports published in Oviedo's *Historia* include Gonzalo Jiménez de Quesada's *Relación del descubrimiento del nuevo Reino de Granada* [*Account of the Discovery of New Granada*] which treated events unfolding in the territory that later became Colombia around the year 1540. In another expedition originating in the northern Andes, the friar Gaspar de Carvajal, in the company of the Spaniard Orellana, navigated the length of the Amazon River in 1541–1542 and recorded his experiences in the *Relación del nuevo descubrimiento del famoso río Grande de las Amazonas* [*Account of the Discovery of the Great River of the Amazons*]. Both these texts reveal the extent to which fantastic myths of American riches and customs had penetrated the European mind by 1530, the naming of the great river for the legendary Amazons being a case in point.

We will return to the *relación* later in its seventeenth-century version. The early narrations of South American exploration mentioned above are the predecessors of two histories of Peru published in the decade of the 1550s: Pedro de Cieza de León's multi-volume work *La crónica del Perú* (Seville, 1553) [*Chronicle of Peru*] and the *Historia del descubrimiento y conquista del Perú* (Antwerp, 1555) [*The Discovery and Conquest of Peru*] by Agustín de Zárate. Of the two, Cieza's is the more extensive and better-known work, and the one we will examine more closely. It is significant to note that while Cieza calls his work a chronicle, and Zárate refers to his as a history, each writer feels authorized to narrate events as he saw them; indeed, Cieza uses the terms "crónica" and "historia" interchangeably. Despite readily apparent stylistic and rhetorical differences in the writing, these two texts represent similar historiographical stances on the part of their authors, combining personal observation with research.

Cieza de León's *Crónica* is considered the earliest history of the viceroyalty of Peru, encompassing territory stretching from Cartagena to Potosí. Only the first volume was published during Cieza's lifetime, for he died at about thirty-four years of age in 1554 (his exact date of birth remains unknown). As a teenager, he crossed the Atlantic to explore the New World and join family members who had emigrated earlier. Years of travel and military participation gave him a broad view of events in the region, particularly the internal struggles for power raging among different Spanish factions. At some point, Cieza began to write down an account of current events, simultaneously carrying out the tasks of "my two jobs of writing and following without fail my captain and my country" (p. 59). After the revolt of Gonzalo Pizarro was put down and a new colonial government established in Lima (1548), Cieza was named *cronista oficial de Indias*. The last two years of his stay in Peru, from 1548 to 1550, were devoted to writing and research, as he traveled the viceroyalty gathering information for his history.

Though Cieza admits to being a relatively uneducated man, it is clear that his drive to write overcame the doubts that lack of schooling inspired. Indeed, the *Crónica* flows prolifically to fill four volumes, the first three book-length and the fourth comprised of five additional books. Volume I, known today as *La crónica del Perú*, describes the region's land and inhabitants in geographical and cultural terms, similar to other general histories of this era. Volume II, *El señorío de los Incas* [*The Domain of the Incas*], goes back in time to examine the empire the Spanish had conquered. The third volume picks up from that chronological point to narrate the *Descubrimiento y conquista del Perú*, and in the lengthy fourth volume of *Las guerras civiles del Perú* [*The Peruvian Civil Wars*], each of five important factional conflicts among the conquerors is afforded separate treatment. Volumes II, III, and IV remained unpublished until the nineteenth century, although the manuscripts were consulted by other colonial historians, such as Antonio de Herrera in the early part of the seventeenth century.

The *Crónica* is a passionate text and in this bears a resemblance to Las Casas's work. Cieza, though not of the clergy himself, shared many of the religious values of the friar; one instruction of his will (which was never carried out) was to deposit the still unpublished portion of the *Crónica* with Las Casas. This is history as written by a young man with deep feelings toward his subject which, as we saw with Las Casas, he made no attempt to disguise. Cieza recognized his deficient training in rhetoric, but believed it to be more than compensated for by personal involvement and observation. His inspiration for the astounding number of pages he wrote in a short period of time sprang from both religious and nationalist conviction; perhaps in no other history of this period do we see depicted with such complete sincerity the Spanish belief in the providential role of Spain in God's master plan for the universe. Cieza's unfaltering faith in the process of pacification, rather than violent conquest, is evident throughout the work. The customs and beliefs of Indians are treated with the characteristic disdain afforded to non-Christian rituals by Spanish observers, but there is a Las Casas-like sense in the *Crónica* of the natives' humanity, a respect for them as human beings.

The narrative voice describing the regions of New Granada and Peru in Volume I is strong and sure, often punctuated by assertions of eyewitness evidence. It is interesting to consider Cieza's assumption of authority – despite his confession of weak preparation – at such a young age, before receiving an official commission years later. Unlike Bernal Díaz, Cieza does not write as an old man reliving past glories and disappointments, nor does he take issue with prior historians. He does feel empowered, however, by his status as a member of the conquering Catholic forces of the Crown, and by his own youth and ideology.

Of the historians we have encountered thus far, Cieza is the youngest, of a generation that reached adolescence after the conquest of Mexico at a time when Spain's power was reaching its height. The *Crónica* is a product of that moment in time when all things were still possible. Against a backdrop of internecine struggle, Cieza idolized no one conqueror, but looked toward Las Casas, Charles V, and Philip II for guidance. These were the spiritual fathers whose creed underlies this first chronicle of Peru, a document of youthful passion spent exploring the New World. Zárate's *Historia del descubrimiento*, in contrast, could not be more sober. It records the observations of a Spanish bureaucrat in Peru from 1544 to 1545, and is in essence a political history. Somewhat older than Cieza, Zárate came from a Castilian family of high-level functionaries with important connections to the church and Court establishments. He was sent to Peru in the capacity of *contador*, or accountant, in order to review the accounts of colonial officials of the royal treasury located there. Educated in the humanist tradition, Zárate was prepared to write history in the classical sense, placing the events of the New World in the context of European tradition. In the *Historia*, there are echoes of the writing of earlier historians, such as Oviedo, whose frame of reference was always Europe and Spain. The Indians and their culture, along with the American landscape, are constantly measured according to that particular standard of civilization and beauty.

But what constitutes the core of Zárate's 300-page work is the struggle for power between the Pizarro and Almagro factions, and the subsequent revolt of Gonzalo Pizarro. On this score Zárate clearly sides with the Pizarros, yet this history is not made into a biography of the sort that Gómara composed, though the latter work may have served as a model for the *contador*. There is no one figure in the Peruvian conquest compelling enough to serve as a center, no hero emblematic of the Spanish triumph. Instead, the discourse of Zárate's text records in measured, learned prose what by mid-century is taken for granted: the greed and violence of the conquerors.

For though the arrival of Spaniards in Tenochtitlán inspired heroic narration and the personal aggrandizement of Cortés, the myths that had been spun about South America, of El Dorado and the Land of Cinnamon, were of a more material nature. They invented fabulous riches for a New World to which the Spanish by now felt wholly entitled. While Cieza's *Crónica* reflects the idealism of a young man on a mission, Zárate's *Historia* demonstrates the politics of conquest as accounted for by a representative of the Crown with no illusions.

Conquest in the margins of empire: Valdivia and Landa

Pedro de Valdivia's *Cartas de relación de la conquista de Chile* (1545–1552; published Paris, 1846) [*Letters*] and Diego de Landa's *Relación de las cosas de Yucatán* (c. 1566; published Paris, 1864) [*Yucatan Before and After the Conquest*] provide an interesting counterpoint in style and content to round out our survey of historical writing at mid century. The very different narrative approaches taken by these works to the description of cultures encountered at distant ends of the Spanish American empire may also be read as the final chapter in the story of conquest from a European perspective, the last marginal notes to a history already written. In many ways, these works echo those of the earlier part of the century, resonating with the ruthless pride of a nation that now assumed its right to expansion into all American territories.

Valdivia, as both a writer and a man, is most often mentioned in the company of an elite cohort of conquerors including Cortés and Pizarro. This makes perfect sense from a formal point of view, for the bulk of Valdivia's official letters, like those of Cortés, were addressed to Emperor Charles V (one of the last, dated 1552, was written to Philip II). Moreover, other letters were directed to Gonzalo and Hernando Pizarro, to whom Valdivia professed loyalty after the death of their brother Francisco. Valdivia's relationship to the latter was that of vassal to lord – Pizarro having been named a marquis – and it is in courtly language that Valdivia's references to his "*señor*," or lord, are couched.

Thus Valdivia's connection to the men who led the grandest of imperial gestures, the campaigns of Mexico and Peru, has been stressed by modern readers of his official correspondence. Born in the early part of the century, he had participated in the conquests of Venezuela and Peru and gone on from there to found Santiago de Chile in 1541, in the territory known as Nueva Extremadura. Around the year 1554, Valdivia died a dramatic death at the hands of the Araucanian Indians he had conquered, a martyrdom lastingly portrayed by Alonso de Ercilla in the epic poem *La Araucana* (1569). This was the figure of brutal yet heroic conquest known to nineteenth-century readers when the *Cartas* were first published, a romantic image of passion and death. Along with Ercilla's lengthy epic, the *Cartas* became a foundational work for Chilean literature.

Yet these letters, apart from their formal characteristics, have little to do with those written by Cortés twenty-five years earlier. Cortés writes as a pathbreaker, an impatient egotist who resists the control of the bureaucrat Diego Velázquez in order to pursue his own plans. It is from this stance of semi-renegade that he must convince the Emperor of his loyalty to the Crown. His letters, written shortly after the action they depict had taken place, give a vivid account of events that principally aggrandizes Cortés himself. There is little to be found here of the *courtier*: Cortés works alone.

Valdivia, in contrast, is the counterpart to Ercilla's own figure of a renaissance man, combining military service to the King with an educated rhetorical style. His letters flow with ease and even grace, as he continually places his own deeds in the context of the courtly hierarchy. Moreover, he also defers to the authority of the "Marqués," Francisco Pizarro, who is named frequently as Valdivia's patron.

Valdivia knows his place in the accepted order and his writing reflects that knowledge, yet this loyal soldier writes to his sovereign without intermediaries. Reading in particular his long letters of 1545 and 1550, it becomes clear that Valdivia bases his authority as a conqueror and as a writer on the eccentric qualities of his enterprise. Rewarded for his service to Pizarro with land and riches in Peru, he left that comfortable situation in order to strike out into territory where one expedition – that of Diego de Almagro – had already failed. "No había hombre que quisiese venir a esta tierra," he states in the letter of September 4, 1545: no man wished to come to this land. Such had been the case in 1540 when Valdivia embarked on his quest into Chile. Five years later his letters to Charles V attest to his perseverance and loyalty, and to the value of continued funding for what might have been interpreted as a futile war in a marginal territory. Valdivia uses that marginality to his advantage in the context of a conquest carried out solely for the glory of the Empire and the church, never for himself. His expedition has a deeply spiritual aspect to it, for Valdivia knew that he would face in Chile a hostile indigenous population and few material riches.

Little is to be found here of the Araucanian culture Valdivia and his men encountered, for the *Cartas*, legal documents that they were, are written for other purposes. They set out the details of the conqueror's actions and decisions, his victories and defeats. Where an indigenous presence appears, it is only to demonstrate the power of the enemy, and the need to fund further military operations in Chile.

Cortés and Pizarro were captains of the first wave of conquerors, gaining aristocratic titles and great wealth as they established the Mexican and Peruvian centers of conquest. Valdivia, writing from the margins of empire, the unusual Santiago and Concepción, represents the extension of that first wave in letters written some twenty-five years after those of Cortés. His foray into Chile describes the already-known rather than the starkly new, as the Conquest produced its second generation of chroniclers. The *Cartas* set forth the program of an Empire determined to expand to the ends of the hemisphere, convinced of its divine mandate to do so at any cost.

Diego de Landa's *Relación de las cosas de Yucatán* tells a similar story of conquest in a marginal territory, carried out at great cost to all concerned. Landa, who had risen through the hierarchy of the Franciscan order to occupy the position of provincial of Guatemala and Yucatán in 1561, had arrived nearly fifteen years earlier to begin his missionary work. The area was one of the most difficult for the Spaniards to conquer, since there was no centralized power to be divided through tribal warfare as was the case in Mexico and Peru. Though the campaign had begun in 1527, it was almost two decades later before political authority could be established. Landa was part of a group of Franciscans brought in by that fledgling colonial government in order to assist with the imposition of Spanish power.

The *Relación* narrates the conquest of Yucatan and describes in great detail the culture of the Mayan peoples of the peninsula, including their writing, religion, calendar, agriculture, and architecture. Its model is the natural history of the Indies written in the first part of the century by Gonzalo Fernández de Oviedo, to whom Landa refers at the end of his work. Landa's own prose is considerably rougher than Oviedo's, especially in the first chapters which bear more resemblance to a listing of items than to the kind of polished rhetoric produced by the author of the *Natural Historia*. Yet the later chapters, describing the indigenous practices and customs, take on a richer character; they include illustrations of pictographs and maps.

Without doubt, Landa knew the culture he described well, knew its language and the importance of illustrated codices, knew its religion and the significance of ritual objects. Yet all of this he ordered to be destroyed in the famous persecutions of 1562, when great numbers of texts, idols, and ceramics were burned in a frenzy of religious zeal. The cruelty of the punishment meted out to those suspected of continuing to observe indigenous rites was so extensive that Landa found himself accused of harming, rather than furthering, the Christian mission. He had left himself vulnerable to attack by the colonists, who for many years had opposed Franciscan efforts to convert the native population, feeling that such activity deprived them of workers. Now the colonists took advantage of a division between the friars themselves – between those who preferred peaceful conversion and those such as Landa who favored more drastic methods – to present their case to the King. Landa, however, was ultimately absolved and made bishop of Yucatan in 1572, after spending nine years in Spain.

Landa loved and hated the civilization he tried to convert; the two emotions alternate in the *Relación*. He writes in the margins of conquest the complementary story to letters such as Valdivia's, carrying out a conquest of minds and hearts rather than bodies. He carries forth the ideological program of conquest and domination the military campaigns only began. Yet he too knows that his actions take place in an area not central to the Empire, a place in which the King is only peripherally interested. He models his *Relación* on a "canonical" text, Oviedo's, much like Valdivia necessarily followed Cortés. These are the narrations of the second string of conquest, the marginal enterprises carried out with difficulty, pain, and little glory.

Sahagún and the "native" voice

Fray Bernardino de Sahagún's *Historia general de las cosas de la Nueva España* (1577; published Mexico, 1830) [*General History of the Things of New Spain: Florentine Codex*] is a multi-volume, multilingual work compiled during various decades of extensive research. Sahagún, a Franciscan who arrived in Mexico in 1529, exemplifies the values of the first groups of missionaries to work in the conquered Aztec empire, who believed that knowledge of indigenous language, customs, and texts was key to the true Christian conversion of Amerindians. His superior, Fray Toribio de Benavente (known as "Motolinía") had written his own *Historia de los indios de la Nueva España* in the early 1540s, and Motolinía was the initial force behind his protegé's massive project.

The gesture of the *Historia general* is one of preservation in the interest of domination. Landa, of course, had been steeped in the same tradition, but in the face of constant Mayan resistance to the exclusive practice of Christianity he elected to destroy, rather than preserve, the material evidence of pre-Hispanic culture, later replacing it with his own text. In Mexico the Conquest was swifter and the resistance less pronounced. Nevertheless, Sahagún's 1536 foundation of an academy for the sons of indigenous nobility (the Colegio de la Santa Cruz de Tlaltelolco) was controversial from its inception – just as such schools in the Yucatan would later be – among Spanish colonizers. Through this institution dedicated to the education of the colonized, Sahagún carried forth a program of research using "native" informants to learn about such topics as the Indians' religious deities, ceremonies, calendars, and beliefs, daily life before the Conquest, knowledge of the natural world of plants and animals, and the native view of the Conquest itself, through poetry, song, and prose. The informants responded to a series of questions set down by Sahagún, and their answers were recorded by the friar's indigenous assistants, students at the Colegio de la Santa Cruz.

Two texts were the product of this research, one written in Latinized Nahuatl and the other a Spanish translation. The double narrative was presented side-by-side in the manuscript as two parallel columns; a third column provides a listing of Nahuatl words. Lacking monetary support for the entire translation into Spanish (as he mentions in the prologue) Sahagún chose not to translate entire sections of the Nahuatl text at all, judging them unnecessary for the intended European or Christianized Indian reader. At present the only complete translation of the original Aztec testimony is that rendered into English.

It is the indigenous voice, then, that is presented in the *Historia general* to explain the world that was destroyed by the Spaniards. That voice is especially compelling and haunting in Book 12, dedicated to the Conquest itself. Some of the poetic laments included here have been made famous among modern readers by Miguel León-Portilla's well-known book *Visión de los vencidos* [*The Broken Spears*]. Through this testimony we see how the fall of the Aztec empire was prophesied through interpretation of events such as the arrival of the Europeans on the mainland and their march to Tenochtitlán. The manner in which the Indians read such signs has been noted as a key factor in their later defeat – despite numerical odds heavily in their favor – by such semioticians as Tzvetan Todorov in his *The Conquest of America* (1982).

Equally important to the consideration of the *Historia general*, however, is Sahagún's own commentary, which forms a frame around the native testimony, appearing in prologues and appendixes attached to many of the twelve books comprising the text. The appendix to Book 1 (a book describing indigenous gods) is particularly important, as it sets the tone for the presentation of a system of beliefs considered inspired by the Devil himself. Sahagún's own very Spanish voice thunders down to indigenous readers as he pronounces the gods of Book 1 to be wicked idols, representing a people living in darkness. The light coming from Christianity and the Pope is shown in quotes from the Latin Bible, subsequently interpreted by the Franciscan author to demonstrate monotheistic Catholicism as the one true religion. Sahagún translates the Latin into Spanish for his indigenous audience: *Omnis dii gentium demonia*, "todos los dioses de los gentiles son demonios" ["all the gods of the Gentiles are demons"]. The refutations culminate in several exclamations: an exhortation to the reader to report any idolatrous activity among the native community, and an anguished plea to God for the continuation of that group's enlightenment through conversion.

The work of transcription and translation in the double narrative of the *Historia general* is thus echoed in the translation and interpretation within Sahagún's own commentary. These were the activities marking his scholarly research, work he saw as equivalent to that of a physician naming and describing a catalogue of diseases the better to treat his patient. As the prologue notes, the friar's efforts not only make better medicine for the soul possible, but also commit to writing for the first time an oral history. In this way indigenous history is saved, even while the civilization it records was being destroyed through acculturation. Indeed, the two actions are as inseparable as the Spanish narrative is from its Nahuatl original. We have Sahagún's text to thank for much of our present-day knowledge of the Aztec world, but as his own commentary demonstrates, it was a world he considered destined for oblivion.

José de Acosta: the natural history in full flower

As the first century of Spanish American colonization drew to a close, a Jesuit priest who had resided in the viceroyalties of both New Spain and Peru published a book which enjoyed immediate and multinational acclaim. José de Acosta's *Historia natural y moral de las Indias* (Seville, 1590) [*A Natural and Moral History of the Indies*] went into several Spanish editions shortly after publication and was translated into most principal European languages as well. The text is divided into seven component books (*libros*), the first four treating the natural side of history in a wide-ranging array of topics, and the last three devoted to moral matters pertaining to the Indians and their culture.

According to the chronology established by Edmundo O'Gorman, a well-known modern editor of the *Historia natural y moral*, Acosta joined the Jesuit order at an early age and was sent to Peru by his superiors in 1571, shortly after taking definitive vows (O'Gorman, "Prólogo"). Arriving in Lima the following year, he would spend the next decade and a half in America: fourteen years in various locations around the viceroyalty of Peru, and one in New Spain's capital city, before embarking on the long return voyage to Europe.

Thus the *Historia natural y moral* was begun in Peru, continued in Mexico, and finished in Spain. Its sweep comprises the whole of the continent, and as was the case with other learned histories of the era, the whole of the universe as well. Much as did the works of Oviedo, López de Gómara, and Las Casas, this history seeks to inscribe America into a cosmic order of things both natural (created by God) and moral (pertaining to human culture). What is different about Acosta's work, as O'Gorman has suggested, is its own historical moment, a century after the actual "discovery" of the New World. No longer was the historian's writing intended to describe the new or the unknown; its purpose now was to explicate for a new generation the place that had been established for the Indies and their original inhabitants in the new world order of the latter half of the century.

As was the case with earlier histories, this place for America implied a providential role for Christianity in general and for Spain in particular. Acosta shows first how America fit geographically into an Aristotelian, geocentric concept of the universe. Reducing his scope to the Earth, he argues against classical theories that the "Torrid Zone" was uninhabitable for humankind, after establishing that the Indians, though their origins are unclear, descended from earlier savages who came to America on foot from other continents (Books 1 and 2). Acosta then goes on to describe in detail the many parts of the natural American world: geography, metals, plants, and animals (Books 3 and 4). The religion of the Incas and Mexicans, as well as their pre-Conquest culture and government, are treated in Books 5 and 6. Finally, the last Book of the *Historia natural y moral* puts the entire story into a providential framework, declaring that a divine plan has brought the Spaniards to the New World in order to Christianize the planet's last and fourth continent. Indigenous culture and religion thus meet their demise in the wake of a justified conquest carried out by the carriers of God's true faith.

Composed by a priest born in Spain after the conquests of Mexico and Peru had been completed, and deceased as the century turned (Acosta's dates are 1540–1600), this natural history represents more clearly than any other we have yet discussed the discourse of Spanish historians during the second half of the sixteenth century. Acosta's work was deeply embedded in a tradition of writing about the New World already established by other Spaniards. Indeed, as O'Gorman documents, nineteenth-century Mexican historians engaged in heated arguments over the accusations of plagiarism lodged against Acosta for his reliance on the work of Juan de Tovar, also a Jesuit and a specialist in pre-Conquest Mexican culture. Tovar in turn had utilized the writing of the Dominican friar Diego Durán, whose sixteenth-century work *Historia de los indios de la Nueva España* [*History of the Indians of New Spain*] was not published until 1867. Acosta acknowledged his correspondence with Tovar in the first chapter of Book 6 of his *Historia natural y moral*, citing the latter's work on indigenous peoples as a source for his own text, but the controversy flared up among scholars in the nineteenth century after Mexico gained independence. The Spanish Jesuit became a symbol of European appropriation of Indian history, the theory being that the original text on which all others were based was an anonymous history written by an indigenous author.

Such indigenist sentiments were common in the decades following Spanish American independence; they reflect a romantic desire to establish literary foundations for the newly freed continent that would pre-date the colonial era. Acosta's *Historia* offers an especially interesting case in point. The information on indigenous culture he relates can ultimately be traced back to indigenous sources, of course, but those sources were oral or pictorial, and had come to him through the filter of others' research.

For a Jesuit historian such as Acosta, trained according to a classical rhetoric in which originality was less important than tradition, and religious values implied suppression of individuality for the advancement of doctrine, using the work of another Jesuit such as Tovar was natural and required no more than the mention it was given. The oral culture from which his material derived, being unwritten in character, for him was not history; it was the vestige of a pre-Christian America now disappearing in order to be replaced by a greater design. Within those limitations we can read the *Historia natural y moral* as an elegantly composed, flowing narrative full of detail, a memorial to one hundred years of Spanish presence in the New World and to the changes wrought through colonization. The indigenous voices within would remain mute for some time longer.

The chronicles of a new generation: Alvarado Tezozomoc and Súarez de Peralta

The final two texts included in this section of our study are intertwined with Acosta's *Historia natural y moral* through both chronology and historical antecedents. The *Crónica mexicana* of Hernando Alvarado Tezozomoc, written about 1598, was first published in full in Mexico in 1878 together with the "Codex Ramírez", a manuscript describing indigenous culture that was later identified as the work of Juan de Tovar, based on that of Durán (O'Gorman, "Prólogo" to his edition of Acosta, *Historia natural*, xix). Juan Súarez de Peralta's *Tratado del descubrimiento de las Indias* [*Treatise on the Discovery of the Indies*] was written nine years before in 1589, but similarly remained unpublished until 1878, when an edition appeared in Madrid of the manuscript, which had been found in Toledo.

These volumes attempt, much like Acosta's *Historia*, to insert the ethnographic work of Durán, Tovar, and Sahagún into a system of meaning relevant to the end of a century of colonization. From the different points of view apparent in these two chronicles, authored by members of New Spain's Indian and creole nobility respectively, emerge the voices of a new group of historians who will begin to re-write the Spanish chronicles from an American perspective.

The *Tratado* of Súarez de Peralta, written in a colloquial, personal style by a cultivated dilettante of history rather than a professional, begins with a rapid survey of the kinds of major philosophical questions that so disturbed the sixteenth century. Where the Indians came from, what their religion was like, why the Spaniards were chosen by God to conquer: all these themes are sounded, yet they are breezed through rapidly for two reasons. First, the author of the *Tratado* has no intention of disagreeing with any historian except Las Casas, whose *Brevísima relación* he criticizes as hyperbole. Suárez does not place himself on the same intellectual level as learned historians, nor does he engage with their arguments. The second reason for not dwelling on prior accounts is that Suárez has another story in mind: that of the actual discovery of New Spain, which he had heard firsthand from his own father, Hernán Cortés's brother-in-law. And beyond the Discovery, the *Tratado* extends its narration to the second generation of colonial nobility, to relate the rise and fall of Martín Cortés, the conqueror's supremely ambitious son, and of the Avila brothers, creole aristocrats publicly executed in Mexico for plotting against the Crown.

Suárez de Peralta's *Tratado* exemplifies a type of creole narrative that would become increasingly important in the seventeenth century: a chronicle mixing documentation with social commentary and gossip, written with oral history, as it reports on the lives lived by the American-born upper class. The *Tratado* is a foundational text for creole historians, in that it takes notice of the work of Spanish chroniclers and missionaries – Columbus, Cortés, Las Casas, Sahagún, and others – synthesizes them, and goes on to tell a story they cannot, for it is based more than anything else on personal contact with the principal players. Much as the first Spaniards in America, such as Bernal Díaz, Fernández de Oviedo, or Las Casas, based their authority in part on firsthand experience, the new generations of creole or *mestizo* historians would claim a privileged space for their own writing.

The *Tratado* is narrated with the ease of one familiar with Indians on a daily basis, in a practical tone devoid of the marvelling quality so prevalent in earlier chronicles. Emotion is saved for scenes such as the recounting of the Avilas' demise and ignoble death, which Suárez considers an excessive and unfair punishment. The *Tratado*, then, chronicles the world of the first-generation Creole, and the beginnings of a society of excess that would later be portrayed so well by baroque poets such as Juan del Valle y Caviedes. Martín Cortés, symbol of the decadence brought on by only a few decades of colonial wealth and power, and the hapless Avila brothers, who meet their fate tearfully but elegantly attired, signal the preocupation of the creoles with ceremony and appearance that would later be represented more fully by the Baroque of the seventeenth century.

Tezozomoc's *Crónica mexicana* tells the tale of the ruling class that was conquered: the vanquished Aztec nobility. The author himself was descended from such imperial ancestors; again, his history is based on the testimony of those with personal knowledge of the events. Tezozomoc, about whom little is known, was apparently born about the time of the

Conquest (1520?) and wrote his chronicle as an old man (Mariscal, "Prólogo" to Tezozomoc, xxxvii). The *Crónica* covers the history of the Aztecs, or Mexica, from their legendary beginnings up to the time of conquest. Tezozomoc refers to a second part of the chronicle which would cover the years since the arrival of the Spaniards, but that manuscript has been lost. What we possess today by this author are two narratives: the one presently discussed, written in Spanish, and the *Crónica mexicáyotl*, composed in Nahuatl.

For a Spanish-reading public, the most notable feature of the *Crónica mexicana* must be its linguistic strangeness. The language is repetitive, sometimes hypnotic, leading one observer to hypothesize that the chronicle published in 1878 in reality is a translation from Nahuatl (Mariscal, xlii). Until a more critical edition of the *Crónica* is published this will remain an uncertain point. What is clear to the reader, however, is that Tezozomoc's chronicle straddles two systems of subjective experience; he is both a descendant of the conquered aristocracy, and the Christianized historian of that conquest.

One important example of the consequences of the dual vision fostered by this position is the manner in which indigenous beliefs are treated. The religious practices of the Mexica are described here in detail, the narrative including many Nahuatl words that remain untranslated. At the same time, moral outbursts against the demonic character of human sacrifice and the idolatry of the Indians form important asides in the narration, a recurrent pattern in the writing of indigenous or *mestizo* historians of the era.

With this Mexican text of colonization and conquest we end our examination of the histories written during the second half of the sixteenth century in the New World, which for someone like Alvarado Tezozomoc was both new and old. In a language existing between two cultures, the voice of an indigenous historian emerges in the *Crónica mexicana* to recast the story of a conquest that had been written before only by the conquerors themselves. It was a voice that would remain silent for many centuries, until post-colonial era scholars "discovered" it anew. In it we have an emblem for the richness, and sadness, of colonial culture at century's end.

Histories and historians of the early seventeenth century: 1600–1620

The early years of the seventeenth century saw the continued writing and publishing of many of the same types of histories that characterized the preceding decades. The legalistic *relación* grew in importance, while the classical *historia* still found practitioners of its art on both sides of the Atlantic. Women, mostly cloistered nuns, wrote spiritual life stories that frequently narrated historical events as well. *Mestizo* and Indian historians wrote in the two principal viceroyalties of New Spain and Peru. And as the limits of Empire extended into Paraguay, the Argentinian territories and the River Plate, new chronicles were written to follow the colonialists' march.

Ovando and the *cronista mayor* school

Juan de Ovando y Godoy, named president of the Council of Indies in 1571, would spend the next five years formulating and refining a list of questions to which the writers of *relaciones* would be expected to respond in their documents. The resultant questionnaires would be used by the *cronista mayor*, or chief chronicler of the Indies, to compile a descriptive book of all the colonial territories (González Echevarría, *Myth and Archive*, Mignolo "Cartas"). After Ovando's death (about 1576), Juan López de Velasco, the chief chronicler of the time, further reduced the obligatory questions to fifty in number.

These two men were thus responsible for the official character and professionalization of two types of historical writing in the late sixteenth and seventeenth centuries: that of the *cronista mayor*, and that of the more humble report or *relación*. The first, following the tradition of Oviedo and López de Gómara, would continue to encase the history of the Indies within a universal and cosmic frame, taking the reports of the *relación* and merging them with a learned rhetoric. A notable example in the early seventeenth century was Antonio de Herrera y Tordesillas, *cronista mayor*, who would publish the *Historia general de los hechos de los castellanos en las islas y tierra firme del mar océano* (Madrid 1601–1615) [*A General History of the Deeds of the Castilians in the Islands and Mainland of the Ocean Sea*]; never having travelled to America, he based his compendious history on the observations of others, re-writing myriad documents both published and unpublished.

The *relaciones* were numerous and with notable exceptions (such as the *Brevísima relación* of Las Casas) are reports that today may be found more frequently in historical or legal archives than in libraries. What must interest us here is the stamp that the official list of questions to which these reports responded left on historical and literary writing as the seventeenth century progressed. The histories composed by the *cronista mayor* school naturally demonstrated this influence. But the ubiquitous *relación*, with its legal rhetoric, was also entwined with the rise of the picaresque novel (González Echevarría, "José Arrom, autor de la *Relación acerca de las antigüedades de los indios*," *Myth and Archive*). From the mid seventeenth century onwards, these strands of legal and literary discourse would combine in the work of authors such as Carlos de Sigüenza y Góngora (*Infortunios de Alonso Ramírez*, Mexico, 1690) to create the heterogeneous prose narratives that characterize the late colonial era.

Writers in the convent: Histories of colonial nuns

Women were important actors in the New World from the beginning of the era of conquest and colonization, exercising many different capacities in both the public and private spheres (Muriel, *Cultura femenina novohispana*, Martín, *Daughters of the Conquistadores*). Women prepared to write history were an extremely small group, for few were educated to a level beyond the basics of reading and writing thought to be sufficient for females. In the later sixteenth and seventeenth centuries, convents founded in the cities of New Spain, Peru, and New Granada (Colombia) would rapidly become institutions important to the upper and professional classes of creoles and *mestizos*. These convents, some housing hundreds of women of all ages and races, were a main locus of prestige in the orthodox, religious society that developed after the Council of Trent. The convents themselves mirrored the outside society, with strict divisions of class and caste dictating who would aspire to the station of a professed nun and who would be servant or slave.

Some women found in the convent a place congenial to the writing of literature, especially poetry and theatre. Sor Juana Inés de la Cruz, who falls chronologically outside the scope of our essay, is but the best-known of these poets. The discovery and publication of colonial women writers is a scholarly task that has only recently begun with the publication of several key books (Muriel, *Cultura femenina*, Arenal and Schlau, *Untold Sisters*). Though poetry, usually of a mystical bent, was the most common vehicle for women writers of that time, spiritual life stories (*vidas de monjas*) were frequently written at the behest of male confessors. These stories, valued for their exemplary character, were read much as the lives of saints had been since the early Christian era.

Thus, nuns who wrote history in the early decades of the seventeenth century did so in the guise of two types of narrative that were frequently combined: the *relación* or *crónica* giving an account of the founding of an individual convent, and the *vida*. The two were meshed, in that the life story of the nun often also encompassed her role as founder of a convent, especially during the decades around the turn of the century when new institutions were springing up rapidly, keeping pace with the growth of colonial society. Among the various religious orders, that of the reformed Carmelites – followers of St. Teresa of Avila – is notable for its emphasis on writing foundational history, as Teresa herself had done in the sixteenth century (Arenal and Schlau, *Untold Sisters*, 19–45).

We will briefly describe the narratives of two nuns who worked together to found Mexico City's first Carmelite convent, that of San José, in 1616. Inés de la Cruz, born in Spain, arrived in America with her family while still a child. Her life story, written during the years 1625–1629, is preserved in manuscript in the library of the present-day convent, as well as within the text of Sigüenza y Góngora's *Parayso Occidental* (Mexico, 1684). Mariana de la Encarnación, a Creole, wrote a *relación* in 1641 recounting her life and the convent's foundation; this too is excerpted within Sigüenza's text, and was copied in manuscript by another nun in 1823.

The two women professed in the Convento de Jesús María (the subject of Sigüenza's history and one of the oldest convents of New Spain). Unhappy with the laxity of religious practice in that institution, they worked together to found San José, which would follow strict Teresian rule. To do so they formed an alliance with the viceregal court, which for reasons both religious and political was especially interested in founding a Carmelite convent in New Spain's capital. The histories of Inés and Mariana tell of the events leading up to the 1616 foundation through first-person accounts, beginning with their own life stories and gradually blending the narration of self into that of the institution.

These writings base their account of events on the very private inner world of religious belief, as miracles and visions reveal a divine plan that will include each nun as central actor in the unfolding drama of intrigue in the arenas of court and church. Along the way, they relate many details of daily life in the convent; in the case of Mariana's account, these details include a description of the tensions present between Spanish-born and creole nuns. These details are fascinating in and of themselves, for they tell us of the separate world inside the convent walls. Equally important and necessary is a consideration of how these women's histories intersect with the dominant rhetorical patterns of their era – and especially with the *relación*, that amorphous vehicle mixing legal document with autobiography. The life stories of colonial nuns should be read in the context of the changing discourse of New World historical narrative, as well as that of a feminine tradition stemming especially from Teresa's works. Just as life within the convents reflected the complexity of the world outside, so do these nuns' narratives participate in the dramatic developments taking place in the writing of history.

Narratives of the native Andean experience

The Mexican historian Enrique Florescano, describing what he calls the uprootedness of the noble Indian chroniclers of New Spain (such as Tezozomoc) and the interpretation of indigenous history that they set down in Hispanicized, written form, differentiates between this process and that which took place in Peru (Florescano, *Memoria mexicana*, 167–81). According to Florescano's analysis, the indigenous historians of New Spain collaborated with the Spanish conquerors, clearly separating themselves from the masses of Indians and assuming an acculturated, Europeanized point of view. For Florescano this suggests a lack of identity and authenticity in the *mestizo* chroniclers of New Spain as they made the transition from oral to written history. The first Andean writers, in contrast, maintained a closer connection to their Indian past and present, and their writing thus provides us with a testimony of colonization in the Andean region more autochthonous in character than that of New Spain.

We may question this scheme as rather too reductive, for all histories written to record a centuries-old oral tradition using the tools of Western rhetoric necessarily displayed the ravages of cultural loss. The translation into static Spanish could never do justice to an indigenous system of meaning that relied on multiple interpretations. However, as we consider the efforts of Andean historians to record the events of the first century of colonial rule in their lands, notable differences with the chronicles of New Spain are evident.

Today the best-known work of an Andean author is that of Felipe Guaman Poma de Ayala, *El primer nueva corónica y buen gobierno* (1615; published Paris, 1936) [*The First New Chronicle and Good Government*]. Guaman Poma's extensive text is one of several from which today's student of colonial Peru may draw information about indigenous culture after the arrival of the Spaniards. The earliest is the *Relación* of Titu Cusi Yupanqui, dictated to a priest about 1570 (published Lima, 1916). A member of the ruling Inca family and a witness to the Conquest, Titu Cusi recorded his account before being executed for his role in the indigenous uprising at Vilcabamba. Another account is that of Juan de Santacruz Pachacuti Yamqui, *Relación de antigüedades deste reino del Perú*, finished about the same time as Guaman Poma's *Nueva corónica* (1613) and published in Madrid centuries later as a volume of the Biblioteca de Autores Españoles.

Both Pachacuti Yamqui and Guaman Poma were members of non-Inca dynasties (Adorno, *From Oral to Written Expression*, 1). Guaman Poma, born about 1535 in the northern region of Andamarca, held various bureaucratic posts in the colonial government of his area and participated in the Spanish campaigns to extirpate Indian "heresies." The *Nueva corónica* first narrates the Andean past up to the time of conquest, criticizing at times the dominance of the Inca over other dynasties. The second part of his work gives an account of Andean life under colonial rule, and here the cruelty of the Spaniards is presented boldly, though always within the tenets of Catholic doctrine.

The study of Andean works such as Guaman Poma's by literary and cultural critics has become progressively more sophisticated since 1980. Semiotic and ethnographic methodologies have enriched the tools of textual criticism, shedding light on these complex narratives that cross cultural boundaries not only linguistically (as in Tezozomoc's work) but through pictorial representation as well. The *Nueva corónica*, for example, illustrated throughout with the author's drawings, presents a double text: that based on the word, argued through the rhetoric of Spanish scholasticism, and that based on the picture, organized symbolically in accordance with Andean use of space (Adorno, *Guaman Poma*, MacCormack, "Atahualpa and the book").

The theme of resistance to acculturation is sounded repeatedly through studies of these narratives, which were but one of the means by which native Andeans struggled to maintain cohesion in the face of disarray fraught through conquest (other battles were joined through the courts, or in actual insurrection). Despite these efforts to combat the despair resulting from what Guaman Poma called a "world upside down," class divisions such as those Florescano cites in the Mexican case ultimately made their way into Andean society as well (Castro-Klarén, "Dancing and the sacred in the Andes," 173). The Hispanicized descendants of the noble classes eventually lost their connection with the masses of illiterate Indians.

The decades that ended the sixteenth century and began the seventeenth were crucial in the formation of a body of written history that would express the catastrophe of conquest as penned by the vanquished themselves. The texts of *mestizo* historians in Mexico and Peru stand as testimony to a resistance to colonialism far from monolithic in character, reflecting the internal complexities of Indian society both before and after its encounter with Europe. What was lost in translation as oral tradition gave way to written history was both material and symbolic: the power to tell one's own story. The historians who tried to bridge the gap and retain that power inevitably lost the battle, as the hegemony of the written word became ever more entrenched.

El Inca Garcilaso de la Vega: the commentary of a *mestizo* Humanist The *Comentarios reales* (Lisbon, 1609) [*Royal Commentaries of the Incas*] and *Historia General del Perú* (Cordoba, 1617) [*General History of Peru*] together form one of the best-known histories of Peru from the origins of Inca society through the Spanish Conquest and decades following. Their author and the circumstances of his life are just as famous: born in Cuzco in 1539 as Gómez Suárez de Figueroa, the illegitimate son of an Inca princess and a Spanish captain of noble family, Garcilaso spent his first twenty years in Peru, growing up among the first generation of privileged *mestizos* and Creoles. He sailed for Spain in 1560 after his father's death, and for the next thirty years struggled in vain to establish his claim to the latter's estate. Garcilaso studied in the library of his uncle's home in Andalusia, fought in military campaigns against the *moriscos*, and eventually retired near century's end to Cordoba, with an inheritance left by his uncle. It was there that he would write the works of renaissance prose so revered today, which also include a Spanish translation of the neo-Platonist Italian author León Hebreo, *Diálogos* (Madrid, 1590) [*Dialogues*] and *La Florida del Inca* (Lisbon, 1605) [*The Florida of the Inca*].

Why the *Comentarios* have been the object of so much attention from historians and literary historians is not difficult to determine: the work is written in an elegant, flowing Spanish prose among the most beautiful of the period, an exemplary text of renaissance measure in writing. The author's bilingual and bicultural subjectivity, moreover, is frequently alluded to, contributing an autobiographical flavor to the narrative. How that subjectivity is brought to bear on the historical dimension of the *Comentarios* is the question at the heart of most – if not all – readings of the work, and the reason Garcilaso has been converted at times into a symbol of the new society of the New World.

The nine books comprising the *Comentarios* begin with the kind of universal situation of America and Peru we have described in other learned histories. Garcilaso makes clear early on that his "commentary" will refer to the work of Cieza de León, Acosta, and others not to correct, but rather to emend them, in order to describe the empire of Cuzco, which he compares to that of Rome. While it was the common gesture of renaissance historians to build upon the texts of other learned writers, thus contributing to the humanist's task of explicating man's place in the Universe, Garcilaso's contribution as a *mestizo* author added a different link to the simple chain of one historian following another. Though his heritage discredited him in the eyes of some as a historian capable of telling the truth regarding his mother's people, he negotiated this dilemma, employing the historiographical tools of European rhetoric (Pupo-Walker, *Historia, creación y profecía, La vocación literaria*).

In particular, his knowledge of the Quechua language was a key element in this claim. The form of commentary was practiced by humanist rhetoricians as a gloss on classical or ancient texts; Garcilaso's exercise takes on a distinct character by glossing the "texts" of the Incan empire, made up of oral testimony and memory (Zamora, *Language, Authority and Indigenous History*). In writing this commentary based on Quechua sources, Garcilaso may expound upon his own vision of the providential role of the Incas in the history of Peru: that they brought civilization to the barbarous Chanca tribes, thus paving the way for the arrival of Christianity.

The books of the *Comentarios reales* thus fit the Incas within the familiar framework of the natural history, examining first the universal, then the local, dedicating chapters to the plants and animals of their author's native land and the character of its inhabitants. Garcilaso's constant desire is to show the rational, monotheistic, just, and civilized nature of his maternal forebears. In this fashion he responded to the reactionary ideological campaign of the viceroy Francisco de Toledo, who, in the last quarter of the sixteenth century, fomented the writing of a series of chronicles designed to portray the Incas as tyrants (Lavalle, "El Inca Garcilaso"). Garcilaso's history, then, is a lament for the harmonious culture that could have been a Christianized Tahuantinsuyo, combining both cultures without destruction, much as Las Casas had envisioned.

The *Comentarios* seek to narrate a native-speaker's history of the Incan empire, "destroyed before it was understood," and to defend the civilization of his mother's land, pulverized by the ferocious armies of his father's nation. The *Historia General del Perú* covers the period of conquest and civil war subsequent to the arrival of those armies. Here it is clear that Garcilaso viewed the Conquest as justified and necessary from a religious standpoint. He relishes the opportunity to wash out some of the dirty linen of opposing factions, detailing such internal power struggles with the authority of an eyewitness.

In the *Historia general*, planned by the Inca as the second part of the *Comentarios* but published posthumously with a different title, Garcilaso endeavors to establish his father as a conqueror loyal to the Crown despite evidence of possible treason, and to defend his own claim to the conqueror's legacy (González Echevarría, *Myth and Archive*). Thus the father's biography combines with the autobiographical narrative of the son, and the narrative of nostalgia and memory blends with a desire for material and legal vindication.

Telling the story from within European discursive boundaries, El Inca assumes the position of a well-born *mestizo* historian attempting to negotiate his own harmonious balance among two cultures. While his history must be differentiated from that of Andean writers such as Guaman Poma who wrote narratives truly indigenous in character and perspective, it shares with those accounts the futility and frustration of a desire for justice between colonizer and colonized that, ultimately, was impossible.

Alva Ixtlilxóchitl: the next generation of native historians

Though the two volumes of the *Comentarios reales* were published in the seventeenth century during the Baroque Era, Garcilaso had begun to write much earlier. Born within the first decade following the conquest of Peru, his personal experience, education, and legal concerns all reflect the changing nature of the Spanish empire at mid-sixteenth century. A code of law establishing the rights of conquerors and conquered was still in the making; the humanist teachings of the first half of the century had not yet disappeared from intellectual life; and the ways of indigenous society before the arrival of Europeans could be culled from memory and oral tradition. Garcilaso had lived in close proximity to his Incan family, and their past was more than an abstraction for him.

Fernando de Alva Ixtlilxóchitl (New Spain, 1580?–1650), son of a *mestiza* mother and a Spanish father, belonged to a new generation of American historians for whom the era of conquest and native empires existed not as cherished memory, so much as archival source. In his *Historia de la nación chichimeca* (written 1608–1625?; published in Mexico in 1891) [*History of the Chichimec Nation*] Ixtlilxóchitl follows a familiar humanist model for historiographical practice, applying it to one branch of his maternal ancestors. Beginning with an account of the origins of the world according to Mesoamerican legend, Ixtlilxóchitl traces the rise and fall of the Olmec and Toltec civilizations, and the subsequent migration of northern tribes into the central valley of Anahuac. Among those migrants were the Chichimecas, who eventually settled in the region of Teotihuacán and Texcoco, adopting the culture and Nahuatl language of the area and thereafter calling themselves the Acolhua. By the end of the thirteenth century they dominated the valley, but civil wars with rival tribes limited their further expansion. During the fourteenth century the Acolhua, Tepaneca, and Mexica emerged as the strongest of the warring groups to form the Triple Alliance; in the latter part of the fifteenth century the Mexica, or Aztecs, would take control of the Alliance (Vázquez, his introduction to Alva Ixtlilxóchitl, 8–15). All of this is narrated in the *Historia de la nación chichimeca*, culminating in the arrival of Cortés and his siege of Tenochtitlán. The work ends abruptly and incompletely at this point, for the manuscript lacks what would have been further chapters relating the establishment of New Spain.

Ixtlilxóchitl, a direct descendent of the rulers of Texcoco, Teotihuacán, and Tenochtitlán through his maternal grandmother, adopted his own indigenous name – that of the Texcocan lord who was his great-great-grandfather – by going back several generations in the family tree. It was common in the sixteenth century for members of a family to use different surnames, and for a person to adopt a name other than that of his or her parents. In this case, Ixtlilxóchitl's gesture established a clear link with his indigenous heritage, despite the fact that he was a *castizo* only one-quarter Indian, and according to documents of the time was regarded socially as white (Vázquez, 33).

What was Ixtlilxóchitl's relationship to his Indian background? Like so many other figures of this period, his personal identification, or lack thereof, with indigenous roots has been a point of controversy for post-Independence intellectuals, themselves passionately embroiled in a modern search for Spanish American identity. The arguments are too numerous to recount here; we will recall only Florescano's dismissal of historians who identified with the collaborating Indian nobility, already discussed in the case of Tezozomoc versus Guaman Poma. The question deserves a serious treatment towards which we will venture some notes.

Ixtlilxóchitl had been educated for several years at the Colegio de la Santa Cruz de Tlaltelolco. The great educational project of Sahagún and other Franciscans had by that time entered its final, waning era, but still offered the descendants of Indian nobility a European course of advanced studies. The Texcocan became a government functionary, working as a judge and later a court interpreter in the bureaucracy that dealt with Indian affairs. He was therefore bilingual, and skilled as well in the reading of Indian codices which served as source material for his historical writing. Indeed, some of his earlier accounts were composed in Nahuatl. His mother inherited the lands of the *cacicazgo* of Teotihuacán at the end of the sixteenth century; the family would struggle to maintain control of their estate for decades to come through extensive legal battles.

The *Historia de la nación chichimeca* bases its account of indigenous history on the codices, and that of Cortés's actions on the texts of Spanish chroniclers such as Gómara, Herrera, and Torquemada (*Monarquía indiana*, 1615). The Chichimecas are cast as a civilized people prior to their arrival in the central valley, though all ethnographic evidence identifies them as nomadic and disorganized. Cortés is the providential envoy of both Charles V and Christ, saving the tribes of Anahuac from idolatry, barbarism, and the savage imperialism of the Aztecs.

Thus the *Historia de la nación chichimeca* broadly follows the model of the *Comentarios reales*: a gloss, really a translation, of indigenous sources to show the importance and civilizing role of the author's ancestors, followed by the arrival of Christians to complete the divine plan. While the *Comentarios* is nowhere cited by Ixtlilxóchitl, he would have been familiar with the work at least through Herrera's compendium.

The Texcocan, though, shared neither Garcilaso's superb rhetorical talent, nor his divided identity. Ixtlilxóchitl was a member of a generation removed in time from the Conquest, and a caste which cooperated fully with the colonial authorities. Yet his fortune, and livelihood, depended on his knowledge of Nahuatl and his legal claim to ancestral land. The *Historia de la nación chichimeca* argues that claim through codified rather than oral sources, for memory had lost its power for the *caciques* of the seventeenth century; their interest was in documentation that would help them retain wealth. Ixtlilxóchitl stood to gain from his noble indigenous ancestry, and he celebrated it as he cheered for the victory of Cortés. By the second decade of the seventeenth century, such a stance posed little if any contradiction.

La Argentina of Ruy Díaz de Guzmán

La Argentina, finished in 1612 and first published in Buenos Aires in 1835, was originally entitled *Anales del descubrimiento, población y conquista de las Provincias del Río de la Plata* [*Annals of the Discovery, Settlement and Conquest of the Provinces of the River Plate*]. Its author, Ruy Díaz de Guzmán, was born in Asunción, Paraguay, about 1560 and died there in 1629; like Ixtlilxóchitl, he was the son of a *mestiza* mother and a Spanish father, and probably bilingual (in Guaraní and Spanish). There the similarity ends, for Díaz de Guzmán was the first chronicler of his province, which was the southernmost frontier of colonization in the late sixteenth and early seventeenth centuries. This product of a second generation of racial blending became himself both an agent of Spanish imperial consolidation, and the founding historian of his region, and as such provides a fitting end for our survey of the time span which roughly coincides with his own life.

La Argentina is the first chronicle written by a pacifier, rather than a conqueror of Indians, for Díaz de Guzmán's actions as a soldier of the Crown contributed to the settlement of colonial society in areas where the initial moment of discovery had long since passed (Gandía, Introduction to *La Argentina*, 32–3). Though not a professional historian – a *letrado*, or educated man – he possessed a keen awareness of history, tradition, and authorship stemming from his own sense of place. For as much as *La Argentina* treats the history of the discovery of the provinces of La Plata, it also is a declaration of lineage and the author's identification with "nuestros españoles" (our Spaniards). Díaz de Guzmán's father was a member of an illustrious noble family; his maternal grandfather was Domingo de Irala, Governor of Paraguay and one of the principal founders of the first settlement of Buenos Aires in the mid sixteenth century. That his mother was a *mestiza*, the illegitimate daughter of one of the Governor's Indian women, is absent from the text. It is not pertinent to the project of *La Argentina*, which is to establish a genealogy through the recounting of past and present deeds of the Guzmán family, using information culled from oral testimony and the chronicler's own eyewitness experience.

Here we must consider the legal character of this history, an aspect overlooked by historians (who emphasize the narrative's value as a foundational, if somewhat erroneous, history) and literary scholars (who have found novelesque aspects in several self-contained "stories" interspersed within the book). Díaz de Guzmán wrote *La Argentina* while residing in the city of La Plata, the judicial seat of the Charcas region of Upper Peru and the location of the *audiencia* (colonial court) which held jurisdiction over Paraguay and Buenos Aires, between 1607 and 1612. At the time he had been waging legal battles with several successive governors, most notably with Hernando Arias de Saavedra. These difficulties, typical of the era, involved Díaz de Guzmán's claim to benefits of land and Indians (*encomienda*) as reward for military actions carried out in the name of the monarchy. The governors, anxious to control the power of the colonizers, harassed him in various ways; each time such incidents occurred Díaz de Guzmán would direct himself in writing to the King, seeking justice (Gandía, 35–9).

The urge to write a history of the provinces of the Río de la Plata, therefore, was not an innocent one simply to be attributed to familial pride, or a desire to save history from oblivion. Díaz de Guzmán dedicated *La Argentina* to the Duke of Medina-Sidonia, a relative in the Guzmán clan, and the narrative constantly draws attention to the brave actions of Díaz's forebears. In other words, it clearly establishes his own claim to the territory, and to the title of *conquistador*, despite the fact that he was following in other people's footsteps by the end of the sixteenth century and breaking no new paths through the South American jungle. *La Argentina* should be seen in this context: it is a document of the descendant of conquerors who argues his claim to territory despite the restrictions of the colonial bureaucrats who thwart that claim, and a plea made directly to the Crown by way of noble relatives. It is the declaration of lineage and claim to privilege made by a *mestizo* wholly identified with Spain and the imperial project.

Thus we conclude this survey of the histories of the years 1550–1620 with three *mestizo* writers, all concerned with the problems of lineage, inheritance and remuneration, and all using history as their vehicle for establishing a claim to the past. For El Inca Garcilaso, the search for balance between the heritage of noble indigenous mother and noble conqueror father leads to an extensive history couched in the rhetoric of renaissance Humanism. Alva Ixtlilxóchitl, writing decades later and several generations removed from the immediate aftermath of the Conquest, defends and records his noble Indian heritage not for love or personal identity, but for gain and the continuation of title to ancestral land. Finally, Díaz de Guzmán's history of the La Plata territories, the southern frontier of the early seventeenth century, mirrors his actions as a pacifier of resistant Indian tribes through an exaltation of his noble father and extirpation of his own maternal, indigenous roots.

Three different *mestizo* historians in three different parts of the Spanish Empire, all defending their claim to the future through an examination of the past: these are the voices of history a century after Europeans first set foot on the American mainland. Theirs was truly an era of colonization and change, and their written work represents a crucial turning point in New World historiography.

Historians of the colonial period: 1620–1700
David H. Bost

Historiography of the seventeenth century reflected many of the patterns of historical writing developed during the earlier age of discovery and conquest. The principal historians of the sixteenth century worked with fundamental models of historical expression that survived well into the seventeenth and eighteenth centuries. We see a continuation of the *crónica mayor*, religious historiography that dealt with the history of religious orders and the spiritual life of the colony, various forms of testimonial literature, works that are primarily descriptive of New World geography, and other narrative modalities that were commonly employed during the era, such as the *relación* and learned commentaries. Yet there were significant developments within these well-defined norms – creative endeavors that have recently interested literary scholars – to communicate a more imaginative interpretation of those events and processes that led to the expansion and stabilization of the colonies. Though somewhat guided by functional models written in the sixteenth century, historical writing of the late colonial period became more complex and varied in style and structure.

Chroniclers of the Indies

A curious irony surrounds the role of *cronista mayor* during much of the seventeenth century. According to some indications, these historians were the most capable of any group of producing comprehensive studies of New World history. Those fulfilling this role had the greatest authority and prestige of any kind of historian in the late colonial period. They possessed the legal charge to petition, read, and censor the work of other historians writing about the American Conquest and settlement. As a representative of the Crown, the Chronicler of the Indies was responsible for synthesizing and interpreting any data he considered relevant to Spain's mission in America. With such an impressive investiture, and with Antonio de Herrera y Tordesilla's legacy in mind, it is surprising that no *cronista mayor* during most of the seventeenth century was able to realize fully the lofty promises made by Juan de Ovando in 1571: to write "a general history. . . .with the greatest precision and truth possible" (Carbia, *La crónica oficial de las Indias Occidentales*, 100), a history whose broad scope would include things "of the land as well as the sea, natural and moral, perpetual and temporal, ecclesiastical and secular, past and present" (pp. 118–19).

The position of *cronista mayor de Indias* was created and sustained throughout much of the colonial period partially as a calculated response to the disturbing propagation of the Black Legend throughout the European community: the *cronista mayor* sought to regiment and control the flow of information from the colonies. The Chronicler of the Indies was, in the words of Herrera, entrusted with showing how unjust it was "that the bad deeds of a few overshadow the good works of many" (Carbia, *La crónica oficial*, 102). The *cronista mayor* was thus in a sensitive political position. His works – and those that carried his approval – were intended to serve the national interest by supporting Spain's legal and moral right to govern a land that she had pacified and Christianized. Writing these histories was thus a legal as well as an administrative act. These official historians had the dual responsibility of writing complete histories of the New World and of restoring Spain's fallen reputation among other colonial powers, particularly France and England, nations that had accused the conquistadors of criminal acts against the American Indians. So although no one after Herrera was effectively able to compose a history made up of all things "worthy of knowing," as Ovando had once hoped, a number of official Chroniclers energetically defended Spain's accomplishments in the New World. Pedro Fernández de Pulgar (1621–1698) was probably the most stridently nationalistic of the seventeenth-century Chroniclers of the Indies. As the title of this work suggests, he was obsessed with reclaiming Spain's past glory as a world power: *Tropheos gloriosos de los cathólicos Reyes de España, conseguidos en la justa conquista de América* (c. 1680). Pulgar's goal was, among other things, to write an extended apology to counter the stories of Spanish atrocities in the New World. Of all the official Chroniclers to follow Herrera, it was Antonio de Solís (1610–1686) who most eloquently argued that Spain had achieved a just victory over the Indians. His *Historia de la conquista de México* [*The History of the Conquest of Mexico*] stands out as an articulate defense of Spain's conquest of the Aztec empire as well as a model of historiography of the *crónica mayor* style; he was, in this regard, Antonio de Herrera's worthiest successor. As Luis Arocena has suggested, Solís's work is one of the last significant historical narratives of the Spanish Golden Age dealing with the conquest of America (p. 216).

Painfully aware of Spain's political and economic decline during the seventeenth century, Solís was one of many who wished to improve his country's image in the international community. The *Historia de la conquista de México* thus functions both as a corrective of earlier narratives and a pointed rejoinder to misinformed and ill-intentioned foreign historians. Solís bitterly chastised those from abroad for their "great audacity and no small perversity in making up whatever they please against our nation" (p. 25). Echoing Herrera's earlier invectives against Spain's many detractors, Solís criticized historians who focused on the mistakes of some "to tarnish the success of many" (p. 25). If popularity is any measure of attainment, then Solís accomplished far more than any other *cronista mayor* during the late seventeenth century: by 1704, sixteen editions of his *Historia* had been published in Spanish, French, and Italian; by the end of the eighteenth century, thirty-six more had appeared, including versions in English, German, and Danish. The *Historia de la conquista de México* almost immediately became the standard reference work on Cortés and the conquest of the Aztec empire, and for many years was held up as an exemplary model of narrative elegance in Spanish. Solís was hardly an unknown in literary circles by the time he was appointed *cronista mayor* in 1661. He was already an accomplished poet and dramatist whose literary production eventually included fifteen plays (one in collaboration with Calderón de la Barca) and dozens of poems. He therefore brought to the office of official Chronicler of the Indies a refined literary sensibility.

With such keen literary acuity, Solís could be a mordant critic of historians who did not meet his standards of expository excellence. Few escaped his acrimonious censures. Francisco López de Gómara was, for Solís, a historian who could not discern the truth from his various sources; "he says what he heard," wrote Solís, ultimately falling victim to his own "excessive credulity" (p. 27). For Bernal Díaz del Castillo Solís had low regard: "although he is aided by the circumstance of having seen what he wrote, it is evident from his own work that his vision was not free of passions...envy and ambition walk in plain view throughout his writings" (p. 27). Bernal Díaz had criticized Hernán Cortés, something Solís considered unconscionable in light of Cortés's principal role in the overthrow of tyranny in the Valley of Mexico. Not even Herrera was immune to Solís's harsh assertions: "we do not find in his *Décadas* all of the ease and clarity needed for comprehension" (p. 26). Only El Inca Garcilaso de la Vega's "smooth and amenable style" seemed to please Solís (p. 27).

Solís's survey of historiography on the Mexican conquest illustrates an important tendency among many historical writers of the later colonial period. By the 1660s – when Solís first began working on the *Historia de la*

conquista de México – the basic events of the expeditionary venture into
Tenochtitlán were widely known. The seminal texts of this adventure
(those mentioned here by Solís and others) had acquired an incipient
canonical status. Consequently, Solís was compelled to write his history
with reference to what had already been in print for many years. Added to
this was his resonsibility as *cronista mayor* to write a "just history" of the
Conquest. Re-appraising earlier historical accounts was, of course, an
operative pattern that had been in place since the early sixteenth century;
recall Bernal Díaz del Castillo's virulent declamations against López de
Gómara's version of the Mexican conquest.

Wholly dependent upon such written sources for his narrative, Solís
made frequent reference to writers who had, in his opinion, shamelessly
distorted the truth to conform to their own biases. In thinly veiled
references to Bartolomé de Las Casas, for instance, Solís vehemently
countered the argument that the Indians were, as Las Casas had once
written, people "with no quarrels, complaints, hatred, or desire for
vengeance." Solís viewed the Mexicans as worthy opponents of Cortés
and his soldiers, fully capable of vigorous opposition and malicious deceit
when dealing with the foreign invaders. Solís was somewhat impatient
with the view that the Indians were ingenuous pacifists and that the
Spaniards were interested solely in their own political and economic
advancement: "They wish to credit the glory of our weapons to greed and
the thirst for gold, without remembering that [the Spaniards] opened the
way for religion, counting on special assistance from the arm of God in
their actions" (p. 150). This providentialist view of history – that the
Spanish were somehow realizing God's plan – is present throughout
Solís's text and is an important rhetorical tool in the "justa defensa" of the
conquest of Mexico. The Crown had earlier requested that *cronista
mayor* Tomás Tamayo de Vargas (1585–1641) write a comprehensive
ecclesiastic history of the New World. In this way the Crown could more
convincingly assert that the conquest of America had been the result of
religious convictions and practices, and that Spain was carrying out its
primary mission (as ordered by the Pope) to Christianize the New World.
Solís's critical remarks were not limited to the issue of the legitimacy of the
conquest of Mexico. We have seen that Solís was an astute reader as well
as writer of history who felt that most historians had failed to discern the
different courses that the history of America had taken since the Discovery. Working within a narrative tradition over a century old, Solís
sensed that it would be beneficial to articulate clearly in hierarchical order
which activities in the New World were worthy of historical consideration: "from this confusion and mixture of reports the pure and simple
truth must appear" (p. 25). Solís argued that the history of the Indies was
made up of three distinct events: the Discovery; the conquest of Mexico;

and the fall of Incan Peru. Other historians had failed in their ambitious attempt to deal with all three events within a single narrative. They lacked the focus and precision that Solís believed was necessary. Solís's own solution to this "labryinth" was to concentrate on the early history of New Spain, a move toward greater specialization that time and distance allowed.

Solís spent over twenty years preparing the manuscript that was to become the *Historia de la conquista de México*, yet was still unable to complete the work he had originally intended. The *Historia* covers the Conquest through the fall of Tenochtitlán in 1521, and heroically pits Cortés and his Christian legions against Moctezuma's demonic battalions. His historical characters – Aztecs and Spanish alike – speak and act in an elevated fashion worthy of classical heroes. In one of his motivational addresses to his soldiers, Cortés spoke with persuasive eloquence to a restive group of men who had not yet seen the fruits of their risks: "We are few, but unity multiplies armies, and our unity is our greatest strength.... I am your commander, and I will be the first to risk my life for the least of my soldiers" (p. 51). Moctezuma is presented as an extraordinarily astute challenger to Cortés. Speaking through an interpreter, Moctezuma perceptively dismantled a number of the myths surrounding the foreign army: "Those beasts that obey you I now know are large deer.... Those arms that resemble lightning I know are pipes made of an unknown metal....and I also find, according to the observation of your customs made by my ambassadors and confidants, that you are kind and religious people" (p. 160). For Moctezuma, the Spanish were not gods but men, different in minor respects but "of the same composition and nature as the rest" (p. 160).

There is little concrete evidence that either Moctezuma or Cortés actually spoke in these exact terms. Solís's intention, however, was to characterize these historical figures in consonance with the political philosophy of the *crónica mayor*. What better way to neutralize the Black Legend than to show that Cortés's principal enemy had the economic, political, and intellectual capacity to hurl the Spanish back into the sea? His convincing depiction of these respective agents of history and their struggle for control of the region draws substantially from literary models: Arocena (*Antonio de Solís, cronista indiano*) notes influences from such writers as Baltasar Gracián, Luis de Góngora, and Garcilaso de la Vega (pp. 164–216). The *Historia de la conquista de México* is, in this regard, a literary elaboration of known historical events. It also represents one of the most successful attempts in the seventeenth century to articulate a coherent response to the varying interpretations of the conquest of Mexico.

Religious historians

Missionaries of the seventeenth and eighteenth centuries compiled, by a wide margin, the largest body of historical writing in the colonies. They wrote extensively about their evangelistic activities among the Indians, histories of their respective orders, biographies of exemplary missionaries, ethnographies, sermons, moral and theological tracts, general histories of the viceroyalties, and detailed geographical studies which were often based on their travels. Like their sixteenth-century predecessors, later missionaries were extraordinarily concerned with the religious conversion of the Indians, and their writings generally reflect this powerful sense of purpose. There was, however, some variance about how best to achieve their evangelistic mission.

Religious historians generally represented one of the five great orders: the Franciscans; the Dominicans; the Augustinians; the Mercedarians; and the Jesuits. The Franciscans were the largest of these five orders, but it was the Jesuits who wrote more than any other group, a startling phenomenon in light of the fact that their tenure in the colonies was comparatively brief (1568–1767). The Jesuits, however, were extremely mobile and highly motivated; historical accounts of their activities in Paraguay and California especially reflect a strong utopian impulse.

Jesuit historiography of the seventeenth century dealt extensively with their work among the Indians and their efforts to convert them, one way or another, into obedient Christian subjects of the Spanish colonial empire. Many religious workers in the seventeenth century had concluded, after much debate, that spiritual conversion of the Indians without the use of some force would have limited success. The idea of peaceful, voluntary conversions gave way to the use of forced compliance with the constraints imposed by the church. Even priests who were sympathetic to the plight of the Indians – those who spoke their languages and understood their customs – spoke out against Indian superstitions and idolatry. A new, more aggressive missionary strategy thus emerged in the seventeenth century that was intended to extirpate Indian idolatry once and for all. The priests felt that as long as vestiges of their old religion remained the Indians would resist both Christianity and the efforts to integrate them more fully into colonial society. A resurgent interest among Peruvian Indians in the late sixteenth century in their ancestral rites and practices prompted the religious authorities to investigate and record these acts of heresy. They felt that in order to conquer the enemy it was first necessary to understand him. Some of the most vivid accounts of the campaign waged against the pagan beliefs of the Indians in Peru were written by Jesuit historians Francisco de Avila (1573–1647), Pablo José de Arriaga (1564–1622), and Hernando de Avendaño (1577–1647). Avila was a *mestizo* who wrote about Incan customs, legends, and history. Avila had personally witnessed the rebirth of interest in native Peruvian cults among restive Indians in his parish in Huarochiri and fought to eliminate these traits from their religious practices. Avila was certainly well prepared to comment authoritatively on the folkways of his ancestors; he spoke fluent Quechua and had spent many years among the Peruvian Indians as a missionary. Avila wrote *Tratado y relación de los errores, falsos dioses y otras supersticiones y ritos diabólicos* (Madrid, 1942), a work intended to expose the heathen beliefs of the Indians. His *Tratado y relación* is unique in that he wrote it first in Quechua. In the tradition of El Inca Garcilaso de la Vega, Avila's *Tratado y relación* and other writings contain many of the myths and legends of their Incan forebears, as well as brief vignettes of religious conversions and manifestations of faith.

Avila's recurring story of Don Cristóbal Choquecaxa, for example, is an entertaining tale of a man who had vehemently renounced the religious practices of his Indian forefathers only to be constantly harassed by spirits from the underworld. Don Cristóbal was able to overcome these visitors – who often invaded his dreams – only by invoking the name of Christ. Don Cristóbal, not unlike El Inca Garcilaso and Francisco de Avila, personally experienced the shift in Peruvian religious culture from ancient pagan cults to Catholicism, a change that priests like Avila and Arriaga were determined to carry out.

Arriaga and Avendaño wrote extensively about the work of the Jesuits to dislodge the ancient beliefs and superstitions from Indian ways. Avendaño's *Sermones de los misterios de nuestra santa fe católica en lengua castellana y en la general del Inca* (Lima, 1648) contains vivid analyses of Indian idolatry that persisted during the early seventeenth century in Peru, and tells of his work to supplant pagan beliefs with a Christian world-view. It was generally felt that the presence of Indian religions prevented their passage not only into Christianity but also into the dominant Spanish culture. The conversion to Christianity thus entailed a broader acceptance of social practices characteristic of Spanish life. Missionary writings by Avila and Avendaño represented an important turn in evangelistic thinking and practice during the early seventeenth century. Once the religious officials had determined that conversion could not take place within the framework of indigenous social and cultural systems, priests were urged to appropriate and dismantle all vestiges of native religions, activities that often resulted in direct confrontations between Indian and Catholic priests. After obliterating the idols, the priests forced the Indians to attend catechism classes intended to indoctrinate them into the practices of Spanish Catholicism. At stake: the spiritual and probable political allegiance of the Indians, a necessary factor in the ultimate supremacy sought by both church and state.

The Jesuits were by no means the only group who attacked what was commonly viewed as the Indians' primitive customs. Franciscans Bernardo de Lizana (?–?) and Antonio Tello (*c.* 1600–1653), though well-versed in Indian languages and culture, were repelled by what they perceived as savage ways. Tello's stance toward the dynamics of the Conquest was especially complex. His evangelistic work in Jalisco from 1619 until his death in 1653 gave him considerable insight into the culture and traditions of the native Mexicans. Yet he felt that many of the conquistadors' excesses were justified since the Indians were initially so hostile toward Christianity. Tello thus admired both Cortés and Las Casas, but quoted the latter profusely. Tello's *Crónica miscelánea* (Guadalajara, 1866) is a history of the Mexican conquest with an emphasis on the spiritual development of the Indians. Lizana wrote in *Historia de Yucatán* (Valladolid, 1633) of Indian idolatry that persisted many years after the Conquest and the problems it posed for missionaries. Characteristic of religious histories of the later colony, these works are also general regional histories and studies of the individual missionaries who had lived there.

One of the most ambitious enterprises with the Indians ever recorded by religious historians was the creation of Jesuit "reductions" throughout colonial Latin America. Jesuit priests founded the reductions, or Indian settlements, as a way of organizing, protecting, and indoctrinating the Indians. Once the Indians were relocated and resettled in a reduction, Jesuit priests educated the Indians, trained them for vocations, and defended them from Brazilian and Spanish slavetraders. This pattern of evangelism was entirely different from existing models since it strove to insulate the Indians completely from those colonists who sought cheap labor. Once isolated from the outside world, the Jesuit missionaries could more effectively educate the Indians and thus improve their economic and social status. The goals of the Jesuits were very ambitious – they began more than 180 of these settlements during the seventeenth century. They were met with a great deal of resistance from settlers, other factions within the church, the civil authorities, and others. The Jesuits in Paraguay (where more Indians were resettled than anywhere else) conscientiously appointed their own chroniclers and thus sustained a continuous record of their activities in this part of the colony. Their histories are records of their struggles in these frontier settlements. *Conquista espiritual hecha por los religiosos de la compañía de Jesús en las provincias del Paraguay, Paraná, Uruguay y Tape*, by Antonio Ruiz de Montoya (1585–1682), is the first full account of life within the Jesuit reductions. Montoya spoke of the successes and failures of their settlements and of the many exoduses that were necessary to escape from the slavetraders, a story he told with a certain tragic quality.

Montoya was keenly aware that by resettling the Indians of the Paraguayan Chaco into reductions, the Jesuits were depriving not only Brazilian slave traders but also Spanish *encomenderos* of a vast, easily obtainable labor pool. Montoya attempted to act as a mediator between the Indians and their many antagonists: "My purpose is to arrange a peace between Spaniards and Indians, a very difficult task, because in the more than one hundred years since the discovery of the West Indies this has not been achieved" (p. 14). Yet Montoya wisely added that it was not his intention "to tell of the offenses the Indians commonly endure," a proposition that would require citing many authors leading to the creation of a "great volume" (p. 40). To deflect the inevitable criticism, Montoya followed a simple rhetorical strategy throughout the *Conquista espiritual*. He focused on the extraordinary needs of the Indian nations – needs generally met by Jesuit missionaries – and highlighted some of the many sacrifices that his colleagues routinely made in carrying out their evangelistic enterprise. Montoya wrote that it was not uncommon to find priests within the reductions who had given away their own shirts and beds to the sick and needy, priests who "suffered an almost intolerable poverty" in a visible sacrifice of their worldly possessions (p. 202). "No one," concluded Montoya hopefully, "will find cause to judge us harshly for teaching the Indians to work for their own gain" (p. 202).

Montoya was unable to avoid political and social entanglements that arose because of their massive relocation of the Guaraní Indians. The reductions were constantly subjected to attacks and harassment, particularly by Portuguese colonists from neighboring São Paulo. Montoya described in vivid detail a number of the assaults that occurred in 1637 against a reduction in Santa María, an attack so fierce that priests as well as Indians came to "the just defense" of the settlement. The raiders were depicted as heathen savages who toppled altars, burned churches, stole cattle and horses, raped women, and enslaved the men. Montoya's discussion of these conflicts had a strong political quality, for later that year he would travel to Madrid to petition the King for permission to arm the Indians to defend themselves against such onslaughts. "These occurrences," said Montoya, "were the cause of my coming to the source of justice" (p. 288). Montoya's underlying intention in his *Conquista espiritual* was thus to acquire the "necessary remedy" – the right to bear arms – to ensure the continued freedom of the Indians. Montoya's narrative is a model of classical rhetoric that culminates in a *petitio* intended to persuade the King to view his case favorably. Montoya included in his text a transcription of a royal decree that had earlier released the Indians of the region from "personal service" to any and all *encomenderos* who sought their exploitation and enslavement. The decree chastised the *encomenderos* for depriving the Indians of their *liberty*, a word that Montoya repeated with frequency in the *Conquista espiritual* when describing the persecution that he and his followers endured.

Montoya ultimately obtained the Crown's permission to arm the Indians within the Jesuit reductions, an endorsement he held until 1661 when Phillip V ordered the removal of all firearms from these establishments. The fact that for many years the reductions were armed camps led to increasing antagonism toward the Jesuits. Historians such as Josep Barnadas have noted that widespread antipathy toward the reductions was one determinant that led to the expulsion of the Jesuits from the Hispanic realm in 1767 (Bethell, *The Cambridge History of Latin America*, I, 534).

Religious writers of the late colonial period were clearly concerned with more than just publishing histories of their orders and biographies of devoted missionaries. They broadened their scope and wrote histories of the New World with eloquent descriptions of American geography and topography. Jesuit Alonso de Ovalle (1601–1651) wrote *Histórica relación del reyno de Chile* [*An Historical Relation of the Kingdom of Chile*] with the stated intention of enlightening Europeans about his homeland. Ovalle had travelled to Spain and Italy as a representative of his order and was astounded that so many Europeans had never heard of Chile. Published simultaneously in Italian and Spanish, the *Histórica relación del reyno de Chile* is an illustrated account of Chile's geography, early history, and the establishment and development of the church, with particular emphasis on the Jesuit order. Ovalle found himself in Rome with few documentary sources to help him construct an accurate historical record of Chile. His work is therefore an impressionistic memorial of his country's most salient geographical and cultural features. Eager to communicate an indelible image of Chile to his European audience, Ovalle included many details in his text intended to distinguish this area from other regions of the New World that had been given greater attention by comprehensive historians such as Fernández de Oviedo and Herrera. His description of the Andes, for instance, reflects a proto-nationalistic hyperbole that would become rather commonplace among Jesuit historians of the later eighteenth century. Ovalle wrote that he did not know of anything in the world that would compare with Chile's mountain range in its visual splendor and mineral wealth, a statement of remarkable partiality when one considers the legendary beauty and opulence of other vice-royalties, especially Mexico and Peru.

Most of the religious historians of this era attributed such unusually spectacular phenomena as visible, authentic manifestations of the auspicious nature of God's worldly designs. Ovalle's text contains a number of personal observations on the diversity of religious life in and around

Santiago, comments that occasionally culminate in anecdotal constructions based on his own experiences and impressions of the Chilean colony. Ovalle's work, among many others, revives a legacy from medieval Spanish literature that focused upon God's interest and periodic intervention in mundane affairs. Ovalle was adept in turning his narrative toward instances of what he interpreted as expressions of a divine presence in the New World. For example, his description of the trees and forests surrounding Santiago leads into a brief account about a famous tree from the Limache Valley that had grown into the shape of a cross. Not only had the tree grown in this most unusual way, it appeared to have a human figure upon it. This tree, wrote Ovalle, was a "true representation of the death and passion of our Redeemer," and was testimony to God's power and omnipresence (p. 80).

Not surprisingly, Ovalle included numerous accounts of religious acts and conversions, remembrances of Marian literature from the Middle Ages. These brief vignettes are highly expressive passages in his narrative that exhibit an imaginative turn from the expository documentation of ecclesiastic appointments and military campaigns. The *Histórica relación del reyno de Chile* contains many episodes where supernatural occurrences were attributed to the Devil's malicious activities. One man, an unnamed noble of Santiago, was visited and tormented by ghostly apparitions. Another was reported to have been carried to the rooftop by flying demons. These and other occasions of diabolical harassment were overcome when the victims simply confided to their priests and accepted their learned catechisms. It was not uncommon for religious historians to incorporate this sort of episode into their historical and geographical discussions, considering the literary foundation and general disposition of their reading public – one nurtured on tales of miracles, conversions, and appearances from the otherworld.

Interest in the landscape is thus a prominent feature of later Jesuit historiography. Bernabé de Cobo (1581–1657) was a priest whose extensive travels prompted him to write a detailed geographical study of the New World. Cobo spent most of his life systematically gathering the information which would embody the *Historia del Nuevo Mundo*. Cobo knew from his own observations and experiences about many of the tribes, mineral deposits, plants, animals, and geological formations of Mexico and Peru. His work is also a valuable source for Indian terminology. Cobo spoke Nahuatl, Quechua, and Aymará, and, whenever possible, included the native names of plants and animals. He often corroborated his etymologies with readings from the Inca Garcilaso, Juan Polo de Ondegardo, and Gonzalo Fernández de Oviedo. A stated desire in his history was to reconcile some of the many varied accounts written by other New World naturalists. He wrote in the tradition of José de Acosta:

his geographical notes were complemented by a study of the Indians and their institutions. Yet Cobo was no disciple of Las Casas. In his view, the Indians were culturally acceptable only when they had converted to Christianity.

Apart from their interest in geography, religious writers of the seventeenth and eighteenth centuries generally found their principal topics in the varied ecclesiastic affairs of the colonies: conversion of the Indians; histories of convents; biographies of evangelists; and the expansion of missionary activities. A few of these writers, however, were more concerned with an imaginative and entertaining depiction of historical events than with a utilitarian, prosaic communication of past occurrences. At times they wrote historical remembrances with a manifest literary intention. This dimension was reflected in their language, style of exposition, and above all, the imaginative quality of the stories they told.

One of the most unusual priest–historians of the colonial era was Juan de Barrenechea y Albis (1669–1707), a Mercedarian missionary who lived in Chile during the prolonged military campaign against the Araucanian Indians. Barrenechea wrote *Restauración de la Imperial y conversión de almas infieles* in 1693 (unpublished), a long, rambling history of the Catholic church in Chile and of the enduring Araucanian wars. Interspersed throughout the text, however, is the love story of two Araucanians, Carilab and Rocamila. This fictional account is about Carilab's unceasing devotion to Rocamila and of the hardships they endured during their extended separation. Told against the backdrop of the Spanish/Araucanian hostilities, Carilab had to fight against rival suitors for Rocamila's hand as well as against his Spanish enemies. Carilab was imprisoned, Rocamila kidnapped, and war constantly raged among rival Araucanians and Spanish soldiers. Carilab was falsely accused by a Spanish governor of inciting his tribe to war and was sentenced to hang for his crime. A Mercedarian friar intervened, however, and convinced the authorities to grant Carilab amnesty.

Barrenechea's manuscript ends at this point; Carilab and Rocamila's love was forever unconsummated. There is little doubt that Barrenechea's intentions in *Restauración de la Imperial* were overwhelmingly literary. His story of life in the Araucanian frontier is an imaginative distillation of the enduring conflict between the Spanish and indigenous forces. Carilab was an idealized hero; though vastly outnumbered by the Spanish, he fought valiantly and fearlessly. Carilab is depicted as a fierce warrior and worthy antagonist to the Spanish army. Like the Araucanians in Alonso de Ercilla's earlier epic, the Indians are often portrayed with a nobility that had little relation to historical fact. The Araucanians, not the Spanish, are the ones who are more fully and artfully developed. His Spanish characters are, more often than not, criminals whose cruelties against the Araucanians go unpunished. *Restauración de la Imperial* contains some pertinent historical information on governmental decrees, Indian customs, and the restoration of destroyed villages and churches. But it is the story of love and adventure that sustains the narrative, not the documentary material (Tomanek, "Barrenechea's *Restauración*," 265).

Literary tendencies are also manifest throughout *Crónica de la provincia peruana de los ermitaños de San Agustín Nuestro Padre* by Augustinian priest Bernardo de Torres (n.d.). Torres succeeded Antonio de la Calancha (1584–1654) as the designated chronicler of Peru's Augustinian order and edited the final volume of Calancha's *Crónica moralizada del orden de San Agustín en el Perú* (Barcelona, 1638). Calancha typified the *cronista de convento*, a religious chronicler interested in recording the events of his order beginning with the early days of the spiritual conquest. Torres relied upon Calancha's notes and documents for his own history which was intended as a continuation of the earlier work. Yet what distinguished Torres from other *cronistas de convento* of his era was his vivid literary imagination.

Torres's work opens with a traditional outline of what his history intends to encompass. There is little within the realm of the human religious experience not included in this *crónica*: "lamentable downfalls ...miraculous conversions, celestial lives, glorious deaths" (p. 3). A tendency toward such hyperbole is a stylistic trait of Torres and other *cronistas de convento* who, in their evangelistic fervor, regarded their historical narratives as opportunities to proselytize further the vast New World.

Curiously, the *Crónica de la provincia peruana* does not begin with a record of one of his order's more notable achievements. The narrative instead describes a crime of almost unimaginable infamy to readers accustomed to quaint stories of saints' lives and religious miracles. The tale is one of sin and deceit, and deals with a defrocked priest who conspired with his brother to commit murder to cover up another unspeakable transgression: an incestuous relationship with their beautiful but powerless and naive sister. The young woman, depicted as a confused, helpless victim of her brothers' lust, became pregnant and ultimately had to face an interrogation from the two concerning her condition. Aware that the two brothers did not know of the other's involvement, she was caught in a classical dilemma: "if she blamed one, he would be wounded by the truth, the other by jealousy" (p. 10). As a consequence of this impasse, she simply accused an innocent man of illicitly fathering her child, an accusation that would lead to a confrontation of honor (p. 10).

The narrator of this story occasionally pauses to remind the reader that God was not unaware of these circumstances and that a just retribution would be forthcoming: "He left them in the hands of their own desires, permitting them to be blinded by their own light" (p. 11). Each the author of his own fate, the brothers killed the faultless man in a primitive gesture of displaced aggression. Yet as they proudly reported their act of honor to their now-vindicated sister, she confessed the truth, revealing to her brothers the other's incestuous relationship with her. They murdered her to maintain a gruesome silence. Rumors of their suspected involvement in these murders soon circulated throughout Peru, and the brothers fled the territory. They both died in their self-imposed exile, but not before one had left a written record of all that had transpired, which, coincidentally, he left with his confessor.

It is upon this Cervantine document that Torres supposedly constructed the story, a tale that is highly emblematic of his literary vision (Arrom, "A contrafuerza de la sangre," 324). His saga integrates features drawn from the Spanish stage: the brothers acted as though they were defending the family's honor, when in reality it was they who had sinned against God and Nature. Their demise would have been expected and encouraged within the moralistic framework of the day, for their offenses were manifest: they were incestuous adulterers; they murdered an innocent man; and they killed their sister and her unborn child. Torres spared no details in describing their deaths. One perished after falling overboard; the other died in Panama of fever, probably malaria. Torres held that God was responsible for carrying out their sentence: "is there anywhere a sinner can go where he will not encounter the wrath of God?" (p. 13).

True to his calling, Torres had an obligation as a religious writer to underscore clearly and persuasively the consequences of such deviant behavior. His literary vision is in marked contrast to earlier, more optimistic views of human conduct, such as the Inca Garcilaso's. The convoluted plot, complex language, emphasis upon the grotesque, and vindictive sense of justice are highly indicative of a baroque mentality thoroughly immersed in the literary currents of his day (Arrom, "Contrafuerza," 322). The story of the two priests represents a powerful moral *exemplum* intended to deter similar iniquities. The *Crónica de la provincia peruana* contains a variety of short tales which are not only historical remembrances of Peru's Augustinian order, but also convincingly potent touchstones of the colony's firm moral codes.

Many of the religious historians in seventeenth-century Latin America found such short anecdotes useful narrative devices to disseminate teachings and opinions regarding the ethical disposition of the colony. Augustinian bishop Gaspar de Villarroel (1587–1665) popularized this literary recourse in his historical analysis of the rights and privileges of ecclesiastical and secular authorities; his *Gobierno eclesiástico-pacífico y unión de los dos cuchillos, pontificio y regio* was written as a study of the various dimensions of the governing bodies of church and state. In many regards, this text can be read as a guidebook for bishops and other clergy. Villarroel considered a number of curious contingencies regarding a bishop's choice of conduct: should a bishop attend bullfights? Whom should bishops visit? What may bishops eat and drink? More seriously, Villarroel examined in considerable detail the range of authority that a bishop had over ecclesiastic and civil matters. He was primarily interested in exploring the legal extension of power invested in the church and Real Audiencia.

Villarroel's stories, like those of Ovalle and Torres, often portray execrable patterns of behavior intended to function as negative models of deportment, an implication that positive lessons could be derived from the impropriety of others. In a section entitled "Absolution without jurisdiction," the narrator tells a tale of horror and despair. A priest was visited by a woman who appeared to be completely aflame; in the midst of her fiery torture she carried a small black baby. She told the priest that she had been condemned to Purgatory until the end of the world. She had become pregnant by her black slave, a condition that caused her enormous torment. Her only solution – kill the father and abort the child, for in this way she could "remove from her eyes the only two witnesses of such an ugly event" (p. 32). Yet this double crime created in her such remorse she felt compelled to confess her sins, preferably to one who was a stranger. She soon had this opportunity, and subsequently lived a pure and devoted life. Yet after her death she found herself in an unusual tribunal. The prosecution was represented by a group of devils who based their case on her two murders. She was defended by her guardian angel, whose legal strategy was to insist upon her confession, a process through which her sins could be expiated. One of the devils pointed out, however, that her confession was null and void, for he had been the one who acted as confessor. The judgment of the court? Although she had confessed in good faith, she had not been sufficiently penitent, and thus was cast into Purgatory.

Religious biographers in seventeenth-century Latin America often focused upon exemplary missionaries of their order or upon the heroic deeds of the early explorers and conquistadors, a legacy inherited from historiography of the first years of the discovery and conquest of the New World. Yet Torres and Villarroel were among a number of writers in the latter era who began to depart from this model in an examination of characters whose activities in the colony represented a darker, more unseemly involvement in the complex dynamics of the historical process. Their view that history could include marginal figures in colonial society differed somewhat from the best examples of the *cronista mayor* school – Herrera and Solís – who envisioned the Conquest as the realization of Spain's noble political destiny. Writers like Torres and Franciscan Pedro

Simón (1581–1630) were among those who felt that some historical events of the sixteenth and seventeenth century were occasionally determined by people of highly questionable moral character, individuals who did not embody the political or ethical ideals implicit in Solís's *Historia de la conquista de México*. In this context, Simón's *Noticias historiales de las conquistas de tierra firme en las Indias Occidentales* contains, among many things, a biographical study of one of colonial Latin America's most astonishing personalities: the legendary tyrant, murderer, and traitor, Lope de Aguirre (1511–1561).

Lope de Aguirre's exploits in Peru, New Granada, and Venezuela had been documented earlier by Juan de Castellanos. Simón inverted the traditional value-laden history of missionaries, finding in Lope de Aguirre a fascinating study of human aberrance and evil.

Historians have generally determined the outline of Aguirre's activities in the northern regions of South America. Aguirre was a member of an expedition down the Marañón River in Peru led by Pedro de Ursúa in 1560. The purpose of the trip: to search for the mythical gilded man, El Dorado. Aguirre was one of several who mutinied against Ursúa, killing their leader for vaguely defined reasons. Gradually, Aguirre acquired control of the expedition through deceit and murder. He led his men through an incredible maze of rivers, tributaries, and jungle paths, eventually emerging on the Venezuelan coast where he and his "marañones" terrorized the local populace. Royal troops put an end to Aguirre's brief reign of terror in October of 1561, an episode presented in graphic detail in Simón's *Noticias historiales*.

Simón's narrative wavers between incredulity and irony when describing Aguirre's unbelievable criminal life. Simón's characterization demonstrates that Aguirre led through fear, not respect or loyalty. One never knew when or why Aguirre would let loose one of his tirades, verbal barrages that would often culminate in a senseless murder. Aguirre, forever fearful of rebellion and treason, incessantly preyed on his own men. Simón wrote that in a span of only five months Aguirre killed sixty Spaniards, including one priest, two monks, four women, and his own daughter.

Simón's presentation of Aguirre is a story of irrationality and collective madness. Simón wrote that one of Aguirre's admirals once warned his leader that waves from the sea were getting him wet. Aguirre answered by cutting off the admiral's arm, and then ordering his death. Simón's narrative wryly adds that "his attention and politeness cost him his life" (p. 131). The world of Aguirre described in the *Noticias historiales* was one whose traditional Hispanic values of Christian charity and just rule had been momentarily suspended. It was a world where Christians were blasphemed, the King cursed, and all codes of acceptable moral conduct ridiculed. Aguirre is characterized as a man of such extreme evil – culminating in his daughter's assassination – that the reader fully anticipates and sanctions the villain's violent sentence. He was beheaded and quartered; his head was placed in an iron cage for public viewing, his body strewn along the roadside, denied a Christian burial.

Such a detailed depiction of historical figures is emblematic of literary biography of the late colonial period. Authors like Simón were interested in creating an image of their subjects that would be comprehensible within the context of the Christian literary tradition. Simón's narrative follows Aguirre's expedition practically day-by-day in a feverish reproduction of his speeches, conversations, and crimes, an analysis so precise that one might easily dispute the authenticity of his portrayal. Historians of this era, however, felt that the re-creation of such experiences – documented or not – was an acceptable recourse in uncovering the intentions and motivations of their subjects. It was thus essential that Aguirre's characterization conform to certain expectations of the Crown as well as the church. Simón created a story of tragic inevitability in his portraiture of the ultimate sinner, who, like the errant priests of Bernardo de Torre's tale or Villarroel's judge-assassin, suffered retribution for his misdeeds.

Pedro Simón's story of Lope de Aguirre reverberated throughout the northern provinces of the colony, eventually attracting the attention of other historians interested in documenting his excursion up the Marañón River and brief reign of insanity along the Venezuelan coast. Lucas Fernández de Piedrahita (1624–1688), a Jesuit bishop from Bogotá, included Aguirre in his biographical study of New Granada's earliest explorers and settlers. His *Historia general de las conquistas del Nuevo Reino de Granada* is an extensive re-elaboration of earlier chronicles by such writers as Antonio de Herrera, Gonzalo Jiménez de Quesada, Pedro de Aguado, and Antonio de Calancha, among others. His study of Aguirre is, in many respects, a condensed re-reading of Simón's detailed portraiture of the madman, retaining the sense of anxiety and urgency that Aguirre's presence evidently caused among the inhabitants of the northern coastal plain. For Piedrahita as well as for Simón, Aguirre's downfall was directly attributable to "having disclaimed not only any obedience to the king, but also fear and respect for God" (p. 773). Piedrahita recorded an incident that dramatically exemplified Aguirre's casual regard for life and utter contempt for authority. After he had one of his opponents quartered – for real or imagined crimes – Aguirre spoke to the lifeless head, asking rhetorically: "Are you there my good friend Alarcón? Why doesn't the King of Spain come to revive you?" (p. 785). Piedrahita noted with no small irony that soldiers loyal to the King finally rallied to defeat the renegade band of traitors, thereby restoring some order and stability to a region that had experienced an unusual measure of restlessness during its first decades.

El Carnero

Juan Rodríguez Freyle's (1566–1640) *El Carnero* (Bogotá, 1859) [*The Conquest of New Granada*] has always posed unique problems for literary historians and critics. On the one hand, it is a traditional chronological narrative of the first hundred years of history (1538–1638) of his native land, New Granada, focusing primarily upon events and personalities in Santa Fe de Bogotá. Much of his work is a routine compilation of names and dates associated with appointments to the most important political and ecclesiastical positions in the city: presidents; judges; solicitors; archbishops; and other members of the various courts and legislative councils – little to distinguish *El Carnero* from other regional and parish histories. Yet on the other hand, its tales of witchcraft, stories of infidelity and deceit, legends of buried treasure, references to classical and biblical history, and lurid accounts of ghastly crimes give *El Carnero* an undeniable literary foundation. In this respect, Rodríguez Freyle was one of the most innovative and engaging writers during the colonial period in Spanish America. Using history as a narrative point-of-departure, Rodríguez Freyle composed a series of anecdotes and *exempla* designed to reveal a dimension of life in the colony that other histories either ignored or understated. *El Carnero* is highly representative of a tendency in seventeenth-century Spanish American historiography toward greater complexity and an increased sense of irony toward events, institutions, laws, and traditions that shaped the colonial experience.

Rodríguez Freyle's motivations for writing *El Carnero* were apparently manifest. He states in the prologue that he wrote his text to keep New Granada history from "the darkness of oblivion," implying that historians had overlooked his homeland in their accounts of the New World; he specifically chides Pedro Simón and Juan de Castellanos for ignoring his region in their histories of the Conquest (p. 50). He thus focuses on New Granada, beginning with the founding of Santa Fe de Bogotá and the fall of the indigenous Chibcha reign. Rodríguez Freyle provides his readers with a set of interpretive keys to unlock the numerous narrative asides and literary allusions that appear throughout his text. Though he initially promises that his narrative will be "succinct and true," without the rhetorical flourishes commonplace in baroque historiography, he finds he must justify his growing number of digressions and departures from this basic plan of history (p. 50). After one of his many references to biblical history (the fall of Adam and Eve), he rhetorically asks: what does the conquest of the New World have to do with ancient history? His response is enlightening: he compares New Granada to an orphaned young lady on her wedding day, one in need of jewelry and fine clothing in order to look her best. To adorn her properly, he must go to the "best gardens" to pick the "loveliest flowers" to place upon the table of her guests (p. 82). Rodríguez Freyle's elegant conceit is an attempt to justify his frequent literary insertions and references to classical authors and texts. The literary vein that permeates *El Carnero* is ostensibly intended to enhance the image of New Granada in this presentation of its first century of history. In this sense, Rodríguez Freyle constructed an entertaining and attractive story of a land that history had undeservedly neglected.

Within this broad context of New Granada history, Rodríguez Freyle wished to tell his own story as well. The autobiographical dimension of *El Carnero* is seen in his many remarks about his own life and experiences, as well as in his countless observations and caustic opinions on the nature of society and humanity. He reinforced the authority of many of his comments by saying that he saw or heard much of what he is presently narrating. Even his account of the rivalry between Chibcha leaders Bogotá and Guatavita came from an Indian informant, "Juan," who apparently witnessed much of what he later told. One of Rodríguez Freyle's major concerns is to present himself as a believable narrator (Foster, "Notes towards reading...*El Carnero*," 7). As a life-long resident of New Granada, he felt that his experiences and observations gave him sufficient authority to talk credibly about the various political and religious administrations, as well as the errant behavior of some of his region's more colorful characters. A direct descendant of one of the founding families of New Granada, Rodríguez Freyle often came into contact with society's highest echelons: *conquistador* Gonzalo Jiménez de Quesada was a frequent visitor in his father's house. Rodríguez Freyle later worked as secretary to Alonso Pérez de Salazar, an official in the Council of Indies, an appointment that kept him in Spain for six years (1585–1591). Yet he never felt quite at home in the mother country. After the death of his benefactor, Rodríguez Freyle returned to Santa Fe de Bogotá, only to find himself in perpetual economic and legal adversity. Old and somewhat disillusioned, Rodríguez Freyle wrote *El Carnero* with the perspective of someone who had not fully benefited from the New World's promise of wealth. El Dorado had eluded Rodríguez Freyle, among countless others. When he looked back upon his own futile quests for riches, it was with the ironic cynicism of personal experience.

The hybrid nature of *El Carnero* – autobiography, chronicle, fictional intrusions – therefore presents problems of genre for traditional literary history. Rodríguez Freyle's frequent reliance upon literary material to enhance his historical exposition is what distinguishes *El Carnero* from works by most of the Chroniclers of the Indies and so many of the minor *cronistas de convento*. Rodríguez Freyle's text is not a simple linear exposition of incidents in and about the New Granada viceroyalty. *El Carnero* is one of a number of narratives from the later colonial period that employs a wide variety of discursive options in its analysis of the New World experience. One must always keep in mind that sixteenth- and seventeenth-century historiographical form was not absolutely fixed, and that the nature of historical truth was quite distinct from today's empirical demands for verifiability and textual evidence. In reality, historical truth for the colonial writer was grounded not only in personal experiences but also in Christian and classical authorities (Zamora, "Historicity and literariness," 338). Many historians of this era thus felt compelled to initiate their discussion of New World events with analogies to this literary heritage. Critics today generally agree that what appeals to modern audiences is not the informative, factual content of works like *El Carnero* or *La Florida* of El Inca Garcilaso de la Vega. Rather, readers are more drawn to the literary, imaginative features of their discourse.

The interior literary aspects of *El Carnero* generally follow two distinct models. On the one hand, Rodríguez Freyle utilized references to classical and sacred authorities to justify and strengthen his frequent passages into the arena of moral conduct. What better resources to draw upon than Old Testament theology, classical Roman and Greek literature, or religious stories from the Spanish Middle Ages? By utilizing literature of such high standing, Rodríguez Freyle was able to present observations and conclusions on social issues that were indisputable. To challenge him would be an affront to the judgment of the ancients. Rodríguez Freyle's other style of interpolated narratives is more contemporary and somewhat more original. His orthodox, dry catalogue of names and official appointments is often invigorated by his own racy tales of greed, lust, and power. He isolates selected individuals in his area and tells about their immoral escapades and exploits, presumably so that his reader would not follow their bad example. *El Carnero* evokes memories of the Arcipreste de Hita's *Libro de buen amor* with its inventory of negative models of social conduct. These creative interludes communicate an intriguing, though somewhat tarnished, image of high colonial society; his characters often represent New Granada's privileged elite. These episodes are frankly the most interesting aspect of *El Carnero*, and are what show Rodríguez Freyle to be one of the most talented story-tellers of the entire Spanish American colonial period.

Juan Rodríguez Freyle's literary culture was quite varied. Exhaustive source-and-influence studies have shown that Rodríguez Freyle was probably conversant with a substantial registry of literary topics and motifs of his day (Martinengo, "La cultura literaria de Juan Rodríguez

Freyle"). There are direct or indirect references to *La Celestina*, the *Libro de Alexandre*, Alfonso X's *General estoria*, and a host of renowned historical and literary figures from antiquity, Spain, and the New World, such as Virgil and Juan de Castellanos. It seems clear that he wished to present himself as a paragon of erudition through such learned allusions and disquisitions. Such references are used to temper his excesses and also to provide a decorative flourish to his prose. It also seems evident that he wanted to put New Granada's history on a par with his classical models. For example, when he speaks of the warfare between rival chieftains Bogotá and Guatavita, he notes that Bogotá's followers engaged in a drunken revelry to celebrate a victory over their enemy. Instead of continuing the narrative in a straightforward, linear fashion, the author seizes the opportunity to present other examples of human frailty taken from the ancient world: King Baltasar of Babylon lost his kingdom and his life by excessive drinking; and Alexander the Great killed his best friend while intoxicated. The author coyly notes that he has many more references to hand to substantiate his case for sobriety. There is little reason to believe that these turns within *El Carnero* are unnecessary addenda or gratuitous displays of scholastic knowledge and expertise. Viewed within the context of sixteenth- and seventeenth-century philosophy of history, Rodríguez Freyle was not only justified but quite possibly obliged to locate his discussion of regional history within the global dimension of Christian providence. Historical occurrences in the New World were often considered the realization of God's plan (Zamora, "Historicity," 338). We have seen that this line of argument was particularly useful for the Chroniclers of the Indies whose official task was to justify the past deeds of the *conquistadors* as the fulfillment of divine providence. Presenting detailed descriptions of the moral transgressions of the inhabitants of New Granada in the light of classical and biblical history was one way of establishing the universality of God's plan. New Granada, like Jerusalem, Rome, or Eden, was part of a world continually opening up to the followers of His sacred design.

One of Rodríguez Freyle's prime intentions in *El Carnero* was thus to examine the various ethical dimensions of his society. A great many of his allusions are designed to illustrate what some have criticized as his incessant moralizing. These often lengthy narrative detours appear, for instance, when the narrator senses the need to make his story more credible to an ingenuous reader. The report of an especially heinous case of fratricide is supplemented by a detailed inventory of similar episodes, again reflecting Freyle's classical upbringing: Tifón and Orsírides; Mitrídates and Herodes; Romulus and Remus; Fernando and García. His secondary references culminate with a note on history's most famous story of brotherly envy and murder: Cain and Abel. The reader simply cannot pass over the horrendous nature of this crime. The tripartite pattern established here – a remark on human weakness, the primary exposition of a crime committed in the colony, followed by references to other historical cases – is repeated over and over again throughout *El Carnero*; this tendency toward narrative framing is a fundamental strategy of didactic literature from the Middle Ages, bringing to mind such texts as *Libro de buen amor*, *El corbacho*, and *Conde Lucanor*, among others.

Rodríguez Freyle's tales of moral deviance often emerge as the structural underpinnings of his historical narrative. His close scrutiny of colonial society's conduct frequently reveals the dark under belly of a world obsessed with appearances and social standing. In cases like Gaspar de Peralta's revenge (Chapter 15) and the escapades of Inés de Hinojosa (Chapter 10), the narrator systematically frames his tales within carefully articulated thematic boundaries that both underscore and intensify the aberrant activities of the individuals in question. There is a strong interdependence among the thematically interwoven elements of these and other episodes. Peralta's enactment is especially illustrative of the logical convergence of a series of ostensibly disparate narrative strands. His story is the culmination of what at first appear to be isolated, divergent remarks.

The story of Peralta's vengeance is initially anticipated by the report of the arrival of his former patron, Alonso Pérez de Salazar, a judge for the Real Audiencia. What is noteworthy about that otherwise routine appointment is that Salazar was a strong proponent of law-and-order, a quality that evokes a nostalgic cry: "Oh, if only he were here now, what a good crop he would reap!" (p. 233). Salazar quickly exhibited his intolerance toward criminal activity; he executed two men who had kidnapped an Indian servant girl and who had violently resisted arrest. The interlude between this account and the Peralta incident contains two curious authorial intrusions. First, the narrator justifies his inclusion of this crime by declaring that he has found history full of similar atrocities. Later, he presents a string of misogynist remarks about the dangers of marrying beautiful women, commentaries that appear to be *non sequitur* ramblings reflecting Rodríguez Freyle's disenchantments with old age. Peralta's episode, however, binds all of these threads together into a coherent tapestry. After more insertions from the author on the dangers of indiscreet gossip, he finally gets on with the story.

A young man known as Ontanera found himself one night among a group of male friends who were bragging about their various amorous exploits. Ontanera, evidently not one to be upstaged in matters of nocturnal activities, boasted that he and an attractive lady broke her bed during their last passionate encounter. The party disbanded and the men, including Peralta, a prosecutor for the Real Audiencia, returned home. Peralta's wife asked him to send for a carpenter, for their bed had somehow collapsed. Peralta instantly realized that his friend Ontanera had shamelessly deceived him. The ensuing development of this story follows the conventions of Golden Age drama. His honor at stake, Peralta sought revenge for the personal injustice that the two had committed against him. Peralta left on an extended trip, fully aware that Ontanera and his wife would consort in his absence. He doubled back to the city, found Ontanera in his wife's bed-chamber, and killed the young intruder. Peralta next turned his wrath on his unfaithful spouse and killed her as well, leaving the two corpses side by side. Rodríguez Freyle closes this macabre exposé with a diatribe taken from Fernando de Rojas's *La Celestina*, one of the most frequently cited texts within *El Carnero*: "Love is a hidden fire, a pleasant sore, a sweet bitterness, a delightful pain, a happy torment, a merry and fiendish wound, and a bland death" (p. 241). This string of oxymorons is a poetic representation of a larger narrative process that similarly combines a set of contradictory elements into a unified discourse. The presentation of Salazar, the hanging judge, the comments on beautiful women, the admonitions of the dangers of unbridled speech, and the defense of honor all lead toward an exposition of the colonial world's view of justice. The first report exemplifies the power and effectiveness of the Real Audiencia when staffed by people of Salazar's caliber, and is indicative of the social indictment of criminality. Peralta's story represents a personal code of honor and propriety. It is significant to note that both men were officers of the court charged with enforcing the legal codes of the Real Audiencia. In either case, justice was swift, certain, and immutable: the punishment for both civil and moral transgressions was death. As Celestina implies, love is at best a risky enterprise.

The stories inserted throughout *El Carnero* often function as dramatic elaborations of ideas and concerns brought up in the presentation of historical or cultural phenomena. Amid such instances of moral wanderings – infidelity is one of his favorite subjects – Rodríguez Freyle occasionally identified particular experiences that were somewhat unique to the American reality. *El Carnero* depicts a number of situations that characterize the distinctive circumstances and opportunities of colonial life. Like many religious chroniclers of the late sixteenth and seventeenth centuries, Freyle was fascinated with the New World's Indian heritage and culture; he was especially interested in tangible manifestations of their religious practice: buried or hidden treasure. He had failed several times in his own attempts to find traces of the legendary wealth of the Chibchas, a confession he made with a measure of chagrin and regret. Yet not all of his countrymen fared so poorly. His story of Father Francisco

Lorenzo's successful treasure hunt is something of an atonement for his own shortcomings; this episode allows Rodríguez Freyle a vicarious enjoyment of an experience that had long frustrated him.

Buried treasure is, of course, a literary topic that was widely diffused in traditional folklore (Pupo-Walker, *La vocación literaria del pensamiento histórico en América*, 150). Rodríguez Freyle placed his motif in an American context by listing the various places that Indians were thought to have hidden their gold. Place names in Latin America frequently reflect a pre-Hispanic heritage: Guatavita; Guasca; Siecha; Teusacá; Ubaque. In this way the narrative establishes a foundation that centralizes the discourse around an event that is singularly American in nature. The various historical components that comprise the story of Lorenzo signify a reality defined by circumstances that distinguish concerns in this part of the colony, thereby fulfilling the stated intentions of the prologue: "To give notice of this New Kingdom of Granada" (p. 49).

Francisco Lorenzo's story is an amusing, lighthearted tale of an enterprising priest who duped an unsuspecting Indian into revealing his hidden cache of gold treasure. Freyle is careful to describe Lorenzo in ways that enhance the development of his story, thus revealing a gift for characterization that is testimony to his literary artistry. Francisco Lorenzo was apparently a popular priest in the town of Ubaque known for his talent for languages. He had close contact with the Indians in the vicinity, a fact that would prove valuable in his plans to divest a particular Indian of his well-hidden gold. Forearmed with a reliable intelligence report, Lorenzo went into the forest with a small entourage on a hunting expedition where he discovered the Indian's home. Careful not to arouse suspicion, Lorenzo ordered his followers to put crosses along the roads, placing the largest one upon a cave where he had earlier found valuable Indian relics. Sometime later, the priest and his flock returned to the countryside in a manifest pilgrimage among the crosses they had placed. Father Lorenzo took brief leave of the group and went directly to the house of the Indian whom he had earlier identified as a follower of the Devil.

Taking advantage of the circumstances and of his knowledge of Indian ways, Lorenzo hid in a tree and called out to the Indian (presumably in his native tongue), pretending to be the Devil, the Indian's master. The narrator includes a lively dialogue between the two in which we learn that Lorenzo ordered the Indian to carry his treasure to the designated cave, for the Christians knew of it and were about to take it. Unaware of the ironic nature of such a statement – it was, after all, true – the Indian obediently took his valuable trove to the designated location. Lorenzo then returned to his group and together they continued their procession, a journey that would culminate at the cave, the site of the largest cross. Here they were witness to an event that Lorenzo had secretly manipulated: the discovery of four pots of gold figurines, whose estimated value was reported as 3,000 pesos, but whose real worth was said to be much higher.

The narrative twist at the end of the story – Lorenzo's underestimate of the gold's value – is in keeping with the irony and ambiguity so highly characteristic of Rodríguez Freyle's interpolated tales. In a number of ways, this particular narrative exemplifies a broad registry of interests and concerns popular among the reading public in the seventeenth century. For example, while a modern reader may disregard the authenticity of dialogues that the author could not possibly have heard, we must remember that this recourse was widely used among historians of this era (Zamora, "Historicity," 338). The reconstruction of such conversations was common practice in colonial historiography as a means to communicate the *appearance* of truthfulness to an audience with clearly defined moral and theological expectations. The actions of a priest who lied and deceived his way into considerable wealth would have been expected and applauded within the given historical and cultural context. This episode is, like the story of Ontanera and so many others in *El Carnero*, the literary culmination of a series of thematically interwoven digressions that precede its revelation. Francisco Lorenzo's story represents the final unfolding of a narrative sequence in which the reader ventures again into classical, biblical, and Spanish history.

Yet, to paraphrase Rodríguez Freyle, just what does the fall of Eve have to do with the account of a local priest-entrepreneur? The narrator indeed begins by reciting the familiar story of Adam and Eve's fall from grace, the result of Eve's unfortunate conversation in the garden with the Devil. Eve, wrote Freyle, was "conquered and deceived," allowing the Devil his most important victory in this world (p. 81). The text documents other such cases of women's failures: Samson and Delilah; Helen of Troy; Florinda and Rodrigo. The story of Francisco Lorenzo may be read, therefore, as a dramatic reversal of these historical cases in which just men were insidiously deceived – in these instances, by women. To trick the Indian out of his gold is, by extension, to conquer the Devil. The theme of deception, directly linked to the biblical antecedent, is placed in a New World context. This time, however, the tables are turned, for God's agent outwits the Devil's agent.

There is a multiplicity of possible sources for such stories of artful cunning; it was a topic of great popularity in medieval literature. Who could forget how the Cid, one of history's most exemplary knights, deftly cheated the two Jews, Raquel and Vidas, out of their wealth? In the American context, writers like Cieza de León and El Inca Garcilaso de la Vega wrote similar tales of devils, hidden treasures, and attempts by the Spanish to uncover the legendary wealth of the Indian nations. It was highly characteristic of colonial historiography to utilize familiar narrative mechanisms in the exploration of a new reality. The narrator could easily tell tales of strange and wondrous places using a language that his readers could easily assimilate. Most of El Carnero's stories reflect a literary heritage that facilitates the apprehension of occurrences that were perhaps beyond the experience of his anticipated reading public. The story of Juana García is the best example of such a confluence of distinct historical and literary currents.

Judging from its presence in anthologies and its overall critical reception, the tale of Juana García is almost certainly the best-known story from El Carnero. It has even inspired a novel: Juana la bruja (1894) by José Caicedo Rojas. Juana García was a Celestinesque character who apparently dabbled in witchcraft and the occult, whose presence in El Carnero gave Rodríguez Freyle his greatest opportunity to amplify the creative vision that flows in varying levels throughout his text.

To many readers of modern Latin American literature, Freyle's use of magic and fantasy in this story will seem quite familiar. A number of critics have pointed to this case as an important antecedent of literary trends and motifs that appear much later in the works of such writers as Cuban novelist Alejo Carpentier: the presence of what Carpentier once termed "a marvelous American reality," and the use of an African descendant as a principal literary character. Freyle's tendency was to attribute history's unexplained phenomena to the presence of the Devil, a stance that he followed fairly consistently while composing El Carnero.

The episode of Juana García is quite an imaginative turn from the chronicle of ecclesiastic appointments that begins this narrative sequence. This story is, by all indications, the most highly developed example of literary expression in El Carnero. The narrator opens the tale by describing a married couple who were separated due to the husband's extended business trips. His attractive young wife, who apparently refused to let her beauty go to waste, became pregnant while he was away. Desperate to rid herself of this unwanted burden, she contacted Juana García, a black midwife, for advice on how to resolve her dilemma. The young woman was naturally afraid that her husband would return and find her in this condition. But Juana García, in a modest display of her powers, assured the woman that he was not on the flotilla that had recently arrived at Cartagena. This unproved assertion offered little solace to the expectant mother who, in open disregard for her cultural mores, asked Juana García to perform an abortion. Knowing that her husband's absence would be fairly extended, Juana García continued to assure the desperate woman that she could safely carry the child to delivery. To prove her authority beyond question, Juana García showed her a tub of water where her husband's image miraculously appeared.

Ironically, his moral conduct was no better than his wife's; they saw him at a tailor's shop in Hispaniola with a woman, his lover, who was being fitted for a new dress. Juana's magical powers were intensely magnified when she reached into the tub and drew out a sleeve from the new dress. Relieved that her indiscretions would for the moment go unnoticed, the woman relaxed, later had her baby, and placed the child "with the name of an orphan" under the care of someone else.

Shortly after her husband's return, the wife became excruciatingly demanding and eventually confronted him with evidence that she knew of his infidelity: the sleeve. Enraged that his peccadilloes had been discovered and eager to find out how, the man went directly to the bishop with his case. The bishop was an expert inquisitor and quickly saw that Juana García's involvement had precipitated the outcome of these events. He apprehended the sorceress along with her two daughters and, in the course of his inquiry, found that Juana García had been involved in a number of unsavory activities in the colony involving quite a few people of high standing. The bishop, under pressure from the likes of Gonzalo Jiménez de Quesada to be merciful, simply banished her from the realm. The story ends with the surprising revelation that Juana García can fly. In her confession she said that she customarily flew from a hill that later carried her name.

Despite its incursions into fantasy, the story of Juana García maintains a significant historical and geographical orientation (Alstrum, "The real and the marvelous in a tale from *El Carnero*," 118). The narrator connects the unbelievable account of a flying sorceress with easily recognizable names and places. He mentions the *adelantado* Alonso Luis de Lugo, the two judges Góngora and Galarza who presumably drowned in a shipwreck, Gonzalo Jiménez de Quesada, the islands of Hispaniola and Bermuda, Cartagena, and others. This tale flows in and out of fictional and historical accounts in apparent disregard for finite boundaries between these two discursive forms. Modern scholarship has shown that such a confluence of what we now term history and fiction was common during this period. Historical writers frequently relied upon recourses from literary models to invest their accounts with a more expressive language. There was often no clear distinction between the two forms of writing with regard to truth or reliability; it was not uncommon for historians like Rodríguez Freyle or Pedro Simón to create portraitures and characterizations with little or no textual evidence. Historians were free to speculate about people and occurrences; their narratives thus reflect frequent turns toward an imaginative, inventive depiction of the American scene.

It is not surprising, then, that Juana García has a parallel literary model in *La Celestina*. Juana was, like Celestina, a tawdry character who used midwifery as a cloak for her unseemly activities. She was apparently known in the community as a woman to whom one came with personal problems that were not easily (or legally) resolved. Like Celestina, Juana García conducted her business with the assistance of her two daughters, literary equivalents of Areusa and Elicia. The episode from *El Carnero* follows the general pattern of Fernando de Rojas's classic from Spanish literature: a young person comes to an older, vastly more experienced woman with an indecorous request; the midwife arranges what appears to be a satisfactory resolution of the dilemma, only to be caught in her own web of deceit and transgressions – the victim of her own iniquity. In both cases, figures of authority deliver severe judgments of finality: the bishop rules to banish Juana García; Pleberio laments a world that for him has lost all meaning.

El Carnero is riddled with allusions and quotations from *La Celestina*. In another section Rodríguez Freyle says: "woman is an arm of the Devil, the head of sin, and the destruction of paradise" (p. 287), an echo of Sempronio's famous speech in which he attempts to dissuade his master Calixto from pursuing Melibea (Act I). Such misogynist remarks from *La Celestina* found a sympathetic reader in Rodríguez Freyle who consistently held women up to criticism and ridicule throughout *El Carnero*. The intersection of these two texts provides the author an avenue into some of the darker, seedier parts of the colony. The woman who approached Juana García was evidently a person of some presence in the community who wished to avoid the appearance of impropriety that an illicit pregnancy would provide. Like Calixto, she crossed social lines in her dealings with the midwife. There is a strong suggestion in *El Carnero* that other well-born residents of the colony had also ventured into the underworld of New Granada for wanton reasons. Yet the communal desire for a virtuous public image within this region was such that Quesada and others of his station implored the bishop to act with restraint. A full exposé of all of Juana García's consorts would "stain" the otherwise new and pure land. Juana García was the classic scapegoat through whom the sins of the many were expiated. Juana García was painfully aware of her sacrificial condition and at her trial cried: "everyone did it and only I pay!" (p. 143). Yet how effective would exile be for an individual with such demonstrable powers? This tale ends on a note of speculation and ambiguity with references to her supernatural ability to fly, a talent that would render her sentence meaningless. The name of Juana García passes from history into myth with the author's emphasis on her legendary capacity to defy natural and civil laws.

El Carnero is, by all indications, a text of texts. It is a rich repository of classical, medieval, and renaissance literary and historical motifs. Such a congeries of dissimilar narrative traditions in Spanish American historiography was not uncommon by the seventeenth century, a period of increasing introspection and reflection on the complex nature of the shifting American reality.

Francisco Núñez de Pineda y Bascuñán's Cautiverio feliz

Stories of captivity and extended residence among the Indians were not unknown among seventeenth-century Latin Americans. Bernal Díaz del Castillo had written years earlier in his *Historia verdadera de la conquista de la Nueva España* of a case in which a Spaniard, Gonzalo Guerrero, survived a shipwreck from an early expedition off the coast of New Spain. Guerrero had managed to forge a new life among a group of Indians who regarded him as their *cacique.* Alvar Núñez Cabeza de Vaca had described in *Naufragios* his own experiences among the Indians of the North American Plains, an eight-year adventure that he narrated with a remarkable sense of literary refinement. Shipwrecks, isolation, and acculturation into the ways of the Indians had become standard motifs of the historiography of the colonial period, as seen in *Cautiverio feliz* (Santiago de Chile, 1863) [*The Happy Captive*] by Francisco Núñez de Pineda y Bascuñán (1607–1682) and *Infortunios que Alonso Ramírez natural de la ciudad de S. Juan de Puerto Rico padeció* [*The Misadventures of Alonso Ramírez*], by Carlos de Sigüenza y Góngora (1645–1700), among other texts of the later era.

Cautiverio feliz is the story of Pineda y Bascuñán's seven-month captivity among the Araucanian Indians of Chile in 1629. Bascuñán was held by the Araucanians essentially as a political hostage used to coerce the Spanish into releasing some of their own Indian prisoners. The autobiographical narrative describes in considerable detail Bascuñán's ordeal during his enforced stay among a people whose ferocity and resistance to domination had been treated earlier by poets Alonso de Ercilla and Pedro de Oña. *Cautiverio feliz* is a surprisingly optimistic recollection of his experiences among the tribe as well as his views concerning some of the Araucanian's stranger customs and traditions. Written over forty years after the event, *Cautiverio feliz* is a distilled summary of his activities in the wild that contains a number of extraordinarily acerbic observations on what he viewed as the mismanagement of Indian affairs by both secular and religious authorities.

Bascuñán's story of captivity forms the nucleus of a much larger work of history whose complete title is *Cautiverio feliz y razón individual de las guerras dilatadas del reino de Chile.* The overall work contains a wide variety of discursive typologies that were commonly found in colonial historiography: descriptive ethnographies of the Araucanians; religious and meditative poetry; moral and political disquisitions; and learned references to classical and biblical authorities (Pollard, *Rhetoric, Politics, and the King's Justice*). Bascuñán's overall purpose was to examine the causes of the warfare against the Araucanian nation that had persisted throughout the seventeenth century. This was, of course, a topic of no small interest to historians of the Crown; in 1625, almost fifty years before Bascuñán's work, *cronista mayor* Luis Tribaldos de Toledo (1558–1634) had written about the difficulties that had arisen in the Araucanian territories regarding their subjugation and religious conversion (*Vista general de las continuadas guerras, difícil conquista del gran Reino y provincias de Chile* [Santiago, 1864]). Bascuñán's autobiographical segment reflects a similar concern with the hostilities and violence among the Araucanians. Unlike missionaries or historians of the Crown, however, Bascuñán criticized not only the savage and unruly among the Araucanians, but also those priests and soldiers who had repeatedly abused the Indians.

Pineda y Bascuñán tells an exciting tale of adventure and intrigue. In the winter of 1629 the young Francisco Núñez was a captain in the army in the frontier town of Chillán in southern Chile. Bascuñán and his company of infantry were ordered to defend Chillán and the surrounding areas from Indian raids and harassment. It was after such a raid that the young captain and some of his men were captured. His story describes in detail his capture, his experiences among the Araucanian people, and the complex negotiations that were necessary to bring him back. When he finally returned to his family some seven months later, it was with the perspective of someone whose attitudes about the Indians had changed forever. He had seen, perhaps for the first time, that Araucanian culture was complex and subtle, and that many among this enemy nation were capable of extraordinary generosity and benevolence. Bascuñán wrote of friendships he had established with Indians such as Lientur and Maulicán, men who defended the young prisoner against fellow Araucanians who sought his execution. It is his friendship with Maulicán in particular that stands out in his story as an exemplary relationship between individuals otherwise destined for continual warfare. While being transported deeper into Araucanian territory, Francisco had rescued Maulicán from the rain-swollen Bío-Bío River. Maulicán felt indebted to the Spaniard for this act of bravery and vowed that he would return Francisco to his father, a promise he ultimately fulfilled.

Yet unlike the romanticized presentation of the Araucanians in the *Restauración de la Imperial* by Juan de Barrenechea y Albis, Bascuñán's view of this tribe was not overly idealized. He kept in mind that the Araucanians were capable of almost unspeakable atrocities. *Cautiverio feliz* differs from much of the historiography of the colonial period in that it presents an image of the Indian that balances the good with the bad. For every Maulicán there were other Indians who were anxious to see Francisco suffer the same fate as the following Spanish captive:

He hit him in the head with such a large blow with the club that he knocked his brains out. At this moment the acolytes with knives in their hands cut open his chest, took out his beating heart, and handed it to my master, who sucked its blood. (p. 11)

The passage brings to mind countless other historians who had commented upon the savagery of the Indians. And what should we think of Maulicán, who appears to have compromised himself by participating in the bloody ceremony? Maulicán's portraiture in *Cautiverio feliz* is very complex. On the one hand, he extended the hand of friendship across cultures to Bascuñán. On the other, he could not deny his traditions and heritage – he was an Araucanian warrior whose people had been persecuted by the Spanish for many generations. Maulicán presented a defense of his actions here by telling his captive that he had no choice but to join in the cannibalistic rite. He knew that he was among his own enemies as well as Francisco's, and that he needed to participate in the ceremony in order to buy time to escape to his father's land. Maulicán was presented as a Machiavellian hero who knew that certain behavioral compromises were necessary to achieve the long-term goals of returning Bascuñán to his people and a lasting peace with the Spanish colonial powers.

Cautiverio feliz counterbalances such negative depictions of the Indians with portrayals of some of the Araucanians' more virtuous practices. Bascuñán observed that the Indians were accustomed to daily bathing, a habit he too acquired while under their custody. He was invited to wear their clothing, eat their food, and join in their festivities, all of which he was glad to do except when he would have compromised his own beliefs and morals. A staunch Catholic, Bascuñán steadfastly refused to engage in many of the bacchanalian pleasures that the Indians apparently enjoyed.

The religious question is one of the most serious issues in *Cautiverio feliz*. Bascuñán knew that Spanish missionaries had worked for many years among the Araucanians yet had not completely succeeded in bringing these people into the ways of the church. Wisely, the narrator allows the Indians themselves to tell why they had resisted so many for so long. Through a series of interpolated narratives, the Indians revealed that their experiences with Catholic missionaries had been mixed. They told of some Jesuits whose own morals were so despicable that they could not possibly have persuaded the Indians to convert. Their only positive memories were of some Franciscans who appeared to embody the virtues they attempted to preach. The Indians were highly critical of any priest who made no effort to communicate in Mapuche, the language of the Araucanians. It was not surprising that the Indians had held on to their own religious practices for so long. They were unwilling to cede what was to them both a political as well as a moral victory to a group that had not distinguished itself in basic ethical conduct.

As a Catholic, Bascuñán faced formidable opposition from Indian healers and magic men. He wrote of a *curandero* who performed an intricate series of dances and recitations over a dying Indian, a description that dramatically contrasts an earlier scene in which Bascuñán prayed for the soul of one of his own young converts who had died after a short illness. The juxtaposition of these two scenes is a clever rhetorical strategy designed to contrast the wild, ineffectual ministrations of the shaman with the quiet displays of Christian faith of the young soldier. Bascuñán was modestly successful in his attempts to proselytize some of his captors, a small victory amid a long history of institutional failure. Having grown up on the frontier, Bascuñán had acquired a basic knowledge of Mapuche and thus was able to impart Catholic doctrine in a language intelligible to the Araucanians. Much like some of the early missionaries from the sixteenth century, Bascuñán integrated strands of indigenous religious beliefs into his message. He told them that their concept of a supreme spirit was similar to the Christian view of a deity. Bascuñán's work as a secular missionary symbolized a reciprocal gesture of accommodation between the two traditionally hostile cultures. Both groups tolerated significant qualities from each other in their process of mutual comprehension.

Among the Indians Bascuñán found severe critics not only of missionaries but also of political and military leaders. Recent scholarship by Raquel Chang-Rodríguez has suggested that Bascuñán used criticism by the Indians as a way for him to attack policies and procedures of the colonial government of Chile (*Violencia y subversión*, 63–83). There is evidence to imply that Bascuñán was quite dissatisfied with his political appointment as a minor official of law enforcement in Valdivia, and that he wrote his text to attack those responsible for his secondary status in colonial society. Eager to reclaim what he viewed as lost prestige, Bascuñán spent a number of years in a frustrating quest to convince the viceregal authorities of his value and numerous contributions to the stability of the colony. He felt that a man of his experience and talent was worthy of an appointment that would grant him his deserved measure of honor and authority. We may approach certain passages of *Cautiverio feliz* with the suspicion that many of the complaints voiced by the Araucanians may be a form of displacement of Bascuñán's own grievances against the State.

Other historians of the colonial period had used their texts similarly as critical explorations of various events of the historical process. Bernal Díaz del Castillo, for example, had earlier examined the role of the common soldier in the conquest of Mexico in deliberate contrast to what he viewed as López de Gómara's sole focus on Hernán Cortés. And, of course, Bartolomé de Las Casas vehemently attacked the armies of the Crown for their excessive violence in dealing with a group he once characterized as "humble, patient, calm, quiet people." Such historians allowed their profound personal convictions to erupt with considerable frequency throughout the course of their narrations. A possible interpretive posture regarding *Cautiverio feliz* is to view the Indians as manifestations of Bascuñán's fundamental desire to criticize a corrupt government that had allowed him to live in poverty during the last years of his life. Ironically, when Bascuñán finally acquired a satisfactory appointment from the viceregal government in Lima, a job as magistrate of the Peruvian town of Moquegua, he died *en route* to his new assignment.

Cautiverio feliz contains quite a few speeches from Indians who felt unjustifiably victimized by unscrupulous Spaniards. Bascuñán is often presented as an intermediary between the two warring groups, an odd posture for one who was in actuality held for so long as a political hostage. In the following passage Bascuñán acted as the confidant of an old *cacique* who talked about the early days of the Conquest, a time when Indians actually fared worse than the present:

> "Did the old folks not tell you," he asked, "their way of collecting tribute with their cruel punishments for any who failed to pay up each month? Did they not tell you how they would let them die like animals, giving no more thought to them than if they were a dog, not allowing them to hear mass or to confess? Did they not show you how their women folk were so cruel and avaricious they would have our wives and daughters working day and night for them for their private gain and indulgence?" (p. 73)

Whom, if anyone, did the Araucanians admire among the Spaniards, if such behavior during the conquest and settlement of Chile was so widespread? *Cautiverio feliz* documents many examples of bad rulers among the Spanish, men who either abused the Indians unjustly or simply used their influence and authority for self-aggrandizement. Pineda criticized any and all Spaniards who allowed their corrupt nature to undermine what he viewed as the will of the king to have justice prevail in his trans-Atlantic realms (Pollard, *Rhetoric*). Yet he had in mind a model ruler who embodied the characteristics necessary for a government of equanimity and vision. On several occasions *Cautiverio feliz* makes reference to Francisco's father, Alvaro Núñez, a feared but respected *maestre de campo* in the occupying colonial army. Revelation of this lineage had actually once saved young Francisco's life. Certain that the Indians would kill him if they knew that he was the son of such a renowned military figure, Francisco tried to hide his true identity from his captors. But, to his genuine surprise, he discovered that the Araucanians thought highly of his father, for he was considered a man of justice and fairness when dealing with the Indians. When many Araucanians called for Francisco's death Lientur interceded on his behalf, saying that the captive's father had always treated the Araucanian people with dignity and respect.

The last few pages of *Cautiverio feliz* suggest a transitory phase for Francisco. Like the heroes from ancient romance cycles, Bascuñán had undertaken a circular journey of adventure, self-discovery, and personal triumph. It is a significant moment in the text when Bascuñán sheds his Indian clothing to dress once again as a member of Spanish society. He experienced a moment of symbolic passage from one world to another. Like Cabeza de Vaca almost a century earlier, Bascuñán returned from his quest with a wealth of knowledge and experience that colonial authorities could have used effectively. Francisco in fact met with the governor of the province in Concepción and reported that the only reason that Indians might attack would be as a result of Spanish provocation. Such accusations of the government were, perhaps, thinly disguised censures of an administration that had long neglected his requests for equitable recompense for his services. The passage from prisoner to mediator was complete when Francisco once again saw his father. The young Bascuñán was saddened to find his father bedridden and very ill – clearly unable to function any longer in the heroic manner described earlier in the text. It seems appropriate at this point to regard Francisco as a successor to his father as a soldier of integrity and high moral standing concerning the Araucanians. The image of a young, vital, informed, and compassionate man contrasts drastically with the presentation of his father, suffering from a crippling paralysis. As an autobiographer, Pineda y Bascuñán fashioned such scenes with the intention of portraying himself as positively as possible within the realms of reasonable credibility.

Bascuñán's self-depiction was primarily as a mediator between two groups whose political animosities were profound. Yet both groups, wrote Bascuñán, had ample reason to mistrust one another. The Araucanians had suffered enormously during the political and economic expansion of the Spanish colony in Chile. The Spaniards, on the other hand, considered the Indians little more than godless savages who rejected all attempts to civilize them. Bascuñán found it difficult to resolve the conflict between his affection for certain members of the tribe who had protected him, and his loyalty to the expansive mission of church and state. When the negotiations for his release were finally secured, he brought back to his world a message of hope and reconciliation, a pronounced desire on the part of the Indians for a cessation of hostilities. One Indian implored Bascuñán to tell his people "we are not so bad or perverse as they make us out" (p. 94). Bascuñán reported his findings to the appropriate authorities, but apparently to little avail.

Cautiverio feliz is an autobiographical narrative that goes beyond the predictable lines of more doctrinal histories written by priests, bishops, or commissioned historians of the Crown. The narrative voice employed by Bascuñán reflects his years of military and administrative experience; it is a voice of maturity and self-assurance, not the tentative utterance of a man in his early twenties.

Bascuñán's defense of the Indian, however, should be viewed in the context of self-interest. When Bascuñán allowed the Indians to criticize military and religious leaders, criticisms that often go unchallenged by the author, he was in all likelihood permitting the Araucanians to articulate his own concerns over the corruption of Spanish society. The positive image of Indians whom he met during captivity is in opposition to the negative examples of Spanish clergy and government leaders from outside Chile who were interested primarily in their own welfare. Bascuñán found in the Araucanians a warrior class who exemplified an ethos of honor and integrity, virtues which he found rare among rulers in the contemporary Peruvian viceroyalty.

Carlos de Sigüenza y Góngora

In the early spring of the year 1690, Conde de Galve, the Viceroy of New Spain, began hearing remarkable stories about a young man who had recently been washed ashore upon the beaches of the remote Yucatan peninsula. This unusual wayfarer, Puerto Rican by birth, had apparently spent the last two years as a prisoner of British pirates. But what made his story truly unique was the fact that in the course of his travels, the hapless mariner had succeeded in circumnavigating the planet, an extraordinary accomplishment in those days. Anxious to learn more about this individual, the Viceroy sent for him, paying his passage from Mérida to Mexico City. The Viceroy listened attentively to Alonso Ramírez as he talked about his work and travels in Mexico and the Philippines, a sojourn culminating in his untimely capture by ruthless English brigands. The Viceroy commended Alonso Ramírez for surviving this tortuous ordeal, and then sent him to Carlos de Sigüenza y Góngora to record his exceptional adventures. Sigüenza interviewed Ramírez extensively, and later helped him secure a position as a sailor with the Royal Armada in Veracruz. In the summer of 1690, *Infortunios* [*The Misadventures of Alonso Ramírez*] was published in Mexico City, an autobiographical narrative describing the numerous misfortunes throughout his life that had led him so far from his island homeland. *Infortunios* is one of the last examples in the seventeenth century – and possibly the best – of a literary adaptation of a historical event.

That the Viceroy sent Alonso Ramírez to Carlos de Sigüenza y Góngora to tell his tale is not surprising. Sigüenza was a well-known scholar of baroque Mexico, probably the most learned historian, mathematician, and astronomer of the entire colony – only Sor Juana Inés de la Cruz could rival his intellectual breadth and capacity. Sigüenza held a number of official posts in Mexico City that were testament to his scholastic accomplishments: chair of mathematics and astronomy at the University of Mexico; cosmographer for the Viceroy of New Spain; corrector of the Inquisition; cartographer; hospital chaplain; accountant; and others, titles that "sound good but pay little," Sigüenza once noted with ironic self-effacement. Sigüenza kept abreast of the latest scholarly trends from abroad; his reputation as a scientist extended throughout America and Europe, a renown that led to no small number of debates, oppositions, and learned polemics. His well-known quarrel with Jesuit Eusebio Kino (1644–1711) over the nature of comets, for example, exemplifies Sigüenza's command of the scientific discourse of his day. Sigüenza y Góngora was the quintessential scholar of the later colonial period; virtually nothing under the sun escaped his curiosity and scrutiny: science; religion, history; geography; and the culture of the ancient Mexicans.

Sigüenza's writings reflect a contemporary, encyclopedic vision of his world. His scientific literature reveals a solid grounding in the "new science" originated by such luminaries as Galileo and Copernicus, an epistemology marked not by tradition and authority but by observation. The *Libra astronómica y philosófica*, is one of a number of his scientific tracts dealing with comets and their peculiarities. Here we see that Sigüenza was highly skeptical of any scientific commentary that simply repeated ancient beliefs or phony assertions about the cosmos. Determined to divorce science from superstition – no small challenge for a seventeenth-century Mexican – Sigüenza disputed conventional wisdom throughout the *Libra astronómica* regarding celestial bodies and movements. Sigüenza even boldly attacked Aristotle, the dean of the ancients, as one whose teachings should be ignored when not grounded in observation and reason. Sigüenza openly and caustically refuted a number of popular notions about comets, particularly that they were ominous harbingers of future calamities sent by God.

This is not to say that Sigüenza y Góngora had suffered a loss of faith or even a crisis of doctrine. Sigüenza was a lay priest who fully accepted the church and its central role in creole society. Even though he had been expelled from a Jesuit seminary (for undisclosed indiscretions), Sigüenza maintained a close relationship with this order and with the more prominent prelates of Mexico City during the late seventeenth century: Archbishop Aguiar y Seija was one of Sigüenza's most influential and generous supporters. Sigüenza once assumed the role of *cronista de convento* by writing *Parayso Occidental*, a work written to commemorate the one-hundredth anniversary of the founding of Mexico City's Convento Real de Jesús María, a cloister for poor *criollas*. Written against the backdrop of post-Conquest sixteenth-century Mexico, the *Parayso Occidental* tells of the convent's founding and of its more admirable nuns, a story based upon archival sources and interviews with some of the older residents of this cloister. Kathleen Ross has recently shown that *Parayso Occidental* is a complex work that in many ways surpasses the simple *crónica de convento* or *vida de monja*. Sigüenza constructed this text upon the elaborate conceit that the creation of the convent represented the Conquest of America and the establishment of a paradise in this, the western hemisphere. Yet the main protagonists of this history – women – were not commonly placed in positions of such historical prominence. These exceptional women, it has been noted, were instrumental in the creation of a New World paradise by transcending their traditional roles as wives and mothers and working toward the spiritual transformation of this land (Ross, *Carlos de Sigüenza y Góngora*, 31–75).

Parayso Occidental may be viewed as one of several texts by Sigüenza that reassesses foundational events and figures of the sixteenth century from the perspective of a *criollo* interested in writing in a uniquely American idiom. The text opens with a chapter on Aztec maidens, native American analogies to the nuns who would later inhabit the Convento Real, a place that had been built upon the ground where Malinche had once lived. Sigüenza was an unrivaled expert in Mexico's pre-Columbian civilizations and used this erudition in a revisionist expression of early American history. By interweaving Aztec history and culture with the history of the convent, Sigüenza established a context that was distinctively *American* in nature. Sigüenza looked back to the Conquest again in *Piedad heroyca de Don Fernando Cortés* (Mexico City, 1693?), an interpretive re-reading of Bernal Díaz del Castillo and other historians of the sixteenth century who neglected to credit Cortés with one of his more noteworthy accomplishments: the founding of the Hospital de la Inmaculada Concepción.

Sigüenza y Góngora's narrative domain was America, a subject over which he claimed considerable authority. Sigüenza could be rather testy about what Europeans thought of his homeland. In the *Libra astronómica*, for example, he bitterly chastized Kino for what he viewed as insufferable arrogance toward Americans: "In some parts of Europe, especially in the more remote north, they think that not only the Indians, original inhabitants of these countries, but also those of Spanish parents who by chance were born here, either walk on two feet by divine dispensation, or that there is little rational to be found in us, even if we were examined with English microscopes" (pp. 312–13). Sigüenza's feisty attitude in *Libra astronómica* is reminiscent of Alonso de Ovalle's earlier incredulity over Europeans who were totally ignorant of the distinct provinces and regions of South America. Sigüenza was intensely interested in exploring all aspects of the American experience, a concern that is manifest throughout his historical and geographical texts. *Glorias de Querétaro*, a history of the creation of Querétaro's Church of the Virgin of Guadalupe, begins with a study of Querétaro during the days of pre-Conquest, a narrative strategy he would employ a few years later in *Parayso Occidental*. *Glorias de Querétaro* presents in some detail the ceremonies held to commemorate the construction of this church. This gala event was marked by a series of processions in which the local populace – mostly Indians – reenacted scenes from their own history and traditions. Sigüenza described in minute detail the symbolism of the numerous costumes and headgears, pedantically noting that such an inventory of Aztec minutiae would probably bore anyone with no knowledge of Nahuatl. The procession, known at the time as a *mascarada*, culminated with the presentation of an image of Guadalupe, around which danced Indians still dressed in their ancestral raiments. This was Sigüenza's Mexico: a land inhabited by people of wildly opposing cultures who had peacefully convened to honor their uniquely American patron saint.

Sigüenza y Góngora was an astute analyst not only of American and Indian history but also of events and issues that he witnessed or experienced in New Spain. His most important and widely studied texts today are those that explore contemporary occurrences within this vast colonial viceroyalty. Works such as *Infortunios* and *Alboroto y motín de los indios de México* are extensive narrative portrayals of significant incidents that took place during his own lifetime. *Infortunios* is the account of Ramírez's oceanic passage around the world, while *Alboroto y motín* relates the infamous food riots in Mexico City during the summer of 1692.

It is useful to view *Alboroto y motín* in light of such texts as *Glorias de Querétaro* or *Parasyo Occidental*, works that show some admiration for the cultural monuments of Aztec civilization. It is evident in these historical studies that Sigüenza had considerable regard for the accomplishments of several of the tribes that had inhabited the valley of Mexico in the pre-Conquest era. Yet history and texts safely distanced Sigüenza from the rancor and violence that had periodically erupted between the dominant Spanish regime and the Indian masses. *Alboroto y motín* describes an occasion on which the tenuous political control the Spanish held over the Indians momentarily dissolved. The fear and anarchy that prevailed in the capital during the days of the riot prompted Sigüenza to record what he referred to as Mexico's "pitiful fate," a night that would remain "infamous for many centuries" (p. 95).

What caused the Indians to burn, loot, and plunder the jewel of Spain's colonial crown? Apparently the spring rains of 1692 had been excessively heavy, a condition that caused a number of unfortunate circumstances to arise: flooding in the valley was much worse than usual; distribution of foodstuffs was exacerbated; and the corn and wheat crops were severely damaged. Fear of food shortages spread rapidly throughout the capital even as city officials set up centers for the equitable distribution of grain. It was in such a granary that the first disturbance actually began, a mêlée that ultimately involved thousands of Indians and other groups who felt disenfranchised from the economic and social currents of the Spanish and *criollo* state. At the peak of the riot the mob had almost complete control of Mexico City's main square and had succeeded in burning a number of official buildings and residences.

Alboroto y motín is a complex text that far exceeds the discursive limitations inherent in a simple narrative of this violent event. Sigüenza included this report in a long letter to Admiral Andrés de Pez of the Spanish Royal Navy that includes a paean to the Viceroy Conde de Galve, a report of Mexico City's celebration to honor the recent wedding of Carlos II, meteorological and astronomical studies, and accounts of civil engineering projects in and around Mexico City. His account is, in this respect, a layered text that is representative of Sigüenza's baroque taste for verbal density and narrative complexity. Yet this is not to suggest that Sigüenza's textual selections were either arbitrary or random. Viewed as a unit, the letter to Admiral Pez builds slowly and deliberately toward the exposition of the riot, an event presented as both the historical as well as the literary climax to a sequence of seemingly inchoate happenings in the Valley of Mexico.

The work on drainage canals and the weather had a direct causal relationship to the riot, but what of Sigüenza's praise of Galve, account of the wedding celebration, and study of a solar eclipse? The brief study of Galve's major accomplishments was simply a way of deflecting any criticism the Viceroy might have received because of the riot. Sigüenza's laudatory remarks about Galve artfully and rhetorically undermine censures of his patron before they might occur.

The festival in honor of the King's wedding was probably reminiscent of the *mascarada* reported a few years earlier in *Glorias de Querétaro*. People were dressed in festive attire, saw bullfights, and viewed fireworks. "How happy the common people were," wrote Sigüenza, a situation that would change as abruptly as the weather (p. 101). Sigüenza ended his brief exposé of this joyous occasion on a note of inevitable expectation. "How true are the scriptures when they say that laughter is mixed with crying and that pain follows the greatest joys" (p. 101). The celebration was a momentary diversion for people who were about to experience a situation

of grave consequences. Sigüenza referred to both Christian as well as
pagan gods for bringing this situation upon them. At one point he wrote
that Fate had regarded Mexico City with scorn. He later alluded to God as
the prime agent responsible for their precarious welfare: "Oh holy and
most just God, how removed from human discourse are your incomprehensible and venerable judgments" (p. 101). In either case, the Mexicans
are presented as people subject to the capricious will of divine or
meteorological forces beyond their control or understanding.

And when confronted with a phenomenon that was well within human
comprehension – an eclipse of the sun – how did the common folk react?
They responded with great fear and went flying to the cathedral for
protection and solace from what they viewed as a menacing heaven. We
see at this and other points in *Alboroto y motín* that Sigüenza's story of the
riot becomes his own story as well. Amid the panic created by the celestial
alignment, Sigüenza went calmly about his work as an astronomer
viewing "one of the greatest [eclipses] that the world has ever seen" (p.
108). His smug self-portrait here is in dramatic contrast to the frightened
Indians inside the great cathedral and the angry rabble destroying the
monuments of Spanish supremacy in the New World: the viceroy's
residence and city hall. Sigüenza wrote briefly of his work in clearing the
canals leading out of Mexico City, and of his heroic efforts to save
valuable archival documents from the fires set by the mob. Sigüenza
depicted himself and other creole elites as the ones who created, preserved, or sustained the instrumental figures and symbols of the civilized
world: the viceroy was hidden away and protected from the hordes;
Sigüenza saved Mexico's written past from certain oblivion. The Indians,
on the other hand, fell too easily into a chaotic anarchy fueled by the
insidious *pulque*, an alcoholic beverage of the lower classes. Sigüenza
bitterly characterized these rebellious Indians as "the most ungrateful,
unthankful, grumbling, uneasy people God created and the most favored
with privileges" (p. 115).

This would not be the last time that Sigüenza y Góngora would write
about Indian uprisings. In 1693 he published *Mercurio volante con la
noticia de la recuperación de las provincias del Nuevo México*, a short
pamphlet on the successful suppression of an Indian rebellion in the New
Mexican territory far to the north. Here he once again reported on "the
innate hatred they have for Spaniards," an animosity that would lead to a
collective resistance and confrontation (p. 146). It is interesting to see in
these two works the dichotomy established between the Spanish rulers
and the indigenous classes. The Indians apparently had not been fully
assimilated into the dominant Spanish culture; during their insurrection
they spoke out loudly and expressively against this alien presence. In
Alboroto y motín Sigüenza reported hearing conversations among Indian

women concerning the presence and possible annihilation of the Spanish people who lived in the Indians' land: "let us go happily to this war, and if it is God's will that the Spaniards be finished in it, it does not matter if we die without confession. Is not this land ours?" (p. 123).

This animosity was neither trivial nor transitory; Sigüenza cited evidence that Indian hatred of the Spaniard was long-standing and profound. Apart from such invectives as "death to the Spaniards" and "death to the Viceroy and all who defend him" (p. 123), Sigüenza found other proof to substantiate his conviction that the Indians abhorred the Creoles. Earlier when Sigüenza was working on the canal-clearing project, they had unearthed some small clay figurines representing Spaniards. These tiny effigies had knife punctures and had been painted blood-red. The significance of this discovery: because they found the clay statuettes where Cortés had fled the city many years before during the "Noche Triste," Sigüenza felt that the superstitious Indians wished the same fate for present-day Spaniards. *Alboroto y motín* therefore re-examines – and reenacts – some of the events of the Conquest. Though on both occasions the Indians initially overcame the Spaniards, the superior political, social, and economic power of the occupying forces would allow them ultimately to prevail. Incisive scholarship on *Alboroto y motín* has signaled a number of parallels to texts that deal with the Spanish victory in Tenochtitlán, suggesting that Sigüenza's narrative is, among other things, an intentional re-writing of the Conquest (Ross, "*Alboroto y motín de México*," 188). Sigüenza appropriated the seminal text of the Conquest – the second letter to the monarch by Cortés – and cast his story in a similar heroic mold. From the perspective of a late seventeenth-century Creole, Cortés had become the quintessential hero of the New World, an important model for the continual struggle for political dominance in the Valley of Mexico.

Yet if we view Sigüenza's historical work in its entirety, it is difficult to sustain the image of the Indian as a barbaric savage. There is little doubt that Sigüenza had a serious scholarly interest in the high cultural and political achievements of the Aztec and Chichimeca civilizations. His *Teatro de virtudes políticas*, for example, interweaves dozens of references to Aztec monarchs and gods with his views on what constitutes an able and just ruler. Sigüenza found enviable qualities of leadership and valor among such Mexicans as Moctezuma and Cuauhtémoc. Why the turn away from such studious equanimity in *Alboroto y motín*? It is hard to overstate the importance of Sigüenza's own involvement in this occurrence. He witnessed first-hand the frightening power of a hungry, angry mob intent on destroying any and all vestiges of control that the opposing camp had established. Sigüenza saw their destructive capability and heard their hateful insults. He realized that these people had no regard whatsoever for the institutions and symbols of authority that had been firmly in place since the 1520s. After experiencing the intensity of such a turmoil, it was difficult to return to the serene study of the ancestors of the unruly hordes who had burned his beloved city. Gone in *Alboroto y motín* is the cultural harmony found in *Glorias de Querétaro*; Sigüenza's later voice is one born of harsh experience and the sobering disillusionment of social conflict.

Infortunios is, like *Alboroto y motín*, the story of a contemporary circumstance that Sigüenza y Góngora constructed from observation and interviews. Among all of Sigüenza's extant works, *Infortunios* has attracted by far the most attention from literary historians and critics. It is a text that invites a number of varying readings and interpretations. It has been viewed over the years as a novelesque chronicle, an ersatz autobiography, a proto-novel of either the picaresque or byzantine genre, a geographical study of Spain's colonial empire and beyond, and a political commentary on Spain's declining presence in the shifting world economy of the late seventeenth century. The general lack of consensus regarding this text's literary genre suggests that it, like so many other historical narratives of the later colonial period, is a work for which there is no modern analogy. *Infortunios* contains such a confluence of rhetorical and discursive tendencies that any efforts to arrive at a concrete generic label are undermined. Besides, as Aníbal González has noted, to view *Infortunios* as primarily fiction or history would be to misunderstand the rhetorical resemblance of historical and fictional language during this era ("*Los infortunios de Alonso Ramírez*," 190). While the categories of "history" and "fiction" may have induced distinct patterns of literary reception, the expressive modalities of historical and fictional discourse were remarkably similar.

In some regards, it is easy to see why the picaresque mode comes to mind with *Infortunios*. Alonso's life – as depicted by Sigüenza – bore some similarities to a Lazarillo de Tormes or Guzmán de Alfarache. Alonso began life in San Juan, Puerto Rico, the son of a poor carpenter. He left his home at an early age in search of a better life and made his way to Mexico where, unfortunately, he "experienced more hunger than in Puerto Rico" (p. 8). Alonso went through several jobs, each with a different master, before his life took a fortuitous turn: marriage. His young wife, however, died in childbirth before they had been married a year. Desperate to make something of himself, Alonso shipped off to the Philippines, the place where delinquents like him were "sent into exile" (p. 10). This decision had both auspicious as well as untimely consequences. Alonso had a reasonably successful, if brief, career as a sailor travelling widely throughout the southeast Asian Pacific. Compared to his years of extreme economic necessity in Puerto Rico and Mexico, his life in the Far East had dramatically improved: he had finally found constant and apparently amenable employment; and he was able "to see diverse cities and ports of India on different trips" (p. 12).

Pícaros, however, often experience rapid changes of fate. On one of his maritime trips out of Manila Bay, Alonso Ramírez and his small crew were taken prisoner by heavily armed English pirates. Here began the most difficult and painful stage of his life. While under the custody of the British, Alonso and his men suffered repeated instances of abuse, humiliation, and adversity. The English were depicted as little more than godless cannibals who lived to plunder the rich ports of the East Indies. They had no regard for their captives, whom they treated as slaves. Alonso's men rapidly perished under the severity of their English oppressors; out of twenty-five original crew members, only eight survived the duration of captivity. The pirates finally gave Alonso and his men their freedom, though a precarious one. They gave them a small boat with minimal provisions and arms and thus parted company. The now diminished and debilitated company of sailors began their trek homeward and sailed from Madagascar toward the west. They were shipwrecked on the beaches of Yucatan where they eventually found their way back to civilization. It was here that Alonso was called to the viceregal capital and his meetings with Galve and Sigüenza took place.

Though it is clear that *Infortunios* uses a number of motifs from the picaresque genre – first person narration, poverty, quest for fortune – it is a text that embraces a wide spectrum of narrative traditions. It is possible to see in *Infortunios* a number of social and political commentaries on Spain's presence in the world community. It is important to remember that Alonso travelled through great expanses of the far-flung Spanish empire and acquired a significant critical perspective on Spain's decline as a world power. Alonso was clearly impressed by the firepower on the English ships and his own inability to stage an adequate defense; Sigüenza would record another case a few years later in *Alboroto y motín* when lack of armaments led to an embarrassing defeat. The soldiers guarding the Viceroy's palace had no bullets for their guns, an inadequacy the Indians quickly noted and exploited. Though Spain's global empire in the 1690s was still quite extensive, Alonso's experiences suggest that the cracks in the wall had widened considerably. Alonso's humiliation and defeat was, by extension, Spain's.

Alonso's intimidation by the English buccaneers, however, did not lead to an admiration of a people he considered beneath his contempt. These were, after all, people who had rejected Catholicism. *Infortunios* contains several narrative sequences of graphic detail that characterize the pirates as bestial savages. Alonso told of an incident in which an Englishman offered him a piece of human arm that they had been savoring. Alonso's refusal was viewed as cowardice. If he ever expected to equal them in valor, he would have to "be less prudish," said the English (p. 16). Although they demonstrated superior technology and considerable military skill, Alonso viewed the British as culturally and morally void. Worse, perhaps, was his opinion of a Spaniard named Miguel who had signed on with the pirates. Alonso saved his sharpest criticism for him: "There was no intolerable task given to us, there was no occasion in which they mistreated us, no hunger that we suffered, nor risk of life that we endured, that did not come from his hand and his instruction" (pp. 24–5). It is a strong and bitter irony that Alonso and his companions suffered more from a fellow Spaniard than from the English. But Miguel had long ago abandoned his religious moorings, a decision that would eventually lead to his "dying a heretic" (p. 25). The religious discord between the captors and their prisoners was so pronounced that Alonso was certain that Nicpat, one of two sailors who showed him the slightest compassion, was a Catholic.

Although Alonso was grateful upon his return to be among people who shared his faith and traditions, not everyone in this world measured up to his standards of conduct. Alonso told of several incidents that took place in Yucatan that offended and disillusioned him. Among the survivors was a black servant of Alonso's named Pedro. Shortly after their arrival in Tixcacal a man approached Alonso and, pretending to be an old and cherished friend, tried to swindle Alonso out of his servant. "Rumor has it," the man said, "that you are a spy for a corsair," for which the governor of the province was bound to seize him (p. 36). Yet the man – old friend that he was – volunteered to intervene on his behalf. He generously offered to take Pedro as a gift to the governor, adding this admonition: "Consider that the danger in which I see you is quite extreme" (p. 36). Alonso, of course, recognized the sham. After all, he had travelled around the world, witnessed unspeakable perversions, and miraculously survived a shipwreck. Nobody's fool, he responded: "I am not so simple that I do not recognize you as a great liar who could give even the greatest pirates lessons in robbery" (p. 36).

Alonso took this episode in stride, referring to it as "a very witty story" – nothing lost, nothing gained (p. 35). Yet Alonso was somewhat disturbed when city officials in Tixcacal denied him permission to return to the beach so he could salvage some of his possessions. If he left the village in the direction of the beach, the mayor warned him, he would suffer "grave punishment" (p. 36). The suspicion is, of course, that the corrupt officials would confiscate the remains for themselves. Alonso drew a sharp and significant parallel with someone from his recent past when he said "remembering the Sevillian Miguel, I shrugged my shoulders" (p. 36). Alonso had travelled the world to find that these government officials were no better than the English, that corruption was a form of piracy.

Alonso's re-entry into this world was thus quite difficult. Called upon to tell and re-tell his story many times, Alonso said that when it came to mealtimes he was always dismissed, never fed. His main support during this difficult interim came from Indians who generously shared their simple fare with him, for which he was genuinely grateful. With these recent misfortunes in mind, all of which happened upon Alonso's return to Mexico, it is easy to see that *Infortunios* functions as a classical *relación* in which an individual presents his claim to a higher authority. Dispossessed of his most fundamental belongings, Alonso's story is one of a plaintiff who demands justice and fair consideration. In this light, *Infortunios* shares similarities with a number of reports from the sixteenth and seventeenth century in which an individual sought a legal judgment from the highest possible authority – the King, if necessary – for what was viewed as a serious miscarriage of justice. In a strictly juridical context, the narrator of a *relación* attempts to construct a story whose rhetorical disposition will lead to a persuasive argument regarding the point in question. Recall Francisco de Pineda y Bascuñán's concern implicit throughout *Cautiverio feliz*: disenchanted with his own financial and political situation, Bascuñán criticized current governmental policies as a way of self-elevation. Similarly, Alonso, disillusioned but never corrupt, would take his story directly to the Viceroy and his learned secretary. It is, perhaps, a painful irony that Alonso simply traded one type of adversity for another. The outcome of Alonso's legal quandary? He was awarded custody of his ship's contents, and, as something of a bonus, was recruited by the Royal Navy in Veracruz, a final turn of Fortune's capricious wheel.

Not surprisingly, *Infortunios* has elicited studies that attempt to document with some precision the many historical and geographical references included by Sigüenza (Cummins, "*Infortunios de Alonso Ramírez*"). Though it would be a mistake to view *Infortunios* solely in terms of its historical and geographical accuracy, it is a consideration of some scholarly interest. In this sense some critics have considered *Infortunios* a basically factual text that accurately reflects a number of situations during its era. The most important historical reference in the work is the running commentary on piracy, scourge of Spain's world-wide trade interests during the seventeenth century. British and Dutch pirates, who appear in the *Infortunios*, were a constant threat to Spanish ports and outposts in the East Indies. This area of the world was a region of intense economic competition for the important European powers of the day. Alonso spoke of some Portuguese soldiers in Siam who had their hands cut off, a story that can be verified by contemporary French and Dutch accounts. Alonso also told of English operations in Borneo, a presence that can be confirmed in contemporary historical records. People mentioned by Alonso such as Antonio Nieto, Leandro Coello, and Gabriel de Cuzalaegui were historical personages. Yet for some of the people in *Infortunios* there is no record whatsoever of their existence. Apart from his story here, Alonso Ramírez disappeared from sight after Sigüenza's interview. His appointment with the navy in Veracruz has never been substantiated. The English pirates (Donkin, Bel, Nicpat) were unknowns as well. Sigüenza was thus creatively selective about what and whom to include in this work that consistently masquerades as a story of truth and verifiability. While many of Alonso's experiences appear to be truthful, it has been impossible to document with certainty the authenticity of some of the incidents of his life. Alonso spoke about his legal battle with the officials in Tixcacal, a situation that should have produced a deluge of notorial manuscripts. Yet no one has yet found any evidence of Alonso's presence in this village or of his legal assertions to reclaim his property (González, "*Los infortunios*," 193–5).

However tempting a historicist reading of *Infortunios* – in which one accepts uncritically the factual basis of the work – it is advisable to consider that there was often little to distinguish historical writing from prose fiction during this era. It is also important to remember that Alonso's narrative voice (however realistically portrayed) is the direct or indirect product of Sigüenza's own creative process. Though *Infortunios* assumes the form of an autobiography, Sigüenza was responsible for the genesis and ultimate realization of the text, a situation that makes unraveling the chorus of narrative voices an extremely difficult task.

It seems clear that Sigüenza came to Alonso's aid with the names and locations of the many places he encountered throughout his experiences on the high seas. The creative process that led to the formation of this book thus included Alonso's oral report about his own life as well as Sigüenza's interpretive guidance regarding chronology, narrative sequencing, emphasis or omission of certain details, and basic information on the layout of the world. In both a figurative as well as a literal sense, Sigüenza wrote himself into the story. Gimbernat de González has noted that there is an occasional confluence of identities within the singular narrative voice of *Infortunios* ("Mapas y texto," 390). We see glimpses of Alonso the historical character as well as Sigüenza, who organized and possibly supplemented the story with data gleaned from his years of historical and geographical research. While Alonso supplied the essential information about his experiences, Sigüenza made carefully deliberate choices about the composition of this text. After Alonso spoke of the pirates' decision to free them, for example, the text regresses a bit and presents a brief character study of some of Alonso's captors. This is a narrative technique that adds variety to the presentation of this life-story.

It is a turn away from the otherwise chronological linearity present elsewhere in *Infortunios*, and represents a moment in which Alonso re-evaluated some of his captors. The text intersperses a number of action sequences with a chapter on Alonso's thoughtful recollections on this period of his life. This fictional construct allows us to view Alonso as both an intriguing historical character as well as a credible narrator who could tell his story with a convincing degree of perspective on human nature. Alonso closed his thoughts on Miguel with the hope that God grant him a pardon for his sins. Alonso thus sought redemption for his enemy, an act of Christian charity that dramatically elevated him above the scurrilous English.

Sigüenza's presence is thus sensed in such instances of narrative choice and closure. We also find Sigüenza at the end of the book depicted humorously as a man of many titles, none of which earned him anything. Alonso, speaking through Sigüenza, told of his encounter with his author. The Viceroy sent him to "Don Carlos de Sigüenza y Góngora, cosmographer and professor of mathematics of our lord the king in the Mexican Academy, chaplain of the royal hospital Amor de Dios of Mexico City.... Taking pity on my hardships, ... he formed this *relación* in which they are contained..." (p. 38). Sigüenza is depicted here as an Unamuno-like author coming face to face with his own creation. Alonso had a story, but alone was unable to tell it. It is in the final paragraphs that we detect most significantly the collaborative enterprise that led to the genesis of *Infortunios*. Here we also see how Sigüenza converted the narrative into his own story. He was, in the end, the most important character that Alonso ever encountered during his eventful life. Without Sigüenza, there would be no *relación* and thus no Alonso Ramírez, as far as history was concerned. Sigüenza's role in this regard is very similar to his self-portrayal in *Alboroto y motín*. In both cases through an intentional act, he rescued history from oblivion: the documents would have burned up without his intervention; Alonso Ramírez would have disappeared from history without Sigüenza's written record of his activities. Their meeting in Mexico City, during early April 1690, was thus propitious for both of them. Alonso found an enduring historical identity. Sigüenza placed himself into a foundational role in the text as the creator of this identity. Sigüenza apparently felt justified in acknowledging his own pivotal role in converting Alonso's oral statement into a record of permanence.

Although both Alonso Ramírez and Sigüenza y Góngora left a historical imprint, their collective voice in *Infortunios* is an adapted function of the narrative. In this sense, the narrator of the text – though a product of both personalities – is a reflection of the fictional disposition of the narrative. The "I" of Alonso Ramírez probably has more in common with the picaresque narrator than with the historical individual who acted as a model for this composition (González, "*Los infortunios*," 199). From Alonso's first utterance to the end of the text, the narrator's voice generally follows a literary mode of discourse rather than "realistic" historical speech. Alonso spoke out as an ironic narrator (a picaresque trait), one who wished to reveal certain things about himself and conceal others (González, "*Los infortunios*," 200). What actually determines the shape and outcome of the story is related as much to the exigencies of literary form as to the real-life experiences of a man named Alonso Ramírez. The latest critical readings of *Infortunios* – and of colonial historiography in general – have sought out the literary dynamics of the text rather than the historical referents. As José Arrom has suggested, *Infortunios* is perhaps best read as a fictionalized biography of adventure. What matters, writes Arrom, is that the author has directed the chaotic events – real or imagined – into a text with consistent literary patterns and coherence ("Carlos de Sigüenza y Góngora," 46). It is "Sigüenza the fabulator who confers upon *Infortunios* the organic nexus with the novelesque genre" (Arrom, "Carlos de Sigüenza y Góngora," 35). Sigüenza y Góngora is one of many figures from the colonial era whose historical works are currently studied for their rhetorical techniques and discursive modalities.

[6]

Colonial lyric

Roberto González Echevarría

Spain occupied the New World as the Spanish language was undergoing its last significant linguistic revolution and Spanish poetry its most profound and lasting change. Perhaps this coincidence explains the pervasive presence of poetry during the Conquest, as well as in the viceregal societies created as a result of colonization. In the sixteenth century, Spanish poetry was in the midst of a feverish renewal, adopting the style and spirit derived from Petrarch and the Italian Renaissance, and elevating its traditional forms, notably the *romancero*, to written and printed expression. At the same time as the Italianate style was being adopted, the inherited medieval poetics of the courtly *cancioneros*, and the ballads of the *romancero*, endured, proliferated, and contaminated the new poetry. Changes in poetry, as in all else in the Spanish sixteenth century, meant more often than not an uneasy coexistence of medieval and renaissance ideas and practices. The resiliency of the Medieval is one of the elements that led, in due time, to the style that characterizes colonial lyric, which is the Baroque.

But the renewal was radical enough. Perhaps the most profound change, because it affected the very rhythm of poetic language itself, and its distinction from everyday speech, was the adoption of the eleven-syllable line. The hendecasyllable became the standard for cultivated poetry, in contrast to the shorter lines used for ballads, other popular verse, and in *cancionero* poems, like the ones written by Hernando Colón, the Discoverer's son (Varela, "La obra poética de Hernando Colón"). The eleven-syllable line became the feature of high art, of cultivated poetry or *arte mayor*, while the shorter ones were left for popular or occasional verse, called *arte menor*. The hendecasyllable was quickly brought to the New World, where its use was also the hallmark of all aspiring serious poets. Along with the hendecasyllable several stanza forms were imported from Italy, most notably *terza rima* [*tercetos*], *ottava rima* [*octava real*], the *lira* (also *lira* in Spanish), and the *silva*. Both

191

the *lira* and the *silva* used combinations of eleven and seven syllable lines. Larger units of poetic expression also came from Italy, such as the sonnet, the pastoral eclogue, the elegy, and the verse-letter or *epístola*. With the pastoral mode, as a generalized feature of renaissance poetics, classical models, particularly Virgil, Horace, and Ovid, became the object of admiration and imitation, and classical mythology's vast reservoir of poetic allusion, nearly like another language for poets. With these new forms there also arrived an abiding interest in poetic theory itself, mostly drawn from Neoplatonism and the commentaries on Aristotle (with a good dose of Horace) that proliferated after the middle of the sixteenth century (Terry, "The continuity of renaissance criticism").

The vast poetic renewal in the peninsula and colonial expansion throughout America unfolded simultaneously. The dates of the first are well known, but need to be recalled to observe the synchronicity of events. The Caribbean was settled between 1492 and 1519, Mexico between 1519 and 1543, Peru between 1532 and the 1560s. Or, to frame the period with the dates in which the *audiencia*, that most significant judicial institution, was founded in each territory: the Audiencia of Santo Domingo was established in 1511, that of Mexico in 1529, the Guatemalan in 1544, and the one in Nueva Galicia in 1549. In the south, the Audiencia of Panama was created in 1538, the one in Lima in 1542, Santa Fe in 1549, Charcas 1559, Quito 1563, Chile 1565 and 1609. One can now place over this grid the meaningful dates in the disemination of the new poetry, with 1525 being perhaps the first and most important. This is the year in which the poet Juan Boscán (?–1542) had a momentous conversation with the Italian diplomat Andrea Navaggiero, in which the latter encouraged him to try his hand at the kind of poetry Italian poets in the Petrarchan tradition were writing. Navaggiero's advice, soon taken up by Boscán and his friend Garcilaso de la Vega (1500?–1536), was in great measure formulated within the climate of ideas that informed Pietro Bembo's *Prose della volgar lingua*, published that same year, 1525. Boscán also translated Baldasare Castiglione's *The Courtier* (1518), which appeared posthumously in 1543. It was a book that outlined not only a poetics, but a whole way of being, and that had a wide-ranging impact on the deportment of Spanish-language poets on both sides of the Atlantic.

Can such transcendental historical consequences be attributed to a mere conversation, even in the realm of literary history? The intellectual milieu of Charles V's Spain was clearly ripe for the sort of program proposed by Bembo, which included the study and imitation of the Greek and Latin classics. But Boscán's initiative cannot be discarded either. It was a watershed. So 1525, barely four years after Hernán Cortés conquered Mexico, must remain a significant date. In the most tangible and documentable way, however, the crucial date is 1543, when Ana

Girón de Rebolledo, Boscán's widow, published the poems of her late husband and his friend Garcilaso, himself killed in southern France while on active duty with the imperial army in 1536. By 1543 the Caribbean and Mexico had been largely settled, and the conquest of Peru was in full swing. The impact of Garcilaso's poetry after the 1543 book is as swift and pervasive as it is indisputable. By 1574 a notable Salamanca professor, Francisco Sánchez, "el Brocense" (1523–1601), published an annotated edition of Garcilaso's poetry, as if it were already a classic text. And in 1580 Fernando de Herrera, "el Divino" (1534–1597), a major poet himself, published his own edition of Garcilaso with *anotaciones* that constitute an influential statement on poetics and literary history. Sebastián de Córdoba, a minor poet, on the other hand, published in 1575 a "Garcilaso a lo divino," in which the Toledan's verses were given a religious cast, a rewriting which had a lasting impact on the great mystical poetry of the second half of the sixteenth century, namely that of St. John of the Cross (1542–1591). The Garcilaso fashion crossed the Atlantic at once, and shaped cultivated poetic activity in the viceregal capitals.

But Italianate or *culto* poetry is not the only one that highlights the period. Other important dates in the history of Spanish poetry of the sixteenth century are: 1511, publication in Valencia of Hernando de Castillo's *Cancionero general*; 1550, which saw the publication in Antwerp of the *Cancionero de romances*, reprinted in Antwerp again in 1555 and 1568, and in Lisbon in 1581; 1550–1551, when the *Silva de varios romances* was published in Zaragoza; 1584, publication in Seville of Lorenzo de Sepúlveda's *Cancionero de romances*; 1600–1601, printing of the *Romancero general*; 1516, date of the *Cancionero general*. The practice of compiling anthologies of this kind, often including cultivated poetry, was a common one throughout the period, and was also to influence poetic activity in the colonies. The *romances* in particular acquired a life of their own, both through the more typical oral transmission, as well as in printed *pliegos sueltos*, and spread to all corners of the colonial world. *Romanceros* were shipped often to the New World, as Leonard has shown (*Books of the Brave*), and *romances* were sung by Spanish musicians in viceregal courts, as well as recited by actors performing plays. Popular and cultivated poets, as they still do, wrote *romances*, and they had a strong influence on popular music, most notably the *corrido* (Simmons, *The Mexican Corrido, A Bibliography of the Romance*). As with most popular poetry, change, if any, is very slow, and beyond the date of publication of major anthologies at the outset of Spanish colonization, there is very little history to relate, except to distinguish thematic trends such as *romances* dealing with independence, or with specific figures such as Simón Bolívar (*Romancero colombiano*).

A question that immediately arises is whether there is a relationship between the ideals embodied in renaissance poetry, and the colonizing enterprise of the Spaniards, whether Garcilaso's courtly "tomando ora la pluma ora la espada" ["wielding now the pen, now the sword"] was an ideal held by the conquistadors. There is no doubt, particularly in the popularity of Renaissance-style epics, such as *La araucana* (1589–1590), and authors such as Alonso de Ercilla (1533–1594), that there is clear evidence of a commingling of poetic and martial activity. The same is true, though naturally in a less developed way, on the side of lyric poetry, as in the case of leaders such as Cortés, who is reputed to have written some poems. But the spirit that led Garcilaso, the ideal courtier, to give his life at Fréjus, was certainly alive among many conquistadors by the 1520s. Whereas the debate over the treatment of the natives of the New World clearly pitted renaissance and medieval conceptions of humanity against one another, and the mind-cast of many a historian was still scholastic, in poetry, renaissance ideas, concepts, attitudes, and forms prevailed. After the Conquest, the poets aspired to be courtiers, and were, indeed, in their own fashion in the highly formal atmosphere of the viceregal courts. The practice of government, from the highest posts held by viceroys, to the most menial bureaucratic ones, replaced the *espada*, in Garcilaso's felicitous phrase. Poets now brandished only the pen, but for two different purposes: government, including that of the church, and poetry.

Garcilaso's poetry, then, is the dividing line between medieval and modern lyric in Spanish. All the poets who make up the Spanish Golden Age – St. John of the Cross, Fray Luis de León, Fernando de Herrera, Lope de Vega, Luis de Góngora, Francisco de Quevedo, Sor Juana Inés de la Cruz, as well as countless others – are his followers, as is every poet since then in the Spanish language. The *cancioneros* and *romanceros* are the cultivated manifestation, preserved in print, of courtly and popular poetic forms respectively that enjoyed widespread familiarity among conquering Spaniards of all social classes. The *romances*, along with the minor forms of occasional love poetry represented in the printed *cancioneros*, survive to this day in Spanish America. Their presence in the eighteenth and nineteenth centuries, for instance, can be observed in investigations into Latin American culture of the magnitude of Alonso Carrió de la Vandera's *Lazarillo de ciegos caminantes* (1773), and Domingo Faustino Sarmiento's *Facundo* (1845). Cultured poetic forms, such as the sonnet and the *décima*, also survive at all levels of social life. From the time of Gutierre de Cetina (1514?–1557?) and Francisco de Terrazas (1525?–1600?) in Mexico, to Nicolás Guillén (1902–1988) and Severo Sarduy (1937–1993) in contemporary Cuba, and including the likes of the Nicaraguan Rubén Darío (1867–1916), who in his time also brought about a poetic revolution of his own, the sonnet, the *décima*, and the *romance*, continue to be the preferred metrical forms for poetic expression. Garcilaso's lyrical voice can still be heard in the love songs of the Chilean Pablo Neruda (1904–1973), and his most somber tones resonate in the anguished verses of the Peruvian César Vallejo (1892–1938). The colonial lyric is not an array of forgotten poetic forms only preserved in histories of literature, but is still the dynamic origin of modern Latin American poetry.

All this poetry came to the New World in the same galleons that brought firearms, Christianity, and horses, and its role in the make-up of the new society was as deep as it was durable. Because of this continuity it is somewhat misleading to speak of a history of Spanish lyric, if by this one means the uninterrupted chronicle of a series of substantial changes in poetic form, each one canceling out the previous one. There are changes, of course, in the poetry written in Spanish throughout the last 500 years, but since the sixteenth century, poetic form has varied but little in the language, except for the practice of free verse and the iconoclastic strophic arrangement introduced by the *Vanguardia* [Avant-Garde]. If they were alive today, Garcilaso and Góngora would find a sonnet by Nicolás Guillén odd because of its subject matter, and some of the figures, but they would recognize it as a familiar poetic form, used in a slightly different way. Vicente Espinel (1550–1624) would perhaps be surprised by the popularity of the *décima* he is purported to have perfected among popular poets, particularly in the Caribbean, but he would have no quarrel with their use of the exacting ten-line stanza.

The lack of an abrupt or radical change is due in part to the absence of a powerful romantic movement in Spanish, comparable to the ones in German, English, or even French poetry (Paz, *Children of the Mire*). The transformations that those poetic traditions underwent, beginning in the late eighteenth century, are comparable to that which the Spanish went through in the sixteenth and seventeenth centuries. Spanish reached the romantic period having already turned transgressions against form into tradition, and having incorporated popular poetry, lyric, and narrative, into its canon. This is perhaps the reason why the Baroque, which is but a variation of renaissance aesthetics, stands as the last truly significant violation of poetic norm in Spanish until the Avant-Garde, and also for the turn to the Baroque by modern poets in search of predecessors who had committed a substantial transgression. Hence the history of Spanish-language poetry, including particularly that poetry produced in the New World, does not fit comfortably into the patterns of literary history devised for English, German, French, or even Italian poetry. From the perspective of those traditions, Spanish-language poetry appears anachronistic, either late or ahead of its time. Hence a scheme appropriate to the dissemination of Spanish-language poetry must be devised, one that accounts for its own rhythm of transgression and continuity.

Such a scheme, at least for what is here called colonial lyric, would emphasize the preeminence of the Baroque as the first period in which a kind of mediated originality appears in the poetry written in the New World. In the most general terms, colonial lyric is part of Golden Age Spanish poetry, inasmuch as it shares with it not only poetic form but the core of themes typical of Garcilaso's version of Petrarchism and its consequences. The nationalism that led to and followed independence in Latin America provoked a series of polemics about the "Americanness" of various poets, like Gutierre de Cetina, Hernán González de Eslava, Francisco de Terrazas, and most notably the playwright Juan Ruiz de Alarcón, that today seem unproductive. I shall consider as American, hence as producers of colonial lyric, those poets who participated in what could be called the poetic activity of the colonies. Such activity involved not so much publishing in the New World, a rare occurrence indeed for poetic works, as the exchange of texts with other poets in the region, writing about them or with them in mind, and generally joining in the cultural life of the viceregal capitals. From the perspective of this textual exchange it is of little importance if a poet was born in Salamanca or Lima, if his or her activities were carried out in the New World. Juan de la Cueva, who was of Spanish birth, spent time in New Spain, and wrote poetry there, including an epistle containing a remarkable description of Mexico City that certainly enters into the kind of textual exchange suggested here (Capote, "La epístola quinta de Juan de la Cueva"). The same, but even more so, can be said of Gutierre de Cetina's poetic activity in Mexico, which had a great influence on Terrazas, González de Eslava, and others (Peña, "Poesía de circumstancias"). I use the adjective "colonial" here simply to indicate that all this poetic activity was carried out with a sense, sometimes vague, sometimes keen, of distance from the source, one that is not necessarily Spain, but Europe, and more specifically (classical) Rome.

By the seventeenth century these activities, and the cultural life of the viceroyalties in general, had attained enough autonomy to generate a thematic of estrangement that coincides and is consubstantial with the Baroque. In other words, viceregal societies felt distant from the metropolis, which it emulated, but also autonomous because of the increasing differences that were making them something new and distinct. The so-called "Barroco de Indias," which I will call Colonial Baroque for the same reasons stated above, issues from such preoccupations and the tropes that they generate: its centerpiece is the poetry of the last great Golden Age poet, the Mexican nun Juana Ramírez, known as Sor Juana Inés de la Cruz (1648–1695). But colonial lyric extends beyond the usual temporal boundaries of the Baroque, reaching into the eighteenth century to include, among others, the works of Pedro de Peralta Barnuevo (1664–1743). Poetic renewal did not really arrive in modern times until the towering figure of Venezuelan Andrés Bello (1781–1865) loomed on the horizon, and with him both the concerns of the Enlightenment and of Romanticism.

There was poetry, of course, in the New World before the arrival of the Europeans, much of it very difficult to account for because of the lack of writing among most pre-Columbian civilizations (see Ch. 1 above). However, what the conquistadors, but mostly the friars, collected, reveals, not surprisingly, the importance of poetry in most of those civilizations, particularly, but not exclusively, in connection with religious ritual. Non-European poetry continued to flourish after the arrival of the Europeans, both among the indigenous people of the New World, and among Africans brought to take their place as labor. Such poetry even continued to exist among the Europeans and their descendants, who incorporated it into their own, both for aesthetic and missionary purposes. Alfonso Méndez Plancarte helpfully notes that there is a tradition of poetry in indigenous languages beyond the Conquest, that such poetry

> was not totally muted by the cacophony of the Conquest, but spreads into Christian works, such as the Guadalupan *Cánticos* by the Azcapotzalcan don Francisco de Plácido (1535), attains an unexpected opulence in the wide-ranging poetico-missionary production by Fray Andrés de Olmos, Fray Juan Bautista and Fray Luis de Fuensalida (amongst many others) and acquires more literary resonances in the Nahuatl poems that alternated with those in Greek and Latin in the poetic contest of 1578, in the Aztec translations of plays by Lope, Calderón and Mira de Amescua during the seventeenth century, or in the *Villancicos* (also in Nahuatl) lovingly composed by the Tenth Muse (Sor Juana)
> (Méndez Plancarte, *Poetas novohispanos*, vi–vii)

Eventually, indigenous and African poetry became a part of the aesthetics of the rare and strange during the Baroque. It is not until the Avant-Garde in the 1920s that such poetry undergoes a revival in which a true effort to glean its own essence is made.

The first European poetry to be uttered in the New World was most probably that of the *romances*, surely known and recited by Columbus's sailors. It is clear from an often-cited passage in Bernal Díaz del Castillo's *Historia verdadera de la conquista de la Nueva España* (Chapter 36) that Hernán Cortés and his men invoked a *romance* at a propitious moment in the early stages of their campaign, and the Pizarros certainly used popular poetry to celebrate their triumphs and the Civil Wars of Peru. Garcilaso de la Vega el Inca remembers that, upon achieving victory, "Gonzalo Pizarro and his captains [...] organized many solemn festivities with bullfights and games of canes and the ring. Some wrote very good poems on these, and others maliciously satirized them. They were so satirical that though I remember some of them, I thought it better not to include them here."[1] In the Caribbean, *romance* forms were soon employed by Blacks in their songs, as in the case of Teodora Ginés, a free Black who lived in Cuba in the latter part of the sixteenth century, in her "Son de la Ma' Teodora." The dissemination of these Africanized popular poems must have been significant when they can be found already parodied in the poetry of Góngora and the theatre of Lope de Vega. Instances such as these reveal that Spanish popular poems were incorporated by those at the base of the social pyramid. Popular poetry of this kind continued and continues to exist today in rural and urban areas of Latin America, as well as in manifestations of popular culture such as the *bolero*, and most importantly, the Mexican *corrido* (Simmons, *The Mexican Corrido*). The *romance* was and is also practiced by cultivated poets, like Sor Juana, following the example of Spanish poets, and most prominently Góngora.

The new poetry introduced in Spain by Garcilaso was first cultivated in the New World, particularly New Spain (today's Mexico), by poets who were, for the most part, born in the peninsula. Among these the most notable was the Sevillian Gutierre de Cetina (1520–1557), whose place in the history of Spanish poetry is secure mostly because of his famous madrigal "Ojos claros, serenos...", but who was a well-known courtier, and the friend of influential poets like Diego Hurtado de Mendoza (1503–1575). Cetina was, in other words, an active agent in the development and spread of Italianate poetry, not only through his own writings, but through his literary connections. His activities in Mexico were no doubt instrumental in the adoption and practice of the new poetry. Cetina belonged to the Sevillian school of Italianate poetry, if the standard division of Spanish sixteenth-century poetry into two schools is followed: a northern one whose real or symbolic seat was Salamanca, and a southern one whose center was Seville. It would be reasonable to think that, given the sustained contact between Seville and the New World, it was the second school that most affected the transmission of the new poetry throughout the viceroyalties. The general style of this school, given to a heightened classicism, the cultivation of wit, and a whole code of conduct involving courtesy and linguistic polish, is very much in keeping with the atmosphere of the viceregal courts, first in New Spain, and later in New Castille (Peru). Creoles in these capitals were proud of their elegant discourse, fraught with a formulaic politeness and artificiality that became emblematic of their speech patterns, and has endured in the Spanish of Mexico (Schons, "The influence of Góngora on Mexican literature," 23).

---

[1] *Royal Commentaries of the Incas and General History of Peru. Part two*, trans. Harold V. Livermore, foreword Arnold J. Toynbee (Austin, University of Texas Press, 1966), II, p. 1011.

The clearest evidence of the literary relations between Seville and New Spain is *Flores de baria poesía*, an anthology compiled in Mexico City in 1577, whose manuscript was masterfully edited by Margarita Peña. This collection contains over 300 poems by more than 30 poets, nearly all from the Sevillian school. Among them are found Fernando de Herrera (1534?– 1597), Cetina, Baltazar del Alcázar (1530–1606), Juan de la Cueva (1543– 1610), Francisco de Figueroa (1536–1617?), Diego Hurtado de Mendoza, as well as several natives of New Spain, like Francisco de Terrazas (*c.* 1525–1600), Carlos de Sámano (no dates available), and, none other than Martín Cortés (1532–1589), son of the *Conquistador*.[2] The connection with the Sevillian school is evident in the poetry written by the first New-World-born poets, as well as by the quick turn to the Baroque that poetry took in the viceroyalties. It is a well-known fact of literary history that Fernando de Herrera and his followers in Seville, wrote in a poetic style that can already be seen as a transition to Góngora, himself a southerner from Córdoba, and other baroque poets, who were also from southern Spain.

Terraza's best known sonnet shows him to be not only one of the many disciples of Garcilaso, but a follower of the Sevillian school, because of the richness of his imagery, the complexity of the central conceit, and his penchant for the colorful:

> Dejad las hebras de oro ensortijado
> que el ánima me tienen enlazada,
> y volved a la nieve no pisada
> lo blanco de esas rosas matizado.
>
> Dejad las perlas y el coral preciado
> de que esa boca está tan adornada,
> y al cielo – de quien sois tan envidiada –
> volved los soles que le habéis robado.
>
> La gracia y discreción que muestra ha sido
> del gran saber del celestial maestro,
> volvédselo a la angélica natura;
>
> y todo aquesto así restituido,
> veréis que lo que os queda es propio vuestro:
> ser áspera, crüel, ingrata y dura.
>
> [Give back the golden curled threads
> in which my soul is entangled,
> and return to the unsullied snow
> the whiteness colored by those roses.
>
> Give back the pearls and coveted coral
> that so adorn that mouth,

---

[2] This is not the son Cortés had with Doña Mariana, but a legitimate one he had later and to whom he impartially gave the same name.

and to the heavens – who envy you so much –
return the two suns that you have stolen.

Return to angelic nature the grace and
discretion that have given proof of
the celestial master's great knowledge.

and having thus all that finally relinquished
you'll be left only with what is truly yours:
rancour, cruelty, ingratitude, and harshness.]

Terrazas's sonnet could not be more characteristic of Spanish renaissance poetry, and of the kind of poem that was being written in the colonies during the second half of the sixteenth century. For this reason it is, in fact, somewhat ordinary, though not lacking in wit. The shaping conceit, a pained lover's complaint to a beautiful, but hard, woman who spurns him, is right out of the courtly [*cancionero*] tradition. The lady's true self, which is characterized by harshness and disdain, is also quite in keeping with the conventions of the courtly tradition, in which women are nearly always inaccessible and cold. The second major conceit, that the lady has stolen from nature her various attributes is more in keeping with renaissance ideas. Nature appears as a perfect realm ordered by God, a vast machinery where He displays His Knowledge by making things not only beautiful, but in synchrony with each other. The more conventional elements appear in the description of the lady's face, where teeth are inevitably pearls, lips coral, and eyes suns. But it is in his predilection for the colorful and bright that Terrazas also shows his affinity to the Sevillian school, particularly to the poetry of Herrera, as already noted. Another conventionality is the rhythmic structure of the poem's unfolding, which is based on an escalation of repetitions leading to a resolution that is recollective and also cumulative.

A good example of the poetic milieu of the colonies in the late sixteenth century is the Academia Antártica, a group of poets living permanently or episodically in Lima, who organized themselves in the manner of the academies that had sprung up in Spain during the period. Some of the more notable academies had their seat in Seville, probably the source of the impulse behind the foundation of the Academia Antártica. Like its Sevillian counterparts, the Antártica "had a marked Italianate orientation because of the influence of poets from the Sevillian school, such as Avalos, born in Ecija, Mexía, Motesdoca, Hojeda, Gálvez, Duarte Fernández and others. Antonio Falcón himself, according to the anonymous voice of the *Discurso*, imitated Dante and Tasso. Some poets, on the other hand, took their inspiration from the Greek, as the "poetess" (of the *Discurso*) reveals in her praise of Gaspar de Villarroel, Luis Pérez Angel, and Cristóbal de Arriaga himself" (Cheesman, "Un poeta de la Academia Antártica," 344). The "poetess" alluded to here is the feminine voice in the *Discurso en loor de la poesía*, of uncertain authorship, but one of the most characteristic products of the Academia.

It does not matter if the Academia Antártica was really the University of San Marcos, as Cisneros claims, the point is that a group of Humanists and poets operated in Lima, sharing interests and texts (Cisneros, "Sobre literatura virreinal peruana," 227). Knowledge of poetic activity in the New World must have been widespread in the metropolis, at least among those attuned to the latest developments in literature. Evidence of this can be found in one, no less than Miguel de Cervantes's praise of American poets in his *Canto a Calíope*, included in his pastoral romance *Galatea*, written in 1583. Cervantes's long list of poets from the New World includes names from both New Spain and New Castille, and speaks eloquently of the intensity of literary activity in the colonies, as well as of the close relations among the viceroyalties and Spain itself.

The production from poets associated with the Academia Antártica is considerable. During this period, Miguel Cabello de Balboa finished his *Miscelánea antártica* (1586), Diego de Avalos y Figueroa published the *Miscelánea austral* (1602), and Diego de Mexía his *Parnaso antártico* (1608). The programmatic and anonymous *Discurso en loor de la poesía* (1608) is one of the most celebrated products of the Academia Antártica, and the riddle of its authorship remains as alluring as that of the identity of "Amarilis," the Peruvian poetess who wrote a long love epistle to Lope de Vega. Since the poetic voice of the *Discurso* is a woman, some have wondered if she was not really "Amarilis," but there seems to be no definitive proof and no consensus among scholars. In any case, both the *Discurso* and the "Epístola a Belardo" are redolent of the commonplaces of Spanish Petrarchism, and constitute evidence of the activities of the Academia Antártica, regardless of who wrote them. The *Discurso* betrays a great familiarity not only with the poetry, but with poetic theory, as Antonio Cornejo Polar details in the informative introduction to his fine edition of the poem (Cornejo Polar, *Discurso*).

But perhaps the most characteristic of poetic doctrine in late sixteenth-century poetry in the colonies is Mexía's *Parnaso antártico*. Even the bare bibliographic information provided by the title page of this entertaining volume is eloquent:

> *Primera parte del Parnaso Antártico, de obras amatorias, con las 21 Epístolas de Ovidio, i el in Ibin, en tercetos.* Dirigidas a do Iuám Villela, Oydor en la Chancillería de los Reyes [i.e. Lima]. Por Diego Mexia, natural de la ciudad de Sevilla; i residente en la de los Reyes, en los riquissimos Reinos del Piru. Año 1608. Con Privilegio; En Sevilla. Por Alfonso Rodríguez Gamarra.

There is also a kind of Antarctic emblem on the cover, whose motto is: "si Marte llevó a ocaso las dos colunas; Apolo llevó al antártico a las musas y al parnaso" ["If Mars bore the two columns [marking the end of the known world] off to the West; Apolo carried off the muses to Parnassus and to the Antarctic [the way in which Peru was known poetically]"]. The book not only contains Mexía's sedulous translation of Ovid, but a biography of the poet, as well as a very interesting story about the translator's travels through the burgeoning Spanish Empire ("El autor a sus amigos"). It is during his protracted meanderings that Mexía, to while away the time, began his translation of Ovid. Mexía's classicism, his Sevillian origins, and his contacts with Lima poets such as Pedro de Oña, mark him as a representative figure of colonial literary history. His choice of the difficult Ovid also makes him a transitional figure between renaissance and baroque poetry.

But Diego Dávalos de Figueroa's *Miscelánea Austral* is truly the fullest and most revealing product of renaissance poetic activity in Peru. Alicia de Colombí-Monguió says, in her magnificent study of Peruvian Petrarchism ("Las visiones de Petrarca"), that the *Miscelánea* was, "with the *Flores de Baria Poesía* compiled in Mexico, the most authentic document of American Petrarchism; unique, no doubt, in the Viceroyalty of Peru" (p. 11). She adds:

> The Colony had already been exposed to Enrique Garcés's Petrarchism, but the *Miscelánea austral* was quite a different thing. The volume is not a translation, but an original work, with poems embedded in a prose that runs copiously, and which must have seemed a true prodigy of refinement and learning. Lima turned out in unprecedented fashion to celebrate a work that was also without precedent. The men of letters are joined by a General, don Francisco de Córdova, an Admiral, don Lorenzo Fernández de Heredia, a government official such as don Diego de Carvajal, who was Correo Mayor de las Indias, Leonardo Ramírez Moreno de Almaraz, the "solemn religious man" already celebrated in *Arauco domado* as well as a good friend of Dávalos, and who also lived in La Paz, and by don Juan de Salcedo Villandrando, eulogized by Cervantes. A total of fifteen writers contribute to the front matter of the *Miscelánea*, making of it a true Parnassus of colonial Peru (compared to only three for Diego Mexía's volume and eight for Enrique Garcés's). (p. 87)

†Dávalos wrote all of his poetry and prose in Peru, where he married Francisca de Briviesca y Arellano, whom Colombí-Monguió believes was the author of the poems attributed to "Cilena," that is, the "poetess" of the *Defensa* mentioned before: "In this Peruvian Parnassus, the *Miscelánea austral*, woman is, without doubt, the best artificer" (p. 67). Colombí-Monguió proves beyond dispute that the *Miscelánea* is based on a Petrarchan model, not only in the poetry, but also in the *coloquios*, whose source is Renaissance Neo-Platonism. She demonstrates that Dávalos

imitated Petrarch or the Petrarchan model drawn from the *Canzonieri* also in his own life. With regard to the dialogic form, she rejects the Erasmian connection, claiming that it is an imitation of Ficino and León Hebreo. She also maintains that the work is a quilt of quotations drawn from Mario Equícola's *Libro de natura d'amore* (p. 103).

For all the poetic activity already present in the two principal colonies (the viceroyalties of New Spain and New Castille) during the sixteenth century, poetic production was for the most part ordinary; the work of pious imitators of Garcilaso, or even directly of his Italian sources, as well as much *poesía de ocasión* collected in *cancioneros*. One must add to this that a good part of the production also consisted of fairly uninspiring religious poetry, with the exception of González de Eslava's *Coloquios espirituales* and *Canciones divinas*, and the famous sonnet "A Cristo crucificado," whose authorship has been one of the more hotly debated issues in the scholarship. Distinctive, even original, lyric poetry really began in the New World at the end of the sixteenth century and beginning of the seventeenth, in what has been called the "Barroco de Indias."

This Colonial Baroque differed from its European counterpart mostly in the themes that it dealt with, and the contextual elements that it incorporated into the New World. But, as in Europe, it was essentially a variation of renaissance aesthetics. The change was mainly in the interpretation and practice of the theory of *imitatio* or imitation. Whereas in renaissance painting, architecture, and literature, there was a concerted effort to reproduce the symmetry, balance, harmony, and propriety of classical models, the Baroque exaggerated formal elements to the point where those features were severely threatened. Clearly, imitation went into crisis, made more acute in America by the representation of objects that lay outside the received register of the classical age, and by the growing feeling among American artists that they were something new, therefore not so severely bound by the doctrine of the imitation of models.

Some art historians claim that the convolutions of baroque form are also the result of a return to medieval features whose upward thrust, particularly in the Gothic, distorted the horizontal symmetries of classicism. In addition to this, the iconographic frenzy of the Gothic reappeared, based on a vast system of symbolic correspondences, and on the possibility of assimilating signs from variegated origins that clashed with each other. In Spain and its dominions the Council of Trent and its strategies to combat the Reformation not only fueled the religious spirit that led to this revival of the Medieval, but contributed to an art that had as its aim conversion and persuasion. Such a trend was destined to have a strong impact in the colonies, where the conversion of the native populations was still an important issue. As a result, the Baroque represented with persistent predilection a clash between the sensuality it inherited from the Renaissance, and the rejection of the tangible and worldly inspired by asceticism and militant religiosity. If anything, the Baroque was a style that reflected a crisis. It was through it that colonial society played out its own crisis of historical, cultural, and artistic identity.

The first important figure in this style is a poet also known for his accomplishments in the epic, Bernardo de Balbuena (1562–1627), whose *Grandeza mexicana* (Mexico, 1604) stands as the first significant American poem. It is an ambitious work both formally and thematically: a laudatory description of Mexico City, by then already rebuilt as a great metropolis, rivaling the capitals of Europe. Balbuena is on the threshold of the *Barroco de Indias*, a period that has gained in importance enormously in the past thirty or forty years because it has been seen by major modern writers like Alejo Carpentier (1904–1980), José Lezama Lima (1910–1977), Octavio Paz (b.1914), and Severo Sarduy, as their distant, yet powerful origin. This attention on the part of contemporary writers of such stature has given new currency to figures like Sor Juana Inés de la Cruz, and by extension others like Juan de Espinosa Medrano, *el Lunarejo*, and even Balbuena.

The crucial role the Baroque played in the cultural and artistic history of Latin America has been a gradual discovery, whose most distant origin is perhaps the revisionist reading of Góngora by the Generation of '27 poets in Spain. The restitution of Góngora to a high place in the history of Spanish poetry removed the taboo with which the Baroque had been seen since the Enlightenment. Previously the Baroque had been the epitome of bad taste, the embodiment of excess and lack of harmony, the antithesis of true art. From a romantic perspective it was viewed as decorative, external, superficial, and these prejudices were carried sometimes well into the twentieth century by followers of such romantic ideas, including Existentialists and some who claimed a Marxist perspective. For these, the Baroque seemed to have been an apology for Spain's Empire. From a Latin American perspective the Baroque offered a further distasteful element: it came to be associated, during the era of independence movements, with the period of Spanish domination. The Baroque was seen as a kind of dark age before the coming of Independence, a world dominated by religious fanaticism, the Inquisition, and the obsolete and oppressive political system on which the Spanish Empire was propped up. To rescue the Baroque from such anathema was no small task.

The first step was the discovery that, in architecture, the elaborate decoration of Spanish churches in the New World contained a surprising array of elements drawn from the very rich native iconography. Given that many of the artisans employed to build these churches were indigenous, their mental world and crafts imprinted on buildings figures that were alien to the European imagination. The most imposing symbol of this symbiosis, which took place literally from the bottom of the social pyramid up, is the imposing cathedral in Mexico City, built on the ruins of the major Aztec temple of Tenochtitlán. But the visible presence of indigenous iconography was everywhere, in New Spain as well as in New Castille. Mixture, contamination, became the very emblem of the Baroque, and as such a possible expression of unease, subversion, and movement toward change. The possibility of such a combination of Christian and "pagan" icons opened a gap between the cultures involved and their representation in various codes, including the literary. The bond between belief and representation had to loosen up a little to accept elements from an alien code, which, itself, had been displaced in the process from its own relationship with a referential world. If the syncretic process observable in the religious sphere – no matter how slight, or how dominated still by a Catholic vision – required a certain amount of tolerance in the acceptance of alien beliefs and icons, the same, only more so was true in the artistic realm. Once the insidiousness of this process of mutual contamination in the fabric of colonial society was observed, the Baroque came to symbolize the Americanization of culture in the New World, even in its most apparently European manifestations, such as the viceregal courts. Baroque society was, by its very exaggerated "bad taste," the acme of a mixed society, where elements of disparate and even inimical worlds coexisted to shape a new conception of beauty. This beauty was now seen to be made up of precisely those elements for which the Baroque had been anathematized before: artificiality, excess, superficiality, and disharmony.

The artificiality of the Baroque, really its artfulness, is the result of the uneasy relationship between representation and that which is being represented or expressed. The most common device to express this break is accumulation, where the piling up of various elements replaces appositeness or propriety, and where the play of diversity takes the place of harmony. An Incaic demon-like figure with bulging eyes cannot really be part of the decoration of a Christian church, if religious or artistic doctrine are pressed to the limit. The systems of belief from which the figure and the surrounding Christian ones evolve are not easily harmonized, as was painfully clear to the Indians in many instances. Yet, in the realm of art, they can share the same cultural space. Belief or theological cogency is no longer at the center, leaving a gap that is filled with the proliferation of figures. As the seventeenth century progresses, this commingling of mythologies, this survival of pagan gods in the same space with the Christian one, may very well lead to the Enlightenment, instead of impeding it.[3] The proliferation of gods may have contributed to their collective demise as purveyors of truth, including, of course, the hegemo-

[3] Jean Seznec, *The Survival of the Pagan Gods. The mythological tradition and its place in renaissance Humanism and art* (New York, The Bollingen Series, 1953; French original, 1940).

nic one. Ritual turned play could be the harbinger of philosophical doubt and worldly self-assertion on the part of Creoles who were at once far from God and the metropolis.

The second step in the vindication of the Baroque was the discovery that by questioning the central renaissance doctrine of *imitatio* it opened the possibility of the new, not only at the level of art, but also at the political, social, and ontological levels. At its most elemental, the theory of imitation meant the imitation of classical models, but later the imitation of those imitators, above all Petrarch. Was Góngora taking the doctrine of imitation to the limit by mimicking the very syntax of Latin in his Spanish poems, or was he breaking altogether or at least significantly from it? The Baroque widened the space between the model and the new creation, between the European and the American. This was heightened in the case of the Colonial Baroque because of a redoubled feeling of distance. The feeling of exile, of being out of place and time, meaning Rome and the classical period, making necessary to recapture them what Thomas M. Greene has called the humanist hermeneutic, had to be felt with greater force by American poets.[4] Rome was faraway in time, but truly remote in space. This is the point of departure for the Baroque, which makes of the necessary bridge, of the mediation, its own essence. Writers of the Colonial Baroque thus reveled in American artificiality. It is what made them distinct.

Apologists of the Baroque have also seen in the proliferation of gods, and in the incorporation of a cornucopia of American products, a clear break with renaissance aesthetics, brought about by the difference inherent in what was represented. It was not the same to paint or describe a European landscape, with its flora and fauna predictable in shape and color, and an American one, full of strange animals, plants, and, particularly, fruit. The Baroque has come to be seen as an aesthetics of the strange, of the rare, representing what was new in the New World, including the people. To Lezama Lima the *señor barroco* [the baroque gentleman] was someone already at ease within his new realm, possessed of the self-assurance of being unique (Lezama Lima, *La expresión americana*). The American artist was the most strange of creatures, his practice of *imitatio* bordered on being a parody rather than a copy of earlier models. Paz sees the Creole as his own most elaborate and baroque self-creation (Paz, *Sor Juana Inés de la Cruz*). Hence in the battles over Góngora that raged in Spain, creole society sided with Góngora and consumed his poetic products with an avid appetite. It found in the Cordoban's complicated verses a mirror to reflect its own complexity. In this sense, the Colonial Baroque exemplified a quest for knowledge, one

[4] Thomas M. Greene, *The Light in Troy. Imitation and discovery in renaissance poetry* (New Haven, Yale University Press, 1982), pp. 81–103.

that may seem hopeless to us today given the philosophical and literary instruments available, but one that nevertheless examined the essence of being colonial.

An important element of the complexity of Creoles was a heightened sense of self-parody and criticism, a satirical vein that provided an inverted image of the pretentious and artificial colonial society. This kind of self-reflexiveness mirrored that of the spaces within which colonial lyric was produced. Viceregal cities, with their vast plazas, official palaces, churches and mansions, were designed for representation, not for life. Social pretension was tempting to Creoles, far from their places of origin, where family histories were known and verifications could be made. Suddenly enriched men and women of uncertain lineage covered their past with lavishness and a frenzy of pomp. Colonial life became a theatrical society, for which the liturgical splendor of the church and the elaborate rituals of the state and its immense bureaucratic apparatus provided the model. Viceregal society could be more pompous than the Spanish court itself, which it was supposed to represent. The distance between pretension and the foibles of human life, between ornate representation and its often tawdry object, was exploited by satirists of varying talent and accomplishment. Social satire became a constant in colonial literature.

Juan del Valle y Caviedes (1651–1697) is the most exalted exponent of this trend, but he had a precursor in Mateo Rosas de Oquendo (1559?–1621), a Spanish-born traveler and observer who spent time in Tucuman and Lima. The discovery and intense exploitation of silver mines in New Castille, particularly in Potosí, had turned Lima into a bustling city which could boast not only of literary academies, but of ample opportunities for extravagant expenditure and the pursuit of sin. Rosas de Oquendo's *Sátira hecha por Mateo Rosas de Oquendo a las cosas que pasan en el Pirú año de 1598*, recently authoritatively edited by Pedro Lasarte, is a counterpart to Balbuena's *Grandeza mexicana*, written at about the same time. Where Balbuena lauds, Rosas de Oquendo deprecates. His *romance*, over 2,000 lines in length, exploits the usual ambiguity of satire: to criticize, yet to revel in the negative aspects of the object of criticism. As can be expected, Rosas de Oquendo focused primarily on the sexual mores of the women, but also of the men, of Lima, a topic that allows him to show off his wit and ability to play with the amphibological possibilities of the language of love. The poem is full of fake virgins, cunning adulteresses, cuckolded husbands, pimps, whores, cardsharps, and *pícaros*. Their deceitful activities are matched by the poem itself, which may ostensibly be depicting a card game, while indirectly alluding to the most lewd sexual acts. Or, it may even turn what appears to be a geographical allusion into a contrast between anal and vaginal intercourse by exploiting the resonances of the names of the ports of Panama and Buenos Aires, as Lasarte has shown. In its best moments, the *Sátira* reminds one of Spanish medieval masterpieces like *Celestina* and the *Libro de buen amor*, as well as countless medieval poems like the *Coplas de Mingo Revulgo* and the *Coplas de ¡Ay Panadera!* This medieval aspect, accentuated by the *romance* meter, is part and parcel of the Baroque's renewed emphasis on the difference between seeming and being, the fragility of the material world, and the impossibility of distinguishing between the transient and the eternal, the apparent and the real (Gilman, "An introduction to the ideology of the Baroque in Spain"). The trend reaches its unsurpassed apogee, of course, in the poetry of Quevedo, and its ascetic undertone will find echoes in later colonial poets like Hernando Domínguez Camargo (1606–1656), and, in a religious vein, Matías de Bocanegra (1612–1668). In prose, Juan Rodríguez Freyle's *El Carnero* (Bogotá, 1636) is the best known exemplar. In verse, however, Caviedes, is Rosas de Oquendo's most direct and successful heir in America.

But Rosas de Oquendo's, for all its wit, was a minor poem. This is not the case with Bernardo de Balbuena's ambitious *Grandeza mexicana* (1604), the first true major American poem. Born in Valdepeñas, Spain, around 1562, Balbuena pursued a religious career that took him, after prolonged sojourns in various parts of the New World, to the bishopric of Jamaica, and later to Puerto Rico, where he died. But his aspiration seems always to have been the great city of Mexico, where he spent comparatively little time. He did squander some years in provincial Mexican towns, like Culiacán, an experience that he did not relish. The viceregal capitals were the magnet for all social, religious, or literary hopefuls. Balbuena was an elegant, though scant lyricist, who wrote a few good sonnets (Entrambasaguas, "Los sonetos de Bernardo de Balbuena"). But if his production in the lyric was not copious, even counting *Grandeza mexicana*, his *El Bernando o victoria de Roncesvalles* (1624) was a huge achievement, and his pastoral romance *Siglo de Oro en las selvas de Irífile* (1608) one of the highpoints of the genre in Spanish. José Carlos González Boixo has recently published excellent editions of *Grandeza* and *Siglo de Oro*, which, together with earlier work by Alfredo Roggiano ("Instalación del barroco hispánico en América") and Angel Rama ("Fundación del manierismo hispanoamericano"), are giving Balbuena the important place he deserves in the history of Latin American literature.

Grandeza mexicana's central conceit plays precisely upon the heterogeneity of the New World, and thus it is the first expression of a dominant topic in Latin American literature: the equivalence of all cultures, and the celebration of their commingling in America. This will be one of the chief concerns of Garcilaso de la Vega, el Inca (1539–1616), and will inform the theories of modern writers like Carpentier and Lezama Lima. Balbuena praises Mexico City because it is at the center of the world, a position it holds not because of tradition or any kind of inherited superiority, but because in Mexico City all the important cultures of the world meet, impelled by a craving for economic well-being:

> México al mundo por igual divide,
> y como a un sol la tierra se le inclina
> y en toda ella parece que preside.
> [...]
> Con todos se contrata y se cartea;
> y a sus tiendas, bodegas y almacenes
> lo mejor destos mundos acarrea

> [Mexico divides the world in equal parts,
> the earth bows to it as if were a sun,
> and it seems to rule over the whole orb.
> [...]
> It [Mexico] trades and corresponds with all of them,
> and its stores, warehouses, and cellars
> hold the best that all those worlds can offer]

The ties of commerce, of greed turned to good purpose, bring to Mexico City a cornucopia of products whose accumulation provokes a kind of Baroque sublime, expressed through repeated enumerations:

> La plata del Pirú, de Chile el oro
> viene a parar aquí y de Terrenate
> clavo fino y canela de Tidoro.

> De Cambray telas, de Quinsay rescate,
> de Sicilia coral, de Siria nardo,
> de Arabia incienso, y de Ormuz granate;

> diamantes de la India, y del gallardo
> Scita balajes y esmeraldas finas,
> de Goa marfil, de Siam ébano pardo;
> [...]
> al fin, del mundo lo mejor, la nata
> de cuanto se conoce y se practica,
> aquí se bulle, vende y se barata.

> [Peruvian silver and Chilean gold
> wind up here, as do, from Terrenate,
> fine cloves and Tidorean cinnamon.

> From Cambray come fabrics, wealth from Quinsay,
> coral from Sicily, from Siria aromatic nard,
> incense from Arabia, and garnet from Ormuz;

> diamonds from India, and from the noble
> Scythia rubies and fine emeralds,
> from Goa ivory, from Siam dark ebony;
> [...]

in short, the best from the whole world,
the pick of all that's known and practiced,
swarms here, to be sold and bartered.]

These "verbal catalogues," as Leonard called them (*Baroque Times in Old Mexico*, 66), do provide, in spite of their deliberate artificiality, an authentic image of Mexico City. Leonard writes in his classic work: "As a halfway station between Europe and the Far East, and a point of convergence of the trade with outlying provinces of New Spain, including Guatemala, Yucatan, Tabasco, Nueva Galicia, Nueva Viscaya, and others, Mexico City was an emporium of the most assorted goods, from the fine laces and textiles of Europe to the silks and chinaware of Asia, and from the exotic fruits and herbs of the provinces to the expertly wrought handicrafts of its own artisans" (p. 76). Abundance of attributes furnish substance in the world of *Grandeza mexicana*, a world deliberately made up, precisely, by the products of artifice. Art, industry, and craft, define each place and culture, in the same way that the poem itself is the result of art. *Grandeza mexicana* is a tribute to the artificial, to the artful, and the artful's most elaborate product is the city.

This mirroring betwixt city and art, each the product of the other, is reflected in the very elaborate structure of the poem. *Grandeza mexicana* appears as a letter that Bachiller Bernardo de Balbuena writes to the lady Doña Isabel de Tobar y Guzmán, "describiendo la famosa ciudad de México y sus grandezas" ["describing famous Mexico City and its greatness"]. The "letter," that is to say, the poem, is preceded by an *octava real* that tells its "argumento" or subject matter. The *octava*'s eight hendecasyllables, in their sequence, become the titles of the poem's eight cantos and determine its arrangement. *Grandeza mexicana*, then, is built upon a poem; in fact, technically it is a gloss, a play between the discrete *octava* and the potentially unending *Grandeza*. The text of the poem is made up of reflections, of attributes, like the products of the city, and the city itself. It is representation to the second power. The curious dialectic between movement and stasis is rendered by the clash between the tercets in which the poem is written, which are typical of narrative poetry, and its dominant descriptive mode. Such a contrivance, like all the elements of *Grandeza mexicana*, is accounted for by its own self-description as a cipher. The last hendecasyllable of the opening *octava* reads "todo en este discurso está cifrado" ["everything is encoded in this discourse"].

Cifrado means encoded, but also encrypted. Balbuena, as Rama has noted ("Fundación," 18), creates a scaled-down model, an emblem, small yet paradoxically designed to contain all, a kind of Aleph. Such a process also proclaims the autonomy and self-containment of his creation. But *cifrado* suggests much more. As inscription, it refers to a hidden, encrypted meaning, that proclaims poetry to be an enigmatic language defying ordinary reading. Reading has to appeal to the poem's own self-reflection, not to an outside referent, and its ultimate meaning has to be difficult. The mystery here has to do perhaps with the etymological meaning of *cifra*, which is "figure," in the mathematical sense, and in the original Arabic "zero" or "emptiness." Given Balbuena's penchant for enumeration, *cifrado* may very well mean here "subordinated to a numerological scheme beyond our grasp." The essence of Mexico City's greatness is inscribed in the poem in enigmatic signs whose materiality we can perceive, as we do the streets of a city, but in whose labyrinthine arrangement we are lost. Here Balbuena juggles the infinitesimal and the infinite, the contingent and the eternal. As Gilman writes in "An introduction to the ideology of the Baroque in Spain": "the infinite is continually applied to the finite in order that the latter may suffer by contrast. But the process does not destroy; it distorts... The resultant distortion naturally takes place in the horizon-bound perceptive world, in the relativity of time and space. When contrasted to the absolute, time undergoes rapid acceleration and space is foreshortened, becoming confused and illusory" (p. 93). "Grandeza" means "greatness," but also immensity, and "incommensurateness." The piling up of attributes from various cultures yields a confused identity, made up of superficial qualities whose aggregate is beautiful truly beyond description and comprehension. This projection of the New World to an incommensurate aesthetic realm, and this postponement of understanding and self-understanding are emblematic of a baroque self. It is a self distinguishable by its strangeness, by its monstrosity, in the sense of being spectacular and made up of disparate, contrasting elements that cause admiration (González Echevarría, "El 'monstruo de una especie y otra'").

But Balbuena was a strict contemporary of Góngora, hence his style is more a parallel development than an imitation. Besides, for all the splendor of his descriptions of Mexico City, and for all the complexity of *Grandeza mexicana*'s design, the poem is tame in comparison with the metaphoric, neologistic, and rhetorical complications of Góngora's major poems, the *Fábula de Polifemo y Galatea*, and the *Soledades*. This is not the case of the poets that follow Balbuena, for Gongorism in all its force will be the prevailing style in colonial poetry for over a century, as well as the object of protracted polemics. In addition to the reasons given above, Góngora's linguistic refinements fell on fertile ground, for as stated before, Creoles had developed a taste for such a manner in their speech. As Schons ("The influence of Góngora") and Leonard (*Books of the Brave, Baroque Times*) report, Góngora's works figure decisively in book shipments to the New World, and it is likely that, as in Spain, his poems circulated in manuscript form in the New World before their publication. What is beyond dispute is that Gongorism became the rage among New

World poets (Carilla, *El gongorismo en América*). Gongorism was a style, according to Alan S. Trueblood,

> steeped in the by now very familiar cultural idiom inherited from antiquity and enlarged upon by the Renaissance, whose points of reference are Greco-Roman myth, history, legend, and law, variously updated; commonplaces of philosophy and Ptolemaic cosmology; rarities of natural history and varied spoils of other branches of learning, all often applied more decoratively than organically. Glitter is added by imagery in which values placed on persons, objects and feelings are underscored by the munificence or refinement of their metaphorical equivalents: precious metals and stones, splendid fabrics and materials, rare fragrances, the ever-present rose and rarer blooms, peacocks, phoenixes, and nightingales, often with inherent symbolic significance. Precisely because of the familiarity of this idiom, a premium is placed on novelty and ingenuity in its handling. Wit expressed in conceit, wordplay which startles and diverts by unexpected couplings of terms usually far apart or belonging to different orders of phenomena, is the fundamental figure of thought. Paradox, antithesis, hyperbole, and periphrasis are constant props. Patterns of scholastic logic, parallelisms, inversions, plain or incremental repetitions, are favorite ways of disposing concept syntactically. Governing all is a rhetorical tendency that highly prizes ingenuity in unraveling variant expressions of an unvarying conceit.
>
> (*A Sor Juana Anthology*, 11)

An excellent example of this is the work by Bogotá-born Jesuit Hernando Domínguez Camargo, the author of an epic *Poema heróico de San Ignacio de Loyola*, which provoked the admiration of Gerardo Diego, one of the Generation of '27 Spanish poets who revived interest in the works of Góngora (Diego, "La poesía de Hernando Domínguez Camargo").

In many instances Domínguez Camargo's poetry is a barely disguised pastiche of Góngora's, as was that of many of his contemporaries in the New World. But Diego and more recent admirers found in him an unrestrained sensuality, particularly in the description of succulent dishes, an unrepentant pleasure in creating verbal beauty, that made him akin to modern practitioners of pure poetry.

But the *Poema heróico* has few readers today, and Domínguez Camargo is mostly celebrated by a relatively brief poem that displays all of the features of the Gongorist style mentioned in Trueblood's quotation. This is the *romance* "A un salto por donde se despeña el arroyo de Chillo," a poem whose sustained metaphor is that of the river as a bolting horse, which ultimately crashes as it leaps (*salto* meaning both leap and a waterfall), against some rocks. A cornucopia of poetic devises, from alliteration ("Corre arrogante un arroyo") and synesthesia ("da cristalinos relinchos") to the most elaborate metaphoric linking, the *romance* is a poetic *tour de force*, almost a boast of skill.

Estrellas suda de aljófar
en que se suda a sí mismo,
y atropellando sus olas,
da cristalinos relinchos.
Bufando cogollos de agua,
desbocado corre el río,
tan colérico que arroja
a los jinetes alisos.

[It sweats stars like pearly drops of dew,
through which it sweats itself,
and jostling its own waves,
utters limpid neighs.
Snorting water shoots,
the river bolts and runs
with such a rage that it throws
the riding alders.]

The most significant line here is "en que se suda a sí mismo" ["through which it sweats itself"], for it reveals the core of the baroque machinery of tropes. If the river is a horse, then when it sweats, it cannot but sweat itself, for it is made of water. This means that, though the river is metaphorically turned into a horse, it does not cease having the qualities of a river. There is a porosity between realms, as it were, a continuity and lack of boundaries among substances once they have been transformed by metaphor. This simultaneity also pertains to the meaning of the poem. At the end, the river-horse's headlong crash onto rocks, a horrible event that strews the animal's brains about, is metamorphosed into beauty, like Polyphemus becoming a river once he is crushed: "vertiendo sesos de perlas,/ por entre adelfas y pinos" ["pouring out brains like pearls/ among oleanders and pines"]. But, at the same time, the *romance* contains a moral that, retrospectively makes it allegorical:

Escarmiento es de arroyuelos
que se alteran fugitivos,
porque así amansan las peñas
a los potros cristalinos.

[This is a warning for brooks
that turn furious as they flee,
because this is how rocks
tame translucent steeds.]

Throughout the poem several adjectives describe the river-horse's rushing in moral terms: it is *arrogante* and *colérico*. The last lines bind these into a moral allegory: to lose self-control, to rush blindly through life, may have dire consequences. This meaning is perfectly unambiguous, even while at the same time the reader feels that without the loss of control there could not have been such a splendid display of beauty, one that, like the exhibition of skill involved in writing the poem, causes *admiración*, one of the effects sought by baroque art.

In Mexico, another Jesuit, Matías de Bocanegra (1612–1668), wrote a poem that became part of the canon of the Colonial Baroque, "Canción a la vista de un desengaño." It is one of the most imitated and anthologized pieces in the period, as well as later (Colombí-Monguió, "La 'Canción famosa a un desengaño'"). Written mostly in *liras*, save at the end where it becomes a *romance*, the "Canción" issues from a literary tradition that goes back to Petrarch's *Canzone delle visioni*, through Fray Luis de León, Quevedo, and other Spanish poets of the seventeenth century (Colombí-Monguió, "El poema del padre Matías de Bocanegra"). Bocanegra, the author of a play derived from Calderón, *Comedia de San Francisco de Borja*, writes what is essentially a narrative poem. In the "Canción," a troubled priest finds a garden, the topical *locus amoenus*, where he tries to alleviate his anxieties. These, which manifest themselves as an inchoate yearning for freedom, have a vaguely erotic origin. The priest, it seems, is troubled by a love that his calling denies him. In the evocative garden, the cleric nearly decides to give up the cloth when he witnesses a horrible scene. A goldfinch whose song he has been enjoying is suddenly killed by a falcon that swoops down from above. The fate of the goldfinch's short-lived enjoyment of freedom and the pursuit of beauty makes the religious man take stock of the fleetingness of earthly life and he gives up his plan to escape his condition. The ascetic element of baroque ideology, as seen in Gilman, underlies this somber ending, where the real is mere appearance or contingency in a fragile world cast against the permanence of infinity.

Bocanegra, like Domínguez Camargo, is a derivative poet, whose borrowings from the entire baroque tradition are obvious, to the point where Colombí-Monguió calls his poem "nearly a compendium of the commonplaces of our baroque lyric" ("El poema," 13). The most obvious source is Calderón, not only in the part of the "Canción" that is a pastiche of Segismundo's famous soliloquy in *Life is a Dream*, but in the entire metaphoric and allegorical cast of the poem. Calderón's popularity in the Spanish Indies was only second to Góngora's, and perhaps greater if one takes into account that in theatrical performances his verses were recited before large audiences including people from all social classes (Hesse, "Calderón's popularity"). To the tropological richness of Góngora Calderón added a cosmic vision, a metaphoric universe that expressed, through the received scientific and theological notions of the time, a truly all-encompassing concept of creation. This conception not only embraced the whole of history, from Genesis to the present, but the very material make-up of the universe, from stars to rocks, from flowers to clouds, from dew drops to pearls. Every instance of human existence was connected to this vast universe, whether it be through actions that repeat historic designs, or through the material composition of the body. Edward M.

Wilson has shown, in a classic article on "The four elements in the imagery of Calderón," how these, represented by their characteristics (heat = fire), or by creatures (bird = air) or things that belong to them (flower = earth), an ordered or disordered universe. When birds are haughty they may soar so high that they become fire (lightning) as they leave their normal sphere (air); flowers on very high mountains turn to stars. The combination of elements, sub-elements, and creatures is nearly infinite, and not as mechanical as it may seem. It gives Gongorist poetics a meaningful, if wholly artificial universe of allusions that make stories possible and comprehensible. Bocanegra, as Domínguez Camargo had in a lesser way in his *romance*, adopts this cosmologico-tropological scheme for his poem. It is one that endures and informs the poetics of Sor Juana Inés de la Cruz, as well as that of countless minor poets (there was no shortage of these, as Leonard has shown in his landmark study *Baroque Times in Old Mexico*).

It is difficult from a modern perspective to imagine how this combination of outdated science, mythology, and penchant for the turgid and obscure could conceivably be affiliated with a quest for knowledge, but underlying all the convolutions of the Colonial Baroque there is an urge to know, as Paz (*Sor Juana Inés de la Cruz*) and Arrom (*Esquema generacional de las letras hispanoamericanas*) have asserted. I would add that the passion is really to self-knowledge and definition. The self-reflexiveness of Gongorist poetry, the admixture of elements from competing cultural systems, the absence of a central, defining essence, are all motivations for this desire to know. The rarity of the baroque self is what begins to give the Creole a sense of how he is separated from nature and tradition, where the perimeter lay between his self and the Other. Lezama Lima (*La expresión americana*) expresses this in a characteristically oracular definition of the above-mentioned *señor barroco*:

> That American baroque gentleman, the first to be authentically established in what is ours [...] is the man who comes to look out of the window, who carefully sorts out the sand in front of the devouring mirror, who stands near the lunar cascade built in the dream of his own self-belonging. When he enjoys language, it braids itself and multiplies, savoring his life becomes rushed and fervent. Living has become for him like a subtle ear, which from the corner of the salon untangles the imbroglios and scrambles the simple fallen leaves.   (pp. 32–3)

The "subtle ear" that can untangle imbroglios and make the simple difficult characterizes the major writers of the Colonial Baroque, Juan de Espinosa Medrano, the *Lunarejo*, Juan del Valle y Caviedes, Carlos de Sigüenza y Góngora, and Sor Juana Inés de la Cruz, all motivated by the passion to know. It also identifies Juan del Valle y Caviedes, the major satirist of the period, and an important poet himself.

Lunarejo, so called because of a prominent birthmark on his face, was not a poet. But the "Sublime Doctor," as he was also known, was a theoretician of Gongorist poetics, as well as a major baroque preacher. A now outdated critical tradition had wrought an Indianist fable around the figure of Espinosa Medrano, who was supposed to be a pathetic *mestizo* autodidact. Recent research has uncovered that there is no reason to believe that he was an Indian, and much that suggests that he was in fact a man of some financial substance, much like Lezama Lima's *señor barroco* (Cisneros and Guibovich Pérez, "Juan de Espinosa Medrano"). Espinosa Medrano's erudition was prodigious, and his wit and verbal capacity phenomenal. *Lunarejo*'s sermons were posthumously collected by his followers in a volume entitled *La Novena Marauilla Nvebamente Hallada en los Panegíricos Sagrados que en varias Festividades dijo el Sor Arcediano Dor D. IVAN de Espinosa Medrano* (Valladolid, 1699). But Espinosa Medrano is known primarily for his *Apologético en favor de Don Luis de Góngora príncipe de los poetas lyricos de España* (Lima, 1662), a polemic against Manuel de Faria, one of Góngora's many detractors, who had written half a century before. The *Apologético* is a manifesto of baroque American poetics from quite a modern perspective. *Lunarejo* defends Góngora's right to allow his poetry to be complicated and devoid of transcendental meanings because, he contends, Góngora's poetry is erotic in theme, not religious or epic. Through appropriately convoluted arguments, Espinosa Medrano denies that Góngora's poetry is fraught with hyperbatons, and celebrates the artificiality of poetic language. But *Lunarejo* goes even further, proclaiming that Góngora is better than the ancients in some ways, that his *Fábula de Polifemo y Galatea* is a better treatment of the subject than Homer's and Ovid's. If Góngora can surpass the models of renaissance poetics, then there is a space for the emergence of the new, which for Espinosa Medrano means that American poets from his remote Peru can also have a place in history. The polemic against Faria, an obscure Portuguese defender of Camões, is a pretext to mount his defense of an American poetics, but an important one because *Lunarejo*'s own text is necessarily built upon that erased text of Faria's. This is an important feature of its own baroque poetics, of its own "monstrosity," as defined before. This characteristic is even more prominent bearing in mind that there is a kind of cypher in the *Apologético*, a hidden key to its own make-up. The very first chapter of the *Apologético* opens with an allusion to an Alciato emblem depicting a dog barking at the moon. The ostensible meaning is that those who criticize the magnificent Góngora are like the dog, barking uselessly at a much greater star. But one soon discovers that there is a complex, self-referential game of allusion involving *Lunarejo*'s own alias (*luna* in Spanish means moon, *lunar* birthmark), as well as that which distinguished Peru: silver, the color of moonlight. This game also includes the proclamation of American poetics, for the moon is the celestial body known for its reflected light, in the way that Peruvian poets would reflect European poetry. There may even be an allusion to madness, with which the moon is associated, and poetic inspiration (González Echevarría, "Poética y modernidad en Juan de Espinosa Medrano"). Be that as it may, the *Apologético* is not only about baroque poetics, but is itself an example of those poetics in actual practice.

The modernity of *Lunarejo*'s formulation and the actual composition of the *Apologético* is found in his insistence on the metaphoric essence of poetry, its detachment from given meanings, and its right to a kind of obscurity and complexity with no apparent end other than pleasure or beauty. If the given meanings and themes of the European tradition, the classics that the Renaissance imitated, were not sacrosanct, if others could be found (as Góngora did in his *Soledades*, whose story is not based on any previous model), then the new, the American, the strange and rare being that was the Creole could have an essence based on its own eccentricity. *Lunarejo* makes of his own physical deformity, his *lunar*, the emblem of such eccentricity, availing himself of a common baroque conceit: the body as sign. This investigation of poetics, knowledge, and self-knowledge is fundamental to the Colonial Baroque.

At roughly the same time and in the same Viceroyalty of New Castille, a Spanish-born shopkeeper, Juan del Valle y Caviedes (1645–1697), obsessed with the body's deformities and dysfunctions, wrote his caustic poetry and theatre. His works remained forgotten in dusty colonial archives until 1873, when they were rediscovered and published by Manuel de Odriozola and Ricardo Palma. He was touted by these originators of nationalist mythologies as the first *criollista*, or propounder of creole autonomy, and, because he depicted American realities, as one of the first American poets. An all too literal reading of his poetry also led to a critical fable about his life as a syphilitic, impoverished, and resentful misanthropist. Many of what were believed to be the facts about Caviedes's life are now questioned, and a less literal reading of his works is revealing a more versatile poet, with a broader range of themes and poetic technique.

But Caviedes's fame will rest on *Diente del Parnaso*, the collection of forty-seven poems Palma and Odriozola published in 1873. These are, for the most part, satirical, indulging in a blunt, often vulgar language, and focused on the foibles of doctors, which gave Caviedes the chance to gratify his predilection for the body and its fluids. A follower of Quevedo, and an heir to Rosas de Oquendo, Caviedes is the symmetrical counterpart of poets in the Petrarchan tradition who idealized the body, particularly of the woman, and who conceived the human in terms of abstract desires and transcendental aspirations. His is the ascetic side of the Baroque, bent on displaying the fragility of life, and the tawdriness of this world. But, as in Rosas de Oquendo and the medieval tradition behind this kind of literary manner, Caviedes relishes the vulgar and the physical too much to be a convincing censor. In his poetry the squalid is idealized as in a kind of countercult. Caviedes is a poet who transgresses all boundaries of repugnance and revulsion in his depiction of humanity. As Frederick Luciani puts it, his is "a pornographic wit" (Luciani, "Juan del Valle y Caviedes," 337). It is this sadistic and even masochistic side that makes him attractive and modern. Like the *Lunarejo* Caviedes seems to have found the boundary of meaning in his own body, and the body's "expressions" to be no more than urine, feces, and pus.

The "interpreters" of those "expressions" were the hapless doctors of the time, depicted by Caviedes, much as Molière did in France, as quacks. It has been a topic in Caviedes criticism to see his portrayal of doctors as merely social satire, perhaps even as an allegory of society's ills. But Caviedes is a much more interesting poet than that. His relentless critique of doctors is really a broader critique of scholastic knowledge as such, which was still the prevailing philosophical doctrine in the Spanish Empire, permeating all institutions of learning, government, and the church. The doctors' helplessness before death is also elevated, if such a term can be used in reference to Caviedes, to a statement about the helplessness of human agency before the disintegration of the physical world. Caviedes drives a wedge between the rhetoric of medicine, elaborated to cover its own uselessness, and the inexorable reality of bodily decay and death. Caviedes's own discourse is a re-naming of the body and its functions, a new rhetoric and poetics of the physical.

Critics have played down the baroqueness of Caviedes, claiming that his poetic language is not as prone to conceit and tropological over-abundance as that of his contemporaries, but this is simply because Caviedes does not often appeal to classical mythology, rarely uses the commonplaces of the Petrarchan tradition, and avoids the world of luxury and sensuality preferred by other poets of the Colonial Baroque. Because Caviedes deals with the base and vulgar it does not necessarily follow, however, that his discourse is less fraught with poetic devices. In fact, it is the opposite. It was none other than *Lunarejo*, in one of the many insights of his *Apologético*, who established a correlation between the language of *germanía*, that is, the speech of thugs and *pícaros*, and poetic language. He complains that poets are criticized for "Calling the sea 'marble,' and oars 'shears' [while] rogues are luckier, for they are allowed and even praised for calling in their jolly slang the jail 'clink'. . .the gallows *'finibus terrae'* and an infinite number of crazy terms. . .that define their style as that of thiefs, picaroons, and pilloried men. . .why should anyone be alarmed if poets have their own kinds of phrases, a different ensemble of locutions" (p. 108). Caviedes often takes recourse to the slang of the day, already made up of tropes analogous to those of poetry (metaphor, metonomy, etc.), to create amphibological games involving sexual matters. The discourse of sexuality is always one of indirection, whether to be euphemistic, or to indulge in repulsive vulgarity. Caviedes puts face to face two tropological systems: that of poetic tradition and that of everyday life and the result is both hilarious and pitiless.

A perfect example is Caviedes's "Pintura de una dama que con su hermosura mataba como los médicos de Lima" ["Portrait of a Lady Whose beauty Killed Like the Doctors of Lima"]. Here Caviedes parodies the poetic convention of painting a portrait of the beloved with words, or better, with the conventionalisms of the Petrarchan tradition. He follows the commonplace description, beginning with the face and moving down the body, comparing each part to a given thing: lips to roses, eyebrows to bows that shoot deadly arrows, and the like. But Caviedes has enlisted, in addition to all those commonplaces, the names of notorious Lima quacks, under the general banner of the conceit that the lady's beauty kills. The poem, then, has the same complicated intertextual layering common to baroque poems in general, though the conceit is quite original, and its execution a veritable *tour de force*.

> Lisi, mi achaque es amor,
> y pues busca en ti remedio,
> y cual médico me matas,
> hoy te he de pintar con ellos,
> pues, según flechan,
> tienen tus perfecciones
> dos mil recetas.
>
> [Lisi, my infirmity is love,
> and it seeks in you its remedy,
> but since like a doctor you kill me,
> I will paint you with them,
> for, like your terminal darts
> they have two thousand prescriptions.]

Lisi is the lady in Quevedo's love poems, hence her name has immediate literary resonances. The conventional malady of love is here rendered as an *achaque*, which in Spanish means not only an illness, but one typical of old age. The lover, then, is a dirty old man with real maladies, not a handsome and ardent suitor. To seek remedy in the lady herself, the tragic error of all lovers in the courtly love tradition, is like taking poison instead of medicine. This paradox is literalized by using the quacks to paint the lady, because the "con ellos" may mean that he wishes to paint her along with them, but also that he will use them to paint her. This is what Caviedes does, playing on the doctors' names (Bermejo, "red"), their skin color (two doctors are black), or their greed (for silver). Caviedes's poem is as "ciphered" as Balbuena's, and the conceits are sometimes as recondite as Góngora's:

> Dos Rivillas traes por labios,
> que es cirujano sangriento,
> y aunque me matan de boca
> yo sé que muero por cierto,
> si muchas vidas
> saben quitar sangrientas
> con breve herida.
>
> [Your lips are like two Rivillas,
> a very bloody surgeon indeed,
> and even if they kill with words
> I know that I die for real,
> for they know how to take
> many lives with a bloody
> but small gash.]

Rivilla, the name of the surgeon, sounds like the diminutive for riverbank [*rivera*], so there is a comical contradiction in having lips like riverbanks described by using a diminutive. This counterpoint between the small and the large (the wound is small), the fact that in Spanish the word for lips and labiae is the same, plus the repeated allusions to blood, hence possibly to menstruation, suggest a rather obscene subtext here. This is Caviedes at his best or worst.

Caviedes's obsession with the body, and with the efforts of men and women to disfigure it, is in line with a peculiar characteristic of baroque poetry and drama, one that is very far removed from contemporary poetic doctrine and practice. In baroque drama and poetry the self appears always on the outside, in view, as it were, leaving no implicit interiority to explore. In other words, Caviedes's turning out of the body is a representation of all there is to see of man or woman. This is a feature of Calderonian drama, where the protagonists' psyches are always visible or audible, with no inner core assumed to rule mysteriously. There is, in fact, no mystery in baroque poetry, as Espinosa Medrano emphasized in his *Apologético*, everything that is exists in language and hence can be represented. It is the same with institutions and systems of belief, which can be represented through elaborate allegories. If the Baroque is theatrical, it is so because it is an art that deals with surfaces, colors, and appearances. The most intricate of these is the self, and also the most theatrical.

This tendency culminates in the poetry of Sor Juana Inés de la Cruz (1648–1695), who is the major poet of the Colonial Baroque, the last major figure of the Spanish Golden Age, and one of the classics of Spanish-language literature. Sor Juana's work is varied and rich, spanning poetry, prose, and theatre. Her famous "Response to Sor Filotea" stands as one of the earliest modern feminist tracts, and her plays are among the best in the Calderonian school. Sor Juana's fascinating life, which took her from being an illegitimate child and *wunderkind* to the viceregal court and later to the convent, has inspired many a commentary, most recently Octavio Paz's remarkable literary biography (Paz, *Sor Juana Inés de la Cruz, o las trampas de la fe* [*Sor Juana or, The Traps of Faith*]). Contemporary feminist criticism has made Sor Juana one of its favorite subjects, and has created through research of conventual life almost a whole subfield of study (Arenal and Schlau, *Untold Sisters*). In the context of the Colonial Baroque, Sor Juana towers above all other poets; she is really the only major figure in the period.

As a poet, Sor Juana is a lyric, as well as a philosophical and sometimes satirical poet, and is equally at home with popular forms like the *romance* or the *villancico*, and cultivated ones like the sonnet and the *lira*. Her long poem, "Primero sueño" ["First dream"] is the most ambitious poetic composition in Spanish since Góngora's *Soledades*, and will find no equal until this century in the works of Federico García Lorca, Pablo Neruda, and Octavio Paz. Sor Juana's love poetry is witty, intricate, playful, and at the same time profound. She brings to a close the Petrarchan mode which, in Spanish, had begun with Garcilaso. One of her central conceits, of course, is to write Petrarchan poetry from the highly unusual perspective of a woman, traditionally the object of love in that poetic tradition. She is thus able to turn upside down many of the commonplaces of renaissance lyric. Her baroque rarity is, precisely, being a woman who is the intellectual and artistic superior of most men (certainly of all who were around her), in a society where men not only embodied social, ecclesiastical and political power, but also the poetic voice. Sor Juana, however, is not content with the exploitation of this vantage point to rewrite the tradition, she competes with the major poets that precede her on their own ground, as can be seen in this remarkable sonnet, where the echoes of Garcilaso, Góngora, and Calderón can be easily heard:

> Rosa divina que en gentil cultura
> eres, con tu fragante sutileza,
> magisterio purpúreo de belleza,
> enseñanza nevada a la hermosura.
> Amago de la humana arquitectura,
> ejemplo de la vana gentileza,
> en cuyo ser unió naturaleza
> la cuna alegre y triste sepultura.
> ¡Cuán altiva en tu pompa presumida,
> soberbia, el riesgo de morir desdeñas,

> y luego desmayada y encogida
> de tu caduco ser das mustias señas,
> con que docta muerte y necia vida
> viviendo engañas y muriendo enseñas!

Alan S. Trueblood has rendered this sonnet thus in his excellent *A Sor Juana Anthology*:

> [Rose, celestial flower finely bred,
> you offer in your scented subtlety
> crimson instruction in everything that's fair,
> snow-white sermons to all beauty.
> Semblance of our human shapeliness,
> portent of proud breeding's doom,
> in whose being Nature chose to link
> a joyous cradle and a joyless tomb.
> How haughtily you broadcast in your prime
> your scorn of all suggestion you must die!
> Yet how soon as you wilt and waste away,
> your withering brings mortality's reply.
> Wherefore with thoughtless life and thoughtful death,
> in dying you speak true, in life you lie.]

There is no question but that this is a remarkable display of poetic skill, and that Sor Juana has juggled the commonplaces of baroque poetry in a witty and original way. The theme, the fleetingness of life, as exemplified by the rose's brief moment of splendor, and the play of opposites (cradle–tomb) is turned into a rhetorical accomplishment, an eloquent warning. But the poem's most profound statement centers on the first line of the second quartet, "Amago de la humana arquitectura" ["Semblance of our human shapeliness"]. *Amago* is, as Trueblood correctly translates, a "semblance," but it is more the threat of a semblance, or the suggestion or fake of a semblance than a semblance. The rose is a suggestion of being, a contrivance that will resemble being and deceive us for a moment. *Arquitectura* is a very Calderonian word that expresses the Baroque's view of the psyche as a machinery of competing forces. Hence, if the rose resembles being, being manifests itself as visible form, in the way that baroque theatre allows theatrical props to be visible. The make-up of being's illusion is perceivable; in fact, being is that perceivable specter, that momentary fabrication. The self appears thus with the geometric awkwardness of an orthopedic contraption, but also with the lightness and faintness of the celestial lights. Being, then is the semblance of shapeliness, a shapeliness that defines its perimeter with sharp lines and whose dynamics are visible and mechanical. This is all implicit in the line "Amago de la humana arquitectura," which then gives the rest of the poem added meaning. It is not just beauty, but being itself that is fragile and vulnerable, the announcement of something that may or may not appear. Sor Juana's perception of self as fragile and vulnerable is in line with her own self-representation in both the "Respuesta" and "Primero sueño."

But it is in "Primero sueño" that Sor Juana makes a full display of self and takes to the limits the baroque impulse to knowledge and self-knowledge. Sor Juana's long (975 verses) and ambitious poem relates the story of the intellect's quest for knowledge in the space of a night of dreaming. It is a description of the inner self, made up of a body laid out in medical detail and a soul that leaves it momentarily in slumber, as it seeks to know the forces that shape the universe and itself.

> El alma, pues, suspensa
> del exterior gobierno – en que ocupada
> en material empleo,
> o bien o mal da el día por gastado –,
> solamente dispensa
> remota, si del todo deparada
> no, a los de muerte temporal apresos
> lánguidos miembros, sosegados huesos,
> los gajes del calor vegetativo,
> el cuerpo siendo, en sosegada calma,
> un cadáver con alma,
> muerto a la vida y a la muerte vivo,
> de lo segundo dando tardas señas
> el del reloj humano
> vital volante que, si no con mano,
> con arterial concierto, unas pequeñas
> muestras, pulsando manifiesta lento
> de su bien regulado movimiento.

> [The soul now being released
> from outward governance, activity
> which keeps her materially employed
> for better or for worse the whole day through,
> at some remove although not quite cut off,
> pays out their wages
> of vegetable heat only
> to listless limbs and resting bones
> oppressed by temporary death.
> The body in unbroken calm,
> a corpse with soul,
> is dead to living, living to the dead,
> the human clock attesting
> by faintest signs of life
> its vital wound-up state,
> wound not by hand but by arterial concert:

> by throbbings which give tiny measured signs
> of its well-regulated movement.]
> (Trueblood, *A Sor Juana Anthology*, 176)

The "Primero sueño" has all the trappings of Góngora's poetics, particularly hyperbatons and a highly recondite vocabulary (Perelmuter Pérez, *Noche intelectual*), but it is essentially an intellectual, not an erotic poem. Hence it is more akin to the work of Fray Luis de León, and to the dramatic poetry of Calderón, particularly his *autos sacramentales*, than to any other tradition. In fact, the make-up of the universe and the self are strictly Calderonian, for it was Calderón who had best translated into poetic language the theology, psychology, and physics of Spanish scholasticism. There are Calderonian echoes in all of Sor Juana's poetry, but particularly in the "Primero sueño," as is evident in lines like "un cadáver con alma" ["a corpse with soul"]. Yet, in spite of the classical and contemporary sources ably outlined by Georgina Sabat de Rivers (*El "Sueño" de Sor Juana Inés de la Cruz*), Sor Juana's poem is a strange one by the standards of the Spanish Golden Age. Though written in *silvas*, is not a pastoral, like the *Soledades*, and it is not the retelling of a myth, like the *Fábula de Polifemo y Galatea*. It is not a moral poem, like many of Quevedo's, nor an epic, like Ercilla's. Though thematically it is linked to a long tradition of visionary tracts and texts, its true genealogy appears to be the hermetic tradition that reaches back to the early Renaissance, as Paz has argued persuasively (*Sor Juana Inés de la Cruz*). The flight of the intellect (not just the soul) as it soars up to meet and know the origin of all, an abstract entity never called God, and with no references to Christianity, it encounters many enigmatic and cabalistic symbols. The main image seems to be that of the Egyptian pyramids, a perfect ascending form that emblematizes the intellect's quest for knowledge. In fact, the "Primero sueño" opens with an allusion to the pyramid shape:

> Piramidal, funesta, de la tierra
> nacida sombra, al Cielo encaminaba
> de vanos obeliscos punta altiva,
> escalar pretendiendo las estrellas

> [Pyramidal, lugubrious,
> a shadow born of earth
> pushed heavenward its towering tips]
> (Trueblood, *A Sor Juana Anthology*, 172)

A hermetic symbol too, and a reference to the hermetic tradition that Sor Juana knew so well, the poem is a lavish display of knowledge in all its seventeenth-century guises. The range of Sor Juana's erudition is stupendous, and the probe into the limits of knowledge as daring as was possible with the instruments available to her. But the quest of the nameless voice is frustrated, and as light returns to earth the self is awakened by it, body and mind reunited again.

> mientras nuestro Hemisferio la dorada
> ilustraba del Sol madeja hermosa,
> que con luz judiciosa
> de orden distributivo
> a las cosas visibles sus colores
> iba, restituyendo
> entera a los sentidos exteriores
> su operación, quedando a luz más cierta
> el Mundo iluminado, y yo despierta.

> [when the beauty of his golden locks
> brought luster to our hemisphere.
> Dealing judiciously with his light,
> by orderly distribution he dispensed
> to all things visible their colors,
> restoring to every outer sense
> full functioning,
> flooding with light whatever had been opaque
> throughout the world, and summoning me awake.]

The ending of the poem has led to a variety of interpretations, all having to do with Sor Juana's intellectual and religious beliefs. To some the frustration of the quest turns the poem into a moral allegory: absolute knowledge is impossible outside religion, therefore the end means a chastised return to the fold of the faith. Paz, whose interpretation is the most thorough and original, maintains that, on the contrary, Sor Juana remains defiant. To Paz the "Primero sueño" pits the obsolete Ptolemeic conception of creation implicit still in scholasticism, one in which the cosmos is finite and though large, measurable, against a modern view of the universe as infinite. It is the same dilemma observed in *Grandeza mexicana* and that Gilman has pointed out as one of the features of the Baroque. The end of "Primero sueño" is a truly modern predicament, according to Paz, that will shape poetry from the Romantics on: the poet is faced with an infinite reality that overwhelms him and reduces him to silence. The silence at the end, therefore, is a form of defiance, not of submission:

> The cosmos no longer has shape or measure; it has become unfathomable, and the Intellect itself – not even Neoplatonism can rescue her at this point – has experienced vertigo confronting its abysses and myriads of stars. Sor Juana is awe-struck. But this emotion soon becomes a different sentiment that is neither the jubilant elation of Bruno nor the melancholy depression of Pascal. The sentiment appears in the last part

of the "First Dream," when everything seems about to end on a Pascalian note. It is rebellion. Its emblem is Phaeton.

(*Sor Juana or, The Traps of Faith*, 383)

Paz's interpretation reveals how strong the presence of a keen critical element is in the Colonial Baroque. Sor Juana's poem would be not only a harbinger of the Enlightenment but of Romanticism and the whole modern poetic tradition, from Blake to Mallarmé, from Valéry to Gorostiza. One wonders, however, how much Paz has projected his own poetics onto Sor Juana. He tends to overlook Calderón among the various sources of "Primero sueño" by correctly rejecting a mechanical comparison of the poem with *Life is a Dream*, and the platitudinous contrast of dreaming and reality. This is a straw man, however. It was not the Calderonian masterpiece that Sor Juana drew from, but, as already mentioned, the *autos sacramentales*, which she not only knew well but imitated in her own theatre. These *autos* were a minute and complete poetic rendition of the scholastic conception of the universe. The *autos* tested the limits of such discourse but always returned to reaffirm their resiliency. They asserted, therefore, the limits of the universe, and the ability of the scholastic method to contain it and express it. Sor Juana, according to Paz, seems to have pushed this discourse farther, contaminating it with Neoplatonism and hermetic doctrines that provide a more disturbing conception of the universe. But the poem itself is so measured in its structure and inner world as if to affirm the limits, the order, and the security of a shaped cosmos with reassuring boundaries of space and time. For instance, the fictive duration of the intellect's flight is a night, a predictable unit of time framed by the appearance and disappearance of heavenly bodies, gives the impression of finiteness. In the "Primero sueño" the time-span of night is the correlative and symmetrical opposite of the day the action usually takes in eclogues. The "Primero sueño" is an inverted eclogue. Symmetries such as these etch the outline of a structured universe. Sor Juana's penchant for geometry belies the notion of an infinite, unknowable universe. Method appears in Sor Juana both as a prison and a refuge, like the convent. Besides, there is not a hint at the end of "Primero sueño" that the cosmos "has no shape or measure," on the contrary, as the sun returns it dispenses its light "orden distributivo" ["by orderly distribution"], which invokes a scholastic formula that is lost in the English. Furthermore, there is no change in the poetic voice; no despair and no hint of having been altered by the experience. Something is missing to make the poem modern: a time that is not measured by outward mechanisms be they man-made or cosmic, but by incommensurate human feeling.

It is in the minute representation of her inner being, literally from the functioning of the body to the intellect's itinerary in search of fulfillment, that Sor Juana pushes the limits of the Colonial Baroque's conceit of the self as theatrical representation. "Primero sueño" is not so much a confession as a form of psychological exhibitionism, one in which Sor Juana's spatial and methodical display of the inner workings of her self manifests the acute estrangement implicit in the Creole's self-definition. It is perhaps in this extreme expression of the self as not only caught but made up by the very bars that grid his or her own prison that Sor Juana announces a more modern conception of self. For in "Primero sueño," as in her famous play *Los empeños de una casa*, the self, her own self, is seen as the intersection of social forces and beliefs, not at all as her own creation.

Sor Juana's baroque obsession with the appearance of the self is manifested in her several poems, mostly but not exclusively sonnets, that are portraits of beautiful women. These culminate in her own self-portrait, and in the "Ovillejos," her critique of the Petrarchan tradition of poetic portraiture, a parallel of the Caviedes poem discussed above. In her self-portrait, one of her most famous poems, Sor Juana avails herself of the anti-tradition, mainly Góngora and Quevedo, of underlining how art lies in representing as permanent what is transient. In a way, her self-portrait is an anti-portrait, a painting that undoes itself in the same way that the "Primero sueño" is a negative revelation of her psyche:

> Este, que ves, engaño colorido,
> que del arte ostentando los primores,
> con falsos silogismos de colores
> es cauteloso engaño del sentido;
> éste, en quien la lisonja ha pretendido
> excusar de los años los horrores,
> y venciendo del tiempo los rigores
> triunfar de la vejez y el olvido,
> es un vano artificio del cuidado,
> es una flor al viento delicada,
> es un resguardo inútil para el hado:
> es una necia diligencia errada,
> es un afán caduco, y bien mirado,
> es cadáver, es polvo, es sombra, es nada.

> [These lying pigments facing you,
> with every charm brush can supply
> set up false premises of color
> to lead astray the human eye.
> Here, against ghastly toils of time,
> bland flattery has staked a claim,
> defying the power of passing years
> to wipe out memory and name.
> And here, in this hollow artifice –

frail blossom hanging on the wind,
vain pleading in a foolish cause,
poor shield against what fate has wrought –
all efforts fail and in the end
a body goes to dust, to shade, to nought.]
    (Trueblood *A Sor Juana Anthology*, 95)

If the body's image is a mere artifice, it is nevertheless the ultimate cipher or key to self-identity. The poem's pretext is to replicate the already failed effort of painting to be truthful, except in denying itself. It is a failure that depends in some measure on the conventionality of the poem's figures, and even its overall movement toward that resounding ending which cancels out what precedes it, where the echoes of Garcilaso, Góngora, and Calderón are loudest.

It is in the "Ovillejos" that Sor Juana takes the critique of representation to its ultimate consequences. The *ovillejo* is a demanding composition made up of eleven- and seven-syllable lines with a rhyme scheme which is much more demanding than the *silva*. The point is that the *ovillejo* is a technically demanding form, a kind of boast of poetic skill. The word itself, ultimately derived from the Latin *ovum*, egg, refers to a spool of thread or wool. An "ovillejo" is a kind of unraveling of poetic tradition that is itself quite entangled with it and with itself. In the poem, Sor Juana pretends to be driven by a mad desire to paint a portrait of Lisarda, a stock name in the gallery of lady-subjects in the tradition, but is faced with the exhaustion of poetic language:

¡Oh siglo desdichado y desvalido!
en que todo lo hallamos ya servido,
pues no hay voz, equívoco ni frase
que por común no pase
y digan los censores:
¿Eso? ¡Ya lo pensaron los mayores!

[Oh luckless, helpless century!
where we find everything already spent,
for there is no word, pun, or turn of phrase
that does not make the critics cry:
The elders have already thought of that!]

She proceeds to condemn contemporary poetry for being nothing but a quilt of quotations from earlier poets, and to compose the portrait of Lisarda as she mocks every one of the conventions she is forced to use. The result is a poem that is at once a description and critique of its own composition, as it is being carried out. It is a technique by which Sor Juana portrays herself in the act of composition, restoring her own authority in the very process of denying it. Frederick Luciani writes the following, in one of the best articles on Sor Juana's poetry:

In spite of the shifting linguistic levels of the "ovillejo," its bizarre texture, and its dialogue of voices and perspectives, what gives unity and coherence to the poem is the authoritative voice of the poetess. It is in this that one can understand Sor Juana's rhetorical motives in attempting a literal transcription of the theme of ineffability. Within a courtly tradition in a state of decay, in which the stylization of the feminine portrait by baroque poetics had reached almost the point of incoherence, the only way in which Sor Juana could assert her own originality was through an antipoetic, heterodox, and even subversive composition. In feigning to write a failed poem, a poem that winds up disfiguring what it attempts to express, Sor Juana creates, in effect, a work that refers constantly to herself...

> (Luciani, "El amor desfigurado," 47)

"Ovillejos" is another self-portrait, but one of the poet in the act of being a poet, as the "Primero sueño" was a portrait of the intellect in action. Both have a common theme: exhaustion, and the desire for something new whose nature is not yet clear.

Sor Juana's companion in intellectual ventures, the indefatigable Don Carlos de Sigüenza y Góngora (1645–1700) distinguished himself as a scholar, cultural promoter, and editor of poetic anthologies. He organized and participated in many of the poetic contests that characterize baroque society, was involved in various polemics, and wrote history and fiction. He is known mostly for his quasi-picaresque romance *Infortunios de Alonso Ramírez* (1690), and increasingly for works such as the *Teatro de virtudes políticas* (1683), in which he provides a series of biographies of Aztec rulers, and evinces a syncretic conception of history that would include them, along with the Europeans, as the builders of Mexico. But Sigüenza was also a poet, not only in his religio-historic *Primavera indiana* (1662), about the Virgin of Guadalupe, but also a not unworthy writer of sonnets and other such compositions, with which he often won prizes. A descendant of Don Luis de Góngora, a fact in which he took pride, Sigüenza y Góngora's true vocation was not poetry, however, but the ardent pursuit of knowledge as historian, astronomer, and even cartographer. Because of the bombastic titles of some of his treatises, such as *Libra astronómica*, and the polymorphic complexity of his works, Irving A. Leonard, his best critic and biographer, has called him "a Baroque Scholar" (Leonard, *Baroque Times*).

The poets that followed Sor Juana were very minor. She had imitators, like Sor Francisca Josefa del Castillo y Guevara (New Granada, modern-day Colombia, 1671–1742), known as Mother Castillo, whose search took a more mystical and tortured turn. And then there was the Peruvian polygraph Pedro de Peralta y Barnuevo (1664–1743), who practiced all genres, including poetry. But as a poet he is known mostly for his grandiloquent epic *Lima fundada*, not as a lyric. In his omnivorous quest for knowlege and multifarious assault on all intellectual ventures available, Peralta y Barnuevo resembles Sigüenza y Góngora. But he lacked the latter's originality.

Sor Juana was the culmination of a poetic movement that began with the introduction to the colonies of Italianate forms during the second half of the sixteenth century, but really took hold with the evolution of renaissance into baroque aesthetics. Baroque aesthetics were quickly, widely, and profoundly adopted in viceregal America because they contained, in their worrying of form, a venue for a critical spirit that questioned the central tenet of imitation, which bound poetry and poets to long for and repeat a past that receded into an unreachable horizon. By pushing form, and therefore language to the limit, poets of the Colonial Baroque tested the limits of their own personal, social, and political beings, and in fact founded such a being on their mixed temporal, geographical, and cultural make-up. The gap between the inherited form and their status was wider than in Europe. Rome was further off in time and space. One had to compose with new elements that were not apposite to the poetic task as defined by the Renaissance. Harmony gave way to the play of opposites, which was not as frivolous in the New World as in the Old. Being for the Creole belonged to a present not connected to an onerous and defining past. To leap out of the strictures of poetic tradition, to break the molds of scholastic reasoning, was implicit in the writhing forms of the Colonial Baroque. To allow for this it was imperative in conceiving of the real as something that impinged directly on consciousness, impregnating language and thought with its own form. Such a break was not possible until language was rethought from the ground up, and literature was conceived as the expression of contingent, historical beings, who reflected the contours of their here and now. The grandeur of American nature, new, majestic, both frightening and promising, opened the way. Such a task was left to Venezuelan Andrés Bello (1781–1865), philologian, pedagogue, and poet, and to the first great American Romantic, the Cuban José María de Heredia (1803–1839).

Epic poetry
Margarita Peña

Historical context

The sixteenth, seventeenth, and eighteenth centuries in Spanish America witnessed the flowering of the genre of epic poetry which, like the chronicle and the Mission drama, was a literary product of the encounter between the Old World and the New. In addition to its artistic aspirations, the sixteenth- and seventeenth-century epic poem frequently had a pragmatic intention, in which case it would turn into a long narrative of the merits of the author or of his friends. Like the chronicle, the epic would document the conquistador's astonishment at the wonders of the new lands. Unlike the chronicle, the epic poem would arrange its eight-line hendecasyllabic stanzas around the individual hero – Hernán Cortés, Garcí Hurtado de Mendoza, or Francisco Pizarro – or the collective hero – Araucanian Indians and Spaniards, in the work of Alonso de Ercilla y Zúñiga, Spaniards, in Juan de Castellanos. The sixteenth- and seventeenth-century colonial epic is the genre that belongs to the moment in history when Spain dominated the world and her captains embodied the ideal of the heroic knight. The survival of the genre into the eighteenth century evinced a desperate effort to keep that ideal alive.

Medieval and renaissance epic

Epic poetry was cultivated in Spain from the fifth century, beginning with the Visigothic conquest. In heroic narrative verses, anonymous authors wrote of the "pursuit of honor through adventure." The poems were possibly the work of jongleurs who wrote at the very moment of the events they narrated. Two types developed: the heroic epic, aimed at a popular audience (*Cantar de Mío Cid*, *Siete infantes de Lara*, *Poema de Fernán González*), and the literary epic (*Libro de Alexandre*), directed to an elite audience and inspired by Virgil. The genre began to decline in the fifteenth century (Deyermond, *Historia de la literatura española*, I, 65–101).

Represented by the works of Ludovico Ariosto (*Orlando furioso*, published in 1516), Matteo Boiardo (*Orlando innamorato*, translated into Spanish in 1555), and Torquato Tasso (*Gerusalemme liberata*, translated about 1585), the Italian epic would give rise to a new literary epic, more in tune with renaissance tendencies and the classic precepts of Aristotle, Homer, Horace, and Virgil, than with the medieval tradition. Educated men must have read the nineteen editions of *Orlando furioso*, translated into Spanish by Jerónimo de Urrea in 1549, as avidly as the Spanish version of Virgil's *Aeneid*, by Gregorio Hernández de Velasco (fourteen editions after 1555). Echoes of Ariosto in Garcilaso's *Eglogas*, between 1533 and 1536, have been pointed out (Chevalier, *L'Arioste en Espagne*, 61–70). The publication in 1555 of *La segunda parte de Orlando*, by Nicolás Espinosa confirmed the popularity of Ariosto's poem in Spain. The Spanish epic and, by extension, the colonial epic owe to *Orlando furioso* the chivalric–miraculous elements, the idealized feminine portrait, and occasionally, the pastoral subject. Lucan's *Pharsalia*, translated into Spanish early, in 1520, would also leave its mark on the epic in Spanish.

To paraphrase Frank Pierce's definition, one may say that epic poems are narrative texts with one or more heroes, distributed into more than one canto, that develop their themes in the manner of the ancient epic or the contemporary Italian epic (*La poesía épica del Siglo de Oro*, 264). They are written in *ottava rima* (hendecasyllabic eight-line stanzas or octaves), the meter of Ariosto and Boiardo, which Juan Boscán and Garcilaso introduced into Spain. In accordance with the precepts of Aristotle, the epic poem represents an heroic action; the plot should center on a single man; it should allow room for fantastic elements without disregarding the principle of verisimilitude; it portrays the final triumph of the hero, and it should, at once, both delight and instruct (Pierce, *La poesía épica*, 13–14).

Parallel to the epic whose subject is an episode in the conquest of America and whose hero is an historic personage is the epic of religious subject, the sacred epic. Christ, the Virgin Mary, or a saint occupies the position which corresponds to the valiant conquistador, the intrepid captain, in the profane epic. There is, likewise, an epic in Latin which developed, both in the peninsula and in America, along lines parallel to the epic in Spanish, and whose plot is either the life of a famous saint or some outstanding historical event.

Colonial epic

Authors and works: sixteenth century

Because it deals with a conquest subject, or because the author was born or the work was written or published in the New World, the colonial epic is linked to America during the period of the Spanish domination, from the sixteenth to the seventeenth centuries.

Alonso de Ercilla y Zúñiga

The first and most noteworthy sixteenth-century representative of the genre is Alonso de Ercilla y Zúñiga (Madrid 1533–1594). A man of arms and letters, a poet and soldier following the model set forth by Baldassare Castiglione in *Libro del cortegiano*, Ercilla went to the Indies in 1556 and, with Governor Garci Hurtado de Mendoza, left Lima for Chile, where he was to remain until 1560. A product of that sojourn on the American continent was *La Araucana*, of which Bartolomé José Gallardo lists eleven editions between 1577 and 1776, in addition to the 1569 first edition (vol. II, cols. 931–4). The poem tells of the conflict between the Spaniards and the Araucanian Indians in the conquest of Chile. From the author's prologue on, two characteristics of the poem stand out: Ercilla's admiration for the courage of the Araucanian Indians, and the cathartic function of the text. Driven by events, Ercilla wrote irresistibly, feverishly, on whatever he had at hand – the bark of trees, the leather of his boots. In the *exordium*, at the opening of the poem (which in accordance with Horace, is divided into the *invocatio*, *propositio*, and *narratio*), he declares his poetic intentions: "I will deliver my pen to the fury of Mars." He presents himself to Philip II as an eyewitness of the events he is relating. Throughout the text, the poet expresses in hyperboles his amazement at the new and unknown world he sees. He refers, among other things, to the geography and to the social organization and military practices of the Araucanians. The bucolic renaissance setting has echoes of the pastoral novel and also of Ariosto and Garcilaso. At times hyperbole gives way to direct and energetic description. At other times, the poet alludes to idolatry and condemns it. The second part, in the 1597 Madrid edition we have consulted, narrates the Battle of Lepanto which appears to the author in a vision. The third part relates the founding of Carthage and, returning to the Chilean scene, the imprisonment of Caupolicán. Relegating Garci Hurtado de Mendoza to a secondary position (possibly because of his personal quarrels with the author), the hero in the poem is personified by the conquistador Pedro de Valdivia. But in its thirty-seven cantos, the poem actually portrays a collective hero, the Araucanian Indians, although not without taking care to justify the imperialist policy of Philip II, whom Ercilla had served in his childhood as a page.

When he went to Chile in 1554, Ercilla was twenty-one years old. He was to stay in America for seven years, devoted to military service and to the writing of his poem. *La Araucana* was published in 1569. During the following twenty-five years, Ercilla married Doña María de Bazán, he was granted the honor of the Order of Santiago, and he inherited a good

fortune from his brothers. From his childhood as an intimate of the
Spanish Court to his death in 1594, he embodied – like Garcilaso de la
Vega, Diego Hurtado de Mendoza, or Gutierre de Cetina – the renais-
sance ideal of "the courtly knight."

If in the sixteenth century *La Araucana* was to become the favorite
book of all who aspired to write epic poetry, in the seventeenth it came to
be considered a classic, celebrated in the manner of the *Iliad* or the *Aeneid*.

Hoping perhaps to take advantage of the fame Ercilla had won, Diego
Santisteban Osorio published in 1597 *La Araucana (partes IV y V)*, in
thirty-three cantos, a work that did not achieve the success of its model.

Francisco de Terrazas

In the second half of the sixteenth century, the first of the poems which
would constitute the so-called "Cortés cycle" was written in Mexico.
Unified around the charismatic figure of Hernán Cortés, the works of the
cycle would find their best exponents in the sixteenth and eighteenth
centuries. Born before 1550, Francisco de Terrazas was the son of Cortés's
steward. He was a member of the first generation of *criollos* (Spaniards
born in the New World), and an Italianate poet celebrated by Miguel de
Cervantes Saavedra in *El canto de Calíope*. He wrote an epic poem
entitled *Nuevo Mundo y conquista*, but apparently he did not manage to
finish it. The fragments we have come from the work of another illustrious
criollo, Baltasar Dorantes de Carranza, who printed them in his *Sumaria
relación de las cosas de la Nueva España* (Mexico, 1612). Without a
predetermined sequence, titles, or numbers, the cantos of the poem relate
episodes of the beginning of the conquest of Mexico. The setting is the
south coast of the Gulf of Mexico; the characters are Quetzal, Huitzel,
Jerónimo de Aguilar, the chieftain Canetabo, Cortés himself, and many
others. There is no formal *exordium* with an invocation to the muses or to
the Virgin, as in other poems. There is only a laconic declaration: "I will
tell in passing only what is necessary." Lacking the emphatic grandiloquence characteristic of the epic, the poem has instead a tender lyricism,
an expressive gentleness – a style characteristic of Terrazas who was also
the author of excellent Petrarchan sonnets published in the book of lyrics
Flores de baria poesia. Twenty-one cantos portray the contradictory
image of the conquistador, whom Terrazas accuses of having slighted his
soldiers. One hears the voice of the resentful *criollo* who will also
reproach his homeland, Mexico: "Stern stepmother you have been to us,
and sweet, pious mother to the strangers..." The complaining tone
alternates with nostalgia for times past (reminiscent of the Jorge Manri-
que of the *Coplas*), and with a messianic sense of the Conquest apparent in
Cantos 8 and 9. Altogether, the poem gives the impression of a disorderly,

disconnected narrative, which is why we think Dorantes de Carranza may have published only those cantos that served his own purposes – redressing the grievances of the *criollos* – perhaps leaving out other cantos which did not suit his intentions at the time and which have, therefore, been lost.

Wogan points out thematic and textual relationships between Terrazas and Ercilla, of whose work the New Spanish poet appears to have been an avid reader ("Ercilla y la poesía mexicana," 371). The exact date of Terrazas's death is unknown, but he must have died early in the seventeenth century, since Dorantes refers to him as alive in his *Relación*.

Gabriel Lobo Lasso de la Vega

An example of an epic poem in the Cortés cycle written on commission is the *Cortés valeroso*, composed between 1582 and 1584 by Gabriel Lobo Lasso de la Vega at the request of Martín Cortés, second Marquis of the Valley of Oaxaca and son of the conquistador. Lasso de la Vega was born about 1558 in Madrid and died in 1615. José Amor y Vázquez points out that the unpublished manuscript of Terrazas's *Nuevo Mundo y conquista* may have been his source of inspiration (Lobo Lasso de la Vega, *Mexicana*, xviii). The poem contains a total of 1,115 octaves in twelve cantos that recount the lineage of Cortés, his arrival in Cozumel and entrance into Cholula, the episode of Gualca and Alvarado, and Cortés's reception by Moctezuma. The historical sources of the poem are several: Francisco López de Gómara, Luis de Zapata (in some cantos of his epic poem *Carlo famoso*, 1569), Ercilla, Jerónimo de Zurita, Pero Mexía, and Gonzalo Fernández de Oviedo, among others.

Because he wishes to exalt the conquistador, Lasso de la Vega creates a magnanimous, serene, intrepid, able, and persuasive Cortés. He even goes so far as to justify the cases of fraud of which Cortés was accused, in verses which attest to the author's exaggerated loyalty to his Maecenas, Martín Cortés, the hero's son.

As in other epic poems, the long lists of soldiers' names and deeds indicate the poet's intention to secure recognition from the Crown for services rendered. On the other hand, the novelistic episodes are important; they include the beautiful Indian maiden Claudina and the apotheosis of Cortés in Canto x, as well as the god Tezcatlipoca's visit to the House of Envy in Canto XII.

Eight years later, in 1594, Lasso de la Vega published the *Mexicana*. Dedicated to Fernando Cortés, son of Don Martín and grandson of the conquistador, the poem treats the same events and time period as the *Cortés valeroso*. It has 1,682 octaves, divided into twenty-five cantos; a commendation by Ercilla and a sonnet by Francisco de Aldana appear among the approbations. One can detect the influence of Luís de Camões, whose epic poem *Os Lusíadas* had been translated into Spanish in 1580 in two versions (one by Benito Caldera published in Alcalá de Henares and one by Luis Gómez de Tapia printed in Salamanca) and which, like the Italian epic authors, was avidly read by the Spanish. Canto XI, "Cortés's dream of the battle on the River Tabasco," appears to combine the influences of Camões, of passages from the *Diana enamorada* by Gaspar Gil Polo, and of an earlier source, Virgil's *Aeneid*. In the work as a whole, Canto XXIV is particularly noteworthy; its spirited and colorful description of the Spaniards' retreat on the "Noche Triste" ["Sad night"] reveals the author's imaginative talents as he describes the battle as an eyewitness. As far as we know, Lasso de la Vega did not travel to America. He also wrote *Primera parte del Romancero y tragedias* (1587) and *Manojuelo de romances nuevos* (1601; 1603).

Juan de Castellanos

Juan de Castellanos, a priest in the city of Tunja in New Granada (Colombia), published in 1589 the *Primera parte de las elegías de varones ilustres de Indias*. Like *La Argentina* by Martín Barco Centenera, or *El Arauco domado* by Pedro de Oña, the book itself is judged to be an heroic undertaking. The publication of the work was preceded by rumors of the great effort it cost Castellanos to write it, and the license for its publication granted by the King states: "that you had composed a book [...] that had cost you much travail..." (Castellanos, 3). The approbation by the examiner Agustín de Çarate provides important facts about the poem: it was originally composed in prose, Castellanos spent ten years translating it into *ottava rima*, and the author's basic purpose was to rescue the deeds of the Spaniards from oblivion. The work summarizes a life spent in the conquest of the Indies. The accumulation of knowledge about mathematics, geography, astrology, the tangled indigenous languages, and many other things, make the time invested and the hardships suffered worthwhile.

Veracity and realism are the basic premises of the poem: "I thought to tell the pure truth, using neither fiction nor contrivance" (p. 12). Castellanos's primary concern is to narrate important matters, gathered during his wanderings in the Indies from direct observation and from what he took from other chroniclers. In Canto 1 he criticizes the renaissance mythological motifs, and in a mood of Marian exaltation, setting Clio and Calliope aside, he invokes the aid of the Virgin Mary for his literary enterprise. The poem is made up of fifty-five cantos and is one of the longest in the genre of the historical epic, together with Zapata's fifty-canto *Carlo famoso*. The themes of the work include the earthly paradise, the image of the "locus amoenus," and the eulogy of the native woman. It describes as well the heterogeneous humanity with whom Castellanos was well acquainted; his characters, as in Bernal Díaz del Castillo's *Verdadera historia de la conquista de la Nueva España*, take on picaresque contours: "fulana de Torralba," "Ledesmica," Mosén Pedro, Fray Buil. One also finds the lamentations, the "elegies," for those who perished on the way in the Indies: Pedro Gorvalán, Pedro Margarit the mayor, Francisco Bobadilla, Diego Velázquez, Francisco de Garay, Diego de Ordás, Hyerónimo de Ortal, and Antonio de Sedeña, among many others.

Castellanos devotes ample space to the figure of the discoverer Christopher Columbus. He refers to his life in Portugal on the island of Madeira, to the "royal favor" granted him by the Crown of Castile and León, and to his visionary stance. Cantos II and IV narrate respectively Columbus's first voyage to the Indies and the discovery of the New World. He tells how Columbus is replaced in the government of the discovered territories by the man who pronounced judgment upon him, Bobadilla, Commander of Calatrava, who was to die thereafter. He draws the physical and moral portrait of the navigator, of whom he affirms that "he suffered great travails," and whose memory he restores in two definitive lines: "He was a noteworthy man in his aims, and admirable in his relinquishment of them" (p. 89). The noble figure of Columbus opens the poem; it closes with the formidable image of the despotic Lope de Aguirre, executed in Tocuyo. In between are scattered the elegies and the quartets and quintets in Latin and Spanish alluding to the death of the valiant soldiers which alternate with the narration in royal octaves. Also in between is the parade of places Castellanos knew in person or by hearsay – Hispaniola, Jamaica, Cibao, Borinquen, New Granada – and, of course, the Indian personages intermingled with the Spanish: Coanabo, Guarionex, Uxmatex, the Ciguayo Indians, and the Caribs.

More than an epic poem, Castellanos's work is a colossal chronicle in verse, comparable in its effect to Díaz del Castillo's chronicle and, as a poetic text, like Barco Centenera's historical epic.

Antonio de Saavedra y Guzmán

Ten years after Castellanos's *Elegías*, in 1599, the fourth sixteenth-century work of the Cortés cycle appeared in Madrid: *El peregrino indiano*, by Antonio de Saavedra y Guzmán. We know that the author was a great-grandson of the Count of Castelar, and he was born in Mexico. Baltasar Dorantes de Carranza mentions him in several parts of his *Sumaria relación* together with Terrazas, and the Sevillian Mateo Rosas de Oquendo, which is why we know he must have participated in an occasional literary conversation group. The fact that he chose the figure of Cortés as the protagonist of his poem suggests that he was very probably a member of the group of *criollos* resentful of the Spanish Crown. Cortés easily came to be the bulwark of support for a *criollo* generation hopeful of "taking over the land," a group Cortés's son Martín attempted to lead, during his stay in New Spain in the second half of the sixteenth century, in a failed plot. The bibliographer Beristáin y Souza says of Saavedra y Guzmán:

> He dedicated himself to the study of the fine arts, especially poetry and history, and in his country's literature he added the assistance of the Mexican language, which he knew to perfection. He was married to a daughter of Jorge de Alvarado, another of Cortés's captains and a brother of the famous Pedro, founder of Guatemala. He went to Spain at the end of the sixteenth century, and in the seventy days of his journey, with the materials he had gathered in seven years, he wrote the following work: *El Peregrino Indiano.*
> (*Biblioteca hispanoamericana septentional*, 325)

In addition to the customary approbations and licenses, the work is prefaced by laudatory sonnets by Vicente Espinel, Juan de Tarsis y Peralta, Count of Villamediana, Lope de Vega, and Miguel Iranzo, a relative perhaps of the Iranzo who was the poet of the *Flores de baria poesía*. The poem is developed in twenty cantos. The first deals with Cortés's departure from Cuba with his armada and the vicissitudes of the journey and concludes with the siege of Tenochtitlán and the imprisonment of Cauhtémoc. Canto III relates what happened to Jerónimo de Aguilar, a captive of the Indians since long before the arrival of Cortés. Canto X describes Mexico, Cortés's entry into Tenochtitlán and the imprisonment of Moctezuma. Canto XIII refers to various battles, and an element of the fantastic is introduced in a dream of Cortés. Canto XV relates the episode of the "Noche triste," the Battle of Otumba, and the Spaniards' arrival at Tlaxcala. Wogan sees Ercilla's influence in his eulogy of the Indians, the repetition of archetypal characters (the wise old man, the chieftain, the warlike youth), and in the handling of the feminine portrait ("Ercilla," 372–3). Important as one more link in the chain of poems about the conqueror of Mexico, the work of Saavedra y Guzmán has not been re-edited in modern times, as far as we know. One copy of this rare book is in the New York Public Library.

Pedro de Oña

Almost at the end of the sixteenth century, in 1596, a book was published which owes much of its motivation to Ercilla's *La Araucana*. *El Arauco domado* by Pedro de Oña attempted to pay the debt to the conquistador

Garci Hurtado de Mendoza, whom Ercilla relegated to a secondary position in his epic poem on the Araucanians. Oña belonged to the group of educated Spaniards and *criollos* who were around Lima at the turn of the century and who felt an injustice had been done to Don Garcí Hurtado de Mendoza. Besides Oña, this circle included Luis de Belmonte Bermúdez, author in the epic genre; Rodrigo de Carvajal y Robles, who, in 1627, published in Lima the epic work *Poema del asalto y conquista de Antequera*; and Fray Diego de Hojeda, author of *La Christiada*.

Pedro de Oña was born about 1570 in Ongol, Chile. He studied at the Colegio de San Felipe y San Marcos in Lima and he received his licentiate from the University of San Marcos. His *Primera parte del Arauco domado* appeared in Lima in 1596, with a dedication to Don Hurtado de Mendoza, son of Don Garci Hurtado de Mendoza, Viceroy of Peru, and of Doña Teresa de Castro y de la Cueva, marchioness of Cañete. The edition was withdrawn because of allusions to the Quito tax revolt (1594). A second edition, published by Juan de la Cuesta in Madrid in 1605, appropriately censored, was the one which circulated. There are several modern editions, including that of J. M. Gutiérrez in 1849. When José Toribio Medina revised the Chilean Academy edition, the 1605 edition was a true bibliographic rarity. Only six copies are known to exist. Oña died, possibly in Cuzco, in 1636.

Pedro de Oña (who should not be confused with Fray Pedro de Oña, author of sacred prose, whom Medina referred to frequently in the second volume of his *Biblioteca Hispano-Americana*) was acquainted with the classical sources. His models were Virgil's *Aeneid* and the work of Ercilla, his own contemporary. This first part of the *Arauco domado* (he did not, ultimately, write the second part because of the unhappy fate of the first), a poem of some twenty cantos, contains several outstanding episodes: the Battle of Biobío, the Quito rebellion against the royal tax collectors, and the naval victory of the pirate Richarte Aquines (Richard Hawkins) over Don Beltrán de Castro y de la Cueva. Likewise, there are cantos which refer to dreams and prophecies (XIV, XV, XVI, and XVIII), others in which the pastoral element is evident (XIII), others which relate in a lyric tone the love of Tucapel and Gualeva (XII). In Canto IV, classical mythology appears in the figure of Megera, the power of evil, allied with the Indian Caupolicán. The identification of the Devil with the "barbaric" Araucanian Indians corresponds to a Manichean Christian mentality. For the rest, Oña's vindicatory intention is apparent in the *exordium*, in which he addresses Hurtado de Mendoza, the son of the Viceroy, and in which he alludes to the rivalries among his contemporaries.

Pedro de Oña also wrote the *Temblor de Lima de 1609* (Lima, 1609), *El Vasauro* (Cuzco, 1635), and a sacred epic, the *Ignacio de Cantabria* (Seville, 1639).

Authors and works: seventeenth century

If in the sixteenth century the colonial epic captivated readers of the Old World and the New in the pages of *La Araucana* and in the works of talented authors writing in America (Oña, Castellanos) or who appeared on the American scene from Spain (Lasso de la Vega), the seventeenth-century colonial epic flowered, enriched by a powerful baroque style and the addition of religious themes.

Martín del Barco Centenera

The first work of the genre in the new century is *Argentina y conquista del Río de la Plata*, by Martín del Barco Centenera, which appeared in Lisbon in 1602. A Spaniard born in Extremadura in 1535, Barco Centenera died in Portugal, according to Ricardo Palma, toward the end of 1605. Of the first edition, now extremely rare, at most six copies were known. There was a second edition by Andrés González Barcia, in *Historiadores primitivos de las Indias Occidentales* (Madrid, 1749), and four more editions (Medina, *Biblioteca Hispano-Americana*, IV, 15), including Jacobo Preuser's more recent facsimile edition.

The life of Barco Centenera was long and rich in adventures. After studying theology in Salamanca, he enlisted in Juan Zárate's expedition to Río de la Plata, securing the title of Archdeacon of the Church of Paraguay. After numerous vicissitudes, he set sail in 1572. Ortiz de Zárate founded the city of Zaratina de San Salvador, on the east coast, where Barco Centenera took office in the Archdeaconry and preached the gospel. In 1579 he joined Juan de Garay on an expedition to pacify the Indians in the interior, the Xoxontobyas and Urambiambias, whom he attempted to evangelize. He devoted more than ten years to travel between Santa Fe, Santiago del Estero, Tucumán, Chuquisaca, and Peru, carrying out religious and political tasks. In 1590 he suffered an enormous setback when a trial was held to investigate alleged misdeeds in his office as Commissary. This office was taken from him and he was fined. He moved from Peru to Asunción, where the church was without a head. In 1592, he exercised the office of Archdeacon and occupied himself in the rebuilding of the main church in the city of Trinidad. He managed to earn the esteem of the inhabitants and he traveled along the River Paraná. He embarked for Spain, where he was in residence from 1594. In 1598, he requested that a report be filed on the services he had rendered since he reached the Indies with governor Ortiz de Zárate. Beginning in 1572, he worked for more than twenty years on his poem, which was published in Lisbon in 1602 (*La Argentina*, pp. ix–lii).

The poem contains twenty-eight cantos on extremely varied themes, and it is plagued by marginal notations, in Spanish and in Latin, which bear witness to the Archdeacon's infinite concerns regarding the materials of the work. Written in royal octaves, it constitutes an exuberant portrait of the Conquest in the "austral" regions of America. When the author refers to the flora, fauna, geography, the ferocity of the Indians, and marvelous events, the tone changes from that of an epic poem to a rhymed chronicle. An eyewitness of the Conquest, the epic singer merges with the materials he is singing, lingering from time to time to treat the theme of avarice, or that of Fortune: "...mad, unhealthy, treacherous ingrate, cruel tyrant" (f. 224). At times he speaks of what he has heard: "they told me," "I found out." In his verses resounds the voice, broken by hardship, of the anonymous conquistador: Juan Gago, tortured by the Indians, who cut off his feet and hands and gouged out his eyes; Chavarría, riddled by Indian arrows like a new St. Sebastian; Juan de Barros, a monk tortured by the natives, whom a beautiful maiden receives in heaven upon his death. The emotional tone of the poem is linked to a plain realism which distances the poem from Ercilla's elevated tone and places it closer to Castellanos's historical narrative. The world in which the young theologian was to end his life is woven of many threads: unredeemed Guaraní Indians and mermaids, butterflies that turn into worms and carbuncles, Charrúa Indians, Spaniards of the ilk of Magellan and the Pizarro family, the bad government of Diego de Mendieta, and the "raw hunger" which afflicted Don Pedro de Mendoza's soldiers. The poetic material seems never to be exhausted. In the last stanza of the last canto, the author warns: "Here I want to leave it, promising elsewhere very appetizing matters, for I am in my old age writing about the Argentinian realm..." (f. 230 r.). Death cut off the Archdeacon Barco Centenera; he was not able to finish a second part of that epic poem which was a great fresco of the conquest of Argentina, Brazil, and Peru.

Silvestre de Balboa y Troya de Quesada

The first text of Cuban literature can be dated to about 1608, and it is an epic poem: *Espejo de paciencia. Donde se cuenta la prisión que el capitán Gilberto Girón hizo de la persona del Ilustrísimo Señor Don Fray Juan de las Cabezas Altamirano, Obispo de la Isla de Cuba, en el Puerto de Manzanillo, Santa María de Puerto Príncipe*. With regard to the bibliographic chronology of the work, Cedomil Goic informs us:

> The text is preserved thanks to the fact that the Bishop of Santiago de Cuba, P. A. Morell de Santa Cruz, copied it into his *Historia de la isla y catedral de Cuba* (1760) [...] from where it was copied [...] by J. A. Echeverría and published in the second edition of the *Biblioteca Cubana de los Siglos XVII y XVIII* (Havana, 1927; reprinted in 1965 by Carlos M. Trelles y Govin). There are modern editions of the poem by Felipe Pichardo Moya (Havana, 1941), a critical and facsimile edition by

Cintio Vitier (Havana, 1962), and a recent edition (Las Palmas, Canary Islands, 1981).   (p. 207)

The author, Silvestre de Balboa y Troya de Quesada was born on Grand Canary Island and he lived in Puerto Príncipe, Cuba, from the end of the sixteenth century until the middle of the seventeenth. He may have participated in an early literary academy like that which certainly was by that time meeting in the capital of New Spain, in imitation of the Spanish custom. Roberto González Echevarría points out about the poem: "In slightly more than 1,200 hendecasyllabic verses (not all of which scan perfectly), grouped naturally into royal octaves, Balboa narrates the kidnapping of the Bishop of Cuba, Fray Juan de las Cabezas Altamirano, at the hands of the French pirate, Gilberto Girón; the liberation of the Bishop by payment of ransom; and the revenge of the inhabitants of Bayamo, who ambushed, defeated, and beheaded the buccaneer" ("Reflexiones sobre *Espejo de paciencia*," 573). Mention has also been made of motifs originating both in the epic tradition (a physical description of the combatants) and in devout literature (the extreme "patience" of the Bishop, the protagonist). The influence of Ariosto's *Orlando furioso* has been pointed out, as well as that of a poem by Luis de Barahona de Soto, *Las lágrimas de Angélica* (p. 574). The *Espejo* exhibits a curious fusion of Greek and Taíno mythologies, which in a few descriptions is reminiscent of images in Fray Ramón Pané's chronicle of the Taíno Indians (*Relación acerca de las antigüedades de los indios*). "They came down from the trees scantily clad, the beautiful nymphs with siguapa and macagua fruits and many sweet-smelling pitajayas. . ." (González Echevarría, "Reflexiones," 573) – these lines evoke the passage of Pané's chronicle in which the Hermaphrodites come down out of the trees to console the Taíno Indians who have been left without their women. The delight Balboa takes in mentioning tropical fruits reminds one, for example, of the enjoyment with which Fernández de Oviedo describes the pineapple in his *Historia*, judging it with the help of the five senses. It has been noticed, likewise, that the *Espejo de paciencia*, discovered in 1838 by José Antonio Echeverría, may have been used by nineteenth-century Cuban intellectuals to establish a national literature (González Echevarría, 'Reflexiones," 577). The poem has been the subject of studies and debates to which have contributed, at various moments, José María Chacón y Calvo, Felipe Pichardo Moya, Cintio Vitier, José Lezama Lima, and González Echevarría himself.

Juan de Miramontes Zuázola

Although the exact publication place and date is not known, it is presumed that the poem *Armas antárticas* may have been written at the beginning of the seventeenth century. The date of birth of the author of the poem, Juan de Miramontes Zuázola, is unknown; he died sometime after 1614. The title of the manuscript cover reads: *Armas antárticas, hechos de los famosos capitanes españoles que se hallaron en la conquista del Perú*. It is dedicated to Don Juan de Mendoza y Luna, Marquis of Montesclaros, Viceroy of Peru (Gallardo, III, cols. 810–11). It has been included in the Ercillan cycle, to which the works of Terrazas and Lasso de la Vega also belong, and it appears to have been published for the first time by Félix Cipriano Coronel Zegarra, in *Revista Peruana*, 3 (Lima, 1879). It was re-published by Jacinto Gijón y Caamaño and by Rodrigo Miró (Goic, "Alonso de Ercilla y la poesía épica," 203).

The dedication to the Marquis of Montesclaros makes explicit Miramontes Zuázola's intention in undertaking to write his poem: "lest the shadows of oblivion dim the deeds of many valiant Spaniards who in conquering, pacifying, and defending this kingdom, in the service of your Excellency, accomplished works worthy of their nation..." (*Armas antárticas*, 3). The basic pragmatic and vindicatory purpose prevails in the work, as in the case of Castellanos or Barco Centenera. The poem begins *in medias res*, in accordance with the precepts of the renaissance epic, and the invocation to Erato, the muse of poetry, is not given until Canto III, in a deferred *exordium*.

The work is structured into twenty cantos. Canto I relates how Pizarro captures and beheads the Inca Atavaliva, conquering Peru, and founding the City of the Kings (Lima). Violent hyperbatons and hyperboles, now baroque, mark the theme of heresy and the "fantastic–marvelous" theme. The unbridled imagination of the author becomes grandiloquent, giving the poem a sense of demonic grandeur. Verbs of motion abound – "trembled," "overthrew," "brandishing," "tramples," "contends," "cleave," "collide" – which make the narrative dynamic. An idea of predestination is apparent – it was God's will that the barbarians be converted to Christianity and reduced to captivity. This notion was already audible in Ercilla and it was to resound in the eighteenth-century epic, in Ruiz de León and in Escoiquiz. As a consequence, the Devil, as embodied in the natives and their deities, will act only insofar as God allows, as a necessary antagonist within the Christian dialectic of good and evil.

The text is poetically distilled; it uses enumeration as a stylistic device to emphasize and capture the vigor of the enumerated elements, creating verses of great plastic beauty:

> El zodíaco cinto tachonado / cinco veces pasó el luciente eterno, / cinco veces vistió de flor el prado, / cinco veces nevó la sierras el invierno...
>
> (Canto I, stanza 144)

The star-studded girdle of the zodiac / five times passed by the eternal light, / five times the meadow dressed in flowers, / five times the winter capped the mountains with snow...

Faithful to his basic intention, Miramontes does not focus his poem on a single protagonist but on the group of Spaniards who accomplished the conquest of Peru and who became the collective hero. The octaves narrate the strife between the Spanish captains – the Pizarros, the Almagros, the Governor Vaca de Castro, the Viceroy Blasco Núñez Bela. Thereafter are recounted the deeds of Francis Drake, whom Miramontes admires, and his adventures in the South Sea. The action focuses on three groups – Spaniards, Indians, and English – and at times it becomes somewhat erratic, moving from one to the other. Classical mythology appears in Cantos XI and XIII. The myth of Andromeda and Perseus merges with and dominates the native reality. The same occurs with the renaissance motifs ("locus amoenus"), the settings reminiscent of the chivalric novel ("triumphal arches," flageolets, sackbuts, hornpipes...), or the materials which recall the constructions of the world of peninsular literature: "alabaster, porphyry, crystalline rock." In the numerous stanzas which constitute its twenty cantos, the poem of Miramontes Zuázola's early seventeenth-century poem reproduces a world that moves from the diaphanous Renaissance to a Baroque formed of light and shadow. The latter is to triumph, years later, in Hernando Domínguez Camargo and his "baroque rebellion." Together with him, Ercilla, and possibly Hojeda, Miramontes Zuázola carries the epic enterprise to its highest poetic expression.

Gaspar Pérez de Villagrá

Author of an epic poem, *Historia de la Nueva México* [*History of New Mexico*], Gaspar Pérez de Villagrá was born in Puebla de los Angeles in 1555. He received his Baccalaureate degree from the University of Salamanca. In 1596 he was named Solicitor General of the Army that was to attempt the conquest of New Mexico. He served the King for thirty years. José Toribio Medina summarizes his biography as follows:

In 1605 he reported on his services in Guadalajara, in New Spain. From there he went to Spain and spent five years seeking office at the Court; he had to return to Mexico to respond to the charge made against him that he had killed Captain Pablo de Aguilar... He returned once again to Spain with his wife, Catalina de Sotomayor, and five children... In 1619 he succeeded in being granted the office and jurisdiction of Mayor of the Suchitepequis, and to assume that office he embarked anew, but he died on board during the crossing, the 20th of September of 1620.

(*Biblioteca hispanoamericana*, II, 107)

Ernesto Mejía Sánchez discovered two letters in which Villagrá, before the Tribunal of the Holy Inquisition, charges Francisco de Porres Farfán, priest of Sombrerete, in Zacatecas. The letters show him to be an educated man, but ambitious and arrogant, litigious and scheming, finicky in matters of racial purity, and obsessed with ferreting out heresy and Judaism, which he calls "a plague and a cancer" at one point in his poem. He was, in short, a typical example of the intolerance of the era ("Gaspar Pérez de Villagrá en la Nueva España," 7–21).

The opposite of this rather disagreeable personality is manifest in his poem *Historia de la Nueva México* (Los Angeles, 1933), printed in Alcalá in 1610 and dedicated to Philip III, which restores him as a poet of merit, familiar with the Italian fashions and meters, and friend of well-known literati: Maestro Espinel, Doctor Cetina (not to be confused with Gutierre de Cetina, poet in the Italian fashion), Luis Tribaldos de Toledo, and Doña Bernarda Liñán, a lady given to the cultivation of letters. The majority of the laudatory poems are directed both to Villagrá and Juan de Oñate, conqueror of New Mexico and protagonist of the poem. The poem is composed of thirty-four cantos. In the first canto, within the *exordium*, the author declares the argument of the poem. In the body of the work he will relate the discovery of the territories later to be called New Mexico; the exploration of the Río del Norte; skirmishes with the Indians; the vicissitudes that beset Polca, Milco, and Mompel, barbaric Indians; the hardship the Spanish soldiers suffered and the ill-fitting recompense they received for their services; the discord among the Acomeses Indians; the death of the warriors Zutacapan, Tempal, and Cotumbo; and the final victory of Governor Juan de Oñate. Wogan has pointed out parallels with *La Araucana* (a bombastic rhetoric, stories of native lovers, the idealization of woman) as well as Villagrá's presumed blood relationship with the Villagrán who is one of Ercilla's characters ("Ercilla," 374).

Although several copies of the 1610 first edition are in existence (we have been able to locate three of them), we know of no modern edition in Spanish. Curiously, it is the only epic poem in Spanish which has been translated into another language (English). Because of its documentary value, its considerable literary merits, and the representative personality of its author, a typically ambitious *criollo*, it deserves to be rescued from oblivion.

Fray Diego de Hojeda

The Viceroyalty of Peru was the scene of the first great religious epic poem to be written in America. Fray Diego de Hojeda's *La Christiada* appeared in 1611, with a dedication to Don Juan de Mendoza y Luna, Marquis of

Montesclaros and Viceroy of Peru. Although it was published in Seville, the poem was conceived and written on American soil. It remained unknown for two centuries until Manuel José Quintana published a few fragments in a book which was central to the definition of the genre: *Musa épica, o colección de los trozos mejores de nuestros poemas heroicos* (Madrid, 1833). A century later, in 1935, Mary Helen Patricia Corcoran prepared a critical edition based on Manuscript 8312 of the Bibliothèque de l'Arsenal in Paris. That Hojeda was unknown before 1833 seems to be owing to the poet's humility and to a lack of interest in the epic genre. There are, however, references to him by some of his contemporaries. He is mentioned in the *Discurso en loor de la poesía*, an anonymous work similar to Cervantes's *Canto de Calíope*, and both Lope de Vega and Mira de Amescua must have been familiar with it, since they dedicated to it laudatory verses which are included in the first edition of *La Christiada*. His biography was reconstructed by Fray Juan Meléndez (*Historia de la gran provincia de San Juan Bautista del Perú...*, Rome, 1681), and it was reprinted in the 1848 Chilean edition of the poem. From that biography we know that Fray Diego de Hojeda was born in Seville around 1571 and he professed in the Dominican order in Lima. During his years as a novice he distinguished himself for his penitence and self-mortification. He was a reader of theology, he wrote laudatory verses for Oña's *Arauco domado*, and in 1602 he granted the publication license for the *Miscelánea austral* by Diego Avalos y Figueroa. In 1609 *La Christiada* was published and he was elected Prior in the Convent of Santo Domingo in Cuzco. In spite of his kindness and devotion to study, he was unable to escape the intrigues of his order. He was humiliated in 1612, together with other monks, by Father Armería, Ecclesiastical Inspector. Complaints against the latter were to multiply, leading to the later rehabilitation of Fathers Agüero, Lorenzana, and Hojeda. The rehabilitation arrived too late for Hojeda, who died in the distant convent of Huánuco on October 24, 1615, at the age of forty-four (Corcoran [ed.], *La Christiada*).

He was a person who fulfilled the duties appropriate to a religious man, and he also participated in the literary life of his time. Together with Diego Avalos y Figueroa and others, he belonged to the Academia Antártica. In *La Christiada* one can detect the influence of the Renaissance (Tasso), of the classics (principally Virgil), and of contemporary authors (echoes of Góngora). But the strongest presence is, without doubt, the Bible and the Apochrypha (Pierce, *La poesía épica*, 271–2). Hojeda accomplishes his "poetization of the Passion" of Christ in twelve cantos or "books," prefaced by a royal octave which summarizes the plot. In the first stanza of the *exordium* he invokes the Muse, and in the third stanza he invites the Viceroy of Montesclaros to listen to "...the brief story of the God Man." The story begins *in medias res*, when Christ washes the feet of the disciples at the Last Supper. He describes the different moments, and in lingering octaves he portrays the attitudes of the future apostles, in a tone of evangelical–mystical fervor that portrays the disciples' love for their Teacher. The expression of the disciples' attitudes to their relationship with Christ connects with the expression of mystic love in sixteenth- and seventeenth-century religious texts. Hojeda takes delight, furthermore, in exalting the physical beauty of Christ: "...with those white, soft, pure and beautiful hands, of lovely skin and superhuman fingers" (Spencer in Hojeda, *La Christiada*, 37). The description is tinged with sensuality, for example, when Jesus washes the feet of Judas: "And he began to wash him, caressing his feet with clean water and soft touch. The beautiful, bathed hands of Jesus shone white as if wounded by the sun, and touched by those unworthy feet, they glistened with a certain vivid light: precious stones thrown into the mud..." (pp. 38–9). The metaphorical language alternates with a realistic, almost prosaic tone, when Christ shares out the supper. In this epic-mystic context, Christ becomes a knight conscious of his magnificence in the manner of Roland, Cortés, and Pizarro: "If there were a God equal to my grandeur and different from my own essence, [...] would not I, God, celebrate his generosity and his immense, magnificent gift?" (p. 49). Christ's reflections throughout his Calvary are a fusion of mystic fervor and hard realism. His self-contemplation and his morbid delight in his own suffering are reminiscent of the private calvaries, sketched in biographical and autobiographical texts, of nuns and priests in the era. They are rooted, perhaps, in Hojeda's own personal experience.

The poem ends with Christ's descent from the cross and burial. On the theological and the discursive levels, the basic intention of the work has been achieved: the magnification of the hero in his absolute triumph over the antagonist Lucifer in an epic battle, rendered in excellent poetry.

Bernardo de Balbuena

In a genre such as epic poetry, in which the life of the author and his work are so intimately intertwined as to be almost one and the same (Ercilla, Castellanos, Pérez de Villagrá, Barco Centenera), it would seem that a fantastic poem, in which the hero is a knight errant and the setting is the wide world of the novels of chivalry, would bear little relationship to its author – a doctor in theology, a priest in the province of Mexico, an abbot and archbishop on the Caribbean islands. Nevertheless, *El Bernardo*, the epic poem of Bernardo de Balbuena, bears more relationship to its author than one might think.

Quintana provided news of Balbuena in the introduction to his *Musa épica* and in the preface to volume XVII of Rivadeneira's *Colección de Autores Españoles*, in which *El Bernardo* was reprinted. Gallardo, Beristáin y Souza, and Medina also turned their attention to him. The most complete biographies of Balbuena are those of John van Horne and José Rojas Garcidueñas, in 1940 and 1958 respectively, although the second includes only a few facts about the poet in Puerto Rico. Basing ourselves on Rojas Garcidueñas, we can say that Bernardo de Balbuena was born out of wedlock in Valdepeñas (Spain), around 1562, to Bernardo de Balbuena and Francisca Sánchez de Velasco. His father, a member of the Royal Tribunal of New Galicia, took him to New Spain when he was two years old. Around 1580 he was a student, apparently of theology, at the University in the City of Mexico. In 1585, 1586, and 1590 he won prizes in literary contests held for religious occasions or to celebrate the arrival of viceroys in Mexico.

From being Chaplain of the Royal Tribunal of New Galicia, he moved on in 1592 to occupy the parish of San Pedro Lagunillas. It has been said that the following ten years were to be the most fruitful as far as his literary career was concerned. Possibly in that period he revised and polished *Siglos de oro en las selvas de Erifile*, written previously, and composed *El Bernardo*. In 1603 he wrote *Grandeza mexicana*, at the request of Doña Isabel de Tobar y Guzmán, a friend from his youth, who wanted to know what the City of Mexico was like. Eager to have an ecclesiastical career, and having received no answer to his insistent request for a canonry in Mexico or Tlaxcala, he decided to take his request directly to the metropolis. In mid-1601 he embarked for Spain. There he obtained a doctorate at the University of Sigüenza, he published his pastoral novel, *Siglos de oro...*, and he devoted himself to seeking an important office. In 1608 he was elected Abbot of Jamaica, where he headed in 1610. He would remain on that island for ten years, always requesting to be transferred, with a higher office, to Mexico or Lima. In 1619 he was granted the Bishopric of Puerto Rico. In 1622 he left the Abbey of Jamaica and travelled to Santo Domingo to attend the Provincial Council; he stayed there about ten months. In 1623 he moved to Puerto Rico, where he remained until his death on October 11, 1627. In 1624 his favorite work was published, *El Bernardo*, or *Victoria de Roncesvalles*, and in 1625 he suffered one of the greatest calamities of his life: the devastation of the Archbishop's Palace and the burning of his library by Dutch pirates commanded by Bodouyno Enrico. Several unpublished works may also have been lost in the looting, and no trace of them has been found.

Besides Balbuena's evident ambition, one must also emphasize his "great Christianity, virtue, and letters." His comments about Puerto Rico give an impression of magnanimity. Of the gentlemen he thought: "The citizens of the rank of gentlemen who are in this city, many are of known quality although they are poor, since the land is not of greater substance. They carry themselves with excessive pomp, with elegance and exuding authority about their persons, they attend well to their obligations, and in their duties in divine worship, they take most noteworthy pains..." (Cuesta Mendoza, *Historia eclesiástica de Puerto Rico colonial*, I, 115–16). A pungent ten-line stanza is attributed to him: "Here are the escutcheons of Castile, many gentlemen in few houses, all of them dealers in ginger and leather, the Mendozas, Guzmanes and Padilla" (p. 116), but his judgment of governor Juan de Vargas reflects his benevolence: "The case of Juan de Vargas is typical. Constantly concerned for the fate of the Puerto Ricans [...] he did not hesitate to cheat the royal treasury and bring into the island more slaves than were allowed when they were truly needed. Should we censure him?" (Villa Vilar, *Historia de Puerto Rico 1600–1650*, 79).

With regard to *El Bernardo*, if indeed Balbuena composed it around 1595, it became a kind of compass for his life; when it was not published on the first two attempts, in 1608 and 1615, it came to incorporate, in successive retouchings, the author's avatars. There is much of him in the epic poem. A projection of his personal identity was his choice of a legendary figure – Bernardo del Carpio – whose name was also his and that of his father and who, like him, was illegitimate. Mexico is present in allusions to the landscape ("The great volcano of Xala, horrible monster, [...] serves as a clear torch to what I write"). There is a portrait of the sailors of the fleet that carried him to Spain in 1606. There is in Canto XVI a transfiguration of Viso del Marqués, his father's birthplace near the Sierra Morena, in the heroic countryside of the magician Malgesí. Some episodes of Balbuena's life appear to correspond to a fantastic context: the unreal journeys he made between Santo Domingo and Puerto Rico, with a five-person retinue carrying his library on their backs across unhealthy swamps and unknown mountains; or his enforced ten-year seclusion on a remote island, and the notion of his being victim of a magic will, which he speaks of in the dedication to *El Bernardo*: "Now its author, who may say that he has emerged anew into the world from the solitude of Jamaica, where for a time he was as if enchanted..." More biography enmeshed with literature would be found in the poem were one disposed to track it down. It would seem that the fate of *El Bernardo* was to become its author's guardian book, to accompany him as an unpublished manuscript during nearly the whole of his life, and to reach publication in 1624, just in time to escape disappearance at the hands of the vandal Boudoyno Enrico. It was an errant text, like its author, wandering across the marvelous landscape of Mexico, Spain, and the Caribbean.

Dedicated to Don Francisco Fernández de Castro, Count of Lemos, the poem contains twenty-four books, each of which finishes with an allegory. This fantastic epic, in the words of Marcelino Menéndez y Pelayo, recreates in an avalanche of characters the world of the traditional epic (Bernardo del Carpio, Charlemagne, Don Gayferos, Count of Saldaña) and the world of the chivalric novel (Hada Alcina, Morgante, Malgesí). It introduces the world of Mexico into the Nineteenth Book when the wise man Tlascalán relates the deeds of Hernán Cortés in the New World. There is an idealization of the countryside, a personification of nature: "Red trees of esteemed coral." There is also an array of feminine types: beautiful maidens (Angélica and Florinda) and repugnant harpies (Arleta), as well as the familiar retinue of fairies and enchantresses: Alcina, Morgana, Iberia. There are, of course, magic weapons (the sword Belisarda) and the miraculous water of the Fountain of Marvels. The imagery of the worlds of the Italian renaissance epic and the peninsular pastoral novel merges with reminiscences of Virgil and the chivalric presences to make this heroic poem, in the opinion of Menéndez y Pelayo, the principal fantastic epic composed on American soil.

Hernando Domínguez Camargo

Author of the heroic poem entitled *San Ignacio de Loyola, fundador de la Compañía de Jesús*, Hernando Domínguez Camargo lived, like Balbuena, in remote places, far from the company of educated men. Like Fray Diego de Hojeda, he created a great protagonist of the sacred epic. Like the baroque native of New Spain, Carlos de Sigüenza y Góngora, his life was marked by his expulsion from the Jesuit order. Perhaps following in the footsteps of the Cordovan Góngora, he created the finest and most polished baroque model of an epic of religious subject.

The son of tradesmen, Hernando Domínguez Camargo was born in Santa Fe de Bogotá in 1606. He entered the Company of Jesus in 1621 and professed in 1623. He suffered a spiritual crisis which obliged him to resign, and thus, in 1636, he began a life of wandering through various parishes: San Miguel de Gahetá, Paipa, Turmequé, and finally Tunja, where he was given a "benefice." At that time, he was engaged in business, acquired properties, and lent money, like Alonso de Ercilla, at interest. He attended to his worldly tastes: to found a picture gallery, to display a varied wardrobe, to accumulate jewels, to enjoy a good table, to converse with books, to indulge a refined spirit. In 1657 he recorded his last wish (to be buried in the church of Santo Domingo, in Tunja), and he died in February or March of 1659 (Torres Quintero in *Obras*, xxxii–liii).

The poem was published posthumously in Madrid, 1666, with additions and corrections by the editor Antonio Navarro Navarrete; strangely enough, it was not re-edited until the present century. In this poem, easily the greatest in the Ignatius cycle, Domínguez Camargo drinks from the fountain of Gongorism toward which his personal sensibility inclined him. The poem is interwoven with the customary Gongoristic elements:

neologisms, alteration of syntax, audacious metaphors, and mythological allusions. Divided into five books, each of which is divided into cantos, the text is dominated by a pure baroque style from the opening lines. Like Jesus, Ignatius is fed by the Virgin, whose breasts are quivers that shoot, toward the child's lips, milk like stars that is not silver from Potosí, but pure ambrosia. He plays with ideas of whiteness (star, spark, silver), creating sparkling visual metaphors. Domínguez Camargo traces the biography of the Saint, from his birth and baptism until his founding of the Company of Jesus, giving us a portrait of a charismatic personality, both admired and reviled by the men of his time. The renaissance context is apparent in the allusion to Ignatius's two professions, consecrated by Baldassare Castiglione in *The Courtier*: war and poetry ("be soft iron, or haughty pen"). On occasion, the baroque style becomes dense and the verses so hermetic that they seem to be in code. As in *La Christiada*, we witness the exaltation of the protagonist and a strain of passionate love vibrates towards the hero. But unlike Hojeda, Domínguez Camargo speaks not in a mystic tone but in one of intense, admiring exaltation. Once again we find ourselves in the dazzling world of self-imposed torture, schizoid miracles, and delirious masochism so frequent in the stories of the lives of religious persons of the era. The poet's taste for luxury, of which his critics have spoken, is apparent in the description of Ignatius's clothing: "With emerald carded into the garment, green pool the undulating camlet..." The narrative follows the saint's bitter penitence in the Cave of Manresa, where the lexical field is one of blood. The extremes and the contrasts are, finally, inscribed within the parameter of a morbid sensuality.

The contradictory and chiaroscuro St Ignatius emerges as an admirable figure. Because of the author's fascination for his character and his expression of that fascination in poetic terms, the poem may be considered a monument of the baroque epic.

Domínguez Camargo also wrote an *Invectiva apologética* (1657), and several compositions gathered by Jacinto de Evia in *Ramillete de varias flores poéticas* in 1676, among them a famous *Romance a la muerte de Adonis*. Domínguez Camargo deserves a modern reading of his work as a whole, of the sort that Gerardo Diego has given one of his poems.

Luis Belmonte Bermúdez

Other epic poems written or published in America appear throughout the seventeenth century. Also within the Ignatius cycle, the *Vida del Padre Ignacio de Loyola*, by Luis Belmonte Bermúdez (Seville, 1577?–1650?), was published by Gerónimo Balli in Mexico in 1609. Written possibly between Lima and Mexico, the poem is a testimony to Belmonte's travels through the two major Viceroyalties of America. In Peru he was acquainted with Fray Diego de Hojeda, Pedro de Oña, and Rodrigo de Carvajal; in Mexico, with Juan Ruiz de Alarcón, possibly with the Bachelor Arias de Villalobos, and with Mateo Alemán. An author of epic poetry, he composed *La Hispálica* in Seville between 1617 and 1618. Likewise an author of "comic plays," in collaboration with Ruiz de Alarcón and seven other playwrights, he composed the epic play, *Algunas hazañas de don García Hurtado de Mendoza*, which was performed in the chambers of the sovereigns in 1623.

Fernando Alvarez de Toledo

Fernando Alvarez de Toledo's *Purén indómito*, more esteemed as a history of the conquest of Chile than as an epic poem, narrates the uprising of the Araucanian Indians against Martín García de Loyola in 1598. Cited by Alonso Ovalle, Diego Rosales, and González Barcia, it was thought to be lost. A copy of the original manuscript found in the Biblioteca Nacional of Madrid was published in 1862 by Diego Barros Arana. It was probably written at the beginning of the seventeenth century by an obscure soldier, the dates of whose birth and death are unknown.

Arias de Villalobos

In *Canto intitulado Mercurio*, Arias de Villalobos tackles the figures of Cortés and Moctezuma in his octaves. Of the author it is known that he was born in Spain around 1568, that he travelled to Mexico, became a Bachelor of Arts in 1585, and in 1607, a priest. The date of his death is not known. The original manuscript of the work is lost and we have only a copy published in Mexico by Genaro García in 1907. The poem, composed for the welcome of the Viceroy Marquis de Guadalcázar, deserves a detailed analysis, since if it falls within certain parameters, it may enlarge the Cortés cycle.

Rodrigo de Carvajal y Robles; Diego Avalos y Figueroa

Because it was published in the City of Lima, 1627, the poem entitled *Poema del asalto y conquista de Antequera* has been considered part of the colonial epic (Goic, "Alonso de Ercilla," 207). The subject is the battles between Spaniards and Moors for the town of Antequera. Its author, Rodrigo de Carvajal y Robles (1580?–?), a Spaniard resident in Peru, was probably acquainted with the writers of the Academia Antártica. Another member of this group was Diego Avalos y Figueroa, whose *Defensa de damas*, an epic composition, was included in his *Miscelánea austral*, published in Lima in 1602. The poem of Carvajal y Robles has been edited and studied in modern times by Francisco López Estrada.

Melchor Xufré del Aguila; Juan de Mendoza Monteagudo

The *Compendio historial del descubrimiento del reino de Chile*, by
Melchor Xufré del Aguila, published in Lima, dates from 1630. Marcelino
Menéndez y Pelayo launched a damning indictment of it:

> It would seem impossible to sink any lower, but there was in the Colony
> still another poet, justly categorized as macaronic, who gave a good
> name to Hernán Alvarez de Toledo. This was Captain Melchor Xufré
> del Aguila, a native of Madrid, who in 1630 published in Lima one of the
> rarest books in the world, so rare in fact that no more than one single
> copy of it is known. It has as its title, 'Compendio historial del
> descubrimiento, conquista y guerra del Reyno de Chile, con otros
> discursos' [. . .] His book has everything; but particularly a memorial of
> ill-rewarded services. The three treatises that compose the work are in
> free verse. . .   (p. 260)

The dates of birth and death of the author are not known. Both the
maligned work of Xufré del Aguila and the poem entitled *Guerras de
Chile*, by Juan de Mendoza Monteagudo, published later in Chile, 1888,
are part of a cycle which carries on the theme of *La Araucana*.

Pierce mentions a *Relación de la conquista y del descubrimiento que
hizo el gobernador Francisco de Pizarro*, anonymous, possibly from the
sixteenth century, and published in Mexico in 1963 from a manuscript of
the National Library of Austria (p. 360).

Fray Diego Sáenz de Ovecuri

La Thomasiada al Sol de la Iglesia y su Doctor Santo Tomás de Aquino, by
Fray Diego Sáenz de Ovecuri, published in Guatemala in 1667 (Goic,
"Alonso de Ercilla," 199), is not an epic poem in the strict sense, but a
sampler of meters – *romances, décimas, glosas, letrillas* – which eulogize
the figure of the angelic doctor.

Fernando de Valverde; Antonio Hurtado de Mendoza

Among the sacred epics variously dedicated to the Virgin, Pierce mentions
the *Santuario de Nuestra Señora de Copacabana en el Perú, Poema sacro*,
by Fernando de Valverde, written in *silvas* (verses of iambic hendecasyllables and seven-syllable lines) and published in Lima in 1641; and the
Vida de Nuestra Señora. . ., by Antonio Hurtado de Mendoza, with a
Mexican edition in 1668, in addition to editions in Seville, Naples, and
Madrid (pp. 354, 356). Here the chapter of the colonial epic in the
seventeenth century could be closed, were it not that in matters of research
one can never pronounce the final word. Works as yet unknown may be
waiting for us in various archives and libraries.

Authors and works: eighteenth century

The sixteenth and seventeenth centuries contain, without doubt, the great manifestations of the epic genre in America. If we take 1569, the year of the appearance of Ercilla's *La Araucana*, as the opening date of the genre in America, and 1666, the year of the publication of Domínguez Camargo's poem, *San Ignacio de Loyola*, as the date of the last great example of heroic literature on American soil, we have a period of one hundred years. During that period, the genre produced works of the best and in abundance. Its literary style was in turn renaissance (Ercilla), mannerist (Balbuena), and baroque (Domínguez Camargo). In the eighteenth century the epic impulse declined. The heroic saga of the Conquest had become remote and the Enlightenment was in the air, bringing to America the new ideas which would lead to insurgency and emancipation from the Spanish Crown. Legendary figures like Cortés and Pizarro would persist, nevertheless, and religious literature would flower in its turn, finding in the epic poem the ideal vehicle for the glorification of saints.

Francisco Ruiz de León

At mid-century, in 1755, Francisco Ruiz de León (1683–1765?) dedicated to Ferdinand VI the *Hernandía. Triunfos de la fe, y gloria de las armas españolas. Poema heroico*, published in Madrid in the Press of the Supreme Council of the Inquisition. Of this writer, "son of New Spain" as the title indicates, the bibliographer Beristáin y Souza says that he was born in Tehuacán, Puebla, that he graduated as a Bachelor in Theology, married, and "retired to the country." He also wrote *La Tebaida Indiana*, a description of the desert where the barefoot Carmelites of Mexico lived (*Biblioteca hispanoamericana*, 266). Beristáin treats Ruiz de León gently in his critical judgment: "I am far from equating this *Poema Epico* with those which the best poets of the educated European nations have composed in imitation of Homer's *Iliad* and Virgil's *Aeneid*. If grave defects have been found in Tasso's *Jerusalén*, [...] in Ercilla's *Araucana*, [...] how could an American poet's *Hernandía* glory in having lived up to all the laws of the *Epic*, and all the preferences of learned men?" (p. 267).

Divided into twelve cantos, the poem follows the usual itinerary in Cortés poems. It begins with the background of Diego Velázquez and Cortés's arrival in Cozumel. It proceeds slowly amidst the obscurity of a baroque style loaded with mythology, astrology, and history. The character of the conquistador fades into collective action, although the author leaves a clear outline of his biography and draws his moral portrait. The language is full of anachronisms: the Tlaxcalteca warriors are "centaurs of the Tetis"; Cortés's camp is alternately the "Republic" or

the "Senate." Two centuries after the Conquest, and with a full understanding of what the causes were, the author takes a critical point of view
at times. Nature and the Mexican landscape shine in verses reminiscent of
Rafael Landívar in *Rusticatio Mexicana*, also an eighteenth-century
work.

Finally, however, Ruiz de León's poem is anachronistic in his flattering
and hyperbolic royalist sentiment, at a time when nationalistic fervor was
in the pens of the expelled Jesuits: Clavijero, Alegre, Abad, Eguiara, and
Eguren. The primary objective of this literature was, without doubt, an
attempt to fortify the declining Spanish monarchy by evoking one of its
paladins, Cortés, in a colony that soon would enter into political turmoil.
The documentary source of *Hernandía* is the *Historia de la conquista de
México* by Antonio de Solís, of which there were at least seven editions by
1755, in addition to the 1684 first edition. Moratín was to use the
Hernandía as a source of inspiration to write *Las naves de Cortés
destruídas* (1777). Ruiz de León is considered one of the last Gongoristic
poets of New Spain.

Juan Escoiquiz

If the previous poem constitutes the apotheosis of monarchist sentiment in
the declining years of the colonial system, *México conquistada*, an epic
poem by Juan Escoiquiz, published in Madrid in 1798, is a late and
fruitless effort to erase the Black Legend of Spain propagated largely in the
sixteenth-century writings and polemics of Fray Bartolomé de las Casas.
In the prologue Escoiquiz touches on the key points of the Legend: the
injustice committed by Spain in invading innocent and pacific peoples, the
superiority of Spanish arms, and the cruelties which accompanied the
Conquest. As in the poem by Lasso de la Vega, the allegorical figure of
Envy is here the infernal fury which motivates Diego Velázquez against
Cortés. Its twenty-six cantos contain a parade of characters reminiscent of
Ercilla (Glauco, Guacolando, Guacolda, Luxario) in a macaronic mix
with those of the Cortés cycle: Guatemocin, Teutile, Pilpatoe. In the
absence of renaissance adornments and baroque hyperbole, plain and
prosaic expressions abound. The heroic impulse characteristic of the epic
is lacking. The rhythm of the verses becomes insipid and tiresome, and
one misses Ercilla's elegance, Oña's strength, or Terrazas's critical
attitude. For the rest, the author does not hide his sympathy (which often
becomes compassion) for the conquered natives, although he takes the
side of the Spaniards. Escoiquiz imitates devices from *La Araucana* such
as the screams, outcries, and roars in the episode of the fight between
Dulmero and Juan Núñez de Mercado, which paraphrases the story of
David and Goliath. Invocations to the Muse are found not only in the

exordium but also in the body of the poem. But, suffocated by a vindicatory sentiment that even manages to undermine its verisimilitude, the poem does not reach beyond its good intentions. Its attitude is one of Hispanic affirmation, heightened by the imminence of independence in New Spain, which was to take place in 1810. A prominent man in his time, Escoiquiz was born in 1762 and died in 1820. He was the director of the Biblioteca Nacional in Madrid and he translated Milton's *Paradise Lost*, in addition to having been tutor to the Prince of Asturias, the future Ferdinand VII.

Pedro Peralta y Barnuevo

Among the epic works which treated profane subjects in the period of the Cortés poems, one must mention a poem by the Peruvian Pedro Peralta y Barnuevo: *Lima fundada, o conquista del Perú*, published in Lima in 1732. It relates the story of the discovery and conquest of Peru by Francisco Pizarro, Marqués de los Atabillos. While telling the heroic story of the Spaniards, Peralta Barnuevo establishes the lineage of the kings of the Inca Empire, the story of the viceroys and archbishops, and the memory of saints and illustrious men whom the viceroyalty produced. Published in two volumes containing ten cantos, the first proclaims: "I sing of the arms, and the famous Man, who went first from the Hesperian Realm to the vast, never imagined Empire, which is another marvelous World of a New World" (p. 1).

Because of its Peruvian nationalistic tone and its historiographical efforts, the poem is reminiscent of the efforts in historical research and systematization carried out by the Mexican Jesuits in the eighteenth century. Peralta Barnuevo, one of the most illustrious writers of colonial Peru, born in 1663 and died in 1743, is the author of several works whose subject is the city of Lima. The first edition of *Lima fundada*, exhaustively annotated, bears witness to Peralta Barnuevo's erudition.

Carlos de Sigüenza y Góngora

While one does not find in eighteenth-century Spanish America any particularly powerful epic such as those that flooded the American and Spanish presses in previous centuries, there is a superabundance of sacred epics, for example, poems like *Rasgo épico del tiempo de la Compañia de Jesús*, by Diego José Abad (Mexico, 1750), or *Débora zacatecana*, by José Mariano Bezanilla (Mexico, 1797). The heroic tone merges with a baroque rhetoric that will later be swept by the didacticism of the Enlightenment. Let us pause to look at a few of the religious epic poems published in this century.

Carlos de Sigüenza y Góngora (1645–1700), a Jesuit of New Spain, may lay claim to having written the sacred epic poem that opens the eighteenth century. *Oriental planeta evangélico*, published in Mexico in 1700, the year of the author's death, is a sacropanegyrical epic dedicated to the Apostle to the Indies, St Francis Xavier. His octaves fill only nineteen folios, making his poem perhaps the briefest of the genre. Unlike other eighteenth-century epics, it has not been included in the very useful catalog compiled by Pierce, which covers the sixteenth and seventeenth centuries, nor is it mentioned in other catalogs of the subject.

Luis Antonio de Oviedo y Herrera

Luis Antonio de Oviedo y Herrera (1636–1717), a knight in the Order of Santiago and Count of la Granja, wrote *Vida de Santa Rosa de Santa María* [. . .] *de Lima*, an heroic poem published in Madrid in 1711. Oviedo y Herrera follows in verse the outline characteristic of biographies of colonial nuns and female saints: birth, genealogy, early vocation, submission to God, repeated temptations by the Devil. . . The progression is interrupted by a description of the city of Quito, historical digressions referring to Elizabeth of England, and properly epic elements: the appearance of the Inca Yupanqui, Atahualpa, Huáscar, Pizarro, and the necromoncer Bilcaoma (Cantos VI, VII, and VIII); Anne Boleyn, the pirate Drake, and skirmishes in Puerto Rico (Cantos X and XI); episodes from the government of the Viceroy Marquis of Cañete. The poem returns in the final Canto XII to its initial theme with the death and canonization of the saint. A major character in the poem is Luzbel, who is identified with the Lutheran heresy. The epic struggle between good and evil is framed by a mixture of hagiographic and epic–historical–miraculous material.

Miguel de Reyna Zevallos

La elocuencia del silencio, a heroic poem about the life of St John of Nepomuk, appeared in Madrid in 1738. Its author, the Mexican Miguel de Reyna Zevallos, was born in Puebla de los Angeles in 1703 and held in turn the offices of Canon of Valladolid in Michoacán, lawyer of the Royal Tribunal of Mexico, defender of prisoners of the Holy Office, and facilitator of legal proceedings for the Bishopric of Michoacán. He died about 1760. To judge by the number of laudatory verses which precede the work, its author was a well-known and respected man in certain educated circles. The ten-canto poem describes the life and martyrdom of the "proto-martyr of the secrecy of the confessional, most faithful custodian of the reputation and protector of the Company of Jesus, St. John of Nepomuk." We have the description of the heroic battle carried out between good, embodied in the saint, and evil, represented by Wenceslaus, King of Bohemia. Because he refuses to betray the secret of the Queen's confessional, St. John is tortured to death by the despot. The points of contact with previous epics are the exaltation of the hero and the narration of the miracles he works. The author delights in the image of the virtuous man who confronts the all-powerful tyrant in the style of Henry VIII, and there is something in St. John that faintly recalls Sir Thomas More. The poem combines tender ingenuousness with improbable miracles in the style of the medieval hagiographies (*Leyenda áurea*, by Jacobo de la Vorágine). Reyna Zevallos, together with Ruiz de León, has been considered the last Gongorist in New Spain.

Antonio de Escobar y Mendoza

The Jesuit priest Antonio de Escobar y Mendoza (1589–1669) wrote a heroic poem entitled *Nueva Jerusalén María Señora*, which was published in Mexico in 1759, but of which there remains no first edition. Dedicated to the Patriarch St. Joseph, the work belongs to the intense Marian cult which prospered in New Spain during the seventeenth century and continued on into the eighteenth, and to which Sigüenza y Góngora contributed with his *Primavera indiana* (Mexico, 1662) and his *Triunfo parténico* (Mexico, 1683). The title suggests that the poem is the second part of a larger work. *Nueva Jerusalén* is written in twelve sections, divided into cantos. This second part begins with Section VII: "Of the time the Virgin was pregnant..." Sections XI and XII deal with the Passion and burial of Christ. Typical of baroque rhetoric is Escobar y Mendoza's innovative placement of each one of his "sections" under the advocacy of a semi-precious stone whose virtues shall determine the sense of the text. Thus he creates an imagery tinged with mysticism, based on chrysolite, beryl, topaz, chrysoprase, jacinth, and amethyst. The Virgin is visualized as an emissary of peace; her character as protagonist is apparent throughout the poem, which also postulates – like every Marian text – the dogma of Mary's virginity. A poem of great expressive delicacy, *Nueva Jerusalén* is reminiscent of the tender *décimas* the eighteenth-century Mexican poet, Father Juan Joseph de Arriola, dedicated to Saint Rosalía, patron of the city of Palermo.

Of the above-mentioned epic poems, as far as we know neither *La elocuencia del silencio* by Reyna Zeballos nor *Nueva Jerusalén* by Escobar y Mendoza have been re-edited in modern times. Held by the Lilly Library of Indiana University, Bloomington, and the John Carter Brown Library of Brown University, respectively, they constitute true bibliographic rarities.

Finally, one must also point out that the eighteenth-century epic, as significant within its particular context as is the sixteenth- and seventeenth-century epic, lies buried in archives and libraries. Neither the *Hernandía* of Ruiz de León, nor *México conquistada* of Escoiquiz, like other heroic poems, have earned the attention of specialists. Critical editions, simply annotated editions, or studies which approach the text from various angles, would make it possible in the future to assemble the entire panorama of the epic genre in colonial America.

[8]

Spanish American theatre of the colonial period
Frederick Luciani

Historical survey

The sixteenth and seventeenth centuries witnessed a robust and diverse theatrical tradition in the Spanish American colonies. The main component of that tradition, both formally and ideologically, was the Hispanic; most of the theatre written in Spain's New World possessions resembled that of the Motherland. This is not to say, however, that colonial theatre was merely derivative: variations of cultural context and creative disposition ensured it had a distinctive character. Moreover, the influence of indigenous modes of dramatic representation was significant, especially in the sixteenth century. Theatre in the Nahuatl and Quechua languages continued to be composed and performed in the seventeenth century, sometimes coexisting, sometimes commingling with Spanish dramatic themes, dramatic forms, and the Spanish language itself.

The legacy of indigenous theatre

All evidence suggests that theatre, in its broadest sense, was deeply embedded in the consciousness of the native peoples of what was to become Spanish America. The Spanish chroniclers of the period of discovery and conquest testify to the presence of theatres and dramatic spectacles – "*farsas*," "*entremeses*" – among the conquered peoples. What is more, their accounts of the manifold aspects of indigenous life and society indicate that dramatic representation was intimately linked with a full array of cultural phenomena. More than diversion from everyday life, such representation was, for the indigenous populations, an organic part of that life. It gave collective expression to their guiding ideologies – dynastic, theogonic, telluric, and so on – and helped to preserve cultural history and identity in societies for whom writing was either unknown or limited to an elite. While often communal and ceremonial in nature, indigenous drama was neither "primitive" nor one-dimensional. Its technical virtuosity is well attested to in contemporary accounts, and the range of its modes – from religious rite to court spectacle to satire – is broad. Surviving texts often reveal a rarefied lyricism rivaling that of the best European dramatic verse of the time.

Fernando Horcasitas finds evidence of forms of theatrical activity in some thirty-four indigenous American languages, from *achí* to *zoque* (*El teatro náhuatl*, 31–2). A brief review of the kinds of representation practiced by the two major native cultures at the time of the Spanish Conquest, the Aztec and Incan, will serve as a representative summary.

The Aztecs, who held sway over numerous other peoples from their capital on the Mexican *altiplano*, developed a varied theatrical art that is well documented by Spanish chroniclers beginning with Cortés himself. Dramatic representation among the Aztecs was both public, in the form of ritual spectacle involving the populace and taking place in the great open spaces of Tenochtitlán (including theatres built for the purpose), as well as private, commissioned by the Aztec nobility for personal edification or entertainment. Drama served the Aztecs as communal rite, propitiatory ceremony, comical diversion, historical and mythological re-enactment, and even as a form of philosophical expression, as is evident in the somber existential musings of surviving texts. Chroniclers emphasize the mimetic talent displayed in Aztec theatre, which excelled in the imitation of natural flora, zoological forms, and the habits and speech of foreign peoples. Finally, dramatic representation among the Aztecs was closely linked with music and dance, the latter in the form of the *mitote* or *tocotín*.

Theatre in the Incan empire shared many of these characteristics. The Quechuan *taqui* was a kind of collective ritual dance performed to celebrate various aspects of the Incan mythological *corpus* as well as the great cycle of nature/religion/agriculture in the Incan calendar. The Incas also cultivated a full range of theatrical forms, often composed by the *amautas*, official court counsellors and poets, which early chroniclers usually classified according to the European comedy/tragedy paradigm. Such drama often had a pedagogic purpose, and was created for both the general populace and the court.

The fate of indigenous theatre was as varied as the kinds of cultural interaction that took place between Spaniards and Indians after the Conquest. As an art form expressing the collective consciousness of major civilizations, it suffered the same diminution common to all institutions of those civilizations. But this was not tantamount to extirpation: in those areas where Spanish domination was overwhelming, the pre-Conquest theatrical legacy nonetheless survived, at least through much of the sixteenth century, in the cultural memory of Indian and *mestizo* creators of theatre, and even influenced those New World Spaniards who composed theatre in indigenous languages for native audiences. Elsewhere, pre-Conquest theatre sometimes survived in unwritten form, with varying admixtures of Spanish influence. Rather than collaborating with the dominant tradition, the latter kind of theatre could serve as a critical counterpoint to it; such is the interesting case of the Quechua drama *Ollantay*, revived in the declining years of the colonial period as anti-Spanish sentiment intensified. Even today, the revival of folk theatre in some parts of South America often responds to political impulses and draws its deepest nourishment from pre-Columbian roots.

The legacy of Spanish theatre

Theatre was an important part of the cultural baggage that the Spaniards brought to their encounter with the lands and peoples of the New World. The early years of discovery and conquest coincided with the transition in Spain from medieval dramatic forms to the theatrical innovations of the Renaissance. In the Middle Ages, theatrical spectacle had run the gamut from the ridiculous to the sublime: from the buffooneries of street entertainers to the stately pageants celebrating coronations and royal entries into cities; from the liturgical dramas which, within the precincts of the church or cathedral, gave solemn expression to religious doctrine, to their burlesque counterpart, the infamous *juegos de escarnio*.

By 1500, theatre in Spain was beginning to evolve toward the form it would take under Lope de Vega and the other great *comediantes* of the Golden Age. As renaissance artistic notions took hold in the Iberian peninsula, its theatre underwent an increased secularization. Classical antiquity became a source of both thematic inspiration and formal influence, as did the Italian *commedia*, with its emphasis on high dramatic intrigue. Historical theatre, the comedy of manners, romantic comedy, pastoral plays, and court masquerades all flourished in the Spanish theatrical Renaissance. 1517 may be regarded as a watershed year: it marked the first publication of a treatise on dramatic theory in the Castilian language (the prologue to Bartolomé de Torres Naharro's collection of plays entitled the *Propalladia*). The New World encounter occurred, then, as Spanish theatre entered a new phase of expansion, diversification and codification.

Unlike indigenous theatre, which survived only marginally or as a fading memory of past glories, the theatre of the Spanish peninsula continued to exert a dominant influence on colonial theatre. The steady traffic of texts, theatre troupes, and even playwrights, ensured that the dramatic fashions of the Motherland held sway in her overseas possessions. Whether this influence was more invigorating than stultifying is open to debate. On the one hand, the prestige and success of the great Spanish dramatists of the Golden Age may have had an inhibiting effect on colonial authors. On the other hand, the innovative energy of the work of the Spanish masters surely quickened the theatrical pulse of Lima and Mexico City as well as of Madrid and Seville.

Mestizo *theatre*

The early Spanish explorers and conquerors used the decks of their caravels as stages for the representation of dramatic or comical skits, to help relieve the monotony of the long transatlantic voyages. But as the unprecedented spectacle of the new continents was revealed to them, these Spaniards must have come to experience, with great emotion and immediacy, a drama in real life that eclipsed that of any stage. The same decks that had served as a space for theatrical diversion now became the setting for the first meeting of races, as Spaniards and Indians, unable to communicate verbally, engaged in an impromptu pantomime.

The missionaries who followed close upon the heels of the Conquerors also used pantomime as a preliminary way of communicating the rudimentaries of Christianity to the native peoples. Even after becoming proficient in the languages of their flock, they retained a high regard for the pedagogical value of symbolic action and public spectacle. Their experiments in dramatic proselytizing soon evolved into a fully developed form of religious theatre, composed mostly in native languages and drawing upon native histrionic and scenographic abilities.

The missionary theatre that flourished in the mid sixteenth century was the first great artistic product of the encounter of the Spanish and indigenous races. Mixing, as it did, Spanish and native languages, as well as European and indigenous dramatic modes, it may be considered a truly *mestizo* art form. While relatively few texts of the genre survive today, other sources of information are available, including descriptions written by clerical chroniclers who witnessed it. Not surprisingly, missionary theatre was practiced mostly in the areas corresponding to the seats of the former Aztec and Incan empires. In these areas, the genre responded to the exigencies of converting large and concentrated Indian populations, as well as to the opportunities offered by cultures possessing their own vigorous dramatic traditions.

Most current information on missionary theatre pertains to colonial Mexico. The Franciscans were particularly active in the adaptation of Spanish religious drama into Nahuatl, and, in some cases, they composed entirely new dramatic pieces in that tongue. Their subject matter was largely drawn from the Old and New Testaments and from Catholic hagiography. Such drama was performed, usually in conjunction with the celebration of mass, on church feast days and to mark special church events, such as the arrival of a dignitary, the presentation of holy relics, and so forth.

The staging of missionary theatre varied according to period and circumstance, but scholars consider the following venues to be the most likely, at least for sixteenth-century Mexico: the earliest dramas may have used the pre-existing raised platforms that were a common feature of the large, open spaces in indigenous urban centers and provided a stage visible to great multitudes of people; the remarkable *bosques* and *peñones* (artificial forests and craggy hills) that were so much a part of pre-Conquest staging may have been adapted for Edenic or other pastoral scenes from the Bible; closed or open wooden platforms, of varying size and degrees of permanence, and arranged either in sequence or with various levels, were used for the representation of different scenes within a dramatic piece; church interiors were used, albeit rarely, for the representation of plays; finally, the so-called *capillas abiertas* [open chapels], attached to the nave of a church and facing the huge atria that opened before the church façade, were an architectural innovation useful both for open-air masses and for religious drama (Horcasitas, *El teatro náhuatl*, 101–25).

While it is difficult to assess the indigenous contribution to missionary theatre, certain probabilities emerge from a survey of information on the genre. While the Spanish friars were usually the authors (or adaptors) of the dramatic pieces, their Indian proselytes were active in every other aspect of production and staging, and in two areas in particular – scenography and acting – their contribution must have dominated. Scholars of the genre remind us that in the most developed indigenous civilizations, aspects of dramatic representation were both highly specialized and technically sophisticated. One of the many ironies of the Conquest was that the Spanish missionaries, makeshift playwrights, had at their disposal theatre professionals of the highest caliber among their conquered flock.

Whatever the mix of European and Native American elements in any given example, early missionary theatre must have offered a spectacular cultural patchwork: Spanish play, native-language dialogue, Latin hymns, European and indigenous costumes (some speculate that demons in these Christian dramas may have been attired as pre-Columbian idols), native scenography of extraordinary mimetic technique, European mechanical special effects, and so on. The element of spectacle must have been intensified by the collective emotion of the historical moment: if the Spanish friars who composed the plays were motivated by a fervent evangelical impulse, the emotions of their indigenous audiences, who experienced in missionary theatre the dramatic essence of the collapse of their civilizations, can only be surmised.

Missionary theatre in Nahuatl and Quechua declined steadily in importance during the last decades of the sixteenth century, as the conditions propitious to its creation disappeared. By 1600, colonial society had become stratified; the missionary fervor of the first New World friars, which made many of them open to those aspects of indigenous culture, such as theatre, that were useful in the evangelizing process, gave way to the hegemony of an entrenched church, which was less tolerant of pre-Conquest cultural modes. In the seventeenth century, as the native theatrical legacy faded from popular memory, Spanish Peninsular drama experienced a powerful resurgence, and, in both secular and religious form, came to dominate the New World theatrical scene even more. Above all, the kind of mass indoctrinating spectacle that missionary theatre provided became unnecessary, since the indigenous masses were both largely converted to Christianity and horribly diminished in numbers due to war, persecution, and disease.

However, *mestizo* theatre was by no means unknown after 1600. Missionary theatre in the Guarani language was used by the Jesuits in the Misiones region of Paraguay throughout the seventeenth century (Pla, *El teatro en el Paraguay*, 14–31). Some original plays, both secular and religious, continued to be composed in Quechua and Nahuatl, or, as in the case of the Nicaraguan play *El güegüence*, in a mixed dialect. In addition, some Spanish *autos* and *comedias* by the great baroque dramatists were adapted into native languages. Such adaptations, as Angel Garibay has shown, are strongly marked by native poetic traditions dating from before the Conquest (*Historia de la literatura náhuatl*, II, 339–69). Remnants of indigenous theatre, such as the *tocotín*, were occasionally incorporated into creole theatre, written in Spanish for largely white audiences; here native elements were used for picturesque effect, or even, as shall be seen in the case of Sor Juana Inés de la Cruz, in a spirit of historical revisionism. Finally, a different kind of "mixed" theatre occurred in those regions, such as the Caribbean, containing a large black population. Scholars of Cuban theatre, for example, affirm the existence of a mulatto theatre during the colonial period, one which combined African ritual and elements of Spanish drama. Unfortunately, no primary texts of the genre have survived (Leal, *La selva oscura*, 65–97).

Creole theatre

The term "Creole" – a person of unmixed Spanish blood born in the New World – can be extended to the bulk of colonial theatre composed during the sixteenth and seventeenth centuries: theatre in the Spanish language, conforming to European theatrical convention, written by creole playwrights for creole audiences. Such a classification, however, demands immediate qualification: creole theatre was enriched from the start by indigenous vocabulary and dramatic modes; some "creole" authors were in reality of mixed racial origin or born in Spain; the audiences who enjoyed such theatre ran the gamut of races and social classes. In theatre, as in colonial culture in general, no strict line separated Creole from *mestizo*. Rather, a zone of infinite gradations provided ground for a continuing cross-fertilization.

Colonial society inherited from both of the principal lines of its cultural patrimony – the indigenous and the Hispanic – a delight in elaborate public ceremony, tantamount to communal, civic theatre. The resources expended on such ceremony, its colossal scale and the lavishness of the effects achieved, seem astonishing by any standard. Even before the advent of the baroque manner with its strong tendency, as one scholar has noted, "to make of life a drama, and of drama, life" (Leonard, *Baroque Times in Old Mexico*, 117), large-scale dramatic enactment in the colonies was an established custom. All evidence suggests the apparent ease with which the populace donned masks, assumed roles, contrived symbolic action, and immersed themselves in fictional spaces and times.

Mexico City, as seat of the Viceroyalty of New Spain and one of the largest and wealthiest urban centers of the colonial realms, can serve as an example. Less than twenty years after the Conquest, public festivities on an enormous scale involved diverse sectors of the population in mass theatre. The chronicler Bernal Díaz del Castillo describes the public celebrations marking the end of hostilities between France and Spain. One day's events included an enactment, in the city's main square, of the siege of Rhodes. The staging called for a miniature fortified city and rolling ships with working artillery. Hundreds of citizens, from Indians to Spanish nobility, represented warring Turks and Christians, with no less a personage than Hernán Cortés playing the role of the Grand Master of Rhodes. Interestingly, the spectacle represented an event that had not yet taken place, but was anticipated as part of the Habsburg campaign against the Turks in the Mediterranean; Trexler calls the spectacle a "conjurative prayer." He also stresses the ideological implications of such "military theatre" in a nation only recently conquered and whose periphery was still threatened by hostile indigenous peoples.

The Great Auto-da-Fé of 1649, also celebrated in Mexico City, called for the construction of an enormous and elaborate outdoor theatre, with multiple stages, sumptuous decoration, seating for over 16,000 spectators (including luxurious compartments for the nobility), and vast cloth screens to protect the onlookers from the sun (Bocanegra, *Jews and the Inquisition of Mexico*, 40–5). Incalculable effort and expense was lavished on this temporary structure, upon which took place ceremonies lasting but a few days, culminating in the execution of thirteen religious dissidents – additional proof of the value placed on public spectacle as a form of ideological expression in the colonial world.

In his analysis of the viceregal *entrada* [entrance into a city] as a political rite with clear allegorical implications, Octavio Paz makes observations that shed light on the general relationship between mass spectacle and official ideology in the colonial period:

> These festivities constituted a political liturgy. Their function was twofold. In the first place, they were a ritual restatement of the bonds that united the King with his subjects in New Spain; second, they served to join the two nations that, at least juridically, composed the kingdom – the Spanish and Indian nations. In the rite a dual relationship was realized symbolically: that of the lord with his vassals, and that of the people with themselves. In this second sense the celebrations performed a vital function: the fusion of classes, groups and hierarchies. The political ceremony was a true fiesta, by which I mean a collective act wherein symbols were embodied and made palpable. (*Sor Juana*, 141)

Of particular usefulness is Paz's emphasis on the integrative effect of spectacle upon the vertical and horizontal axes of colonial society; while symbolically affirming the rigid vertical hierarchy of the colonial structure (Catholic, orthodox, bureaucratized, racially stratified), mass spectacle brought together, in the same physical space and with unanimity of experience and intent, the varied elements of a society whose remarkable diversity defied the monolithic character of the colonial regime.

In all of the colonial realms, public celebration and theatre were closely related: on the one hand, public festivities had a strong theatrical dimension; on the other, the performance of theatre was often linked to the celebration of some event, such as Corpus Christi and other church holidays, the arrival of a new viceroy or other public official, the canonization of a saint, a significant happening in the life of a member of the Spanish royal family, and so on. Some theatrical works conformed thematically to the public event they celebrated (a hagiographic piece for a saint's canonization, for example), while others, more entertaining than edifying, were simply included as part of a program of festivities.

Such plays were often performed in temporary theatres erected in public spaces for the celebration in question. But as the sixteenth century came to a close, more permanent structures, designed expressly for regular theatrical performances, became increasingly available, especially in the largest cities. The viceroyalties followed the Peninsular Spanish custom of linking theatre with charitable institutions; theatres were erected in the courtyards of hospitals, and their proceeds provided financial support. By 1605, the so-called *corrales* of the Hospital Real de Naturales in Mexico City and the Hospital de San Andrés in Lima were among the first permanent theatrical structures in the Spanish colonies. Other venues for dramatic performances were the *colegios* and universities, where clerics and their students composed and performed religious theatre in Latin and Spanish, and, as the seventeenth century progressed, the viceregal palaces, where secular theatre was performed, often in connection with a civic celebration of some kind.

If Spanish plays dominated New World stages, they also became, in the early decades of the seventeenth century, the predominant form of light reading in the New World. Records of book shipments show that, beginning with the phenomenally popular Lope de Vega, vast quantities of plays arrived on American shores in the form of *partes* (collections of a dozen plays) or *sueltas* (individual plays in pamphlet form) (Leonard, *Baroque Times*, 106). After Lope and his followers, Calderón de la Barca and his school came to dominate colonial theatre in the late seventeenth and eighteenth centuries. The prestige of the Spanish *comediantes* was evidently great; even the accomplished Mexican poet and dramatist, Sor Juana Inés de la Cruz, could remark, in an entr'acte to one of her own *comedias*, that "the plays from Spain are always best." Sor Juana's entr'acte is jocular and self-deprecating, yet seems tinged with the resentment that creole writers must have felt as they competed with the Spanish greats; it is representative of the interesting dialogue that took place in the genre between the metropolitan center and the colonial periphery, between Spaniard and Creole, between Old World and New.

This thematic and formal dialogue, at times barely audible against the background of Spanish domination, was never stifled. The entr'actes that creole writers composed to be performed with Spanish plays could stand in ironic relation to those plays. The theatrical panegyrics that welcomed Spanish dignitaries could present, beneath their baroque effusiveness, a pointed regional or personal agenda. Nor did colonial interests fail to find a voice in Peninsular theatre; in one of the earliest Spanish plays containing New World themes (*Las cortes de la muerte*, by Micael de Carvajal and Luis Hurtado de Toledo, published in 1557), Indians appear as characters who protest the injustices of the Conquest. Later, during the Golden Age of Spanish theatre, peninsular dramatists turned to the wonders of the American continent for thematic inspiration. While creole writers, obedient to the norms of the Motherland, set their "cape and sword" plays in Toledo and Seville, Spanish playwrights like Lope de Vega, Tirso de Molina and Calderón de la Barca recreated the exotic worlds of the Caribbean or the Amazon. Perhaps the final ironic turn that the Old World/New World theatrical dialogue took is that colonial readers and audiences witnessed, on the printed page or the stage, their own hemisphere, filtered through the European imagination, and made fantastic and strange.

Authors and works: the sixteenth century

Most of what is known about sixteenth-century Spanish American theatre is derived from secondary sources: chronicles, correspondence, municipal records, the documents of religious orders, and so on. The few primary texts available in modern editions offer a rather random sampling of theatrical tendencies, and, in most instances, are insufficient to provide a complete literary profile of individual playwrights. Yet these texts do confirm what is known from secondary sources, and largely parallel texts from the Spanish peninsula of the same period. What is more, their number continues to increase, if slowly, as scholars examine archival material and edit new texts for publication.

These texts show that, as in the case of Peninsular Spanish theatre, religious themes predominated in sixteenth-century colonial drama. Even where secular themes made an initial, tentative appearance (as in the works of the Mexican playwright Hernán González de Eslava), the tendency toward allegorization of characters and theme was marked. As in Spain, most "realism" in theatre – linguistic naturalism, psychological observation in characters, social commentary, and so on – was to be found in the *entremés*, or entr'acte. And as in Spain, renaissance modes and motifs formed a constant overlay to popular theatrical elements, as evidenced in the dominance of the pastoral mode, the recourse to classical themes, the stylization of poetic language, and the ascendancy of Italianate metrical forms.

Theatre in Nahuatl

Only a handful of dramatic texts in Nahuatl have been translated and edited in modern times, and these comprise but a fraction of the many titles and performances cited in sixteenth-century accounts of missionary theatre. They have been prepared using manuscripts dating, for the most part, from the seventeenth and eighteenth centuries. Two kinds of evidence, however, suggest that they are of greater antiquity: some are named or described in secondary sources of the period; others contain stylistic or thematic details that seem to place them in the earliest decades of the missionary period.

The earliest known example of missionary theatre in Nahuatl, and the only one whose author can be identified with any certainty, is *El juicio final* [*The Final Judgment*] by Father Andrés de Olmos (?–1571). A number of citations can be found in chronicles indicating performances of a play on this theme – one as early as 1531 in Tlaltelolco. The same Father Andrés was possibly the author of *La adoración de los reyes* [*The Adoration of the Kings*], although the evidence for such an attribution is slender (Garibay, *Historia*, II, 144–45). A play on this theme of the Magi is known to have been performed in Tlaxomulco, Jalisco, in 1587. *La destrucción de Jerusalén* [*The Destruction of Jerusalem*] is an anonymous drama from Tlaxcala, closely related to several known medieval European dramas on the theme of the Veronica. Also of unknown author is *El sacrificio de Isaac* [*The Sacrifice of Isaac*], perhaps the same dramatization of the Genesis story known to have been performed in Tlaxcala in 1539. A sixteenth-century manuscript exists for *La conversión de San Pablo*, which Horcasitas attributes to the hand of an anonymous Christianized Indian.[1]

Three evangelical dramas in Nahuatl that are not derived from Scripture are *El mercader* [*The Merchant*], *Las ánimas y los albaceas* [*Souls and Testamentary Executors*], and *La educación de los hijos* [*Bringing Up Children*].[2] The first is a moral tale hinging on the theme of salvation and damnation. The second deals with the fate of souls in Purgatory. Most interesting of all is the third, a series of dialogues among mortal or divine beings relating to proper ethical conduct and devotional practice. Scholars find this play strongly reminiscent of the pre-Columbian practice known as *Huehuetlatolli*, in which the Aztec youth received oral instruction in ethical and behavioral matters from their elders.

Indeed, scholars have found glimmerings of pre-Conquest indigenous culture in all of these texts. At the very least, the stories they tell give evidence of having been modified to address specific indigenous practices and beliefs that the friars wished to promote or discourage. At most, as in the case of *La educación de los hijos*, the very essence of the drama appears to derive from native custom. The most certain trace of indigenous influence, and perhaps the most compelling aesthetically, is found in details of linguistic expression. The Nahuatl of these dramas incorporates the stylistic properties of Aztec poetry, its syntax, imagery, kinds of metaphor, and so on. Were the Spanish friars so well-versed in Nahuatl that they could compose with the graceful lyrical touches customary in that tongue? Or are those touches the result of a working partnership between the friars and their native assistants? Either hypothesis points to a remarkable and fleeting moment in the history of the Spanish/indigenous cultural encounter.

Theatre in Latin

A considerable portion of the theatre composed in the Spanish colonies during the last decades of the sixteenth century was neither in Spanish nor

---

[1] The texts of these plays in Spanish can be found in Horcasitas, *El teatro náhuatl*. *La adoración de los reyes* is also in Cid Pérez and Martí de Cid, *Teatro indoamericano colonial*. English versions of all except *La conversión de San Pablo* can be found in Ravicz, *Early Colonial Religious Drama in Mexico*.

[2] The English texts of *El mercader* and *Las ánimas y los albaceas* are in Ravicz, *Early Colonial Religious Drama*. The Nahuatl text and English translation of *La educación de los hijos* are in Cornyn and McAfee, "Tlacahuapahualiztli".

in indigenous languages, but in Latin, the language cultivated by the Jesuit order in its institutions of higher learning. The Jesuits, who arrived in Peru in 1568 and Mexico in 1572, were as enthusiastic as the Franciscan missionaries before them in their use of theatre as a pedagogical tool. A scholar of the genre, José Quiñones Melgoza, has calculated that in Mexico City alone, some fifty-two dramatic pieces were composed and performed in the Jesuit schools between 1575 and 1600 (Llanos, *Diálogo en la visita de los inquisidores*, xxvi). Unlike the Franciscans, whose native-language theatre was used in the conversion of great masses of people, the theatre of the Jesuit schools was intended for an educated elite. Their dramatic productions, although religious in content, were above all an exercise in rhetorical skill and humanistic learning; the intended beneficiaries were not only the audiences that witnessed these productions, but also the students who took part in them. This is not to say, however, that Jesuit theatre was a dry academic exercise. Contemporary accounts reveal that the Jesuits had a fondness for lavish visual spectacle that was very much in keeping with the overall tenor of the viceregal societies in which they lived.

As in the case of Jesuit university theatre in Spain, Jesuit theatre in the New World was rarely composed entirely in Latin; dramatic productions mixed Latin and the vernacular in varying degrees, the latter coming to dominate with the passage of time. This is surmised more by secondary than primary evidence: few texts of the genre have survived, although references to texts and performances abound in the *Litterae annuae* of the Jesuit order. Documents point to a continuing effort on the part of Church authorities to ensure propriety and doctrinal substance in Jesuit productions, as well as to maintain the dominance of Latin over the vernacular.

Two surviving texts composed entirely in Latin are the [*Ecloga*] *pro patris Antonii de Mendoza adventu* [*facta*] *in collegio Divi Ildephonsi* and the *Dialogus in adventu inquisitorum factus in collegio Divi Ildephonsi*, both by the Spanish-born Mexican Jesuit Bernardino de Llanos (1560–1639). The works are occasional pieces: the first commemorates the arrival of the Provincial of New Spain, Father Antonio de Mendoza, and was represented in the Colegio de San Ildefonso sometime between 1588 and 1590; the second was performed in the same institution in honor of the visit of a group of church inquisitors in 1589. Both works are eclogues, closely imitating those of Virgil in thematic and formal terms.

Theatre in Spanish

The first known work by a creole playwright, the *Desposorio espiritual entre el pastor Pedro y la Iglesia Mexicana*, was composed by Father Juan Pérez Ramírez (1545–?), son of one of the original *conquistadores* of

Mexico.[3] An occasional piece, it was performed in Mexico City in 1574 to celebrate the installation of the Archbishop Pedro Moya de Contreras – Pérez Ramírez thus anticipating generations of creole playwrights whose pens were to be occupied in eulogizing the ruling class. The play's allegorically named characters, in the guise of shepherds and shepherdesses, celebrate the marriage of Menga and Pedro, that is, the spiritual union of the Mexican church and the new archbishop. Its pastoral framework and linguistic refinement place the play within the tradition of the renaissance eclogue. At the same time, the presence of the comic "Bobo" and the elements of music and dance give the play a sprightly popular quality.

Another occasional drama, but of far greater length and ambition, is *El triunfo de los santos*, first represented by students of the Jesuit schools in Mexico City on November 2, 1578, as part of the eight-day celebration of the arrival in that city of saints' relics presented by Pope Gregory XIII.[4] Both a detailed description of these elaborate festivities as well as the complete text of the *Triunfo* have been preserved. The authorship of the drama, however, is uncertain. It is usually attributed to the Jesuit fathers Juan Sánchez Baquero and Vincencio Lanuchi, distinguished teachers of Latin and rhetoric and holders of high administrative posts.

El triunfo de los santos presents the story of the persecution of Christian martyrs by the Emperor Diocletian. Its five acts weave allegorical characters – the Church, Idolatry, and so forth – with historical ones. Everything about the play, from the bookish sources the authors employed, to the inspiration it found in Senecan tragedy, to its versification, in which Italianate verse forms prevail over traditional Spanish ones, gives evidence of the scholarship of the Jesuit order and the humanistic cast of its artistic tastes. It bespeaks, as well, an urbane viceregal culture, already far removed from a more austere post-Conquest era.

Another extant example of Jesuit theatre is the *Egloga pastoril al nacimiento del niño Jesús*, written in the closing years of the sixteenth century by the Spanish-born Mexican, Juan de Cigorondo (1560–?).[5] The eclogue, as its name indicates, belongs to the pastoral mode; the shepherds in question, however, are not allegorical transformations, but real shepherds, in the vicinity of Bethlehem on the night of Jesus' birth. Remarkably free from the ponderous, doctrinaire quality of so much religious drama of the time, the play is a celebration of both language and

---

[3] The text can be found in Rojas Garcidueñas, *Autos y coloquios del siglo xvi*, and in Ripoll and Valdespino, *Teatro hispanoamericano: antología crítica*.

[4] The text can be found in Johnson's edition and in Arrom and Rojas Garcidueñas, *Tres piezas teatrales del Virreinato*.

[5] The text can be found in Arróniz, *Teatro de evangelización en Nueva España*, 191–238.

the spirit. The shepherds speak in a variety of verse forms as well as in prose. Their speech varies from the rustic to the highly mannered, the latter mode paralleling the verbal brilliance of Cigorondo's contemporary, Bernardo de Balbuena, and prefiguring the preciosity of the Baroque. If the stamp of Jesuit accomplishment is to be remarked on this play, it is not in the form of erudition, but of lyrical virtuosity.

Another Spanish-born Mexican, Fernán González de Eslava (1534–1601?), is considered the most important playwright of the sixteenth century in the Spanish colonies, by virtue of the felicitous survival of a considerable body of his work as well as its inherent interest and quality. On the surface, the profile of his life and theatre resembles that of the authors already mentioned: González de Eslava was a clergyman; his sixteen *Coloquios espirituales y sacramentales* (published in 1610) are primarily of a religious and symbolic nature; many of these are occasional pieces; the element of panegyric, especially in the form of the *loa* (a brief laudatory introduction), is marked.

Such a superficial survey, however, cannot reveal the richness and variety of González de Eslava's dramatic works. To begin with, several of his colloquies are based on secular themes and local events (although, admittedly, they tend to allegorize and spiritualize the secular). Secondly, scholars have noted a distinct New World flavor in González de Eslava's theatre, especially in the use of linguistic peculiarities of Mexican speech. Finally, and above all, the colloquies are enlivened by four *entremeses* (not quite the independent entr'acte of a later era, but intercalated scenes of a humorous nature). It is on this last aspect of González de Eslava's theatre that most critics have focussed, and with good reason: the dramatic tension of the *entremeses*, their very human characters, linguistic verve, and satirical suggestiveness, all move González de Eslava's theatre beyond the predominant dramatic mode of allegorical pageant. The fact that the playwright spent some weeks in prison, implicated (without foundation) in the scandal caused by the performance of an anonymous *entremés* critical of the reigning viceroy, also helps to make of González de Eslava the prototypical creole author (despite his Spanish birth): a restless and creative intellect, often at odds with the very sociopolitical hierarchy that his works praise and sustain.

If satire in González de Eslava is tentative and cautious, not so in the case of Cristóbal de Llerena (?–?), a native of Santo Domingo and author of religious dramas, now lost. One *entremés*, however, has survived, thanks to the scandal it provoked and the difficulties that resulted for its author.[6] The brief piece in question, performed by university students as part of the Corpus Christi celebrations of 1588, uses humor to deride both

6   The text can be found in Icaza, "Cristóbal de Llerena," and Ripoll and Valdespino, *Teatro hispanoamericano*.

the customs of the city and its civil authorities. Llerena paid for his insolence with a year of exile. Even more than González de Eslava, he is proof that sixteenth-century Spanish American theatre was sometimes more than doctrinal spectacle or scholarly exercise; it could be socially engaged, even combative.

Authors and works: the seventeenth century

The extraordinary geographic mobility of Old and New World Spaniards in the seventeenth century makes classification of authors by nation difficult. Juan Ruiz de Alarcón (1581?–1639), one of the major dramatists of the Golden Age, is a case in point. Born in Mexico, Ruiz de Alarcón achieved fame as a playwright in Spain, to which he emigrated as a young man. The critical debate as to his true cultural patrimony has been inconclusive; criteria for classification are subjective and variable. In this survey, the primary criterion for inclusion of a playwright is place of authorship, not place of birth, which leaves several émigrés from the colonies to Spain – Ruiz de Alarcón most prominent among them – outside our purview.

Theatre in indigenous languages

The decline of missionary drama in the seventeenth century is paralleled by a scarcity of secondary sources on theatre in native languages. The authorship of some of the most interesting surviving texts is unknown, as is their date of composition. Scholars have relied on internal evidence – linguistic and stylistic – to place these dramatic pieces in their proper context, but results have been tentative. Such is the case of La comedia de los Reyes, a Nahuatl version of the story of the Magi.[7] The play is dedicated to the Franciscan friar Juan Bautista, and therefore attributable to his Indian assistant and collaborator, Agustín de la Fuente. The garbled date that appears in the manuscript title seems to be 1607, yet certain references as well as details of style and language seem to place the play much closer to the pre-Conquest period. Whether these clues argue for early composition or for indigenous authorship, the play is very much in the tradition of the missionary drama of the previous century.

The Quechua dramas El pobre más rico and Usca Paucar present an even more difficult scholarly challenge.[8] The manuscript of the former indicates authorship (Gabriel Centeno de Osma, about whom virtually nothing is known) but not the date of composition, while the manuscript

---

[7] The text can be found in Horcasitas, El teatro náhuatl.
[8] Both texts can be found in Meneses, Teatro quechua colonial and in Cid Pérez and Martí de Cid, Teatro indoamericano colonial. See also the facsimile edition of El pobre más rico with a Spanish translation (Centeno de Osma, 1938).

of the latter indicates neither author nor date. To place these works within the seventeenth century is conjectural, yet they seem to evoke that era: the impoverished Incan noblemen who are the protagonists of both works seem very much like a new, marginalized generation, at some remove from the trauma of the Conquest, yet haunted by its effects. While maintaining a personal refinement appropriate to their aristocratic lineage, they exist in a kind of existential void. Their situation, and the melancholy lyricism that gives expression to it, elevates these dramas above the superficial didacticism of their plots.

Both *El pobre más rico* and *Usca Paucar* tell the story of a destitute Inca who sells his soul to the Devil in exchange for earthly pleasures and wealth, but who is saved from fulfilling his contract by his faith in the Virgin Mary. Both plays are a call to Christian faith and, in particular, to veneration of the Virgin. They stress, as well, the illusory quality of material wealth, and the permanence and satisfaction of spiritual wealth. Despite their didactic intent, the plays are quite unlike the evangelical drama of post-Conquest Mexico: they take place in Cuzco, not in the biblical world; their protagonists are Incas, not characters from Scripture; references to indigenous culture seem fundamental, not accessory. The plays suggest an established cult of the Virgin – a *mestizo* Virgin, evocative of pre-Conquest divinities. Christianity seems not a foreign system, something to be explained to indigenous masses, but something already synthesized and made familiar, a remedy to cultural dislocation and personal despair. Even the marvelous lyrical passages of the plays seem to be a synthesis: some scholars (e.g. Cid Pérez and Martí de Cid) find them reminiscent of Incan poetry, while others (e.g., Meneses) discern the influence of the great lyricists of the Spanish Golden Age.

One of these greats, Calderón de la Barca, left his imprint on indigenous-language theatre in the form of the *auto sacramental*, a genre of religious drama which, in its Calderonian form, is allegorical in nature and has as its central theme the mystery of the Eucharist. A Nahuatl version of Calderón's *auto El gran teatro del mundo* was composed by Bartolomé de Alva (1604?–?), a secular priest and descendant of a prominent Aztec family. As its title suggests, the *auto* uses the allegory of theatre to represent man's passage through his earthly existence. Its baroque emphasis on life's illusory and transitory nature coincides nicely with similar themes in pre-Conquest Aztec lyric, with which Alva must have been familiar. Indeed, his Nahuatl rendition of Calderón is so free a translation, and so evocative of Aztec literature, that it perhaps deserves to be considered an original theatrical work. A short, untitled farce in Nahuatl accompanies the text of the *auto* in its one surviving manuscript.[9]

[9] The text of the *auto* is in Hunter, *The Calderonian Auto Sacramental*. The *entremés* is discussed by Hunter in his "The seventeenth century Nahuatl *entremés*."

The Peruvian *mestizo* Juan de Espinosa Medrano (1629?–1688), some-times referred to as *el Lunarejo*, composed at least two original *autos* in the Quechua tongue: *El hijo pródigo*, which allegorizes the tale of the Prodigal Son, and *El rapto de Proserpina y sueño de Endimión*, which allegorizes the classical stories of Persephone and Endymion.[10] Both kinds of *autos* – those based on Old Testament passages and those based on Greco-Roman myths – had precedents in Calderón. Was Espinosa Medrano mindful of Calderón's notion that pagan letters contained, in veiled form, the truths of Revelation? By composing these works in the Quechua language, with its concomitant cultural references, Espinosa Medrano was – wittingly or not – adding a third dimension to the cultural amalgam of the *auto*. Most remarkably, *El rapto de Proserpina* joins the Greco-Roman, Judaeo-Christian, and Native American worlds, a synthe-sis that in Espinosa Medrano's Mexican contemporary, Sor Juana Inés de la Cruz, becomes an explicit syncretism, as shall be seen in her Spanish-language *auto El divino Narciso*. This – and other aspects of Espinosa Medrano's largely overlooked theatre – merits further critical attention.

A handful of surviving texts attests to the cultivation of theatrical satire in native or mixed Spanish-native languages. Two brief works from this tradition are the *Loa satírica en una comedia en la fiesta del Corpus hecha en Tlayacapa* (1682), in Nahuatl and Spanish, and the undated *Entremés entre una vieja y un mozuelo su nieto*, in Nahuatl; the author of each work is unknown.[11] Also anonymous is *El güegüence o macho-ratón*, a brief comedy with dancing, in a mixture of Nahuatl and Spanish.[12] Of Nicaraguan provenance, it is roughly attributable to the seventeenth century, although its manuscripts date from the nineteenth. The play consists of a series of conversations between Güegüence, an Indian, and Spanish civil authorities. The humor derives from the lies, linguistic tricks, and salty jokes that the former uses to deceive and appease the latter. Brinton places the play more within the indigenous than the Spanish tradition; among his examples of pre-Conquest elements are the constant repetition of phrases and the comic device of feigned deafness and its resulting confusion (*The Güegüence*, xliii–xliv). The overall tenor of the play, with its waggish Indian protagonist and the overbearing Spaniards who serve as his foil, suggests a popular sense of resentment and resistance cloaked in humor and a show of deference.

---

[10] Both texts are in Meneses, *Teatro quechua colonial*. *El hijo pródigo* is also in Cid Pérez and Martí de Cid, *Teatro indoamericano colonial*.

[11] The text of the *Loa satírica* is in Ballinger, *Los orígenes del teatro español*. The *Entremés* can be found in French translation in Paso y Troncoso, "Comédies en langue naualt."

[12] Brinton's edition contains facing Nahuatl/Spanish and English texts. The text in Spanish can be found in Cid-Pérez and Martí de Cid, *Teatro indio precolombino*.

Theatre in Spanish

Two anonymous pieces, probably although not certifiably of the seventeenth century, are the *Relación de un ciego* and the *Auto al nacimiento del Hijo de Dios intitulado La prisión más prolongada con el más feliz suceso*.[13] The *Relación* is a brief (144 lines) dialogue between a blind man and his Lazarillo, or guide. It was apparently performed in a Mexican convent as part of Christmas festivities, and uses the language of the people, full of irreverent humor and colorful Mexicanisms, to allude to the conventual environs as well as the occasion celebrated within. The *Auto al nacimiento* is a sprawling representation of the Nativity, which combines pastoral characters, characters from the Old and New Testaments, and one allegorical character – La Naturaleza, or Human Nature, whose "prolonged imprisonment" ends with Christ's birth. It mixes, as well, the refined, lyrical language of the pastoral mode with crude humor. Rubén Vargas Ugarte, who discovered the play in a collection of Peruvian manuscripts, admits the possibility that it was not composed by a New World playwright (*De nuestro antiguo teatro*, xxii). Suárez Radillo echoes this doubt and suggests that the play may have been brought to Peru by a Spanish missionary (*El teatro barroco hispanoamericano*, 314).

Another play best characterized as anonymous, although it has been attributed by some to the Mexican Creole Cristóbal Gutiérrez de Luna (?–?), is the *Coloquio de la nueva conversión y bautismo de los cuatro últimos reyes de Tlaxcala en la Nueva España*.[14] The play tells the story of the legendary conversion to Christianity of four Tlaxcalan kings, through the intercession of Hernán Cortés and his companions. With its final emphasis on the Blessed Sacrament, the play qualifies as an *auto sacramental*, in the legendary–historic rather than the allegorical mode. Winston A. Reynolds has demonstrated the considerable debt that the *Coloquio* owes to Lope de Vega's play *El Nuevo Mundo descubierto por Cristóbal Colón* (pub. 1614); even the idol Hongol worshipped by the Tlaxcalan kings prior to conversion apparently derives from Lope's play, and is of Araucanian, not Mexican origin ("El demonio y Lope de Vega"). There are more glaring cultural incongruities: the Indians, with their allusions to Phoebus, Neptune, and Apelles, seem more like European courtiers than aboriginal noblemen.

Another tribute to the Sacrament is found in *El Dios Pan* by Diego Mejía de Fernangil (?–?), who was born in Seville but flourished as a poet, translator and playwright in Peru during the early seventeenth century.[15]

---

[13] Bryant provides the text of the *Relación* along with a brief introduction and notes. The *Auto* is in Vargas Ugarte, *De nuestro antiguo teatro*.

[14] The text is included in Arrom and Rojas Garcidueñas, *Tres piezas teatrales*.

[15] The text is in Vargas Ugarte, *De nuestro antiguo teatro*.

In *El Dios Pan*, the shepherds Damón, a pagan, and Melibeo, a Christian, witness and describe religious festivities in a Peruvian town, probably Potosí. Damón is persuaded by what he sees and hears to renounce his devotion to the pagan god Pan and to embrace the Christian God Pan, that is, "bread," the embodiment of Christ in the Eucharist. The description that the characters offer of the altars, banners, and processions that they observe are iconographically and anthropologically significant; despite the pastoral framework of the play, with its Arcadian characters and allusions, *El Dios Pan* gives interesting glimpses of popular Christianity in colonial Peru.

The *Auto del triunfo de la Virgen y gozo mexicano* (1620) by the Mexican Francisco Bramón (?–?) is an *auto virginal* rather than *sacramental*; it culminates in the exaltation of the Virgin Mary, who triumphs over *el Pecado*, or Sin. The play is actually a play within a novel, the pastoral novel *a lo divino* entitled *Los sirgueros de la Virgen*. Enrique Anderson-Imbert has argued that the shepherd Anfriso who "composes" the play is a dramatic transmutation of Bramón, and that, indeed, the entire novel has a secondary, autobiographical dimension (*Crítica interna*, 19–37). This kind of baroque embedding of works within works and authors within characters antedates by a half-century similar devices in the theatre of Sor Juana Inés de la Cruz. Bramón is also a precursor of Sor Juana in the dramatic incorporation of Aztec dance; his play concludes with a *tocotín* performed in honor of the Virgin by a character representing Mexico and others in Indian attire.

The *Comedia de Nuestra Señora de Guadalupe y sus milagros* was designed to propagate the cult of the Spanish Virgin of Guadalupe in the colonies. Composed by the Hieronymite priest Diego de Ocaña (1570?–1608), who took orders in the monastery of Guadalupe in Cáceres, Spain, before embarking for the New World, it was first performed in Potosí in 1601. The play is an early example of a *comedia a lo divino*, that is, a religious play that is, in essence, a *comedia*, with the standard characters, situations and themes of that genre. Father Ocaña weaves together stories of miracles performed by the Virgin of Guadalupe with the tale of Roderick, the last Visigothic king of Spain, whose illicit passion for Florinda was, according to legend, the origin of the Moorish conquest. The Roderick/Florinda plot allows for the incorporation of amorous intrigue and the honor theme, standard elements of the Spanish *comedia*, and gives the play moments of dramatic exuberance. But the fit between the various plots is bad, and the play, with its huge number of speaking parts and enormous chronological leaps – covering, eventually, more than seven hundred years – is ponderous and disjointed.

Another example of the *comedia a lo divino* is the *Comedia de San*

Francisco de Borja, by the Mexican Jesuit Matías de Bocanegra (1612–1668).[16] Composed and performed in 1640 in honor of the newly arrived viceroy, the Marquis of Villena and Duke of Escalona, it tells of another marquis, duke, and viceroy (to Catalonia), Francisco de Borja, who a century earlier had renounced his titles and riches to become a Jesuit priest. Woven into the story of Borja's religious conversion is an amorous subplot of a purely fictional nature: Belisa and Flora are two ladies of the court, both of whom are enamored of the noble protagonist and endeavor to win his love. As Arrom notes, the allegorical significance given to these characters, the former representing Beauty and the latter Vanity, is superficial; their real purpose seems more dramatic than didactic. They are stock figures of the *comedia*, and the love triangle they create is standard fare (*Tres piezas teatrales*, 229). Interesting to note, as well, is the choice of Borja as dramatic subject: a high-ranking administrator in the order, Borja had been instrumental in the introduction of the Jesuits into the New World; a titled grandee of Spain who chose a life of humility and devotion, he was a paragon of both civic and religious virtue. Thus, the play both glorifies the Jesuit tradition and provides the viceroy with a model of public and private conduct. Finally, it should be noted that, like Bramón's *Auto*, Bocanegra's *Comedia* concludes with the performance of a *tocotín*.

The genre of the *comedia a lo divino* appears to have enjoyed enduring popularity in the Spanish colonies throughout the seventeenth century. Near the century's midpoint, the already cited Peruvian author Juan de Espinosa Medrano composed a biblical drama entitled *Amar su propia muerte*.[17] The play is a massive and elaborate – yet dramatically effective – retelling of a cryptic story from Judges 4. Amorous and political intrigue serves, not to embroider an edifying tale, as in the *comedias* by Ocaña and Bocanegra, but as the very dramatic fiber of the play. A fine level of suspense is maintained throughout, and, despite constant plot complications, the thread of the story is never lost. The *culteranismo* of the play's verse is worthy of its author, who was best known for his *Apologético en favor de D. Luis de Góngora* (1662). Later in the century, the Mexican Francisco de Acevedo (?–?) was rather less successful in the genre of the religious *comedia*. His *El pregonero de Dios y patriarca de los pobres* (1684), a recounting of the life of St. Francis of Assisi, enjoys the baroque exuberance of Espinosa Medrano's play, but not its dramatic discipline. The imprudent fictional additions to the hagiographic story earned the play official censure from the Inquisition, and, it would seem, a somewhat

---

16 The text is in Arrom and Rojas Garcidueñas, *Tres piezas teatrales*.
17 The text is in Vargas Ugarte, *De nuestro antiguo teatro*, and in Ripoll and Valdespino, *Teatro hispanoamericano*.

sullied literary reputation for its author: Francisco Monterde identifies him as the Acevedo lampooned by Sor Juana in the second entr'acte to her play *Los empeños de una casa* (*Cultura mexicana: aspectos literarias*, 75).

Elements of the *comedia* also appear in a *coloquio* entitled *La competencia en los nobles y discordia concordada* by the Spanish-born resident of Cartagena de Indias (in present-day Colombia) Juan de Cueto y Mena (1604–?). In this work, the four elements Earth, Water, Air, and Fire are personified as gentlemen and ladies engaged in amorous dispute; the play combines Aristotelian cosmology with the rhetoric of love. The four are attended by a *gracioso* and a maid, stock *comedia* characters. Despite the play's final religious theme (the elements ultimately compete for the honor of serving as abode for the Virgin Mary), the play is really an ostentatious display of erudition and of dense, *culterano* poetic language. Cueto y Mena was also the author of the *Paráfrasis panegírica en forma de coloquio de la milagrosa vida y muerte del Ilustrísimo Señor Santo Tomás de Villanueva, Arzobispo de Valencia*, in which the personifications of Time and four Spanish cities eulogize St. Thomas of Villanueva. Both plays were composed and performed in Cartagena in 1660 as part of the festivities commemorating that saint's canonization.

There are a few extant examples of purely secular *comedias* written by New World playwrights in the closing decades of the seventeenth century. With the exception of those by Sor Juana Inés de la Cruz, they show little of the dramatic genius and intellectual verve of Calderón, to whose school they belong. For example, the anonymous *Sufrir para merecer*, probably by a Mexican Creole or transplanted Spaniard, is a *comedia de enredo amoroso* in which the *enredo*, or entanglement, is so thorough that the play is practically unreadable and, presumably, unactable as well.[18] The play reiterates themes of jealousy and amorous suffering without achieving the novelty within convention that characterizes the best baroque drama. Schilling also notes defects in the play's versification and inconsistencies in characterization (*Teatro profano en la Nueva España*, 184–96).

Just as unreadable, if for different reasons, is *También se vengan los dioses* by the Peruvian Lorenzo de las Llamosas (?–?). The play – actually, a *zarzuela*, that is, a dramatic work that alternates spoken dialogue and song – was performed in the viceregal palace of Lima in 1689 in honor of the birth of the viceroy's son. Set in an Arcadian world of gods, nymphs, and shepherds, the play is more spectacle than drama. Like the decadent post-Calderonian theatre of Spain, it substitutes lavish visual effect and linguistic preciosity for coherence of plot and substance of idea. *También se vengan los dioses* was part of a complete theatrical program; it was preceded by a *loa* in praise of the viceroy and was followed by a *sainete* (a

[18] The text can be found in Jiménez Rueda's edition.

light, one-act piece). It is representative of the kind of court theatre performed in Lima and Mexico City in the late seventeenth century, a theatre intended to flatter a patron and provide sumptuous entertainment for the court elite. Llamosas was the author of two other *comedias*, both of which were composed and performed in Spain, where the playwright, spurred by courtly ambitions, spent most of his adult life. Neither play is available in modern editions.

Another interesting example of late baroque theatre in the New World is the *comedia* entitled *La conquista de Santa Fe de Bogotá* by Fernando de Orbea (?–?). Nothing is known about the author, not even his country of origin. There are some indications that the play was composed in Peru; most notably, the final lines of the play address the city of Lima. The period in which the play was written – the late seventeenth century or early eighteenth – is surmisable from its *culterano* language and from the spectacular visual effects, so typical of the theatre of the time, that it calls for: earthquakes, elaborate battles, and even a fire-breathing dragon. The play's subject is the Spanish conquest of Bogotá, but inaccuracies abound: Bogotá is conquered by water, a geographic impossibility, and the Indians who appear as characters are transmutations of prototypes from Greek mythology. Even the sung snippets of their "indigenous" language are apparently an invention of the author. With its overlay of classical mythology, supernatural elements and fantastic American geography, the play is a late baroque reprise of the Spanish *comedia* set in the New World, composed by playwrights like Lope de Vega, Tirso de Molina, and Calderón de la Barca. But unlike the best examples of the genre, *La conquista de Santa Fe de Bogotá* is all spectacle and grandiloquence, with little dramatic substance.

The ascension of the baroque aesthetic in literary language and theatrical tastes in the Hispanic world, which led to such extreme examples of stylization as the theatre of Llamosas and Orbea, also left its mark on theatrical satire of the period. In the sixteenth century, González de Eslava and Llerena had composed satirical theatre aimed at social types and practices. In the following century, anonymous playwrights in native or mixed languages wrote lively, popular farces. But surviving examples of seventeenth-century satirical texts in Spanish seem more concerned with language itself, particularly the extravagant literary language in fashion. In 1628 or 1629, Fernando Fernández de Valenzuela (1616–1685?), a seminary student from Bogotá, composed the *Laurea crítica*.[19] This humorous skit satirizes several social types, who present themselves before an examiner to petition official decrees. The greatest attention by far is given to the figure of the *crítico*, who is unable to converse except in

---

[19] The text is provided by Arrom and Rivas Sacconi, "La *Laurea crítica*." It also appears in Camacho Guizado, *Estudios sobre literatura colombiana, siglos XVI–XVII*.

the inflated style of the Gongorist school. In this character's speeches, satire becomes linguistic parody, and the play becomes another in a long series of partisan texts in the great polemic regarding Góngora's mode of poetic discourse.

Some decades later, the Peruvian Juan del Valle y Caviedes (1645?–1697?), well-known for his large body of satirical verse, composed three short dramatic pieces: two *bailes*, or skits with dancing, entitled *El Amor médico* and *El Amor tahur*, and an *entremés* entitled *El Amor alcalde*. In form, they are not unlike Fernández de Valenzuela's skit; in each, several characters enter and converse (or sing) individually with a figure of authority. In Valle y Caviedes's skits, the central figure is Love, in the guise of a doctor, a gambler, and a magistrate; his interlocutors are lovers, whose amorous vicissitudes are expressed, appropriately, in terms of disease, chance, and transgression. The raw material for these skits is more literary than social; what is satirized, above all, is the rhetoric of love in its most stylized forms. Love is poetry and delirium, and the lovers and their mentors engage in a dialogue that alternates between compressed wit and sheer nonsense. In the *bailes*, the characters seem to partake in a kind of choreographed frenzy, a Dance of Folly. Verbal brilliance becomes madness, dynamism becomes derangement, and familiarity with mannered forms of discourse becomes an awareness of their absurdity. If the young Fernández de Valenzuela was a conventional parodist of baroque excess, the theatre of the mature and more talented Valle y Caviedes can be regarded as its dramatic apotheosis.

The theatre of Sor Juana Inés de la Cruz (1651?–1695) is the epitome of seventeenth-century Spanish American drama, in two senses: it summarizes major theatrical trends and brings them to their most perfect state. The Mexican nun composed both religious and secular theatre: three *autos sacramentales*, two *comedias*, eighteen *loas* (five of which precede her *autos* and *comedias*), two *sainetes* (entr'actes to one of the *comedias*), and a *sarao* (a short piece with singing and dancing that follows the same *comedia*). Her major patrons were the church and the viceregal palace, and her theatre reflects the self-promotion, barely disguised beneath a rhetoric of modesty, deference, and praise, that characterizes so many creole writers of the colonial period. Her literary models were Peninsular – in theatre, mostly Calderón and his school – but like the best colonial writers, Sor Juana was not content with imitation; subtle differences in outlook, heritage and inflection give her theatre an accent of its own. Typical, as well, is the presence of a satirical element in Sor Juana's theatre, one that gives a refreshing critical edge to a talent employed in the service of orthodoxies and hierarchies of power.

Each of Sor Juana's three *autos sacramentales* belongs to a distinct subcategory of the genre, with clear precedents in Calderón. *El mártir del*

Sacramento, San Hermenegildo is allegorical/historical: its subject is St. Hermenegild, a Visigothic prince of Spain who, according to Catholic lore, was martyred for his refusal to accept communion from an Arian bishop, represented in the *auto* as Apostasy. *El cetro de José* is allegorical/biblical: it tells the story of Joseph and his brothers in terms of prefigurations of Christ and the Eucharist. *El divino Narciso* is allegorical/mythological: it allegorizes the Ovidian myth of Echo and Narcissus. This play appeared in *suelta* form in 1690 and in the first volume of Sor Juana's *Obras* in 1691; all three *autos* were published in the second volume of the *Obras* in 1692.

El divino Narciso has received far more critical attention than Sor Juana's other two *autos*. The overriding reason may be the daring reach of its allegorical design. There is little in the classical myth to suggest Eucharistic parallels, but Sor Juana's *auto* finds striking allegorical possibilities. Narcissus is Christ, who contemplates the face of Human Nature – his own face – in the waters of Grace, becomes enamored of it, and dies, but remains for mankind in the form of the Narcissus flower, that is, the Chalice and Host of the Eucharist. Echo is Satan, who attempts to seduce Narcissus/Human Nature, but is rejected and reduced to linguistic mimicry. True to her inclinations, Sor Juana makes explicit the intellectual underpinnings of her allegory: following the precedent of Calderón, she states, at the outset of the *auto*, the syncretic harmony of Pagan letters and Scripture. The characters Synagogue and Paganism are asked by Human Nature to join forces in the representation of the *auto*; Paganism provides the allegorical "cloak," Synagogue the fundamental truth.

Of Sor Juana's eighteen *loas*, brief allegorical and laudatory dramatic pieces, the one that precedes *El divino Narciso* is perhaps the most interesting; it adds a dimension to the syncretic thinking that underlies the *auto*.[20] This *loa* has rightly been called a miniature *auto sacramental*: it allegorizes the Conquest, finding parallels between indigenous rites and the Catholic Eucharist. The *loa* begins with a *tocotín* sung and danced before the characters Occident and America, native monarchs. The ceremony honors the God of Seeds, an idol made of grain and blood, consumed in a sort of "communion." The characters Zeal and Religion, in Spanish dress, enter and force their Indian counterparts to submit, Zeal (a male) using force of arms, Religion (a female) using force of persuasion. Religion notes the similarity between the worship of the God of Seeds and the Eucharist, and offers to explain more fully the mysteries of the latter by means of the representation of an *auto sacramental* (*El divino Narciso*) whose combination of Paganism (Greco-Roman) and Christianity can

---

[20] An English translation of the *loa* can be found in Sor Juana Inés de la Cruz, *Poems*.

serve as an exemplary bridge between Aztec and Christian systems of thought and worship. *El divino Narciso* is thus framed as theatre-within-theatre; Sor Juana reveals a respect for the tradition of evangelical drama in the New World, a respect that derives not only from its pedagogical efficacy, but also from its philosophical integrity – the cross-cultural resonances and syncretic parallels that such theatre can reveal.

Sor Juana was the author or co-author of two *comedias*: *Los empeños de una casa*, whose first performance was most likely in a private residence in Mexico City in 1683, and *Amor es más laberinto*, probably first performed in the viceregal palace in 1689. Both works are *comedias de enredo amoroso* – comedies of amorous intrigue – in the Calderonian vein. *Los empeños* derives its title, its principal characters – two ladies and three suitors – and the basic configuration of its plot, from Calderón's *Los empeños de un acaso*. *Amor es más laberinto*, whose first and third acts are by Sor Juana, its second by Juan de Guevara, is based on the legend of Theseus and the Minotaur. Its mythological content, however, is a mere pretext for a rather typical *comedia de enredo*, Theseus being involved in a complex five-way courtship with two princesses of Crete and their respective suitors.

Both *comedias* develop variations on the theme of love through a series of plot complications: mistaken identities, misunderstood intentions, messages gone astray. Indeed, both plays seem intended as spectacles of entanglement, aesthetically compelling, above all, for their ingenuity and intricacy of design; in *Amor es más laberinto*, the Cretan labyrinth seems to serve as a metaphor both for love and for the play itself. Such meta-theatricality finds expression in the two *comedias* in other ways as well. There are moments in each when theatrical illusion is broken in a near-Pirandellian fashion. Commonplaces of the genre are deliberately inverted, such as the character of the female in masculine attire (the *gracioso* in *Los empeños* dons a woman's clothing). Finally, the author herself subtly intrudes into the dramatic fabric of both works: Leonor's famous autobiographical soliloquy in *Los empeños* seems a thinly disguised version of Sor Juana's early life, and Theseus's entrance speech in Act I of *Amor es más laberinto*, which develops the theme of the superiority of self-made to inherited nobility, has been viewed by some as a self-referential allusion made by the author to her aristocratic audience.

The second *sainete* of *Los empeños*, performed as an interlude between Acts II and III, takes the meta-theatricality and self-referentiality of the larger *comedia* to its conceptual extreme. Two characters, playing actors, pretend to rest between acts and comment on the play being performed. Noting its defects, its facile novelty, and the superiority of tried and true works by Calderón and other peninsular playwrights, they decide to assume a new role: they will pretend to be *mosqueteros*, standing spectators from the pit, and whistle in protest. This, they hope, will bring the production to a speedy end. Their commotion causes the alleged author of the *comedia*, Acevedo (perhaps the ill-fated Francisco de Acevedo discussed earlier), to emerge, distraught, and accept his deserved abuse. The tone of the *sainete* is playful, its humor lively, yet with its unflattering authorial masquerade, dislocation of represented spaces, dialogue of illusion and disillusion, and awareness of the timeworn and confining prestige of the Spanish greats, it seems to announce the end of an era. Sor Juana's theatre stands on the brink of the exhaustion of convention, the self-consumption of form, while maintaining, nonetheless, a level of wit, lyricism and imagination comparable to the best examples of seventeenth-century drama on both sides of the Atlantic.

[9]

Viceregal culture
Asunción Lavrin

The greatest challenge to the concept of a universe in which humankind was central to the explanation of history took place during the sixteenth century. The nature of the relations between peoples across the world took a new turn as European states embarked on unprecedented commercial and colonizing ventures in areas of the world inhabited by people of different races, beliefs, and social organizations. Those undertakings entailed a cultural exchange of political, social, and religious values through a process that was never peaceful, and that implied either the imposition of values by one dominant society on the other, or the displacement of the weaker group. While Europeans found a powerful cultural resistance in India and China, and were unable successfully to establish their culture there, the indigenous societies of the Americas became vulnerable after their military defeat. Spain, the main beneficiary of the first allocation of the newly discovered hemisphere to its west, through the Treaty of Tordesillas (1493) had an explicit interest in replicating its society and in furthering its religion there.

This goal implied a massive and long-term cultural enterprise. Cultural transfer involved many processes, some of which took place simultaneously and began to unfold from the time Christopher Columbus set foot on land in 1492. Others took time and developed through trial and error. Three hundred years of historical evolution meant that none of the peoples who met in the Spanish Indies escaped from change and no institution remained static. The indigenous cultures, a mosaic of expressions and different stages of evolution throughout the continent, sometimes bent to, sometimes resisted, the intrusion of European molds. They put up formidable opposition to the Spanish ambition of self-replication. The physical defeat of the Amerindians did not mean the obliteration of their traditional customs or their world view for throughout the colonial period indigenous and Spanish cultural elements mutually affected each other. In addition, African demographic and cultural elements were

286

introduced in the mid sixteenth century, when the slave trade began to supply the labor demanded by the intensive cultivation of tropical products. The degree of success that each of these elements of the population achieved in the process of retaining its own identity depended on the opportunities they had to maintain a relative independence from one another. In remote geographical areas, the indigenous world was able to retain many of its own features. In the midst of colonial cities, Spanish culture left an indelible trace. In the circum-Caribbean areas and the lowlands of New Granada and Peru, African cultural traits imprinted their own mark within the cities, and in the rural areas where Blacks labored.

The viceroyalty of New Spain, established by Antonio de Mendoza in 1535, ended the period of experiments in administrative schemes, and firmly placed the state and its bureaucracy in charge of colonial destiny. The viceroyalty of Peru, finally in place by 1548 after a bloody civil war among the conquerors, signalled the supremacy of the Crown and the beginning of a viceregal period that ended in 1825 with the final defeat of the last Spanish troops in South America. Two other viceroyalties were created during this period: that of New Granada, which after a trial in 1717 was recreated in 1739, and that of Buenos Aires, created in 1777.[1]

Throughout the long viceregal period in Spain and its colonies the cultural landscape experienced important changes. The humanism of the central European Renaissance was transformed by the protestant religious schism into a staunch defense of Catholicism during the counter-Reformation period after the end of the Council of Trent in 1563. The years between the mid sixteenth and mid seventeenth centuries were the zenith of Spanish culture, evolving from Italian and Moorish influences to become the expression of the conflicts within Spanish society and those created by its European and American empires. In the American continent the Spanish colonies set their own style of life in the seventeenth century, a period of erudite conceptualism, sensuality in form, and an emotional religious atmosphere flowering in a mercantilist society defined by deep class divisions. The dynastic change from the Habsburgs to the Bourbons at the turn of the eighteenth century brought important changes that culminated in administrative revisions and a reordering of the intellectual

[1] C. H. Haring, *The Spanish Empire in America* (New York: Oxford University Press, 1947); Mark A. Burkholder and Lyman Johnson, *Colonial Latin America* (New York: Oxford University Press, 1990); James Lockhart and Stuart B. Schwartz, *Early Latin America: A history of Colonial Spanish America and Brazil* (Cambridge University Press, 1983); Lyle N. McAlister, *Spain and Portugal in the New World, 1492–1700* (Minneapolis: University of Minnesota Press, 1984). For Spain, see, Antonio Domínguez Ortiz, *The Golden Age of Spain, 1516–1659* (New York: Basic Books, 1971); Stanley G. Payne, *A History of Spain and Portugal*, 2 vols. (Madison: The University of Wisconsin Press, 1973).

universe under the "lights" of the Enlightenment, the last cultural chapter of the viceregal period.

An attempt to synthesize the many forms of cultural expressions of viceregal Spanish America in a limited space would be self-defeating. It seemed appropriate to privilege several expressions of thought and art as the backdrop to a survey of the "high" culture which is the object of other chapters in this volume. Because sixteenth-century Spaniards regarded the city as the locus of culture, urban planning, architecture, and the plastic arts introduce other cultural expressions in this essay. Of the latter, none could be as important as language, as the foremost means of human communication, paramount vehicle of ideas, and a political tool managed by Crown and church to impose Hispanic culture upon their newly acquired subjects. The quality of daily life changed radically for Europeans settling in the Indies, and for the aboriginal populations. The exchange of animals and plants, the introduction of new techniques for the exploitation of natural resources, the concept of trade and profit, leisure activities, and daily rituals of social life are all forms of material culture that injected meaning into the life and history of the colonial people, and will be noted here.

Religion and conversion, and firmly held concepts of moral and political imperium are key themes in the history of the first 200 years of colonial life. There was, however, no firm consensus among the Spaniards on how to solve the ethical problems of ruling and the many problems encountered in the administration of the colonies. The debates revolving around these topics were critical elements of colonial culture. This essay will reflect the highlights of the process of cultural transfer and exchange between Spain and its colonies as expressed by notable figures and its key intellectual trends without pretending to exhaust all topics.

The cities: foci of art

Spanish culture was, above all, urban. In the cities the settlers and their descendants defined their personal and social goals, reaffirmed their rights through the use of Spanish legislation, asserted their religion, and expressed in architectural form their own concept of the world. The sixteenth century was a century of city-founding hardly rivaled anywhere else. As they drew up plans for the first cities, the Spaniards began the substitution of one form of understanding the living space – the indigenous – by another, the European. There was no homogeneity in either of these two conceptions. Indigenous cities reflected a variety of cultures. The Spanish model had deep historical roots. Few of the Amerindian urban complexes survived the Conquest for long. Tenochtitlán was razed during the final struggle between the conqueror Hernán Cortés and the Aztec leader Cuauhtémoc. Cuzco was slowly dismantled to serve as the foundation of a new Spanish city. Some of the great urban centers of Peru and the Maya cities of Mesoamerica had been either abandoned before the Conquest, or collapsed shortly thereafter.

The new cities followed the artistic canons fashionable in Spain in the early sixteenth century. Spain was then adopting architectural styles developed in Italy and France in the late fifteenth century and adapting them to the peninsula's Muslim and Romanesque heritage. Styles such as the late Gothic, still used in the early sixteenth century, and the *plateresco*, (decoration in imitation of the art of the silversmiths [*plateros*]), *mudéjar* (the Christianized version of Muslim art), and *herreriano* (a stern and solid renaissance style named after architect Juan de Herrera [*c.* 1539–1597]) dominated the sixteenth century, and influenced the unfolding of civic, religious, and private architecture in the first cities of the Spanish colonies.[2]

The plans of the New World cities show influence of the Roman *castrum*, a type of walled city with straight streets and a plaza used throughout Roman times and revived by the Catholic Kings in the building of the Spanish city of Santa Fé. The cities were to be constructed following precise orders from the Peninsula, already spelled out in the 1513 instructions for the plan for Panama (1519) and in the instructions given to conquerors Francisco de Garay for Tierra Firme (present-day Venezuela) and Hernán Cortés (1485–1547) in 1523. Philip II's 1573 *Ordenanzas de Población* reiterated the rules for the foundation of cities that prescribed the choice of sites and the exact location of the main buildings. The gridiron plan adapted for planning the cities had a civic and religious center and rejected the labyrinthine design of Arab and Christian medieval cities. The exceptions are found in mining towns such as Potosí and Guanajuato that were adopted to the contours of the terrain, or in cities built on previous indigenous cities, such as Cuzco. Central planning was also adopted for the Amerindian towns founded after the Conquest. Throughout the colonial period the municipalities controlled the growth of the cities, the height of the buildings, the location of

---

2 Useful as general surveys of art in Spanish America are, Leopoldo Castedo *A History of Latin American Art and Architecture: From pre-Columbian times to the present* (New York: Praeger, 1969); George Kubler and Martín Soria, *Art and Architecture in Spain and Portugal and The American Dominions: 1500–1800* (Baltimore: The Johns Hopkins University Press, 1959); Mario J. Buschiazzo, *Historia de la arquitectura colonial en Iberoamérica* (Buenos Aires, 1961); José de Meza and Teresa Gisbert, *Arquitectura andina, 1530–1830* (La Paz: Embajada de España en Bolivia, 1985); *Summa Artis: historia general del arte* (Madrid: Espasa-Calpe, 1986), vols. 28 and 29, with essays by Santiago Sebastián López, José de Mesa, and Teresa Gisbert.

markets, provision of water, the maintenance of the streets, the garbage and sewage, the movement of animals, and even the manner of celebrating popular and religious feasts.[3]

The first buildings, whether private homes, markets, government offices or churches, were modest wooden or adobe structures with thatched roofs. They were slowly replaced by stone as soon as municipal means permitted and rich patrons began sponsoring religious buildings. Most of the original sixteenth-century homes and churches were subsequently destroyed by earthquakes or fire, or were replaced by more sumptuous structures in the seventeenth century. The 1541 destruction of the capital of Guatemala was the first of several disasters to affect the location of its capital throughout two centuries. The building of cathedrals such as those of Lima and Cuzco was affected by the time it took to build them as much as by earthquakes, resulting in the redrafting of original plans and numerous changes over time. What remains today of sixteenth-century architecture are the solid fortress-like Dominican Order churches in central Mexico, churches such as that of the convent of San Gabriel, Cholula or San Agustín, Acolman; some mid-sixteenth-century churches like the parish church at Ozumba, state of Mexico; and the most solid of the domestic and religious buildings constructed at the end of the century, such as the Montejo house and the Cathedral of Merida, and the Cathedral of Santo Domingo.

Colonial civil and religious architecture resulted from the combination of European design with indigenous labor. Spanish and other European architects and craftsmen drew up the plans and brought to the task the technical knowledge required to build the new cities. Before the end of the sixteenth century, however, American-born masters were already working on several constructions. The great demand for masons, architects, and designers in the sixteenth century explains the extensive travels of some European architects of repute. Angelico Medoro, a Neapolitan, visited Quito in the late sixteenth century, and left for Lima in 1600, staying there for two decades. Francisco Becerra, a notable Spanish architect, was appointed by New Spain's Viceroy Martín Enríquez (1568–1580) to build the Cathedral of Puebla in 1575. Subsequently Becerra traveled to Quito in the early 1580s, where he drew up the plans for the churches of Santo Domingo and San Agustín, and the choir of the church of San Fransisco. He then left for Peru, where he undertook the construction of the cathedrals of Cuzco and Lima. When he died in Lima

[3] *El proceso de urbanización en América desde sus orígenes hasta nuestros días*, XXXIX Congreso Internacional de Americanistas, Lima, 1972, 2 vols. (Lima: Instituto de Estudios Peruanos, 1972). Selected essays by Woodrow Borah, Jorge Enrique Hardoy, Edwin W. Palm, Graziano Gasparini, and others are useful as summaries and sources of current debate; Ramón Gutiérrez, *Arquitectura y urbanismo en Iberoamérica* (Madrid: Cátedra, 1983).

in 1605, he had spent twenty-three years working in the viceroyalty of Peru.

Civic architecture never rivaled that of the church either in number of buildings or availability of funds. In smaller towns the church building was often the most important edifice, no matter how modest. While the viceregal palace of Mexico underwent several reconstructions and was an imposing building, some lesser cities did not have properly finished civic buildings until the eighteenth century. Such was the case of Santiago de Chile, where the Audiencia (Appellate Court) building was not finished until 1714, and where even the cathedral, built in the seventeenth century, was a modest and ill-appointed building in dire need of repairs by the mid eighteenth century.

Military architecture developed between the late sixteenth and the late eighteenth century, due to numerous attacks by pirates and corsairs on the coastline of the Caribbean Sea in the east and the Pacific Ocean in the west. Spanish or European military engineers left excellent examples of the state of their art, in Havana, Veracruz, Cartagena, Panama and Valparaíso. The Spanish style for domestic architecture, greatly influenced by Muslim and classic Roman models, was repeated in the New World regardless of location. Intimacy and seclusion dictated one- or two-story buildings flush to the street, with inner patios where various dealings with the outside as well as family recreation took place. The walls, built of adobe, stone or brick according to location, were often thick and crowned by tiled roofs. Special features were covered or open balconies on the façades of the houses, that reflected *mudéjar* taste.

The church as patron of the arts

The church was the main patron of the arts during the colonial period. Religious orders, more than the episcopal church, became key factors in the transmission of architectural styles. While there was only a cathedral church in the administrative urban centers, the male and female orders built hundreds of churches in the cities and the countryside that rivaled the cathedral churches in sumptuousness. The consolidation of wealthy elites in the viceregal capitals and provincial cities in the seventeenth century sustained the extraordinary proliferation of religious building and its attendant arts. The pious endowments of merchants, miners, and large landowners for the construction or decoration of churches and chapels were the mainstay of religious art. Sculptors and painters were surrounded by master carpenters, silversmiths, and gilders in charge of embellishing the interior of the temples.

In the viceroyalties of New Spain and Peru, a new architectural development prompted by the needs of the evangelizing church were the sixteenth-century open-air churches constructed to hold large numbers of converts and neophytes. Walled courtyards accommodated the church-goers, while roofed altars stood against one wall. This model had variations, such as the *posas*, open altars in the four corners of the courtyard to serve as stopping-places for prayers during processions. There were also small chapels at one end of the courtyard, big enough to accommodate the priests and the Spanish settlers while the Indians stood outside. Several open chapels were also constructed in the Andean region, with examples in Cuzco and Huamanga (Ayacucho). Examples of *atrios* or open space squares and *posas* are found in Bolivia.[4]

For the construction of churches the religious orders, such as those of the Franciscans and the Jesuits, quite often used their own friars as designers and craftsmen. Some of them were not Spaniards, but came from other European Catholic states. Franciscans Fray Pedro de Gante and Fray Juan de Alameda were among the first builders in New Spain. In 1564 the Franciscans of Quito brought two Flemish friars, Fray Jodoco Ricke and Fray Pedro Gosseal, and the German Jacome Germán to help in the building of their main church and cloister. These men brought with them important non-Spanish artistic influences. Dutch, Italian and French art was copied extensively in South America in the seventeenth century, while Central America and Mexico were closer to Spanish influence. After a destructive earthquake in 1647, the Jesuits obtained permission to bring in Dutch and French carpenters to rebuild their church in Santiago de Chile. They also introduced the Italian Baroque into South America. The plan for the Chiesa di Gesú in Rome, designed by Giacomo Barozzi, served as a model for their Colegio de San Pablo in Lima. The Peruvian building later served as an inspiration for Jesuit constructions in Chile and Buenos Aires. Plans for Jesuit churches were sent to Rome for approval where they received final touches from Italian architects.

The predominant religious themes of most art speak of the profound influence of the church as the main patron of this period. While English and Dutch arts were eminently civic and focused on homes and portraiture, colonial Latin American art was devotional, with the predominance of religious themes over any other. The influence of the church as a cultural venue for the arts was even more significant in peripheral areas, where it was the most important patron of high culture. In Chile the artistic contributions of the Jesuits between 1720 and 1776 were paramount. Johan Bitterich, a Tyrolean master sculptor, requested artistic help from Bavaria and a number of southern German Jesuits arrived in Chile in 1723. Following standard practice, the Jesuits built their own schools and temples, employing American-born *criollos*, Indians, and

---

[4] José de Mesa and Teresa Gisbert, *Iglesias con atrio y posas en Bolivia* (La Paz, 1961); John McAndrew, *The Open-Air Churches of Sixteenth-Century Mexico* (Cambridge, Mass.: Harvard University Press, 1965).

mulatto craftsmen. In 1748 Charles Haymbhausen, Profesor of Theology in Concepción and rector of the College of St. Michael brought books, tools and Jesuit artists and artisans from Europe to train a generation of artisans in Santiago. The influence of these German Jesuits on the creation of a tradition in Chile is important enough to be called Bavarian Jesuit Baroque.[5]

Another example of ecclesiastical influence in peripheral areas are the Franciscans and Jesuits communities known as *reducciones* or *misiones* where Indians were grouped to work, live, and worship under their direction. While this type of community existed throughout Spanish America, only some areas displayed a special artistic style of their own. The best-known are in Paraguay and northwestern Mexico.[6] This style acquired its personality in the late seventeenth century, when stone and adobe buildings with wood roofs erected by the friars were complemented by wooden doors decorated by the Indians. The best-known missions in the distant provinces of California, New Mexico and Texas, were built by the Franciscans, who expanded into these areas after the expulsion of the Jesuits in 1767. This is yet another example of the varied cultural sources of Spanish American colonial art, and of the importance of the church in the creation of an artistic identity almost everywhere in the continent.

European models and colonial creativity

The traffic of artistic models between Europe and the Indies was the mark of colonial art.[7] Copies of original European paintings, engravings, and altars, were already on their way by the early 1520s. Spanish, Dutch, and Italian artists and master craftsmen were sought after, and they became the mediators between Europe and the Americas, helping to maintain a vibrant intellectual exchange among several cultural centers in Europe and the Spanish colonies. The capital cities of the Viceroyalties and Audiencias served as the centers from which art and artists traveled to provincial towns everywhere in Spanish America. Lima and Cuzco acted as centers of artistic influence for Santiago, Alto Peru (Bolivia), and Buenos Aires from the early seventeenth century onwards. By mid seventeenth century Quito and Cuzco had become well-known centers of art, influencing the rest of Andean South America. In New Spain, Mexico City, the first nucleus of artistic production, was joined by Puebla in the seventeenth century, owing to the temporary artistic collapse suffered by the former during several decades after the devastating 1629 flood.

[5] Eugenio Pereira Salas, *Historia del arte en el reino de Chile* (Buenos Aires: Ediciones de la Universidad de Chile, 1965).
[6] Alberto Armani, *Ciudad de Dios y ciudad del sol: el "Estado" jesuita de los guaraníes (1609–1768)* (Mexico: Fondo de Cultura Económica, 1988); Kurt Baer, *Architecture of the California Missions* (Berkeley: University of California Press, 1958).
[7] George Kubler and Martín Soria, *Art and Architecture in Spain and Portugal, passim.*

In the sixteenth century master craftsmen founded guilds to protect their economic and artistic interests. Sculptors, painters, gilders, and others competed for contracts from private and religious patrons and attempted to control the admission into their group. The silversmiths of Mexico City were organized as early as 1537, and the retable painters, gilders, and the painters' guilds in 1557. Apprenticeship and exams were required to become a master craftsman, and elected officials regulated the price of labor. Although a great number of guilds were founded primarily to suit the needs of religious art (gilders, silversmiths, altar carpenters, blacksmiths), others catered for objects of daily use, such as leather garments and coaches. Guild regulations were revamped whenever necessary. New *Ordenanzas* for painters and gilders were written for Mexico in 1686, and for Chile in 1776. Their regulations appeared to be restrictive and exclusive, barring admission of non-Whites, but they could not be carried out in full or applied thoroughly.

Restrictions notwithstanding, indigenous and mixed-blood craftsmen obtained exemptions or carried out their work unmolested by the authorities. The initial training of Indian artists was provided by the religious orders. By the mid sixteenth century, Franciscan friars had founded schools of arts and crafts which prepared the Indians in all the practical occupations necessary to recreate Spanish culture. The indigenous population showed special aptitude for European arts. For example, they excelled in music, introduced by the friars as an appealing venue for religious conversion. The 1583 Lima Provincial Council recommended that church services be carried out with pomp, including music and singing. By the mid sixteenth century, all teachers of music in Quito were Indians, and their services were in demand in most religious and civil ceremonies.

If throughout the sixteenth century Indian and *mestizo* craftsmen copied European models, important American elements such as fruits and trees, and local costumes were introduced in the seventeenth century. These artists produced mostly religious works for churches, but countless artisans produced "popular" religious art for private homes and chapels. In Mexican and Andean cities some of the most notable artists were either Indian or *mestizos*. Quito was particularly rich in Indian artists.[8] In seventeenth-century Quito, master painter Antonio Gualoto and sculptor Gabriel Gaullachamin were much sought after, and equally famed was the *mestizo* Miguel de Santiago. Jorge de la Cruz and his son Francisco Morocho, possibly trained in the school founded by Flemish Fray Jodoco, built the choir of the church of San Francisco in that city in the late sixteenth century. Also well-known were Indian architects Carlos and

---

[8] Fray José María Vargas, *Arte quiteño colonial* (Quito: Litografía e Imprenta Romero, 1944), *passim.*

Antonio Chaquiri, and Manuel, Juan and Diego Criollo. Cuzco was another city where Indian painters excelled. The best known were Diego Quispe Tito (1611–1681) and Basilio Santa Cruz Pumacallao (1661–1699), both of whom left a school of followers.

In the eighteenth century, Bernardo de Legarda (d. 1773) was a much-feted *quiteño* master wood sculptor. Manuel Chili, better known by his Quechua name of *Capiscara* carved in marble as well as in wood. Another notable Indian painter and sculptor of this region was Gaspar Sangurino, known as *Iluqi* [Lefty]. He lived at the turn of the nineteenth century and is reputed to have inspired Simón Bolívar to found a School of Fine Arts in Quito in 1822 for Sangurino to direct. All these masters of the arts were directly inspired by Spanish, Italian, and Dutch arts, pointing to the constant exchange between Europe and America.

The Baroque as a style of art and life

Around the first quarter of the seventeenth century – it is impossible to pinpoint the dawn of any style with precision – a new world view, the Baroque, began to develop across Spanish America. For some scholars the Baroque represents not an artistic style, but a mentality or outlook that dominated the sensibility of colonial culture in all its manifestations. As such, while I will refer to art in this section, it should be understood that most of the mental outlook of the seventeenth and part of the eighteenth centuries, should be considered idiosyncratically Baroque. To quote Irving Leonard, the term "has come to designate an historical epoch and, subsequently, a way of life."[9] The Baroque could be artistically and culturally stretched into the 1750s. Art critics see a "late Baroque" in the first half of the eighteenth century, while the beginnings of a renovating mentality in the sciences and learning can be traced to the middle of the eighteenth century. Blurred boundaries rather than precise borders mark the transition of one period to the other.

The Baroque marked apotheosis and decline at the same time. By the early seventeenth century the most arduous problems of discovery and exploitation of resources, territorial occupation, administration, and evangelization seemed to have been overcome. The administrative structures of the Spanish colonies were in place, and both church and Crown were in control. Yet, these achievements were accompanied by a perilous decline in the indigenous population that began as early as the 1500s in the Caribbean islands, and the 1530s in the continental areas. This decline did not affect every region with the same intensity but the native population

---

[9] Irving A. Leonard, *Baroque Times in Old Mexico* (Ann Arbor: University of Michigan Press, 1971), p. viii. Mariano Picón Salas also refers to the Baroque of the Indies, in literature, learning, and the general outlook of culture. See Mariano Picón Salas, *A Cultural History of Spanish America* (Berkeley: University of California Press, 1963).

reached its nadir between 1620 and 1650. As early as the 1550s the first attacks of French, Dutch, and English pirates began a relentless assault on vulnerable coasts, while Portuguese raiders assaulted the Jesuit establishments on the Uruguay River. Beginning in the 1620s the fabulous wealth of the Potosí and Zacatecas mines suffered a decline in output which, in the case of the Peruvian mines, was hard to overcome. The Mexican production began to recover in the 1680s, but Peru lagged behind in production until the 1720s.

In Europe, Spain began to decline as a world power after the death of Philip II in 1598. Its role as champion of Roman Catholicism in the European Counter-Reformation forced a centralization of its political system and drained much of its economic energies. Torn apart by internal political strife, the English and French challenges, and the loss of the Dutch provinces, the once powerful nation was only a shadow of its former glory at the outset of the eighteenth century. Spain was, nonetheless, successful in maintaining its colonies firmly within its hold, and the Baroque expressed the style of life of its different areas. The great fortunes made in mining and trading in the seventeenth and eighteenth centuries created an affluent elite with a firm hold on the wealth of the land, and a proclivity for patronizing the church and religious art. The indigenous population began a slow but sustained demographic recovery by mid seventeenth century that, while not compensating for the great losses of the sixteenth century, assured its ethnic presence in the colonies. At the same time, the growth of a mixed population throughout the empire provided the labor necessary to sustain the economic expansion experienced by the 1730s.

For the church there was no protestant Reformation challenge in Spanish America. Indeed, the Counter-Reformation had one of its strongest pillars in the spiritual life of the colonies, where its official hegemony was complete. The expansion of religious building and rebuilding throughout the seventeenth century was extraordinary. Hundreds of churches, chapels, and shrines were built as the religious orders expanded into new areas, and the secular church ministered in the cities and some of the rural doctrines previously held by the orders.

The *Barroco de Indias* [Spanish American Baroque] was mostly religious, exuberant in color and shape, visually rich, and emotional. It was a clear expression of the cycles of regional economies and family wealth, the rivalry among members of society, and the tension between the demands of the world and those of the spirit. In addition to its European and some East Asian influences – developed through trade with the Philippines – the Baroque had many regional nuances in Spanish America. It was capricious and colorful in New Spain, a viceroyalty in which a steady economic expansion throughout the late seventeenth and eighteenth centuries supported a magnificent development of the arts. South American religious architecture was more severe in conception, although equally heavy and imposing. The massive buildings, mostly religious, of the seventeenth century were emblematic of the power of a church supported by the state. During the time of Bishop Manuel de Mollinedo's episcopacy in Cuzco, (1673–1699), there were over fifty churches built in the diocese. Temples were symbolic of the world of the spirit; yet they could be luxurious and sensuous in the representation of religious themes.

The architectural form took extravagant forms such as salomonic columns, *estípites*, pseudo-supporting elements shaped as upside-down columns, applied decoration covering most of the architectonic surfaces, and complex cupolas. Local stones, such as the red porous lava *tezontle* of Mexico, or the white lava stone of Arequipa (Peru), gave those cities a special character of their own. The threat of earthquakes forced the construction of heavy walls that added mass to the buildings in some areas, such as in Central America and the Andean highlands. Sculpture and relief became an intrinsic part of the architectural design, leaving little empty space on the surface. The Jesuit church of Arequipa and the cathedral of Zacatecas are excellent examples of this *horror vacui*. Art historians see the clear imprint of indigenous imagination in the architecture of some Andean cities such as Postosí, Pomata, Julí, Arequipa, which has been defined as "*mestizo*" or the product of adaptation of European architectural concepts with strong indigenous traces in the decoration and iconographic meaning.[10] On the other hand, some areas, directly connected to the peninsula, such as Cuba and Venezuela, developed a much more sober Baroque.[11]

Within the church, the Baroque expressed itself in *retablos*, altar pieces holding the sacred figures for worship in niches holding one or several figures. They were especially important in the seventeenth century as a medium to teach and express the intense religiosity of that period. Murals

[10] Art historians Angel Guido, Harold Wethey, José de Mesa and Teresa, Gisbert de Mesa and Pál Kelemen favored, at one time or another, the term "mestizo art." "Andean Baroque" is more frequently used at present. This style developed between 1690 and 1780. See a brief summary of the debate in *Arte Iberoamericano desde la colonización hasta la independencia* in *Historia General del Arte*, Sené Summa Artis, 29 (Madrid: Espasa-Calpe, 1988).

[11] While Pál Kelemen extolls the originality of baroque art in Spanish America, Graziano Gasparini and Erwin W. Palm refuse to accept the validity of a *mestizo* art or the existence of "schools" of painting, especially in the Andean area. They consider colonial art to be a pale reflection of European artistic centers, lacking in true creativity. See, Pál Kelemen, *Baroque and Rococo Art in Latin America*, 2 vols., 2nd. edn. (New York: Dover Publications Inc., 1967); Graziano Gasparini and Erwin W. Palm, "La ciudad colonial como centro de irradiación de las escuelas arquitectónicas y pictóricas" in *Actas y Memorias: XXXIX Congreso Internacional de Americanistas, Lima*, 2 vols. (Lima: Instituto de Estudios Peruanos, 1972), II, 373–86 and 387–92.

had performed that role in the sixteenth century, but as time advanced the greater realism of the polychromed wood carvings, with their melodramatic expressionism, became the favorite medium for conveying the religious message. During the first quarter of the seventeenth century, altars became the centerpieces of churches, employing more sculptors and allied craftsmen than painters. It was an architect designer of *retablos*, José Benito Churriguera (1650–1723), who introduced the style later to take his name, which represented the extremes of light-and-shade, twisted movement and excessive decoration known as *churrigueresco*. The best examples of this style are in Mexico, where the expanding economy of the first half of the eighteenth century allowed the construction of outstanding churches in this style. The most representative architect of this period is the Spaniard Lorenzo Rodríguez (1704?–1774), builder of the *Sagrario* of Mexico City (1749).

Baroque painting was best represented in South America by the Cuzco school of painting. With a distinct character of its own, it catered to the wealthy and more European in taste, as well as to the less educated in more folkloric tones. Largely the reinterpretation of European sources by Indians and *mestizos*, its homely virgins and life-size archangels dressed in colorful court clothes and engaged in several occupations, including the martial art of shooting, were unique expressions of colonial local art. The Spanish painters Bartolomé E. Murillo (1618–1682) and Francisco Zurbarán (1598–1669?) influenced much of the religious paintings of the urban centers of New Spain and South America.

Portraiture expanded in the eighteenth century to relieve the crushing dominance of religious art, and it was especially notable in New Spain. As such, this viceroyalty could boast of Mexican-born artists of recognized merit. The Mexican Rodríguez Juárez family produced several generations of painters between the seventeenth and the eighteenth centuries, masters of religious and lay art. A similar path was followed by José de Ibarra and Miguel Cabrera, who represented a continuous line in the painting tradition stretching from the mid seventeenth to the mid eighteenth century. Cabrera was the author of a well-known portrait of Sor Juana Inés de la Cruz, and a collection of *mestizaje* paintings, a theme that was very popular in New Spain in the second half of the eighteenth century.

After the end of the war of the Spanish Succession (1700–1713), a branch of the French Bourbon family succeeded the Habsburgs, who had ruled Spain since Charles I of Spain. The Bourbons opened a new chapter in the history of Spain and its colonies. While the reigns of Philip V (1700–1746) and Ferdinand VI (1746–1759) were not marked by forceful changes, a major administrative reordering of Spain and its colonies was undertaken by Charles III (1759–1788). During this period an intellectual renovation guided the artistic taste from the last stages of the *churriguer-esque* towards a new style, Neoclassicism, which was fully accepted by the 1790s. Imitating the Greek and Roman architectonic models, Neo-classicism responded to the Enlightenment's desire for clarity and ration-ality. Charles IV (1788–1808), favored a clear separation of church and state that would allow the revitalization of urban centers and the strengthening of civic architecture.

Neoclassicism was supported by the San Fernando Academy of Fine Arts in Madrid that encouraged the foundation of other academies in the Americas and approved of plans for the construction of civil and religious architecture in the colonies. A Royal Academy of Arts was founded in Mexico City in 1785, and another in Guatemala in 1795. The cathedral churches of Bogotá and Potosí, constructed in the late years of the colonial period, are among the best examples of neoclassic architecture.

As in previous centuries, European masters were instrumental in bringing Neoclassicism to the colonies. For example, architect Joaquín Toesca (1745–1799), born in Palencia of Italian parents, a student of Francisco Sabatini, became the royal architect of the Spanish court in 1760. Appointed to undertake the reconstruction of the city of Guatemala after its disastrous 1773 earthquake, Toesca went to Chile instead, at the request of the Bishop of Santiago, to take charge of the rebuilding of the cathedral. There he spent the rest of his life, designing and beginning the construction of the cathedral, and the Palacio de la Moneda, still in use as the presidential palace today. Neoclassicism was introduced in Mexico by Gerónimo Antonio Gil, appointed chief engraver for the Royal Mint in 1778, and promoter of the Academy of Fine Arts. The appointment of Manuel Tolsá (1757–1816) a Valencian sculptor appointed to the Mexi-can Academy in 1790 and director of architecture in 1810 was the turning point for the acceptance of the neoclassic style in Mexico. Neoclassicism was eagerly taken up in cities such as Buenos Aires, which lacked a strong baroque tradition. Thus, its cathedral, begun in 1754 and completed in 1823 is a perfect example of French-influenced Neoclassicism. The wars of independence created a small hiatus in artistic production, which began reviving in the early 1820s with new themes in painting – a new appreciation of nature, patriotic themes and eventually a new bourgeoisie – but as yet without a definite break with Neoclassicism in architecture or painting.

The Conquest: theological and philosophical issues

The sixteenth century was a century of intellectual controversy in Spain. The hopeful flowering of Humanism in the early decades of the century had to contend with the religious conservatism resulting from the conquest of the territory under the rule of the last of the Muslim kingdoms, and the wish to achieve a unity of faith in the peninsula. The discovery of the New World would add yet another element to the debate by posing the question of the rationality of the indigenous people, their potential for conversion, and the right to establish sovereignty over them.

The justification of imperium

The issue of the Spanish title to rule over the newly discovered lands was also under scrutiny. In the bull *Inter Caetera* (1493), Pope Alexander VI invoked his God-given authority to divide the world and granted the task of spreading Christianity to the Spanish Catholic Kings. Several years later this authorization began to be questioned by some theologians who searched for a better definition of authority. The debate created by the definition of physical and spiritual authority over the newly discovered lands and peoples became one of the main philosophical preoccupations of the sixteenth century. The religious orders were intimately involved in the definition of political and philosophical guidelines. The Dominicans argued the bases of political rule and the rights of the new subjects, while the Franciscans inherited the visionary hopes of the renaissance Humanists *par excellence*, Erasmus (1466–1536) and Thomas More (1478–1535). Erasmus, the expounder of a return to Christian principles within the framework of classical and patristic knowledge, had numerous readers and followers in Spain. But Erasmian advocacy of the authority of the Bible became suspect after Protestantism took root in Europe, and his writings were systematically banned from Spain and its possessions. Before this took place, however, the nucleus of his ideas had been adopted by men such as Fray Juan de Zumárraga, first bishop of Mexico and writer of a book of indoctrination (*Doctrina Christiana*, 1543–1544) for the Indian subjects. In 1559 this work was censured by the Archbishop of Mexico because it contained theological statements of dubious orthodoxy.

Thomas More had a more tangible influence in the New World. The man who attempted to follow the model of *Utopia* in Mexico was Vasco de Quiroga (1470?–1565), member of the second Audiencia and first bishop of Michoacán. Quiroga was a sixty-year-old lawyer in 1530 when the Crown requested his services in Mexico. Having helped restore order in the Mexican capital, he founded the hospital-city of Santa Fé, as a social experiment. It was a place where the Indians were evangelized and trained in various trades. In 1533 he introduced a similar system among the Tarascan Indians, founding several towns, each one of which specialized in a different trade or in an agricultural crop. In 1535 Fray Juan de Zumárraga proposed him for the bishopric of Michoacán, and after taking holy orders, he was consecrated in 1539. There he founded schools for boys and girls, and a hospital.[12] This was the most successful planned social experiment in the New World. The separation of the Indians and Spaniards in two republics, a socio-political concept underlying many of the Crown's policies and the church's hopes would never be a reality except in planned communities such as the *pueblo-hospitales*. To some extent Quiroga's success served as a model for the confinement of Indians in special towns in the last quarter of the sixteenth century, but for demographic and labor reasons which were absent from Quiroga's plan. The *pueblo-hospitales* supported the arguments of those who believed in the perfectibility and rationality of the Indian, but they also demonstrated the capability of the colonizer to redraw the features of indigenous life.

The theological debates carried out in the first half of the sixteenth century between the Dominicans and their opponents had an important political objective: the justification of Spanish sovereignty over the indigenous peoples. Most of the men who participated in this debate had little or no experience in the Indies. But, the thrust of the arguments debated had nothing to do with reality. They were a test of the principles rooted in European philosophical traditions against the political necessity of justifying power. The touchstone of the argument was whether or not the Indian was a "natural man", incapable of assimilating civilized life, and therefore best off living under the rule of more civilized people. This argument turned on the Aristotelian assumption that some people were "by nature" slaves.[13] Thus, the Spanish settlement could be justified by the nature of the Indians themselves rather than by the dictum of any human authority. The theory of the natural slave had been refined by Thomas Aquinas and in *c.* 1513 by Juan López de Palacios Rubios, who used it to elaborate a justification of conquest based on the Indian's barbarism. To justify the wars waged against resisting Indian groups all *conquistadors* were ordered, in 1526, to call on them to accept Spanish sovereignty. This formula, known as the *requerimiento*, gave Spanish occupation a gloss of legality, but as a much-abused device during the first decades of the Conquest it fueled indignation in the conscience of several influential theologians.

The first set of laws regulating the relationship between Indians and Spaniards was issued by Dominican theologians in Burgos (1512). It assumed that the Indians were lazy and unmotivated, but this assumption was mollified by the desire to impose order in the new settlements and establish a modicum of peace and respect for the indigenous peoples

---

[12] Fintan B. Warren, *Vasco de Quiroga and his Pueblo-Hospitals of Santa Fe* (Washington: Academy of American Franciscan History, 1963).

[13] See Antony Pagden, *The Fall of Natural Man* (Cambridge University Press, 1982); Silvio Zavala, *Filosofía de la conquista* (Mexico: Fondo de Cultura Económica, 1984).

conducive to their conversion. The legislation had been stimulated by the 1511 excommunication of the settlers of Hispaniola by Dominican Fray Alonso de Montesinos, who claimed for the Indians the status of free subjects of the Crown and objected to their physical mistreatment. The discovery of Mexico and Peru changed the philosophical and theological debate. The complexities of the Aztec and Inca societies destroyed the basis for the assumption that the Indians were wild humans liable to servitude.

Francisco de Vitoria: challenge and accommodation

It was the task of the Dominicans of the Salamanca school, Fray Francisco de Vitoria (1486–1546) and Fray Domingo de Soto (1494–1560) to shake the arrogant intellectual self-confidence of the conquistadors and early settlers by questioning not only the warped premises of the *requerimiento*, but also the assumption of papal and royal authority to determine the destiny of other peoples. Between 1532 and 1539 Domingo de Vitoria developed an important body of thought on the right of the Spaniards to rule and evangelize. Vitoria used sharp logic in his arguments, basing his assumption on Thomist rules of natural laws, and the consensus reached by the human community on what is true and ethical. To resolve the most important ethical controversy of his time, he shattered old assumptions in order to build the only ones acceptable to him as a Christian. A link between past and present had to be established in a manner which, without denying the existence of the new reality, could accommodate it into accepted patterns of thought. Vitoria put to the test the claim of savagery over the Indians by explaining their civilization. They had cities, and laws, trade and religion, but, in his opinion, they had failed to achieve a satisfactory stage of development in their legislation and social life. Taking the Aztecs as his example, he acknowledged that their religion was marred by practices such as cannibalism which defied natural laws. Their lack of sophistication in certain aspects of technical development, such as metallurgy, the lack of the wheel, the perceived imperfection of their writing – or lack of it altogether – cast doubts on their having achieved a true state of civilization. They had, however, the potentiality to achieve higher stages of development. By living with Europeans and becoming Christians the Indians, like peasants, would realize their highest potential. The Spaniards had the right to exercise *imperium* over the Indians for the latter's benefit.

Destroying all currently used arguments, Vitoria attempted to establish a principle of law acceptable to all peoples. It was the principle of freedom of access. Spaniards and Indians would enjoy the freedom to travel, to trade, and to preach. Indians would respect the freedom of the Spaniards to the same degree that Spaniards were to respect theirs. However, the

Indians would not have the option of preaching their own faith. Vitoria was a Roman Catholic friar in troubled times, and the word of Christ admitted no questioning. Spaniards would preach peacefully. Furthermore, Vitoria granted to Spaniards the exclusive right to preach the Gospels, upon the authority of the Pope, admissible in that instance, but solely for that purpose. Christianized Indians should be protected from hostility, but aggression would be repelled.

Vitoria eroded the claim of the universal rule of the Pope and the papal donation, but did not remove the foundation for occupation, although he humanized and Christianized it. Vitoria illustrates the dilemma posed to the early sixteenth-century Christian Humanist facing the development of the use of force against peoples that did not form part of his previous mental universe, and who had never been exposed to Christianity. The ethical quandary was resolved by resorting to preaching for conversion. The practical implications of Vitoria's thoughts were limited. By the time he had polished and published his thoughts the effective conquest of the key areas of the New World had already taken place. His influence was intellectual. Among his followers were Alonso de la Vera Cruz (1507–1584), the first philosophy professor in New Spain, Bartolomé de Ledesma (d. 1604), who went to Peru, and Tomás de Torre, who lived in Guatemala. These men helped to soften the rough edges of the Indian–Spanish encounter.

Other voices: the Las Casas-Sepúlveda controversy

The Dominican school found its most versatile and vocal exponent in Fray Bartolomé de Las Casas, whose ideas evolved slowly as a layman and as member of the order, after he took the religious vows in 1522.[14] A man of an intensely religious and combative nature, Las Casas practiced what he preached and attempted a peaceful conquest in Chiapas (then reached from Guatemala), although he spent most of his life traveling and arguing his points as a man of letters in the pursuit of a utopian society. *De unico vocationis modo* (1537), written at the time Vitoria was in the final stages of his own intellectual understanding of the Conquest, argued for a conversion carried out without violence, through persuasion and good examples. Like Vitoria, Las Casas never questioned the right of the Indians to defend themselves. The principle of natural rights, belonging to the individual as such and to all people living in organized societies, was the backbone of Vitoria's and Las Casas's thought. Natural rights gave the Indians the free will to choose to become subjects of the Spanish King and to accept Christianity. There was never any doubt in Las Casas's mind that the Indians would do so. God had a universal plan and history

---

[14] Juan Friede and Benjamin Keen, eds. *Bartolomé de Las Casas in History: Toward an understanding of the man and his work* (DeKalb: Northern Illinois University Press, 1971).

was unfolding it. The role of Spain was not questioned by those who continued to regard the papal donation as a valid entitlement, and who were willing to justify war as a vehicle by which to impose political rule and to spread Christianity. Their argument was best expressed by Juan Ginés de Sepúlveda (1474–1557), a well-traveled expert on Aristotle and educator of Prince Philip (later Philip II). In the 1530s Sepúlveda developed a theory of justification of war for Christian conversion in his *Democrates primus*, which he later extended to the specific case of the New World, *Democrates secundus* (1544). The Indians had committed crimes against nature, such as enslavement and subjection, which deserved punishment. The Indian was considered an Aristotelian "natural slave," a person without freedom for personal action. Drawing a warped picture of Indian societies as having innumerable social and personal defects, he angered the intellectuals of the Salamanca school and, above all, Fray Bartolomé de Las Casas. Sepúlveda's and Las Casas's arguments had a hearing in Valladolid in 1550 before members of the Council of the Indies and several theologians who heard both men argue their case at the request of Charles I (V) of Spain. Las Casas's arguments were geared to demonstrating that the indigenous societies satisfied Aristotelian standards of civility. Their governments followed their own customs and laws, and they could not be blamed if they were different from those of Europeans. The Indians were simply at a different stage of development than other peoples. While redeeming the Indians from the stigma of being inferior, his arguments did not relieve them from the state of being in a "growing" stage, just like children. Las Casas's thought prevailed but his was an intellectual triumph that changed little in reality.[15]

The Sepúlveda–Las Casas controversy represented the moral and legal dilemma that occupied the best minds of the sixteenth century, and the limits of any intellectual dispute of that time. In 1542 the Crown enacted the *New Laws* restricting the possession of *encomiendas*, and the right that the holders of those titles had to exact tribute from the Indians. But the *New Laws* were not immediately enforced in the New World. Eventually, a bowdlerized version of the legislation that protected *encomienda* holders for two generations was enacted. By the end of the sixteenth century the demographic and economic realities of the settled areas had changed enough to make the intellectual debate outmoded. In the last quarter of that century many royal ordinances eliminated the

---

[15] Lewis Hanke, *All Mankind is one. A study of the disputation between Bartolomé de Las Casas and Juan Ginés de Sepúlveda on the religious and intellectual capacity of the American Indians* (DeKalb: Northern Illinois University Press, 1974); and with Manuel Giménez Fernández, *Bartolomé de Las Casas, 1574–1566. Bibliografía crítica* (Santiago: Fondo Histórico y Bibliográfico José Toribio Medina, 1953).

word "war" and encouraged peaceful settlement and coexistence. Yet, these are the same years that witnessed the effective dismantling of the Incas' political and social organization in Peru, the beginning of the waning of the influence of the regular orders in the definition of social policies, and the ascendancy of peninsular formulas in the administration of the colonies and the execution of the law.

Philip II had none of the ethical doubts of his father Charles V, and adopted a straightforward policy of royal centralization that removed the remnants of any freedom of interpretation from members of the church. In Peru, Viceroy Francisco de Toledo (1515–1582) represented the reaction against the broad Humanism of the first friars, the counter-Reformation spirit, and a new type of militancy in the imposition of a new world view. Between 1570 and 1572 Toledo gathered information (*Informaciones*) among the Indians to prove that the Incas had been tyrannical and not the natural lords of their people. As the immediacy of the Conquest receded in time, historians and lawyers consolidated the view of the just title of Spain to the New World, and its duty and mission to lift up the Indians from their condition.

Post-scriptum to the sixteenth-century debates

In the seventeenth century Spain was effectively challenged on the high seas and its hopes to restore the Roman Catholic Church to its former unity were permanently shattered. Having lost ground to the Dutch in the Netherlands, Spain also lost its claim to and possession of the Portuguese Crown. But the apparent breakdown of the European scenario and the *raison d'être* of Spain in Europe did not affect the consolidation of its dominions in the Americas. The seventeenth century produced the most solid forensic works of the colonial era, reaffirming the supremacy of Spain and its just title to the portion of the New World it had succeeded in occupying effectively. Erudite studies of contracts, taxation, and juridical procedures suggest a mentality concentrated on the final definition of political, economic, and social structures. These features characterize the best legal minds of the period, including its earliest representative, Juan de Matienzo (1520–1579), author of *Del gobierno del Peru*, (written in the 1560s), and the mid seventeenth-century baroque erudites, Antonio de León Pinelo (1590–1660), author of *Tratado de las confirmaciones reales de encomienda y casos en que se requieran para las Indias Occidentales* (1630), and Juan de Solórzano Pereira (1575–1655), author of *La Política indiana* (1629, 1639) and co-worker with Pinelo in the massive legal compilation known as the *Recopilación de las Leyes de Indias* (1680). The *Recopilación* crowned the movement towards the consolidation of the laws, and represents the systematization of a forensic literature that had been developing since the late sixteenth century. The discussion of the rights of the Indians still occupied an important place, although it boldly asserted the right of Spain to its possessions. Matienzo and Solórzano examined the issue of the individual freedom of the new subjects of the Crown, with Matienzo reasserting the unfitness of the Indians for self-rule, and Solórzano arguing that regardless of their cultural level, they deserved to be ruled with justice. Neither of them, however, had much respect for the indigenous people, but Solórzano could reflect on the subject with the advantage of time. For his part, Antonio de León Pinelo was an avowed supporter of Spain's rights and rejected all theories of Inca and Aztec abilities. Self-justification won the ultimate victory in a debate that took over 150 years to find its resolution.

Conversion and religious life in the colonial setting

The conversion of the inhabitants of the New World to Roman Catholicism was one of the stated goals of its "spiritual conquest," and one of the most ambitious and controversial cultural agendas of its colonial history.[16] The juxtaposition of these spiritual ends with the material pursuits of the settlement created contradictions in theory and practice still under debate today.

The task of evangelization was not carried out with equal fervour or thoroughness everywhere in the continent. The Antillean period of the Conquest was marked by a lack of ecclesiastical influence. Despite condemnations as strong as those of Fray Antonio de Montesinos (d. 1515) against the Spanish abuse of the Indians in Hispaniola, the church was poorly equipped to set up an effective conversion effort in the first decade of the sixteenth century, while it was still engaged in a similar task among the conquered Muslims in Granada. The conquest of Tenochtitlán in 1521 provoked the first serious attempt to convert the inhabitants of the expanding new world.

New Spain was fortunate in having received a distinguished contingent of talented and exemplary Franciscan friars who carried out a daunting exercise in spreading Christianity among the Indians. Peru, involved in a civil war for many years, had a less favorable experience. There, the task of conversion was carried out in a less methodical manner and without the educational zeal present in Mexico. Even under the best circumstances, conversion was a painful and trying process for both parties involved. Zeal could lead to obfuscation. The trial for idolatry and ultimate execution of *cacique* Don Carlos in 1539, under the inquiry of Fray Juan

---

[16] See the classic work by Robert Ricard, *La conquista espiritual de México* (Mexico: Editorial Jus, 1947).

de Zumárraga (1468–1548) was highly criticized by the Crown. Zumárraga, despite his affiliation to renaissance Humanism, as the first episcopal inquisitor of Mexico favored the inclusion of the Indians under the Inquisition's jurisdiction. Bishop Diego de Landa's ruthless persecution of Mayan "infidels" in Yucatan was also a regrettable incident for which he had to account in Spain.[17] Their personal campaign against idolatry, while not shared by other men of the cloth, expressed the non-negotiable nature of the Christian conversion by early sixteenth-century evangelizers. The acceptance of Christianity was a *sine qua non* of Spanish settlement in the New World, and the investigation of idolatry extended into the seventeenth century.

Inculcating orthodox Christian beliefs in the indigenous population was no easy task, given the enormous obstacles in communication and the difficulties in grasping each other's cosmological views. Destruction of the symbols of the existing religions was accompanied by mass conversions in an initial raw process of Christianization carried out by men such as Fray Toribio Benavente (*Motolinía*, 1499?–1569), who believed in this method. Others, such as Fray Bartolomé de Las Casas (1474–1566) opposed mass baptisms, and believed that Christianization required a process of indoctrination. By the end of the 1530s the newly appointed episcopal and the regular ecclesiastical authorities in New Spain began to refine conversion through the education of children and neophyte indoctrination through the teaching of the articles of Christian faith.

It is nearly impossible to ascertain how the Indians experienced the process of conversion and assimilation of Christianity, since most of the testimonies available emanate from the conquerors or from Christianized Indians. Under the direction of the members of several key regular orders, conversion seemed to have progressed rapidly in the second half of the sixteenth century, incorporating most easily those born in that period, and closer to the centers of indoctrination, the *reducciones*. These were either newly founded towns or older ones used as centers to gather together several communities. The friars of several orders remained popular among many rural communities who resisted their slow substitution by secular priests, ordered by the Crown after the Council of Trent (1545–1563).[18]

---

[17] Richard E. Greenleaf, *Inquisición y sociedad en el México colonial* (Madrid: José Porrúa Turanzas, 1985); *The Mexican Inquisition of the Sixteenth Century* (Albuquerque: University of New Mexico Press, 1969); Inga Clendinnen, *Ambivalent Conquests: Maya and Spaniard in Yucatan, 1517–1570* (Cambridge University Press, 1987).

[18] The friars belonged to orders who lived by rules (*regula*). The secular priests were the members of the church who traditionally administered the sacraments of baptism, marriage, and extreme unction. Their hierarchy was presided over by the Pope, and comprised cardinals, archbishops, and bishops, in charge of specific administrative units.

Evangelization, learning and religious syncretism

Evangelization was accompanied by a process of learning about the indigenous people carried out by different individuals for different purposes. A Dominican friar, Diego Durán (1537–1588) compiled a history of the Aztecs, but he was overshadowed by Franciscan Fray Bernardino de Sahagún (1500?–1590), whose compilation of a vast amount of information on the Aztecs throughout several decades had no parallel elsewhere. His work, *Historia general de las cosas de Nueva España* covered all aspects of daily life and beliefs, political and social organization, technology, and scientific knowledge. Sahagún and his companion Fray Andrés de Olmos (*c*. 1491–*c*. 1571), another early student of Aztec culture, based their work on oral sources and complemented them with illustrations which constitute one of the earliest sources of visual history resulting from the encounter of two cultures.[19] The Bishop of Yucatan, Diego de Landa (1524–1579), wrote the only available Spanish contemporary source for the Mayas (*Relación de las cosas de Yucatán*), a poor substitute for the countless codices he burned in 1562 to destroy such sources of superstitions.

In Peru, Pedro Cieza de León (1518?–1569) in his *Crónicas del Perú* satisfied his own curiosity in learning about the Incas and furnished one of the best accounts of that civilization. Later, in 1559, Polo de Ondegardo, a royal official in Cuzco was the first to carry out an enquiry into Indian beliefs. His results were first published in 1585 in *Instrucción contra las ceremonias y ritos que usan los indios* ... and *Tratado y averiguación sobre los errores y supersticiones de los indios*. Knowledge of each other's culture did not necessarily contribute to mutual understanding at this early date. In fact, works such as Polo de Ondegardo's had the purpose of demonstrating the cruelty of the indigenous rule. Due to the Inca's resistance to Spanish settlement under the leadership of Titu Cusi Yupanqui and Tupac Amaru, Viceroy Francisco de Toledo (1515–1582) began a thorough "Hispanization" program that arrested the process of mutual knowledge.

Despite the monopoly of belief enjoyed and enforced by Roman Catholicism, the effectiveness of the Christianization process remained questionable. Once the first generation of missionaries died and the secular church rooted itself in the New World, the task of evangelization declined in inner strength except in those border areas such as northern New Spain and Paraguay, where missions under the direction of the regular orders continued to thrive. Just as the church began to feel confident that Roman Catholicism had been accepted by the Indians,

[19] Munro S. Edmonson (ed.) *Sixteenth-Century Mexico: The work of Sahagún* (Albuquerque: University of New Mexico Press, 1974).

news of "pagan" cults in border areas and in established dioceses shook that certainty. In 1608 a priest in Cuzco discovered the cult of a *waka* (Andean sacred place or god) during the feast of the Assumption. Campaigns to uproot such practices (*extirpaciones*) were carried out in key areas of Peru, Central America, and New Spain in the ensuing half-century.[20] Even within orthodoxy some forms of Catholic worship remained close to indigenous sources. For example, the Señor de Huanca in Calca (Cuzco) and the Virgin of Guadalupe, in Mexico, "appeared" to Indian believers in sites of ancient pre-Hispanic worship.

The Spaniards themselves came to the New World with a baggage of hagiography and religious lore that allowed them to see mysterious and miraculous signs all throughout the Conquest. The chronicles of the Conquest and the histories of settlement, as recounted by participants and historians, repeat stories of divine apparitions of Santiago, the Virgin Mary and the saints, instantaneous acquisitions of the gift of tongues, sudden conversions of the heathen, and similar experiences. Spain had its own lore of hidden and dark arts that were taken to the New World and, joining forces with African and indigenous beliefs, created an underground layer of popular culture preserved in ecclesiastical records throughout the colonial period. Part of the Inquisition's task was to survey any belief that might undermine Christian orthodoxy by challenging the sacraments. Those practicing, or accused of practicing, such arts were members of all ethnic groups.[21]

Counter-Reformation Catholicism became intolerant of syncretic practices, although it was unable to uproot them. Seventeenth-century clerical reports of hidden unorthodox practices express disgust at such obstinate unwillingness to see the truth of Christianity. The first evangelizers' desire to see the goodness and nobility of the indigenous population was replaced by a harsher seventeenth-century mentality unwilling to accept deviations from dogma. Even eighteenth-century students of indigenous cultures such as Francisco Javier Clavijero (1731–1787) showed ambivalence in judging the religious practices of pre-Columbian peoples and although his analysis achieved a fair degree of understanding,

[20] Fray Pablo Joseph de Arriaga, *The Extirpation of Idolatry in Peru* (Lexington: University of Kentucky Press, 1968); Francisco de Avila, "A narrative of the erroneous false gods, and other superstitions and diabolical rites in which the Indians of the provinces of Huarochirí lived in ancient times" in *Narratives of the Rites and Laws of the Yncas* ed. and trans. Clements R. Markham (London: Haykluyt Society, 1973), 121–47; Hernando Ruiz de Alarcón, *Treatise on the Heathen Superstitions that Today Live Among the Indians Native to This New Spain, 1629*, trans. J. Richard Andrews and Ross Hassig (Norman: University of Oklahoma Press, 1984).

[21] Solange Alberro, *Inquisición y sociedad en México, 1571–1700* (Mexico: Fondo de Cultura Económica, 1988); José Toribio Medina, *Historia de la Inquisición de Lima 1569–1820*, 2 vols. (Santiago, 1887); Ruth Behar, "Sexual witchcraft, colonialism, and women's powers: views from the Mexican Inquisition" in Asunción Lavrin (ed.) *Sexuality and Marriage in Colonial Latin America* (Lincoln: University of Nebraska Press, 1989), 178–206.

it did not preclude condemnation.[22] The problem lay in the limited number of priests available for the outlying areas, neglect in the care of their flock, and the fact that the translation of doctrine allowed for many mistakes that perpetuated indigenous misunderstandings.

The problems of religious syncretism and the weakness of religious orthodoxy must be countered by mentioning the social and cultural mechanisms that eased the transition to a new set of beliefs. Confraternities involved the laity in religious worship in familiar terms, gathering people of the same ethnic group, or the same occupation, neighborhood or town, around the worship of a special male or female saint. Urban and rural, rich and poor, mono- or multi-ethnic, these institutions mediated between the church and the parishioners and strengthened the bases of Roman Catholicism, although they also served to conceal syncretic cults. Nonetheless, they were useful in incorporating Indians into the body of the Roman Catholic church. By attracting worshippers from all ethnic groups, these saints and virgins helped to coalesce, at least under the ecclesiastical umbrella, the varied social mosaic of the colonial period. The crowning experience of the New World church was the canonization of several men and women in the seventeenth century, as part of a process of religious consolidation not lacking in political connotations. Santa Rosa de Lima was canonized in 1671, while Francisco Solano and Toribio de Mogrovejo were beatified in 1675 and 1679 respectively. Martín de Porres (1579–1639), Juan Macías, and Teresita de Jesús were eventually successful candidates for sainthood among several other *beati* whose causes did not come to similar ends.

Language as a cultural medium

Language, as a means of expression and communication among people, plays a paramount role in the transmission of culture. Conquerors and missionaries were the first to experience the communication problems posed by the myriad languages spoken by the indigenous groups in the New World. This multiplicity became an issue for the Crown, the church, and their respective bureaucracies once the task of conversion and administration began in earnest. Only a few regions in the Americas had a common language understood by a significant number of people. The Aztecs and the Incas, by means of territorial conquest, had established a certain uniformity in communication by imposing Nahuatl and Quechua as official languages in the heart of Mexico and throughout much of the Andean area respectively. A common linguistic root made communica-

---

[22] Francisco Javier Clavijero, *Historia Antigua de México* (Mexico: Porrúa, 1968).

tion in the Maya area less difficult than in others, and a similar situation prevailed in the highlands of New Granada.

The preponderance of Castilian in Spain and its adoption as the official language of the unified peninsula prior to the period of discovery, had solved the problem for the conquerors, who were able to utilize it as their most effective tool in the acculturation and political domination of the newly gained territories. Latin, the *lingua franca* of renaissance high culture, was used in the New World until the end of the seventeenth century for the diffusion of scientific and theological knowledge, and beyond the independence period for religious ceremonial and prayer.

A language policy for the Indians

The challenge of how to communicate with the indigenous population remained a key cultural problem. Language policies changed throughout the colonial period, as a result of modifications in the perception of how best to cope with the integration of indigenous cultures into a Spanish framework. Communication with African slaves did not pose the same challenge because they were neither free nor subjects of the Crown. Slaves were to learn the language of their masters.

The church had a virtual monopoly on the means of communication with the Indians, and counted on royal support to back its decisions. The initial problem was how to convey the Gospels to the Indians with accuracy, avoiding the dangers of misinterpretation by the neophytes. The friars had several ways of solving this problem. They could learn the Amerindian languages and translate the Christian concepts into those languages or they could impose Castilian on the native peoples. Teaching the Indians Latin, the language of high learning in the sixteenth century, was yet another option devised for a potential elite.

The first evangelizers experimented with these three choices. The task of learning the Indian languages was solved by pragmatic means, either by mingling with the Indians or learning from the children. The issue of translation was thornier, however, and gave much thought to sixteenth-century theologians, eager to obtain the right nuance in the translation of Castilian into indigenous languages which sometimes lacked words for Christian theological concepts.

While learning the Indian languages, the first missionaries began teaching Latin to the indigenous neophytes at the Colegio de la Santa Cruz de Tlaltelolco in New Spain. The experiment showed the willingness of the Franciscans to take the Amerindians into their humanistic fold, and the latter's aptitude for assimilating and excelling in European culture. The example of Mexico was followed in other areas. By the mid sixteenth century, Juan del Valle, bishop of Popayán, had also established schools of Latin and European culture for the Indians. Similar examples of schools for Indians, and for both Indians and Spaniards were founded in Nueva Andalucía (Venezuela), Quito, and Peru.

In the face of enormous theological challenges in Europe, and suspicious of experimentation with untested peoples, church authorities prohibited the use of Latin with the Indians. This linguistic decision was accompanied by the prohibition of the ordination of non-Spaniards issued by the first Council of the Mexican church (*Concilio Mexicano*, 1555), a meeting of ecclesiastics in charge of defining the means and objectives of the conversion of the Indians. This cultural and ethnic rejection was a blow to the process of assimilation, and determined the exclusion of the majority of natives from the world of high culture. By the turn of the sixteenth century only a handful of Indian scholars could still read and write Latin, even though up to the eighteenth century some convent schools still taught the elements of that language to the neophytes.

In the 1540s the Crown decided that until the Indians learned Castilian, their conversion would be carried out in their own languages. The reasoning behind this policy was that teaching the Indians both a new faith and a new language, imposed a burdensome intellectual obligation on them. Most missionaries had doubts about the capacity of the common Indians to learn both at the same time and agreed to royal policy, with some expressed misgivings and even opposition. The preservation of their languages could, in theory and practice, create a cultural barrier between the Indians and the rest of the population, propitiating the control of the church over indigenous people and their isolation from other social elements. The Provincial Councils and the Diocesan Synods celebrated in the sixteenth and seventeenth centuries continued to lend their support to indoctrination in Indian tongues. Royal policy revalidated the ecclesiastical policy. In 1577 Philip II ordered the creation of university chairs to teach native languages.

The adoption of the use of native languages was not favored by all. In 1596, the Council of the Indies proposed the abolition of this practice. Yet Philip II, not wishing to depart from his previous endorsement, opted for a conciliation of opinions and decided that those Indians who wished to learn Castilian should be taught the language, while letting previous legislation stand. The most astute Indian leaders realized the value of Castilian in gaining good will and in learning the technological skills of the conquistadors. Official translators were always available, while either leaders of the communities or those who lived near urban centers managed at least two languages with ease.

To ensure the learning of the languages and to convey the new religion, two forms of books appeared in the sixteenth century: the grammars of Indian languages and catechisms and confessionals that served as pedagogical tools to teach the faith. The grammars were one of the most significant intellectual accomplishments of the colonial period, a living testimony to the tenacity of the church in its pursuit of knowledge of the Indian world as a means of spiritual conquest. These works followed the grammatical pattern established for Castilian by Antonio Nebrija's *Arte de la Lengua Castellana*, published in 1492. Nebrija had used Latin to define the linguistic pattern of Castilian, and the missionaries used the same methodology as a model to construct – or reconstruct – the basic structure of all indigenous languages. The first Nahuatl grammar was written by the Franciscan Fray Andrés de Olmos (*c.* 1540s) although it was not printed until the nineteenth century. Fray Andrés de Molina's Nahuatl grammar was published in Mexico in 1571, the first in a long list of grammars and vocabularies of native languages to appear throughout the colonial period. Among the most notable were the Quechua grammar and vocabulary by Diego González Holguín (1607, 1608), a 1607 Christian doctrine in Aymara by Luis Jerónimo Ore, and the eighteenth-century compendium of Maya languages of Fray Ildefonso Joseph de Flores (1753). For all practical purposes no indigenous language lacked its grammar, and members of all religious orders participated in this task.

The cultural effect of this decision was very important. Despite the fact that royal policies again began to encourage the learning of Castilian (the royal decrees of 1636 and 1769, for example), no amount of legislation succeeded in reversing the *status quo*. At the end of the eighteenth century many parish priests, especially in the rural areas, complained bitterly about the Indian reluctance to adopt Spanish as their own language. The farther Indians lived from an important urban center, the more likely it was that they would speak their own language. While Indian languages were thus preserved for posterity, they only exceptionally produced any written literary expression.

The mixture of language and culture was best expressed by Felipe Guamán Poma de Ayala, author of *Primer corónica y buen gobierno* [*Letter to the King*], written partially in Spanish and partially in Quechua, and thus representing the blending of two different cultures. A reinterpretation of world and Andean history, and a close description of life in the Viceroyalty of Peru at the end of the sixteenth century, makes this work emblematic of the conquest and colonization experience.[23] On the other hand, Garcilaso Inca de la Vega (1539–1616) represents the assimilation of

---

[23] Rolena Adorno, *Guamán Poma de Ayala: Writing and resistance in colonial Peru* (Austin: University of Texas Press, 1986); Abraham Padilla Bendezu, *Huamán Poma, el indio cronista dibujante* (Mexico: Fondo de Cultura Económica, 1979). The dates of Guamán's birth and death are unknown; Felipe Guamán Poma de Ayala, *Letters to a King*, trans. Christopher Dilke (New York: 1978); Garcilaso de la Vega, El Inca, *Royal Commentaries of the Incas and General History of Peru*, trans. Harold V. Livermore (Austin: University of Texas Press, 1966).

European culture with a nostalgia for the ancestral traditions which were no longer part of his life.

More like Garcilaso than Guamán Poma de Ayala, all cultivated Indian intellectuals of the late sixteenth and early seventeenth centuries lived in the penumbra created by the use of the Spanish language and the practice of Roman Catholicism to recreate a past that had already escaped them. Such was the case of Hernando Alvarado Tezozomoc (1525?–1610?) author of an Aztec chronicle, who claimed to descend from Moctezuma and the king of Ecatepec. Domingo de San Antón Muñón Chimalpáin (1579–1660), born in Amecameca, New Spain, wrote a chronicle of Chalco, and Fernando de Alva Ixtlilxóchitl (1578–1650), of the Tezcocan and Mexican royal families, and educated by the Franciscans, wrote a chronicle of his people and a history of the Chichimecs. In Peru, Juan de Santa Cruz Pachacuti fulfilled the same role of mediator between two worlds and two religions. These men used oral and visual indigenous sources, and expressed better than anybody else the superposition of cultures taking place throughout the sixteenth century.

Despite the problems posed by the incomplete assimilation of Spanish by the indigenous population, Spanish prevailed as the language of the Empire, enriched by numerous words of Indian origin. The physical transfer of Castilian to the New World determined changes in its pronunciation and the adoption of numerous local linguistic corruptions. In many rural areas remnants of sixteenth-century Castilian continued in use throughout the colonial period. The result was the development of a language that while remaining true to its origins was a richer and more flexible instrument of expression for the needs of the inhabitants of the New World.

The technological exchange

Material culture and daily life

Alongside language, another profound cultural change was brought about with the introduction of the technological apparatus of Europe to indigenous societies. Some of these groups were in an advanced neolithic stage; others had achieved extraordinary engineering feats with the most rudimentary tools, and had gained considerable knowledge of nature by persevering observation. The diffusion of the wheel, not used among the indigenous people, was the most important technological contribution to daily life in the New World. Coupled with beasts of burden, the wheel allowed the eventual elimination of human beings as a means of transportation, as had been the custom prior to 1492. The exploitation of mines on a large scale, and especially the use of mercury to refine silver, created a totally new economic base, upon which the Spanish Empire rested.

European knowledge of physics allowed for the construction of large buildings, military installations and aqueducts using principles unknown among the indigenous cultures. Handwriting and the system of counting introduced in the New World supplanted indigenous means of computation and glyph script.

Firearms, restricted to Spaniards, had a great impact on the process of colonization and settlement as tools of conquest and control. But while firearms inspired terror and subservience, new plants and domestic animals helped to build a broader food base for the indigenous people. By the end of the sixteenth century new techniques of cultivation and of producing cloth, pottery, and metals had created a regional market network never envisioned before 1492. On the other hand, certain techniques of weaving and food preparation, such as the use of *metates* [stone grinders] to grind corn, the technique of freezing potatoes in the Andean region, the manufacturing of corn and maguey-based alcoholic beverages, and the back-strap loom used by women throughout the continent remained unchanged.

In the routine of daily life the concepts of wages, private property, individual inheritance, commercial profit, and litigation through new legal notions, were among the most important intellectual changes to which the indigenous communities had to adapt. They did not take long in learning the ropes of European life, which eventually formed a mixed system with some of the institutions for community rule they succeeded in preserving. There is no question, however, that the process of adaptation created significant dislocation. The distortion of tribute systems demanding labor without any social compensation to the community or to the individual created enormous tensions in the indigenous communities, forced social and physical mobility, and changed forever many of the values by which they had lived. For their part, peninsular Spaniards also experienced a significant change in their daily routines, having a permanent labor force and a newly gained confidence in their privileged elite position in society.

Books and the printing press

For the purposes of cultural diffusion, the introduction of the printing press was of primary importance to initiate the exchange of ideas between Europe and the Americas. The press carried the vast array of European traditions and beliefs that were to be superimposed on those of the native societies, although it ultimately also served to preserve their culture and memory. The production of books in the Spanish colonies was not as copious as in Europe, and it was narrowly focused on several themes. The earliest book published in the Spanish possessions was *Doctrina Cristiana en lengua mexicana* by Fray Juan de Zumárraga (1468–1548), produced by the Italian printer Juan Pablos in 1547. This book exemplified the intertwining of the many cultural threads of the New World. The latest European technology for cultural circulation was used to impose a new religion using the language of the conquered. In Peru where, due to the civil wars among the conquistadors, the introduction of the press had been forbidden, the printing of the first books took place in 1584. Under church auspices, a trilingual Christian Doctrine, a catechism for Indians, a confessional manual for priests, and the official adoption of the Gregorian calendar were printed in Lima by the Italian Antonio Ricardo. Germans, French and Italians were the first printers, and the business and art of printing remained in the hands of Europeans and their descendants during the colonial period.

The themes of the books printed during the sixteenth century were predominantly religious, and they were mostly published in New Spain, with Lima in second place. The tools of indoctrination such as catechism, confessionals, Indian grammars and vocabularies, and the books of Roman Catholic rituals, were the most numerous titles. Compilations of laws applicable to the colonies and books of medicine began to be published toward the end of the century, when the thematic spectrum broadened its narrow boundaries.

Printing presses and publishers worked closely with the religious orders, within whose premises they were often installed. Among the orders, the Jesuits rose above the rest as patrons. The demand for printing presses rose with the foundation by several religious orders of colleges for learning and universities in the main urban centers (Santo Domingo, in 1538; Mexico, 1551; Lima, 1553). Slowly, the presses found their way into Puebla de los Angeles (1643), Guatemala (1660), Asunción (*c.* 1700–1705), Havana (1723), Santa Fé de Bogotá (1738), Santiago de Chile (*c.* 1754), Quito (*c.* 1754), Córdoba (1765), Buenos Aires (1780), and Guadalajara (1793), reflecting the growth of those urban centers.

Popular culture

Leisure and recreation in daily life

Popular culture, as a legitimate expression of values, traditions, social symbols and rituals, is a vast topic that would demand a separate essay. Some of its most obvious expressions in the indigenous world, such as rituals associated with the life cycle or the celebration of important community events continued to be practiced by them throughout the colonial period. Planting or gathering crops, naming newborns, welcoming yearly cycles, and similar events were marked by procession, offerings, and ceremonies. The Roman Catholic church astutely used such events to introduce and reinforce Christian rites such as baptism, marriage, and death rites, which in Andean areas and indigenous Mesoamerica, for example, partook of native and European elements. In urban centers the civic and lay celebrations either for recreation, or for marking events such as the marriage of the Kings, the birth of princesses, and the arrival of viceroys and archbishops were important ceremonies observed since the earliest days of colonization to reinforce the authority of the Crown and a political bond with the overseas subjects.

The Spanish population recreated the forms of leisure practiced in the peninsula by introducing hunting, bullfights, ball games, and tournaments in which the ability to ride on horseback was essential. Hunting men with dogs was, unfortunately, a form of "sport" that was also practiced against the indigenous population during the Antillean and Central American conquest period (1495–1530). Falconry, cards, and chess joined some New World forms of entertainment – like the Aztec *totoloque* and *patolli*.[24] Despite the prohibition of certain forms of card games, this leisure activity was so widely practiced that the income derived from the tax levied on cards was one of the most profitable for the Crown. Cockfights became a popular pastime among the rural population, and were practiced professionally in the cities. The betting that accompanied this game contributed to its diffusion. Bullfights, which in the sixteenth century were the entertainment of the elite, lost that connotation during the seventeenth century, and by the eighteenth they had become a form of "mass entertainment". Entrance tickets to the spectacle earned the royal government a handsome income for building roads or constructing buildings.

Other forms of popular amusement included chess, billiards, and dice, always accompanied by betting. Indian "hockey" (*chueca* in Spanish or *huino* among the Indians) was very popular in South America, particularly among Chilean Indians [*mapuches*], although it was adopted by Spanish settlers. Several ball games predating the Conquest, and similar to soccer in nature, continued to be played by the Indians in places such as the Orinoco River missions and the Guaraní area along the River Plate and the Paraguay River. These team games could involve both genders and rival towns. The *volador* game, of pre-Hispanic roots, was another game that remained popular throughout the colonial period. Beginning in the seventeenth century the popular mock confrontation of *moros* [moors] and Christians, adapted a peninsular experience to that of the Conquest, while symbolic re-enactments of the Conquest in Indian towns

---

[24] *Totoloque* was a game in which gold pellets were aimed at tile-markers. It involved betting on the winner. *Patolli* was a game with dice played on a table shaped like a cross and divided into squares, and played with beans. Jacques Soustelle, *Daily Life of the Aztecs on the Eve of the Spanish Conquest* (Stanford University Press, 1961). Luis Weckmann, *La herencia medieval de México*, 2 vols. (Mexico: El Colegio de México, 1984).

probably served as a satirical critique of colonial authorities. Religious processions in honor of important saints involved the entire community. The confraternities organized in most churches had a paramount role in the religious festivals. They spent much money in contracting for music, fireworks, and masses to celebrate their patron saint's day. Special celebrations, such as Corpus Christi, were punctuated with a procession in which a rigid hierarchy regulated the order of the participants, with the royal officers, higher clergy, and elite associations always leading the way. The *paseo del pendón*, a civil municipal celebration in which the royal emblem was carried in a procession by the municipal officers, was an important ceremonial occasion in most cities, as it served to render homage to the Crown.

Theatrical performances began as soon as urban life was organized. They served as a tool for the conversion of the Indians, and became an essential part of the religious celebrations of some important dates in the Christian calendar, such as the Epiphany, Lent, and Corpus Christi. The adaptation of Judeo-Christian traditions and European sagas to colonial theatre by Indian or *mestizo* authors was the crowning experience of cultural diffusion and adaptation, whether those pieces were written in Spanish or in Indian languages. This cultural tradition persisted in small towns beyond the end of the colonial period. In New Spain, the Spaniards found a tradition of theatrical representation among the natives that was fully utilized for conversion and that, in turn, influenced to some extent the European tradition. The rich variety of dances recorded in Peru by Bishop Baltasar Jaime Martínez Compañón (1735–1797) in the third quarter of the eighteenth century, attests to the blending of cultural strains, and the use of dance as a theatrical expression of strong popular flavor.[25]

The secular theatre was a strong cultural component of colonial life. Inside and outside viceregal palaces, it fulfilled more than an artistic role. In New Spain, for example, the Royal Hospital for Native Peoples depended heavily on the income of its theatre. During the late sixteenth and the seventeenth centuries plays had to suffer the ecclesiastical censorship of the Inquisition before they could be performed. As a potential threat to "good public customs," the theatre remained under the scrutiny of the church until after mid eighteenth century. At that point, censorship passed to the jurisdiction of the state, but surveillance was still exercised by a priest designated by the viceroy. Towards the end of the eighteenth century, the lay theatre was absolved from suspicions of helping to corrupt the good customs of the inhabitants and, in fact, began to be regarded as a means of education. In 1786, a carefully designed set of

---

[25] Archbishop Baltasar Jaime Martínez Compañón, *Trujillo del Perú a fines del siglo XVIII* (Madrid: n.p. 1936).

regulations was issued in New Spain, to maintain propriety and order among the actors and in the spectacle.

Higher learning in the colonies

One important aspect of the cultural transfer was the foundation of centers of higher learning, reflecting the settlers' concern for the education of their children. Imperial decrees ordered the foundation of universities in Mexico City and Lima. Since 1538 a theological school in the Dominican convent of Hispaniola had been raised to the status of university by the Pope. The universities depended on endowments rather than foundation decrees, and the University of Mexico was more fortunate than Lima's or Hispaniola's in its beginnings. It began operating in 1553, while that of Lima had to wait until 1577.

Learning at the universities was philosophical, legalistic, and theological. Chairs in Theology, the Scriptures, Rhetoric and Logic, Philosophy, Canon and Civil Law, and Indigenous Languages in some instances, formed the core of the curriculum. Several degrees were offered (*licenciado, bachiller, doctor*) which entitled the recipient to proceed to the priesthood or the exercise of the law. At the end of the sixteenth century, the University of San Marcos in Lima had fifteen chairs [*cátedras*], nine of which were directly concerned with religion. The predominance of theology over the experimental sciences was complete within the academic world, but this dominance began to break down with the establishment of chairs of medicine. In Lima the study of medicine was officially established by royal order in 1638.

Theological trends

On the theological and spiritual levels, there was no challenge to the canons established by Aristotle and St. Thomas Aquinas. Scholasticism prevailed in the New World throughout the seventeenth and part of the eighteenth centuries, although the popularity of St. Thomas Aquinas was challenged by the followers of John Duns Scotus, largely Franciscans, and those of Francisco Suárez, mostly Jesuits. Since these dissents fell within the parameters of orthodoxy, they were simply squabbles within the family.

The universities were not the only sites of higher education, however. Religious orders established their own "colleges" offering stiff competition. The Jesuits excelled in the education of the elite, founding chairs in their own institutions that rivalled those of the royal universities. Privately endowed colleges, such as the Colegio de San Martín in Lima, founded by the Peruvian viceroy Marín de Esquilache in 1582, challenged the University of San Marcos as the main center of education. The Jesuits taught theology, jurisprudence, and philosophy at San Martín, while sustaining their own College of San Pablo. Other regular orders also infiltrated the university by endowing chairs. In addition to these institutions the secular church, following the recommendations of the Council of Trent, fostered the foundation of private colleges [*seminarios tridentinos*] to educate young men for the clergy.

Aristotle, St. Augustine, St. Bonaventure, St. Gregoy, Duns Scotus, and other early and late medieval theologians provided the texts discussed and officially approved in all educational institutions. The Jesuit *ratio studorium* was very popular, and followed throughout the seventeenth century in all centers of higher education. This education pursued a dual goal of instructing men in the observance of the law of God and the law of the land. As late as 1774, the royal order requesting information for the foundation of the University of Guadalajara described its purpose as the "formation of the spirit as well as the knowledge of those rules necessary to govern oneself, rule the people, educate the youth and instruct the faithful, while promoting the law of God, and obedience, recognition and love to the sovereign."[26] A renovation in the curriculum would not take place until the eighteenth century.

Within the parameters established by scholasticism, colleges and universities nurtured a small intellectual elite of distinguished theologians, such as Peruvians Juan Pérez de Menacho, Alonso de Peñafiel (1594–1657), Diego de Avendaño (1594–1688) and Martín de Jáuregui, all Jesuits. Avendaño was also a knowledgeable jurist who wrote an essay proclaiming the natural right to freedom of all peoples, although he condoned the forced evangelization of the Indians in his *Thesaurus Indicus* (1668–1686). In Mexico Tomás Mercado (1523–1575) and Bartolomé de Ledesma (1525–1604), both born in Spain, were unflinching defenders of Thomism in the sixteenth century. More influential were the Jesuits Pedro de Ortigosa (1547–1626), whose academic career in Mexico lasted forty years, and Antonio Rubio (1561–1615), who taught in Mexico and ended his days at the University of Alcalá, and whose expositions of Aristotle were used as texts in Mexico and Spain. These men helped create a veritable common intellectual ground between Spain and its colonies, strengthening the new scholasticism characteristic of Spanish thought after the Council of Trent.

Scholasticism was the philosophical marker of intellectual knowledge, but the theological bent of the seventeenth century moved between the mystic and the ascetic. Kindled by the emphasis placed on direct knowledge of God by sixteenth-century Spanish mystics, the religious

---

[26] Carmen Castañeda, *La educación en Guadalajara durante la época colonial, 1555–1821* (Guadalajara: El Colegio de Jalisco y El Colegio de México, 1984), 340.

experience of *recogimiento*, a reliance on internal prayer and meditation, gained acceptance as an orthodox practice. It could, however, come dangerously close to the experience of the *alumbrados*, and the near-heretical position of *quietism*, both of which denied the validity of deeds to receive grace, and believed in receiving it directly from God. The Tridentine position favoring the reception of grace through deeds created a tension within Spanish and Spanish American Catholicism reflected in the lives of many of their saints. Many male saints were activists who earned their sainthood through preaching, if not martyrdom, beyond the frontiers of the mother country. Apart from St. Teresa, who had the privilege of mobility, female religiosity achieved its goal through denial and daily practice of devotion and self-punishment.

A widely accepted theological path by which to obtain the fruits of mysticism and ascetism was delineated in the three *vías* or paths recommended for orthodox practice: purgative, illuminative, and unitive. The purgative stressed discipline and sacrifice; the illuminative allowed the soul to gain a vision of God, and in the unitive one achieved the final experience of God. Spanish American religious writings bear the imprint of these guidelines. They can be traced in the devotional literature written for the religious elite as well as that written for the confessionals used by priests for the guidance of the common penitent. Religion was made accessible to the masses through displays of acts of penitence and charity, and the cult of the saints, an agenda set at the Council of Trent, with a special regard for Mary as an intercessor for humanity.

The significant support given by urban and rural communities to the construction of churches, the founding of convents and nunneries, and the organization of confraternities can be attributed to the prevalence of a religious sensitivity that regarded these institutional vehicles as necessary in order to sustain the individual's daily struggle between temptation and virtue. The imagery of the Baroque, whether artistic or verbal, stressed the conflicts of the soul, and a dependency on its formal expression as evidence of faith and orthodoxy. The mediators between God and the people, the priesthood and the members of the regular orders, gained considerable weight in a church in which the personal soul required direction and guidance in order not to lose itself in the traps of heresy. In Spanish America, the influential role played by the regular orders in the evangelization of the Indians came under question with the entrenchment of the secular church, politically closer to the directives of the Crown after Trent. The internal conflicts between the friars and the priests did not affect the general observance of the faithful, but by the end of the colonial period the secular church was more influential in policy-making decisions than the orders. Political and economic circumstances influenced the relationship between church and state, as demonstrated in the fate of one of the key intellectual forces in the colonies, the powerful Company of Jesus (Jesuits), which was expelled from Spanish America in 1767.

Nature as the source of knowledge

The walls of convents and the lecture halls of universities and seminaries did not contain the sum of all knowledge. The prevalence of scholasticism in the centers of higher education, and of a religion that relied on obedience and authority, did not preclude the study of nature or society, and the development of scientific and historical curiosity. Bacon, Descartes, and Newton would not be officially studied in Spanish America until the mid eighteenth century, but in the cultural world of the mid-colonial period these European innovators were known by a select group.

Also free from any challenge to theology was a vast accumulation of knowledge based on the observation of nature. This knowledge could have fostered a flowering of science, had it not been for the unfailing censorship of Crown and church, and the emphasis on description and cataloguing over explanation. The close scrutiny given by the Crown to all works of law, science and history printed in its kingdoms, and the similarly meticulous scrutiny given by the church to all works of a spiritual or philosophical nature, contrast with the pursuit of detailed geographical knowledge, the weighing of evidence in historical writing, and the fascination with the observation of flora and fauna, as well as with astronomical observations prevalent among the intellectual community since the very first years of the colonial period.

Geographical knowledge was encouraged from the early sixteenth century onwards, given the task of reconnoitering the vast unknown territories. The challenge of nature sustained geographical expeditions to the end of the colonial period. The telluric attraction of the land enticed hundreds of fearless men into deserts, jungles, and remote mountains. Their reports slowly revealed the configuration of the land, and underscored the wealth of native plants and animals.

The first grand descriptions of the natural world, triggered by a similar desire to gather information for economic and political purposes, are those of Gonzalo Fernández de Oviedo (1478–1557) who, after six trips to the Indies between 1514 and 1530, produced the *Sumario de historia natural*, in 1526, and the *Historia general y natural de las Indias* in 1535. Fernández de Oviedo began the formidable task of describing the continent. His quest for completeness was picked up later in the century by Francisco López de Gómara (1510–1560) in his *Historia general de las Indias*, by the Jesuit José de Acosta (1540–1600) in his *Historia natural y moral de las Indias* (1590), and by another Jesuit, Bernabé Cobo (1580–

1657) in his unpublished *Anales de ciencias naturales*. The latter, carried out between the late 1590s and 1636, comprised a full description of the Spanish possessions with the emphasis on New Spain and Peru.

These works expressed the consuming interest of sixteenth-century men in the unfolding of a world that challenged the definitions of antiquity and raised far more questions than answers. In his work Acosta began to supply some inferences which contradicted classical knowledge. The world was a wonderful scientific puzzle which these men knew would eventually yield some of its mysteries to the enquiring mind. In its discovery inquisitive minds found an alternative to the experimental sciences.

The "discovery" of the natural world was pursued throughout the ensuing 200 years. Unfortunately, the efforts of many men to expand the frontiers of knowledge would be stranded in the bureaucratic quagmire of a court that delayed publication of works that would have had a ready and eager cultural market in Europe. Such are, for example, the undated "Relaciones" of Fray Juan de Rivadeneira, describing the Río de la Plata region, and Pedro Sotelo de Narváez's description of the Tucumán (Argentina) area, written towards the end of the sixteenth century, and the "Descripción breve de toda la tierra del Perú, Tucumán, Río de la Plata y Chile," written at the beginning of the seventeenth century by Monsignor Reginaldo de Lizarraga, and not published until 1908 in Lima.

Since the early sixteenth century Spain had a school of cosmography and mapping, an essential tool for its expansion. The early maps used by the captains of the Discovery period were either destroyed or lost, and many others remained in manuscript in the royal archives. Spain was not interested in disseminating knowledge of its territories to other competing nations. The progress of cartography and map-making followed the exploration of the natural world. Throughout the sixteenth century the task of measuring longitudes was carried out under the orders of the Council of the Indies and the compliance of numerous aficionados and technicians. Curiously, the geocentric system was not challenged by this or other enquiries into the natural world. Geographical knowledge was well patronized by Philip II, who fostered a vast study of the land and the people with requests for geographical and demographic reports, and the creation of the post of cosmographer and chronicler of Spain's possessions in 1571.

The union of history and geography that typified many of the works published in the late sixteenth century and thereafter was not simply the result of royal policy, but also responded to the nature of the task ahead of the scholars of the period. Among the outstanding geographers of the sixteenth century was Alonso de Santa Cruz, author of a geographical treatise on the world's islands, and the first royally appointed cosmographer. Juan López de Velasco succeeded him in 1571, and attempted a synthesis of geographical knowledge based on many of his own publications and those of others that remained unpublished. The same motivation was behind another encyclopedic work authored by the Carmelite friar Antonio Vázquez de Espinosa (d. 1630), the *Compendio y descripción de las Indias Occidentales*, not published until 1942, the result of a trip from Mexico to South America between 1612 and 1621. Both authors conceived a grandiose scenario in which weather, climate, river systems, mines, flora, and fauna, interlocked with the social and political systems developed by the human actors. This brand of erudition was the only one appropriate to convey the awe and wonder that the New World still aroused in the intellect of Europeans. Vázquez de Espinosa, like historians of the period, was proud of the fact that his knowledge derived from his own personal experience of the Americas.

Descriptions and accounts of voyages, explorations, evangelizing enterprises and military expeditions, along with bureaucratic reports, form a vast body of writings impossible to account for, not just because of their numbers, but because of their diversity of purposes and styles. Jesuit father, Eusebio Kino (1645–1711), whose interpretation of comets was colored by theology was, at the same time, a royal cosmographer, mapped the territory of the northern frontier of New Spain, and having carried out dozens of exploratory expeditions, became convinced that California was a peninsula. Kino is living proof that neither scientific curiosity nor the spirit of enquiry was choked by the scholastic nature of theological and philosophical discourse. The colonial geographical accounts are rich in ethnograpic information and answer the need for intelligence from church and Crown. This need did not abate with the years and, in fact, had an invigorating renaissance in the second half of the eighteenth century with works such as José Gumilla's *El Orinoco ilustrado*, (1741), and Fray Antonio Caulin's *Historia coro-gráphica natural y evangélica de la Nueva Andalucía* (1779).

One of the incentives behind the discovery of plants was an interest in incorporating indigenous pharmacopeia into European medicine. Medicine, on both sides of the Atlantic, was much preoccupied with cures, and the need for remedies and treatments was magnified by the catastrophic consequences of the exchanges of diseases that took place after 1492. Nahuatl knowledge of herbs and their pharmaceutical applications was gathered in a codice known as the *Códice Badiano* (1552), compiled by two Mexican natives but never published. A similar fate awaited the fifteen volumes describing plants and animals of New Spain by the physician Francisco Hernández (1517–1587), who went to the Indies commissioned by Philip II, and whose outstanding work was accomplished with the cooperation of a team of Indians and Spaniards. After his death in 1578 his work was tangled in a bureaucratic muddle. Summarized in part by several authors in Europe and Mexico throughout the seventeenth century, a significant part of the original was lost in a fire in 1671.

By the end of the seventeenth century, the intellectual world of colonial Spanish America was struggling to bring about a synthesis of all the knowledge gathered by direct observation and the conventions of scholasticism. The notion of a new concept of the universe was available to a chosen few, but would not be accepted officially. The tension caused by the results of scientific inferences and the boundaries imposed by faith would cause some contradictory results. The debate between Father Eusebio Kino and the erudite Mexican scholar Carlos de Sigüenza y Góngora (1645–1700) between 1681 and 1690 over the nature of comets, was a dialogue between what people should think and what they should not, and reflected the official policy of suppressing some aspects of knowledge while leaving others open and following its natural course, as illustrated by the geographical works cited before. Cartesian rationalism was hardly a generation old when Kino and Sigüenza exchanged their opposite views about celestial bodies. As a cartographer, mathematician, and student of history, a man who had explored the coasts of the Gulf and shared his contemporaries' spirit of discovery of the natural world, Sigüenza was compelled to challenge the anachronistic views held by Kino. The irony was that Kino was capable of making keen observations about places and peoples despite his beliefs, while Sigüenza still retained a modicum of the restraints imposed by his faith, and respected its dogma as the will of God. A historian of the royal convent of Jesús María, in Mexico City, he wrote an exemplary hagiographic work in the true spirit of the seventeenth century (*Paraíso occidental*, 1684).

The Spanish Crown made little use of the prodigious knowledge of the physical world accumulated by some of its best minds throughout the first 200 years of colonial rule. A dynastic change that took 15 years to consolidate would eventually allow a slow release of this control over the intellectual life of the minds on both sides of the Atlantic.

The Enlightenment
The eighteenth-century transition to intellectual change

Although it is difficult to trace the evolution of one mental attitude to another, the transition from the Baroque into the Enlightenment is made less difficult to understand due to the replacement of the ruling dynasty – the Habsburg – by the French Bourbons – after the War of the Spanish Succession (1700–1713).[27] The advent of the Bourbon dynasty to the Spanish throne, marked by the official end of the war, also brought about a change in the cultural axis of Spain. Closer to France than ever before, Spain visibly began to change its administrative, political, and cultural outlook by the 1730s. The Bourbons adopted a policy of increasing independence from the Papacy in the appointment of ecclesiastical dignitaries that eventually matured into the limitation of many privileges [*fueros*] previously held by the church and its members. The objective was a demarcation of jurisdictions that would strengthen the state and allow the Crown to take over such privileges. This policy is known as *regalismo* or *jansenismo* [Jansenism] a term of seventeenth-century French origin. It reached its climax in the second half of the eighteenth century, supported by the eminent advisers of Charles III as well as by some of the church prelates. Spiritual orthodoxy remained, but it expressed itself in reforms within the church that sought to revive the models of earlier Christianity by improving religious discipline under pastoral guidance. The Inquisition, more remote than ever from its original role of authority for social and religious control, found itself pursuing orthodoxy in books rather than in behavior.

Alongside such new concepts of state–church relations, and the revitalization of the power of the monarch, came a revamping of the structure of government in Spain and its colonies, the loosening of the grip of scholasticism in higher learning, and the eventual development of new artistic styles. Rather than a revolutionary change in the modes of thinking, the effects of the Enlightenment in Spanish America were an expansion of the curiosity of the educated elites towards the natural sciences, and the possibilities of new forms of political and economic change. The roots of such change were in the seventeenth century, but the scope of interest was broader, encompassing larger numbers of persons in the eighteenth century. Furthermore, this intellectual challenge was fostered by the Crown itself.

The imprint of the Bourbon dynasty on Spanish life took at least three decades to develop in the peninsula and the colonies. Political conflicts with England in which France was an ally of Spain paved the way for a growing French influence that was a catalyst for change. The most important critique of dogmatism and conservatism in Spain was the publication of *Teatro crítico universal* (1726–1739) by the Benedictine friar Benito Gerónimo Feijóo (1676–1764). His attacks against traditionalism, prejudice, and bigotry were well received in Spain and patronized by the Court. Feijóo voiced the need to join the mainstream of contemporary

---

[27] For a history of this event, see, Henry Kamen, *The War of Succession in Spain, 1700–15* (Ontario, Canada: Fitzhenry & Whiteside Ltd, 1969). Two basic books for Spanish history during the Enlightenment are, Richard Herr, *The Eighteenth-Century Revolution in Spain* (Princeton University Press, 1958), and Jean Sarrailh, *La España ilustrada de la segunda mitad del siglo XVIII*, trans. Antonio Alatorre (Mexico: Fondo de Cultura Económica, 1957).

science and philosophical critique, to discard Aristotle and Descartes and to study Locke. His writings began to arrive in the New World by 1735. Another important influence was that of Portuguese educator Luis Antonio Verney, an advocate of Locke and Condillac, who became well-known in the Americas in the second half of the century.

The break with a traditional Aristotelian interpretation of the physical and intellectual world, and the diffusion of late seventeenth- and eighteenth-century European philosophical and theological tenets was slow in Spanish America. Traditional philosophy persisted in many centers of higher education and in many minds throughout the eighteenth century. Few centers of learning began to reexamine their curricula before the 1750s, although some concessions were made earlier; for example, the University of San Marcos in Peru accepted the scientific explanation of blood circulation in 1723. Though slow at first, the reception of the new "lights" of knowledge and interpretation that sparkled in the eighteenth century was warm and positive. This process was launched, in part, by the Jesuits. Far removed from the intrigues of the Spanish court, the Spanish American Jesuits in Mexico, Quito, New Granada, Chile, and Buenos Aires followed guidelines already adopted by the Seminary of Nobles in Madrid in the 1720s. Descartes, Leibnitz, and Newton began to be taught in Quito by the Jesuits in the third decade of the century. In New Spain the Jesuit Colleges also nurtured change in the teaching of philosophy. Notable among the reformers were Rafael Campoy and Francisco Javier Clavijero (1731–1787), who launched the attack on scholasticism.[28] They introduced Descartes, Leibnitz, Malebranche, Newton, and Franklin to their students.

Unfortunately, regalism had some dire consequences for the Jesuits as official upholders of papal authority. They were expelled from Spain and its colonies in 1767, an event that removed a key ingredient of intellectual life from the colonies for the last quarter of the eighteenth century, precisely the period during which the Enlightenment reached its zenith. However, the Jesuits never had a monopoly on education, and their absence did not delay the acceptance of modern philosophies. In Lima, both the University of San Marcos and the Convictorio of San Carlos (founded in 1770) introduced Newton and Descartes after the expulsion of the Order. In New Spain Benito Díaz de Gamarra was the main proponent of "modern" philosophy, which discarded the antiquated tenets of scholasticism and adopted the natural sciences as the bases for human knowledge. Two other men, José Antonio Alzate and José Ignacio Bartolache (1739–1790) helped prepare the ground for the cultivation of

[28] Pablo González Casanova, *El misoneísmo y la modernidad cristiana en el siglo XVIII* (Mexico: El Colegio de México, 1948).

science. Alzate propounded numerous practical applications of science, while Bartolache was more interested in the theoretical sciences.

By the 1770s hardly any respectable intellectual remained unacquainted with the new science. Newton and Condillac were known and explained as emblems of knowledge derived from observation and experimentation, and the rejection of innate ideas or deductive knowledge. The winds of change affected the church itself. Some of the most important intellectual reformers of the late eighteenth century came from its ranks. Canon Juan Baltazar Maciel (1727–1788) distinguished himself in the Viceroyalty of La Plata, supporting the adoption of the sciences and modern philosophy as the regent of the Real Colegio de San Carlos, which took over the teaching of theology and philosophy after the expulsion of the Jesuits. Viceroys Caballero y Góngora in New Granada (1782–1789), Revillagigedo in New Spain (1789–1794), Manuel Amat y Junient in Lima (1761–1776), and Juan José Vértiz (1770–1777) in Buenos Aires, favored reform in university studies to introduce the teaching of useful exact sciences.

The intellectual renewal of the eighteenth century had a pragmatic bent. For the state this translated into the adoption of policies that sought efficiency in the administration of its resources. The power of any state was measured by the productivity of its subjects, and towards that end, people had to be educated in the disciplines that helped to promote wealth. A penchant for regularization, efficiency and productivity was behind the schemes to revamp trade, fiscal policies, industry, and the agricultural production. The Bourbons had a clear understanding of the goals of the state, as different and separate from the spiritual pursuits of the church, and they relied on men of significant intellectual strength to define the policies they considered likely to achieve those goals.

Spanish political economists such as José del Campillo (1693–1743), Bernardo Ward, Gaspar de Jovellanos (1774–1811), and Pedro Rodríguez de Campomanes (1723–1803), who developed theories to overhaul the economy of the peninsula, had a clear concept of the role the colonies would play within their schemes: they should be useful sources of wealth to the mother country. The first changes adopted in the eighteenth century in the colonies were not, however, in tune with the most advanced political economies of the period. The tightly controlled commercial companies that replaced the sixteenth- and seventeenth-century fleets in areas such as Venezuela and Cuba (founded in 1728 and 1740 respectively) expressed mercantilist concepts running against the growing acceptance of commercial freedom. A revised version of free trade with friendly nations was not in place in the colonies until the last quarter of the century, being preceded by commerce through registered ships. The gradual opening of trade and communication supported the exchange of ideas and cultural change.

Scientific expeditions: continuing the rediscovery of nature
The study of nature was placed in a positive light of social usefulness. Unlocking its mysteries would put them at the service of humankind. Medicine, physics, botany, chemistry, and other sciences would help develop techniques for curing illness, developing industries, increase production, and create a society where people would live in greater harmony with others and would see usefulness as a worthwhile objective. The late eighteenth century nurtured a utopian belief in the perfectibility of humankind and society. The state had an increasing role in steering its subjects towards desired goals, and a greater responsibility in creating the appropriate means to achieve them. Many royal bureaucrats developed their own inquiries and reports on the flora, fauna, society, and administrations of their jurisdictions. These works are extraordinarily detailed and precise in their information, revealing a keen spirit of observation and a sustained interest in reform emblematic of the period. The *Relación* and the *Descripción* of the Viceroyalty of Santa Fé de Bogotá, written by governor Francisco Silvestre (1734–1806) in 1785 and 1789 respectively, are good examples of such texts.

Scientific expeditions and scientific writings differed from past curiosity in the New World in that they showed a truly modern interest in the practical applications of their findings. They were also more cosmopolitan in their membership and purpose. The French expedition to measure the geographical degree of latitude that began in 1735 resulted in a thorough description of Peru, and numerous physical and astronomic observations. The two Spanish scientists who accompanied the expedition, Jorge Juan and Antonio Ulloa, also made a thorough report of the social and administrative conditions of the viceroyalty. While their observations were not published until 1748, this expedition not only opened the path for others in the future, but resulted in the residency of two French scientists (Godin and La Condamine) in Peru and the Amazonian basin, respectively.

No other expedition took place for two decades. The Spanish–French expedition of Hipólito Ruiz, José Pavón and J. Dombey began in 1777 and focused on Peru, resulting in a treatise on quinine and several volumes on Peruvian and Chilean plants and animals. New Granada was the subject of an expedition carried out by the physician José Celestino Mutis (1732–1808), a doctor to the new Viceroy, who began it 1782. Mutis served for twenty-five years in his official duties before being able to devote himself totally to the study of the flora of New Granada. He also taught mathematics and astronomy in Bogotá. The Inquisition charged him with heresy for teaching the Copernican system, an incident that represented the last attempts of that institution to control intellectual orthodoxy.

Ironically, ecclesiastical inquiries and episcopal visits, carried out by bishops in their dioceses, gathered much information of a socio-economic and anthropological nature in the late eighteenth century. The best example of such visits is that carried out by the Bishop of Trujillo, Baltasar Jaime Martínez Compañón (1735–1797) who, in six years of diocesan visits that began in 1782, gathered together a complete collection of paintings depicting the daily life of his parishoners.

Other important expeditions fulfilled the Linnean imperative of classifying the natural kingdom, and the challenge of learning about the remotest corners of the continent. Significantly, the religious orders carried out part of this work in their renewed efforts to reach the peoples not as yet christianized in the great waterways of South America. Such a man was fray Antonio Caulín (b. 1719), author of *Historia coro-gráphica* ... *de la Nueva Andalucía* (1779), which described the Orinoco basin. The anthropological knowledge of aboriginal cultures initiated in the sixteenth century by the first missionaries thus flowered again in the eighteenth century.

Martin de Sessé (d. 1809) led an expedition to Mexico, where he gathered animal and plant specimens in 1788 and 1789 aided by the Mexican José Mariano Mociño (1757–1822). This venture was prolonged by subsequent visits to Central America and Cuba. Other significant voyages were those led by the Italian Alejandro Malaspina, who was accompanied by one French and one Bohemian scientist. They collected specimens in southern South America and the southern Pacific. Another important source of knowledge was the series of expeditions commissioned to determine the true boundaries between the Spanish and Portuguese colonies in mid eighteenth century. Félix de Azara (1746–1821), a self-taught scientist and professional soldier, spent years studying nature in the riverine areas of Paraguay and the River Plate between 1781 and 1800, partly to survey the Portuguese–Spanish boundary. The culmination of these explorations was the trip made by Alexander Von Humboldt (1769–1859), who between 1799 and 1804, under the auspices of the Spanish Crown, visited the Venezuelan interior, Havana, New Granada, Quito, the Andean cordillera, and Peru. The last place he traveled to was New Spain, producing the best-known of his studies. Thirty volumes of natural description and analysis published in Paris beginning in 1809 could earn Humboldt the title of the true discoverer of the Americas.

The flurry caused by these international expeditions were but one facet of the many activities of a scientific nature that took place in the last decades of the century. Patronized by the Crown to develop and refine any technology applicable to the extraction of natural wealth, scientific research and scientific institutions were finally incorporated into the educational scenario of Spanish America. The experimental sciences had only slowly been introduced into the universities in the second half of the century. Mining, one of the most productive sources of wealth in the New World, was targeted for technical improvement by Charles III and his advisers. The *Real Cuerpo de Minería*, a recommendation of the royal visitor José de Gálvez (1729–1786) and Mexican scientist Joaquín Velázquez de León (1732–1786), was formally established in New Spain in 1777 to regulate the industry and to teach new technological improvements. Fausto de Elhuyar, trained in Saxony and Sweden, was appointed in 1786 as its first head. The Mexican institution which began to function in 1792, served as a model for others in Peru, Chile, northern South America, and Central America. Several other European scientists interested in botany and mining came with Elhuyar, and they were responsible for the foundation of the Royal Mining School and the Botanical Garden.

Education: the possibility of change and reform

Interest in education at all levels increased, with special attention being paid to "popular" education, the forerunner of the concept of state schools. Book circulation, especially scientific books, increased significantly. The eagerness of Spanish American subjects to participate in the process of learning that was unfolding in the older continent was expressed through the foundation of societies of persons interested in science and its practical applications, variously called *Sociedades Económicas de Amigos* or *Amantes del País*.[29] Spanish societies accepted Spanish American members. Out of 1,268 members of the *Real Sociedad Vascongada de los Amigos del País*, 522 resided in the American continent. Of those, 469 lived in New Spain, Peru, and Cuba. The Society published proceedings of its meetings to keep its non-resident members informed of its activities. In Spanish America Societies were founded in Buenos Aires, Havana, Quito, Guatemala, Bogotá, and Caracas. It should be noted that those cities had been on the periphery of the colonial empire until the eighteenth century, and that their openness to the Enlightenment was possibly due to their lack of deeply rooted traditional centers of knowledge.

Renovation in the curriculum of institutions of higher education took place only in the last decades of the eighteenth century. The teaching of science found many obstacles, not the least important being the lack of a budget for the purchase of scientific instruments. If religious orthodoxy proved to be an obstacle to change in science teaching in some universities during the first three quarters of the century, it was the lack of facilities that weighed much more heavily at the end of the century. Curriculum

[29] Robert J. Shafer, *Economic Societies in the Spanish World* (Syracuse University Press, 1958).

reform aimed at making university instruction a practical means by which to solve social and economic problems. Typical of such reform was that promoted by José Pérez Calama, a dean of the Michoacán church who was appointed Bishop of Quito in 1788. In New Spain Pérez Calama had attempted to found a learned society for the development of the province, and had written an essay on how to plant corn and prevent scarcity of grain. As bishop of Quito from 1790 to 1792, he wrote numerous essays on subjects ranging from the design of bread ovens to a plan for the reform of university curriculum that would add history, politics, and economy to the theological base of the University of Santo Tomás. Pérez Calama underlined the utilitarian objective of all learning, and wished the university to open its lectures to all. Other members of the church shared the hope that learning would build a strong foundation for a better society. Canon Juan Baltazar Maciel distinguished himself in the Viceroyalty of Buenos Aires, supporting the adoption of the sciences and modern philosophy as the regent of the Real Colegio de San Carlos, which took over the teaching of theology and philosophy after the expulsion of the Jesuits.

Not all hopes for cultural and technological change had a firm foundation or fulfilled an innovative role, and many achievements of this period were undone during the period of independence. The Chilean University of San Felipe, founded in 1738, added mathematics to the classic subjects in 1758, but on an informal basis. Neither this nor the Universities of Córdoba and Tucumán, founded in 1784, played any role in the development of the Enlightenment. Quito did not have teachers of mathematics or physics until 1789, when the Copernican theory was first taught. At the Chilean Academy of San Luis, the mathematics chair was occupied in 1799 by the engineer Agustín Cavallero, who focused on the teaching of mining machinery, calculus, and surveying. The Academy had to close in 1813 due to the tensions caused by the political situation in the Captaincy.

Intellectual opposition to scientific and philosophical renovation was by no means absent from the colonies. Added to the difficulties of promoting scientific research and implementing curriculum plans, they posed a formidable challenge to change. In New Spain, the Jesuit scholar José María Vallarta opposed all innovation while Dominican theologian Cristóbal Mariano Coriche scorned the writings of Jean Jacques Rousseau for exalting the natural man, in disregard of Christianity and civilization. Lima was a bastion of conservatism, and it was there that men such as José Baquíjano and Toribio Rodríguez de Mendoza were investigated by the Inquisition, which by that time had as its main occupation keeping watch over unorthodox ideas in science and philosophy. The *Mercurio Peruano* was targeted by Bishop Juan Domingo

González de la Reguera for publishing "unorthodox" materials. In New Granada José Celestino Mutis succeeded in personally teaching mathematics and astronomy and the Copernican theory from 1762 to 1767 against the wishes of the Dominican order. But the Dominicans succeeded in helping to suppress those subjects between 1778 and 1786, when they were restored.

The press and the diffusion of knowledge

For the interested reader, European technological and scientific news became accessible in the periodical publications that began to appear in some capitals as early as 1722. In that year the *Gaceta de México y Noticias de Nueva España* appeared for six short runs, to be followed by another *Gazeta de México* between 1728 and 1742. The second half of the century was the true period of flowering for similar vehicles of information. Mexico, the site of the first press in the Americas, published more journals than any other capital. Antonio de Alzate ran the *Diario literario de México* in 1768. He also published two other ephemeral scientific journals in 1772 and 1787, Alzate succeeded in publishing *Gazeta de literatura de México* between 1788 and 1794. He translated Benjamin Franklin's works and was in touch with North American and European centers of research. Another brief but important publication was *Mercurio Volante*, appearing in Mexico in 1772 and carrying mostly studies on physics and medical matters. In Guatemala the *Gazeta de Guatemala* published scientific information from European and North American sources. Of the latter, the influence of the College of Philadelphia and the American Philosophical Society were felt in more than one important Spanish American city.

Lima's *Sociedad Económica de Amantes del País*, published the *Mercurio Peruano* between 1791 and 1793. The stated purpose of the *Mercurio Peruano* expressed goals common to all these publications. The *Mercurio* wished to be a vehicle of useful knowledge, such as a better acquaintance with the Viceroyalty, a popularization of medical, engineering, and mercantile knowledge. Its collaborators wrote on Feijóo and Newton, as well as on "free" trade and mining techniques. Among other notable publications were the *Semanario del Nuevo Reino de Granada*, published between 1808 and 1881. Behind these journals were the most astute of the *criollo* notables, men such as Francisco José de Caldas in New Granada, Francisco Javier Eugenio de Santa Cruz y Espejo (1747–1795), José Baquíjano, and Hipólito Unanúe (1755–1833) in Peru, and Manuel de Salas (1755–1841), a member of the Consulate of Santiago de Chile. The latter was a promoter of numerous civic buildings and the force behind the founding of the Academy of San Luis, a center for the study of design, geometry, and mathematics in 1796. It should be noted that an increasing number of intellectuals were American-born, and their interests were geared towards the improvement of what they vaguely felt was "their" turf, in opposition to an increasingly regulatory and self-centered Crown and royal bureaucracy.

Despite its importance in opening the mental doors of Spanish America to the modernity of science, economics, and administration, the Enlightenment remained an evolutionary process that directly influenced only the social elite of the colonies. Only a tiny percentage of the urban population could or would read the journals of the period. The reform of the university curriculum broadened the range of knowledge of the students, but the inclusion of philosophical theories created in Europe in the seventeenth century meant that the colonies were simply updating. Although change and openness came without much opposition, detractors of revisions and "modernization," scored important victories in their efforts to stall the adoption of new methodologies.

The colonial setting caved in under the aegis of the Enlightenment. The men who took advantage of the opportunity of the Napoleonic invasion of Spain in 1808 to begin shaping a political destiny of their own, had matured in the last two decades of the eighteenth century, and had assessed the potential of the "lights" of modern thought. The possibility of progress and betterment, they felt, was open to anyone with education and will. The philosophical winds of the French and the American revolutions had brought seeds of equality which could and should be applied, at least among those at the top. They had also become aware of a distinct feeling, nourished by Jesuit writers in exile, which exalted the positive side and the good of their own *patrias chicas*. The Americas could become as great as Europe under the aegis of liberty, supported by the intellectual achievement and natural intelligence of its people. Men such as Juan José de Eguiara y Eguren (1696–1763), author of *Biblioteca mexicana*, a catalogue of Mexican authors, praised the achievements of the *criollo*. The greatness of an Indian past, remote and mythical, was useful in asserting roots that were comfortably detached from their own present, but which could be used to embarrass Spain and claim legitimacy through a history different and separate from that of the mother country. Finally, the naked dislike of Creoles shown by several enlightened Spanish bureaucrats, and the obvious benefits for Spain resulting from administrative and commercial reforms, lent a material basis for separation. This break would take on different degrees of resolution and shades of participation, but that story belongs elsewhere.

Conclusion

The panorama of Spanish American viceregal culture in its 300 years of development offers a picture of movement and debate which goes beyond a simple reflection or imitation of European models. Although one of its sources was, and remained, European, and specifically Iberian, the reality of the American continent imposed its presence in the development of a culture in the Spanish colonies. Its original inhabitants and its ecology asserted its personality from 1492 onwards, forcing the Iberian source to adapt itself to a new reality that could not be totally assimilated. This became obvious in the development of a legislative and administrative system that had to respond to the new colonial circumstances. The process of adapting the models was slow and contrived, but when it matured in the late seventeenth century, it bore its own distinctive features.

The American society gave Europe new elements to rethink universal human values and to recast its material life. The solution to the challenges presented by the new geographical scenario and the variety of human actors, engaged in constant and necessary intercourse with the Iberian philosophical and theological culture, forced Spain into a self-analysis of important repercussions. While it did not yield constructive or beneficial results in all cases, and was hotly contested by many, the answers Spain gave to itself led to the debate on the rationality of human kind, the meaning of justice in dealing with non-Europeans, and the laws that should rule all peoples.

Cultural exchanges are never simple. Under Spanish rule, the weight of a Christian and European world view and technical knowledge reshaped the basic structures of life of the aboriginal inhabitants. However, the picture of a passive colonial subject whose main role was to reiterate and adapt an Iberian model is inoperable in the Spanish American context. The dynamics of viceregal culture lay in the constant challenge that Spain found in its colonies producing a new and truly distinctive society.

10

The eighteenth century: narrative forms, scholarship, and learning

Karen Stolley

Introduction

In the year 1737, as an epidemic raged in and around Mexico City, its inhabitants carried out desperate acts of devotion to a number of holy images in a series of unsuccessful attempts to halt the disease's mortal progression. Finally, after the city formally declared the Virgin of Guadalupe as its official patron, the epidemic subsided. Recounting this miraculous turn of events in his four-volume *Historia de la Provincia de la Compañía de Jesús de Nueva España* (1767; Mexico, 1841–1842), Francisco Javier Alegre (1729–1788), a Jesuit himself and the acclaimed historian of the Order, observed that it appeared the exterminating angel was only waiting for the declaration of patronage in order to sheath his sword (Lafaye, *Quetzalcóatl and Guadalupe*, 86; see also Deck, *Francisco Javier Alegre*). Jacques Lafaye points to this moment as the occasion for the "belated flowering for the Guadalupe cult," two centuries after its apparition, a flowering he relates to incipient Mexican national consciousness and, more generally, to a period of creole triumphalism in the early 1700s. Even discounting these later developments, Alegre's account preserves for us a striking example of colonial hagiolatry.

Almost half a century later, in 1779, a smallpox epidemic was declared in Mexico City. Dr. José Ignacio Bartolache (1739–1790), who had edited the *Mercurio Volante* (which some consider to be America's first medical journal) during its brief appearance from 1772 to 1773, presented to the viceroy a plan for combatting the disease. Although Bartolache's text has unfortunately been lost, his recommendations were preserved in the Cabildo's official approval of the plan. Bartolache called for city streets to be lit and perfumed and any churches where corpses were kept to be well ventilated; he also suggested that music be played whenever food and medicine were ministered to the sick and that bands of musicians roam the streets at night to alleviate the fear and worry of Mexico's citizenry (*Mercurio Volante* xxxvi–xxxvii). Although Bartolache's suggestions may strike today's reader as quaint or even misguided, they clearly reflect a rudimentary understanding of the issues involved in disease control, an intuitive appreciation of the psychological effects of a catastrophic epidemic, and an enlightened concern for matters of public health.

This brief foray into eighteenth-century pathography suggests the difficulties inherent in any attempt to categorize eighteenth-century prose writing in Latin America. Is it possible to articulate a coherent characterization of the eighteenth century based on the aforementioned writers? Where do the works by Alegre and Bartolache – a history of the Jesuits in Mexico and a proposal for public health reforms – fit into the Latin American literary tradition? How are we to weigh the importance of eighteenth-century narrative forms, scholarship, and learning against the marvelous accounts of sixteenth-century chroniclers or the *modernista* [modernist] renovation of poetic language?

These questions are meant to convey some sense of why eighteenth-century prose has traditionally been regarded as a literary no-man's land. For many readers of Latin American literature, the eighteenth century represents not a bridge but rather an abyss between the Colonial Baroque and nineteenth-century Romanticism. It is not only literary historians who retreat before the eighteenth-century challenge: even José Lezama Lima, in *La expresión americana* (1957), jumps from the baroque *señor* to the persecuted Romantic (pp. 89–97). And while neoclassical verse enjoys a respected niche in most literary histories and anthologies, eighteenth-century prose ends up being a "peje entre dos aguas" (to use Concolor-corvo's phrase in Carrió de la Vandera's, *El lazarillo de ciegos caminantes*) that is to say, a fish out of water...infrequently studied and even less frequently read.

This critical uneasiness can be explained to a point by historical factors. The final years of the seventeenth century saw the death of three major figures of the colonial baroque period: Sor Juana Inés de la Cruz (1648–1695), Juan del Valle y Caviedes (1652–1697), and Carlos de Sigüenza y Góngora (1645–1700). Sigüenza y Góngora's death came the same year that the Bourbon dynasty ascended to the throne in Spain. But literary history rarely evolves in tidy, hundred-year periods. Lafaye goes too far, perhaps, when he speaks of the "tragic ambiguity" of the early part of the century (*Quetzalcóatl*, 97); however, it is difficult to dispute his conclusion that the first decades of the eighteenth century were "hardly distinguishable from the closing ones of the seventeenth century, except in developing and accentuating trends begun in the latter" (Lafaye, "Literature and intellectual life in colonial Spanish America," 695). The persistence of baroque tendencies meant that Neoclassicism and then Romanticism appeared later than in Spain and, indeed, vivid traces of Romanticism appear in fiction produced in the early part of the twentieth century. There is a longstanding debate about when – if at all – the Enlightenment arrived in Latin America; questions regarding the significance of Catholic enlightened thought, the degree to which the Inquisition affected the dissemination of new thinking across the Atlantic, and how to characterize the relationship between the Enlightenment and Latin American independence movements have tended to marginalize the Ibero-American world in Enlightenment scholarship, even in more recent studies. Nevertheless, Arthur Whitaker has argued that the revisionist focus on the Enlightenment's diversity and pragmatism (while qualifying earlier claims of unity and idealism) is particularly relevant to the Ibero-American world (Aldridge, *The Ibero-American Enlightenment*, 42–3).

The definition of the Hispanic Enlightenment represents a Gordian knot requiring far more drastic whacks than can be wielded within the limited confines of the present study. However, the classic collection of essays edited by A. Owen Aldridge on the Ibero-American Enlightenment takes as its starting point a traditional understanding of the key elements of the European Enlightenment: the commitment to scientific discovery and rejection of superstition; a spirit of critical inquiry; and dedication to social and economic reform (Aldridge, *Ibero-American Enlightenment*, 8). Most contributors to the volume stress the dual importance of reason and experience in understanding and appropriating the world and point to the "intellectual revolution" (to use John Tate Lanning's phrase) which had completely transformed Hispanic academic culture by the end of the century.

Charles Griffen acknowledges that eighteenth-century Latin Americans were often hostile to Enlightenment ideas such as popular sovereignty and anti-clericalism. At the same time they advocated the promotion of useful scientific knowledge and the liberation of philosophic thought from scholasticism. In this respect, their position is not unlike Fray Benito Jerónimo Feijóo's (1676–1764) concept of "classic modernity," and several Latin American writers carried on a lively trans-Atlantic exchange with the ideas of the Benedictine scholar (Griffen, quoted in Aldridge *Ibero-American Enlightenment*, 27).

When does the sympathy to enlightened ideas develop in Latin America? The chronology is a matter of some debate, but certain dates stand out: 1759, when the enlightened and reformist reign of Charles III begins; the Jesuit expulsions of 1767; 1778, when the *flota* system is abolished and a new system of *comercio libre* is put into place (Lerdo de Tejada). The reform programs initiated by the Bourbon king and his ministers during the second half of the century, while aimed primarily at economic and administrative structures, had far-reaching implications for the intellectual life of the viceroyalties. And although their significance would not become clear until well into the Independence period, the reforms served as a catalyst for the formation of a creole identity, the consolidation of the "imagined communities" which Benedict Anderson sees as the forerunner to a nationalist consciousness ("Creole pioneers," 6–7). Undeniably, at some point after mid century a sea change took place which is reflected in the account of Alegre and Bartolache's very different responses to the threat of epidemic in Mexico City with which this chapter opened.

One of the factors that makes this shift so difficult to evaluate in conventional literary terms is that it often evidenced itself in cultural production (as opposed to textual production) concentrated in the rapidly growing urban centers – Lima, Mexico City, La Plata, Caracas, Havana. The late colonial period witnessed the emergence of new centers of population and prestige, as the balance of power shifted from Lima and Mexico City to the newly created viceroyalties of New Granada (1739) and La Plata (1776). Throughout the colonies, the proliferation of printing presses and the publication of gazettes and newspapers, the formation of Sociedades de Amigos, ["economic societies of friends of the country"], the organizations of scientific expeditions, the founding of libraries, universities, and academies, the sponsorship of reform projects and a seemingly endless series of debates and polemics on a number of topics are as much manifestations of eighteenth-century thinking as any one volume or author. Perhaps this explains why to date the most interesting work on eighteenth-century Latin America has been done by economic and social historians, or by cultural historians such as Antonello Gerbi, David Brading, or Lafaye.

Eighteenth-century prose writing in Latin America encompasses works which are now inaccessible or out of literary fashion. The reader must often deal with marginal genres – the scientific or philosophical essay, the travel journal – whose "literariness" is in some ways problematic, or with hybrid texts which resist facile generic categorization. Enlightenment scholarship has been characterized to date by what Lester Cocker calls a "compulsion to define" ("The Enlightenment," 336). Yet there is a certain irony in the fact that, despite the eighteenth-century fascination with Linnean classification, the authors and works discussed here defy systematic organization. I will attempt instead to suggest the wide range of scholarly, literary, and civic activity which the eighteenth century produced in Latin America.

I must add a parenthetical comment about eighteenth-century women writers. While studies of the eighteenth century in Europe have yielded important additions to the canon by women writers, the same cannot be said at this time for Latin America. Several factors are at work. One is that the sixteenth-and seventeenth-century historiographical tradition which is central to early Latin American literary history was for the most part closed to women's experience. Another is that women, traditionally marginalized in European literary culture, were even more so in the developing colonial literary culture, where the possibilities of urbanization, trade, and travel were limited until late in the colonial period. An exception, of course, is the rich tradition of Hispanic convent writing; we must turn to historical studies or anthologies (Lavrin, Schlau and Arenal, Muriel, Myers) for information about these "untold sisters." Francisca Josefa de le Concepción del Castillo y Guevara's spiritual autobiography is an important eighteenth-century contribution to this tradition.

For the reasons outlined above, a thematic approach to eighteenth-century prose proves more useful than one based on genre, chronology or region. The sections I enumerate below will serve to organize my approach to scholarship and learning in the eighteenth century:

From scholasticism to new thinking
Trends in historiography
Scientific observation and travel
The organization of knowledge

A final caveat: many eighteenth-century writers, considered minor figures within the larger context of Latin American letters, are fiercely held up within their own countries as the founding fathers of a national culture. To omit them would strike some readers as an egregious oversight; to include them will no doubt strike others as excessively generous. Much was written about the continent by European travellers, some whose stay spanned more than a decade and who became intimately familiar with the regions they were describing. Other Creoles, like the Jesuits exiled in 1767, left Latin America to relocate in Europe and resumed their writing in Latin or Italian. The conventional means by which we measure literary history – national origin, language, dissemination of a given work – fall short of capturing the complexity of the eighteenth century. I have tried to steer a judicious middle passage that will provide the reader with criteria for reaching an appreciation of the period and its major figures without resorting to a mere laundry list of authors and works.

From scholasticism to new thinking

The gradual shift in thinking which occurred during the eighteenth century manifests itself perhaps most dramatically in the areas of religion and philosophy. These two disciplines are closely linked during the early part of the century but thereafter take increasingly divergent paths. In 1700, academic culture was firmly anchored in Thomistic thought and cultural production dominated by spiritual or contemplative writing. Although the second half of the century brought a sharp increase in the number of printing presses in the Spanish colonies (see works by Toribio Medina), in 1700 there were only five (in Mexico, Lima, Puebla, and Guatemala), and their output was largely limited to works of a religious nature – sermons, novenas, funeral orations, and devotional tracts. The sheer abundance of such publications provides us with a glimpse of how thoroughly public life in the Spanish colonies was dominated by the church (Lafaye, *Quetzalcóatl*, 84–5). One of the first works to be published by the Bogotá press after its installation in 1739 was the funeral eulogy for Madre Castillo, signalling both the end of an era in religious textual production and a new era of secular publishing which will be discussed later in this chapter.

Madre Castillo stands out as the most important figure of religious letters in the early eighteenth century. Both her poetry and prose writings reflect the persistence of baroque tendencies well beyond the close of the seventeenth century and mark the continuation of the Spanish mystic tradition almost a century after the deaths of San Juan de la Cruz and Santa Teresa. The daughter of a prominent family in Tunja, in the viceroyalty of Nueva Granada, she was educated at home and entered the Convent of Santa Clara at the age of eighteen. She took her vows in 1694 and thereafter played an active role in the life of the convent until her death, serving on three occasions as Mother Superior. She left behind a scattering of lyric poetry, and two prose works: the *Afectos espirituales* and the *Vida* (both unpublished at the time of her death).

Given the scarcity of women writers during the colonial period, comparisons with Sor Juana Inés de la Cruz are inevitable, although perhaps unjust. As in the case of Sor Juana, critical attention has focused until recently on the biographical, with excessive attention paid to Madre Castillo's own accounts of hysterical illness and self-doubt. Certainly the circumstances of these two nuns are quite different: Sor Juana lived in the center of viceregal life in Mexico City; Madre Castillo spent her days in a forgotten convent in a melancholy town in a marginalized region of the colonies. Her surroundings were austere and her daily routine monotonous (Achury Valenzuela, *Análisis crítico de los "Afectos espirituales,"* clxxxvii). And while Sor Juana's writings reflect a wide variety of both secular and religious themes, an astonishing range of genres, and an acknowledged mastery of baroque imagery, Madre Castillo's literary project must be defined, on a much smaller scale, as devotional literature. The degree to which Sor Juana casts a shadow over the younger nun's literary reputation is evidenced by the fact that three of Sor Juana's poems which Madre Castillo had copied into one of her notebooks were for a time attributed to her (Achury Valenzuela, *Análisis crítico*, cxcii–cxciii).

Madre Castillo began writing the *Afectos espirituales* after entering the convent, perhaps in 1694, and at the time of her death had completed 196 spiritual exercises. The *Afectos* use biblical imagery and baroque language to describe a mystical journey of the soul. The manuscripts show much evidence of revisions and corrections, some by her own hand and others apparently by the series of Father Confessors who encouraged her to write. Unconcerned with documenting her biblical sources, Madre Castillo frequently links biblical phrases and original thoughts in a seamless manner which Achury Valenzuela calls "el arte del enlace" ["the art of linkage"] (*Análisis crítico*, clxii). At other times the style of the *Afectos* is so distilled as to verge on aphorism.

Madre Castillo undertook the composition of her spiritual autobiography at the request of her confessor, Father Francisco de Herrera, who encouraged her to use Santa Teresa's spiritual guides as a model. The *Vida* purports to chronicle the progression from childhood to adulthood in a straightforward manner and emphasizes throughout the dichotomy between the spiritual and the mundane (Antoni, "Women of the early modern period," 156). Yet one must resist the temptation to view the *Afectos* and the *Vida* as both stylistically and thematically opposed; the two works are intimately related and must be read against each other in order to be fully understood.

Madre Castillo herself saw them as a continuous text. She moves quickly at the outset of the *Vida* from the autobiographical to the spiritual, describing her aversion to matrimony and the intense pull she feels toward contemplation and prayer (*Vida* [1968], 4). In one of her more surprising revelations, she assures the reader that she miraculously learned Latin without ever studying it (p. 3), but most chapters of the *Vida* contain only the most fleeting reference to the outside world. Spiritual crises are experienced and conquered over and over again in what might be characterized as a narrative of monotony: "I will write only one thing or another, because otherwise I would never finish telling them all, and they have been almost all the same" (p.144). Another narrative strategy frequently employed by Madre Castillo is prophecy: she foresees events which are confirmed later in her life (often the departure or transfer of one of her confessors; see pp. 135–6); in this way the narrative structure constantly reaffirms itself, even in the face of protestations of self-doubt by the narrator.

The most striking passages are those in which Madre Castillo inscribes her own *Afectos* within the narrative framework of the *Vida*, reinforcing at the same time both her spiritual and writerly vocations. Chapter 34 of the *Vida* explains how she is consoled on one occasion by an inner light:

> But this will be better explained by a few words which I heard then, or rather that I wrote (not because they were actual words, but rather a

light which impressed itself on my soul and convinced it, having received Our Sacred Lord), as if to say: "Look, if all the world were pure gold, pearls and precious stones, and you were able to acquire it and bring it all to you, merely by desiring and wishing it to be so, you could not be transformed; but in me, true and ineffable richness, love can transform you."   (pp. 130–1)

The rich and glowing images of the mystic vision come from *Afecto* 39 and saturate this text from the *Vida* with undeniable authority.

While Madre Castillo is clearly the most outstanding representative of eighteenth-century convent writing, many other nuns wrote spiritual autobiographies or devotional exercises. *Letras de la Audiencia de Quito* (edited by Hernán Rodríguez Casteló), for example, includes many previously unpublished works which have been transcribed from the original manuscript. One of the most striking pieces in the collection is a brief fragment, entitled "Secretos entre el alma y Dios," from the spiritual autobiography of the Ecuadorean nun Catalina de Jesús Herrera (1717–1796). Unlike Madre Castillo's *Vida*, the brief fragment makes reference to a number of gripping events in Catalina de Herrera's life. But what is most striking about the fragment is its insistence on a feminine, even feminist, consciousness. On three separate occasions the writer describes her father's abusive behavior, taking care to open and close each anecdote with pious affirmations of his Christian character and essential goodness: "The first time was when I was recently born and all swaddled ... Because my mother did not come quickly when I cried, he took me in his arms and was about to throw me out of the window, and if my mother had not hastened her step he would have done so violently" (p. 118). The contemporary reader is struck by the description of child abuse, the physical violence brought on by the child's crying, and the fortuitous maternal intervention.

Later Catalina de Jesús Herrera confesses that her first meditations on the divine were occasioned by having witnessed the birth of a younger sibling. The childbirth scene leads her to imagine an almost infinite regression of women born of other women, until she must ask her mother to explain the origin of the first woman. Although Catalina de Herrera is again careful to credit God with enlightening her mother so that she might answer all the daughter's questions, what is actually described in the text is a deep and extended theological discussion between mother and daughter, made even more remarkable because its scenario is the lying-in room shortly after the birth itself (pp. 119–20). Catalina de Herrera's autobiography, while firmly rooted within Hispanic mystical tradition, is unique for its matter-of-fact treatment of issues of female sexuality and women's experience.

I close this section on convent writing with a brief mention of María

Ana Agueda de San Ignacio (1695–1756). Although her works have long been largely inaccessible, she is considered to be an important mystical writer and one of the few women who turned her attention to theological matters. Selections of her writings have been included in Arenal and Schlau's *Untold Sisters* (353–5, 387–96).

While nuns' writing tends to be of a private nature, either for themselves or for a confessor, men wrote for a wider audience. Early bibliographies contain many mentions of sermons and funeral elegies delivered by clerics too numerous (and too minor) to mention. They form part of the cultural landscape of the early part of the eighteenth century, but most are seldom read and only rarely re-edited.

Francisco Javier Conde y Oquendo (1733–1799) was known as the best orator of his day, despite the fact that only three of his sermons had been published at the time of his death. Born in Cuba, he later spent several years in Spain before returning to Mexico; like so many eighteenth-century figures of letters, he moved from one vice-royalty or geographical area to another, and both Cuba and Mexico claim him as part of their literary history. During his years in Spain he wrote the "Elogio a Felipe V," which was printed in Madrid in 1779 (where it received a prize from the Real Academia Española) and reprinted in Mexico in 1785.

Conde y Oquendo left three volumes of unpublished *Piezas oratorias*, preceded by the *Discurso sobre la elocuencia*, a treatise on eloquence which reflects eighteenth-century distaste for baroque oratorical excess. Like the eponymous protagonist of the satiric novel *Fray Gerundio de Campazas, alias Zotes, Historia del famoso Predicador* (1757–1768) by Father José Francisco de Isla de la Torre (1703–1781), Conde y Oquendo in his treatise attacks pretentious sermonizing and attempts to explain its prevalence in the Spanish viceroyalties. Just as the rays of the rising sun first illuminate Europe before moving westward to America, the new enlightened spirit in arts and letters has been slow to reach New Spain: "it seems that gerundism, finding itself already dethroned in the Metropolis, decided to move to these vast colonies in order to rule longer and extend its iron scepter with greater dominion and authority" (p. 380).

Conde y Oquendo also wrote the *Disertación histórica sobre la aparición de la portentosa imagen de María santísima de Guadalupe de México* (1794), a two-volume refutation of Bartolache's essay on the same topic ("Manifesto satisfactorio anunciado en la *Gazeta de México. Opúsculo Guadalupano...*," 1790). Beginning with a critique of the artistic merits of the image which had supposedly miraculously appeared on the Indian Juan Diego's blanket in December of 1531, Bartolache had gone on to question the authenticity of many details of the Guadalupan legend itself. In his prologue, Conde y Oquendo promises his readers "a complete history of Our Lady of Guadalupe, as called for by our times;

that is, a history which is at the same time critical and apologetic, which will satisfy the devout, the curious and the incredulous" (p. xxvii). His lengthy disquisitions on indigenous, Spanish, and creole accounts of the occurrence alternate with pointed rebuttals of Bartolache's arguments, and he concludes with an analysis of the image based on his own training as a painter.

This exchange is, at most, a bibliographical curiosity which reflects the intellectual and religious tenor of the times, as well as the central role played by Guadalupism in the cultural life of New Spain. Despite their differences, Conde y Oquendo and Bartolache share a genuine commitment to their Catholic faith; research on the historiographical foundations of the Guadalupan legend was not necessarily at odds with devotion. Even Fray Servendo Teresa de Mier (1763–1827), whose 1794 sermon linking St. Thomas with Quetzalcóatl and the Virgin of Guadalupe with Tonantzin led to his trial for heresy, sought primarily to ground New World theology in indigenous polytheism (see Lafaye, *Quetzalcóatl*, 262–71). The Guadalupan debates provide a glimpse of the particular character of the Latin American Enlightenment, in which scientific observation is not necessarily at odds with belief. (A similar case is the Virgen del Cobre, or Copper Virgin of Cuba, whose miraculous apparition was chronicled by Onofre de Fonseca [no dates available] in a 1703 manuscript which was lost and later reconstructed in 1782, and more recently by the Cuban critic José Juan Arrom [*Certidumbre de América*, 184–214].)

I now turn to two thinkers who represent the break between traditional scholasticism and what is often called the new thinking or modern philosophy: Juan Bautista Díaz de Gamarra y Dávalos (1745–1783) and José Agustín Caballero (1762–1835). In his seminal work, *Cultura mexicana moderna en el siglo XVIII*, Bernabé Navarro discusses the influence wielded by a small group of Jesuits in mid-century as they challenged the supremacy of scholastic thought in New Spain. Gamarra was a central figure in this group. A professor of philosophy at a Franciscan college in Michoacán, he published three works: *Elementa recentioris philosophiae* (1774), a plan for the reform of philosophical education and a critique of peripatetic thought; *Errores del entendimiento humano* (1781), a critique of scholastic philosophy written in Spanish for a popular audience; and *Memorial ajustado*, a satirical account of a judicial ruling against the proponents of the new philosophy which was first published in 1790 in José Antonio Alzate y Ramírez's *Gazetas de Literatura de México*. The *Elementa* is a *cursus philosophicus* of uneven quality (see Navarro, *Cultura mexicana moderna en el siglo XVIII*, 135–67 for a detailed account of the work); in order to appreciate fully the role Gamarra played in disseminating modern philosophy, we must turn to the *Errores del entendimiento humano*.

Gamarra's decision to write the *Errores* in Spanish underscores his didactic and utilitarian aims. The work was originally published under a pseudonym, "Juan Bendiaga," and consists of responses, based on logic and experimentalism, to a wide range of common errors. The discussion of health and hygiene is common-sensical and enlightened; Gamarra recommends that his readers take cold baths, wear loose-fitting clothes, and drink great quantities of water. He also includes many comments directed specifically at women and at one point rails against the current custom of girdles: "Those learned in anatomy know very well how many illnesses can be caused by these unnatural garters... We might be forgiven if the circulation of the blood hadn't already been discovered" (p. 15). He also attempts to persuade women to breast-feed their babies by appealing to their maternal instincts: "What a shameful spectacle it is to see a mother deny her child her own substance, and then endanger herself by the unworthy spilling of it elsewhere" (p. 24).

But the bulk of the work is devoted to questions of human wisdom, the tenets of modern thinking, simply stated and framed for a popular audience. Gamarra praises moderate thinking informed by experience and reason, criticizes obscure speech and announces: "Happy those eclectic philosophers who, imitating the bees, search from flower to flower for the sweet nectar of science!" (p. 45).

José Agustín Caballero is Gamarra's Cuban counterpart; he was one of the first thinkers there to distance himself from scholasticism and actively advocated the reform of public education. He was one of the founders, with Luis de la Casas, of the *Papel Periódico* and exerted considerable moral and intellectual influence on his contemporaries (Henríquez Ureña, *Panorama histórico de la literatura cubana*, 121). Caballero was a Latinist who wrote his *Lecciones de filosofía electiva* in Latin but his approach to philosophy may clearly be characterized as modern, as demonstrated by the following dictum: "It is better for the philosopher, even the Christian philosopher, to follow various schools of thought than to elect only one to which to subscribe" (quoted by Henríquez Ureña, *Panorama histórico*, 122).

Another key eighteenth-century thinker is the Peruvian Pablo de Olavide y Jáuregui (1725–1803). After the Lima earthquake of 1746, Olavide played such a central role in assisting the surviving population and gathering funds for reconstruction of the city that the viceroy put him in charge of all restoration projects. But rumors soon began to circulate regarding the proposed construction of a public theatre and a new cathedral, and Olavide was eventually forced to flee to Madrid to avoid charges of corruption and defaulting on his debts.

Once in Europe he married well and adapted so completely to French enlightened tastes and ideas that one critic refers to him as "el afrancesado" ["the Frenchified one"]. Olavide was chosen by Charles III to oversee an ambitious project to populate and develop the Sierra Morena region in Andalusia but, despite his efforts between 1767 and 1775, the project was a failure. When political fortunes changed in Madrid, Olavide was brought up on charges by the Inquisition and sentenced to eight years in a convent during which time his activity was closely restricted (undoubtedly a heavy price to pay for an enlightened thinker; see Menéndez y Pelayo, *Historia de la poesía hispanoamericana*, 228). In 1780 Olavide escaped and fled across the Pyrenees to France, where he quickly became the darling of Parisian salon society, famous as much for his persecution at the hands of the Spanish as for his own wit and intelligence. Imprisoned once again in 1794, he began to draft the *Evangelio en triunfo o Historia de un filósofo desengañado*. He once again returned to Spain, where his final years were spent in rural retirement writing the *Poemas cristianos* (1799) and working on a translation of the Psalms, *Salterio español, o versión parafrástica de los Salmos de David, de los cánticos de Moisés*...(1800).

As is the case with many eighteenth-century writers, Olavide is more discussed than read, and the misfortunes and triumphs of his life in the New World and in Europe are unequalled by any other figure except Fray Servando Teresa de Mier. Even Diderot was captivated by the story and wrote a brief biography of Olavide (Defourneaux, *Pablo de Olavide*, 471–2). Olavide's poetry is forgettable; Menéndez y Pelayo, with his characteristic directness, describes Olavide's poetry as "badly rhymed prose, without nerve or warmth or the liveliness of fantasy" (p. 224). Notwithstanding the publication by Estuardo Núñez of Olavide's *Obras narrativas desconocidas*, and his *Obras dramáticas desconocidas*, Olavide's best known work is his epistolary novel, *El evangelio en triunfo, o Historia de un filósofo desengañado* (1797–1798).

El evangelio en triunfo is a monumental work, comprising four 400-page volumes of Christian apology set within a loose narrative framework. The plot can be summed up by the work's subtitle: a philosopher, fleeing a duel gone wrong and the vicissitudes of his dissolute life, takes refuge in a monastery where he begins a series of long discussions with one of the monks about religion, philosophy, and morality. He eventually renounces his earlier beliefs and accepts Christianity. The story is told in epistolary form, in a series of forty-one letters the prodigal son (or disabused philosopher) writes to his friend Teodoro, with an introduction where the author sets forth his reasons for writing: the tragic events of the "frightful revolution in France" (*El evangelio en triunfo* [1808], iii) and the subsequent abandonment and abolition of religion, blaming both on the "modern sophists" (p. v).

The work was an instant success and was translated into French and re-published several times (ten editions before the close of the century, fourteen editions of the French translation and six editions of a – mercifully – abbreviated version), although four letters which mention the French revolution were initially omitted by the censor of the French edition (Goic, "La novela hispanoamericana colonial," 394–5).

Critics differ on whether or not the professions of faith of the protagonist can be taken as indicative of the author's own conversion. However, the outcome of the conversations between the philosopher and his Christian mentor is never in doubt, since the narrator uses the fiction of a manuscript which has fallen into his hands to introduce the series of letters (which he himself has put in order) and anticipates the philosopher's ultimate conversion. In introducing the manuscript, he refers to its exemplary nature, utility, and also to its accessible style.

As Enid Valle (*La obra narrativa de Pablo de Olavide*) has suggested, the philosopher has two voices in the letters, that of his libertine self and his newly converted self; in this sense the *Evangelio* can be read as spiritual autobiography (in which the author has experienced a conversion which separates him from his former self and provides him with the authorial perspective necessary to write) and as an attempt at persuasion (the philosopher hopes to convert not only Teodoro but also the reader). The final letters discuss education and public works ("the people are convinced by deeds, not by speeches," p. 147) and conclude with a discussion of the study of religion and the important mentoring role played by fathers in the upbringing of their children. These letters serve not only to attest to the depth of the philosopher's conversion but to set forth the community's *plan de reformas* – a reform plan based on Christian enlightenment and a Virgilian evocation of rural life. Valle suggests that the letters are both a proposal and an accomplished project: it is in these social, commercial, agricultural and educational reforms that the triumph of the Gospel ["el evangelio en triunfo"] is ultimately witnessed.

Olavide's *Evangelio*, both an epistolary novel and a philosophical or religious meditation, is typical of many eighteenth-century works in that it crosses over generic and disciplinary boundaries. Another such work is the *Sueño de sueños* (first published in Mexico in 1945) by José Mariano de Acosta Enriques (?–1816). Because of its reflections on the human condition and its emphasis on the opposition of appearance and reality, it seems reasonable to discuss the *Sueño* in the present context as a philosophical work.

The work, which refers to itself as a "satiric fantasy," is informed by Acosta's readings of Quevedo, Cervantes and Diego de Torres Villarroel (1693–1770), author of the *Sueños morales*. In the prologue, imaginatively titled "Levadura del sueño de sueños" ["Leaven for the Dream of Dreams"], Acosta establishes an intertextual narrative framework:

inspired by a recent edition of Quevedo's *Sueños*, the narrator falls asleep and dreams "the dream of dreams" which enables him to meet with Cervantes, Quevedo, and Torres Villarroel in the New World (Goic, "La novela," 399). Together the four traverse an imaginary landscape peopled with fantastic "figurachos," or visions. The New World is seen, therefore, as a *locus* of unlimited possibilities for intellectual and literary exchange, where the sleepy narrator can include his own text with those of his distinguished companions. An implicit concern with the commercialization of literature runs through their discussions, as Cervantes, Quevedo, and Torres Villarroel eagerly question the narrator for news of how their works are faring in the eighteenth century (pp. 139–40) and ask him to explain the meaning of a periodical subscription (p. 142). The conclusion reiterates the author's utilitarian intentions: the narrator awakens, dresses, and goes to his office to write down his dreams, "fantasies which, if for some serve as a diversion, perhaps for others will be of some usefulness" (p. 211).

Trends in historiography

Historiography in its many forms – chronicles, *relaciones*, histories – accounts for the vast majority of colonial prose works before 1700, and it is not surprising that much of eighteenth-century letters also so can be thus categorized. Yet several trends are worth noting which serve to differentiate eighteenth-century historiography from what comes before: the emergence of urban or regional histories; a growing number of indigenous histories; and the publication of encyclopedic works which blur the boundaries between historiography, travel accounts and scientific writing.

There is a shift away from the compendious "Historias de Indias" such as those written by Gonzalo Fernández de Oviedo (1479–1557) toward local histories which chronicle the discovery, exploration, and settlement of a region or even a specific city. Urban histories become increasingly common as new demographic centers in America become more clearly established. Even without accepting the notion of any real nationalist consciousness during the eighteenth century – an anachronist notion, to be sure – one notes that many authors do seem to identify closely with a particular region. This identification is expressed through the titles of their works (more geographically restrained than those of their sixteenth- and seventeenth-century counterparts), their portrayal of *hijos ilustres* or native sons, and their interest in economic and administrative reforms.

One exception to this general trend is Juan Bautista Muñoz (1745–1799), although it is worth noting that Muñoz was a Spaniard who in 1770 was appointed Cosmographer of the Indies by Charles III. His unfinished (and probably unfinishable) project was to organize the Spanish archives. Muñoz only published the first volume of what was clearly to be a monumental undertaking, the *Historia del nuevo mundo* (Madrid, 1793). However, in the course of his exhaustive research he did manage to bring some order to the archives, which facilitated the work of nineteenth-century historians and proved to be helpful in promoting Spanish-funded archaeological expeditions to the New World. Interestingly, Muñoz's archival research also served as the basis for an address, "Discurso histórico-crítico sobre las apariciones y el culto de Nuestra Señora de Guadalupe de México," which he presented to the Real Academia de la Historia in 1794. While he is able to cite numerous instances of historiographical inaccuracies, the historian refrains from making a final judgement regarding the legend, which he describes as "a very reasonable and just cult, with which individual opinion on the subject of the apparitions has nothing to do" (quoted in Lafaye, *Quetzalcóatl*, 270).

Muñoz himself never left Spain, and his temerity in attempting to write a comprehensive history of America was looked at askance by some creole historians. He defended the enterprise by reminding critics of his solid grounding in documentary evidence, writing in the first volume: "I assumed an attitude of radical doubt with regard to all that had been published on these matters, with the firm intention of verifying the facts by reference to authentic and irrefutable documents" (quoted in Lafaye, *Quetzalcóatl*, 267). The issue of Muñoz's legitimacy as historian of the New World points both to the continuation of earlier tensions between the chronicler eye-witness of events and the Court-appointed historian who viewed those events from afar (I am thinking, of course, of Bernal Díaz del Castillo [1492–1581] and Francisco López de Gómara [1512–1572]), and to increasing resentment on the part of Creoles at being unfairly represented by European writers.

Thus the second trend, a focus on indigenous or pre-Hispanic history, which can be seen as an attempt to define New World history in terms which differentiate it from Europe, anticipating (though it would be foolish to suggest any causal relationship) the independence movements of the early nineteenth century. This impulse is in part a response to what Gerbi has called (in his book of the same name) "the dispute of the New World," a debate about the supposed inferiority of the New World's climate, flora and fauna. The writings of George Buffon and Guillaume-Thomas Raynal fueled the debate in the mid-eighteenth century; the *Recherches philosophiques sur les Américains*, published in 1768 by Cornelius de Pauw, shifted its focus to the indigenous inhabitants of America, and William Robertson's *History of America* (1777) later served to popularize their ideas (see bibliography). The charges made by Buffon, Raynal, de Pauw, and Robertson incensed Creoles, who attempted not only to challenge their arguments but to counter allegations of New World inferiority with proof of its superiority. The counter-claims often took the form of descriptions of pre-Hispanic cultures which implicitly or explicitly challenged European notions of civilization and barbarity.

These indigenous histories appear predominantly in Mexico, where the sixteenth-century savant Sigüenza y Góngora had acted as "a vital, indispensable link" between Fernando de Alva Ixtlilxóchitl (1578–1650) and eighteenth-century historians by preserving Ixtlilxóchitl's papers (Brading, *The First America*, 371). The relative paucity of indigenous history in eighteenth-century Peru suggests that the key factor was not so much a large indigenous or *mestizo* population, but rather a tradition of scholarly interest in the field of pre-Hispanic culture. It may also be the case that in the Andean region, where a revolt led by José Gabriel Condorcanqui Tupac Amaru (1738–1781) against a plan to increase taxes raised the specter of an incendiary link between the indigenous past and the present, Creoles found themselves less anxious to resurrect that past in their writings (Brading, *The First America*, 483–91).

The encyclopedist impulse which is the third trend I have mentioned is related, of course, to French Enlightenment influences, but also to the need for data about the Spanish colonies in order to move forward with Bourbon reforms. The chronological framework of earlier writings about Latin America which generally had as their goal a providential account of the Spanish Conquest proved insufficient or unwieldy when attempting to describe colonial American reality; we shall turn to these descriptive writings later. However, one area where a linear progression continued to serve a purpose were those histories which chronicled the founding and evolution of a particular colonial institution. Institutional histories flourished during the eighteenth century as convents, universities, and religious orders gained an increasing sense of security and entitlement. Of course, the Jesuit expulsion order in 1767 radically altered the cultural landscape; thus Alegre's work on the history of the Jesuit order in New Spain becomes both a chronicle and a eulogy to a reality that had passed even as it was being recorded.

Juan Luis Maneiro and Manuel Fabri, in their *Vidas de mexicanos ilustres del siglo XVIII*, offer the most complete account of the group of Jesuits sometimes referred to as the Generation of 1750. Accomplished scholars all, the group was characterized by an acceptance of new scientific theories (always, however, within the limits of their faith), rejection of scholastic thinking and an acceptance of ecelectisism and experimentalism. Some were writers, like Alegre, Francisco Javier Clavijero (1731–1787) or the Latinate poet Rafael Landívar (1713–1793). Others, like José Rafael Campoy (1723–1777), left few extant writings but played an important role as mentors and proponents of educational reform, especially in the fields of physics and mathematics. Gamarra, as we have already seen, is another key representative. The expulsion order of 1767 splintered the group and sent its members to live and work in exile in various European cities; it also deprived Mexico of its brightest and most committed students and teachers.

It is curious that Navarro, who has studied the eighteenth-century Jesuits extensively, barely mentions Alegre's historical writings, focusing instead on his "humanistic" and theological works and calling him "the greatest scholar of classical languages and the most agile Latin poet of his generation" (*Cultura mexicana*, 83). Yet it is the histories, with their wealth of information, which hold interest for today's reader.

The *Historia de la Provincia de la Compañía de Jesús de Nueva España* (later edited by Carlos María Bustamante and published, 1841–1843) ends with the events of 1763. Longer and much more detailed than the *Memorias*, and obviously directed to Alegre's fellow Jesuits, it reflects the extensive archival research the author had done in preparation for writing. The *Memorias para la historia de la provincia que tuvo la Compañía de Jesús en Nueva España* are an extraordinary compendium written almost from memory after Alegre had settled into exile in Italy. Maneiro and Fabri relate that to the astonishment of his colleagues, with the aid of his "stupendous memory," Alegre was able to recall "not only events and everything that happened, but also dates and the most minor circumstances" (p. 231).

One of the most powerful passages in the *Memorias*, excerpted by Gabriel Méndez Plancarte in *Humanistas del siglo XVIII* (77–81), tells of the events surrounding the expulsion of the Jesuits. It recounts how the Visitador Joseph de Gálvez (who had come to deliver the expulsion order) was stunned by the simplicity and poverty of the Jesuit quarters. One of the priests, finding a small silver coin and a hairshirt, showed them to the Visitador, saying, "These are the riches and treasures of the Jesuit Fathers" (p. 78). Alegre also records the Jesuits' request for permission to take communion before leaving and concludes by describing the general state of shock and dismay which reigned everywhere: "Meanwhile the entire city felt the greatest consternation, the streets were occupied by soldiers and patrols making their rounds, churches were closed and their bells were silent, people went along the street in a solitary and confused fashion, and it was forbidden to form groups or speak among themselves" (p. 80).

Alegre was not the only Jesuit who was obliged to continue his work in exile. Clavijero wrote his masterful history of the Aztec culture and civilization, *Historia antica di Messico* (1780–1781) [*The History of Mexico*] in Italian in Bologna; it was soon translated into a Spanish version which arrived in New Spain in 1778. Clavijero's passion for the indigenous past of his long-lost country is not merely an indignant reaction to the theories of American degeneracy put forth by European writers such as Buffon, de Pauw, Raynal, and Robertson (see Gerbi, *The Dispute of the New World*). Clavijero had also had extensive contact with the modern Indian population and had even learned Nahuatl at one point so that he could hear confessions in a Mexican Indian prison.

The *Historia* is divided into ten books. In the prologue, Clavijero declares that his aim in writing has been to serve his country and preserve the truth about ancient Mexican civilization. The first seven books deal with the natural history of Mexico, Aztec religion, and politics, with appendixes on the Aztec calendrical and numerical systems. The final two books consist of nine dissertations which Clavijero considered to be the heart of the work and which represent a systematic refutation of de Pauw's claims about the American Indians (Ronan, *Francisco Javier Clavijero*, 130).

Clavijero's sources included many Spanish histories of the New World (which he lists as the beginning of the work), as well as ancient Mexican codices and picture collections. Writing from exile, he uses the opportunity to make a plea for the preservation of documents relating to indigenous history, and in the 1780 letter which he wrote to the Directors of the Royal Pontifical University of Mexico (and which is included with the Spanish translation of the *Historia*), he proposes the creation of a museum of Mexican antiquities. Like El Inca Garcilaso (1539–1616), he uses his experience and linguistic prowess to solidify his legitimacy as an author. Yet it has been suggested that the significance of Clavijero's use of primary sources has been exaggerated. Ronan, in fact, argues that the *Historia antigua* is important not because of its originality but because Clavijero brought together and synthesized a wide body of information for an eighteenth-century audience, while Gerbi cites the forcefulness of Clavijero's response to De Pauw and the "rich array of arguments" which he marshals in support of his cause (*The Dispute*, 208).

Clavijero's defense of the Mexican Indians represents an important stage in the project of cultural differentiation which would ultimately provide a foundation and rationale for political independence. As John Leddy Phelan notes, "The outstanding feature of Clavijero's text is his contribution to the development of neo-Aztecism. He brought out for the first time its anti-Spanish implications, and he related the cult of Aztec antiquity to the social problems of the contemporary Indians" ("Neo–Aztecism in the eighteenth century," 763). Later, Fray Servando Teresa de Mier and Carlos María Bustamante would make that connection explicitly.

Another eighteenth-century thinker who expressed keen interest in Mexican antiquities was Antonio de León y Gama (1735/6–1802), who was, like Sigüenza y Góngora, a scholar of astronomy and mathematics. In 1790, when the main plaza of Mexico City was cleared in preparation for renovations, workers uncovered two pre-Hispanic monoliths: one represented the goddess Coatlicue, elaborately decorated with carvings of skulls and serpents which caused horror among the onlookers; the other was the Sun Stone, a great disc carved with calendrical markings.

The story of what happened to these monoliths once they were uncovered sheds interesting light on eighteenth-century ambivalence regarding the indigenous past. The Viceroy ordered that the stones were to be preserved intact, as part of Mexico's cultural heritage. However, since they were considered too frightful to be looked upon, especially by the youth of Mexico, they were buried in a courtyard of the University, but only after drawings and measurements had been made to facilitate their study. When Alexander von Humboldt visited Mexico City in 1803, he pleaded that the monoliths be unearthed. The stones were finally excavated, only to be reburied after the Prussian visitor had gazed to his heart's content (Bernal, *A History of Mexican Archaeology*, 81).

León y Gama wrote his *Descripción histórica y cronológica de las dos piedras* (1792) on the basis of the drawings made before the Sun Stone was buried. He began his analysis by learning classical Nahuatl and systematically reviewing the writings of sixteenth-century indigenous writers for clues to the stone's glyphs. His interpretation, which proved to be remarkably accurate, was the "first systematic interpretation of the Mexican calendar" and opened the door for a reconstruction of Aztec chronology (Brading, *The First America*, 462). And Ignacio Bernal, in his history of Mexican archaeology concludes: "His work on the Indian methods of measuring time and also on their chronology, is without a doubt superior to anything previously done, and corrects many a misunderstanding not only on the part of his immediate predecessors in the seventeenth century and the first half of the eighteenth, but also among the sixteenth-century chroniclers, who did not understand how the calendar really worked" (*A History*, 80). The *Descripción histórica* was translated into Italian by Pedro José Márquez (1741–1820), another member of the Jesuit Generation of 1750 and read widely throughout Europe.

With the *Tres siglos de México*, written by the Jesuit Andrés Cavo (1739–1803), we move from the indigenous past to the viceregal present. Cavo originally planned to entitle his manuscript *Anales de la ciudad de México desde la conquista española hasta el año de 1766*; the shift in title reflects a change in focus from the urban to the regional or national which may have been a result of the Jesuit expulsion. In the prologue Cavo explains that he writes out of a love of country and a desire to serve his nation, and the municipal government of Mexico collaborated on the project by sending pertinent documents to him in Italy. According to Cavo, while others had written of ancient Mexico, no one had written a history of the city of Mexico from the time of the arrival of the Spaniards until the present. He writes, therefore, so as not to "leave buried in eternal forgetfulness the monuments of the first city of the New "World" (p. iii); the metaphor reminds us of the archaeological foundations of the study of indigenous antiquity in the eighteenth century. What is most notable about the long-delayed publication of Cavo's work in 1836 is the supplement added by Carlos María Bustamante (which more than doubled the length of the history), and the extensive explanatory notes.

Unfortunately, the literary merits of Cavo's work are limited; the author allows himself few digressions or reflections on the relentless march of municipal affairs. Even potentially shocking events such as the burning at the stake of several sodomites or the numerous plagues which visited the city are recounted without commentary, in sharp contrast to the urban histories to which I will return shortly. But Cavo does include several sections which reflect his deep concern over the unjust treatment of the Indians in viceregal Mexico, offering at one point this observation about miscegenation: "In effect, if from the time of the Conquest matrimony between both nations [that is, the Indians and Spaniards] had been promiscuous, after some years, with great pleasure on the part of the Mexicans a single nation would have been formed from both" (quoted in Méndez Plancarte, *Humanistas del siglo XVIII*, 105).

The *Historia del reino de Quito en la América Meridional* was also penned by an exiled Jesuit, Juan de Velasco (1727–1792). The three-part work ("Historia natural," "Historia antigua," "Historia moderna") was written between 1789 and 1791, but the author was unsuccessful in his attempts to have it published in Spain. Subsequent editions in French and Spanish were either incomplete or flawed, and the definitive edition of the work did not appear until 1960. In order to write the *Historia*, Velasco drew heavily on earlier histories by the Inca Garcilaso, Pedro Cieza de León (1518–1554) and José de Acosta (1539–1600); his defense of the pre-Hispanic culture of the Andean culture was aimed at European writers, Raynal in particular. Despite the frequent errors that appear in his work, Velasco is considered "the creator of Ecuadorean historical prose" (*Historia* [1981], xlv; see also Brading, *The First America* 447–8). The *Historia geográfica, natural y civil del reino de Chile* [*The Geographical, Natural, and Civil History of Chile*] by Juan Ignacio Molina (1740–1829) is yet another salvo fired in the battle between European thinkers and New World apologists: Molina devotes several chapters to the Araucanian Indian in addition to describing the current economic and political situation of Chile.

Historia de la conquista y población de Venezuela (1723) [*The Con-*

quest and Settlement of Venezuela] by José de Oviedo y Baños (1671–1728), although written relatively early in the eighteenth century, is another example of the trend toward urban and regional histories. Indeed, this work has long been considered the founding text of Venezuelan history (despite vitriolic accusations of plagiarism by some historians and Oviedo y Baños's own references to a mysterious second part which has never been located). Oviedo y Baños's life is often read as a symbol of viceregal unity: born in Bogotá and raised in Lima, he moved to Caracas at the age of fifteen, where he was educated by his uncle, Bishop Diego de Baños y Sotomayor, and later took an "active part in municipal affairs (Parra León, "Oviedo y Baños," xlvi; Morón, "José de Oviedo y Baños").

The prologue to the *Historia* reveals Oviedo y Baños's acute awareness of the challenges posed by historiographical tradition, and he frequently laments the fact that there are so few histories of the province of Venezuela. Such laments about the absence of sources, which are a familiar topic in colonial historiography, become a surprising *leit motif* in Oviedo y Baños's work, given the later charges of plagiarism. His sources, as the author explains in his prologue, include written documents (though he does not specify them in the text), oral traditions and his own observations. The legends and anecdotes he includes, ostensibly to lighten the tone of the history, reflect his intention to represent the whole of Venezuelan reality, not just the deeds of the conquistadors or the founding of cities. He makes this observation about a particular kind of small bird which is rumored to give off a ghostly light:

> No one in these times has seen them: I fulfill my obligation as historian by telling it, leaving the reader free to judge for himself, although I have no difficulty believing it, since we see the same property in fireflies, or *cucuyes*, as we call them in the Indies, and some twenty years ago I saw in this city a piece of wood which the rising Guaire River had tossed up on its banks, which at night or if placed during the day in a dark place, threw off light as if it were burning in flames, and, having given this virtue to the vegetable, why should not Providence give it to the animal?
>
> (pp. 470–1)

Oviedo y Baños takes a complex stance here: the responsible historian who is at the same time skeptical and apologetic, the scientific observer working through a process of deductive reasoning, the captivated witness to Venezuelan natural phenomena. His explanation of the word *cucuyes* calls to mind the lexical imperative of all colonial authors. Although they are clearly writing for their fellow *criollos* (as Arrom notes, the term took on greater importance in the period leading up to independence, see *Certidumbre*, 11–26), like their sixteenth- and seventeenth-century predecessors, they are also writing for Europeans (and not just Spaniards). Therefore they must translate, explain and define their terms continually.

It is possible to understand the encyclopedist impulse (a constant in Latin American narrative even before the Enlightenment – we have only to think of Fernández de Oviedo) as part of a continuing effort to represent the New World to the Old. Angel Rama has suggested that the penchant for translating indigenous words is a clear reflection of the postulation of a European reader. With Oviedo y Baños translation is an occasional project; as we shall see, it becomes a monumental undertaking in Antonio de Alcedo's five-volume *Diccionario geográfico-histórico de las Indias Occidentales de América*.

The title of Oviedo y Baños's work reveals its double thrust: to narrate the conquest and settlement of the province of Venezuela. The historian recounts the prolonged struggle to complete what he calls the "unhappy discovery and ill-fated conquest" of Venezuela (p. 210). He is clearly troubled by the rivalries which spring up among the conquistadors and includes frequent moralizing admonitions regarding their carelessness and hotheadedness. Brading wonders why Oviedo y Baños would have risked quoting in its entirety the text of Lope de Aguirre's letter to Philip II, given that the letter had the potential to remind readers of a "defiant challenge to royal authority" in the past (*The First America*, 311). I would argue, however, that the treatment of Lope de Aguirre is central to the work, both thematically and structurally, and ultimately consonant with the historian's aims. Oviedo y Baños presents Aguirre as the terrible and inevitable result of the process of conquest (a Facundo *avant la lettre*) – opposed to, but ultimately overcome by, the institutionalizing process of colonization and settlement.

This process culminates in the *Historia* in the founding of Caracas, and critics agree that the chapters devoted to the founding are the most original part of the work. One notes the lovely description of the countryside surrounding the city (pp. 420–2), the detailed list of churches, convents, and hospitals (pp. 422–30), and the proud characterization of the citizens of Caracas. The praise of the city forms part of a long tradition in Latin America which includes *Grandeza mexicana* (1604), by Bernardo de Balbuena (1562?–1627), and *Historia de la villa imperial de Potosí* (written between 1705 and 1736), by Bartolomé Arzáns de Orsúa y Vela (1676–1736).

Arzáns was born at the moment when Potosí's fortunes had begun to fail. As he surveyed the history of the "imperial city," he was clearly torn between admiration for its past grandeur (the city had flourished from 1572 to 1650) and the clear recognition that its moment of greatest glory was over. In fact, there is evidence that Arzáns originally planned to entitle the work "Tres destrucciones de Potosí," a reference to the civil wars of 1622–1625, the collapse of the Caricari dam in 1626 which left the city flooded, destroying both lives and property, and the devaluation of

Potosí's coinage in the 1650s. Arzáns's perspective – retrospective and undeniably elegiac – signals to us that Latin American historiography has entered a new phase.

There are marked similarities between Oviedo y Baños's work and Arzáns's account of Potosí. Both share an apparently rigid chronological organization (which pulls, nevertheless, toward the present moment in which the historian is writing and which clearly reflects the preoccupations of the early eighteenth century). Arzáns's sources, like Oviedo y Baños's, were varied: both authors refer to an earlier history in verse as well as other written and oral materials (1965 edn., xc), although the reader notes a shift in Arzáns's text after 1715 to more reportorial writing based on Arzáns's own observations rather than published or manuscript sources. It is clear that we cannot speak of chronicles of discovery at this late date; rather, both Oviedo y Baños and Arzáns write of the prolonged struggle to create colonial institutions, of the founding of cities, the consolidation of colonial administrative power.

Arzáns's history covers an enormous range of subjects: information on the mines (p. 31), a pious and enthusiastic interest in the church (p. 34), an emphasis on wealth and prices which gives the work a marked materialist tone (p. 36), commentaries on the injustice of forcing Indians to work in the silver mines and – like *El Carnero* (1636), by Juan Rodríguez Freyle (1566–1640), before it – a gossipy, sensationalist taste for the scandals and outrages of everyday life. These "interpolated stories," as Enrique Pupo-Walker has called them, have served as a true Potosino gold mine for later chroniclers of Peruvian society such as Ricardo Palma (Pupo-Walker, *La vocación literaria del pensamiento histórico en America*).

The fourth chapter of Book I, "In which an account is given of the monarchy of the Incas of Peru with the same brevity as in preceding chapters, with the description of the Tarapaya Lagoon," offers an instructive example of the different elements at work in Arzáns's history. The chapter begins with a familiar commentary on indigenous historiography: "it is a well-known fact that the Indians in this entire New World were lacking letters," but Arzáns then adds that Peruvian Indians are gifted graphic artists whose *quipocamayos* recorded Inca dynastic history on *caytos* (p. 20; note the translating function here). Arzáns begins an enumeration of the Inca kings which he breaks off to give a detailed description of the Tarapaya lagoon, a natural hot spring discovered by one of the Inca monarchs.

In striking fashion the contemporary soon displaces the historical in Arzáns's text as he remarks, "its depth is such that, until today, many, through lack of experience, insist that no one has touched bottom" (p. 22). Arzáns describes the many scientific experiments which have been carried out to measure the lagoon's depth and informs the reader – in a moralizing aside – of the presence of yet another hot spring nearby, "where one could construct another lagoon if Spanish curiosity were not so fixed on the greed of wanting to earn money for its purse rather than spend it to close off the water" (pp. 23–4). This aside is typical of Arzáns's capacity to distinguish between his Spanish and his Potosino self.

The author's own experience of the hot springs involves the near drowning of a young visitor which is recounted in frightening detail as a warning to his readers: "I found myself so near to him that I was not more than five yards away, seeing the situation with my own eyes so that the horror I had of this lagoon grew as a result of this event" (p. 24). Once the boy has been saved (due to the miraculous intervention of St. Joseph, it is suggested), Arzáns returns somewhat reluctantly to his announced task of listing the Inca monarchs; one notices a change in tone, a return to the subdued and distanced historian of Potosí's ancient past.

Like its Venezuelan counterpart, the *Historia de la villa imperial de Potosí*, as the title clearly indicates, can be read as urban history, a subgenre which is an outgrowth of the explosion of settlement and building which took place in the final century of the colonial period. Pedro de Peralta Barnuevo (1664–1743) attempts a poetic version of the urban history with *Lima fundada o la Conquista del Perú. Poema heróico en que se decanta toda la historia del descubrimiento y sujeción de sus provincias por Don Francisco Pizarro* (1732) – without great success, it is agreed. Nevertheless, the extensive notes that accompany the poem function almost as a gloss and reveal Peralta Barnuevo's gifts as a historian even as they obscure his modest skills as a poet.

As Lewis Hanke points out in his introductory volume to the Brown University publication of Arzáns's manuscript, the work represents a "new inclusive kind of history...exemplifying a 'conciencia de sí', a New World feeling of independence and separateness growing through the Indies" (p. 12). Both Oviedo y Baños and Arzáns de Orsúa y Vela demonstrate an enthusiastic interest in the history they are living as they write and a mixture of creole pride and loyalty to Spain that is typical of the mid-eighteenth century. While Oviedo y Baños may be read as a cautionary tale for administrators of the late colonial period, Arzáns's history transcends its historical and sociological importance to offer us a moving account of late colonial nostalgia, written in a moment of extreme historical crisis (Mendoza edn., cxxxiv).

Cuba flourished during the eighteenth century, despite (or perhaps because of) the British invasion of the island in 1762–1763 and more general concerns about piracy in the Caribbean. Histories of Cuban literature faithfully mention a number of early historians, although it is clear that only the *Llave del Nuevo Mundo* (1761), by José Martín Félix de Arrate y Acosta (1701–1765), can be considered of lasting literary importance. Shortly before Arrate penned his history, Nicolás Joseph de Ribera (1724–?) wrote a *Descripción de la isla de Cuba*, which was lost and forgotten until 1883. Regardless of its place in the evolution of Cuban historiography, Ribera's work focuses on geographical and economic questions; the author recommends closer supervision of the economy, defense, and administration, an increase in both the white and the slave population, and more commercial activity. The work also includes a defense of slavery, leading one scholar to call it "a most faithful expression of the creole landed class at the moment it is preparing itself to leap forward with the growing sugar industry" (Saínz, *La literatura cubana de 1700 a 1790*, 196).

Ignacio José de Urrutia y Montoya (1735–1795) is another figure frequently mentioned among Cuba's early historians because of his *Compendio de Memorias: teatro histórico jurídico y político militar de la Isla Fernandina de Cuba*, written between 1785 and 1787, but not published until 1876. Raimundo Lazo suggests somewhat unkindly that Urrutia's only literary value is to have served as the target for the first piece of Cuban literary criticism: a critique of his excessively baroque style written by José Agustín Caballero and published in the *Papel Periódico*. But others, perhaps more inclined to be gentle with a compatriot, laud the attempt to write a complete history of the island and the exhaustive archival research which the work represents.

Pedro Agustín Morell de Santa Cruz (1694–1768) is even less successful with his *Historia de la Isla y Catedral de Cuba*, written around 1760 (although not published until 1929 and only preserved in incomplete form). One suspects that Morell found it difficult to maintain the balance promised in the title between a discussion of the island and an account of its major cathedral. Without a doubt the author's most important contribution to literary history is to have included in the *Historia* the complete text of Silvestre de Balboa y Troya de Quesada's (1563–1647?) epic poem, the *Espejo de paciencia*: "This is in sum the tragic end of a case so worthy of memory; and so that the reader may enjoy himself, I will insert the page that in those times a poet of the island, from Puerto-del-Príncipe, produced in octavas" (I, 143).

José Martín Félix de Arrate y Acostas studied law in Mexico, as the University of Havana had not yet opened its doors. Like Oviedo y Baños in Caracas, Arrate participated in municipal government and was a member of the Havana aristocracy. He too laments in his prologue the general neglect of Cuban history, which he hopes to remedy with his work. He notes, however, that the task is a difficult one as many of the island's early archives were destroyed in a fire in 1538.

The *Llave del Nuevo Mundo, antemural de las Indias Occidentales* takes its name from a 1634 royal proclamation naming the city. Only the first six of its forty-nine chapters deal with the discovery and early colonization of the island; the rest deal with the growing importance of Havana and its inhabitants. Arrate's "Cubanness" – the phrase used by Lazo is "cubanía" (*La literatura cubana*, 408) – is evident in his repetition of Christopher Columbus's comments on the beauty of the Cuban landscape and the detailed descriptions of the customs of different racial groups on the island.

Is it possible to come to any conclusions regarding the status of historiography in the late eighteenth century? The previous hundred years had been characterized by a growing consolidation of the discipline, which is reflected in the creation in 1738 of the Real Academia de la Historia to replace the royal administrative position of "Official Chronicler." The works I have been discussing mirror the changing reality of the late colonial period, providing a link between the chroniclers of the Discovery (ever-present in the eighteenth-century historian's mind) and the essayists of the Independence period. These histories reflect the author's growing creole consciousness, their heightened appreciation of the immediate context (both geographical and historical) in which they are writing, and a preoccupation with the institutionalization of the Conquest itself. Their project is to write the history of the structures of colonial culture, and their intended reader is no longer a lofty and distant monarch, a peninsular authority, but rather an audience of creole peers.

Scientific travel and observation

Much as the sixteenth-and seventeenth-century chronicles and *relaciones* were a response to the jurisdictive imperative of imperial discovery and conquest, eighteenth-century narrative was often driven by the Bourbon reformist bureaucracy. In the latter part of the century, Charles III's ministers put into place a plan to reform the postal system in the New World. A number of Visitadores ["Overseers"] were named and charged with the task of surveying the established postal routes. Alonso Carrió de la Vandera (1715?–1783), an itinerant functionary of the Spanish Crown one of whose earlier missions had been to accompany a boatload of exiled Jesuits on their voyage to Europe, travelled from Montevideo to Lima by mule and wrote an extensive account of his trip. He entitled the work *El lazarillo de ciegos caminantes* [*El lazarillo. A guide for inexperienced travelers between Buenos Aires and Lima*] a reference both to the celebrated picaresque novel *Lazarillo de Tormes* (1554) and to Cosme Bueno's *Descripciones de provincias* (also known at the time as *Lazarillo de los ciegos*). Carrió de la Vandera published his work under an Indian pseudonym, Concolorcorvo, and with a false place and date of publication (Gijón 1773, but actually Lima 1775 or 1776).

El lazarillo de ciegos caminantes has been described as a travel journal, a novel, a satire, and a diary. Most importantly, it is a dialogue between a Spanish bureaucrat and his Indian companion about colonial Latin America. The narrative fiction which structures the work is that Concolorcorvo is writing his account of the trip based on notes taken by his master, the Visitador, who periodically reviews Concolorcorvo's manuscript, challenging and correcting what he reads there. Through their impassioned and argumentative discussions, the encounter between the Old World and the New is dramatically represented.

Some readers have suggested that Carrió de la Vandera's decision to publish under a pseudonym stemmed from a poor relationship with his superiors in the postal administration. But the same Concolorcorvo (literally, "with the color of a crow") also refers the reader to "The Tale of the Crow" in Ovid's *Metamorphosis* and provides a context for understanding the pseudonym as an indication of the work's preoccupation with the ambivalent and violent nature of language. It is also an explicit reference to the character's racial background which carries with it the implicit recognition of the relation between race and power in eighteenth-century Latin America. The Spanish author's decision to mask his own identity with an Indian pseudonym in fact points to the increasingly complex nature of the social, political, and cultural milieu he is attempting to describe. Thus it can be argued that despite the author's declared intention of defending colonial institutions, *El lazarillo de ciegos caminantes* reflects the inevitable ambivalence of colonial discourse and the progressive disintegration of Spanish imperial authority during the final decades of the eighteenth century.

Carrió de la Vandera's text shares the ironic tone of much late eighteenth-century narrative, written within this context of a colonial structure which was beginning to crack and crumble despite many well-intentioned efforts at reform and modernization. This ironic impulse appears in the work's prologue, in which Concolorcorvo mocks the insistent claims to legitimacy and authority which characterize sixteenth- and seventeenth-century chronicles: "I am pure Indian, save for my mother's tricks, to which I cannot testify" (Carilla edn., 116). It informs the reductionist rewriting of the Spanish discovery of the Caribbean islands and conquests of Mexico and Peru which are the subject of lengthy conversations between Concolorcorvo and the Visitador. And it enables one to read the appropriation of the picaresque suggested by the work's title as a commentary on the relationship between historians and travellers in representing American reality. According to this reading, the historians are "ciegos caminantes," blind wayfarers who must depend for their source materials on the "viajero" [traveller], a wily and sometimes untrustworthy guide.

Not all guides mean to deceive, however. I referred earlier to the *Descripciones de provincias* (also known as the *Descripciones geográficas del Virreinato del Perú*), published by Cosme Bueno (1711–1798) in a series of Lima almanacs from 1763 to 1772, and again from 1774 to 1778. Bueno was born in Aragón and studied Latin in Spain before travelling to Peru in 1730. He was also a well-known doctor in Lima and Europe, though his extant written work is not abundant. He is best remembered for the *Descripciones*, written at the request of the Viceroy of Peru, Antonio José de Mendoza Camaño y Sotomayor. In order to gather his material, Bueno undertook a slow and extensive process of research, writing to colleagues and acquaintances to request information from throughout the territory which presently makes up Peru, Chile, Argentina, Uruguay, Paraguay, and Bolivia. Not surprisingly considering their functionality, the *Descripciones* show little expository unity and their tone is often somewhat arid (though the reader is struck by the vehement patriotism which emerges when the author is discussing Portuguese or British incursions into viceregal territory (Buesa Oliver, "Sobre Cosme Bueno y algunos de sus coetáneos," 339). Nevertheless, they provide a wealth of information; the most entertaining sections for today's reader are the ones dealing with indigenous life, customs, and superstitions.

Carrió de la Vandera, Bueno, and the other writers discussed in this section reflect the fact that scientific writing in eighteenth-century Latin America tended to the technical and practical rather than the theoretical, perhaps because technical subjects were less likely to incur inquisitorial wrath, or perhaps because of the perceived urgency with which the changing situation called for practical applications for science. Indeed, Latin America was the proving ground for many scientific theories generated in Europe, a *locus* of constant observation and experimentation, a forum for Newtonian observation rather than Cartesian intuition. The gaze of these enlightened scientists was an active, investigative appropriation of Latin American reality. José Celestino Mutis's botanical expedition of 1783 gathered over 20,000 specimens and resulted in over 5,000 carefully drawn plates of almost 3,000 species of plants; the plates are Mutis's most lasting contribution to Latin American cultural history. (I am referring only to those which survive in the collection of the Botanical Gardens of Madrid: Mutis's expedition gives new meaning to Sartre's observation that "To see is to deflower.")

Another impassioned observer of Latin American flora and fauna was Félix de Azara (1742?–1821). A self-taught naturalist whom Buesa Oliver calls "the Humboldt of America" ("Sobre Cosme Bueno," 339), Azara trained as a soldier and fought in Algeria before travelling to Paraguay in 1781 as part of a diplomatic mission to clarify the borders between Spanish and Portuguese territories there. He confesses that he "decided to begin some geographical work to fill the time which he did not care to waste" ("Sobre Cosme Bueno," 340). He describes himself as "a soldier who has never looked carefully at an animal until now. I have neither books nor the means to acquire information and instruction. I am an original naturalist, who doesn't even know the right vocabulary, and many of my notes are taken without a chair, table or bench..." (quoted in Buesa Oliver, "Sobre Cosme Bueno," 341). Azara's responsibilities included making periodic visits to different regions, travelling by horse or canoe, and in this way he familiarized himself thoroughly with the area (Buesa Oliver, "Sobre Cosme Bueno," 345). His stay in America, which lasted twenty years, was spent making zoological, cartographic, ethnographic, geographic, and botanical observations. He founded a number of Spanish colonies and identified several species of animals which were subsequently named after him; for example, *Canis azare*, the fox or *aguarachay*. Azara wrote constantly, frequently revising and editing his work; his best known volumes are the *Apuntamientos para la historia natural de los quadrúpedos del Paraguay y Río de la Plata* and the *Apuntamientos para la historia natural de los Páxaros del Paraguay y del Río de la Plata*.

Dedicating the *Apuntamientos para la historia natural de los quadrúpedos* to his brother, Azara voices this lament, reminiscent of Columbus or Bernal Díaz: "I have spent the twenty best years of my life in the farthest corner of the earth, forgotten even by my friends, without books or human contact, and travelling continually through deserts and immense, frightening forests, communicating only with the birds and the wild beasts" (quoted in Buesa Oliver, "Sobre Cosme Bueno," 342). This evocation of the solitary feelings provoked by the vast expanses of South American geography anticipates the geographically determinist premise of Domingo Faustino Sarmiento (1811–1888) in *Civilización y barbarie* (1845).

Another Jesuit to visit America and write about it was José Gumilla (1687–1750), who arrived in Santa Fe de Bogotá in 1705, spent ten years studying there and then thirty-five more as a missionary in the Orinoco basin (with brief respites to fill administrative positions at the Colegio de Tunja and a return visit to Spain from 1741 to 1743). *El Orinoco ilustrado y defendido. Historia natural, civil y geográfica de este gran río y de sus caudalosas vertientes: gobierno, usos y costumbres de los indios, sus habitantes: con nuevas y útiles noticias de animales, árboles, frutos, aceytes, resinas, yerbas y raíces medicinales: y sobre todo se hallarán conversiones muy singulares a N. Santa Fe, y casos de mucha edificación* (1741) is noteworthy for its rich detail and graphic descriptions, prompted by – as the author himself admits – an "insatiable and natural curiosity."

Gumilla did not set out to write natural history, but rather to transmit the "curiosidades" that had been omitted from earlier accounts of the region; his gaze is keen, but not necessarily scientific.

Gumilla is by no means a defender of Indian culture, yet he is clearly fascinated by it. When he transcribes his conversations with the Indians, he goes to great lengths to reproduce indigenous vocabulary in his text. He includes a long and detailed explanation of how the Indians make *curare*, a poison with special blood-clotting properties which Gumilla believes to be the work of the Devil. He is also shocked to learn that the *curare* fumes are so toxic that old women are traditionally used to prepare the potion: their labor will scarcely be missed once the fumes kill them (as they inevitably will). Gumilla also describes marriage rituals among the Guayquirí. He uses direct dialogue which makes the ceremony come alive for his reader and includes slight touches of humor: according to tradition, the bride is required to fast before the wedding and thus on her wedding day appears looking "more moribund than radiant" (pp. 141–3). Gumilla's intended readers seem to be his fellow Jesuits and, as a Spaniard, he defends his country vehemently against the *leyenda negra*.

Charles-Marie de la Condamine's 1737 expedition to Quito typifies scientific inquiry in the eighteenth century. A perfect marriage of the scientific and the political, the theoretical and the practical, his international delegation was sponsored by the French Academy of Sciences under orders from Spain's Bourbon king, Phillip V, "to conduct astronomical and physical observations designed to measure the precise limits of the degrees of latitude at the arc of the earth's meridian" (Brading, *The First America*, 422). The members of the expedition hoped finally to resolve the controversy over Newton's contention that the earth bulged slightly at the poles. Six years later, after numerous misadventures and much hardship, they had demonstrated that Newton was right.

The La Condamine expedition fortuitously led to a series of works written by two young Spanish naval lieutenants who were sent along to represent their country and challenge French prejudices about the stagnation of Spanish science. Jorge Juan (1713–1773) and Antonio de Ulloa (1716–1795) collaborated in writing the *Relación histórica del viaje a la América meridional* [*A Voyage to South America*] and the *Noticias secretas de América* (1749), a confidential report on the state of the colonies compiled at the request of the Marquis of Ensenada (first published in 1826 in England and translated into English as the *Discourse and Political Reflections on the Kingdoms of Peru*). Ulloa was the principal author of the *Relación histórica* and the *Noticias secretas*, and later wrote a natural history, *Noticias americanas*.

As Peninsular authors, Juan and Ulloa fall outside the scope of this essay. Nevertheless, it is important to note that the 1826 publication of the *Noticias secretas*, with their account of colonial corruption and mismanagement, gave rise to a raging controversy reminiscent of the one surrounding the *Brevísima relación de la destrucción de las Indias* (1552) by Bartolomé de las Casas (1474?–1566). The authors discuss topics ranging from smuggling and contraband to abuses of the clergy and tyrannical *corregidores*; their observations and suggestions for reform are presented within an enlightened framework of what is reasonable and natural (*Discourse*, 31). Mindful of the explosive material contained in the report, they caution "private matters in this treatise are secret information for ministers and others authorized to know and must remain confidential" and insist that their aim has been "to restore religion and justice to their proper place; to make all subjects, even those far away, aware of the benevolent influence and vital warmth of their sovereigns' wise rule; and finally, to shape the best government and the most just administration for these subjects" (p. 40).

Finally, Alexander von Humboldt (1769–1859) merits a brief mention as the region's preeminent scientific traveller, even though he comes late in the century and is neither creole nor Spanish. However, the impact of his *Personal Narrative of Travels to the Equinoccial Regions of the New Continent during the years 1799–1804*, and his *Ensayo político sobre el reino de la Nueva España* (1807–1811) [*Political Essay on the Kingdom of New Spain*] was enormous. As Brading has observed, "At one stroke the fissure which had opened between the European Enlightenment and American reality was effectively bridged by the intervention of a qualified, critical observer" (*The First America*, 517). Humboldt's observations frequently touched on political life in America, as when he warned of the potential for creole unhappiness after the economic reforms of 1728 (Minguet, "Alejandro de Humboldt," 72). It should be stressed that Humboldt, like many other eighteenth-century travellers, was an observer of facts and concrete reality who was disinclined to theorize on the basis of his observations.

These eighteenth-century experiments and expeditions were not carried out in the name of imperialist expansion, as will be the charge made against nineteenth-century European travellers. Rather they are a scientific *modus operandi* for the creation of an independent cultural consciousness. Rama has argued that the early colonial cartographers and urban planners hoped to fix and order reality in writing. The eighteenth-century authors, on the other hand, aspired to create a new enlightened reality through writing and knowledge; in this regard the *proyecto*, or plan, is perhaps the genre *par excellence* of the second half of the century.

The organization of knowledge

I have already noted that the eighteenth century is characterized as much by diverse manifestations of cultural activity as by any one literary form. In fact, one might argue that the organization and dissemination of knowledge in all its rapidly expanding dimensions through the establishment of academies, *sociedades de amigos*, reform plans, periodical literature, and other publishing projects constitutes a master plan which is entirely consistent with the encyclopedic impulse of the Enlightenment. At the same time, these activities reflect the particular circumstances of the Spanish colonies: a growing realization of the relationship between knowledge and incipient patriotism or nationalism, and the postulation of a new kind of creole reader.

Perhaps no other work embodies these elements as does the *Biblioteca mexicana*, initiated around 1735 by Juan José de Eguiara y Eguren (1696–1763). The *Biblioteca* was conceived as an extremely ambitious biographical and bibliographical project: an extensive catalogue of Mexican authors (not only those born in Mexico but others considered Mexican by virtue of residence as well). The first volume appeared in 1755. It begins with a long series of prologues or *Anteloquia* discussing the development of Mexican culture and follows with entries and key institutions and individuals for the letters A, B, and C. Predictably, the project was only half-finished at the time of Eguiara's death, although the volumes corresponding to the letters D through J have been preserved in manuscript form.

Eguiara was a Jesuit of Basque descent who served for a time as professor and rector of the Real y Pontificia University of Mexico City. Despite a brilliant career as a student and administrator, he declined to accept the bishopric of Mérida when it was offered to him in 1752, claiming poor health and voicing a desire to devote his remaining years to his bibliographical endeavors. He was renowned during his day as a theologian and sacred orator, although he is remembered principally as the author of the *Biblioteca*.

The project began in response to the twelve *Epístolas* (1756) written by Manuel Martí, Dean of Alicante, in which the Spaniard at one point discourages his young reader from visiting Mexico, characterizing it as a cultural wasteland inhabited only by barbarous Indians (Brading, *The First America*, 388). The charge was a familiar one: in fact, Feijoo's essay, "Españoles americanos," is a rebuttal of the belief that the intellectual capabilities of Spanish Americans diminish with age. Eguiara's indignation at this slanderous evaluation of his homeland may best be seen in the polemical and apologetic prologues which defend indigenous culture against European criticisms; it is as if he cannot bring himself to begin the bibliography before setting to rest the much-debated question of his compatriots' intelligence. Eguiara's contribution to the dispute of the New World is to have reiterated (following in the tradition of Sigüenza y Góngora) that Mexican culture is characterized precisely by the fusion of pre-Hispanic and Spanish traditions (*Biblioteca*, II: ccxxxviii).

A passionate advocate of the Mexican educational system, the author devotes the first sixteen chapters of his work to a panegyric to the University of Mexico, with specific mention of "a very few things from among the many which give lustre to our University and which can no more be contained in these pages of ours than the Ocean can be contained in a tiny shell" (II, 203). At other moments he admits the existence of serious material obstacles to creole intellectual achievement. One such difficulty was the scarcity of good presses, and Eguiara eventually imported a press which he named the "Biblioteca Mexicana" and which began to function in 1753 (II, xciv).

Eguiara wrote to his compatriots (as Bueno had also done), asking them for assistance in compiling the *Biblioteca* and, according to his own calculations, garnered information for more than 3,000 entries. Unfortunately, notwithstanding the editor's declared intentions of widely disseminating the results of his investigations, the work (entirely written in Latin – even book titles – and organized alphabetically according to the authors' Christian name) proved difficult to read and did not circulate widely. Nevertheless, the *Biblioteca mexicana* represents the founding initiative of Mexican bibliography. Its importance is evidenced by the recent re-edition of the *Biblioteca* by the Universida Nacional Autónoma de México, translated into Spanish with a long introductory study, copious notes, and appendixes of documents relating to Eguiara's life and eighteenth-century culture (1986–1990).

As a point of comparison with Eguiara's bibliography, one must mention the *Biblioteca hispanoamericana septentrional* published in 1816 by José Mariano Beristáin de Souza (1755–1817). Although Beristáin echoes Eguiara's indignant rebuttal of Martí's criticisms of Mexican culture, he is a much less fervent and committed apologist for indigenous traditions, and his principal aim seems to be to defend Spain from attacks by European writers. Though he proposes his work as a continuation of Eguiara's, he criticizes Eguiara's style, research methods, and decision to write in Latin: "It is imprudent to deprive a thousand Spaniards of the chance to read of their literary figures in Spanish just so that half a dozen foreigners may read of them in Latin; these, if the work merits it, will know how to find it and read it even if it is written in the language of the Chichimecas" (p. iii). Yet for many years all that was known of Eguiara's text came to us through the *Biblioteca hispanoamericana septentrional*, and together the two works represent an important milestone in creole cultural awareness.

Another project of encyclopedic proportions is the *Diccionario geográfico-histórico de las Indias Occidentales o América* (1786–1789) by Antonio de Alcedo (1735–1812). As a young man Alcedo, born in Ecuador, frequently assisted his father, Dionisio de Alcedo y Herrera, President of the Real Audiencia de Quito, with his research on government and commerce in the Spanish colonies. Later, Alcedo continued his father's work while pursuing a military career; his *Diccionario* "was considered by his contemporaries to be the most important reference work concerning America, and...still remains the most accurate compilation of historical and geographical documenttion of the Spanish eighteenth century" (Lerner, "The *Diccionario* of Antonio de Alcedo," 72). Both the Spanish edition and an early English translation (London 1812–1815) were banned by the Spanish government because of the wealth of strategic information contained therein.

In his prologue, Alcedo demonstrates his awareness of the encyclopedic tradition of both early Latin American narrative and enlightenment letters, explaining that although the vast amount of material he has amassed calls for a universal history of America, "one has already seen what a difficult and complicated matter that is; it seemed to me less arduous to reduce it to a Dictionary ..." (p. 6). Although his tone is restrained and his declared intentions modest, the scope of Alcedo's project is impressive. Not only does he provide referential information; like the French *philosophes*, he uses the encyclopedic format to present contentious issues of the time such as slavery, differences between European and American character, and the treatment of the Indians ... clearly establishing his own position in the course of the exposition (Lerner, "*Diccionario*," 72).

At the end of the work Alcedo included what may be considered the first known dictionary of Americanisms, the *Vocabulario de las voces provinciales de la América* (Lerner, "Sobre dialectología en las letras coloniales," 118). About half of the 634 items included are indigenous words; the rest are either Spanish words whose meaning has evolved or foreign words. Alcedo's explanations are fluid and vivid, reflecting his extensive familiarity with American flora, fauna, and customs.

In addition to these bibliographies and dictionaries, the eighteenth century witnessed a veritable explosion of periodical literature. Toward the early part of the century, colonial gazettes were published when newsworthy events dictated – earthquakes, deaths, visits by viceregal authorities, or the arrival of commercial vessels – but during the latter part of the century a new form of scientific journalism began to emerge. The new gazettes were edited by Creoles and expressed a clear commitment to public service and reformism (see works by Tavera Alfaro).

José Antonio Alzate y Ramírez (1737–1799), who was mentioned earlier, is perhaps the best-known Mexican representative of these fledgling journalists. His interests ranged from philosophy and medicine to chemistry, geography, agriculture, mining, and education, leading some critics to label him an intellectual dilettante. No one questions, however, his key role as a disseminator and polemicist of scientific knowledge. During his lifetime Alzate published four separate journals: the *Diario literario de México* (March 12, 1768–May 10 1768; eight issues); *Asuntos varios sobre ciencias y artes* (November 2, 1772– January 4, 1773; 13 issues); *Observaciones sobre la física, historia natural y artes útiles* (May 21, 1787–October 30, 1787; 14 issues); and the *Gazeta de literatura de México* (January 15, 1788–October 22, 1795; three volumes of 48, 47, and 44 issues). In the remarks that follow I will focus on the *Gazeta de literatura*, which for obvious reasons of longevity and continuity is of the greatest historical and literary importance.

Azate sets forth his reasons for founding the gazette in a prologue to the first issue, calling for the broadest possible understanding of the word "literatura" (understood as knowledge of any kind), expressing a strong interest in pre-Hispanic culture and reiterating his desire to be of use to his country. The prologue clearly reflects the desire to establish an "imagined community" of interests between editor and readers; this intellectual affinity would eventually develop into the intense creole patriotism of the Independence period (Anderson, "Creole pioneers," 62–5). At the same time one notes the adherence to enlightenment principles of didacticism, utilitarianism, and experimentalism. The *Gazeta* published plans for a flood control project, an account of Alzate's observations (with José Ignacio Bartolache) of Venus's transit across the path of the sun, a detailed description of an English auger or borer for use in the mining industry, and a highly informative treatise on the cochineal dye industry.

Many of the articles reflect Alzate's keen interest in commerce, mining, and agriculture. Others (often included as supplements to the *Gazeta*) stem from his study of Mexican antiquity; for example, the "Descripción de las antigüedades de Xochicalco dedicada a los señores de la actual expedición marítima alrededor del orbe" (1777), in which he rebutted European theories of American degeneracy in terms that – to his pleasure – closely matched arguments previously made by Clavijero. The publication of León y Gama's *Descripción histórica* sparked a long-running polemic in the pages of the *Gazeta* regarding the decipherment of the Sun Stone carvings; however, Alzate's attempt to challenge León y Gama's interpretation proved unconvincing.

Yet even during the course of a debate on the merits of Linnaeus's system of plant classification, Alzate draws on his knowledge of ancient Mexican culture. He argues that, following Mexican custom, plant names should include some reference to their possible uses: "With the Linnaean system, you know that the plant belongs to a given class or genus. What do you gain from all that?...Plants are useful to the extent that they serve as food, to cure disease, or are used in the various Arts such as dyeing or carpentry. So if Botany does not instruct us in this, what good is it?" (quoted in Luque Alcaide, *La educación en Nueva España en el siglo XVIII*, 352).

We have already seen examples of Dr José Ignacio Bartolache's commitment to public health and epidemiology and his fervent interest in the legend of the Virgin of Guadalupe. A colleague and frequent opponent of Alzate's in the numerous polemics which appeared on the pages of Mexican gazettes, Bartolache is best-known as a popularizer of scientific knowledge and the founding editor of *El Mercurio volante con noticias importantes y curiosas sobre varios asuntos de física y medicina* (October 17, 1772–February 10, 1773; 16 issues).

The journal's importance transcends its limited span due to the wide-ranging selection of topics. Issues 3 and 4 contain detailed instructions for assembling a thermometer and barometer, since these instruments were rare in Mexico. Another issue discusses the "mal histérico" ["hysteria"] which tended to afflict women in communal living situations. Bartolache cites three likely causes: excessive sweets and chocolate, restrictive clothing, and the habit of going to bed and rising late. The essay responds implicitly to proposed reforms of convent life which had recently caused an uproar by calling for a return to more spartan forms of communal living. Bartolache avoids dealing directly with the political issue, preferring instead to address it from a medical and psychological point of view (*Mercurio volante*, xlvi–xlvii).

Bartolache also includes a lengthy discussion of the medicinal value of *pulque* (an indigenous alcoholic beverage) in three successive issues of the journal. Referring to the quintessentially eighteenth-century debate on whether this regional liquor represented a vice or a virtue, he announces that he has personally conducted a series of eleven experiments on the topic. He advises his readers that he had planned to initiate a second series of experiments on the "quantity and quality of urine produced from pulque," but that, lamentably, he has been prevented from doing so by a recurring stomach ailment (p. 108).

Finally, another issue uses the pretext of a letter from a fictional Indian *cacique* who writes to criticize both Alzate's and Bartolache's journals. The tone of the letter is informed and witty; referring to the above-mentioned issue on thermometers, the *cacique* writes: "I have told my wife and daughter-in-law not to bathe in the *temazcalli* until I check, as soon as I have my thermometer, how many degrees of heat there are in the water so that the *temazcalli* can be carefully regulated; I wouldn't want their blood to heat up too much" (p. 70).

Although Mexico was an important center for journalistic production, gazettes were founded in other urban centers as well. The *Gaceta de Lima*, perhaps the oldest periodical in South America, appeared regularly beginning January 18, 1744 (p. xiii). During the 1790s, Hipólito Unanúe (1755–?), whom Lockhart and Schwartz call "Alzate's Peruvian equivalent" (*Early Latin America*, 345), edited the *Mercurio Peruano* which had been founded by Lima's "Sociedad de Amantes del País." The society also conducted a survey of archaeological ruins in the region; this project, although admittedly lacking the depth of similar Mexican endeavors, reflects some degree of interest in indigenous history by educated eighteenth-century Peruvians (Macera Dall'Orso, "Imágenes del indio," 315). Unanúe's *Observaciones sobre el clima de Lima* are a painstaking record of meteorological conditions in the city which he hoped would help put to rest European notions about the pernicious American climate (see Barding, *The First America*, 448–50).

A Cuban patriotic society also played a key role in establishing the *Papel Periódico de la Habana* in 1790. The journal was characterized by an early focus on commerce and economic activity, although short *costumbrista* pieces describing colonial manners and customs were often included. In New Granada, Francisco José de Caldas (1770–1816), the distinguished naturalist who had taken part in Mutis's botanical expedition, functioned as the driving force behind the *Semanario del Nuevo Reyno de Granada*, which appeared intermittently during 1808 and 1809. All of these early periodical publications reflect the close link between economic and cultural developments in the Spanish colonies during the latter part of the eighteenth century. Both economic societies and gazettes served to provide readers with a sense of local identity and spur their commitment to better their communities.

The Peruvian satirist Francisco Javier Eugenio de Santa Cruz y Espejo (1747–1795) produced a body of work which embraces many of the areas that have already been discussed. A *mestizo*, Espejo studied medicine and wrote an important treatise on communicable diseases in the Spanish colonies, *Reflexiones acerca de las viruelas* (1785). He was instrumental in organizing Quito's patriotic society, director of its public library and in 1792 was the founding editor of the city's first newspaper, *Las Primicias de la Cultura de Quito* (Greer Johnson, "*El Nuevo Luciano* and the satiric art of Eugenio Espejo," 67–71).

The titles of Espejo's work point quite obviously to Lucian's satiric dialogues as a model: *El Nuevo Luciano de Quito o despertador de los ingenios quiteños en nueve conversaciones eruditas para el estímulo de la literatura* (1779); *Marco Porcio Catón o Memorias para la impugnación del Nuevo Luciano de Quito* (1780); and *La ciencia blancardina* (1780). The *Nuevo Luciano* first circulated in manuscript form under a pseudonym, "don Javier de Cía, Apéstegui y Perochena." In this work Espejo uses a dialogue on the merits of different oratorical styles as a point of departure for suggesting reforms of the Peruvian educational system. The interlocutors are Mera, an enlightened thinker, and Murillo, a pompous and pedantic doctor. Their discussions range from the question of "el buen gusto" (understood in the broadest sense as a scientific, enlightened and fashionable sensibility) to ethical questions and scholastic rhetoric (Astuto, "Espejo: Crítico dieciochesco y pedagogo quiteño," 516). The author chooses a critique of religious rhetoric as a structuring device for the narrative because of his conviction that the sermon, as a genre, represents the rigid, static nature of colonial institutions.

Espejo uses his next work, *Marco Porcio Catón*, to articulate criticisms he had received of *El Nuevo Luciano* and then responds to those criticisms in *La ciencia blancardina*. Unfortunately, his writing style lacks grace and subtlety, leading one critic to remark that, though a master of irony and sarcasm, "Espejo was no literary giant" (*Obra educativa*, xxii). His volumes are ill-suited to the demands of satiric humour by virtue of their length and tendency to repeat the same themes and stylistic flourishes (Greer Johnson, "*El Nuevo Luciano*," 81). Yet Greer Johnson reminds us that Espejo's satire, like other philosophical writings discussed earlier, is always closely linked to a sincere utilitarian impulse; his dialogues set forth concrete plans for reforming Peruvian education (p. 67). He goes far beyond the Jesuit Generation of 1750, however, both in the aggressive tone of his writings and the degree of his political engagement.

Espejo ultimately proved unable to maintain the delicate balance between reformism and revolution and was persecuted for his political beliefs. In this sense he serves as a link between eighteenth-century scholarly thinkers and the essayists of the Independence period to follow – Fray Servando, Juan Pablo Viscardo y Guzmán (1748–1798), and even José Joaquín Fernández de Lizardi (1776–1827). Espejo's words in the final issue of the *Primicias de la Cultura de Quito* were prescient: "We are already partners, we are already *quiteños* (that is, not Spaniards), we are already entering the School of Common Consent, from us the Fatherland will be reborn, we are the arbitrators of its success" (quoted in Velasco, *Historia del reino de Quito*, 1981, ix–x). His exhortation reflects the degree to which the failure of Bourbon reformist efforts in the Spanish colonies had as its price the loyalty of the creole scholars who came to intellectual and political maturity at the close of the eighteenth century.

I conclude by returning to the question posed at the beginning of this essay: how are we to assess eighteenth-century narrative forms, scholarship and learning? We must begin by re-evaluating our own critical stance, by questioning our critical point of departure. Who are the authors we have singled out as representative? What kinds of texts have we focused on, and in what terms have we attempted to define (or defend) their "literariness?"

We must abandon the generic and nationalistic criteria which have tended to dominate eighteenth-century criticism; the debate over when the first novel appeared in Latin America, the insistence on traditional literary forms or the search for a point of origin for national literatures only serve to distract us from a close reading of the voluminous writings produced during the closing decades of the colonial period. We must renounce the cherished stereotypes of eighteenth-century narrative – rational, logical, clear, measured...boring – as distortions which are in large part the product of nineteenth-century Romanticism. This will free us to enter a lively polemic with eighteenth-century texts, to accept as our project what Laura Brown and Felicity Nussbaum have called "the problematization of period, canon, tradition and genre in eighteenth-century literary studies" ("Revising critical practices," 14). The eighteenth century, in its historiography and its early attempts at anthropology, in its fledgling periodicals and its scientific essays, reveals its enlightened impulse best (as Cassirer has seen) "where it is in the process, where it is doubting and seeking, tearing down and building up" (*The Philosophy of the Enlightenment*, ix). The same can be said of our own critical project as readers of the eighteenth century.

11

Lyric poetry of the eighteenth and nineteenth centuries
Andrew Bush

From the early fiction of Jorge Luis Borges, where Cervantes is writ large of course, but where Quevedo, too, appears in the fine print of the *oeuvre* of Pierre Menard, to José Lezama Lima's life-long commitment to a Gongorine aesthetic in the lyric, to Octavio Paz's more recent essay on Sor Juana (*Sor Juana Inés de la Cruz*), the leading figures of Spanish American letters in the twentieth century have set their writing in a direct relation to the Baroque. They have done so with the clear precedent of their peninsular forerunners, who, particularly in the area of the lyric, identified avant-garde activities with the reading of Góngora. But just as the commemorative acts surrounding the tercentenary of Góngora's death in 1927 may be read as a deflection or defense, a willful nationalistic redefinition of vanguard influences crossing into Spain from France and elsewhere, so too, the immediacy of the baroque heritage in twentieth-century Spanish America calls for a critical assessment. Following the lead of Borges, Lezama and Paz, amongst other practitioners of the Neo-Baroque, has brought important benefits to contemporary criticism, it is true, most notably the recuperation, if not to say reinvention of colonial letters in our time through the valorization of the *Barroco de Indias*, a period obscured by nearly 200 years of the ideology of independence. Nevertheless, the emphasis on baroque ancestry, whether in lyric style or literary scholarship, has, like T. S. Eliot's attachment to the English metaphysical poets and the corresponding literary historical orientation of the American New Critics, had the deleterious effect of obscuring in turn that very period – the late eighteenth and the nineteenth centuries – in which both political and literary independence took their shape.

The characteristic statement of this position in its most influential articulation is that of Paz in *Los hijos del limo* [*Children of the Mire*] where he asserts that Spain had no Romanticism for lack of a true Enlightenment to react against and that the situation was still more acute in Spanish America, a mere simulacrum – "reflection of a reflection" (Paz,

Los hijos, 122) – in this regard. In short, for Paz, and for a century of literary criticism, Latin America, like Spain, had no modernity (p. 119), at least not until Rubén Darío invented it belatedly under the banner of *Modernismo* [Modernism]. The re-evaluation of eighteenth- and nineteenth-century letters in continental and Anglo-American studies in the present generation raises questions for this blanket dismissal. Commenting on Schiller's essay "Naive and sentimental poetry" (1795), for instance, Herbert Lindenberger has remarked that this text "as well as many other theories of Romanticism contemporary with it, should be called a theory of modernity" (*The History in Literature*, 66). The terms might be reversed, I suggest, to declare that *Children of the Mire* and the many efforts to define modernity contemporary with or subsequent to it are but theories of Romanticism, and like Schiller before them, take up a position within rather than beyond the movement that, in Hispanic letters, Paz and others would efface. The relation of twentieth-century Spanish American literature to Romanticism may take the form of a continuation of fundamental concerns, such as one discovers in the *novela de la tierra*; or one may find in the reaction of *modernista* [modernist] or *vanguardista* [vanguard] poetry the process that Ortega y Gasset referred to as "negative influence" (*La deshumanización del arte*, 43–47) in Hispanic literature long before Harold Bloom elaborated his theory of revisionism on the basis of the reading of English Romanticism (e.g. *The Anxiety of Influence*). But irrespective of the polarities of the relations between the literature of the twentieth century and its eighteenth- and nineteenth-century past, it may be stressed that literary history itself, as practiced diversely by Paz in *Los hijos del limo* and the contributors to the present volumes, participate in the romantic enterprise (see González Echevarría, "Albums, ramilletes, parnasos, liras y guirnaldas," 875–6). In a word, the twentieth century is incomprehensible in unmediated juxtaposition to the Baroque. And if this is not the proper context to put forward a broad theory of modernity that would embrace Hispanic Romanticism in its complex relationship to the Enlightenment that preceded it, this can be the occasion to recuperate some of the texts from which that statement might emerge.

The century dates that organize these volumes represent an obstacle to that reclamation project which calls for some preliminary meditation. Lost between the traditional period designations of literary history and the realities of social change, the calendrical abstraction called the eighteenth century has become a true hundred years of literary solitude, all but unremarked even on García Márquez's map of death. The new colonial literary studies rarely reach up to the Wars of Independence in the first decades of the nineteenth century: a blatant disregard of political reality. Yet the temporal boundaries associated with the Baroque in

Peninsular letters – boundaries that demarcate a Siglo de Oro that closes, in Spanish America, with the death of Sor Juana in 1695 – commonly exclude the eighteenth century from treatment. On the other hand, the dates implied by a Siglo de las Luces are falsified by literary practice in a period in which the Baroque continues to predominate; the Age of Reason, too, leaves the larger part of eighteenth-century Spanish America out of account. And if there has been some headway with respect to prose in such recent work as Julie Greer Johnson's discussion ("*El nuevo Luciano* and the satiric art of Eugenio Espejo,") of the satirical writing of Francisco Javier Eugenio de Santa Cruz y Espejo (Ecuador, 1747–1795) (see Santa Cruz y Espejo, *Obra educativa*) or the odd travelogue of Alonso Carrió de la Vandera, alias Concolorcorvo (Spain, 1715 – fl. Peru, 1783) (see Stolley, *El Lazarillo de ciegos caminantes*, along with her contribution to these volumes), as well as the burgeoning attention devoted to the reports of the scientific expeditions to the Americas (e.g., the special issue of *Revista de Indias* coordinated by Del Pino Díaz; for a broader account, see Stafford's monumental study, *Voyage into Substance*) the present state of knowledge concerning the poetry of the period is abysmal (see the Bibliographical note at the beginning of this chapter's bibliography).

Almost the only lyric poet to escape the general neglect has been Juan Bautista Aguirre (Ecuador, 1725–1786) (see Zaldumbide, "Estudio preliminar", and Rodríguez Castelo, *Letras de la Audiencia de Quito (Período jesuita)*, wherein one also finds the complete poetry of Aguirre, and Cevallos Candau, *Juan Bautista Aguirre*). The exception may be explained by reference to the narrow interests of canon formation; the evaluative standards applied to the baroque poetry of the preceding centuries of colonial literature will not find Aguirre wanting. My own purposes are altogether different, however. Canonization means reduction and the study of eighteenth- and even nineteenth-century Spanish American literature is in need, on the contrary, of expansion, beginning at the level of the most basic editorial functions. Moreover, the needs of these studies will not be served by exempting the best poets from their own periods – customarily judged cold and prosaic with respect to the eighteenth century or over-heated and bombastic for the nineteenth – and thereupon casting them backwards into the more limited domain of colonial studies or forward as precursors of *Modernismo*. Hence, I would set aside the issue of an evaluative judgment of Aguirre – inferior to Sor Juana, surely, but superior to, say, Hernando Domínguez Camargo (Colombia, 1606–1656?) – in favor of a mapping of his historical coordinates.

First, Aguirre was among the generation of Jesuits who suffered the expulsion from Spanish lands under the orders of Charles III in 1767. While it would be untrue to make this date, any more than the death of Sor

Juana, a terminal point in the history of the Gongorine lyric in America, the predominance of the Jesuits in the colonial educational system had been a significant factor in the prolonged life of the Baroque. The latinate substratum of the baroque style, which Elias Rivers ("Góngora y el Nuevo Mundo") has referred to recently in Bakhtinian terms as the fundamental diglossia of the Gongorine lyric, was wounded by the departure of the most influential expositors of classical languages in the colonies. A process of linguistic change was thus initiated. Still, it needs to be emphasized that the process was slow, lest a cap be placed too hastily on the succeeding period of the Enlightenment and its characteristic neoclassical expression. Hence, the reformation of the curriculum in Cuba in the first decades of the nineteenth century, inaugurated by José Agustín Caballero (Cuba, 1762–1835) and pursued by Félix Varela (Cuba, 1788–1853), that led to the shift to Spanish-language instruction in philosophy may well represent a convenient milestone to mark a potential borderline between Neoclassicism and Romanticism, and indeed their contemporaries recognized the moment as a watershed (see, for instance, the eulogy by philosopher José de la Luz y Caballero [Cuba, 1800–1862] on the occasion of his uncle J. A. Caballero's death in 1835). Yet half a century later, the same José Martí (Cuba, 1853–1895) who proclaimed in his crucial essay "Nuestra América" (New York, 1891), that "the governors, in the republics of Indians, learn [to speak] Indian" (*Obras completas*, II, p. 525), was himself informed rather by Latin than Arawak or Quechua.

Returning to the Jesuits, then, it must be remembered that they were also the leaders among the colonists in acquiring the native languages through their work in the missions. Thus, at one blow, the expulsion undermined the bases of baroque poetry preserved in the Jesuits' combination of conservative religiosity and strong Latin, and at the same time foreclosed upon the most important eighteenth-century philological and anthropological researches into American indigenous cultures. The exile of the Jesuits did not preclude all further contact with the colonies, of course. Francisco de Miranda (Venezuela, 1750–1816), for instance, sought them out in Italy as he prepared himself ideologically for revolution against Spain. But the publication history of the great work of Francisco Javier Clavijero (Mexico, 1731–1787) is indicative of the delay of a full generation in the integration of the indigenous cultures into an independent American identity: the research conducted in Mexico prior to the expulsion was first published in Italian as the *Storia antica del Messico* in Cesena, 1780–1781, and only translated into Castilian a quarter of a century later by the Spanish man of letters José Joaquín de Mora (Spain, 1783–1864), whose interventions in Spanish American literary history are best remembered in connection with his conflicts with Andrés Bello (Venezuela, 1781–1865).

As a Jesuit exile, then, Aguirre is but one among many, including a distinguished group of neo-Latin poets such as Rafael Landívar (Guatemala, 1731–1793) and Diego José Abad (Mexico, 1727–1779) (on the Latin poetry of the Mexican Jesuits see Menéndez y Pelayo, *Antología de poetas hispano-americanos*, I, lxxviii–lxxxiv, as well as Jiménez Rueda, *Letras mexicanas en el siglo XIX*, and on the Jesuits in exile more generally, Batllori, *La cultura hispano-italiana de los jesuítas expulsos*). But Aguirre's posthumous literary fortunes take a more singular turn that make him an exemplary case for the interrelations between the eighteenth and nineteenth centuries. For we owe the reading of Aguirre to the researches of Juan María Gutiérrez (Argentina, 1836–1896), Latin America's greatest literary critic of the period, whose investigations brought to light most of the poetry by Aguirre now extant (see Gutiérrez, *Estudios biográficos y críticos sobre algunos poetas sud-americanos anteriores al siglo XIX*, 237–67). Gutiérrez himself understood his overarching literary project as an "act of patriotism", as he stated in his brief and anonymous prefatory remarks to *América poética/colección escojida/ de composiciones en verso,/por americanos en el presente siglo* (p. iii), the first continent-wide verse anthology in Spanish America, which he edited. And there is a special poignance in his recuperation of Aguirre, since his inclusion as an early avatar of a recognizably American identity required a breadth of vision that surpassed the post-Independence aversion to the long colonial epoch. It may further be added that Gutiérrez's mixture of literature and patriotism links him both to Bolívar's prior pan-American ideal and to the most acute and enduring of romantic stances in the history of Spanish America literature: the very notion of an independent and original literary identity.

The work of Gutiérrez, discovering Aguirre's manuscript pages, reclaiming the last great flowering of the baroque lyric from oblivion through the twin efforts of literary critic and editor, has still another relevance here. The persistence of the Baroque throughout the eighteenth century is easy to document – from the fine religious verse of Madre Castillo (Francisca Josefa del Castillo, Colombia, 1671–1742) that was appended to her spiritual tract, *Afectos espirituales* (not published until 1896 in Bogotá; see Castillo, *Afectos espirituales*) to the ponderous satire of Esteban Teralla Landa (b. Spain, fl. Peru, late eighteenth century), that is his *Lima por dentro y fuera* (Lima, 1797; see also Meehan and Cull, "El poeta de las adivinanzas"), reactionary in its politics, its racism and misogyny, and in its unflinching devotion to a baroque manner as late as the last decade of the century – but the phenomenon requires explanation. And recent studies of the sociology of literature (see esp. Kernan, *The Imaginary Library* and *Printing, Technology, Letters and Samuel Johnson*, and for Latin America, the distinct and illuminating study of Rama,

La ciudad letrada) underline the presence of such figures as Gutiérrez, that is literary professionals independent of the traditional patronage system, as evidence of a change in the social institution of literature and as promoters of that transformation. Gutiérrez is not altogether without precedent. In different ways both Bello and José María Heredia (Cuba, 1803–1839), the two outstanding figures in the nineteenth-century lyric, were representative products of a sociological shift within the institution of literature. But the evolution of a print culture that Alvin Kernan ties to the exemplary case of Dr. Johnson (England, 1709–1784) in mid-eighteenth-century England is a literal impossibility in Spanish America at that time. The printing press itself did not appear beyond the vice-regal centers until the century's end, or even later: e.g., Quito, 1760; Buenos Aires, 1780; Veracruz, 1794; Puerto Rico and Caracas, 1808 (see Martínez Baeza, "La introducción de la imprenta en el nuevo mundo"). And inasmuch as Kernan is able to argue for institutional change as a cause of stylistic change, the protracted predominance of an oral culture in Spanish America vis-à-vis Europe and North America may be understood to be a significant factor, perhaps the most important, in the slow arrival of Romanticism.

The breadth and vitality of Spanish America's oral culture, or rather cultures, present a further distinction with regard to the West more generally that no literary history of the region has yet to consider adequately, namely the presence of indigenous languages and literatures at the margins of print culture from the Conquest to our times. Even within the narrower confines of written literature, Jesús Lara complained nearly half a century ago with respect to the otherwise estimable work of Marcelino Menéndez y Pelayo and Luis Alberto Sánchez: "[they] synthesize a broad spectrum of historians and poets who made use of the language of Castille for the expression of their work. But neither of them presents a formal proposal to verify if the indigenous languages were used or not by any writer of those times. In that sense, they construct a Castilian history of America, not an American history" (Lara, *La poesía quechua*, 126). An institutional perspective is again illuminating. When Gutiérrez returned to the Spanish-language poetry of the colonial period, from the seventeenth-century Sor Juana to Manuel de Lavardén (Argentina, 1754–1809) on the brink of Independence, he recuperated them for literature. In contrast, research on the status of the couplet in Mayan, including such broad assertions as Munro S. Edmonson and Victoria R. Bricker's conclusion that "Perhaps the most distinctive quality of Maya literature is that it is all poetry" ("Yucatecan Mayan literature," 59, although note Gossen's reservations ["Tzotzil literature"] for a text as important as the *Popol Vuh*) are conducted within the discipline of anthropology.

Needless to say, this disciplinary division of labor, of literature versus anthropology, corresponds to a division into us and them, and so mimics, authorizes, and disseminates the prejudices of cultural hegemony. For a case in point, one might contrast the literary fate of Mariano Melgar (Peru, 1791–1815) and Juan Wallparrimachi Maita (Bolivia, 1793–1814). Melgar approached the racial boundary from the side of the hegemonic language, transposing a popular indigenous form, the *yaraví*, into Spanish. The results, far superior to his verse in traditional Castilian forms, have had great impact, especially in his native Peru, and, buoyed by his place in political history – he was executed by the Spanish in the course of the Wars of Independence – have gained Melgar a lasting renown across the continent (e.g., inclusion in such standard anthologies as Menéndez y Pelayo, *Antologia*; Flores, *The Literature of Spanish America*; and Carilla, *Poesía de la Independencia*; and for the complete poetry, see Melgar, *Poesías completas*). Not so his contemporary Wallparrimachi, a Quechua poet, who, in addition to developing the resources of his own literary tradition, also experimented at the cultural border from the other side; that is, according to Lara (*La poesía quechua*, 141), Wallparrimachi also appropriated the Castilian *décima* for verse in Quechua. Yet for all their ideological tendentiousness, cogently explained by Julio E. Noriega ("Wallparrimachi"), the various versions of his heroic actions in the Wars of Independence have not sufficed to promote Wallparrimachi to the pantheon of Spanish American literature – the encyclopedic notes of Pedro Henríquez Ureña (*Literary Currents in Hispanic America*), for instance, pass over Wallparrimachi in silence.

Literary scholarship in the Andean countries has long since concentrated attention on the native languages so as to recuperate the indigenous poetry for literature rather than anthropology (in Bolivia, for example, in addition to Lara, see Cáceres Romero [*Nueva historia de la literatura boliviana*]). And there is evidence that the concern has begun to spread: Antonio R. de la Campa and Raquel Chang-Rodríguez include a section on pre-Columbian literature in their anthology [*Poesía hispanoamericana colonial*]; and the Biblioteca Ayacucho has dedicated several volumes to indigenous texts (e.g., Bareiro Saguier, *Literatura guaraní del Paraguay*). But this is an effort that requires considerable expansion and, as with Spanish-language verse, the eighteenth and nineteenth centuries are especially under-represented. The extraordinary collection of poetry compiled in the eighteenth century and known as the *Songs of Dzitabaeche*, a Mayan text, but available in both the Spanish version of Alfredo Barrera Vásquez (*El libro de los cantares de Dzitbalché*) and the English of Edmonson ("The songs of Dzitbalché"), remains as yet a topic in the anthropological journals alone.

The marginalization of the indigenous cultures notwithstanding, the transformation from an oral to a print culture does begin to take place at the close of the eighteenth century through the establishment of periodical publications. In addition to official government organs of longer standing (e.g. the *Gaceta de México* in its various incarnations [see Urbina, *et al.*, *Antología del centenario*, for a brief history], newspapers began to arise in response to the fundamental impulse of the Enlightenment, dedicated, that is, to the diffusion of knowledge for the purpose of social progress (the preeminent periodical of the day, the *Mercurio peruano*, is available in a facsimile edition [1965]). Particularly attentive to the interests of local commerce, these journals published new findings in the pertinent sciences of metallurgy and meteorology, botany and zoology, and many others, along with discussions of economic issues and news items strictly related to trade. But the enlightenment faith in the infinite perfectibility of mankind through the exercise of reason extended to the moral sphere as well. In this context, poetry, chastened by the rationalizing principles of the great aesthetic codifiers of the Continent – Nicholas Boileau-Despréaux (1636–1711) above all (translated by the Mexican Jesuit Javier Alegre [1729–1788], among others; Alegre's interesting, Hispanizing version is included in his *Opúsculos* [1889]), but also Hugh Blair (England, 1718–1800) and Ignacio Luzán (Spain, 1702–1754) – held its place in the overall enlightenment project and found its place in new periodicals of the American colonies.

The dimensions of the newspapers mandated short verse forms; the moralizing context favored satire; the social custom tended to cover authorship in anonymity or pseudonyms made impenetrable, generally, with the passage of time. Literary history, driven by the romantic presuppositions that attended its birth, namely, the concentration on individual identities and unified bodies of work, has had neither the interest, nor the theoretical wherewithal to address this copious material. Once again the basic editorial tasks remain (although among the exceptions, see Miranda and González Casanova, *Sátira anónima del siglo XVIII*). But if the very topicality of the satirical verse in the ephemeral publications of the colonies renders their reading problematic today, the debunking purpose and popular venue lent themselves to an experimentation with everyday diction that make these texts a lexical treasure trove. The verse of some of the more readily identifiable and at least somewhat more accessible figures, such as Francisco del Castillo Andraca y Tamayo (Peru, 1714–1770) in his poems (see the edition of 1948) recounting the experience of Blacks and Indians, or the aforementioned Teralla Landa, when he turns his hand to his forte, invective, may also serve to exemplify the role of satire in enlarging poetry's social purview. In this respect the eighteenth-century satirists, both known and anonymous, may be ranged alongside the "Coplas del jíbaro" of Miguel Cabrera (Puerto Rico, dates unknown; Rivera de Alvarez and Alvarez Nazario [*Antología general de la literatura puertorriqueña*] include the text, and note that it circulated in manuscript prior to its first publication in the periodical *El Investigador* [1820] in an article attacking his poem) or the far more familiar, early gaucho poetry of Bartolomé Hidalgo (Uruguay, 1788–1823) (on the tradition of gaucho poetry, see Ludmer in these volumes, and for a selection of texts, including poetry by Hidalgo, see J. B. Rivera, *Poesía gauchesca*). The urge to allow new voices to speak in Latin American verse would have a long resonance in the nineteenth century and beyond. And satire itself would of course live on, finding such able nineteenth-century practitioners as Felipe Pardo y Aliaga (Peru, 1806–1868; see Luis Monguió's excellent critical edition [Pardo y Aliaga, *Poesías*]).

Nevertheless, the limitations of satire came to be felt acutely when their modest prods in favor of social change were overwhelmed by the call to revolution. "Querer salvar los Estados / Con remedios paliativos, / Con versos y reglamentos," writes Camilo Henríquez (Chile, 1769–1845), "Cosa es que el diablo no ha visto" ["To want to save States / With palliative remedies / With verses and with rules / The devil has never seen the like"] (Ghiraldo, *Antología americana* III, 212). The advent of the Wars of Independence set poetry on the course of political expression, which is to say that the patriotic ode came to the fore. To say as much is all but to name a new tutelary figure for Spanish American verse as revolution came and with it the poetic burden of exalting the local heroes of military exploits: the name is Manuel José Quintana (Spain, 1772–1857). Quintana would have recommended himself particularly for his own American sympathies (for an expression in verse, see "A la expedición para propagar la vacuna en América," included in the 1813 edition of his *Poesías completas*, 301–6; see also Carilla, *Poesía de la Independencia* xxiv and n. 7), and his verse, ranging from a strict Neoclassicism to a suggestive Pre-Romanticism – to employ a term to which Marshall Brown (*Preromanticism*) has given new critical vigor – found emulators from Juan Cruz Varela (Argentina, 1794–1839; see Varela, *Poesías*) in the Southern Cone for the former style, to Heredia in the Caribbean for the latter. But it was the pair of poems that Quintana published under the heading of *España libre. Odas* (Madrid, 1808) (see *Poesías completas*, 318–33) that became the virtually inevitable model for patriotic poetry as the long era of colonial rule came to a close.

The emergence of Quintana, however, needs to be measured not so much against the satirical mode, as against the influence of his mentor, Juan Meléndez Valdés (Spain, 1754–1817). As Quintana himself recognized, Meléndez was the outstanding poet of eighteenth-century Spain, and the praise may be expanded by noting that he had many imitators, but no peer in Spanish America either. Nevertheless, neither Quintana's unflagging support in the prologue to the posthumous edition of Meléndez's poetry, nor the excellent editorial and critical attention that John H. R. Polt and Georges Demerson (see Demerson's biography *Don Juan Meléndez Valdés y su tiempo* and Polt's companion study *Batilo* to their jointly edited text of Meléndez Valdés [1981–1983]) have devoted to his work in our times have sufficed as yet to redeem his literary reputation from his political mistakes – unlike Quintana or Nicasio Alvarez de Cienfuegos (Spain, 1764–1809), Meléndez capitulated to Napoleon. I simplify matters here. For in fact, Meléndez's extraordinary popularity upon the publication of the first edition of his collected poems in 1785 diminished significantly with the augmented second edition of 1797, as Quintana attests (*Obras completas*, 114). As his poetry developed, he posed a challenge that his contemporary readers were unable to meet. This is not the place to reevaluate Meléndez's achievement, but neither can I allow the moment to pass without asserting that a proper literary history of Hispanic Romanticism depends upon reading him aright.

It is fair to say that, by and large, the Spanish American poets of the period did not do so. Rather, like their peninsular contemporaries, they chose the facile point of access through Meléndez's Anacreontic odes, forming, in his wake, poetic Arcadias for the propagation of an artificial eroticism, erring twice over; first, for being less adept in their artifice than their distinguished model, and second, for being less boldly erotic. The typical results are especially evident in Mexico, where the activities of the Arcadia are well-documented by Luis G. Urbina, Pedro Henríquez, and Nicolás Rangel in their superb *Antología del centenario* (Mexico, 1910 and 1985).

The Mexican case is also noteworthy for offering some atypical successes, poets who, if underestimated, are nonetheless the identifiable authors of recognized bodies of work: Manuel de Navarrete (Mexico, 1768–1809) and Anastasio de Ochoa (Mexico, 1783–1833). Navarrete was Meléndez's most able follower and perhaps, altogether, the best poet in late eighteenth-century Spanish America, combining a delicate musicality in his amatory verse with a willingness to undertake the challenge of what Meléndez referred to as his philosophical poetry, exploring the thematics of melancholy at the heart of Western literature from Rousseau onward through the Romantics, particularly in the poems that Navarrete gathered under the heading of "Ratos tristes" (see *Poesías profanas* 145–62). Ochoa merits attention for his accomplishments in a variety of modes that cover the gamut of the poetry of his times, from the Anacreontic to satire, including the striking juxtaposition of traditional erotic themes and patriotic hymns in the series of sonnets in the first volume of his *Poesías de un mexicano* (New York, 1828). The epigraph to that same volume taken from the poetry of Sor Juana is an unexpected testament to the continuity of her appeal even as the Baroque cedes its place to Neoclassicism. And as he looks back to the foundations of a national literary tradition – that epigraph is attributed to "*La Mexicana* Sor Juana Inés" (my emphasis) – Ochoa also measures the pulse of change in a poem like "El paseo de las cabras en S. Angel." There the trappings of pastoral idealization, imbibed in the neoclassical veneration of antique authors, yield to the pressure, equally epochal, of direct observation, as the familiar perspective of "la dócil comitiva / Animada del júbilo inocente / Que lejos de la corte se respira" ["the docile retinue / Animated with the innocent / joy that one breathes when far from the Court"] (*Poesías*, 180) at the outset comes to concentrate itself in the individualized experience of "mis ojos" and "mis oídos" ["my eyes", "my ears"] (p. 183) whose perceptions are more singular:

> El alto *tejocote* entre mil hojas
> De oscurísimo verde allí convida
> A contemplar sus frutos, que agrupados
> Muy más que el oro a centenares brillan.
>
> > (p. 182)

> [The tall *tejocote* amidst a thousand leaves
> Of darkest green invite one there
> To contemplate its fruits, which, massed
> By the hundreds, shine more brightly far than gold.]

New science timidly meets old literary models in these verses. Ochoa strikes a difficult balance: the "almo jugo / Del maguey mexicano" ["white juice / Of the Mexican maguey"] of his Anacreontic ode, "Mis delicias," is paired with the "Trémulas alabanzas / A Lieo soberano" ["Tremulous praises / of sovereign Bacchus"] (pp. 26–7), much as the exaltation of the native fruit in the "Oda a la piña" (composed before 1821) of Manuel de Zequeira y Arango (Cuba, 1764–1846) is rife with classical allusions (Zequeira y Arango, *Poesías [de] Zequeira y Rubalcava* 191–4). The balance will soon tip, however, in favor of the Enlightenment appreciation of the minutiae of local circumstance as Bello comes to provide just such a paradigm for a strictly American literary identity, eclipsing the influence of Meléndez and Quintana.

The trajectory from Meléndez to Quintana to Bello is well illustrated in the career of one of the few canonical names of the period: José Joaquín de Olmedo (Ecuador, 1780–1847). Olmedo is remembered almost exclusively for his patriotic ode, "Victoria de Junín, Canto a Bolívar" (Guayaquil, 1825), but it is well to note that before he took up the greater burden, he was rather the author of Anacreontic verses which were a feeble imitation of Meléndez. Olmedo himself casts the shift in poetic manner under the aegis of Pindar (see Olmedo, *Poesías completas*, 125 and his own n. 3), but this is misleading. As regards the classical world, it is the precedent of Virgil, in particular Book VI of the *Aeneid*, that lends Olmedo's "Victoria de Junín" its principal narrative strategy. Virgil, that is, inserted a brief compendium of Roman history into his epic – a retrospective account from the point of view of the poet that becomes a prophecy in the mouth of the shade of the Anchises in the underworld, since the events would come only after the life of his hero Aeneas. Olmedo likewise resolves the chronological dilemma posed by historical events – Bolívar was present at Junín but not at the subsequent and decisive battle at Ayacucho – by bringing forth the shade of the Inca Huayna Capac to review American history and foretell the course of imminent events. The narrative sleight-of-hand has been often noted, but further emphasis is called for with regard to the Virgilian source, which projects forward in Spanish American literary history with continuing relevance up to *One Hundred Years of Solitude*; it may also be traced back well beyond Olmedo. Pedro de Peralta Barnuevo (Peru, 1663–1743), not only draws self-consciously on the same episode in the *Aeneid* to solve his own temporal bind, recounting colonial history as a prophetic vision presented to Pizarro in thousands of verses of his *Lima fundada o Conquista del Perú* (Lima, 1732; see Peralta Barnuevo, *Lima fundada*, [1863], 85–273, and Leonard, "A great savant of colonial Peru"); he also offers an exemplary disquisition on the uses of the marvellous, as derived from Virgil, in a fascinating introduction to so dull a poem (see esp. Peralta Barnuevo, *Lima fundada*, xii).

Olmedo's "Victoria de Junín" must also be viewed in its contemporary context as the most familiar example of the poetic effort to celebrate the triumphs of the revolution. The broad impulse stretches from Andrés Quintana Roo (Mexico, 1787–1851) in the north, to recall another relatively well-known figure, to the largely forgotten names to the south which constitute an invaluable anthology published in the wake of Independence, the *Lira argentina, o colección de las piezas poéticas dadas a luz en Buenos Aires durante la guerra de su independencia* (Paris, 1824; available in an outstanding scholarly edition, Barcia, 1982). In this case, as in most others, Quintana as the closest model is a palpable presence. I might also add that Olmedo's preeminence in this poetic vein owes much to the success of his hero in gaining the paramount position as the Liberator in the historiography dedicated to the wars of Independence. The patriotic odes of the aforementioned Juan Cruz Varela or Esteban de Luca (Argentina, 1786–1824), for example, may have been subordinated to Olmedo in the formation of a Spanish American canon for much the same extra-literary reasons that San Martín himself was subordinated to Bolívar. Or, to turn to the testimony of the *América poética* anthology, against, say, the standard account of Emilio Carrilla (*La literatura de la independencia hispanoamericana* and *Poesía de la Independencia*), who

claims that the canon of the independence period was essentially limited
from that time forward to but three names – Olmedo along with Bello and
Heredia – J. M. Gutiérrez dedicated more pages to José Fernández
Madrid (Colombia, 1789–1830) than to Olmedo.

Whatever place is to be assigned to Olmedo in an evaluative hierarchy,
his "Victoria de Junín" is most notable for its ambitions to deploy the
classical resources of Virgil and the neoclassical style of Quintana in the
context of a historical theme of emphatically American character. It is in
this sense that he passes from the ambience of his precursors in the
Salamanca school to the compass of Andrés Bello. Indeed, quite literally:
the poem was begun in Peru, but completed amidst Bello's literary circle in
London (see Berruezo León, *La lucha de Hispanoaméricana por su
independencia en Inglaterra*, for a comprehensive account of the all-
important interrelations between Spanish Americans that took place in
England). Bello's activities were manifold – literary critic, political
propagandist, grammarian, educator among other areas of achievement
in a long and fruitful career. Concentrating here on his role as a poet, two
productions of crucial importance stand as a temporal frame around
Olmedo's ode. In 1823 Bello published his "Alocución a la poesía" in the
first issue of *Biblioteca Americana* that he edited in London along with
Juan García del Río (Colombia, 1794–1856). The programmatic status of
the poem was immediately apparent and further enhanced when Gutiérrez published it at the head of the *América poética* anthology. Generations
of readers have reduced the long *silva* to its opening stanzas, with their
famous invitation to poetry to quit its ancient haunts in Europe, shed its
unwonted veneer of civilization and settle in uncultivated America:

> Divina Poesía
> tú de la soledad habitadora,
> a consultar tus cantos enseñada,
> con el silencio de la selva umbría;
> tú á quien la verde gruta fué morada,
> y el eco de los montes compañía;
> tiempo es que dejes ya la culta Europa,
> que tu nativa rustiquez desama,
> y dirijas el vuelo adonde te abre
> el mundo de Colón su grande escena.
>
> > (Bello, *Obra literaria*, 20)

> [Divine Poetry,
> You, a denizen of solitude.
> Raised to consult your songs
> With the silence of the shady wood;
> You, who in the verdant grotto made your home,
> And of the hillside echo your companion,

It is time you abandoned courtly Europe,
Who loves not your native rusticity,
And turned your flight to where Columbus's
world unveils to you its grandeur.]

Pedro Henríquez Ureña's critical assertion that this invocation constituted a "declaration of literary independence" (*Literary currents*, 99) has given this reading of the poem a concise statement of the greatest force and influence. It will be useful to recall, however, that this pronouncement has had the unfortunate effect of appearing to obviate the reading of several generations of self-consciously American poets and prose writers who preceded Bello. It reduces, much in the romantic spirit, a broad movement to a single personality. Moreover, the claims for Bello's originality are overstated without some reference to the vogue for "progress pieces" such as Gray's "Progress of poesy" (1757) that had yet to die out in England at the time of Bello's long sojourn there (see Griffin, "The progress pieces of the eighteenth century").

Having said this, I can only reinforce the position taken by Gutiérrez, Henríquez Ureña, and many others. The impact of an authoritative voice speaking from the influential setting of London in favor of American themes for American poets was undeniably great. And Olmedo's "Victoria de Junín," whether a direct response to Bello's summons or a spontaneous and coincidental expression of the same impulse may be seen as one highly visible example of the enthusiasm in the period to take up the mantle that Bello denominates as that of "algún Marón americano" ["some American Virgil"] (Bello, *Obra literaria*, 24). But Bello himself will soon shift the terms of that assignment. A competitive response, perhaps, to Olmedo's accomplishments which had improved upon him in a certain way? Or does Bello determine to foreclose on a particular misreading of his original call? The speculation is inviting, but a more neutral approach will recognize that in the long portion of the "Alocución" that has largely escaped critical attention, Bello focuses on American history as the proper subject for the Muse upon her arrival in her new home, and Olmedo's ode clearly shares that conception. When Bello reissues his proclamation of the true task of American poetry as the *silva* "La agricultura de la zona tórrida" in his later London journal *El Repertorio Americano* in 1826, the new Virgil is understood to be more the author of an American *Georgics* than an American *Aeneid*. Despite the late date, relative to the English poetry that surrounded him as he wrote – the *Lyrical Ballads* had been in print since 1799, and the younger triumvirate of Byron, Shelley, and Keats had all died by 1826 – "La agricultura de la zona tórrida" is the acme of the Enlightenment in Latin American verse, and a bulwark for the aesthetics of mimetism. Or, to refer to the argument of Oscar Rivera-Rodas (*La poesía hispanoamericana del siglo XX*), who has analyzed this crucial moment in the history of the Spanish American lyric with more acuity than anyone before him, it is precisely in light of the late date of the second of Bello's *silvas americanas* that one ought to read the poem as a deliberate defense of the mirror against the lamp, in the terms of M. H. Abrams (*The Mirror and the Lamp*) that serve as the basis of that discussion. The antagonist, then, is not Olmedo, who belongs to the neoclassical cohort, but rather, as Rivers-Rodas sees, José María Heredia, whose first edition of *Poesías completas* had been published in New York the previous year (see Bello's review, *Obra literaria*, 270–7).

On Bello's side in this debate, one reads in "La agricultura de la zona tórrida" that nature rather than culture, that is the land itself and not its history, constitute the distinctive character of Spanish America, and with that recognition, a conviction that the poet's role is that of a new Adam in a new Eden: the poet must name American objects by their American names. The endurance of this frankly anti-romantic stance in the history of Spanish American literature is well known, but its import for the development of Romanticism itself, which is to say, once again, modernity, still requires investigation. The attractions of the myth of an unmediated relation to nature, not in some remote past, but as part and parcel of the Spanish American experience at any given moment, mitigate against the central romantic mythology of a fall. And the procedure that places the poet as a recorder in the wilderness, detached from his observations by a certain scientific objectivity, stands against the romantic view that perceives the world only in relation to and as an expression of the isolated self. Bello's aesthetics will not often withstand some degree of admixture in the century and a half and more to come – though Gregorio Gutiérrez González (Colombia, 1826–1872) writes one of the great poems of the nineteenth century, "Memoria sobre el cultivo de maíz en Antioquia" (1866), by attempting to follow Bello's neoclassical program as closely as possible (note, in this regard, the quotation of Bello's "Alocución" as an epigraph to Gutiérrez González's earlier poem of 1845, "Al salto del Tequendama"; see Gutiérrez González, *Poesías*). It may be more useful, however, to approach the issue from the opposite point of view, and to note not so much that a pure Neoclassicism is quickly eroded, but rather that the quasi-solipsistic outlines of the romantic self are rarely to be encountered in Spanish American verse, due, in some measure, I am suggesting, to the heritage of the objective perception of a world not fallen and for that very reason more strange and wondrous than the ego itself, a heritage whose exemplary poet is Bello.

In this light one may return to the century that preceded Bello with a renewed interest and a research plan that surpasses the obstacles presented by Henríquez Ureña's great divide. However, rather than look to such efforts in verse as Lavarden's "Oda al Paraná" (Buenos Aires [in the *Telégrafo Mercantil*], 1801), often cited as a pioneering poem in its objective descriptions of an American landscape – though this is false: Peralta Barnuevo, in the descriptive passages of his *Lima fundada*, along with his own prose notes, may serve once again as long-standing precedent to the more canonical example – one might take a hint from the author's notes to the text. The prose, in short, is superior to the verse. Bello's true forebears are not Spanish America's neoclassical poets, whether in the Anacreontic or the patriotic mode, but rather the prose writers of the many reports of the scientific expeditions of the eighteenth century – his own early contact with Alexander von Humboldt (Germany, 1769–1835) is often noted, though the broader consequences require further study.

The proposal risks going awry on theoretical and practical grounds. First, one may recall the argument of Clifford Siskin (*The Historicity of Romantic Discourse*) to the effect that the effacement of differences in kind, such as the generic distinction between poetry and prose, in favor of differences in degree is itself a typically romantic strategy. It was Shelley, for instance, who claimed in his *Defence of Poetry* that "The true poetry of Rome lived in its institutions," not in its verse (*Selected Poetry and Prose*, 508). Insofar as Siskin's theoretical point can be sustained, it breeds caution. It would be better to recuperate the eighteenth century in some fashion than not at all, but to remake it in the image of the nineteenth century would be but a small critical advance. The more pragmatic obstacle is simply that the availability of prose texts is as limited as that of poetry. The greatest of the expeditions to sail under the Spanish flag, the voyage of Alessandro Malaspina from 1789 to 1794, is a prime case in point. Malaspina ran foul of the Court upon his return. He was imprisoned and his papers impounded; they have yet to be edited and published in full. On the other hand, recent investigations of scientific expeditions spearheaded by the Real Jardín Botánico in Madrid (e.g., *La botánica en la expedición Malaspina* [1989] are far in advance of the study of the contemporary poetry, with publications on voyages reaching well up into the nineteenth century (e.g., Puig-Samper, *Crónica de una expedición romántica al Nuevo Mundo*). The intersection between the disciplines has already produced some unexpected results: Guillermo Hernández de Alba and Guillermo Hernández Peñalosa (*Poemas en alabanza de los defensores de Cartagena de Indias en 1741*) have discovered important samples of poetry from among the papers collected by José Celestino Mutis in his expedition in Nueva Granada from 1783 to 1810. But in addition to such valuable editorial work, the demand for literary analysis of the prose texts themselves remains a major undertaking. For instance, discussion is called for with respect to the predominant tropes by which the objects under observation were habilitated for textual transmission; Mary Louise Pratt's *Imperial Eyes* is of signal importance here.

If the literary history of the eighteenth century must move forward to the dates of Bello's *silvas* in the mid 1820s, the history of the nineteenth century must be pushed back from the generally recognized starting point for Latin American Romanticism: the return of Esteban Echeverría (Argentina, 1805–1851) from his sojourn in the Paris of Victor Hugo (1802–1885). It has been convenient for French criticism to seize upon the opening of *Hernani* on February 25, 1830, as an inaugural date for Romanticism, particularly since the time of the eye-witness account of Théophile Gautier (France, 1811–1872) (published originally in 1872, see Gautier, *Oeuvres complètes*, 109–21); and more convenient still for Spanish American critics to note that Echeverría brought the testimony of his own experience of that atmosphere back to Buenos Aires upon his return in June of the same year. But the personal influence of Echeverría in the River Plate area is more important with respect to sociological questions in the history of the institution of literature in that region than as a literary point of departure for the writing of poetry. Not that sociology should be dismissed. On the contrary, the organization of an institutional identity, first through the *Salón literario* of Buenos Aires and thereafter through the *Asociación de mayo* for a group of writers sharing a political program and certain literary presuppositions, is a fact of the first order of magnitude (for pertinent texts, see Echeverría, *Dogma socialista*). Nevertheless, it is significant that Echeverría's literary reputation today rests most securely on his short story, "El matadero" (written *c.* 1838, first published Buenos Aires, 1871), just as the other leading poet of the group, José Mármol (Argentina, 1817–1871), is best remembered for his novel *Amalia* (Montevideo, 1851). Echeverría and his circle make their most substantial contribution in prose and politics – witness the careers of his fellow Argentinians J. M. Gutiérrez, Juan Bautista Alberdi (1810–1884), Bartolomé Mitre (1821–1906), and their great contemporary, Domingo Faustino Sarmiento (1811–1888). While they need to be studied in relation to the history of the lyric, that relation is no more, though also no less, straightforward than that which I have outlined for the interconnections between the prose of the scientific expeditionaries and neoclassical verse. I limit myself here to noting that the prosaic quality of the poetry has been over-emphasized; what is needed is an investigation of the poetic procedures of the prose.

The formative period for the new poetic sensibility that will challenge Bello and Neoclassicism more generally precedes Echeverría, then, and is to be dated instead to the brief span from 1820 to 1832, from the putative date of Heredia's composition of "Fragmentos descriptivos de un poema mexicano," to the publication of the second and last collection of his poetry edited in his lifetime, the Mexican edition of his *Poesías completas* (Toluca, 1832), in which the same poem appeared, augmented and thereby substantially altered, under the title of "En el teocalli de Cholula." I can be more precise: there is a change of epoch from Neoclassicism to Romanticism between the neoclassical introduction of a timeless landscape description in that text and the insertion of an isolated poetic self, identified in history and defined by loss. When the poem is rewritten for the Toluca collection by the added recounting of a nightmare (Heredia, *Poesías completas*, includes the complete text of both versions), Heredia is already fully in the romantic world that not merely anticipated, but rather produced, Freud and our modernity.

Like Olmedo, Heredia advances towards mature poetry over the course marked by Meléndez and Quintana, imbibing with these the influence of Cienfuegos; this last often disparaged for undermining the young poet's neoclassical decorum – an attitude that does disservice to Heredia and Cienfuegos alike. Heredia distinguishes himself from his Spanish American contemporaries, in any case, by carefully exploring Quintana's work beyond the patriotic themes, and by overcoming the latter's reticence in the face of the sublime. Spurred on by Cienfuegos's extreme expressions of anguish, Heredia surpasses Quintana as a reader of the melancholy of Meléndez, who was, already in the late eighteenth century, the author of texts that correspond to the definition of the "greater romantic lyric," in Abrams's terms (*The Mirror and the Lamp*), or even Bloom's "crisis poems." I dwell for the moment on these intertextual relationships in order to recall, first, that if the Napoleonic invasion of Spain stymied the development of the lyric there, the Salamanca school continued by correspondence course, as it were: their proper heir was Heredia. Furthermore, it is important to set Heredia into that broad pan-Hispanic context precisely because he will be the last Latin American poet for whom it will be necessary, at least until the close international contacts of the early twentieth century. Heredia himself, along with Bello – to limit the question to poets of a continent-wide reach – will come to replace such forebears as Meléndez and Quintana as the inevitable reading in the formation of Spanish American poets in the nineteenth century.

Heredia's particular contribution was the development of a poetic melancholia: not merely the commonplace of bathos by moonlight only slain in the Spanish American lyric by the *modernista* Leopoldo Lugones (Argentina, 1874–1938), but rather a specific resistance to the therapy of the elegy. In Heredia's poetry, Spanish America will not give up the ghost of its own history. The effect is most clear, though not necessarily most profound, in his transformation of the political reality of exile into a major trope for poetry. A comparative perspective may be illuminating.

Wordsworth discovered, or perhaps became the *genius loci* of English poetry by walking the breadth of the national identity on foot. If his chosen scene in the Lake District was a wilful anachronism in its rejection of industrialized England, Whitman proved it possible to march into modernity within the broad compass of his native land. Heredia's itinerary carried him far from Cuba, and he conceived his national identity – he becomes a national poet – from afar, recognizing the severance without accepting the loss. The oft-cited fantasmagoria at Niagara Falls may stand as a familiar example:

> Mas, ¿qué en ti busca mi anhelante vista
> Con inútil afán? ¿Por qué no miro
> Alrededor de tu caverna inmensa
> Las palmas ¡ay! las palmas deliciosas,
> Que en las llanuras de mi ardiente patria
> Nacen del sol a la sonrisa, y crecen,
> Y al soplo de las brisas del Océano
> Bajo un cielo purísimo se mecen?
>   (I cite the 1832 version, Heredia,
>   *Poesías completas*, 227)

> [But what does my longing gaze search out
> In you with vain desire? Why find I not
> 'Round your enormous cave
> The palms, oh! the delicious palm trees
> That upon the plains of my ardent homeland
> Are born in the smile of the sun, and grow
> And rock in the breath of sea breezes
> Beneath an immaculate sky?]

Exile of course is not an uncommon fate in the long era of political turmoil from the wars of Independence to the close of the twentieth century, both under continuing colonial rule in the Caribbean, as in the case of fellow Cuban Juan Clemente Zenea (1832–1871) or Lola Rodrí-guez de Tío (Puerto Rico, 1843–1924), and throughout the continent, e.g., the whole of Echeverría's circle in the River Plate region. The local precedent of Heredia as poet–exile was reinforced, particularly in the context of the far stronger affinity of nineteenth-century Spanish America to France than to Anglo-American culture, by the example of Hugo – still the most widely read contemporary poet through the time of Darío. And the popularity of both figures, foreign and domestic, may best be understood against the backdrop of a belated print culture in Spanish America that had never cordoned off a social institution of literature from other spheres of public discourse. Hence, when a pan-American delega-tion made an excursion to the site of "Niágara" (composed 1824 and included, with variants, in both of the collections of poetry that Heredia edited in his own lifetime) and there a spontaneous chorus formed, as Martí relates in his Hardman Hall address (New York, 1889) – "and hearing the stupendous falls resound, 'Heredia!' said the son of Montevideo, getting to his feet; 'Heredia!' said the one from Nicaragua, baring his head [. . .] 'Heredia!' said the whole of America" (the text is included in its entirety in Heredia, *Poesías completas*, II, here p. 457) – they single out neither poetic achievement nor political resistance, but rather reaffirm the trope of the poet as exile, whose distant perspective, moreover, can comprehend a visionary American unity.

I might append a further speculation. Political conditions notwithstanding, in the literary realm, the dominion of the neoclassical principles fostered by Bello's *silvas* wedded national identity to national landscape, but only through a strict mimeticism that excluded the active agency of the poetic ego. It may well have been, therefore, that even where domestic tranquility reigned, the poetic self had nowhere to go but out. Exile, I am suggesting, may have been nineteenth-century Spanish America's necessary fiction – even as it was, and continued to be, a political reality. Darío's subsequent expatriation, as well as the centrality of travel, imaginary or real, for the succeeding vanguard generation (see Grünfeld, "Cosmopolitismo modernista y vanguardista") may be but avatars of that disjunctive poetics that ceded the native land to mimetic reflection while obliging the imagination to seek its fortunes far from home. This division may in itself constitute Spanish America's version of the literary fall which in turn produces Romanticism.

And Romanticism does come to Latin America. When it does, especially in those cases where it is worn as a foreign fashion, the melancholia that Heredia establishes as a foundation for a native lyric tradition will often collapse into mere nostalgia on the one hand, or an ungainly triumph of Positivism on the other. It would be well to note, nevertheless, that even so apparently tired a topos as the faded rose of Fernando Calderón (Mexico, 1809–1845), writing directly under Heredia's influence, is reinvigorated if it is read not so much as an exhausted metaphor, but rather as a melancholic demetaphorization, a deliberate wilting of the flowers of rhetoric.

One discovers so fine a poet as Gertrudis Gómez de Avellaneda caught on the horns of the dilemma of the legacy of Heredia in the poems in which she confronts him most overtly, only to succeed when she shifts the ground to the issue of a woman's refusal to accept her loss of, her exclusion from, the poetic word. One compares, for instance, the unexpected praise of Yankee ingenuity – "oh aéreo, indescriptible puente" ["oh indescribable, airborne bridge"] (Gómez de Avellaneda, *Obras literarias*, 374) – at the close of her "A vista del Niágara," an unsuccessful attempt to secure the freshness of her vision in a heavily burdened tradition to the subtlety with which she analyzes the complicity of all poetic discourse with the masculine point of view. Gómez de Avellaneda's strategies of silence and anxieties of authorship, well-documented for nineteenth-century women writers of other literary traditions (e.g., Gilbert and Gubar, *The Madwoman in the Attic*), find ample corroboration amongst the little-read poets of the anthology edited by José Domingo Cortés, *Poetisas americanas/Ramillete poético/del/ Bello sexo hispano-americano*, the best collection of Hispanic women's poetry of the nineteenth century. Susan Kirkpatrick's *Las Románticas* is a major contribution in this respect.

The permanent suspicion that poetic language cannot heal ideological wounds, that poetic language is itself symptomatic of those wounds, is by no means the universal lyrical stance of the nineteenth century. And yet such creative melancholia will appear consistently in some of the most interesting poets and poems of the period, enough to discern amidst the commonplace expression of yearning a critical current in Spanish American Romanticism that meets the test of a properly modern consciousness as it has been posed at least from Kant to Paz. Hence, one finds José Eusebio Caro (Colombia, 1817–1853; see Caro, *Antología. Verso y prosa*) returning to the crossroads between the erotic and the funereal at which Garcilaso introduced the classical elegy into the language. In doing so, he undermines the healing effect of love, demonstrating that what Freud would come to call libidinal reinvestment (The Standard Edition, XIV, 243–58) may be a process for burying the dead alive, rather than mourning their loss (see Abraham and Torok, *L'écorce et le noyau*, esp. 259–75; also available in Spanish as "El duelo o la melancolia"). To choose a more limited example, the powerful elegy of José Antonio Maitín (Venezuela, 1804–1874), "Canto fúnebre" (in Menéndez y Pelayo, *Antología*, II, 523–32), among the finest Latin American poems of the period, needs be read not in spite of but rather precisely because of its deliberate hamstringing of the genre. The poem closes, as Heredia or Gómez de Avellaneda often do, by preferring textual suicide to resignation and renewal, in the mode – if less spectacularly so – of Shelley's "Adonais" (1821) at the very boundaries of the elegiac genre, as Peter Sacks argues (*The English Elegy*), or in fact beyond them. It is representative of poetry that is funereal without being teary-eyed, to revise Mariano Picón Salas's apt characterization of the cloying sentimentality of the early verse of José Antonio Calcaño (Venezuela 1827–1894), typical of a certain stylized Romanticism ("he began funereal *and* teary-eyed like all the Romantics of the 1840s. . ."; Picón Salas, *Formación y proceso de la literatura venezolana*, 121, emphasis added).

The point may be expressed more simply, perhaps, by stating that the most exciting poems of the period tell ghost stories. One may recall in this respect Albert Dérozier's valuable discussion (*Manuel Josef Quintana et la naissance du libéralisme en Espagne*) of Quintana's role in importing the Gothic tale from English into Spanish literature in the theatre. But in Spanish America, removed from the European Middle Ages and their late eighteenth- and early nineteenth-century revival in continental taste, the literature is haunted primarily by the victims of its own colonial history. Bolívar pointed out in his letter to Olmedo, the resuscitation of an Inca as the mouthpiece of *criollo* ambitions was an ideological dodge: "it doesn't seem proper," he wrote, "that [the Inca] praises indirectly the religion that destroyed him; and it seems even less proper that he would not want to reestablish his throne and instead gives preference to foreign intruders, who though they may have avenged his blood, remain the descendants of those who annihilated his empire" (Bolívar, *Cartas del Libertador*, 38). But if a poet of the succeeding generation, like Carlos Augusto Salaverry (Peru 1830–1891), might preserve the topos of a supposed "venganza … de Atahualpa" [revenge … of Atahualpa"] in his "El sol de Junín" (*Poesía*, 91), he could nonetheless raise a critical question in the same text that overthrows Olmedo's facile identification of *criollo* independence with indigenous aspirations. Salaverry's indigenous soldiers at Junín descended inexplicably from their freedom in the mountains to a war that did not truly concern them. The mystery is not dispelled by revolutionary history. He might as well have described his contemporary indigenous countrymen as "oculto en sus selvas de verdura" ["hidden in their jungle greenery"] (Salaverry, *Poesía*, 97) – hidden, but perhaps also buried in the jungle: a ghostly presence in the national conscience. Much nineteenth-century verse is expended in the effort to exorcise that ghost or lay it to rest through a proper elegiac distancing. The elegy, that is, takes its own revenge upon the restless spirit of melancholia, as when the royalist sympathies of Rafael María Baralt (Venezuela, 1810–1860) lead him to arrest the image of a satanic fall of imperial Spain in favor of a concluding nostalgia for lost grandeur in "Oda a España" (originally published in *El Tiempo* [Madrid], 1846; see Baralt, *Obras literarias* esp. the final two stanzas, p. 46).

Experiments in this area were widespread and varied. One finds the exploration of Indian themes directly under the aegis of Bello in the poetry of Salvador Sanfuentes (Chile, 1817–1860), for example (see his verse tale *Inani*, originally published in Santiago de Chile, 1850; included in Sanfuentes, *Obras escogidas*). Other instances arise rather from the influence of Heredia, as in the case of the "Profecía de Gautimoc" of Ignacio Rodríguez Galván (Mexico, 1816–1845) (for selected texts of his poetry, that of F. Calderón, mentioned above, and other Mexican writers of the period, see Pacheco, *La poesía mexicana del siglo XIX*). And Echeverría, too, finds his way from the mode of Hugo to the *indigenista*

[Indigenist] theme, though with neither sympathy nor admiration for the indigenous peoples, in "La cautiva" (originally published in Echeverría's *Rimas* [Buenos Aires, 1837], for text, see Echeverría, *"El matadero" y "La cautiva"*). In Mexico, José Joaquín Pesado (1801–1861) published a collection of Nahuatl songs in his Castilian version in *Los aztecas* (Mexico, 1854), while in Cuba José Fornaris (1827–1890) founded a *siboneista* movement, intent on reproducing the lost indigenous culture in theme and spirit.

For all the differences that might be noted between the productions of these and other individuals and groups, the fundamental motives are relatively stable and familiar from poetry of the more adequately studied Afro-Antillean movement of the twentieth century. The concerns form a sometimes self-contradictory jumble. There was a lust for the exotic in reaction to the emerging bourgeois culture on a European model, and the associated drive to recover from the fall into civilization by a return to the primitive. And yet, transferring Bello's poetic argument from the realm of nature to that of culture, there was also a promotion of the Latin American identity as itself exotic – again as measured against the European standard – that allowed for a separation of the newly established nations and their corresponding literary traditions from the former metropolis. Sarmiento will argue forcefully for civilization against such barbarism in the same period, of course, where the gaucho takes the marginalized cultural position of the indigenous peoples elsewhere in Spanish America, but the internal evidence of the work, not to mention the success of the gaucho poetry of José Hernández (Argentina, 1834–1886) and others (again, see Ludmer in these volumes), suffice to suggest that a triumphant ideology parts company here with a predominant literary stance. One further factor may be cited in explaining the diverse and powerful wave of *indigenista* [indigenist] poetry. While would-be reminiscences of the lost *areito* favored short forms in Cuba, and such a poem as Plácido's "Jicotencal" (i.e., Gabriel de la Concepción Valdés, Cuba, 1809–1844; see *Los poemas más representativos de Plácido*), was highly esteemed, Indian themes as treated in "Anacaona" of Camila Ureña de Henríquez (Dominican Republic, 1850–1897; the poem was included in the first edition of her *Poesías* [San Domingo, 1880]; see *Poesías completas* 241–328, along with Paravisini-Gebert, "Salomé Ureña de Henríquez") as well as several of the poems already cited, provided the material for very extensive verse forms. Walter Scott is as much the model here as he was for developments in prose, and the mixture of history and fiction that he inspired brought the nineteenth-century lyric to the borders of the epic in the deliberate attempt to found a national mythology apart from the evidence of the chronicles of the Conquest and the long era of colonial administration. Romanticism itself, as Alejandro Losada points out, commenting specifically on the early post-Independence period in Peru, "is an aspect of the process of nation-building" (*La literatura en la sociedad de América Latina*, 36).

Doris Sommer ("El otro Enriquillo") has examined the ideological concomitants of this attempt in the Dominican context with regard to *Enriquillo* (Santo Domingo, 1882) the historical prose romance of Manuel de Jesús Galván (Dominican Republic, 1834–1910), offering a model for needed studies of the verse romances of the period. Here, too, research into the contemporaneous poetry by indigenous peoples and in the indigenous languages will be invaluable as a counterpoint to the ideological tendentiousness of the literature of the hegemonic class, much as the reading of the verse of the ex-slave Juan Francisco Manzano (Cuba, 1797–1844), and still more so his *Autobiografía* (written in 1839, first published Havana, 1937; see reprint, 1970), provide crucial references for such poems by white authors as "La madre africana, oda" by Francisco Acuña de Figueroa (Uruguay 1790–1862) (see Falcao Espalter, *Antología de poetas uruguayos*, I, 63–5, for the text, as well as Soler Cañas [*Negros, gauchos y compadres*] and more recently Carullo ["Una aproximación a la poesía afro-argentina de la época de Juan Manuel de Rosas", for an introduction to the poetry of River Plate Blacks).

The perspective of the present day, that is, may find that the assimilation of Indian themes, aided by the nascent disciplines of philology and historiography, are primarily elegiac, to use the terms of the preceding discussion, closing off the indigenous cultures as past and lost at some paradisiac origin, thereby allowing *criollo* culture to mend its own sense of rootlessness or usurpation in Spanish America. I might add that such critical suspicions are not limited to the twentieth century. Miguel Luis and Gregorio Víctor Amunátegui, in their *Juicio crítico de algunos poetas hispano-americanos* (Santiago de Chile, 1861), one of the most significant efforts at literary criticism in nineteenth-century Spanish America, denounce the *indigenista* poetry of Juan León Mera (Ecuador, 1832–1894) as a superficial exploitation: "it is a poor originality that consists only of words. The fact that the Ecuadoran poet may have pretended to be an Indian poet while entoning the songs in which those exotic words appear does not justify their use; because, if he has taken some of the expressions of the indigenous peoples of America, he has not known how to assimilate with the required perfection either their ideas, or their sentiments, their customs, or their beliefs, which alone would have authorized that language" (Amunátegui, *Juicio crítico de algunos poetas hispano-americanos*, 101–2).

The lyric response to such a critique is not an enhanced sociology, but rather, more characteristic of the age, an improved philology. Juan Zorilla de San Martín (Uruguay, 1857–1931) is explicit about his labors with the Tupi language in his notes to *Tabaré* (Buenos Aires, 1886 is often cited as the first edition, which I have been unable to examine, while others argue for Montevideo, 1888; for a recent edition, see Zorilla de San Martín, *Tabaré*), for instance. And his poem is particularly important for endeavouring in the vein of Heredia to deny its dead the consolation of consecrated ground, preserving a fantasmal presence through the curious, hybrid language of the poem no less than in the characterization and suicidal drive of the protagonist.

This melancholic note, I reiterate, is within the range of only the strongest voices, whereas the other strains touched upon here are ubiquitous. Indeed, one may turn almost at random to a poet like Ricardo Gutiérrez (Argentina, 1836–1896) and discover a complete compendium: from the religious poetry that is a constant in Spanish American literature, to the gaucho of "Lázaro," cast at once as a Byronic Cain and also a distinctly American identity – "soy el hombre americano / sin más Dios ni soberano / que su propio corazón!" ["I am American man / with no more God nor sovereign / than his own heart!"] (R. Gutiérrez, O. V. Andrade, *Selección de poemas*, 47), including in this broad compass a certain sympathetic identification with the Indians in the same poem "Lázaro," an open reliance on the centerpieces of contemporary Peninsular literature (the clear presence of the final act of *Don Alvaro o la fuerza del sino* [first performed Madrid, 1835] by Angel Saavedra, Duque de Rivas [Spain, 1791–1865] in Gutiérrez's "La fibra salvaje"), and even a modest engagement with the trope of the wandering ghost in "El cuerpo y el alma." Yet the later Gutiérrez coincides with the early Darío, and the characteristic postures of the nineteenth-century lyric show evidence of alteration in even so typical a product of Romanticism, as for instance, when Gutiérrez states with *modernista* cosmopolitanism – the romantic declamatory style, notwithstanding: "Patria es palabra de ambición y guerra: / si te oyes preguntar – ¿cuál es tu patria? / ¡dirige al cielo tu inocente mano / y la infinita bóveda señala!" [Fatherland is a word of ambition and war: / if you hear yourself asked – where is your fatherland? / raise your innocent hand to the heavens / and point to the infinite vault!"] (*Selección*, 8).

It would be no more difficult to document a mass of such anticipations of *Modernismo* in the poetry of supposed Romantics than it is to point out the initial romantic steps of the poets who would be *modernistas*. But the distinction, however deeply rooted in Spanish American literary historiography, is no more tenable than the supposition of an impermeable boundary between the closely associated French Parnassians and their own romantic sources. The received opinion of the originality of Darío, indisputedly great poet though he may be, is not only an unnecessary barrier to a proper assessment of the eighteenth and nineteenth centuries, but also in and of itself a romantic pronouncement that proves rather the persistence of the literary frame of mind that it purports to replace. It is with regret that I throw down this gauntlet upon a field whose allotted space and concomitant methodological limitations prohibit that I be bold in my own defense. Perhaps for that very reason I allow myself a further rash remark in conclusion. A growing body of theoretical discussion defines our own contemporary literature in terms of the dispersion of the self, of the unimpeded crossing of national boundaries and crossing out of national histories, of the triumph of pastiche, superabundant citation and other forms of explicit intertextuality over originality and the integrity of the individual imagination, in short, of Postmodernism. This may well be no more than a claim that we are finally taking a first step beyond Romanticism – but the jury is still out.

12

Spanish American theatre of the eighteenth century
Frederick Luciani

Theatre in eighteenth-century Spanish America reflected the contradictions of what was, for most of the Hispanic realms in the New World, the last century of colonial rule. Like other aspects of colonial culture, theatre followed closely the dictates of the Spanish peninsula; accordingly, it tended to support and defend the colonial regime, while adhering to the anachronistic, late baroque repertoire that remained popular in Spain through most of the period. Yet the very conservatism of colonial theatre ensured its participation in the changes that peninsular drama underwent during the century, changes that corresponded to the reformist spirit of Neoclassicism and the critical perspective of the Enlightenment. It was inevitable that these changes would acquire their own kinds of momentum in the colonies, given the energy and diversity of the Hispanic realms beneath the official veneer of ideological and bureaucratic uniformity. Conformism in colonial theatre guaranteed change, and change moved irrevocably in the direction of individuation and disengagement.

Records of plays performed throughout the Hispanic world in the eighteenth century show a remarkable consistency of repertoires. The most popular playwright, through to the very end of the century, remained Calderón de la Barca (1600–1681), followed by other, lesser playwrights of the Calderonian school. Yet, by virtue of its close connection with the theatre of France, Hispanic theatre experienced a gradual and uneven acceptance of the neoclassic aesthetic: traditional Golden Age plays were often revamped according to the "new rules," which demanded a closer adherence to the classical unities; tragedies and comedies of manners by Racine, Voltaire, Corneille, and Molière were translated or adapted for Hispanic stages, and original plays in the French neoclassic mold by Hispanic playwrights were written and performed. Neoclassic sensibilities also underlay the royal decree of 1765 that banned the performance of *autos sacramentales* and "saints' plays" in the Hispanic realms.

The popularity of the *sainetes* of the great Spanish playwright Ramón de la Cruz (1731–1794) was coetaneous on both sides of the Atlantic. The *sainete*, a short, humorous theatrical piece that depicted social types and customs, became a favorite genre among colonial writers, and the one in which they most successfully competed with their Peninsular counterparts. The works of these New World *sainetistas* mirrored, of course, New World realities: the Mexican *charro* and the Argentinian gaucho made early appearances on the colonial stage. Given the increasingly restive nature of colonial society, such "local color" was not without larger political implications. It reflected – and probably was an agent of – a sharpening sense of cultural difference and national identity, important factors in the movement toward independence.

The official tone of colonial theatre was set by traditional Peninsular repertoires, *loas* that gave praise to viceroys and prelates, and lavish dramatic festivals that celebrated coronations and royal births. Yet other kinds of theatre, which responded to the critical spirit of the age, coexisted – if precariously – with the dominant tradition. Satirical drama, for example, was by no means unknown in the colonies; it was an effective instrument of ridicule in the factional squabbles that often arose in the viceregal regimes. Indigenous dramatic themes and forms, long marginalized by European theatrical modes, were revived in conjunction with Indian rebellions against Spanish rule. Pseudo-historical dramas based on themes of the Discovery and Conquest – progeny of the New World dramas of Lope, Tirso, and Calderón – stirred nationalist impulses in creole audiences; Olavarría y Ferrari notes that *México rebelado*, a play about the Conquest performed in Mexico City in 1790, was suspended by civil authorities for this reason (*Reseña histórica del teatro en México, 1538–1911*, 83–7). A kind of "underground" theatre, corresponding to the beginnings of agitation for independence, may have existed among the creole class in large urban centers; Trenti Rocamora discusses the manuscript of an anti-Spanish theatrical piece purported to date from 1776 and linked to the clandestine Sociedad Anti-Hispana, founded in Buenos Aires in 1775 ("El teatro porteño," 419–20).

As in Spain, the utility of theatre in public life became part of cultural debate in the Spanish American colonies. While the fortunes of the theatre varied greatly according to the disposition of the civil and ecclesiastic authorities in any given period and region, the overall trend was toward the consolidation and regularization of theatrical activity. Period documents suggest that encouragement for the construction of Spanish America's first *coliseos* – large, solid and attractive theatres – often came from high places in the colonial hierarchy; some viceregal administrations saw such theatres as an opportunity to express civic pride and to provide honest and morally instructive entertainment. As the century came to a close, pragmatic political considerations came to the fore: the rehabilitation of Mexico City's *coliseo* in the 1790s was part of the program of public works undertaken by the Viceroy Revillagigedo with the express purpose of diverting the populace from seditious impulses (Leonard, "The 1790 theatre season of the Mexico City Coliseo," 104–7). The governor of Montevideo was similarly motivated to establish that city's first *coliseo* in 1793 (Rela, *Breve historia del teatro uruguayo*, 5–6).

While the theatrical venues of preceding centuries – the atria of churches, open air *corrales*, the viceregal palaces, convents and *colegios* – continued to be used in the Spanish American colonies throughout the eighteenth century, the *coliseos* became the center of dramatic activity in the largest cities: Mexico City (1753), Lima (1771), Havana (1776), Caracas (1784), Montevideo and Bogotá (1793), Guatemala City (1794) and La Paz (1790) (Suárez Radillo, *El teatro barroco hispanoamericano*, III, 655). Permanent, roofed structures with interior illumination, the *coliseos* represented a major step toward theatre as practiced in the modern age. Theatrical performances were given on a regular schedule throughout the year – not just on festive occasions – and evening performances became increasingly common. Theatrical activity enjoyed a greater professionalization: a dramatic company, composed of male and female actors who were regulated both by contractual agreement and by the vigilance of church and state authorities, was attached to each major theatre. The commercial success of the *coliseos* also guaranteed the gradual liberation of colonial theatre from the patronage system.

It might be thought that the eighteenth century, which brought Spanish American theatre to the very brink of modernity, would be viewed as a high-water mark in the history of colonial theatre. Yet modern critical opinion has given general approval only to a few native-language dramas, poignant symbols of an indigenous consciousness threatened with extinction, and to the *sainete*, with its promise of new national identities; most of the rest of eighteenth-century colonial theatre is often judged as derivative, aesthetically muddled, or servile. Such judgments inevitably reflect modern critical perspectives: a secularism unsympathetic to religious theatre; a Eurocentrism that tends to view colonial culture as imitative and inferior; its converse, an Americanism hostile to the political and cultural hegemony of Spain; remnants of both the neoclassic disdain for the excesses of baroque art and the romantic impatience with the academicism of the neoclassic age; indeed, a positivistic faith in the very validity of these traditional periodizations of literary history.

The reevaluation of such critical perspectives – which are neither absolute nor immutable over time – may offer important new insights on the field. For example, the late baroque theatre of the colonies, often dismissed as extravagant and unreadable, has seldom been studied within its own contexts: viceregal court etiquette, the representation of power hierarchies in the Hispanic empire, the hybridization of genres, the diversification of sensorial experience in theatre, and so on. Similarly, colonial experiments in Neoclassicism have been judged almost exclusively by comparison with Spanish and, above all, French models, with little regard for the varying historical and cultural resonances of the movement in the New World.

The difficulty of realizing such a critical reevaluation is compounded by a dearth of primary data: while the record of actual performances in major colonial theatres is clear and extremely useful, the number of titles by colonial playwrights is relatively small, and many of the actual texts have not survived. Biographical information on playwrights is often minimal, or even nonexistent. The geographical dispersal of the archival record – and the perennial difficulty of archival work in many Spanish American countries – means that the body of data is likely to grow at a slow pace. The challenges faced by the next generation of scholars of eighteenth-century Spanish American theatre are considerable. If met, they may lead to the kind of revitalization that has occurred in the fields of colonial narrative and poetry.

Theatre in indigenous languages

By the eighteenth century, religious theatre in Quechua and Nahuatl had become largely independent of the mendicant orders which had introduced it in the early decades of evangelical fervour. It endured, in some places, as an essentially folkloric art form, often at odds with a church anxious to preserve doctrinal purity and unhappy with the unorthodox, even atavistic elements that such drama sometimes displayed. The cycles of Nahuatl Passion plays in central Mexico studied by Horcasitas are an example. Eighteenth-century manuscripts exist for *La pasión del Domingo de Ramos*, composed in Tepalcingo, Morelos, and the very similar *La pasión de Axochiapan*, composed in Axochiapan, Morelos.[1] While the precise origins of these dramas are obscure, Horcasitas observes a high degree of "mestization" in the characters as well as other details that suggest a folk theatre at a considerable remove from early missionary drama (*El teatro náhuatl*, 340–2). Horcasitas also cites an eighteenth-century source that reports the translation of such Passion plays from Nahuatl into Spanish and their subsequent performance by Creoles and *mestizos*. This important item of information gives support to the theory that some present-day forms of popular theatre in Mexico – *moros y cristianos*, *pastorelas*, Passion plays, and so on – have their source in early

---

[1] The text of *La pasión del Domingo de Ramos* and a description of *La pasión de Axochiapan* can be found in Horcasitas, *El teatro náhuatl, épocas novohispana y moderna*.

missionary theatre, and therefore, ultimately, in indigenous as well as European dramatic forms (*El teatro náhuatl*, 428–30).

La invención de la Santa Cruz por Santa Elena [*How the Blessed St Helen Found the Holy Cross*] is a Nahuatl drama that was "put in order," as its manuscript indicates, by Father Manuel de los Santos y Salazar (?– 1715) in a small parish of Tlaxcala, Mexico, and completed on May 31, 1714.[2] Opinions vary as to whether Santos y Salazar was the author of this drama, its adaptor, or merely a copier of a preexisting manuscript. Among the play's characters are two *graciosos*, who bring comic relief to the drama of Constantine, his conversion, and the subsequent finding of the Cross by his mother, St. Helen. Ravicz, who sees the manuscript as a copy, notes that the *graciosos* "teach, through dramatic satire, the negative value of human sacrifice, ritual warfare (for non-Christian purposes) and cannibalism" (*Early Colonial Religious Drama in Mexico*, 179). Her reading of the *graciosos'* interventions, if correct, may argue for an early date of composition, since early missionary drama was often designed to combat certain, specific practices of the indigenous cultures. Horcasitas, however, finds evidence that the play is a largely original, eighteenth-century work. The presence of the *graciosos*, of musical interludes in Nahuatl, and of a celebratory *tocotín*, corresponds to a baroque sense of theatre, interested in the amusement of the audience as well as its indoctrination. References to pre-Hispanic deities, and to indigenous foods and customs, suggest to Horcasitas an "incipient nationalism" very much of the eighteenth century (*El teatro náhuatl*, 516).

The kind of truly collaborative missionary theatre that had existed in sixteenth-century Mexico and Peru endured in the eighteenth century in the Misiones region of Paraguay, where the Jesuit missions among the Guaraní Indians preserved a frontier, evangelical spirit. Such theatre was employed by the Jesuits as a catechistic tool until their expulsion from Misiones, and all the Hispanic realms, in 1767. Despite the lack of extant examples of such theatre, a considerable body of information survives in the form of eyewitness accounts and the *carta annuae* of the Jesuit order. This information suggests that, as in Mexico and Peru some centuries before, the Spanish friars adapted existing European plays or composed original ones in the native language. These plays were then performed by the Indians themselves, who drew on their own musical, choreographic, and histrionic traditions in their interpretations. The large plazas of the mission towns, as well as the porticoes of churches, were the venues for these dramatic productions, which ranged from simple devotional songs and dances to full-scale *autos sacramentales*. There is also a hint of Jesuit worldliness in the record of the theatre in the Misiones region: profane

[2] The Spanish text can be found in Horcasitas, *El teatro náhuatl*, and the English text is in Ravicz, *Early Colonial Religious Drama*.

comedias and *entremeses* in Guaraní were also, apparently, part of the repertoire (Pla, *El teatro en el Paraguay*, 14–31).

In the Andean region, forms of pre-Conquest indigenous drama appear to have survived into the eighteenth century in a more unadulterated and vigorous state than in other regions of Spanish America, as a result of a lesser degree of racial mixing and a subsequent greater indigenous consciousness. This consciousness took form in political action: the Tupac Amaru rebellion, led by the Peruvian Indian *cacique* José Gabriel Condorcanqui in 1780, represented a real threat to Spanish control. His execution and the suppression of the rebellion by Spanish authorities was accompanied by a ban on secular Quechua-language theatre – proof of the potency that such theatre retained for the indigenous sense of identity.

Nowhere is that sense of identity more powerfully expressed than in *La tragedia del fin de Atahualpa*, a Quechua-language play that tells the story of Atahualpa, the last Inca, his defeat by Pizarro, and the latter's subsequent punishment by the King of Spain, represented as *España*. The play is known only through manuscript versions dating from the nineteenth and twentieth centuries, as well as in variants still performed in the Andean region as folk theatre. Some scholars (e.g., Arrom, Gisbert) find evidence of an eighteenth-century revamping of the play, at least in the so-called Chayanta manuscript which formed the basis of Jesús Lara's well-known translation into Spanish and edition.[3] Nonetheless, much in the play bespeaks a sixteenth-century origin, especially the presence of non-Spanish, presumably pre-Conquest dramatic modes: the use of a chorus that announces and comments on events, elaborate formulas of address among the characters, the continuous repetition of words and phrases, and the rapid changes of scene within the same dramatic sequence. Likewise, the moral and epistemological perspective offered by the play is completely indigenous. Pizarro and his fellow Spaniards are represented as cruel, avaricious, and hypocritical. Their instruments of war, their writing, and their language – which is silently mouthed by the Spanish characters and translated by their indigenous interpreter – are viewed as sinister and incomprehensible. Only the final scene, in which a spoken dialogue occurs between Pizarro and a shocked and wrathful "Spain," offers some vindication of Spanish authority; it suggests, interestingly, a fealty to the Crown as opposed to the colonial regime.

A different dynamic of loyalty and rebellion is expressed by the Quechua-language drama *Ollántay*, a play whose earliest extant manuscripts date from the eighteenth century, and that is known to have been performed for the *cacique* Condorcanqui in 1780.[4] It tells the story of

---

[3] José Cid Pérez and Dolores Martí de Cid (eds.), *Teatro indoamericano colonial*, reproduces Lara's text, while José Meneses (*Teatro quechua colonial*) offers an original translation.

[4] The numerous versions of the play in Spanish and other languages use several orthographic variants in the title and characters' names. This spelling of the title corresponds to the often cited and anthologized Spanish translation by Pacheco Zegarra (Madrid, 1886, and Buenos

Ollántay, a prominent warrior of the Incan empire, his illicit love for an Incan princess, his punishment by the Inca and his subsequent rebellion, along with the people of his ancestral lands, against the empire. Defeated after some ten years by the armies of the Inca's son and successor, Ollántay is reunited with his beloved and the daughter of their union, is pardoned by the Inca and restored to his place in the kingdom.

Ollántay's link with the Condorcanqui rebellion provides important clues about its origin and meaning. Although based on legendary material with roots in pre-Conquest history, the play seems to respond to the circumstances of the moment. Its very revival as a cultural artefact suggests an awakening and an affirmation of indigenous consciousness, and the story's emphasis on the evils of tyranny and the legitimacy of insurrection have obvious significance for a people in revolt. At the same time, the play's resolution underscores the virtues of clemency and conciliation – virtues which, for a rebellion about to be brutally crushed by the colonial regime, must have had an immediate appeal.

Despite these ties to a particular era, the exact provenance of the *Ollántay* drama remains obscure: critics have long debated the degree to which the play retains dramatic and textual elements dating from before the Conquest. A few questions seem resolved: the division of the play into acts and scenes, for example, is accepted as a colonial-era modification. Some fundamental questions, such as the era to which the Quechua of the play belongs, have given rise to the most varied opinions. Other elements that would seem to argue either for a pre-Hispanic origin, such as the use of a chorus, or for a colonial-era origin, such as the presence of a *gracioso* character, have proved inconclusive in the critical debate. Arrom, for example, finds that the *yaravís* sung by the chorus are replete with images and metaphors common in the lyric poetry of the Spanish Golden Age (*Historia del teatro hispanoamericano (época colonial)*, 124–5). Cid Pérez and Martí de Cid argue that the *gracioso* is a universal character type, and that Incan culture did not exclude comical entertainment (*Teatro indio precolombino*, 297). Many other examples of ambiguous evidence could be cited. Such ambiguity, while problematic for the literary historian, has positive aesthetic and cultural implications. Of all the extant colonial-era theatrical texts in native languages, *Ollántay* manifests the most perfect integration of Hispanic and indigenous dramatic elements.

Theatre in Spanish

Spanish-language religious theatre in eighteenth-century Spanish America took a variety of forms, from lively folk theatre to the theologically

Aires, 1942). Cid Pérez and Martí de Cid (*Teatro indio precolombino*) base their translation on Pacheco Zegarra's French version (Paris, 1878). Ripoll and Valdespino use the Barranca version while Meneses uses an original translation in his anthology. English translations of the play include those by Markham and Halty and Richardson.

complex dramas of the Jesuit schools. An example of the latter is the *Coloquio de la Concepción*, performed at some point in the century in a Jesuit *colegio* in Santiago, Chile in conjunction with the Feast of the Immaculate Conception.[5] The probable author of the *Coloquio* is Juan Antonio Tristán y Doyague (?–?). The play presents a dispute between the characters *Devoción* and *Escuela* as to which of the two has the greater right to praise the Immaculate Conception, a dispute in which elaborate scholastic arguments are brought to bear, and which ends, predictably, with a call for the reconciliation of faith and learning. The allegorical characters are complemented by the character "types" of the *Estudiante*, the *Poeta*, and the *Beata*, all of whom receive satirical treatment; they are lampooned, respectively, for their pedantry, bombast, and false piety. The caustic humor of the *Coloquio* barely provides comic relief from its dense theological dialectic.

The *decuria* was a genre of religious theatre that was intended as a rhetorical and histrionic exercise for the students in the Jesuit schools. Unlike the theologically ambitious kind of Jesuit theatre represented by the *Coloquio de la Concepción*, the *decuria* presents a brief, exemplary story. Two extant examples of the genre from Lima, Peru, are the *Decuria de Santa María Egipcíaca*, whose probable author was Father Vicente Palomino (?–1741), and the *Decuria muy curiosa que trata de los diferentes efectos que causa en el alma el que recibe el Santísimo Sacramento*, composed in 1723 by Father Salvador de Vega (1682–?).[6] Both works include a *gracioso* among their small group of characters.

The Capuchin nun Sor Juana María (Josefa de Azaña y Llano, 1696–1748) was the author of five religious *coloquios*, written for her conventual sisters in Lima. Only one of these plays, the *Coloquio a la Natividad del Señor*, has been published.[7] The *Coloquio* tells the story of the Nativity with a simple lyricism – seasoned in the rustic speech of the shepherds, with Peruvianisms – that contrasts with the prevailing, late baroque dramatic mode of expression. The *Coloquio*'s editor, Father Vargas Ugarte, attributes this contrast to a certain innocence of spirit in the author, which found expression in a spontaneous, untutored style (*De nuestro antiguo teatro*, xxiv). Arrom, with broader historical perspective, notes the *Coloquio*'s affinity with the sixteenth-century religious theatre of Encina and Gil Vicente; he views Sor Juana María's work, then, as a felicitous anachronism (*Historia del teatro*, 105).

The *Historia de la Comberción de San Pablo* is an anonymous Guatemalan drama composed in 1772.[8] It elaborates on the story of Paul's

---

[5] The text is in Vargas Ugarte, "Un coloquio representado en Santiago en el siglo xviii."
[6] Both texts are in Vargas Ugarte, *De nuestro antiguo teatro: colección de piezas dramáticas de los siglos XVI, XVII y XVIII*.
[7] The text is in Vargas Ugarte, *ibid*.
[8] The text is in Johnson, "La *Historia de la Comberción de San Pablo*, drama guatemalteco del siglo xviii."

conversion as told in the Acts of the Apostles, with an interesting mix of baroque *cultismo* and rough, colloquial language, the former in the speech of the characters Saul and Ananias, the latter in the speech of the *graciosos* Hormiga and Zompopo. The plot of the drama, with its opposing bands of Jews and Christians, offers the opportunity to incorporate the popular dance of *moros y cristianos*: the play's characters are arranged in symmetrical groups, whose actions are carefully choreographed. In fact, virtually all movement on the stage is done in the form of dance.

The *loa* was a genre of the theatre that embraced both secular and religious themes in colonial Spanish America. While most *loas* preceded full-length plays by colonial, or, more frequently, Peninsular playwrights, they rarely, by the eighteenth century, served merely as an introduction to the larger piece. Rather, they were independent works of a panegyric nature; the object of their praise was usually the Virgin, a saint, the Spanish monarch, or persons of high rank in the colonial hierarchy. Stylistically, the *loa* was the last redoubt of the high baroque manner in colonial theatre. Its characters were almost always mythological or allegorical, its language was highly euphemistic, and its metaphors and imagery were of an extreme preciosity. Colonial *loas* also abounded in a variety of metrical tricks: acrostics that spelled the name of the personage lauded, echo devices, *glosas* (sequences of verses that expanded upon the lines of an initial stanza), *laberintos* (blocks of verses that retained sense when divided internally), and so on. A chorus of singers, providing brief musical interjections, was another standard feature.

Among the *loas* that fit this conventional mold are those by the Peruvian Pedro de Peralta Barnuevo (1664–1743) written to accompany his *comedias Triunfos de amor y poder* (1711), *Afectos vencen finezas* (1720), and *La Rodoguna*. All three *loas* praise reigning Spanish monarchs and viceroys of Peru. The *Introducción al sarao de los planetas*, by Jerónimo Fernández de Castro y Bocángel (1689–?), was written and performed in Lima in 1725, also in honor of the Spanish king.[9] Another Peruvian author of *loas* was Félix de Alarcón (?–?), who composed a *Loa al cumplimiento de años de la señora Princesa de Asturias doña Luisa de Borbón* (1744) and a *Loa ... para la coronación de ... Fernando el VI* (1748), whose eight characters represent the letters of Fernando's name, and who join verses and voices to form a spectacular quadruple acrostic near the *loa*'s culmination.[10] Other conventional examples of the genre include a *loa* by Jacinto de Buenaventura (?–?) in honor of Fernando VI performed in Ibagué, Colombia, in 1752, and the religious *loas* by Father

[9] The text is Lohmann Villena, *El arte dramático en Lima durante el Virreinato*.
[10] The *Loa al cumplimiento de años*, is in Vargas Ugarte, *De nuestro antiguo teatro*, and the *Loa para la coronación* is in Lohmann Villena, *El arte dramático en Lima*.

Diego Molina (?–?), of Quito, Ecuador, represented between 1732 and 1740.[11]

A few extant *loas* of this period deviate sufficiently from the standard form to suggest that the genre was not unaffected by the changes in dramatic taste that took place during the century. A *loa* composed by the Argentinian Antonio Fuentes del Arco (?–1733) celebrates the decree by Philip V in 1717 exempting Santa Fe from payment of tax on merchandise entering that city.[12] The style of the *loa* is largely free of the extreme artificiality common in the genre: the characters are three *caballeros*, not mythological figures; their speeches contain references to Argentinian geography and products. Another Argentinian *loa*, the anonymous *Loa para cualquier función* (or *El año 1775 en Buenos Aires*) begins in the conventional way, with four mythological figures representing the four elements, who praise the Spanish monarch.[13] But a fifth character, a *gracioso*, intervenes near the end of the *loa* and ridicules the allegorical premise of the play. The self-parody of the *loa* is suggestive of a genre in decline. Finally, two anonymous *loas marianas* from Mexico, the *Loa en obsequio de la Purísma* and the *Loa en obsequio de Nuestra Señora de Guadalupe* represent a significant departure from convention.[14] The primary characters in each are Indians, portrayed in a way that must have been intended as amusing for creole audiences: they are all simpletons or rogues, and are prone to lapse into a kind of fractured Spanish. These two *loas*, written late in the century, reflect the growing preference for works representing local types and customs, a preference most clearly seen in the *sainete*.

Surviving full-length plays of eighteenth-century Spanish America belong to thematic sub-genres that flourished in the seventeenth-century Peninsular repertoire: *comedias* of amorous intrigue, historical dramas, "saints' plays," and so on. Stylistically, as well, these plays resemble Peninsular drama of the preceding century, especially its closing decades, when the lesser followers of Calderón brought drama to its peak – critics traditionally say its nadir – of flamboyance and extravagance. Yet the colonial *comedia* cannot be categorically dismissed as derivative and retrograde. A few plays, sufficient in number to suggests the relative vigor and contemporaneity of colonial theatre, are engaged with political or stylistic polemics very much of their time. Others, of a more conventional mold, are nonetheless of intrinsic merit: deprived (as they are for the modern reader) of the music and visual spectacle that once served as their vehicle,

---

[11] Buenaventura's *loa* is in Johnson, "Loa representada en Ibagué para la jura del rey Fernando VI." Molina's *loas* are summarized in Descalzi, *Historia crítica del teatro ecuatoriano*, VI.

[12] The text is in Trenti Rocamora, "La primera pieza teatral argentina."

[13] The text is in Bosch, *Historia del teatro en Buenos Aires*.

[14] The texts are in Olavarría y Ferrari, *Reseña histórica*.

these few works still retain felicities of characterization, plot development, and lyrical expression.

The *comedias* of Pedro de Peralta Barnuevo (Peru, 1664–1743) suggest an esoteric and irrecoverable theatrical aesthetic. To the elite audiences that saw them performed, they must have seemed richly allusive and sensorially gratifying. Reduced to texts, and removed from the world of the viceregal court, with its elaborate systems of patronage and courtesy, the plays seem inflated and pointless. *Triunfos de amor y poder* (1711) was commissioned by the viceroy of Peru, and was represented in the viceregal palace as part of celebrations marking the victory of Philip V at the battle of Villaviciosa in 1710. *Triunfos* is a play of amorous intrigue; its characters are gods and mortals of classical mythology. Another play of the same genre, *Afectos vencen finezas*, was performed in the viceregal palace in honor of the Peruvian viceroy in 1720; its characters are princes and princesses of ancient Greece, shepherds and shepherdesses, and a sole *gracioso*.

Peralta Barnuevo's *La Rodoguna*, whose dates of composition and first performance are unknown, is an adaptation of Corneille's *Rodogune*. As such, it has drawn the attention of literary historians, who recognize it as an early example of the influence of the French neoclassic dramatic mode on Hispanic theatre. However, as Leonard notes, Peralta Barnuevo's adaptation is a thorough Hispanization of the original. Corneille's alexandrine verse is replaced by a variety of Spanish metric forms, and the tragic tenor of the play is compromised by traditional elements of the Spanish *comedia*: a *gracioso*, an amorous sub-plot, musical interludes, and elaborate special effects ("An early Peruvian adaptation of Corneille's *Rodogune*," 175). An austere neoclassic tragedy recast in the florid baroque manner, Peralta Barnuevo's *Rodoguna* is a literary milestone of somewhat uncertain bearings.

Another Peruvian playwright, Father Francisco del Castillo (1716–1770), mainly composed drama of the conventional, late Golden Age kind. Yet, like Peralta Barnuevo, Castillo's forays into neoclassic tragedy point to a new era in colonial theatre. *Todo el ingenio lo allana* is a *comedia* of amorous intrigue, very much in the Calderonian vein. *El Redentor no nacido, mártir, confesor y virgen San Ramón* is a *comedia de santos* with all the hallmarks of the genre, including a heavy reliance on mechanical special effects. *Guerra es la vida del hombre* is an *auto sacramental* whose allegorical premise recalls the *autos* of Calderón. *La conquista del Perú* (1748) is a New World historical drama in the tradition of Lope, Tirso, and Calderón; despite having been composed by a colonial playwright during an increasingly rebellious age, its vision of the Conquest is decidedly pro-Spanish.

Mitrídates, rey del Ponto, a tragedy set in ancient Rome, differs markedly from Castillo's other full-length dramas. Concepción Reverte Bernal argues convincingly that *Mitrídates* constitutes an attempt at a tragedy in the strict, neoclassic manner. She notes that the play adheres closely to the "new rules" of drama, especially the three classical unities, and employs metrical forms, such as the hendecasyllabic line, preferred in neoclassic drama. She cites Racine's tragedy *Mithridate* as an important antecedent for Castillo's version, while noting the considerable disparities between the two plays (*Aproximación crítica a un dramaturgo virreinal peruano*, 186–95). Reverte Bernal's succinct explanation of *Mitrídates*'s shortcomings as drama can perhaps serve as illustrative of the overall Hispanic failure to excel in the tragic genre: it lacks both the action of the traditional Spanish *comedia* and the profound, conflictive characterization that gives French tragedy its dramatic impetus (p. 191). Like Peralta Barnuevo's *Rodoguna*, Castillo's *Mitrídates* stands as an important – if unimposing – historical marker.

The Spanish-born Mexican Eusebio Vela (1688–1737), an actor, director, impresario, and playwright, dominated the theatrical scene in Mexico City in the early decades of the eighteenth century. Only three of his plays have been recovered. *Apostolado en las Indias y martirio de un cacique* is a historical drama based on the conquests of Cortés and the missionary activities of the first Franciscans in Mexico. *Si el amor excede al arte, ni amor ni arte a la prudencia* is a mythological *comedia* of amorous intrigue, involving mortals, gods, and goddesses, and set on Calypso's isle. *La pérdida de España* is a historical drama based on the legend of Roderick, the last Visigothic king of Spain. All three plays, while relatively free of the most glaring linguistic excesses of late baroque theatre, clearly belong to the Calderonian school; their recourse to the supernatural and to spectacular stage effects is especially evident.

Apostolado en las Indias represents an interesting combination of genres. It recalls both the New World historical dramas of the Golden Age and the *comedia de santos*. The basic historical plot, verifiable in the early chronicles of the Conquest, is recounted within a hagiographic framework, replete with miracles and martyrdoms. The result is a work of extreme religious and political conservatism. Cortés and his fellow *conquistadores* are portrayed as uniformly virtuous, despite their martial disposition; motivated by an evangelical zeal, they use physical violence only when forced to do so. The Franciscan friars are of an unimpeachable sanctity. The Indians are virtuous only to the extent that they accept Spanish and Christian domination; indeed, the rebellious *cacique* Axotencalt is portrayed as in league with the Devil. Such moral reductionism and historical whitewashing surely would have proved unacceptable to a later generation of Creoles. Despite its New World theme, which would suggest, at first glance, an anticipation of cultural and political independence, *Apostolado en las Indias* looks backward, not only to traditional peninsular dramatic genres, but also to a colonial complacency and orthodoxy whose process of erosion had already begun.

If Vela's plays seem to prolong the least attractive dramatic and ideological tendencies of another age, the work of a Cuban contemporary, Santiago de Pita (?–1755), recalls the best of Golden Age theatre. His *El príncipe jardinero y fingido Cloridano* (1730–1733), a *comedia* of amorous intrigue set in ancient Greece, is very much of the Calderonian school. *El príncipe* is based on an Italian play by Giacinto Andrea Cicognini, and shows the influence of Lope de Vega, Moreto, and Sor Juana Inés de la Cruz, as well as of Calderón. The thematic and stylistic conventionality of the play in no way detracts from its merits: a sustained lyricism, deft characterization, and a pleasingly complicated – not convoluted – plot. The humor of the *graciosos*, sprinkled with Cubanisms, retains an engaging quality that contrasts with the wooden cleverness of the comical characters in other plays of the period. The judgment of Arrom, whose scholarship yielded most of the basic information on the play's authorship, date, and sources, is deserving of respect: he considers *El príncipe jardinero* the best surviving example of the eighteenth-century colonial *comedia* (*Historia del teatro*, 103).

The *Drama de dos palanganas Veterano y Bisoño* (1776), usually attributed to Francisco Antonio Ruiz Cano y Sáenz Galiano (1732–1792), a Peruvian of noble birth, is an example of a kind of drama that flourished in the very center of the political intrigue of the viceroyalties, if on the periphery of true theatre.[15] The *Drama* was composed as part of a vituperative campaign against the outgoing viceroy of Peru, don Manuel de Amat, whose administrative agenda and personal life earned the general disapproval of the creole upper class. Dramatic action and plot are virtually absent from the play. It may be considered theatre only by virtue of its dialogic form: two "palanganas," or pedants, engage in a series of conversations that detail the viceroy's faults and crimes. The *Drama* recalls an anonymous Peruvian *Entremés famoso de Juancho y Chepe*, composed some decades earlier, also as an invective against the reigning viceroy. Lohmann Villena's opinion with regard to these satirical dialogues makes good sense: it is likely that they were intended to be circulated and read by interested parties, rather than performed in public (*Un tríptico*, 371). Whatever their true genre and mode of dissemination, these works are another example of the existence of dramatic forms outside the orthodox confines of the palace, religious institutions, and *coliseos*.

The short theatrical pieces of Peralta Barnuevo enjoy considerably

[15] The text is in Lohmann Villena (ed.), *Un tríptico del Perú virreinal: el Virrey Amat, el Marqués de Soto Florido y La Perricholi*, and in the edition by Luis Alberto Sánchez.

more critical favor than the full-length dramas that they accompany. Unlike his ponderous and conventional *comedias*, Peralta Barnuevo's *bailes*, *entremeses*, and *fines de fiesta* possess a compressed energy and corrosive irony. They are, perhaps, as baroque as the *comedias*, but in a different sense: they are conceptually dense, rather than inflated and declamatory, and "patterned" rather than plotted. Even when taking satirical aim at pedantry and verbal bombast, they seem to celebrate an aesthetic of complication. Yet there are glimmerings of something else – a sense of humor that indulges human foibles, an observant eye for social types – that emerges from the intricate machinery of these works, and points ahead to the full-fledged *costumbrista* theatre of the latter half of the century.

The characters and choreography of Peralta Barnuevo's *bailes* recall those of his compatriot Valle y Caviedes, composed some decades earlier. In the *baile* for *Triunfos de amor y poder*, the character Love converses, at times in song, with characters representing various social types, who are variously subjected to Love's critical assessment. Similarly, in the *baile El Mercurio galante*, which accompanies *Afectos vencen finezas*, the character Mercury sustains a spoken and sung dialogue with five gallants and five ladies, each representative of a certain type, who are paired off at the end according to their complementary peculiarities. The *fin de fiesta* for *Triunfos*, based largely on an *interméde* by Molière, is a satirical portrayal of the qualifying examination of a *bachiller* in medicine. The *fin de fiesta* for *Afectos*, which takes its inspiration from Molière's *Les Femmes savantes*, ridicules the sophistry and false erudition of the characters, both male and female, whose intellectual debate is the substance of the piece; interestingly, some of the severest ridicule is reserved for the figure of the poet, whose inflated baroque style is scarcely distinguishable from that of Peralta Barnuevo himself in his *comedias*. The *entremés* for *La Rodoguna* portrays the furtive courtship of four sisters and their corresponding suitors, who represent different professions. The mildly racy repartee of the couples, as well as the ironic commentary of the girls' father, who intrudes on the scene, give the piece a lively humor that sets this *entremés* apart from Peralta Barnuevo's other short works, and seems most in tune with the *costumbrista* theatre of the following decades.

As in the case of Peralta Barnuevo, the short theatrical pieces of Father Francisco del Castillo retain an accessibility that his full-length dramas have lost. Of the handful of such pieces that have been published, Castillo's *Entremés del justicia y litigantes* is the most successful. In this play, a magistrate and his scribe must hastily compose and dispatch a reprieve for a man they know to be unjustly accused of murder, and whose execution is imminent. The two are interrupted by a series of local citizens, each of whom presents some petty complaint, spun out in excruciating – and comical – detail, to the increasingly frantic magistrate. The dramatic tension builds until the condemned man himself, with an officer of the law in pursuit, bursts onto the scene and receives his reprieve in person. Castillo's effective use of suspense, his rapid delineation of characters, and his exploitation of the situation's many satirical possibilities, all suggest a thorough mastery of the genre.

Other short pieces from early in the century include *El amor duende* (1725) by Jerónimo de Monforte y Vera (?–?), of Lima, and the *Bayle o Sainete del mercachifle*, by the same Diego Molina, of Quito, who was the author of religious *loas*.[16] The structure of the first work recalls the *bailes* of Valle y Caviedes and Peralta Barnuevo: the central character is Love, the peripheral characters are mortals. But rather than serve as judge or teacher, Love acts as a mischievous spirit [*duende*]. He instills amorous passions in two gentlemen for two *tapadas*, or veiled ladies, only to substitute the latter, as the play concludes, with an old woman and a black woman, to the surprise and horror of the two gentlemen and, presumably, the amusement of the audience. The speech of the characters in *El amor duende* varies according to class and race. The central character of Molina's work is a *mercachifle* [pedlar], a one-time womanizer who satisfies a bet with three gentlemen by resisting the blandishments of three women intent on carrying off some of his wares. Like Montforte y Vera's work, the *baile* offers a cynical view of love and courtship, expressed in colloquial language and with racial humor.

Examples of satirical *entremeses* and *sainetes* from later in the century include the following: *El baile del tapicero* (1765), composed in Buenos Aires by someone named Lucena, about whom nothing is known beyond the authorship of the piece;[17] the anonymous *Entremés de la vieja y el viejo* (1790), which was composed and performed in Arequipa, Peru, as part of the celebrations marking the ascension of Charles IV to the Spanish throne;[18] the *Entremés gracioso de Juanillo y de Antonio Desaciertos* and the *Coloquio de las comparaciones de doña Elena y el casamentero*, two anonymous plays composed in Quito, probably toward the end of the century;[19] the anonymous *El valiente y la fantasma*, first performed in Buenos Aires in the late 1790s.[20]

Several short pieces from late eighteenth-century Mexico are particularly noteworthy as examples of the *costumbrista* theatrical mode. *El pleyto y querella de los guajolotes*, an anonymous *sainete* from Puebla,

---

[16] Monforte y Vera's play is in Lohmann Villena, *El arte dramático en Lima*, and Molina's play is in both Barrera, *Historia de la literatura ecuatoriana*, and Descalzi, *Historia crítica* vol. VI.

[17] The text is in Bosch, *Historia del teatro en Buenos Aires*.

[18] The text is in Trenti Rocamora, "El teatro y la jura de Carlos IV en Arequipa."

[19] Fragments of the *entremés* and the complete text of the *coloquio* can be found in Barrera, *Historia*.   [20] The text is in Bosch, *Teatro antiguo de Buenos Aires*.

Mexico, presents a legal dispute between a black woman and an Indian woman, arising from the death of the latter's prized turkey. With a brevity characteristic of the genre, the play manages a vivid satirical portrait of the lower-class litigants, as well as of the cynical and self-interested middle-class clerics and judges to whom the women appeal for justice. Two other plays that also excel in the portrayal of the Mexican lower classes are the dramatic monologue *El charro* and the short satirical piece *Los remendones*, both composed by José Agustín de Castro (1730–1814) and published in 1797.

The Argentinian *sainete El amor de la estanciera*, composed, possibly by Juan Bautista Maciel (?–?), some time during the last decades of the century, both captures the essence of eighteenth-century *costumbrismo* and helps to inaugurate the important nineteenth-century movement of "gauchesque" literature.[21] The play's hero, Juancho Perucho, who successfully competes for the hand of Chepa, a country maiden, is a prototype of the countless rough-hewn but amiable gauchos of Argentinian letters. The play's villain is a pompous and cowardly Portuguese, whose rivalry with Juancho prefigures the dialogue between "civilization" and "barbarism," as embodied in European and creole culture, respectively, that was to be the thematic cornerstone of nineteenth-century Argentinian literature. The play's emphasis on Argentinian speech, customs, and psychology seems to reflect both a creole pride and an alienation from Europe and Europeans. *El amor de la estanciera*, perhaps more than any other extant play of the period, is a clear example of the confluence of the *costumbrista* mode in colonial theatre and the regionalist sentiments of the creole class. It heralds the demise of the colonial system and the emergence of the national cultures and political entities of Spanish America.

[21] The Ripoll and Valdespino anthology, *Teatro hispanoamericano*, modernizes the orthography of the text, taken from the 1925 edition published by the University of Buenos Aires.

13

The nineteenth-century Spanish American novel
Antonio Benítez-Rojo

Andrés Bello: nationalism and narrativity

In his article "Modo de escribir la historia" (1848), Andrés Bello (1781–1865) gave the following advice: "When the history of a country exists only in scattered, incomplete documents, in vague traditions which must be compared and evaluated, the narrative method is obligatory." With this judgment Bello disqualified any effort to write works of philosophy of history because he considered it, in the case of Spanish America, premature. He thought the history of a young nation ought to be far removed from theoretical generalizations, that it ought to be a concrete narrative based on the examination and comparative study of those sources which refer to American events since the pre-Columbian era. One may suppose that Bello's intention was to give the new nations ample room to develop historiographical discourse, an enterprise then in its infancy, before it was to be judged by more demanding standards of historiography. Nevertheless, I think there was another motive behind his strategy, a concern related to the question of nationalism. We can see this additional objective in his praise of the work of Bernal Díaz del Castillo: "no synthesis, no collection of historical aphorisms, will ever allow us to conceive so vividly the conquest of America" ("Modo de estudiar la historia," 246). In other words, Bello favored the writing of history in narrative form because such a form, with the vitality of its story-telling, made it possible for the reader to identify with the protagonists of the exploration and conquest of the American territories. The Spanish chronicles were not the only ones that stood out among his preferences. In his note on the publication in Mexico of the *Manuscrito de Chimalpain*, he celebrated the narrative language of the Aztec chronicler and he recommended that the old codices and indigenous chronicles be studied, since they had related incidents of the Conquest "in a manner favorable to the concerns and the interests of the mother country" ("Colección de los viajes y descubrimientos que hicieron por mar los españoles desde fines del siglo XV"). One should not forget that, in accordance with the ideas of Johann Gottfried von Herder (1774–1803), Bello stressed the importance of these works "as products of the earliest period of American literature."

It is no accident that Bello named his Chilean newspaper *El Araucano*. Like the enlightened proponents of independence in his youth, Bello was very conscious of being a participant in the immense task of the creation of nations. He knew as well that one of the most practical ways to consolidate the unstable and divided societies emerging from the wars of liberation was to connect them, by means of the written word, to a common nature, a common land, the pre-Columbian land which had always been there. In this way the National Territory, recently surveyed and described with pride in republican cartography, would seem legitimized by a story that flowed towards an immemorial past; a *utilitarian* story that, following the bifurcated design of a genealogical tree, spoke of Enlightenment, of Renaissance, of Europe, of Spain, of Discovery and Conquest, of Rome and Christianity; but also of Tenochtitlán and of Cuzco, of Moctezuma and Atahualpa, of Cuauhtémoc and Caupolicán, and finally of Quetzalcóatl or Gugumatz, of Manco Cápac and Mama Ocllo, the mythical founders of *Terra Nostra*.

When he questioned the objectivity of the philosophy of history, Bello did not mention that his proposal was aiming toward a predetermined goal; to propagate nationalism. It is true that the term "nationalism" was not yet current in his era, but he understood its meaning as a practice designed to manipulate the differences which are in play in a given sociocultural arena, either in order to include or gather them together as native to the land, or in order to exclude or isolate them as alien. There is no doubt that Bello's judgments on this matter owed much to romantic literature, whose principal objectives had included the search for origins and national identities for prophetic purposes. Exiled in London between 1810 and 1823, Bello had seen the birth of Walter Scott's (1771–1832) cycle of historical novels. His notes and commentaries on the works of Augustin Thierry (1795–1856), and other historians who wrote in a narrative style, indicate that his ideas on the relationship between history, narrative, the search for origins, and nationalism were the product of long reflection.

In any case, one must conclude that none of the cultural promoters of the first half of the nineteenth century – Domingo Delmonte (1804–1854), Esteban Echeverría (1805–1851) – appreciated as did Bello the formidable capacity of an emerging body of writing, both historical and fictional, to spread forms of national identity. In 1841, in his very noteworthy study of the work of Alonso de Ercilla (1533–1594), he had mentioned the foundational role of literature: "we ought to suppose that *La Araucana*, Chile's *Aeneid*, composed in Chile, is familiar to the people of Chile, to date the only modern nation whose founding has been immortalized in an epic poem" ("*La Araucana* por Don Alonso de Ercilla y Zúñiga," 362). Nevertheless, Bello does not write this article in order to propose poetry as the most appropriate genre to promote a Spanish American identity. In spite of the importance of his own work in this regard – *Alocución a la poesía* (1823), *A la agricultura de la zona tórrida* (1826) – Bello understands that his era belongs to the novel: "These descriptions of social life [...] constitute the favorite epic of modern times, and it represents for societies at the present juncture the rhapsodies of Homer's century and the rhymed ballads of the Middle Ages. A particular form of fictional history corresponds to each social era, to each modification of culture, to each new development in intelligence. The form of our time is the novel" ("*La Araucana*," 355).

In effect, closely linked to the rise of the European middle class, the novel had become the preeminent literary genre of modern times, as Bello noted. The revolutions which had taken place in the fields of knowledge, technology, and political and economic ideas, as well as the reorganization of society itself, had opened up enormous spaces which demanded commentary not only encyclopedic and journalistic, but also fictional. At the time when Bello wrote those words, the novel had already become a cultural item of export merchandise that was read with increasing interest by an international, middle-class public which recognized itself in its characters. Although its importation had been subject to restrictions in the American colonies, its spread had not been completely impeded. After independence had been achieved, the new republics began a long and difficult process of reorganization that demanded structural transformations of all kinds. It was time to build nations, to put people on the road of "progress," a word then inevitable. Each educated person had formulated in his mind an impassioned national project, and the printed word, as an essentially urban sign of order and power, would be deployed for many years to expound such schemes. Although it was read in America as a novelty, the novel became the most suitable literary vehicle to carry out these strategies. Its discourse was a kind of inventory of languages which commented on everything and lent itself to everything. The novel contained popularized versions of the new scientific, social, and political theories next to depictions of the virtues, the passions, the vices, and the hopes of the human being; it spoke of the medieval castle as well as of the manufacturing city, and it described both daily life and the exotic landscape. In the grip of its seductive narrative power, the reader imagined, as his own, past times that he was never to see, adventures and experiences that he was never to have. But it must also be noted that in Spanish America the novel served like no other literary genre to reinforce in the reader the idea that he was living immersed in a physical and sociocultural space, recently become independent, that was called Chile, Mexico, or Argentina. Such a space (its geographical and ethnological complexity) had been more or less described in the old chronicles and documents, in the poetry and drama of the baroque period, in the scientific diaries and the travel books, and in the informative articles and the *costumbrista* pieces of recent journalistic prose. Nevertheless, it was only now, as he identified with the characters of local novels, that the common reader had for the first time the illusion that he was really experiencing the National Territory, with its rivers, mountains, valleys, flora, fauna, roads, villages, and cities – a kind of telluric matrix where the collective memory preserved both the ancient toponymy and the traditions of the land. And not only that, as he accompanied the protagonists through the tangles of the novelist's plot, the reader entered into imaginary contact with the voices of a human conglomerate whose races, social classes, and customs could be very different from his own. Moreover, the novel also contributed in no small measure to the reading public's participation in the first debates about what was, what ought to be, what should be included and excluded from the idea of the Argentinian identity, the Chilean, or the Mexican, and even what was and what ought to be the Spanish American identity. But, above all, the novel served as a public platform for the debate over a key issue in the history of Spanish American thought: the relationship between Nationness and Modernness.

Nationness and Modernness in the Spanish American novel

No one finishes the process of becoming a complete citizen of a nation. One is always in deficit, among other reasons because the concept of nationality is constantly manipulated by a country's ideologizing factions and is, therefore, in continuous disequilibrium. As Benedict Anderson points out, it is probably the imaginary nature of words like "nation," "national," and "nationality" that has prevented world-class theoreticians from concerning themselves with an analysis of the question of nationalism. But here the difficulty lies not only in achieving a working definition of the term in multicultural countries, but also in the tendency of nationalist practices to connect an event in the present with a rationally unconnected past. One should observe that in a text that speaks of Nationness, contemporary and past referents are mixed. In this way the nationalist message carries off the imagination of the listener or reader to a prestigious and perfect – although altogether impossible – past. And this without mentioning the openly heteroclitic character of nationalist discourse, especially in Spanish America. As we know, such discourse in Europe is generally dominated by doctrinaire and didactic forms of a monologic kind, such as foundational myths and legends, hymns and civil prayers, biographies of heroes, school texts of history and civics, pieces of oratory and of epic literature that construct a kind of panoply or legitimizing heraldry that refers to the Greco-Roman tradition and to Christianity. In the Americas, however, given the obvious fragmentation of the sociocultural surface, nationalist discourse tends to become dispersed, expressing itself in monologic and dialogic forms. Such forms, in addition to those mentioned above, include important strata of lyric, drama, and essay, as well as the narrative genres (the chronicle, the local color sketch, the short story, the novel) and folklore (proverbs, jokes, popular drama and poetry, songs, lore). These expressions refer ultimately to a sociocultural space furnished both by modern ideas (from the Enlightenment on, *grosso modo*) and by ancient oral traditions originating in indigenous America, black Africa, and medieval Europe. It is no wonder that Miguel Hidalgo proclaimed Mexican Independence under the aegis of revolutionary ideas of the Enlightenment and the advocacy of the Virgin of Guadalupe, nor that the Associations of Veterans of the Independence War in Cuba was the institution that established the Virgin of Caridad del Cobre as Cuba's national patron. The cults pertaining to these madonnas spring from syncretic myths that from early colonial times express a desire, a hope, for racial and sociocultural equality. This yearning to channel toward a common destiny the various ethnological factors coinciding in the country (Indoamerican, European, African) is a necessary antecedent of the more complex desire for nationality. Even more, the fact that Spanish American nationalist practices – including strategies of art, dance, music, and literature – preserve these old integrating desires, corroborates Anderson's opinion that the so-called "national sentiment" is engaged more in cultural discourse than in ideological or political discourse. If to this we add Fernand Braudel's penetrating observation that cultural systems last much longer than social, economic, and political ones, we can better appreciate the tremendous importance of the nationalist phenomenon in general. This importance, ever more visible in the contemporary world, demands not only the study of nationalism within the cultural sphere but also the manipulation of its discourse by other discourses. We are concerned here, of course, only with the study of the relationships between nationalism, modernity, and Spanish American literature, an area that has been brilliantly analyzed in recent years by Doris Sommer (1991), Roberto González Echevarría (1990), Carlos J. Alonso (1990), Gustavo Pérez-Firmat (1989), Julio Ramos (1989), Antonio Cornejo Polar (1989), Josefina Ludmer (1988), and Benedict Anderson (1983). It goes without saying that my opinions owe a great deal to these researchers.

Now then, once the mimetic displacement peculiar to all desire – as

René Girard has seen – has created in the minds of an influential part of the social group those imaginary ties of nationality, it is no longer possible to avoid speaking of it. Among other reasons, for the simple one that no-one is born with a given national sentiment, in the same way that no-one is born with a given culture. It is necessary, therefore, to saturate each new generation with the historico-cultural discourse that speaks of Nationness; its constant propagation guarantees the continuity of the fatherland. Furthermore, considering that Nationness is always under debate, its various versions make it necessary to refer to earlier stories which can serve as centers of legitimation, a practice that tends to diversify in a *utilitarian* way the history of the nation. This cluster of recurring stories is broadcast in a fragmentary fashion through an institutional network which, manipulated by the groups in power, extends from the family to the government, from the school to the armed forces, from the press to the political party and the union. Many of these stories, like the myths of the Mexican and Cuban virgins, have a great deal in common with the stories told by the African *griots* to transmit local tradition, and they are thus a part of the paradigm of a pre-scientific knowledge, or as Jean-François Lyotard so aptly terms it, a "narrative" knowledge. It is therefore no wonder that the varied pot-pourri which speaks of Spanish American identity was seen by the intelligentsia of modernity as an anomaly ("mystery," "enigma") that had to be corrected – Domingo Faustino Sarmiento (1811–1888) in *Facundo* (1845) – or poeticized – José Martí (1853–1895) in *Nuestra América* (1890) – given its reluctance to conform to the scientific canon. Observe that, unlike disciplinary works, the nationalist stories need meet no requirements to prove their competence; they authorize themselves as they speak of autochthonous nature, of the land, of the fatherland, of their mythic or real heroes – in other words, reconstructing the past.

All the above may perhaps help to explain why in Spanish American countries there is so much talk about the writer's responsibility to the people. In fact, I think that what is asked of the intellectual is the same thing that Bello was demanding: a nationalist work, or at least a work that would contribute to perpetuating the debate about national identity. It is an inevitable demand since without the cooperation of patriotic practices (their institutionalization, their authority, their power), it would have been difficult for the unstable and fragmentary societies of Latin America, sunk in the despair of chronic underdevelopment and prevented from leaving the periphery of the world economic system, to maintain the cohesion, however precarious, which it has managed to sustain from colonial times to the present.

Now then, if one may say that demonstrations of nationalism can be seen as absurd because of their need simultaneously to conjugate versions of the past and of the present, one must conclude that the relationship between Nationness and Modernness is equally paradoxical, since the first concept concerns itself with the origins of a sociocultural group in a given territory and the second concept looks towards the future of the world. In that sense, one can say that any attempt to connect Nationness and Modernness on the same hierarchical level, as occurs in Spanish America, calls into question the continuity of the relationships between past, present, and future – in other words, Spanish America as a historico-cultural entity and as a viable socioeconomic utopia. Such a paradox would seem to be irreducible because it is present at the moment of the founding of the Spanish American states. One should remember that the arguments which led the Founding Fathers of Independence to secede from the Spanish Empire were, on the one hand, the unjust secondary role the Creole played within the colonial Spanish system, and on the other hand, the anachronism of the mother country's political, economic, and educational institutions with respect to those of the Enlightenment. Thus in the case of the Spanish American societies one can say that the desires of national identity and those of modernity were expressed within the same proposition. Likely such a paradox came into being when the ideas of the Enlightenment brought influence to bear on the process of the formation of national sentiment. In any case, the confluence of both desires within one discourse, which could be called "Nationness/Modernness" in order to emphasize both its *excessive* character and its internal *tension*, would seem to have been inevitable. Later, throughout the century, the paradox of Nationness was to be debated and supposedly resolved by means of a voluminous and varied register of projects. Among the hundreds of authors who most contributed then to carry forward and to diversify this discourse – which has become the Spanish American discourse – one must cite names such as: Andrés Bello, José de la Luz y Caballero (1800–1862), Esteban Echeverría, Juan Bautista Alberdi (1810–1884), Domingo Faustino Sarmiento, José Victorino Lastarria (1817–1888), Francisco Bilbao (1823–1865), Juan Montalvo (1832–1889), Eugenio María de Hostos (1839–1903), Manuel González Prada (1848–1918), Justo Sierra Méndez (1848–1912), José Martí. Nevertheless, "the Spanish American enigma" – as Martí said in 1890 – could not be resolved by the "European book" or the "Yankee book"; it could not even be resolved by the Spanish Americans themselves, perhaps because they never had within their reach the ability to modernize in an autonomous way, that is to say, to build Modernness on Nationness (the Europe of the Common Market, the United States, Japan). Thus it is that *to be* a Mexican, an Argentinian, or a Peruvian is to be reborn again and again within the tension of Nationness/Modernness, a condition the Spanish American peoples share with those of other economically dependent countries that wish to modernize.

Nevertheless, I think one can agree that behind this pessimistic proposition one can see the shape of a common desire that is productive in more than one sense. Because it preserves the perfection of an epic moment that never existed in the past (the paradise lost of the "first" founding) nor ever will exist in the foreseeable future (the final victory of progress as a positivistic utopia), such a desire or dream not only brings the fatherland and its history to a rebirth through its perpetual discourse of reconstruction, but also helps to regulate institutionally the political and social conduct of the individual through the mechanism of exclusion and inclusion carried within every desire, every project. Thus, behind the contradictory appearance of Latin American expressions of Nationness and Modernness, there lies a hidden order: a community of institutionalized interests that tacitly accepts the contingencies of the imaginary and the unforeseeable for the sake of fending off the danger of social dissolution. It is this community of institutionalized interests, always deployed at the edge of catastrophe, whence the national literatures of Spanish America emerged, especially the nineteenth-century novel.

Now then, the space for legitimization of the national literatures of the Americas is not limited to their respective National Territories. They could not be confined only to the latter because, unlike European literatures, neither their language nor their genres are autochthonous; even more, not even their claims to autochthony are genealogically autochthonous. Thus, as Juan Marinello saw, there is also a means of extraterritorial legitimization that cannot be evaded even within the most radical forms of literary or cultural nationalism. The American referent (let us say, an Aymara Indian, his social life, his culture), before being invested with Nationness, turns out to be *prelinguistic*, since in order to enroll in Nationness it ought to be signified by the language of Europe (not by the Aymara language) within the epistemological, cultural, and literary criteria of Europe. In this way, one could say that the more autochthonous a novel proposes to be (*Enriquillo*, *Cumandá*, *Aves sin nido*), the more exotic it will turn out to be, since it will be narrating autochthonous matters in a language that speaks from outside not only about nature and the Indian (the Eurocentric language of anthropology), but also about the author of the novel itself. But this is only part of the problem, because if our author were to decide to write a narrative proposing a project of social or political reform (*El periquillo sarniento*, [*The Itching Parrot*] *Francisco*, *Facundo*, *Amalia*), the language of the Other, however "liberal" it may be, would exclude the author himself as the only author of the proposal. All of this takes place, I repeat, not only because the Spanish American writer, in order to be *Spanish American*, needs the European language – I do not refer here to the Spanish language in itself – but also above all because such a language has constructed the *epistemé* appropriate to the West (its disciplines, its systems, its strategies, its paradoxes, its blind spots) and claims its legitimacy *only* in European institutions, the novel being one of them. In conclusion, the referents proposed as autochthonous in any novel (the jungle, the volcano, indigenous music, etc.) are mediated by the anthropological discourse of the Other, although the writer may have been born within that particular tradition. But not everything is Otherness in Spanish American literature, since in an analogous manner, the referents of European precedence (Christianity, Progress, the Republic, Science, the Novel, and even Language itself) are mediated by the writer's desire to enroll in the land. I think Marinello was referring to this double mediation or *noise* when he said that finally it was a question of a language that was "ours" in spite of being foreign.

Certainly, I think there is a Spanish American novel distinct from others in the world. But I also believe that such a novel exists not because it constitutes a coherent set of texts produced across the map of Spanish America at a given time, united axiologically, ontologically, structurally, stylistically, referentially or intertextually. Instead, the Spanish American novel as such exists because it has been constructed and is being constructed by an *interplay* of national novels that, although differing from one another, show parallel asymmetries, interferences, and discontinuities, particularly in how they inscribe themselves in Nationness in ways that are non-linear and conflicting. That is to say, these novels reach at the same time for two mutually exclusive sources to legitimize their language, both of which are unattainable. On the one hand, America (the autochthonous, the Mother), and on the other, Europe (the modern, the Father). These novels also reflect a prelinguistic being that identifies with Nature but has been veiled by the language of the Other (Europe), and present a dialogue about modernity with the Other that is in turn obscured by the prelinguistic desire to identify with Nature.

Contexts of the novels of Spanish America

In order to emphasize the influence that French ideas had on educated Creoles, it is customary to say that Francisco de Miranda, after reading *Histoire philosophique et politique des établissements et du commerce des Européens dans les deux Indes* (1770) by the Abbé Raynal (1713–1796), and *Les Incas* (1777) by Jean-François Marmontel (1723–1799), decided to name his utopia of independent American states "Incanato". The anecdote is true, but one must put it in a context where European ideas coexist with autonomous thought that had already been engaged in a critical dialogue with the rigid criteria of the Spanish administration. One ought to remember that the cultural contradictions between Creoles and Spaniards were already becoming apparent at the beginning of the seventeenth century, even in the bosom of the church, as Thomas Gage points out in the case of Mexico. A rivalry of this kind, as it grew stronger with time, in the eighteenth century reached moments of open confrontation. The peasants and artisans did not rebel because they had read Voltaire (1694–1778) and Jean-Jacques Rousseau (1712–1778) or in order to emulate the minutemen of the North American Revolution – as has been suggested on occasion – but because of concrete abuses by the Spanish authorities: the repression of the communal institutions, the commercial monopoly of cacao or tobacco, the increasing taxes, the military draft, the favoritism in legal matters. One must also consider the repercussions of the African and indigenous uprisings, examples of which were the very prolonged resistance of the Palmares Blacks in the seventeenth century and the Túpac Amaru rebellion (1780–1781), whose purpose was to reestablish insofar as possible the ancient Tahuantinsuyo. The Haitian war of liberation (1791–1804) was no less influential. Toussaint Louverture's victories over the French and English troops and, especially, the easy capture of the Spanish Santo Domingo, provided tangible proof to the Spanish American Creoles that independence was viable.

In like manner, in this century of colonial crisis, Jesuit Humanism infiltrated the pedagogical system with an understanding of the indigenous people and of their culture which was, in itself, to have relevant impact on the nationalist thought of the educated Creoles. Furthermore, as is known, before their expulsion from Spanish dominions (1767), the Jesuits drew maps, built missions, created communication networks, studied the native languages, and published important historical works and treatises with information on geography, ethnography, and the flora and the fauna of the most remote regions of the continent. One should remember, among others, the handsome book *El Orinoco ilustrado*, by José Gumilla, with editions published in 1741, 1745, and 1791. Once in exile, the Jesuits wrote such noteworthy books as the *Storia antica del Messico* by Francisco Javier Clavijero (1731–1787). Or, insofar as literature is concerned, the *Rusticatio Mexicana* by Rafael Landívar (1731–1793), whose bucolic vision of rural life constitutes a predecessor to Bello's *Silvas americanas*.

At the time of the appearance of these more or less local examples, which were a prelude to the emergence of Nationness, the Creoles with the most radical ideas (the case of Miranda) read the critics of the Spanish colonial enterprise with the voracity of disciples: Voltaire, Rousseau, Denis Diderot (1713–1784), Etienne Bonnot de Condillac (1715–1780), Jean Le Rond d'Alembert (1717–1783). This period also saw the appearance of the historical works of the Abbé Raynal and William Robertson (1721–1793), which, although prohibited by the Inquisition, were to arouse the lively interest of the generation at the end of the century. In this almost subversive climate, Bartolomé de las Casas (1474–1566) was recovered as a fashionable author. His *Brevísima relación de la destruc-ción de las Indias* was reedited in Paris, London, and Philadelphia, even in Bogotá and in Puebla. In addition, gazettes and newspapers appeared in the principal cities. In them, as Mariano Picón Salas observes, one can trace day by day, from capital to capital, how all the fascinating utopias elaborated by the eighteenth century rose in the creole consciousness. And not only that, the print media above all helped to spread the sentiment of Nationness and the yearning for progress. News from the interior and from abroad, financial and mercantile information, port traffic statistics, scientific and literary articles, notes on cultural activities, government announcements, and statistics of all kinds appeared in their pages. In this atmosphere of foreign books and local newspapers, the discourse of Nationness as a construction of thought emerges as a precursor of independence. Francisco Eugenio de Santa Cruz y Espejo (1747–1795), Francisco de Miranda, Manuel de Salas (1735–1841), Miguel José Sanz (1754–1814), Antonio Nariño (1765–1823), Fray Servando Teresa de Mier (1765–1827), Mariano Moreno (1778–1811) and so many others.

Throughout the century, from the navigation of Amédée-François Frezier (1712–1714) to the journeys of Alexander von Humboldt (1799–1804), a constellation of learned men visit the Americas. As Mario Hernández Sánchez-Barba points out, in their deepest motivation the journeys of the Enlightenment not only represented the impulse of an era but they also, further, shaped projects of uniting the scientific and literary enterprises. The result of these expeditions takes shape in an essential collection of beautifully illustrated books which, in serene, neoclassic prose, combine scientific curiosity and the explorer's tale. But these travelers leave something more: they contribute to the transition of a creole consciousness, limited by a parochial way of seeing the world, to a consciousness we could now call nationalist and modern. One must conclude that without the presence in America of the Spanish astronomer and botanist José Celestino Mutis, for example, it is unlikely that the genius of Francisco José de Caldas (1770?–1816) would have reached the distinction necessary to accomplish his modern work of geography or to publish in 1807 his very noteworthy *Semanario de la Nueva Granada*. Certainly, the emergence of the national, disciplinary discourses in the various colonies owes much to the visits of the European scientists. Furthermore, such studious travels awoke in the cities a curiosity for the landscapes of the interior, for the ruins of indigenous monuments, and for the picturesque customs of the villages. Indeed, when they saw that the hinterland of their own viceroyalty awoke the interest of the most famous scientists in the world – Charles La Condamine, Alexander von Humboldt, etc. – the Creoles of the capital cities began at once to want it for themselves. Because of the mimetic property of desire, they appropriated the Other's desire for the American natural landscape, "their" nature, which they had scorned until then, in the same way as they had scorned "their" Indians. When they took this step, establishing an imaginary connection between the walled enclosure of the city and the indigenous scene of the interior, these Creoles began to construct Nationness.

In summary, already conditioned by a nativistic desire to represent the land with ever-increasing complexity – a phenomenon which can be observed in the trajectory of baroque poetry, let us say from Bernardo de Balbuena (1568–1627) to Rafael Landívar – the creole writers were motivated to write for reasons both internal and external. Or, perhaps, to state the case more concretely: because of the desire to legitimize themselves in autochthonous nature and in local color and, at the same time, because of the desire to imitate, from utilitarian postures, the institutions of modern Europe. It is precisely this bifurcated desire, impossible to summarize dialectically by a synthesis, that defines Nationness in Spanish America and that characterizes its *paradoxical* and *excessive* discourse. Hence the ambiguity and the density of Spanish American novels, with regard to the matter of legitimization.

The first literary manifestations to speak of the nation would be poems idealizing both nature and the native American, historical–cultural essays, travel accounts, satirical verses and dialogues, and theatrical and descriptive pieces exalting local color. Aided by the then recent practice of supplying the reader with graphic images that sought to represent the *picturesque* quality of particular landscapes and human types, such texts contributed a great deal to the formation of a desire for the National Territory. Furthermore, this dense protocol, a great part of which appeared in periodical publications, produced the varied mass of texts that is required, as a referent, by the totalizing and dialogic discourse of the novel. As shall be seen, the first novelists of Mexico, Cuba, Argentina, etc., did not put into their works new ideas about Nationness, but rather ideas which had already appeared in the press, including at times ideas from works they themselves had penned. The novelty of these initial novels lay not in their ideological, political, economic, social, or cultural propositions. All such propositions can be read, scattered here and there in pages that preceded the novel. The novelty, and the truly characteristic thing, was that as the development of the genre in Europe coincided with the emergence of Nationness in Spanish America, the novel constituted the first literary machine capable of *simultaneously* narrativizing such propositions, however heterogeneous they might be, and offering them to the reader in the form of a single story. The effectiveness of the genre, its productivity, its flexibility, and above all its ability to allegorize the most varied situations and to collect voices and materials belonging to different disciplines and systems of knowledge, were the qualities that allowed the genre to become the ideal literary vehicle to represent and debate the tension caused by the desire for Nationness and Modernness.

As far as the innumerable novelistic models offered by European literatures are concerned – the most visible surface of extraterritorial legitimization – one would have to say that they were not unrestrictedly imitated by Spanish Americans. Generally they took from those models what suited the national projects being discussed in each country. A novel like *Atala* (1801), by François René de Chateaubriand (1768–1848), which spoke about American landscapes and indigenous societies, captivated the imaginations of creole readers. For them the pages of the book held not a mere sentimental conflict, but a real question of primary importance within their sociocultural problematics. For parallel reasons, as will be seen later, certain novels by Alain-René Lesage (1668–1747), Oliver Goldsmith (1728–1774), Jacques-Henri Bernardin de Saint-Pierre (1737–1814), Scott, Stendhal (1783–1842), Alessandro Manzoni (1785–1873), James Fenimore Cooper (1789–1851), Alphonse de Lamartine (1790–1869), Honoré de Balzac (1799–1850), Victor Hugo (1802–1885), Alexandre Dumas (1802–1870), Eugène Sue (1804–1857), George Sand (1804–1876), Charles Dickens (1812–1870), Emile Zola (1840–1902), José María de Pereda (1833–1906), Benito Pérez Galdós (1843–1920), and others awakened a similar interest and were taken for the sake of Nationness. In reality, it can be said that they were *nationalized*, understanding here that "nationalization" is the expropriation of a foreign discourse by subjects (writers) of a nation for the purpose of transforming it so that it may serve the nation (the literary tradition). As a result, references to the European novel found in Spanish American narratives ought not to be seen as the result of disinterested, accidental, passive, or merely imitative intertextual relationships, but, on the contrary, as the product of utilitarian relationships (expropriation) providing benefits (prestige, authority, power) to the economy of the national novel.

Now then, the practice of nationalizing foreign texts was not applied in a global manner to the different artistic movements that were sprinkled about in Europe throughout the nineteenth century, but rather it was applied to certain strata of specific works which, written according to such aesthetics, could serve to articulate nationalist mechanisms in Spanish America, depending on the different situations in which the various countries found themselves. Indeed, as the Spanish American writers took these fragments from here and there, from old novels and new, guided often by a utilitarianism in which the national question counted for more than artistic achievement, they did not adjust completely to the successive canons that put the artistic history of Europe in order: Neoclassicism, Romanticism, Realism, etc. Thus it is that Fernando Alegría speaks of the presence of a "romantic realism" and of a

"naturalistic realism" in the Spanish American novel. This particularity –
the artistic anachronism exhibited by the varying materials of one single
work – constitutes the most serious obstacle that must be overcome by any
chronological organization that takes into account the sequence in which
aesthetic movements are expressed in Europe. In a like manner, the
tendency to disregard national literary differences in favor of a unity of
Spanish American literature has contributed to the construction of global
chronological organizations based on a supposedly organic succession of
the "literary generations" of authors. In fact such efforts, although they
may be useful for the unfolding of critical discourse, cannot explain, for
example, why certain neoclassic strategies survived in "romantic" and
"realist" novels, or why Spanish American Romanticism lasted in certain
countries until the last years of the nineteenth century, or why the
"naturalist" novels of the 1890s exhibited characteristics reminiscent of
previous aesthetics, or why the "Generation of 1880" in Argentina wrote
on urban themes while the literary theme of growing currency in Peru was
the Indian.

The study of the relationship among Nationness, Modernism, and the
novel, however, helps to define the problematics of the study of Spanish
American literature and, at the same time, offers partial answers to
questions such as those I have posed above. For example, the long
duration of romantic strata in the novel could be explained by the fact that
until the 1870s – when the most obsessive attempts at institutional and
economic modernization begin in some countries – certain tendencies of
Romanticism (the idealization of nature and of local color, for example)
served nationalist purposes better than those of Realism. Of course, not
all romantic models offered the same possibilities of acting as mechanisms
to consolidate the nation. The Gothic modality, for example, was scarcely
cultivated in Spanish America because of its obvious limitations for
communicating nationalism. The Scott-type historical novel, on the other
hand, given its inclination to construct foundational romances – as
Sommer has seen – and to offer interpretations of past events (the roots of
the nation) from a modern perspective, was a favorite genre of Spanish
American writers (*Guatimozín*, *Yngermina*, *La novia del hereje*, *El
Inquisidor Mayor*, *Enriquillo*). German Romanticism did not have a
direct influence in Spanish America, unlike French Romanticism, whose
two currents – a conservative one (Chateaubriand) and a liberal one
(Hugo, Sue) – aroused a great interest, in particular the latter, since,
because of its late emergence, it brought nineteenth-century social ideas
that suited the tastes of the more radicalized young people. As Cedomil
Goic has observed, the romantic models generally taken were politically
and socially *constructive*, since they ought to have served the purposes of
consolidating and perfecting the nation. Thus it was not so much the
romantic aesthetic in itself but some of its tendencies and themes that

generated in writers the desire to take the European product for the sake of Nationness.

In reality, the 1870s provide an important panorama of changes and discontinuities helpful for the study of the Spanish American novel. In this period, nationalist discourse was transformed by a new manner of desiring modernity that in practice became the so-called "process of modernization." Of course, such a process did not occur simultaneously in all countries, but it did constitute a general, irreversible trend in spite of the resistance it encountered among conservative powers (the church, the *gamonal*, the slave-holding planter). It originated when the rhythm of industrialization picked up in the centers of world capitalism, with a consequent increase in demand for cereals, meat, sugar, coffee, cacao, tobacco, leather, wool, rubber, wood, minerals, and other goods. Such demands required that peripheral economies (among them, those of Spanish America) gain a more visible position in the global system under a new commercial and financial regime – necessarily of a deficit type since the local production was technologically weak – which has been extensively studied under the name of "dependent capitalism," "economic imperialism," and "neocolonialism."

As far as the novel is concerned, the desire for Modernness had been channeled until then via the codes of the Enlightenment, commercial capitalism, utopian socialism, and Romanticism; henceforth it would be channeled via the codes of industrial capitalism, of the new scientific-social discourse – Auguste Comte (1798–1857), Alexis de Tocqueville (1805–1859), Herbert Spencer (1820–1903) – and those of Realism and Naturalism. The interests of this second era, however, would not manage to displace completely those of the first, since the growth of industrial production in the capitalist world did not envision (or rather denied) the possibility that Latin America would modernize its traditional structures in depth. We cannot speak here, thus, of a true substitution of the new for the old, but rather of the critical coexistence of two different manners of desiring modernity. This tension contributed to the even greater fragmentation and dispersal of the nationalist discourse, to such an extent that in the novels of the end of the century – let us say, *La charca* (1895) by Manuel Zeno Gandía (1855–1930) – one can often see the combination of strata of Romanticism (lyricism), Realism (irony), and Naturalism (pessimism). One can appreciate the passage from the first phase to the second of nineteenth-century novelistic production. In order to establish this, I will take the line that speaks of nature and of the "autochthonous" being.

It is easy to see that the ideas of the physiocratic school of political economy, that attributed the exclusive origin of wealth to nature and conferred upon agriculture a prevalence over industry, not only assisted in the Americas in the formation of the discourses of economics, geography, agronomy, and the natural sciences, but had also, beginning with Bello's

Silvas, prolonged prophetic–literary repercussions. Given the economic, scientific, and technological backwardness of the republics that emerged from Spanish colonialism, the relationship between nature and wealth seen by François Quesnay (1697–1774) still seemed exploitable to many Spanish Americans in the second half of the nineteenth century. Furthermore, the ideas the *philosophes* held of the Noble Savage (the Indian, the slave, and the peasant invested with nature) and the dream of achieving a universal civilization, had contributed both to the liberating purposes and to the first constitutional debates that took place in the Americas.

Indeed, Romanticism, far from dismantling the myth of nature and of the innocence of the "natural being," narrativized it sexually in the novels of Chateaubriand (the Indian) and in Hugo's *Bug-Jargal* (the African slave). As a result, with regard to nature and to its Noble Savages, many "romantic" Spanish Americans connected, via *Paul et Virginie* (1788), the ideas of the Enlightenment with those of Romanticism, pouring this construction into their works. In order to confirm this, one need only observe the frequency with which Indians, slaves, peasants, land owners, country dwellings, landscapes, rivers, valleys, forests, fields, pampas, mountains, flora, and fauna appear in literature prior to the modernization process. Even more, notice the abundance of agronomic and livestock references (plantations, cattle ranches, crops, orchards, groves, fruit trees, gardens, flowers, medicinal plants) associated with wealth, knowledge, happiness, romance, and the physical and moral qualities of the characters.

One ought not to be surprised, then, that Echeverría, in his literary program, has idealized the gaucho, or that in *Sab* Avellaneda saw the attributes of Cuban nationality in a slave-born mulatto, or that *Yngermina* (1844), the first national novel of Colombia, took the idyll of a conquistador and an Indian woman as the origin of the fatherland. In those years, Indians, gauchos, and Blacks formed a group exalted by the Enlightenment as well as by Romanticism. Furthermore, these early projects desired in the abstract a future of national unification; that is, a utopia where the factors of nationality would be harmoniously reconciled on the foundation of words such as "liberty," "equality," "fraternity," "civilization," and, of course, "nature". Years later, however, Sarmiento in his *Facundo* and Antonio José Morillas (1803–1881) in *El ranchador* (a Cuban story published in 1856), would include the Indian, the gaucho, the slave, and the *ranchador* (a hunter of runaway slaves) in the territory of *barbarism*. Why? Although they were somewhat disconcerted by their own propositions – as González Echevarría says, the "barbarian" was also *The Other-Within* – both authors simply had gathered in their respective countries the incipient signals of the second modern moment of which I have spoken, a positivistic moment where the Noble Savage would no longer have a real place. In effect, in the 1880s, the untamed pampa would be "pacified" and the slave-holding plantation would be "liberated"; society would begin to be restructured by industrial capitalism, and the Indian, the Indian camp, the frontier fort, the chieftain, the Indian revolt, the maroon, the slave barrack, the *palenque*, the slave hunter and his mastiffs, all would turn suddenly into national icons and soon would begin to illustrate the pages of urban, "white," histories of Argentina and Cuba as if they belonged to a distant past. Nevertheless, in other countries like Peru, Mexico, and Guatemala, where there prevailed an indigenous mass impossible to annihilate or assimilate, and many of the old colonial structures were maintained, positivistic ideas were expressed in projects that saw in education the solution to the "Indian problem." Here, contrary to what happened in Argentina, the Indian came to be ever more present in the novel, although as a factor that had to be transformed in order to be integrated into the modern nation. I should clarify, however, that if indeed I take the 1870s as the more or less general starting point of the new desire of modernization, there are before and after this point abundant literary examples that mediate between the two eras. They are works that serve as an epilogue to the ideas of the Enlightenment and Romanticism, and as a prologue to the impact of industrial capitalism and the ideas of Positivism.

In any case, as noteworthy growth took place in foreign investments and, especially, in exports to the industrial powers, the economic and social structures of the Spanish American countries experienced changes that had repercussions on nationalistic discourse. It is then that writers begin to pay greater attention to the realist models offered by Europe since the time of Balzac. In Chile, with Alberto Blest Gana (1830–1920), a narrative emerges that describes the process of substitutions of new values for old: to have money, to enjoy life, to triumph in society. Certainly the presence of nature will continue in the novel until well into our century, but not consistently. Further, it will no longer be an idyllic scene (*La vorágine, Doña Bárbara, Canaima*), but rather, at most, a nostalgic one (*Don Segundo Sombra, Los ríos profundos, La casa verde*). In truth, nature has ceased to be in style; in the literary climate of the era the modernized city, as well as its institutions, appears with ever greater insistence: the press, politics, the stock market, the business, the factory, the theatre, the café. The rural themes, although they coexist with urban ones, tackle different situations. The process of modernization changes the remote and picturesque region overnight into an economic center tied to the city by the railroad, the mail, the daily newspaper, and the telegraph. Thus it is that a regional novel appears, dominated at first by the small local epic and later by forms of Realism that describe new characters and conflicts. Of course, this modernization process, as I said, is limited both in breadth and in depth. The transformation of the old economic and social structures is a long way from being total and uniform, to the extent that there are countries in which the consequences of the process of change begin to be noticeable at the end of the century. Besides, around the new production zones there are peasant masses who live in a subsistence agricultural economy, or who work the landowners' fields in conditions like those in the times of Independence. In addition, neither are the benefits of modernization general: the flow of immigrants and of people from the country to the cities cheapens labor; social classes become more unequal and, for many, life becomes harder than before; there is an increase in poverty, unemployment, beggary, crime, prostitution, gambling, alcoholism. Furthermore, as the local economies become fully part of the Atlantic system, they are affected by the fall of prices in an ever more competitive market, as well as by stock market crashes and recessions and crises taking place in the centers of industrial capitalism. In reality, many of the old problems do not manage to get solved, at most they transform and coexist with the new difficulties. The Spanish American novel at the end of the century narrates this paradoxical process of change, especially in Argentina and in Mexico. In the same era, French literature offers the naturalist novel of Zola (his series *Rougon-Macquart*, 1871–1893) and, more importantly, his new narrative method based on "scientific" observation (*Le Roman experimental*, 1880). Thus, toward the end of the century, Zola's work will be nationalized by the better-read narrators.

In summary, the preceptive fiction that Bello proposed to speak of the nation was to be cultivated for many years. Except that Nationness, that element that spoke with a vested interest of nature, tradition, and progress in the language and knowledge of the Other, would rarely be represented with the aesthetic quality that Bello would perhaps have demanded. Trapped in the narrative mechanisms of the newspaper serial, oratory, *Costumbrismo*, allegory, and melodrama, the novels written in Spanish America used up in a few decades the simple programmatic outlines to which they subscribed without, for the rest, showing much artistic concern. One must agree that their authors – unlike Machado de Assis (1839–1908) in Brazil – did not achieve a deep understanding of the genre and, as a consequence, they did not contribute to its development. Nevertheless, in their favor, it is good to remember that a great part of Spanish American literary production was subject to political, religious, and social censorship, a situation that affected, among other things, its actual nationalist impact. In any case, beginning in the 1880s, when several countries of economic and demographic substance were involved in the illusory zeal of modernizing in European style, fiction tended to represent national realities with pessimism. Its most frequent characters were the bandit, the bad gaucho, the prostitute, the marginal person. That was perhaps due to the failure of the positivistic ideals that sustained the hegemonic groups in their task of leading their respective nations along the utopian road.

In the pages that follow I will comment upon a substantial group of novels that, with few exceptions, are quite well known. With regard to the much-discussed subject of what materials should or should not be included in the genre, I will take as my basis those critical opinions that seem to me most prudent. On such a controversial point, I have preferred to echo the empiricism of dominant currents rather than to attempt an originality that could turn out to be arbitrary. Certainly, as I work in this way, without adopting precise schemes of a taxonomic or normative sort, I have followed criteria with which I have not always been in agreement, especially because they did not consider certain texts to be novels. But, on the other hand, I think, as do many people, that the genre is still in development and does not lend itself to docile systemizations. Also, given that the Spanish American novel seems to resist any global attempt at chronological organization that takes its aesthetic premises into account – one ought to remember that *María* (1867), which takes a great deal of Chateaubriand's melancholy, was preceded by *Martín Rivas* (1862), that "Chileanizes" the Realism of Stendhal and Balzac – I have resolved to divide my commentary into two sections which allude in a vaguely chronological way to the role of the national novel in the two great socioeconomic moments of the nineteenth century in Spanish America. In truth, such a division, taking as its point of demarcation the 1870s does prove slightly problematic – what systematizing effort does not? – since a careful reading of these novels would recognize inconsistencies with respect to the periods I have indicated, as well as specificities appropriate to different modes and moments in which Nationness was debated in each country. These limitations, although smaller to my way of thinking than those offered by other schemes, make this brief study more useful for comparative purposes than for global ones.

Mexico: the work of José Joaquín Fernández de Lizardi

Repeated efforts have been made to represent as Spanish American novels certain texts written prior to *El periquillo sarniento* by José Joaquín Fernández de Lizardi. These efforts have not achieved a true consensus among critics, not only because of differences in current criteria used to define the novel but also because of the variety in points of view that can be used to judge the "Spanish Americanness" of a particular text or author. With this lack of consensus in mind, I have decided to follow the majority opinion and consider *El periquillo* as the first Spanish American novel properly speaking. I think, however, that although earlier works manifest uneven levels of Spanish Americanness and of narrativity which could indeed render them inadequate as novels, a mere inventory of these suffices to suggest a significant body of more or less narrativized texts which ought not to be ignored in more extensive studies. The apparently anti-canonical and dialogic orientation of some of these works deserves more than a cursory glance. Perhaps the interesting thing is not in wanting to demonstrate, for example, that *El Carnero* or *El lazarillo de ciegos caminantes* are novels, but rather in taking note – as José Juan Arrom and Enrique Pupo-Walker have done – that the organizing dynamics of fiction had infiltrated, beginning even in the conquest period, those various genres that were beginning to speak of America.

In any case, the publication of *El periquillo sarniento* helps to prove that, insofar as the Americas are concerned, the conditions that preceded the birth of the novel included the existence of a narrative tradition responding to a desire to write about the singularities of the New World, the foundation of the printing press and of educational and cultural institutions, the exercise of letters, the formation of the habit of reading among the middle and upper classes in colonial society, the impact of the ideas of the Enlightenment, the development of a creole consciousness, and the practice of a journalism that was nationalistic in character. In 1812, when Lizardi founded his newspaper *El Pensador Mexicano* (a name he would adopt as a pseudonym), Mexico City had about 170,000 inhabitants and it differed from other colonial capitals not only in its riches but also in its long educational, literary, and journalistic experience.

Nevertheless, these reasons alone do not explain the publication of *El periquillo* in 1816. One must keep in mind the critical situation Mexico was in at that time as well as Lizardi's position in the nationalist debate then taking place. As is known, Napoleon Bonaparte's overthrow of the Spanish monarchy had different consequences in Mexico than in the majority of the South American colonies. There the event prompted the Creoles to organize provisional government juntas; although at first they swore fidelity to the captive Fernando VII, they soon looked toward independence. In the case of Mexico, however, efforts to create an autonomous government which would express Creole interests ended in a resounding failure. The Viceroyalty fell into the hands of the conservatives, led by the powerful sector of the Spanish merchants. The Mexican Creoles, thus lacking a transitional form of government to unite them, were divided between separatism and reformism. The latter was supported by the urban group, the most influential, and it was the dominant party until the promulgation of the Iguala Plan (1821). The majority of Creoles, therefore, did not support Hidalgo's insurgence in 1810. It has sometimes been hinted that Lizardi was sympathetic to the independence cause, but there is nothing in his actions or in his strategies as journalist and writer which would suggest that ideal. It is clear, however, that he enthusiastically favored a nationalist reform which, following the liberal precepts of the Constitution of Cádiz (1812), would elevate the Creoles to the heights of political, economic, and social power within the framework of Spain and the Americas.

The first appearance of Lizardi's narrative work coincides with the beginning of his political efforts as a journalist. If he decided to write *El periquillo*, it was surely because he understood that prose fiction had potentially more influence on the creole mentality than the anonymous satires he was publishing in the newspapers. Furthermore, he probably thought that the novelty of the work, as well as its length and fictional nature, would help to fool the censorship apparatus of which he had already been a victim. (In 1814 his articles on the injustices suffered by the Creoles under the colonial system, published in *El Pensador Mexicano*, had earned him a prison term.) Nevertheless, it is also obvious that the plot of *El periquillo* owes a great deal to the picaresque novel *Aventuras de Gil Blas de Santillana* (1787), a translation of Alain-René Lesage's work (1715–1735) done by José Franciso de Isla. The reason why Lizardi felt attracted to a neoclassical novel, and not to one of the romantic works available in Spanish versions, is obvious: the neoclassical codes – the only ones which spoke of bettering the conditions of life through moral rectitude – were the most useful for the liberal Creole to represent optimistically his own economic instability and social marginality with respect to the Spaniard. It is interesting to note Felipe Reyes Palacios's observation that *Gil Blas* expressed in its plot the hegemonic desires of the French bourgeoisie which could, in the conditions of Mexico, be compared to those of the Creoles. One should remember that having repented of his bad life, Gil Blas receives a castle from the hands of a benefactor. Something similar happens to Periquillo: as a reward for reforming, he inherits from his master a tavern and a store. It is here, in this improbable denouement, where Lizardi reveals with the greatest clarity the aspirations of the Creole. Lizardi's Enlightenment ideas are expressed also in the high esteem in which Periquillo holds travel, science, and foreign languages, as well as in the chapters where he holds forth against slavery and makes fun of titles of nobility. Those were the chapters which provoked the censorship of the fourth volume of the novel, not published in complete form until the years 1830–1831.

Given its seminal nature, *El periquillo* was the obligatory point of reference for the Mexican novels which followed it, novels which tended to continue the theme of social marginality as well as its journalistic style, its *Costumbrismo*, its didacticism, and its melodrama. But the importance of *El periquillo* is not limited to what has already been stated. One should keep in mind, as Benedict Anderson notes, that its readers experienced the illusion of accompanying Periquillo along the roads and through the villages and towns of the Viceroyalty, which helped to awaken in them the desire for Nationness. Furthermore, because of Periquillo's varied life – he was student, monk, physician, barber, scribe, pharmacist, judge, soldier, beggar, thief, sacristan, and merchant – readers could associate the universal professions he practiced with the particularities native to the country, in the sense of being able to imagine what it was like to be a soldier or a thief in Mexico, to be in jail or in a hospital in Mexico and in no other place. If one adds to this the catalogue of customs and typical characters Lizardi included in his narrative, we can clearly appreciate the important nationalist role the work has played since then.

With regard to Lizardi's other three novels, the one that has most in common with *El Periquillo* is entitled *Vida y hechos del famoso caballero don Catrín de la Fachenda*. The most notable difference between the principal characters of the two novels is that unlike Periquillo, Catrín does not reform; he continues his bad life until the very day of his death. The didactic orientation of the work is expressed in the fact that Catrín, son of a creole family, aspires to nobility and tries to imitate the dandies of the viceregal court; that is, not to work, to dress elegantly, to gamble, drink, seduce women, and behave haughtily. But this imitation leads him only to poverty, to crime, to jail and to the hospital, where at the age of thirty-one he dies of illnesses contracted through his vices. The most influential European source continued to be the picaresque, but given Catrín's refusal to change his life, the model was the old picaresque genre of *Lazarillo* and the *Buscón*. One should note that the messages of *El periquillo* and *Don Catrín* represent the choices their author saw available to the Creoles: either they could climb the social ladder via a civic and professional apprenticeship, or they could fall, dragged by the weight of moral inertia, until they transgressed beyond the limits of Mexican identity.

In chronological terms, Lizardi's second novel was *Noches tristes*, republished in 1819 with the definitive title of *Noches tristes y día alegre* because of the addition of a new chapter. The philosophical tone Lizardi tried to achieve in this work led him to adopt a rhetoric which had no room for his *Costumbrismo*, his irony, and his popular humor. Furthermore, given the narrowness of its structure and the paralyzing lack of action – five scenes in dialogue – the work scarcely offers the level of narrativity usually demanded of the novel. *Noches tristes* takes as its model the pre-romantic prose of the Spaniard José Cadalso (1741–1782), specifically his *Noches lúgubres* (1798). Lizardi must have referred to that work because it dealt with the theme of the disinterment of the beloved woman, a theme that allowed him to deliver the reader a moral lesson in a fearful setting: a cemetery in the darkness of night. But in Lizardi's nationalistic version, the principal character faces not the pestiferous carrion which the adored body has become, but rather an unknown woman's corpse he has, in his nocturnal fear, confused with his wife. When the protagonist leaves the cemetery, he has the joy of finding his beloved at the gravedigger's house, a situation which leads to the couple's reunion with their children on the "happy day" of the last chapter. This treatment of Cadalso's macabre theme allows Lizardi to write an edifying reflection about the nature of marriage when the couple's behavior is guided by pure sentiments. At the end, the protagonist's wife encounters by chance a rich priest who turns out to be her uncle. Similar to events in *El periquillo*, the good priest gives his niece his entire fortune, and she immediately begins to put it to use in works of charity. It is noteworthy that the beneficiaries of these gifts are neither Indians nor degraded indigents; they are Creoles who bear their poverty with stoicism and decency, as Lizardi never tires of saying when speaking about himself. In summary, Lizardi nationalized the *Noches* because the theme could be manipulated in such a way as to express his desire to build for the Creole a solid bourgeois home.

This work was followed by *La Quijotita y su prima* (incomplete edition 1818–1819; complete edition 1831–1832), an exaggeratedly moralizing and tedious novel. Here Lizardi compares the lives of two women, the cousins Pudenciana and Pomposa. The first receives from her parents an education based on principles of rectitude and prudence, and she thus gets the rewards of a solvent marriage and happy offspring. Pomposa, on the contrary, is a victim of the neglect and indulgence which surrounded her childhood; very soon she develops delusions of grandeur – which is why she is called "la Quijotita" – and she is accustomed to doing whatever her caprice and desires dictate. As an adult, her wayward conduct leads her to the basement of the social scale, for after being dishonored and robbed of her dowry by an impostor, she is forced into prostitution when her father dies. The pages where Lizardi gives information about the literary tastes prevailing in creole homes are also interesting. Quijotita's family library contained, besides *Don Quijote* and *Gil Blas*, Francisco de Quevedo's *Obras jocosas*, the *Novelas amorosas y ejemplares* by María de Zayas y Sotomayor, Samuel Richardson's *Pamela o La virtud recompensada* and *Clarisa o La historia de una señorita*, Gaspar Gil Polo's *Diana enamorada* François-René Chateaubriand's *Atala*, Cristóbal Lozano's *Soledades de la vida y desengaños del mundo*, etc. This sampling of such dissimilar and anachronistic works gives one an idea of the European fiction styles, themes, characters, and plots which influenced Lizardi and his followers.

Cuba: the era of Domingo Delmonte

Literary nationalism, expressing the desire for independence, emerges in the 1820s in Cuba with the anti-scholastic philosopher Félix Varela (1787–1853) and the poet José María Heredia. The idea of separatism did not gain the support of the great majority of Creoles, however, as happened in Mexico. In the circumstances of Cuba, where sugar dominated the economy, the fight for independence could not feasibly be undertaken without granting freedom to the slaves. Given the high number of the latter (about 287,000 in 1827, 41 per cent of the population), the white Creoles thought a revolution of this kind could easily turn into a racial war. They feared that Cuba, like Haiti, would become a black republic with no place left for them. Thus, in the 1830s, when the island's black population was approaching the half-million mark, the creole ideologues adopted a strong reformist path. Their national project included, in the first place, a complete suppression of the slave trade, a measure halting the growth of the black population and allowing for a gradual abolition of slavery. Although this project tolerated the Black as a second-class Cuban, it did not want his presence on the national scene in massive numbers. The proposition was that Cuba be "whitened" through a sustained immigration of cheap labor of European origin. The project also aimed to secure from the Crown a revocation of colonial status in favor of an autonomous regime, to reorganize and modernize sugar cane farming, to renew transportation and communication, to eradicate vagrancy and vices, to promote scientific study, and to reform the educational system. In order to spread their program, the reformist Creoles intended a thorough use of the print resources of the country. Texts soon began to appear which talked about Cubanness in geography, natural sciences, economics, social sciences, education, literature, and literary criticism. The principal figures of this movement were the social scientist José Antonio Saco (1797–1879), the naturalist Felipe Poey (1799–1891), the geographer and lexicographer Esteban Pichardo (1799–1879), the educator José de la Luz y Caballero, and the champion of culture and literary critic Domingo Delmonte.

The intense and varied journalistic activity that took place in Havana from the era of the *Papel Periódico* (1790) prepared an ideal context for the emergence of a national novel. In 1834 the reformist group created the Cuban Academy of Literature, the first autonomous literary institution, dismantled because of planters' and Spanish merchants' complaints. Measures taken up against the group included the closing of the *Revista Bimestre Cubana*, the Academy publication, and the exile of Saco. The literary activity did not cease, however. Delmonte organized a private *tertulia* in which he gathered the most promising young people. During the period of 1837–1844, the members of the circle published a significant ensemble of texts that included legends, historical narratives, travel chronicles, stories, brief novels, and novels, as well as the autobiography of the slave Juan Francisco Manzano (1797–1853). Unlike Mexico, where Lizardi's work stands alone, Cuba produced six novelists: Ramón de Palma y Romay (1812–1860), Cirilo Villaverde (1812–1894), José Antonio Echeverría (1815–1885), Anselmo Suárez y Romero (1818–1878), Gertrudis Gómez de Avellaneda, and José Ramón de Betancourt (1823–1890). With the exception of the last two, all came out of Delmonte's circle.

Some of the works I will consider here were quite controversial in their day. When Palma published his short novel *Una pascua en San Marcos*, which criticized the idleness and dissipated life of the upper classes, he provoked furious protests in Havana. The action takes place in the coffee plantations in the San Marcos zone, near the capital. It is the Christmas season and there are parties one after another at the planters' mansions. The guests dance, eat, drink, and flirt in a luxurious setting; in the daytime they hunt and ride horseback and at night the gold flows on the gaming tables. There are four main characters: Claudio, a carefree playboy of the era; Aurora, a rich planter's only heir; Irum, a clumsy captain in the Spanish army; and Rosa, his beautiful and passionate wife. The plot is simple, constructed with the materials appropriate to the three literary currents coinciding in those years in Cuba: a Neoclassicism in decline, a dominant Romanticism, and an emerging Realism in the style of Balzac. The romantic elements are expressed in the exaltation of nature and the passionate violence of the amorous triangle Claudio/Aurora/Rosa, which shapes the central part of the story. The neoclassical ingredients are in Claudio's moralizing end; he is forced to marry Aurora, he destroys the marriage, squanders his entire fortune in gambling, and dies in a hospital, poor, alcoholic, and alone, very much in the style of Lizardi's Catrín. And the realistic components are in the descriptions and dialogues. The primary Cuban source to which the text refers is *Memoria sobre la vagancia en la isla de Cuba* (1832), Saco's brilliant essay which attacks, from a modern sociological perspective, the destructive consequences of gambling, idleness, and alcoholism. This work of Palma's provided José Ramón Betancourt with a model for his novel *Una feria de la Caridad en 183...*, which, although now little known, enjoyed great popularity in its day.

Antonelli, by José Antonio Echeverría, is one of the most interesting brief novels of the period. What distinguishes Echeverría from the rest of the writers from his group is the interest he shows in historical and literary research. It was he who, searching in the archives, found and copied in 1837 the text of the poem *Espejo de paciencia*, the foundational talisman of Cuban literature. Influenced by romantic poetics of fiction and historiography, Echeverría liked to reveal past events hidden in the old hermitages, in the streets and plazas of Havana, in the walls and fortresses defending the city. In this he was pursuing a clear foundational purpose, which did not work to the detriment of the quality of his prose. *Antonelli's* most immediate European source was Hugo's *Notre Dame de Paris* (1831). The local antecedents are two essays on the historical novel, published by Delmonte and Heredia respectively in 1832. They are two excellent examples of nineteenth-century Spanish American criticism, and they are a reflection of the literary activity that went on in the Cuba of those times.

In any case, the title *Antonelli* refers to a historical figure: Juan Bautista Antonelli, a military architect of Italian origin who fortified the Caribbean area in the sixteenth century. Antonelli worked in Havana (1587–1593) on the construction of the castle of El Morro. Although in Europe and in the viceregal cities of Spanish America the building of greatest prestige is the cathedral, in the Caribbean it is the fortress. Notre Dame illustrates to a great extent the history of Paris; in Havana, the stone book is El Morro. It is significant that in the opening pages of the novel we see Antonelli building a hydraulic sugar-mill on the banks of the Almendares River. In this the double role he plays as builder is emphasized: on the one hand, the fortress; on the other, the production of sugar for export. Antonelli can be read, thus, as a character who represents the European presence in its economic and military role in Cuba. Other characters include Casilda (the beautiful creole girl, daughter of an indigenous woman), Captain Gelabert, and the Indian Pablo. The plot is the consecrated love triangle: Antonelli loves Casilda, but she loves Gelabert. The Indian Pablo, who has been trampled by Gelabert's horse, is the inexorable hand of fate. At Antonelli's instigation, the Indian decides to take vengeance on the elegant Captain. The story ends tragically when Pablo, in Antonelli's presence, pushes Gelabert from the high balustrade of El Morro. Casilda, who was standing by her lover, falls into the abyss as well, in spite of Antonelli's efforts to save her. And so things turn out, as Casilda slips through his hands over the wall he himself built, that Antonelli cannot use romance to consolidate his position as continuer of the Spanish enterprise in America. From this abyss, yawning between the towers of *Notre Dame* and El Morro, Cubanness emerges.

The most prolific and important storyteller of Delmonte's group was Cirilo Villaverde, who published several novels and brief novels, among them: *Teresa* (1839), *La joven de la flecha de oro*, *El guajiro*, *La peineta calada* (1843), *Dos amores* (1843), *El penitente* and *Cecilia Valdés o La loma del Angel* [*The Quadroon or Cecilia Valdés/Cecilia Valdés, or Angel's Hill*]. The laborious and protracted rewriting of the last work, although begun in 1839, places it in another period – as William Luis has seen. It ought to be viewed rather as an example of the Cuban literature written after the abolition of slavery (1880).

Taken in its totality, Villaverde's work harks back to numerous literary sources, which proves that he was a constant reader. One can observe in his fiction, besides the strong impact of the Spanish *costumbrista* writers, the influence of Chateaubriand, Scott, Hoffman, Manzoni, Cooper, Balzac, Hugo, Dickens, and Poe. But for the critic, the interest that Villaverde's work arouses goes beyond the identification of his stylistic and thematic sources. It should be pointed out that he was the first author in Spanish America who, influenced by Balzac, attempted to novelize systematically an entire city; that is, Havana with its harbor, marina, walls, neighborhoods, streets, plazas, churches, and houses, as well as its different social, racial, and professional groups. In his Havana novels, the central characters are abused and tragic women. Their loves generally turn out badly. In his historical novel *El penitente* the protagonist is sacrificed in order to perpetuate the alliance between two patrician Havana families. In a similar fashion, the character of *La joven de la flecha de oro*, daughter of a rich Creole, is persuaded to marry a Spanish merchant. But his most natural characters are mulatto women, like Anacleta in *Dos amores*, Rosario in *La peineta calada* and his masterly *Cecilia Valdés*. Not all of Villaverde's novels, however, have Havana and Woman as their referents. The action of *El guajiro* takes place in the village of San Diego de Núñez, his own birthplace. The protagonist, Tatao, was drawn from real life and can be read as a forerunner of the "good outlaw" type so popular in Latin American literature. Although the plot of *El guajiro* is irrelevant, one should notice that the work inaugurates the *campesino* theme in the Spanish American novel, which was to be picked up by the Uruguayan Alejandro Magariños Cervantes (1825–1893) in *Caramurú* (1848), the first gaucho novel, Pedro F. Bono (1828–1906) in *El montero* (the first Dominican novel), the Colombian Eugenio Díaz (1804–1865) in *Manuela*, the Mexican Luis G. Inclán (1816–1875) in *Astucia*, the Argentinian Santiago Estrada (1841–1891) in *El hogar en la pampa*, and others. It is worth noting that Villaverde introduced into Spanish America several major themes from the romantic school, among them the theme of incestuous love (*El ave muerta*, 1837), taken from Chateaubriand's *René* (1802) and the defiant life of Lord Byron, and the criminological theme (*Sucesos notables del siglo XVIII en La Habana*, 1846), taken from Poe's *The Murders in the Rue Morgue* (1841).

The Cuban novels of this period that have been most interesting to critics are: *Sab* (written in 1838–1839 and published in Madrid in 1841) [*Sab-Autobiography*], by Gertrudis Gómez de Avellaneda, and *Francisco* (written in 1838–1839 and published in New York in 1880), by Anselmo Suárez y Romero. They were the first anti-slavery novels in America, for they preceded Harriet Beecher Stowe's *Uncle Tom's Cabin* (1852). Their European sources are numerous and confused with the theme of the Noble Savage, although the romantic themes of freedom, social marginality, and racial exoticism also served as antecedents. As for Cuban sources, there are texts like Varela's *Memoria sobre la esclavitud* (1822) and, in particular, Saco's remarkable article entitled *Análisis de una obra sobre el Brasil...*, published in 1832 in the *Revista Bimestre Cubana*, where slavery was criticized according to the tenets of the reformist program.

Suárez y Romero's novel, commissioned by Delmonte, deals with the unhappy love affair of two domestic slaves, Francisco and Dorotea. The couple ask their owner, Doña Dolores, to allow them to marry, but she refuses and forbids them to continue their relationship. When they disobey their mistress, Francisco is sent to the family sugar mill to be whipped and shackled for two years, and Dorotea is put to work as a laundress. Meanwhile, Doña Dolores's son Ricardo, who is hopelessly in love with Dorotea, orders the sugar-mill's overseer to arrange for Francisco to die a slow death, assigning him the most difficult tasks and whipping him without mercy. After some time, Doña Dolores takes pity on the slaves and agrees to the wedding. She goes to the sugar mill, accompanied by Dorotea, in order to arrange the affair. But Francisco is a victim of Ricardo's false accusations, and Doña Dolores once again refuses permission for the slaves to marry. Finally, Dorotea resolves to give herself to Ricardo to save Francisco from punishment. Her decision, however, sets a tragic finale in motion. Francisco commits suicide and she dies shortly thereafter.

The writing of *Sab* responds less to a sociological interest than to a literary one. Its most immediate source is Hugo's novel *Bug-Jargal* (1819), to which it bears a great similarity. However, to think that *Sab* is a mechanical plagiarism of *Bug-Jargal* would be an error. Avellaneda used Hugo's prestige to legitimize the first Cuban – and Spanish American – allegorical novel. Indeed, Sab as a character is an imaginary and impossible entity, unlike Bug-Jargal; that is, he refers to the totality of Cubanness. His mother was a princess from the Congo; his father, Don Luis, is the descendant of a patrician family, and his adoptive mother, the old Martina, claims to be descended from an indigenous chief. His physical traits confirm these three origins, furthermore, and his sexuality is obviously hybrid – as Doris Sommer has observed – including masculine and feminine elements. His illegitimacy, like his cultivated manners and his privileged position as sugar mill overseer, make him master and slave at the same time. When he receives his freedom, therefore, he accepts it with indifference and experiences no change in his life. His presence, always associated with autochthonous plants, invests the territory of Cuba with history, represented by the ancient aboriginal site of the caves of Cubitas (small Cuba), the Creole hacienda of Bellavista, and the mercantile city of Puerto Príncipe (today Camagüey). His incestuous love for Carlota, his paternal cousin, is obviously symbolic. The impossibility of the union of the two cousins symbolizes the conflictive relationship between the sugar aristocracy, self-defined as "white," and the unstable color of Cubanness. Enrique Otway, Carlota's triumphant fiancé and usurper of her property, is also an allegorical character. His father was born in England, he was a pedlar in the United States, and he opened a textile warehouse in Puerto Príncipe. Thus Enrique represents foreign commercial capital, the undesirable ally of the creole plantocracy which aspired to displace the latter from the sphere of power. Avellaneda's national project stands thus, as a testimony which is more democratic and expansive than the project of Suárez's book. This is so, furthermore, not only because Sab is made to represent Cubanness, but also because the text displays patriotic ideas which can be defined as critical on political terrain, decolonizing on economic terrain, and antipatriarchal on sexual terrain, since the text compares the situation of women with that of slaves. It is no wonder that Avellaneda, who lived in Spain from 1836, decided to exclude this novel from her *Obras completas* (1869–1871), published when Cuba was fighting for independence.

In 1846 Avellaneda published *Guatimozín, último emperador de México*. At that date the indigenous theme had numerous antecedents in Spanish America, especially in poetry and drama. With regard to fiction José María Lafragua had published his short story "Netzula" (1832), and in Cuba, Palma had initiated national fiction with his short story "Matanzas y Yumurí" (1837). There also existed the text of the novel *Jicotencal* (Philadelphia, 1826), by an anonymous author. But none of these works influenced Avellaneda. *Jicotencal*, although based on the history of the conquest of Mexico, is a rationalist novel whose author – perhaps Félix Varela, in the opinion of Luis Leal – used the historical incident as a pretext to expound his republican ideology in a dry and cerebral language. Jicotencal emerges from the text as the emblematic hero of the Republic and of Reason, while Cortés and Moctezuma emerge as despots driven by low passions. *Guatimozín*, on the contrary, is a novel of romantic rhythms where neoclassical rhetoric appears only in the dialogues. Its pages are profusely annotated, referring to texts by Díaz del Castillo, Cortés, Solís, and Clavijero. There are excellent descriptions of the Mexican landscape and nature, Moctezuma's court, Aztec customs, and battles between natives and Spaniards. As for the treatment of the figures of Cortés and Cuauhtémoc (Guatimozín), Avellaneda emphasizes the positive features of both chiefs. There is an evident tendency, however, to idealize the integrity and courage of Cuauhtémoc, whose dramatic execution closes the novel. Besides fictionalizing the historical episode, Avellaneda dramatized three different kinds of love. Of these three variations, the one which dominates in the end is the relationship between Malinche and Cortés. But Avellaneda makes clear that such a relationship is far from harmonious, as she reveals the ethnological contradictions undermining the foundational moment of Spanish American identity. Furthermore, the interracial pair attain their unstable union by means of Cuauhtémoc's execution (in history, arranged by Cortés) and Gualcazint-la's murder, perpetrated in the novel by Malinche. Thus, for the author, the Conquest constitutes less a celebration than an overthrow of the legitimate regime.

With respect to the authors of the Delmonte group, they were able to maintain their active literary reformism only until 1844. That was the year of the so-called Conspiracy of the Ladder, whose organizers, according to colonial authorities, were planning a general slave rebellion centered in the Matanzas region. Historians have found no conclusive proof that there was such a conspiracy. Very possibly it was, more than a real event, a pretext to terrorize the slaves and to suppress anti-slavery discourse, the spread of which was already beginning to threaten the plantation *status quo*. In any case, pretext or reality, the repression was extreme. As a consequence, the poet Gabriel de la Concepción Valdés (Plácido) was shot, Manzano was tortured, Luz y Caballero was tried, and Delmonte was exiled. During the next three decades the novel was scarcely cultivated again in Cuba. Political stability was shattered in the 1850s by an intense conspiratorial climate, and between 1868 and 1878 the bloody Ten Years War took place, in which Creoles and slaves from the central and eastern regions fought fruitlessly for independence.

Argentina: Esteban Echeverría and the National Program of the May Association

It can be said with all propriety that the Argentinian novel emerged outside of Argentina and that it did so as a consequence of the political exile imposed by the tyrant Juan Manuel de Rosas (1835–1852) on the educated younger generation. Indeed, at the beginning of the 1840s, Vicente Fidel López wrote his historical novel *La novia del hereje o La Inquisición de Lima* while in exile in Santiago de Chile; in 1843, Juan María Gutiérrez finished his brief novel *El Capitán de Patricios* in Turin; in 1844, exiled in Montevideo, José Mármol began to write *Amalia* [*Amalia*] in 1845, Juana Manuela Gorriti (1819–1892) published *La quena* in Lima; in 1847, during his stay in La Paz, Bartolomé Mitre published

Soledad; in May of 1851, Miguel Cané signed in Florence the last page of *Esther*. The criteria of the nationalist program, on which the great majority of these works were based, had been shaped by Esteban Echeverría in his *Palabras simbólicas* of 1837. The importance of this text is crucial, for it constituted the creed of the May Association, founded in Buenos Aires by Echeverría himself at the time when Rosas's despotism was beginning to make itself felt. The Association was organized in the fashion of European secret societies and it had the participation of Alberdi, López, Cané, Gutiérrez, and some thirty more young people who would soon have to go into exile. Once abroad, they would spread the Association program among exile intellectuals and politicians.

The main contradiction dividing Argentina in the 1840s had begun to take shape in the Independence period, a product of the opinion of those who desired a centralist form of government seated in Buenos Aires (*unitarios*), in opposition to those who wanted a decentralized government that would distribute power among the provinces (*federalistas*). After a long period of political upheaval and civil war, Congress had ceded the government to Rosas (1835), who represented the federalist interests. Meanwhile, a desire for Nationness had not developed in a uniform manner among the people of Argentina. In Buenos Aires, on the other hand, influential groups existed for whom Nationness coincided with Modernness; that is, groups who believed in progress and wanted to imitate the institutions of France, England, and the United States. Thus in 1830, when Echeverría landed in Buenos Aires after a four-year stay in Europe, he found there were two modes of "Argentinianness" in his homeland, corresponding to two warring political parties: a federalist-conservative model, and a unitarian-liberal model. Echeverría's genius was to reveal itself not so much in his literary work as in his nationalist vision, for although his sympathies were with the Unitarians, he saw that the most practical way to pull his country out of anarchy was to propose a national reconciliation based on the overthrow of Rosas and the adoption of modern political, economic, social, and cultural forms of European thought. During his stay in Paris he had the opportunity to be present at the awakening of the French romantic school, whose Manifesto Hugo would publish in the preface of *Cromwell* (1827), and to breathe the revolutionary climate of 1830. This rich intellectual and political atmosphere would prove to be decisive in his life. In 1832 he founded Argentinian Romanticism with the poem *Elvira o La novia del Plata*. Influenced by Hugo and Utopian Socialism, he had seen in Romanticism an arena where the free expression of feelings went hand in hand with liberal politics, antischolastic education, and social and economic progress. Nevertheless, when he constructed his national program, he did not adopt the European models word for word. Aiming to reconcile the differences dividing Federalists and Unitarians, he proposed to hark back to the epic times of the Independence period, especially the anti-Spanish thought which had sustained the men of the May Revolution. Of course, it was necessary to oust Rosas from power, but within the new strategy Rosas would be undesirable not because he was a Federalist, but because he was imposing on the nation the semi-feudal principles that had reigned in the colonial era.

Echeverría's program of patriotic reconciliation and national modernization constituted the womb from which other variants of nationalist thought would be born, among them the proposals in Sarmiento's *Facundo* and in Alberdi's *Bases y puntos de partida para la reorganización política de la República Argentina* (1852). In truth, art was for Echeverría a means to educate, a civilizing agent with a task to carry out within the nation. His cultural project, besides disclaiming Spain and proclaiming Romanticism as the aesthetic which best suited the nation's needs, was an invitation to cultivate the study of history and a literature that sought its inspiration in the gaucho, the Indian, nature, and local customs and manners. His story "El matadero" ["The Slaughterhouse"] (*c.* 1840), in which he relates the barbarism of the mobs of Rosa's followers, has aroused a great deal of interest. Although it ends in the romantic fashion, this piece begins with a series of descriptions that are noteworthy for their naturalism. "El matadero" launches the fiction of political denunciation in Spanish American letters and, at the same time, suggests the theme of the dictator.

Excluding *Amalia*, it must be agreed that *La novia del hereje*, by Vicente Fidel López, is the most important narrative effort in the anti-Rosas period. Although his eventful historical plot takes place principally in Lima and on the high seas, his text refers to the program of the May Association, of which López was one of the main members. The action occurs within the framework of Sir Francis Drake's circumnavigation of the globe (1577–1580) and the naval disaster of the Spanish Armada (1588). The first chapters refer to the events of 1578, when Drake captured the annual galleon carrying gold and silver from Peru. It is precisely this treasure-laden ship that provides López with the opening setting for gathering his characters. On the ship is a rich Spanish couple and their beautiful daughter María, born in Lima; there too is María's servant, a *mestizo* girl called Juanita, and also Don Antonio, a Spaniard who is seeking María's hand in marriage. When the ship is taken by Drake, a fictional character named Lord Henderson joins the group, and he falls in love with María at first sight. After hundreds of pages full of intrigues, pirate stories, descriptions of Peruvian customs and sinister machinations by the Inquisition in Lima, the novel ends in England with a domestic scene brimming over with conjugal happiness. To the expected marriage of Lord Henderson and María is added that of Sir Francis Drake and Juanita, who has turned out to be a descendant of the royal house of the Incas. Thus, all ennobled, enriched, and blessed with a healthy progeny, they celebrate England's victory over the Armada sent by Spain.

La novia del hereje is the first Spanish American historical novel with a cosmopolitan setting. Its most immediate antecedent are the articles that López himself published in Valparaiso throughout 1842, in which he initiated – and nourished, together with Sarmiento – the well-known polemic about Romanticism. Its principal historical sources are various English and Spanish chronicles of the era, among them the epic verses of *Argentina* by Martín del Barco Centenera (1544–1605?). It can also be said of *La novia del hereje* that it is the first novel which, through romance, tries to reconstruct world history in depth. One should note that Spanishness is represented by the medieval institution of the Inquisition, while the fertile and happy unions María/Henderson and Juanita/Drake allegorize the desired alliance of the modern Argentinian with Anglo-Saxon capitalism. The desire for Anglo-Saxonness is also apparent in the text of *Esther*, Cané's autobiographical short novel, in the plot of which an Argentinian exiled in Florence carries on amorous relations with a British lady. It is a curious piece, for the romance unfolds amidst works of art that anticipate *Modernismo* [Modernism] at the same time as they underline the "civilizing" ideal of the May Association.

The aspiration to achieve national reconciliation shapes the plot of *Soledad*. Mitre, following the strategy of Echeverría's *Palabras*, organizes the amorous scene of his novel in the Independence period. The action takes place in the interior of Bolivia, a country that received Mitre well. The love of the inconstant Soledad, married to a rich old man, wavers between her bizarre cousin Enrique and the seducer Eduardo. Enrique returns victorious from the Battle of Ayacucho (1824) with the rank of captain; he represents the patriotic and moral principles of the May Association. Eduardo is a man of dissolute life modeled on the Spanish Don Juan; he allegorizes the depravation, egoism, and violent nature of which the Unitarians accused the Federalists. Eduardo has seduced his cousin Cecilia, who has turned up pregnant, and he is now preparing to seduce Soledad. After a scene where the three characters exchange insults, Cecilia faints and suffers a miscarriage, whereby she wins Eduardo's compassion. Finally, Soledad realizes that Enrique has always been her true love. When her aged husband dies, she ends up rich and free. The last chapter, which takes place a year later, finds the four cousins happily married. Enrique and Soledad have served as godparents to Eduardo and Cecilia's new son, so that the romance, begun under the sign of adversity and turbulent passions, concludes patriotically in the most crystalline harmony.

In his short novel *El Capitán de Patricios*, Gutiérrez also sets the action in the heroic Independence period, except that here the amorous scene between María and the Captain is shattered when he dies in a battle. The story ends when María becomes a nun and retires to a convent in accordance with the vow she had made, "either God or him," thus obscuring the differences between God and the man who dies for his fatherland. In spite of its simple plot, *El Capitán de Patricios* reveals polished language and well-executed descriptions of the Argentinian landscape and customs, among them the ritual of drinking *mate*. Cané followed the theme of Independence in *Una noche de boda* (1858), where a patriot and a Spaniard fight for the love of a creole woman. Much later, when the alliance between Romanticism and nationalism proposed by Echeverría had been dissolved, López's *La loca de la Guardia* (1886) appeared. Its overblown romantic intrigue is far inferior to that of *La novia del hereje*, and the only passages of interest are those which describe the Battle of Chacabuco (1817). It is significant that the theme of independence has been handled almost exclusively by the members of the May Association. They were the most interested in taking the war against Spain as the point of origin for Argentinianness, a sacred zone toward which it was necessary to return again and again in order to reconcile the elements of nationality.

José Mármol's intellectual life runs parallel to that of the members of the May Association. In spite of the fact that he was not a member of the group organized by Echeverría, his poetic and narrative work strongly reflects the body of political and literary ideas shaped in the *Palabras simbólicas* of 1837. After being arrested for circulating anti-Rosas propaganda, he fled to Montevideo in 1840, where he became known as a poet and a political activist.

Amalia began to be published in Montevideo in 1851 as a serial in *La Semana*. Its publication was discontinued when the Rosas regime fell in 1852, a circumstance that provoked Mármol's return to his fatherland. Three years later the definitive edition appeared in Buenos Aires. The novel, besides justifying the overthrow of Rosas, proposes a reconciliation of Federalists and Unitarians based in institutionalized, civilized, and progressive Argentina. Its nearest antecedents are the abundant anti-Rosas journalistic pieces written in exile, with *Facundo* in the foreground. With regard to prose fiction, the most immediate antecedent is "El matadero" whose sordid vision of the Buenos Aires of 1840 is expanded and deepened in *Amalia*. Following nationalistic criteria, one could say that *Amalia* is to Argentinian narrative what *El periquillo* is to Mexican narrative. This analogy is also valid if one compares the great defects which mar both works: repetitive situations, authorial intrusion, excessive length, and a tendency toward hyperbole. Nevertheless, as also happens in Lizardi's work, these failings are accompanied by visible successes and, above all, important achievements of a foundational nature: the *costumbrista* point of view, the description of Buenos Aires and the River Plate, and the inclusion of characters taken from reality, Rosas himself among them. The result was so successful that *Amalia* enjoyed tremendous popularity for a century.

Curiously, the couple formed by Amalia and Eduardo Belgrano, as well as the incidents of their truncated romance, are not particularly interesting. The most successfully executed characters are Rosas and Daniel Bello, whose respective contradictions lend them human density. Bello, the hero of the novel, is reminiscent of the cloak-and-dagger adventurers of European serials. Believed by the Federalists to be a solid partisan of Rosas, he conspires against the dictator and helps the persecuted Unitarians to escape to Montevideo. It is Bello who has saved the life of Belgrano, wounded by Rosas's henchmen when he tried to join Lavalle's unitarian army, and Bello who hides him at the country house of his cousin Amalia, a young and beautiful widow. At the end of the variegated plot, Amalia and Belgrano, who have fallen in love at first sight, marry at the farm. Bello, who has facilitated the wedding, arranges for Belgrano to flee to Montevideo that very night. Shortly before the hour of departure, Rosas's agents arrive and engage in a merciless fight. In spite of the fact that numerous literary critics have taken it for granted that the three young protagonists of the novel are murdered by Rosas's constables, the truth is that such a denouement is far from clear in the case of Amalia and Bello. If Amalia survived, it could be read as an icon of the Argentina desired by the May Association. One should observe – as Doris Sommer has said – that she is from the inland country, from the heavily indigenous Tucumán, and she lives in Buenos Aires, where she reads Lamartine and lives in the middle of the most sophisticated examples of European culture. One should note as well that her life transpires between her cosmopolitan parlor – as David Viñas observes – and Rosas's dagger, that is to say, between "civilization" and "barbarism." If we take into account that neither of her husbands has managed to get an heir from her, Amalia/Argentina would remain between life and death, like Sleeping Beauty, waiting for the liberating and fertile kiss of a future prestigious suitor.

The publication of *Amalia* unleashed a thematic line in Argentinian narrative: the anti-Rosas novel. After the government of Rosas had been overthrown, it was necessary to reorganize society around the "civilizing" project the victors had defended. This project required something more, however, to be legitimate: it had to give guarantees that the strong man model of the *caudillo* would never again be repeated in the nation's history. For that reason, the dictatorship of Rosas had to be repudiated repeatedly through the procedure that has come to be called an exorcism of the past. In any case, many of the anti-Rosas novels that followed *Amalia* – *La huérfana de Pago Largo* (1856), *El prisionero de Santos Lugares* (1857), *Santa y mártir de veinte años* (1857), *Aurora y Enrique, o sea la Guerra Civil* (1858) – are lacking in literary value. The only exceptions were the short novels *El guante negro* and *El lucero de Manantial*, by Juana Manuela Gorriti, published in her *Sueños y realidades* (1865), a collection of stories widely read in their day.

The "autochthonous" themes of nature, tradition, customs, as well as the characters of the Indian and the gaucho, were handled basically according to the codes of the Enlightenment and Romanticism. In the works that followed *Amalia*, however, the stereotype of the Noble Savage was already in transition, and thus in those texts "good" and "bad" Indians appear and the gaucho is seen as a contradictory being. For example, the legend of Lucía de Miranda, introduced by Ruy Díaz de Guzmán (1554–1629) in *La Argentina manuscrita* (1612), served as a plot for the novels *Lucía de Miranda*, by Rosa Guerra (?–1894), and *Lucía Miranda*, by Eduarda Mansilla de García (1838–1892), both published in 1860. The coincidence of two women writing at the same time about the same character is not fortuitous: the legend of Lucía Miranda was the only local tradition that spoke in depth of the Indian's sexual desire for the European woman, a very real desire in those years to the creole women living on the frontier, constantly exposed to being kidnapped by Indians. In summary, in dealing with the theme of the legendary Lucía de Miranda, desired by the "noble" Mangore and the "evil" Siripo, the novelists Guerra and Mansilla de García reflected the mixed feelings they had about the Indian, eroding the myth of the "natural man" so apparent in the works Avellaneda had written two decades earlier.

Mansilla de Díaz, a woman of excellent intellectual training, took *The Vicar of Wakefield* (1766) as a model for another of her novels, *El médico de San Luis* (1860). Nevertheless, when she nationalized Oliver Goldsmith's well-known work, both the equilibrium and the moralizing didacticism of the neoclassical prose gave way here and there to the violence common to life in the Argentinian provinces. Next to the serene order of the neoclassical home and its useful and impartial tasks (the exercise of medicine, the cultivation of fruit trees), there appear the disorder of judicial corruption and bureaucratic inefficiency and the violence of banditry, kidnap, and murder. It is worth pointing out that here altruistic principles are maintained by Englishmen joined to Creole women, either in marriage or in love, revealing the desire for Anglo-Saxonness characteristic of the May Association project. Something similar occurs in *La familia de Sconner*, by Cané, a juridical–economic novel where money is the main character – as Myron I. Lichtblau says – concretely the money of an inheritance which has been misappropriated by a scoundrel, dispossessing its legitimate heirs. Justice triumphs in the end, of course, but the interesting thing is the origin of the fortune, which is mythified according to the ideology of the May Association. Indeed, the novel not only describes the deceased Sconner as an upright landowner and entrepreneur who transformed savage nature into a productive cattle ranch, but it portrays him as no less than the founder of the Argentinian wool industry, for it was he who saw before anyone else the usefulness of importing English sheep in order to acclimatize them to the country and export their wool. Thus Sconner, as he nationalizes the British sheep, turns out to be a hero of the new epic: commercial capitalism.

Although the gaucho appears in *Amalia, El médico de San Luis*, and *La familia de Sconner*, he cannot be said to enter fully on the novelistic scene until the publication of *El hogar en la pampa*, by Santiago Estrada. Besides describing in detail country manners and exalting rural over urban life, this work idealizes agricultural economy to the extreme of proposing it, in keeping with Quesnay's old ideas, as the true riches. *Aventuras de un centauro de la América meridional* (1868), by José Joaquín de Vedia, introduces the character of the gaucho as a fugitive from justice, at the same time as it proposes that he will understand his rights and duties as an Argentinian.

Peru: Narciso Aréstegui and Luis Benjamín Cisneros

Although she was Argentinian by nationality, Juana Manuela Gorriti cannot be excluded from Peruvian letters. She emigrated to Bolivia in 1831, married the military man Manuel Isidoro Belzú, future president of the country (1848–1855), from whom she would separate. She finally settled in Lima, where she would devote herself to teaching for three decades. There she wrote her works, founded journals, and organized a famous *tertulia* she recalled in her book *Veladas literarias de Lima*, 1876–1877. Her short novels *La quena*, based on the colonial traditions of Peru, and *El tesoro de los incas*, which offers a compassionate view of the Indian, belong to Argentinian and Peruvian fiction alike. Nevertheless, the originator of the national novel was Narciso Aréstegui (1826–1869) with *El Padre Horán*, published as a supplement by *El Comercio* in 1848. Its plot is based on a real incident: the murder of a girl in 1836 by her confessor, a priest from Cuzco. Aréstegui sought authority in the works of the French storytellers of liberal and anticlerical tendency, particularly in *Le Juiff errant* (1844–1845). The old rallying cry of Liberty and Equality embraced by the protagonist's father, a veteran of the Battle of Junín (1824), is the ideological center on which the novel seeks to base its legitimacy. But Aréstegui's project includes in its demands not only the Creole of the middle class – the group to which the protagonist's family belongs – but also the *mestizo* and the Indian of the lower classes. Thus it is that the indigenous rebellions of Túpac Amaru (1780) and of Pumacca-hua (1814) are considered preludes to Independence. In fact, in spite of its artistic mediocrity, *El Padre Horán* is a work of national interest. In addition to being one of the first novels of political, economic, and social denunciation written in Spanish America, it manifests the desire for a new nation where the colonial structures that survived Independence would not prevail.

Luis Benjamín Cisneros (1837–1904), a lyric poet and author of fiction, wrote two brief novels in Paris: *Julia, o Escenas de la vida en Lima* and *Edgardo, o Un joven de mi generación*. In the first, an ill-advised young woman marries a man who dazzles Lima society, but he is ruined by gambling and abandons her. Later, now a widow, she marries her first suitor. *Edgardo* tells the story of a young officer who observes, on his travels through Peru, the miserable life of the Indian and acquires knowledge of the nation while he perfects his autodidactic education. His aspirations to regenerate society are truncated when he falls in an armed encounter. As in the majority of Spanish American fiction writers of this period, Cisneros's correct prose contains an anachronistic combination of propositions from the European novel of the end of the eighteenth century and the first half of the nineteenth. The neoclassical point of view is seen in the excessive didacticism of his work, the exaltation of the simple life and domestic peace, and his visible desire to "regenerate" society; the romantic perspective is apparent in the sentimental themes, the pictures-que intention, and the early death of the hero; the realist tendency, which carries least weight in Cisneros, is suggested by the zeal of certain characters to attain high social position and by the sporadic naturalness of the dialogue.

Chile: José Victorino Lastarria and Alberto Blest Gana

The combination of Andrés Bello and Argentinian immigration into Chile helped to inaugurate the national narrative there. In 1842 José Victorino Lastarria founded the Literary Society, and in his inaugural speech he outlined the form he judged Chilean literature ought to take. From Bello, his old master and critic, he acquired respect for language; from Sarmiento, an admiration for the French Romantics and the idea that literature ought to have a social orientation; from both, the need to refer to the nation, to its nature and customs, its history and tradition. The following year, Chilean narrative fiction would begin with "El mendigo", a short story by Lastarria which deals with the life of a provincial youth and recalls the Battle of Rancagua (1814). Lastarria emigrated to Peru for political reasons, and together with other exiled Chileans, he contributed to the literary movement there. Among the exiles was Manuel Bilbao (1827–1895), author of the historical novel *El inquisidor mayor*, in which he combined nationalist Enlightenment concepts with ideas from Utopian Socialism and the romantic pamphlet. In spite of these examples, there is no Chilean novel properly speaking until the beginning of the 1860s, when Alberto Blest Gana (1830–1920) published *La aritmética en el amor*, *El pago de las deudas*, *Martín Rivas*, [*Martín Rivas*] and *El ideal de un calavera*. Studies of greater scope than this one ought not to disregard Blest Gana's narrative production between 1853 and 1859, however, for they are works which, in spite of their melodrama, stand above the cheap popular literature of those years.

Blest Gana was the first Spanish American author who proposed to write a thoroughly realist work. For reasons explained above, he achieved this only in part; in speaking of the nation, he could not do without romance and thus Alegría assigns his novels to a "romantic realism." It is worth pointing out that Blest Gana felt no attraction for the theme of nature; his Romanticism is essentially urban, with an occasional brush stroke of local color. His interest in the realist novel arose in France, where, in addition to taking courses in military engineering (1847–1851) and witnessing the revolution of 1848, he read French authors with devotion. On his return he would propose to nationalize some of Balzac's strategies, especially those developed in his *Etudes de moeurs*, which includes scenes of private, metropolitan, political, military, provincial, and country life. On this solid base, Blest Gana wrote a cycle of novels in which he expressed his national project. In the cycle one can study the differences between city and country manners, relations between social classes, and details of the worlds of commerce, business, and politics. Above all, however, Blest Gana's work reflects the formation and rise of the Chilean middle class under the influence of English capital, during which process the old moral code (honor, integrity, honesty, duty, family affections, and sincere love) began to be displaced by the desire to achieve riches at any cost. Blest Gana is the first to warn us that it is not a question of abstract riches; money is desired in order to dress elegantly and shine in social gatherings, to possess mansions and luxurious furniture, to eat and drink well, to flirt and have lovers, and to establish alliances with rich families and achieve political power. Emulating Balzac, he registers the growth of the acquisitive urge in the population as well as the obsession with money and pleasure, as Jaime Concha observes. If there is one message in his novels, it would be this: if you have money, enjoy the good life; if you are poor, gain riches through an advantageous marriage.

The French novel offers three different characters whose dramatic course was controlled by the connections between money and love: Sorel (*Le Rouge et le Noir*, 1830), Rastignac (*Le Père Goriot*, 1835), and Odiot

(*Le Roman d'un jeune homme pauvre*, 1858). In his work Blest Gana would take not only elements of these characters, but also settings, conflicts, and resolutions from the novels in which they appear. In *La aritmética en el amor* the protagonist has much in common with the Rastignac type – so frequent in the *Comédie humaine* – that is, the poor provincial youth who triumphs in the capital without concerning himself much about the means he uses to achieve his ends. The end of the novel, however, recalls the end of *Le Roman d'un jeune homme pauvre*, by Feuillet, where money from an inheritance makes possible the hero's marriage to his beloved. The end of *El pago de las deudas*, on the other hand, is similar to that of *Le Rouge et le Noir*, since the protagonist, his future undone and his conscience troubled, marches inexorably towards death. In *Martín Rivas* one recognizes the presence of Julien Sorel as well.

In the 1850s in Chile there were three national projects in play: the conservative, composed of an oligarchy of landowners allied to the church, which held political power from 1829; the liberal representing mining and commercial interests, whose modernizing ideals were opposed to the hegemony of the church; and the radical, supported by artisans, farmers, and intellectuals influenced by Utopian Socialism. The author would speak about all of them in his work and, in *Martín Rivas*, he would even make the protagonist participate in the failed revolution organized in 1851 by the liberal and radical groups. But Martín's participation in these events lacks ideological importance; it is simply a romantic gesture in the face of amorous frustration, like Marius in Hugo's *Les Miserables*, when he goes to die at the Parisian barricades of 1848. In reality, Blest Gana did not subscribe specifically to any of these projects. As indicated by the love affairs carried on in his works, he wanted for his country a bourgeois alliance of the conservative and liberal factions. *Durante la reconquista*, one of his best works, does not belong to this period.

Colombia: Juan José Nieto, Eugenio Díaz, and Jorge Isaacs

Although in 1841 José Joaquín Ortiz (1814–1892) had published *María Dolores o la historia de mi casamiento*, the national Colombian novel begins with the publication of *Yngermina o la hija de Calamar* by Juan José Nieto (1804–1866). As in the case of *El Padre Horán*, it is a novel whose importance, as Raymond L. Williams has seen, goes beyond its modest artistic value. The work should be seen not only as another historical novel of the period but also as a foundational text that speaks of its relationship to the origins of Colombianness. For Nieto, a *mestizo* author, those origins were to be found on the Caribbean coast of the country, specifically in the area of Cartagena, his birthplace. Thus Nieto writes *Yngermina* in order to legitimize his own genealogy and to present himself as an authorized interpreter of Colombianness. His "progenitors" are Yngermina, an indigenous princess, and the conquistador Alonso de Heredia, brother of Pedro de Heredia, founder of Cartagena; the happy union of Alonso and Yngermina closes the fictional discourse.

After *Yngermina* dozens of historical novels were published throughout the century. Although it is an irrelevant production which generally rewrote the chronicles of the Indies following enlightenment and romantic codes, one may mention Juan Francisco Ortiz (1801–1875), José Antonio Plaza (1809–1854), Soledad Acosta de Samper (1833–1913), and Felipe Pérez (1836–1891). I think the abundance of historical novels in Colombia is explained by the slow pace at which the process of national integration was accomplished there – one of the most irregular in Spanish America. That slowness caused writers to search in the past for causes to explain or mythify the fragmentation of national identity they saw in the present. The practice of *Costumbrismo*, begun with notable success in the 1850s, helped the population gradually to accept a "national reality" stretching beyond the emphatic geographic, ethnographic, economic, social, and cultural boundaries which defined the country. Of all this *costumbrista* fiction, Eugenio Díaz's *Manuela* is undoubtedly the best example. Furthermore, as Seymour Menton has seen, the *Costumbrismo* of Díaz is unique in being more realist than romantic.

The action of *Manuela* is set in 1856 in a small village north of Bogotá. Since the previous decade, Colombia (then Nueva Granada) had already been divided by the confrontation between Conservatives and Liberals, and it had already begun the long period of revolutions and civil wars characterizing the Colombian process of national consolidation. Demóstenes, the protagonist, is a young intellectual from Bogotá who has studied in the United States. Ideologically he identifies with the radical faction of the Liberals, influenced by Utopian Socialism, which has been pushed to the margins of power after an alliance between Conservatives and old Liberals. Disillusioned by politics, he has packed his books and some clothes in a trunk and left the capital, swearing that he will never take public office. Nevertheless, when he reaches the village, Demóstenes attempts an ideological apostlehood that ends in failure, since the majority of the people do not know how to read nor do they understand the impassioned harangues he addresses to them. The principal theme of the novel, however – as Williams indicates – is the conflict between traditional knowledge (narrative) and modern knowledge (scientific). Manuela, a local woman, represents the telluric forces of the country; in spite of her illiteracy, her natural judgment usually triumphs over Demóstenes's bookish word.

Although Eugenio Díaz introduces numerous *costumbrista* scenes into the novel, his purpose goes beyond that of other authors in the sense that the scenes serve to establish a hierarchy for the traditional values of the land, in contrast to the ideas of Demóstenes, mechanically taken from foreign books. As one can easily see, the characters of Manuela and Demóstenes symbolize two extreme ways to conceive of the fatherland. In the novel neither prevails: Manuela dies, as within the sociocultural framework appropriate to the rural setting, and Demóstenes (the voice of modernity) returns to the capital when he runs out of people to talk to. In this manner, more than offering an immediate solution, Díaz's message alludes to the complexity of Colombian structures and to the differences which separate the people of the country.

María [María] by Jorge Isaacs (1837–1895), is the most widely read nineteenth-century Spanish American novel and the one about which most has been written. The reason for its success is explained not only by its artistic level but also by the complexity of its structure, its polyphonic density, and above all, by the universality of its theme: the world of the past (the old order) recollected from the standpoint of the emerging world (the new order). Indeed, however important the idyll between María and Efraín may be in the text, the work cannot be reduced – as Menton, Jaime Mejía Duque, and others have said – to the simple story of the love relation between the two young people. María is thus not only the mellow remembrance of María through Efraín's story, but also something more. What is this more? My reading sees in the text two discourses coexisting problematically without any prospect of synthesis: one mythological–Adamic discourse, and another historical–critical one. The first attempts to legitimize itself in nature and in the patriarchal tradition by means of neoclassical and romantic forms. The second looks to the future and expresses itself in realist and evolutionist terms. Both discourses are well constituted and enriched by interconnected referential fields, for example – and in this I follow Gustavo Mejía's criterion – the worlds of María and Efraín (the aristocracy of the *latifundistas*, landowners of great estates), of Nay and Sinar (slave labor), of Tránsito and Braulio (wage labor), of nature, etc. Here I will speak only about the first.

Who is María? For several years researchers were determined to find the real person hiding behind the mask of María. The results were inconclusive, and no one is now trying to unravel the enigma. Nevertheless, Anderson Imbert relates that in 1880, when the painter Alejandro Dorronsoro sent Isaacs a sketch of María's portrait, Isaacs answered that he had painted a "Spanish nose" and not a "Jewish" one, and he added: "Have you looked at a portrait of me? That is the shape of the nose in our family." In other words, Isaacs had imagined María with his nose. María was not only an exterior reality for Isaacs; she was the representation of one side of himself, or one might say, *The Other-Within*, the Other Isaacs, the son of the landed, slave-holding, and conservative Jew who would evolve within the new order (industrial capitalism) to become a new Isaacs (the modern Creole, the political liberal, the Mason, the Darwinist), potentially represented in the character of Efraín. María was a hysterical, aristocratic Jewess, carrier of spoiled genes – as Sommer observes – and racially inadequate to symbolize the type of heroine demanded by the new order. She had to die in the text so that Efraín's wedding with "progress" could occur. If intercourse between Efraín and María had taken place, the result would have been undesirable: a defective foundation destined to languish within the new economic–social order. Indeed, the sick idyll of María and Efraín, enveloped in heavy scents of flowers and tearful readings of *Atala*, refers to the past of the author and of the nation and ought not to recur. But, of course, there is a paradox here: when Efraín does not die, neither does his desire for María die (Isaacs's prelinguistic desire). Thus María's slow death (the novel *María*) has a double function: on the one hand, to desire the past with desperate nostalgia – as Sylvia Molloy says – lest it disappear (a funerary monument); on the other hand, to exorcise the past so that its ghost should not haunt the utopia of progress.

In 1866, one year before publishing *María*, Isaacs was sent to Congress by the Conservative Party; in 1869, he switched suddenly to the radical wing of the Liberal Party. In this way, *María* is the text that connects and separates the conservative Isaacs from the radical Isaacs; that is, the text which problematizes Isaacs and places him in an ambiguous historical space. But, of course, the referents of *María* go beyond Isaac's paradoxical biography; the unresolvable pathos of the novel is also that of the fatherland, trapped likewise between the past and the future, between nature and progress, between romantic and positivistic interpretations. In that sense one can conclude that more than any other work of the period, *María* demands the institutionalization of the Nationness/Modernness paradox. Even more, I think that the text proposes itself as foundation for such a construction of power. Thus one can say that if *María* is the national novel *par excellence* – Donald McGrady has registered nearly 140 editions up to the year 1967, the date of its centenary – it is because its institutionalized authority has overcome the impossibility of its own project.

Ecuador: Miguel Riofrío and Juan León Mera

The first novel of Ecuador is *La emancipada*, by Miguel Riofrío (1822–1879), published as a serial by *La Unión*. The work was written during the ultraconservative dictatorship of Gabriel García Moreno (1860–1875) and it can be read as a liberal alternative for the country. Its main theme is the equality of woman within the nation. The protagonist, forced by her father to marry an old man she detests, wins her freedom at gunpoint as she comes out of the church where the wedding took place. She goes to live in the city of Loja, where she follows an independent and happy life, confronting civil and religious authorities. In the end, discouraged by the letters from the man she had loved before she married, now a priest who berates her for her behavior, she decides to take her own life. The text seeks its legitimization in the person and the work of George Sand – the protagonist at times dresses as a man – and in the liberal program of García Moreno's opponents.

Cumandá o Un drama entre salvajes [*Cumandá*] by Juan León Mera (1832–1894), earned great praise in its day from Spanish critics but today is scarcely read. Nevertheless, from the point of view of the relationship between Nationness and the novel, the text of *Cumandá* arouses interest because of its anomalous character. Indeed, its project wants the Ecuadorian nation of the 1870s to "evolve" toward the past, or to be exact, to seek modernity in the first half of the eighteenth century, the period of the Jesuit missions and the travelers of the Enlightenment. This peculiarity can be better understood if one takes into account that Mera was an extreme defender of García Moreno's regime, whose ideological foundation recalls somewhat the eighteenth-century Spanish Bourbon model (enlightened despotism), as it combines religious fanaticism and political absolutism with commercial capitalism and the scientific thought of the Enlightenment. In the conduct of his administration, characterized by political persecution and a lack of free expression, he appointed numerous priests to public positions, delivered the field of education to the religious orders, and proposed to unify the fragmented nation under the codes of Roman Catholicism. The Constitution of 1869, written during his rule, demanded adherence to the Catholic church as a condition of Ecuadorian citizenship.

Although the action of *Cumandá* is set in 1808, the principal *locus* of its legitimization is the theocratic power exercised by the Jesuits through their Reeducation Centers (*Reducciones*, settlements of converted Indians) in the eastern region of Ecuador. Even more, the tragic denouement of the work can be read as a consequence of the expulsion of the Jesuits from Spanish domains (1767). Now, as Hernán Vidal has seen, for Mera this theocratic power had found its mirror image in García Moreno's regime, where the Jesuits, besides being called to take charge of secondary, university, and polytechnical education, had enjoyed great official influence. In this way, the text of *Cumandá* follows a double strategy: to establish itself simultaneously as a Jesuit utopia and as an apology for the administration of García Moreno. Mera chose the jungle of the eastern part of the country, watered by the Pastaza and other tributaries of the Amazon, as the scene of his "drama among savages." In doing so he broke not only with the natural setting and the native Quechua tradition of his birthplace (Ambato), but also with the Andean referents of his lyrical work: *Melodías indígenas* (1858), *La virgen del sol* (1861). One cannot but find surprising this abrupt change in literary interests, where the familiar was sacrificed on the altar of the unknown, particularly if one considers that here the unknown was the jungle and its more conspicuous inhabitants: the Jíbaro Indians, hunters and head-shrinkers. I think, however, that there were reasons why Mera was interested in mythifying the Ecuadorian East.

It is easy to see that the rocky geography of the Andes has nothing to do with the teeming, green forests of the novels of Chateaubriand and Cooper, the only novelistic models of prestige to speak decently of America and its Indians. Thus, seeking literary legitimization in the exuberant forest narrated by these writers as well as in the chaste and exotic "natural" idyll conceived by Bernardin de Saint-Pierre, Mera nationalized numerous strata of *Paul et Virginie*, *Atala*, *René*, *The Pioneer*, *The Last of the Mohicans*, *The Prairie*, *The Pathfinder*, *The Deerslayer*, *The Wept of Wish-ton-wish*, etc., as Concha Meléndez has seen. As I have said, these sources serve not only the purpose of proving the prestige of *Cumandá*, but also the intention of García Moreno's project, an attempt to achieve the unity of the nation through a cultural force: Catholicism. This purpose is clearly visible in the relationship between Carlos and Cumandá. Their failed idyll, inevitably impossible because of its incestuous character, does not allude to a racial difference, as happens for example in *Sab*. Kidnapped by the Indians in her earliest infancy, Cumandá is as white as her brother Carlos. Thus what separates the lovers is not the color of their skin but culture, and within that culture, religion. As she suffers the ritual death to which the widows of Jíbaro chiefs were destined, Cumandá is the victim of the culture in which she has lived. Precisely, this "savage" culture is what, in accord with García Moreno's Constitution, excludes Cumandá from the nation.

Mexico: Luis G. Inclán and Ignacio M. Altamirano

The nationalist fiction begun by Fernández de Lizardi was not assiduously cultivated until the 1860s, with the appearance of the figures of José Tomás Cuéllar (1830–1894), Vicente Riva Palacio (1832–1896), and above all, Ignacio Manuel Altamirano (1834–1893). This paralysis was due in great part to the long period of political instability that followed Independence (1821), characterized by continuous armed conflicts between Federalists and Centralists and, later, between Liberals and Conservatives. But, above all, one should bear in mind that in those years the country was bled by a series of wars that embroiled it in political, social, and economic crisis. Such conflicts were provoked by the secession of Texas (1836), by the North American invasion (1846–1848) which cost Mexico half its territory, by the putting into effect of the liberal Constitution (1858–1861), and by the French armed invasion (1861–1864) in favor of the puppet empire of Maximilian of Habsburg (1864–1867).

Nevertheless, some works of interest were produced in those turbulent decades, like *El fistol del diablo* by Manuel Payno (1810–1894), a *costumbrista* pamphlet influenced by the picaresque; *La hija del judío* (1848–1850) by Justo Sierra O'Reilly (1814–1861), a historical pamphlet of anticlerical content; and *Gil Gómez el insurgente o La hija del médico* by Juan Díaz Covarrubias (1837–1859), a historical novel of sentimental strain that recalls the Independence era. But none of these can compare even remotely with *Astucia, el jefe de los Hermanos de la Hoja, o los charros contrabandistas de la rama* by Luis Gonzaga Inclán. The greatest achievement of *Astucia* derives perhaps from its modest literary pretensions, which save it from the artificial language and excessive melodrama characterizing the works of the period. Born in the Mexican interior, Inclán devoted himself to the ranching business, an experience that nourished his novel with an authentic and vital Regionalism. The European source of greatest impact is, as Salvador Novo observes, the popular adventure novel, concretely *Les trois mousquetaires* by Dumas *père*, whose fraternal egalitarian spirit – "one for all, all for one" – unites the band led by Lorenzo Cabello, known as Astucia. The long title of the novel refers to the activities of the band: contraband trafficking in tobacco. Here the profession of smuggler should be read in a positive sense, since around mid century the tobacco trade was an official monopoly of which the authorities took advantage to enrich themselves. The consumption of tobacco should also be read in like manner, that is to say, according to the codes of the era. As Anthony Castagnaro suggests, tobacco was then equivalent to pleasure. The profession of the band of the De la Hoja brothers is ethically justified, therefore, since it helps to make pleasure accessible to the most impoverished layers of society. It is noteworthy that Inclán extends this decentralizing extension to other areas of his novel. In effect, not only is it constructed in the popular language of the rural people, but it places the sociocultural values of the people of the interior in opposition to the law and the corruption emanating from the capital. In the end, these are the values which triumph in the novel, since after twenty years of adventure, Astucia decides to enter into marriage and retire happily to his ranch. It is easy to see that in his novel Inclán complements Lizardi's popular Nationalism. For the latter, the future of Mexico was in the hands of the low Creole of the city; for the former, in the hand's of the *peón* and the rancher, whom Independence and Empire had not benefited.

Once Maximilian's regime was liquidated (1867), Benito Juárez began a process of national reconstruction that is echoed in the novel. The great literary figure of the Restoration is Ignacio M. Altamirano, friend of Juárez and liberal politician, who was to provide a cultural leadership in Mexico like that exercised by Delmonte and Echeverría thirty years earlier in their respective countries, except that in his case this would be done from a position of power. Like Bello, Altamirano believed the novel was not only the most appropriate literary genre of the era, but further, a means of dissemination that, in speaking of the landscape, the history, and the things of Mexico, contributed to the national consolidation. He was a fervent admirer of the work of Lizardi; like him, he thought that the literary profession involved an ethical and educational responsibility. He published two novels, *Clemencia* [*Clemencia*] and *El Zarco* (written in 1888 and published in 1901) [*El Zarco, the Bandit*], as well as several short stories and brief novels, among which *La navidad en las montañas* (1871) stands out. The works of Altamirano, in spite of the artificiality from which his characters suffer, his too controlled style, and his moral didacticism, were the first in Mexican literature to demonstrate an artistic interest.

Of Altamirano's two novels, *Clemencia* follows most closely the models of Romanticism. The action is set in the years of the French invasion preceding the government of Maximilian. The main characters are four: Enrique, Fernando, Isabel, and Clemencia. The first two are officers in the nationalist army and they fight in the same regiment, but they are divided by deep physical and moral differences. Enrique is elegant, blond, gallant, and given to amorous adventures; Fernando is ugly, dark, introverted, and unlucky in love. It is no wonder, then, that Isabel and Clemencia, two beautiful and rich heiresses from Guadalajara, fall in love with Enrique, one after the other, and scorn Fernando. In the final chapters of the novel, however, it is revealed that Enrique is an unscrupulous man and, above all, a traitor who passes military information to the French troops in exchange for being accepted in their ranks as a colonel. Fernando, a sincere patriot who loves Clemencia in silence, discovers Enrique's treason, and against his wishes, denounces him to the leader of the loyal forces. Enrique is condemned to be shot, but knowing that his death would destroy Clemencia, Fernando takes his place in the cell. Finally, Enrique's moral baseness becomes apparent to Clemencia, and she tries to save Fernando, who has been condemned to death for letting the prisoner escape. In the end, Fernando dies before the firing squad, Clemencia dons the habit of a Sister of Charity, and Enrique, ironically, attains his colonel's rank in the army of the invaders.

The nationalist and didactic function Altamirano required of the novel is clearly manifested in *Clemencia*. Although the author says in passing that Fernando is neither Indian nor *mestizo*, his dark color, his timidity, his withdrawn character, his frugality, his straight black hair, and the fact of his having entered the army as a buck private make him an Indian in the eyes of the Mexican reader of the period. In spite of his lack of physical attractiveness, however, he turns out to be the spiritual hero of the novel as he is disposed to die for his ideals, be these the sovereignty of the fatherland or Clemencia's happiness. Altamirano, who was a pure Indian like Juárez, seems to have wanted to indicate to the racist reader that he ought not to judge people by their appearance, as Clemencia had done, but by their moral qualities and their patriotic conscience. Thus, the dark Fernando is placed in the center of Mexicanness, while the blond Enrique is expelled from its boundaries when he prefers the invader's flag to his own.

The historical novel of the Restoration was represented by Vicente Riva Palacio, who published eight books between 1868 and 1896. As happens in the great majority of Spanish American works of this kind, written before the process of modernization took place, the novels of Riva Palacio are lacking both in artistic value and in an intentional interpretation of the past. Several of them refer to the activities of the Inquisition, but they are nothing more than very badly written popular pulp fiction. None is any better than O'Reilly's *La hija del judío*, not even those written in that period by the Guatemalan José Milla (1822–1888). Nevertheless, one must admit that in referring to more or less historical events and people they helped to reinforce the national sentiment. Within the historical novel, the theme of the idealization of the Indian was taken up by Eligio Ancona (1836–1893) and Ireneo Paz (1836–1924).

The *costumbrista* current of urban and picaresque viewpoint, begun by Lizardi and continued by Payno in *El fistol del diablo*, would find its best exponent in José Tomás Cuéllar, author of a series of eleven brief novels entitled *La linterna mágica*. The most accomplished are *Ensalada de pollos* (in serial form, 1869; as a book, 1871) and *Historia de Chucho el Ninfo* (1871). He was interested in photography and painting, and his works emerge from a visualization of the typical characters of the middle class: spoiled children, ambitious military men, corrupt politicians, small merchants, dandies, and coquettes. Influenced by Balzac and by the Spaniards Estébanez Calderón and Mesonero Romanos, Cuéllar's *costumbrista* work is among the most accomplished in Spanish America, above all with respect to precision in details. Although he was attempting a didactic fiction in the Lizardi manner, aimed toward correcting the defects of the society of his time, his taste for satire led him to ridicule the virtuous characters he took as models. In any case – as John S. Brushwood has seen – the target of his attention was the *pollo*, the irresponsible young man who was, in accord with Cuéllar's ideas, at once both cause and effect of the social inconsistency suffered by the urban petite bourgeoise.

Although the weak character and the lack of common sense exhibited by this figure recalls the defects of Lizardi's Catrín, the *pollo* is not a rogue; he is simply a victim of the opportunism and corruption that rule society. In accordance with Cuéllar's tragicomic perspective, at times close to that of Naturalism, the sons and daughters of the *pollo* were to follow the same road in life the *pollo* followed, and their impoverished morality would lead them to do anything to get money and reach social preeminence.

The West Indies: the theme of the Indian in the novels of Eugenio María de Hostos and Manuel de Jesús Galván

Unlike *Cumandá*, the majority of the novels of this period that took the Indian as a referent did so in order to legitimize Nationness. The Indian and his traditions are idyllically confused in them with nature, which thus confers upon them telluric authority. This kind of novel is not abundant in the countries whose modernization process began early, nor in those where it started late. In Argentina, for instance, the Indian was scarcely idealized, for he was the nucleus of "barbarism"; the gaucho, however, being more assimilable into "civilization," was frequently mythified. In the Andean countries, where the semifeudal cultures in the colony were maintained almost intact, the only thing to which the Indian could aspire was to the compassion of liberal writers, a minority made marginal by conservative power. This is not the case in Mexico and the nations of the Caribbean basin. In the first case, the liberals triumphed under the leadership of Juárez, and the Constitution of 1857 crushed the old conservative alliance between the church and the landowners. In this anticolonial and revolutionary context, a series of novels was produced that criticize the Conquest and seek cultural authority in the indigenous people, for example: *La cruz y la espada* and *Los mártires del Anáhuac* by Eligio Ancona, and *Amor y suplicio* (1873) by Ireneo Paz. In the case of the West Indies the inclusion of the Indian within Nationness was accepted not only by the liberals but also by conservative power. There were two reasons for this. In the first place, the Indian had disappeared more than two centuries before and his remote demographic presence did not bother anyone. In the second place, the Indian theme served to diminish the authenticity of the black slave as a citizen of the nation. In Colombia and Venezuela, furthermore, although there were Indians and slavery had been eliminated, the Blacks were much more active socially than the Indian, and they constituted a political danger for conservative power. Thus it is that in these planter enclaves Indianist works appeared, like Nieto's *Yngermina*, *Anaida* (1860) and *Iguaraya* by José Ramón Yepes (Venezuela, 1822–1881), *La peregrinación de Bayoán* by Eugenio María de Hostos (Puerto Rico, 1839–1903) and *Enriquillo* [*The Cross and the*

Sword] by Manuel de Jesús Galván (Dominican Republic, 1834–1910). In Cuba, although antislavery literature based on black characters was written, it could not be published in the country even after Abolition (1880). Nevertheless, the Indianist short story "Matanzas y Yumurí" (Palma y Romay, 1837), as well as the abundant poetry idealizing the island's primitive inhabitants, were widely accepted by diverse social and political groups.

In any case, of the body of works I have mentioned, *La peregrinación de Bayoán* is the most original. Its national project desires the union of Puerto Rico, Cuba, and the Dominican Republic (Santo Domingo) within a commonwealth with Spain. (In 1863 the three countries were Spanish colonies.) The novel is narrated as a ship's log, and it can be read as a counterdiscourse to the old chronicles of the voyages of Christopher Columbus. Indeed, in the novel there are descriptions composed from on board steamships, of the island of Guanahaní (San Salvador, Cat Island), of the site of La Isabela (a settlement founded by Columbus on Hispaniola), as well as features of the coasts of Cuba and Puerto Rico explored by Columbus. A "return" journey to Spain is also recounted, as long and full of difficulties as those of the old caravels. Although they are contemporary with Hostos, the main characters of the work have the following Taíno names: Bayoán, the first Puerto Rican Indian to doubt the immortality of the Spaniards; Marién, a maiden named after a beautiful region of Cuba; Guarionex, a powerful chieftain from Hispaniola in the times of Columbus and Marién's father. The novel presents itself as the personal diary of Bayoán, that is to say, the voice of the Other-Columbus, although Hostos's own voice is also heard as an authentic interpreter of West Indianness, as is the voice of the editor of the diary, a Spaniard who symbolizes Bartolomé de Las Casas in his double role as Protector of the Indians and the true publicist of the discovery and conquest of the West Indies. Although Bayoán and Marién manage to wed in Spain, the marriage cannot be consummated because of the maiden's mortal illness. In the end, alone and embittered, Bayoán decides to return to the islands. This second return leaves open the possibility of a new act of foundation that may constitute the triple West Indian nation. Its premises would be autochthonous nature, the Taíno tradition, and the language and culture of Spain. As Eliseo Colón Zayas has noted, Hostos did not attempt to legitimize his novel in the insular capitals – which he understood to be denationalized because they wanted to imitate European cities – but rather in the canefields, in a manner analogous to that of Avellaneda in *Sab*; that is, in the space most approximate to the telluric. Naturally, Hostos excluded from his project Haiti, already independent, and the other non-Hispanic islands of the Caribbean. In accordance with the autonomic ideas, the European *locus* had to be Spain, specifically the "good" Spain, the decolonizing Spain of Las Casas, the liberal Spain of the Constitution of 1812 and of the Liberal Union (1856–1863), that offered at least some remote hope of change to the colonial situation of the three nations.

Apart from the originality of *La perigrinación de Bayoán*, the most important novel of the group is *Enriquillo*. Among the works of this period, it can also be said to be one of those which represent with greatest fidelity the type of literary Americanism proposed by Bello. I say this not only because its European sources are the chronicles of the Indies, but above all because these sources are thoroughly dominated by the *Historia de las Indias* (1875–1876) by Bartolomé de Las Casas – from which *Enriquillo* took numerous paragraphs – a work that Bello judged to be required reading for Spanish Americans. The *Historia de las Indias* had particular interest for the Dominicans, among other reasons because it spoke of Enriquillo, the chivalric chieftain who between 1519 and 1533 organized a center of indigenous resistance that eventually defeated bands of up to 300 men. Enriquillo had risen in arms in order to demand his rights under the law and to defend his honor as an illustrious Indian. The Spaniard for whom he worked had stripped him of his property, and, later, brutally beaten his wife when she refused to consent to his sexual demands. After exhausting the legal means provided by the colonial system of justice, Enriquillo decided to rise in rebellion in the mountains of Bahoruco. Finally, by express order of the Emperor Charles V, he was pardoned and compensated. He received the title of Don and he was allowed to found his own village, where he retired with his people and his family.

Galván's patriotic zeal has often been questioned because he collaborated with the last government of General Pedro Santana, who had requested and obtained the reannexation of Santo Domingo to Spain (1861–1865). This criticism, seemingly just, should nevertheless take into account that Nationalism is a manifestation of an eminently cultural nature. If Galván supported the annexationist government of Santana, it was because he thought that Santo Domingo ran the risk of being occupied anew by the Franco-African Haiti, that is to say, a *culturally* distinct nation. (In 1822 President Jean-Pierre Boyer had invaded the country, annexing it to Haiti until 1844.) Thus, to be a Dominican and a patriot in the times of *Enriquillo*, presupposed first and foremost a firm rejection of everything that came from Haiti. Although a great part of the population was black and mulatto, coinciding in this with the Haitian people, nationalist practices sought the explanation for the more or less dark color of the people in a fictional indigenous ancestry, an approach which *Enriquillo* strengthened. Thus it is that although popular culture continued to be characterized by an abundance of elements of African origin – and even Haitian (for example, the *merengue*, the national dance) – Dominican literature sought authority in the Indian, whose absence favored his idealization. The popularity that *Enriquillo* has enjoyed up to recent times owes a great deal to this tacit compromise with the realm of the imaginary.

Argentina: Lucio V. López, José María Miró, Eugenio Cambaceres, and Eduardo Gutiérrez

The most ambitious modernization project in all of Spanish America took shape in Argentina where, in a climate of political stability, there emerged a powerful plutocracy of landowners, businessmen, and financiers, a grouping which connected the nation's economy to the Atlantic economy almost completely. Annual wool exports grew from 45 million kilograms in the 1860s, to more than 100 million in the 1870s, and to 211 million towards the end of the century. In like manner the country became a grain exporter on a world scale, to the point where the number of acres of pampa devoted to grain cultivation multiplied by a factor of fifteen between 1872 and 1895. Likewise, as the system of refrigerated ships was put into practice in the 1870s, the exportation of fresh meat began a new stage in commerce. Naturally, the importation of capital, technology, machinery, and manufactured products also grew, and Argentina came to be doubly tied to Europe on the economic front, especially to England.

Within this panorama of changes literature was, of course, no exception. Thanks to the development of the press, publishing, libraries, and other cultural institutions, as well as to the emergence of the professional writer, the production of novels increased notably. This can be seen as an indirect consequence of the substantial rise in the population's living standard (then the highest in Spanish America), the increase in European immigration, and the decrease in illiteracy. The science fiction novel made its appearance in this climate of Positivism and faith in science. Borrowing from Charles Darwin and Jules Verne, Eduardo L. Homberg (1852–1937) published *Viaje maravilloso del Sr. Nic-Nac al planeta Marte* (1875–1876) and *Horacio Kalibang, o los autómatas* (1879). Aquiles Sioen (1834–1904), an immigrant of French origin, wrote *Buenos Aires en el año 2080*. Sioen constructed the fabulous city he describes – and wishes for – thanks to scientific progress, agricultural and commercial development, and the increase in European immigration. Nevertheless, Juan Bautista Alberdi, by then absent from the political scene, was not entertaining false hopes. In his allegorical novel *Peregrinación de Luz del Día, o viaje y aventuras de la Verdad en el Nuevo Mundo*, he included acid criticism of the militarism, *caciquismo*, violence, and corruption which the last two decades had brought to the country. In any case, it can indeed be said that the most significant novels published in this period abandoned the foundational canon of Romanticism, so apparent in *Amalia*, in order to nationalize models of Realism and Naturalism. As I have said above, one can identify romantic details in these works (melodrama, sentimentality, the picturesque) and even neoclassical characteristics (moral didacticism), but such features ought to be seen as metaphors alluding to certain areas of the sociocultural surface which were resisting the modernizing changes.

La gran aldea (a *Sud-América* pamphlet), by Lucio V. López (1848–1894), uses primarily realist models in order to narrate the transformation experienced by Buenos Aires in the brief period of twenty years. Julio, the protagonist, is a kind of outsider who does not sympathize with the priggish, pseudo-patriotic, and militarized society of his childhood (the decade of the 1860s) nor with the bourgeois, civilian, and materialistic society of his adulthood (the decade of the 1880s). Although the text presents itself as a novel of Buenos Aires customs (*costumbres bonae-renses*), its plot transcends *Costumbrismo* in focusing on the conflict experienced by Julio when he cannot adjust to the morally relaxed regime of the new times. In the novel there appear three icons of stylish Buenos Aires which were to reappear again and again in later works: the Colón Theatre, the El Progreso Club, and the Palermo resort. Borrowing from Balzac, López describes with singular precision the mansions, dresses, jewels, dances, opera, parties, banquets, and dissolute customs of the rich, particularly the *parvenu*, determined to outshine others in the material-istic society of those years. The cultural impact of the Europeanization of the country can be seen not only in the fashions and imported articles consumed by those of the "new class," but also in the French and English words they used in their style of speech.

Fruto vedado, by Paul Groussac (1848–1929), was also published in *Sud-América* in the same year. Born in France and an immigrant to Argentina at the age of eighteen, Groussac was to achieve a complete mastery of Spanish. His intellectual importance does not rest on his having written *Fruto vedado*, but rather on his long and productive career as critic, historian, librarian, and cultural promoter. The plot of *Fruto vedado* can be summarized as the story of Marcel Renault, an engineer of French origin who immigrated to the city of San José (Tucumán), who enjoys the love of two sisters, Andrea and Rosita. The first part of the novel intends to do honor to its subtitle of *costumbres argentinas* [*Argentine Customs*], for Groussac lingers to describe the provincial life of San José. However, like the treatment in *La gran aldea*, the *costum-brista* framework is very much transcended, in this case by the intention of depicting how the modernizing changes have reached all the way to the remote province of Tucumán, provoking an ambivalent situation. Although the social and economic life of the city is galvanized, the price of land rises dizzily as it is subjected to endless speculation. Furthermore, the march towards progress is seen paradoxically by the landowners of the place who, at the same time as they are getting rich, ponder sadly that the nation is gradually falling into foreign hands. Marcel's sentiments are also paradoxical, as he falls in love alternately with the beautiful and passionate Andrea – his first love, married for convenience to a blind cousin named Fermín – and the virtuous Rosita. Finally, as all gather in Paris, Marcel and Andrea carry on an adulterous love affair until they are surprised by Rosita and Fermín. Groussac finishes the realist/naturalist conflict with a decidedly romantic end: Fermín commits suicide, Rosita takes refuge in a convent to wait for Marcel, and the latter decides to go off to Africa on a scientific expedition where he dies at the hands of Arab warriors.

The unbridled speculation characterizing the financial climate of the 1880s reached its highest point in 1890. That was the year the Buenos Aires stock market fell and the currency was devalued, causing the sudden ruin of thousands of investors. The economic and moral crisis afflicting the country was a theme for a number of writers, the most distinguished of whom was José María Miró (1867–1896). Under the pseudonym of Julián Martel, he published the novel La bolsa in 1891. The work recounts the rise and fall of Dr. Glow, an upright and brilliant lawyer who succumbs to the speculation craze and passes from wealth to poverty when the crash comes. The novel depicts the financial ambience of Buenos Aires in the style of the Spanish Realists, from the faithful description of the stock-market building with its majestic arcades and its great clock, to the gallery of the new characters whom the economic bonanza has generated within the city: the broker, the banker, the speculator, the money-lender, the winner, the loser. Finally, ruined and dishonored, Dr. Glow goes mad and believes he sees a monster threatening him constantly; the Stock Market.

The financial crisis is also the central theme of Horas de fiebre by Segundo I. Villafañe (1860–1937); Quilito, by Carlos María Ocantos (1860–1949), published in Paris the same year; Contra la marea, by the Chilean immigrant Alberto del Solar (1860–1921). Of these writers the most important is Ocantos, who wrote a series of twenty "Argentinian Novels," basing himself on the works of Pérez Galdós and Balzac, which appeared between 1888 and 1929. It is worth noting that Ocantos rejected the idea of representing in his novels the Spanish spoken in Argentina; his language rarely transgresses the limits of academic Castilian.

The theme of immigration, touched upon directly or indirectly in numerous works, is treated with a certain complexity in Teodoro Foronda, by the Spanish immigrant Francisco Grandmontagne (1866–

1936). Using works by Pérez Galdós as his point of departure, Grandmontagne recounts the paradoxical life of an immigrant – Teodoro Foronda – who, after marrying an Indian woman and making money in trade, is scorned by his children because of his scant education and his negligible social contacts. Taken together, the works which deal with European immigration offer an entire field for sociological research. The immigrant did not always encounter in Argentina a land of promise, as Ocantos and other writers suggest. In the last decades of the century discrimination against the humble immigrant – usually Italians, Spanish, and Eastern European Jews – was already common. For example, in *Inocentes o culpables* Juan Antonio Argerich (1862–1924), taking Zola as his model, recounts the life of an impoverished family of Italian origin – the Dagiores – who do not succeed in escaping from their "inferiority." Argerich's naturalist Fatalism is expressed above all when he narrates the violent and degraded existence of the Dagiore son who, sick with syphilis, ends up committing suicide.

Zola's naturalist canon found Argentinan followers in Villafañe, Argerich, Manuel T. Podestá (1853–1920), Francisco A. Sicardi (1856–1927), and Martín García Merou (1862–1905), but its most significant exponent was Eugenio Cambaceres. The son of rich and distinguished parents, Cambaceres enjoyed an excellent education full of books and travels. His first novel *Pot-pourri* caused a scandal among the upper classes of Buenos Aires. Probably suggested by Zola's *Pot-Bouille* (1881), the title alludes to Argentina as a pot of stew (*olla podrida*). In effect, throughout a monologue disorganized by fragmentation and by iconoclastic fury, Cambaceres proposes to dismantle the image of the nation communicated by positivistic codes. In his denunciation, Cambaceres criticizes the hypocrisy of politics and of marriage; for him, social life is undermined by lies, opportunism, and immorality. But above all – and I think here is where his true literary achievement resides – Cambaceres denounces the vapid language institutionalized by politics, the social chronicle, literary Romanticism, positivistic education, the church and the family, in order to install his own language as a legitimate option; an uneven and contradictory language which, in its disorganization, can be at once both cynical and sincere, intelligent and vulgar, colloquial and mannered, local and open to foreign influences.

In his next novel, *Música sentimental*, Cambaceres approaches the models of Zola more closely, especially *Nana* (1880). Although the narration continues in the first person and he appears as narrator, the plot is much more developed. The action takes place in Paris, a city which Cambaceres knew very well. The main character is Pablo, a rich and dissolute youth who travels abroad in search of new experiences. There he carries on simultaneous love affairs with a countess and a prostitute named Loulou, who falls in love with the young man. When Loulou learns of Pablo's relationship with the countess, she decides to inform the latter's husband. After a duel where the count dies and Pablo is wounded, Pablo is discovered to be ill with syphilis. Far from healing, the wound infects his whole body while it also accelerates the progress of the venereal disease. Finally Pablo dies blind and rotten, while Loulou, who has an abortion, takes up her life as a prostitute once more. The character of Pablo allows for an allegorical reading which questions the authority of the groups in power who were defining the Argentinian nation as a system marching toward progress.

Sin rumbo and *En la sangre* are Cambaceres's best novels. In spite of the fact that his pessimism is nearly absolute, both works achieve an exceptional artistic quality due to the psychological and introspective development of their respective protagonists. Unlike Cambaceres's other novels, the plot of *Sin rumbo* does not have a predictable denouement. For a moment the reader believes that Andrés, repenting from his irresponsible and licentious past, is going to manage to reconstruct his life thanks to the paternal love he professes for Andrea, his illegitimate daughter by a peasant woman now dead. But when she dies of diphtheria after horrible suffering, the girl breaks the only bond linking her father to life. The work ends with the suicide of Andrés.

En la sangre – in my judgment the most interesting novel of the period – does not limit itself to talking about the impact of the environment and of hereditary factors on a child of poor Italian immigrants. Unlike any other more or less naturalistic Spanish American novel, Genaro Piazza, the principal character, has assimilated the sociological codes referring to his inferiority, his violence, and his immorality, in such a manner that he believes himself incapable of redemption. Thus, convinced that he has been and always will be a bad seed, he concocts a repugnant scheme to penetrate the exclusive circles of the aristocracy: to seduce and impregnate the daughter of a rich Buenos Aires family. Having achieved the desired marriage, Genaro acts like a blind and destructive force within the groups of power which he has managed to infiltrate socially. In the last instance Genaro Piazza is much more than the fruit of genetic and environmental determinism; he is at once both victim and executioner of the modality of nation which positivistic Liberalism had constructed upon the "barbarous" Argentina of Rosas. Cambaceres's critique of the social *status quo* was not only more desperate and extreme than Zola's in his *Rougon-Macquart*, but the optimistic intention from which Zola's work emerged is not even found in Cambaceres. In my reading of the Spanish American novel, Cambaceres emerges as the writer who observed with greatest pessimism the paradoxical interplay of Nationness and Modernness.

Although Cambaceres's works attracted middle- and upper-class readers, the most popular and productive writer of the moment was Eduardo Gutiérrez (1851–1889), author of more than thirty novels. Characterized by a combination of artistic objectivity and an urgency in speaking of the nation, the work of Gutiérrez was informed by the truculent reports and the sensationalist chronicles which the most prestigious newspapers of that time did not hesitate to publish. In any case, the work of Gutiérrez contributed enormously to spreading among the humble sectors of society, including the immigrants, an image of the Argentinian nation very different from those offered up by other writers of the period.

The four novels which make up Gutiérrez's Dramas of Terror have reference to the tyranny of Rosas, narrating in macabre manner the persecutions suffered by his opponents and the crimes of his despotic government. The plot of such novels does not differ greatly from that of *Amalia*, and one could well say they hold up the ideals of the May Association. Nevertheless, in the series of four Military Dramas, Gutiérrez defends with passionate conviction the figure of the political boss Angel Vicente Peñaloza (El Chacho), whose band was exterminated without mercy by Sarmiento on the altar of "civilization." In that case, at what ideological pole are Gutiérrez's novels located? I think at neither the one nor the other. His rudimentary narrative simply echoed the anomalous values then current in the popular tradition, where, beyond the ideological reductionism of "civilization versus barbarity," Rosas appeared to be a monster and El Chacho a patriotic Robin Hood from La Rioja. When he spoke of the gaucho, Gutiérrez also followed a paradoxical guide. Although they approach *Martín Fierro* in condemning the unjust treatment suffered by the gaucho during the positivistic governments, his most well-known gaucho novels – among them *Juan Moreira*, *Santos Vega*, and *Hormiga negra* – differ from the work of Hernández in relating the most shocking details of the violent life of the pampa. In short, the triumph of Gutiérrez was due to his capacity to recycle a vision of Argentinianness which simply represented the tastes and desires of the lower classes in opposition to those in authority, in a sense that it was marginal to the ideological interpretations of the nation being debated in the groups in power. His work, although coarse and vulgar, ought not to be underestimated, for among other things, it served to consolidate the national myths of the gaucho and the revolutionary. His *Juan Moreira* – whose protagonist was taken from real life – was incorporated into the pantomimes of the circus and later the stage (1884) with great popular success, marking not only the beginnings of gaucho theatre but also the popular orientation that River Plate regional theatre was to follow.

Uruguay: Eduardo Acevedo Díaz, Carlos Reyles, and Javier de Viana

The process of modernization in Uruguay had a late beginning due to the long and devastating period of civil wars between *Blancos* (the Whites, Federalists) and *Colorados* (the Reds, Centralists). The dictatorship of Lorenzo Latorre (1876–1879) initiated a period of military governments which was to last until 1890. In those relatively stable years the rural areas were finally pacified and the agricultural economy of the country began to be reorganized, leading to an increase in international trade. Uruguay was making itself felt as a reliable exporter of leather, jerked beef, and wool, at the same time as it was attracting ever larger investments of European capital and, above all, immigrants from Italy and Spain. It was about that time that the novel resurfaced with what has come to be called the "Generation of 1890," or more frequently the "Generation of 1900."

The most distinguished writer of those years was Eduardo Acevedo Díaz (1851–1924), author of seven novels. Of these, we are interested here only in *Ismael*, *Nativa*, and *El grito de gloria*, the main part of a historical – patriotic tetralogy which included also *Lanza y sable* (1914). The next after Acevedo Díaz is Carlos Reyles (1868–1938) with *Beba*, and finally Javier de Viana (1868–1926), primarily a short story writer, with his novel *Gaucha* (1899–1901). Besides their artistic significance, the works of these three writers form a particularly interesting group because they offer three different ways of speaking about the Uruguayan nation, each one buttressed by a sociological thesis. The tetralogy of Acevedo Díaz took as its point of departure Bello's texts on history and the novel which we considered in the first part. For him – as for Bello – the novel ought to have an ethical and perceptive function and, above all, it should contribute to the development of the national consciousness. His political ideas – which were federalist until 1903 – not only justified his sympathy for the gaucho and his opposition to the economic and cultural Europeanization of the country, but also his devotion to relevant historical figures of federalist credo such as José Artigas, the forger of Independence and Protector of the Uruguayan fatherland, as well as the deputies Juan Antonio Lavalleja and Manuel Oribe. No wonder then that Acevedo Díaz, who had fought in the ranks of the *Blancos* and was living in exile at that time in Argentina, tried to legitimize in the first three novels of his series the federalist national project, connecting it to the glorious epics which had liberated the country from the domination of Spain (1811) and from Brazil (1825). Years later, as the writer changed his political allegiance, he was to write *Lanza y sable*, where the hero turns out to be the centralist Fructuoso Rivera.

In any case, of the European literary models Acevedo Díaz had to hand in the 1880s, one of those which best fit his project was the one used by Pérez Galdós in his *Episodios nacionales*, of which the first two series had appeared throughout the 1870s. Not only had Pérez Galdós novelized the War of Independence in Spain, narrating the actions of fictional and real characters, he had also regressed stylistically, making a concession to popular taste, in sprinkling his realist prose with *costumbrista* scenes and romantic turns of phrase. Such a model was precisely what Acevedo Díaz was looking for, and it was that model which he nationalized. The principal local source which Acevedo Díaz used in order to legitimize his series of novels was the campaign diary of his grandfather, General Antonio Díaz, memoirs which he used as well for his historical work *Épocas militares de los países del Plata* (1911).

The best novel of the tetralogy is *Ismael*, which begins with a description of Montevideo in 1808 and ends with the triumph of Artigas over the Spanish in the Battle of Las Piedras (1811). The principal character is Ismael Velarde, an earthy and sentimental gaucho who joins the Independence forces. Disregarding the predictable denouement of the amorous triangle constructed by the writer with the characters of Ismael, Almagro, and Felisa, the novel is of great interest for two reasons. In the first place, it admirably describes the customs of Montevideo, particular features of the Uruguayan landscape and nature, and the rural life of the countryside. In the second place, in centering his work on the agitated existence of Ismael Velarde, Acevedo Díaz offers the reader an excellent sociological study of the gaucho. In the remaining two novels of the series the principal character is Luis María Berón, a young aristocrat from Montevideo who joins the forces trying to liberate the country from Portuguese domination. After he is wounded in combat, Luis María convalesces on the ranch Los Tres Ombúes, whose owner has two daughters, Dora and Natalia. Both girls fall in love with him, but Luis María is interested only in Natalia, who is being courted by an enemy officer named Pedro de Souza. *Nativa* ends when Luis María, wounded anew and captured by Souza's detachment, is rescued by the gaucho Ismael Velarde. In *El grito de gloria*, although the star-crossed love of Luis María and Natalia continues, the attention of the plot turns essentially to certain real figures (Lavalleja, Oribe, Rivera) and historical events (the substitution of Brazilian for Portuguese domination in 1824, the liberating "expedition of the Thirty Three," the decisive battle of Sarandí in 1825). The novel ends when Luis María, mortally wounded in Sarandí, dies in Natalia's arms. It is worth noting that with these novels Acevedo Díaz proposed not only to glorify the federalist cause, but also ethnically and culturally to vindicate the gaucho, the *mestizo*, the Black, and the Charrúa Indian as foundational elements in Uruguayanness.

In reading *Beba*, by Carlos Reyles, and *Gaucha*, by Javier de Viana, the reader has the impression of being in a country other than that portrayed by Acevedo Díaz. Of course, they were men with different professional and literary interests. Reyles, for example, was a rich rancher interested in the application of the latest scientific methods to improve agriculture and livestock. The past did not interest him, although the land did; he was a modern man who saw the National Territory as a vast ranch which could achieve progress through science and technology. The city did not interest him either; for him Montevideo was a sort of decadent appendage which had to be transformed from the interior of the country; the true center of Uruguay was the ranch of his era, and the true patriot was the modernizing rancher. There are three key characters in the novel: Gustavo, a modern, enterprising rancher in the Río Negro zone, spokesman for Reyles; Isabel (Beba), his niece, whom Gustavo saves from drowning in the river; and Rafael, married to Beba, a man weak in body and spirit who lives in Montevideo and who allegorizes, in Reyle's eyes, the parasitic life of the city. The love triangle is created when Gustavo and Beba realize their love for each other and have sexual relations. The conflict is resolved when Gustavo, ruined and consumed by remorse, leaves for Europe, and Beba commits suicide when she gives birth to a monstrous son, the product of the incest between uncle and niece. Beyond the fact that Reyles applied here his biological and social pseudo-scientific theories, in its metaphors of incest and the Río Negro the novel portrays the struggle between past and present, between nature and technology, between primitive culture and modern culture, between the instinctive side of human nature and the rational and civilized side. In the final analysis, thus, the allegorical conflict of *Beba* refers – and in a pessimistic way – to the conflict between the new and the old provoked by the process of modernization. Like Sarmiento in *Facundo*, Reyles leaves us the following message: the dark forces impeding the march of progress reside not only in untamed nature – the Río Negro – but also within those people who, as he did, advocate "civilization."

Although Javier de Viana fought in the ranks of the *Blanco* party, as did Acevedo Díaz, his representation of the gaucho is not compatible with the latter's portrayal in *Ismael*. This difference in criteria stems from each writer's fundamental concept of national literature. For Acevedo Díaz, as we have seen, the novel ought to be an instrument of both patriotic and moral education. The figure of the gaucho, therefore, should be designed in an epic fashion out of the nation's past and articulated by means of romantic, *costumbrista*, and realist codes. Javier de Viana, on the other hand, did not believe that literature should have an edifying function; his concern was that it should reflect the good and bad reality of things and, above all, that it should observe the changes taking place in the economic, social, and cultural spheres of the nation. For him the gaucho was not a fixed (foundational) figure, but rather a biological–social entity who, driven by the transformations in the structures of Uruguay, had completed a trajectory stretching from his birth to his adulthood, from his decline to his death. Misunderstood in his time, he was reproached by those who idealized the past for characterizing the gaucho as an animal. In fact, Viana thought the writer's role was to observe reality scientifically and, having nationalized the methods of the French experimental novel, he limited himself to narrating the moment of the gaucho's material and spiritual disintegration under the dynamic pressure of the modernization process.

The principal characters of *Gaucha* come into play in the following way: When her parents die, Juana is taken in by her uncle Don Zoilo, a taciturn and brutish gaucho who has his hut in an isolated spot. The girl loves Lucio, her childhood playmate, who returns her love. But then Lorenzo appears, a *bad gaucho* whose gang of bandoleers roves the area; taking advantage of Don Zoilo's absence, Lorenzo rapes Juana, an event which prompts her to break with Lucio. The lovers are reconciled, but the novel ends when Lorenzo kills Lucio in a knife duel, murders Don Zoilo, and provokes Juana's death by tying her naked to a tree so that she may be raped by the members of his gang.

Besides the three types of gauchos – Don Zoilo, Lucio, and Lorenzo – who occupy the novel's center stage, Viana included other typical frontier characters in his narrative: the boss, the agent, the backward rancher. Of all these, only Juana and Lucio are not morally degraded, although they are both very far from representing the handsome foundational pair of the romantic novel. Lucio is a timid gaucho with a weak character, and Juana is a squalid and neurotic beauty. With keen insight in his analysis of the gaucho, Viana observes that if Lorenzo had been born in earlier times, he would have channeled his earthy violence into the wars of liberation or the battles between *Blancos* and *Colorados*; that is, he would have been a hero of the fatherland as was Acevedo Díaz's Ismael. This relativistic position extends to the nation, of course, since the gaucho is its most powerful myth. Thus for Viana the Uruguayan nation was a changing organism, a biological species that lived, died, and was reborn, transformed by the interaction of genetic impulses and environmental agents; that is, speaking in metaphorical terms, nature and tradition on the one hand, and Europeanization and modernization on the other.

Mexico: Heriberto Frías, Emilio Rabasa, Angel de Campo, and Federico Gamboa

The last quarter of the nineteenth century is dominated by the figure of General Porfirio Díaz, whose dictatorial government was to last from

1876 until 1911. In spite of his *mestizo* origin, his liberal past, and his patriotic military career at the side of Juárez, Díaz was known for the heavy hand with which he punished any outbreak of anarchy, political opposition, and social nonconformity, as well as by the dispossession of lands and the violent repression he carried out against the Indians. At the same time, the prolonged stability of his government, the protection of foreign investments, and the decision to push the country towards progress in accord with positivistic ideas resulted in an era of prosperity unlike any other in the history of Mexico. Independent of the excessive concessions liberally granted to foreign investments, Porfirio Díaz's most serious error was the alliance he established with the clergy, and especially, with the powerful landowning and commercial oligarchy which he showered with privileges; that is, the old centralists and conservative sectors which had supported the Empire and had opposed the constitutional reforms of Juárez. In fact only the rich, the high-ranking members of the army and the official bureaucracy, the career professionals, and the intellectuals were favored by the Díaz government. The Indian and the *mestizo* masses of the peasantry were excluded from the benefits of the economic bonanza and the cultural development. Although literary production was affected by censorship, the Mexican novel of the Porfirio period shows an intrinsic mediocrity in general – banality, thematic poverty, didactisim, dramatic insufficiency – which cannot be explained solely by the restrictions imposed by censors. If one compares these novels with the works of Cambaceres, Acevedo Díaz, Reyles, Matto de Turner, Villaverde, Zeno Gandía, Carrasquilla, and even Mexican writers themselves such as Lizardi and Inclán, the reader will perceive at once an inequality which I cannot define more precisely than in terms of lack of passion, vigor, and conviction. Perhaps, as Manuel Pedro González has said, these deficiencies may reflect a feeling of guilt. It is worth noting that Díaz astutely offered prestigious offices to outstanding writers.

In any case, for one reason or another, the novelists of those years, with the exception of Heriberto Frías (1870–1925) in *Tomochic* (1894), generally did not criticize the dictatorship of Díaz nor did they show any interest in including the Indian as a real part of the nation. The importance of *Tomochic* lies in its documentary value; it is an early example of what today we would call the testimonial novel. The work narrates via realist and naturalist codes the rebellion, capture, and destruction of Tomochic, an Indian village in the north of the country which had rebelled against the authorities for political and religious reasons. Frías, who had participated in the campaign as a second lieutenant in the federal troops, relates the events through his character Miguel Mercado, also an army officer. Although an amorous conflict is presented in the novel, it lacks significance. The most interesting pages of the work are those which describe the semi-pagan cult of Tomochic and the most outstanding characters of the village: Cruz Chaves, who claims to be the reincarnation of San José, and a fanatical and combative woman known as the Saint of Cabora. Also of particular interest are the details Frías gives about the composition and customs of the federal army – for example, the description of the *soldaderas*, the women who followed the soldiers to the battlefields. Although Frías does not criticize the government directly, his sympathy for the Indians of Tomochic is evident. They belonged to the Yaqui nation whose tribes, refusing to be governed by the central authority and to participate in the process of modernization, maintained a state of rebellion throughout the Porfirio period. In any case, after publishing his novel in *El Demócrata* – closed down shortly thereafter – Frías was expelled from the army. Later he published other novels, but none of them equalled *Tomochic* in importance, the thematic materials and the journalistic style of which were to have an influence on *Los de abajo* (1911) [*The Underdogs*] by Mariano Azuela (1873–1952). The similarity existing between the rebellion of Tomochic and that of Canudos (Brazil, 1897), described by Euclides da Cunha (1866–1909) in *Os sertões* (1902) [*Rebellion in the Backlands*], speaks of a more or less common phenomenon in the Americas: the desperate cultural resistance with which the frontier villages met the process of modernization.

The four brief novels of Emilio Rabasa (1856–1930) should be read as parts of one single work. Although the series has been praised widely by literary critics, I think it lacks the originality which has been attributed to it. Its strategy is a replica of Lizardi's: the white middle class carries in its breast the destiny of the nation and, therefore, must be perfected morally lest the nation disintegrate. Although Rabasa criticizes in Lizardi's picaresque and *costumbrista* manner the violence (*La bola*), the politics (*La gran ciencia*), the corruption of the press (*El cuarto poder*) and the delinquency (*Moneda falsa*), his project does not include the peasant masses as a social component, nor the Indian as an ethnological factor in the Mexican nation. Furthermore, the didacticism of Lizardi reflects a vehement sincerity, while Rabasa's is artificial and banal. This same complacency with the *status quo* and with the restricted idea of the nation characteristic of the Porfirio period is to be found in *La Calandria*, the best-known novel by Rafael Delgado (1853–1914). Although *La parcela* (1898) by José López-Portillo y Rojas (1850–1923) deals with the problem of the illegal possession of land, it leaves the matter unresolved; it is, thus, not quite a novel of social denunciation.

La rumba, by Angel de Campo (Micrós), is a brief novel which is reminiscent stylistically of Groussac's *Fruto vedado*. Realistic features predominate in it, but there are also forms belonging to the most important literary currents of the nineteenth century, including *Moderismo*. Its execution is excellent, to the point that I believe it is the best-written Mexican novel of the decade. The title refers to the name of the plaza of a poor neighborhood in the capital and also to one of the meanings of the word *rumba*: a pile of things, a disorderly heap. The author describes with precision the poor spectacle which goes on in the plaza – puddles, mud, garbage, squalid dogs – as well as the sad existence of the neighborhood people, particularly that of a young woman named Remedios. The novel, as can easily be seen, lends itself to an allegorical reading. I agree with Brushwood (*Mexico in its Novel*) that *La rumba* attempts to present to the reader a collective space, that is to say, a marginal pocket of Mexicanness within the splendor of the Porfirio period.

Altamirano's *El Zarco*, published posthumously in 1901, is a typical foundation novel. In reality, it is a perfected variation of the model used by Altamirano himself in *Clemencia*. Here we encounter once again the binary opposition "white/dark" which divides the nation by skin color. At the beginning of the narrative Manuela (negative and white) loves El Zarco (negative and white), at the same time that she is courted by Nicolás (positive and dark), who in turn is loved secretly by Pilar (positive and dark). In her love for El Zarco, the real name of a bandit in the period, Manuela has let herself be dazzled by his appearance – virtually covered by silver ornaments – without taking note of his moral poverty. After rejecting Nicolás, the young woman runs away from her maternal home and goes to live with El Zarco, in whose camp, besides being the subject of humiliations, she realizes the perversity of the *plateados* (the silver-plated bandits). Soon she regrets having joined her destiny to that of the bandit, but, of course, it is too late. Nicolás, for his part, has the opportunity to test the love Pilar feels for him, and he decides to marry her. The novel ends with the capture and execution of El Zarco, the death of Manuela, and the wedding of Nicolás and Pilar. In triumphing over the "white" pair, Nicolás and Pilar define and simultaneously legitimize the "dark" color of Mexicanness. Nevertheless, it is not the Indian of the peasant masses – who was to rise with Hidalgo, Morelos, and Guerrero – to whom Altamirano refers. Although Nicolás is an Indian from a racial point of view, he is not in an economic, political, social, and cultural sense. Thus, the most representative color of the nation is neither "white" nor that of the unassimilated Indian, but rather a "dark" color wrapping like a contradictory peeling, a being who has the European attributes of "civilization." In effect, Nicolás turns out to be an alter ego of Altamirano and even of Juárez himself, who appears at the end of the novel as an example of civility and patriotism. In reality, *El Zarco* is a visibly anachronistic novel. Its allegory, articulated in neoclassical, romantic, and *costumbrista* codes, corresponds to the utopian schemes entertained by writers and politicians in the second quarter of the century. Something similar occurs in the interminable *costumbrista* pamphlet by Manuel Payno, *Los bandidos de Río Frío*, published in serial form in 1889–1891.

Of all the writers of the Porfirio period, Federico Gamboa was the one who most successfully nationalized the French models of Naturalism, although he did it in a much less radical way than Cambaceres and Viana, particularly because scientific determinism had a limited impact on the thought of the Porfirio period. The positivistic tendencies of that era were aimed towards religious positions of the Catholic church – free will on the one hand, hope for redemption on the other. Thus neither Gamboa's naturalism nor, at the bottom, Mexican Positivism was based on a scientific conception of society or the world. It is true that we see in his novels characters and settings taken from French naturalistic narrative – the adulterous relationship of *Suprema ley*, the sinful nun of *Metamorfosis* – but this appropriation is merely thematic, not ideological. *Santa*, his best-known work, relates the story of a country girl who, after being seduced and abandoned, works as a prostitute in a brothel in the capital. Very soon Santa becomes the favorite of the customers and, like Zola's Nana, she rules over the gay, dissipated life of the place. After being the lover of a bullfighter and of a rich man, things go badly for her and she sinks to the depths of her profession and falls ill from cancer. Fallen into physical and moral decadence, she is redeemed by the pure love of Hipólito, a blind pianist who played at the brothel where she had earlier reigned supreme. Although Santa dies at the end, she is at peace with God and with herself; thanks to the transforming love of Hipólito, her death implies a Christian hope, a resurrection. Brushwood (*Mexico in its Novel*) astutely observes that the character of Santa can be read as an allegory of Mexico at the turn of the century, that is to say, when the national values, corrupted by the immorality of the Porfirio period, needed to break down completely so as to be reborn in another historical moment.

Cuba and Puerto Rico: Cirilo Villaverde and Manuel Zeno Gandía

Although in Cuba the process of modernization began during the Spanish domination – one must remember that the island did not achieve independence until 1902 – the process was financed in great measure by the North American demand for sugar. This tendency is seen during the 1860s, the period when the old sugar mill began to be replaced by the modern *central*, with the consequent increase in production and export. Nevertheless, in spite of the high technology used in sugar manufacturing as well as the impressive advances achieved in transportation and communications, Cuban modernization excluded agriculture in general from its reach, even the cultivation of cane sugar. Thus, while sugar productivity in the industrial sector continued to increase, it remained stagnant in the agricultural sector, where labor was basically slave labor until 1880–1886. In the post-slavery period Cuba was unable to overcome this contradiction, and so agrarian structures continued to be obsolete and the rural population scarcely benefited from the industrial modernization. Likewise, since the country continued to depend on sugar exports and on the black cane cutter, the old socioeconomic dynamics of the slave plantation underwent little transformation. These circumstances explain why anti-slavery novels like *Sab* and *Francisco*, written in the decade of the 1830s, aroused interest half a century later, and why the problematics of race were reflected in the works of Francisco Calcagno (1827–1903), Martín Morúa Delgado (1857–1910) and, above all, in *Cecilia Valdés* by Cirilo Villaverde.

When the definitive version of *Cecilia Valdés* was published in New York, Villaverde's political exile in the United States had lasted more than thirty years. Involved in the conspiracies (1848–1851), of Narciso López whose secretary he was, he had ceased writing fiction at the moment when his literary talent was flourishing. In 1849, after having been captured and condemned to death by the Spanish authorities, he had escaped jail and managed to take ship for Florida. Settled in New York as a teacher and translator, both he and his wife would prove to be active propagandists for Cuban independence. Then, in circumstances so inauspicious for literary endeavors, what reasons did Villaverde have to dust off his old novelistic project, interrupted forty years earlier? Certainly it was not for abolitionist reasons, for slavery had been abolished in Cuba in 1880. Neither was it for political reasons, given that the action of the novel takes place in the first quarter of the nineteenth century. Indeed, the modern critic must also face another question: how to classify *Cecilia Valdés*, if it has been said to be a historical novel, a *costumbrista* novel, a testimonial novel, an anti-slavery novel, a romantic novel, a realist novel, a social novel, a pessimistic novel, even a racist novel?

I think these questions can be answered through a single commentary. I read *Cecilia Valdés* as the legacy of a founder of Cuban nationality, born into the generation of Echeverría and Delmonte, who was to die in the generation of Martí and Darío. At the end of the nineteenth century there were very few Cubans who knew the problems of his country as well as Villaverde; the fatherland had always been his topic. This patriotic constancy is precisely what leads me to believe that the completion and publication of *Cecilia Valdés* ought to be seen as the recapitulation of Villaverde's long dialogue with Cuba. I mean to say here that *Cecilia Valdés* is above all a foundational novel – although, I would add at once, it is a foundational novel far more complex and paradoxical than those we have seen, for it celebrates the constitution of Cubanness at the same time as it speaks of the ethnological tensions undermining the coherence of the nation. It is no accident that Cirilo Villaverde shared with the character of Cecilia Valdés a common date of birth (1812) and the same initials (C. V.), nor that in the novel Cecilia Valdés was known in the popular Havana world as the *Virgencita de Bronce* (the little bronze Virgin), that is, the mulatto Virgin, the Virgen de la Caridad del Cobre, the mythic image of the nation itself. In summary, I think the text of *Cecilia Valdés* presents itself as a problematic variant of this myth, in the sense that it desires the racial, social, and cultural integration of the fatherland while at the same time speaking of the impossibility of achieving such a synthesis, not even within the sociocultural space constructed by modernization. The paradoxical center of Cubanness is allegorized several times in the novel, for example in the chapter which speaks about the sugar mill, or also in the chapter which describes the dance the mulatto woman Mercedes gives at her house. In the latter case we see an overflowing crowd of Blacks, Whites, and mulattoes of various social classes, among them the principal protagonists of the novel: Cecilia Valdés, a beautiful quadroon; Leonardo Gamboa, a young White from the sugar and slave-owning aristocracy; and José Dolores Pimienta, a mulatto clarinet player who plays in the little orchestra. There, on the occasion of the festive gathering, Whites and Blacks eat, drink, joke, and enjoy themselves together, dancing to the music which now belongs to everyone, the *danza cubana*. Nevertheless, the sociocultural harmony is irreparably broken when Cecilia, already desired by José Dolores, begins to be desired by Leonardo. "Don't the whites have enough women of their own?" José Dolores complains. "Why do they have to come take ours away from us?" But the problem is much more serious and cannot be reduced to the "Black/White" opposition alone. Leonardo desires Cecilia because of her physical resemblance to his white sister, Adela Gamboa. The incest, however, cannot be avoided, since Leonardo and Cecilia have sexual relations without knowing that both are children of the same father. In this way, the incestuous desire is presented to the reader as a generalized and fatal defect which runs through the Cuban nation, reducing its effectiveness to the extent that it is a slave-owning and patriarchal project. It is precisely the desperation with which Villaverde contemplates the cracks in the Cuban nation which makes *Cecilia Valdés* a turn-of-the-century novel, in spite of his marked *costumbrista* and romantic features. When one reads the novels of Calcagno, Morúa Delgado, and Ramón Meza (1861–1911) the commentary on which would be essential in a more extensive study, one must conclude that none of these writers attempted to reveal the incongruities of Cubanness to the extent that Villaverde proposed to do.

In Puerto Rico, unlike Cuba, the process of modernization hardly developed during the nineteenth century. Although sugar and coffee exports increased, the isolation and economic backwardness suffered by the island under the colonial Spanish administration prevented the formation of strong commercial and financial capital as well as the organization of an infrastructure capable of underpinning the modernizing impulse. For the latter purpose it was essential to raise the education and the productivity of the peasant, a theme which Manuel Zeno Gandía (1855–1930) developed in *La charca*.

The subtitle of Zeno Gandía's novel is *Crónicas de un mundo enfermo*, which illustrates the naturalist perspective of the work. The author, a physician by profession, attempted to make a clinical diagnosis of the rural population, then enmired in backwardness, malnutrition, and poverty. The main character is Silvina, who after having been raped by Galante, a rich and immoral landowner, is forced to marry one of his peons, a degenerate named Gaspar. The plot of the novel revolves around Gaspar's plan to kill the owner of a local store, a man named Andújar, in order to steal the money he kept in a trunk. Gaspar counts on the assistance of an accomplice (Deblás) and of Silvina, whom he forces to participate in the crime. But when Andújar is warned of the plan to kill him, he flees from the store and gives cause for confusion: Andrés and Silvina kill Deblás in the dark, taking him for Andújar. When Andrés runs away, one might think Silvina is left free to join Ciro, the man she always loved, but he is knifed to death by his own brother. Finally Silvina suffers an epileptic attack and throws herself off a cliff.

The secondary characters in *La charca* meet no better fate, and Zeno Gandía's social diagnosis is alarming: the Puerto Rican peasant is a physically and morally defective being; he lives outside the reach of science, religion, education, health, work, and the family, and although there are educated people who would like to see him emerge from his degradation, their good intentions are insufficient for the task.

Peru: Clorinda Matto de Turner

Although the Indian tribute system and the slavery of Blacks were abolished during the second presidential term (1854–1862) of Ramón Castilla, in the following years the oligarchy of landowners and entrepreneurs which dominated Peru proved incapable of transforming in depth the socioeconomic structures inherited from the colonial period. The construction of the railroad brought enormous international debts and, after the conclusion of the War of the Pacific (1879–1883), Peru had lost to Chilean hands the coastal region producing guano and nitrate for export. Mired in economic and political crisis, the country demanded a change. In 1895 Nicolás Piérola founded the Democratic Party and won the presidential elections. But once again modernizing efforts failed to improve the economic and social conditions of the rural peasantry, particularly of the Indians in the Andean region, whose numbers had already reached 2 million and constituted the bulk of the population.

At the end of the 1880s Manuel González Prada (1848–1918), the most important Peruvian intellectual of those years, had begun to criticize the conservative alliance sharply – the church, the army, the state, the landowners, and the business interests – who had lost the war with Chile and brought the country to ruin. In his modernizing proposals González Prada saw the education of the Indian and his social improvement as a necessity, so that he could be incorporated into the nation, ideas which, although they enjoyed little acceptance, established a basis for the renovation of the Indianist literature of romantic stamp still being cultivated at that time. This new direction was characterized by denunciations of the concrete abuses suffered by the Indian in the Andes, the most conservative region in Peru. Clorinda Matto de Turner (1854–1909), influenced by González Prada, introduced this new tendency into the national novel with *Aves sin nido* [*Birds Without a Nest*]. Nevertheless, *El Padre Horán* by Narciso Aréstegui should be considered a romantic–liberal antecedent. One should also not ignore Mercedes Cabello de Carbonera (1843–1909), whose serial urban novels were built on positivistic ideas.

The plot of *Aves sin nido* is set in Killac, a village on the eastern edge of the Andes. The characters are numerous. In the first place there are Margarita and Manuel, the young lovers who are unaware that they have a common father in the Bishop Pedro de Miranda. They are followed by two married couples, Marcela and Juan Yupanqui, a humble pair, and Petronila and Sebastián Pancorbo, who represent the local political and economic power. Both Marcela and Petronila were victims of Bishop Miranda's sexual rapacity when he was the village priest, and thus it is that they turn out to be the respective mothers of Margarita and Manuel. Finally there are Lucía and Fernando Marín, a generous couple of white race and comfortable position who have taken up temporary residence in Killac for business reasons. This exemplary couple, who hold Matto de Turner's positivistic ideas, run into conflict with the local political and religious authorities when they pay the Yupanquis' debts and save them from poverty. Furious about what they judge to be an interference in the internal affairs of the village, Sebastián Pancorbo and the priest Pascual Vargas organize an armed assault on the Maríns' home. The Maríns survive, but not so the Yupanquis, who had run to help their benefactors when they heard the gunfire. Before she dies, Marcela reveals the secret of the illegitimate birth of Margarita, who has by then been adopted by the Maríns; they do not make this public, however, until the end of the novel, when Manuel comes to ask for her hand and reveals that he is, in turn, the illegitimate son of Bishop Miranda.

As Antonio Cornejo Polar says (in *La formación de la tradición literaria en el Perú*), the novel can be seen as an ethical–pedagogical project in the sense that it advocated the education of the Indian as a means of integrating the nation while denouncing at the same time, the immorality of the institutions which regulated the Indian's life. Matto de Turner clarified her ideas even more in *Herencia*, where we find Margarita Yupanqui, educated by the Maríns, shining in Lima society and entering into an advantageous marriage. Although Matto de Turner subscribed to a positivistic national project in her works, it cannot be said that the author looked on the future with optimism. Margarita's adoption by the Maríns is only a casuistic example which cannot by any means be taken as a successful demonstration of her thesis. Indeed, the author herself seems to question the practical value of good individual actions when she wonders, as she refers to the Indian Isidro Champí's's liberation from jail, "And who will liberate his whole disinherited race?" In any case, independent of the naive pedagogical Positivism of Matto de Turner's novels, *Aves sin nido* is an important work in more than one sense. In the first place, it desires the integration of the Indian into the nation in conditions of civil equality; in the second place, in denouncing the colonial practices still oppressing the Andean villages at the end of the century, it speaks of the limitations of the modernization process as an agent for the transformation of the Peruvian nation.

Venezuela and Colombia: Gonzalo Picón Febres and Tomás Carrasquilla

The modernization of Venezuela began under the dictatorship of General Antonio Guzmán Blanco, who governed the country, with brief interruptions, between 1870 and 1888. His administration was characterized, on the one hand, by authoritarianism and corruption, and on the other, by the adoption of liberal measures, among them the organization of a system of public education and the dismantling of the power of the church. During his dictatorship there were frequent uprisings organized by the Conservatives, but they were crushed. He was succeeded by General Joaquín Crespo, under whose government the country once again fell into political and economic chaos. Crespo died in 1898 as he put down the rebellion of a local strong man. A year later General Cipriano Castro took power, initiating a disastrous military dictatorship.

The most important Venezuelan novelist of the period was Gonzalo Picón Febres (1860–1918), author of *Fidelia* (1893), *Nieve y lodo* (1895), and *El sargento Felipe*, his best work. The action of *El sargento Felipe* takes place in the times of Guzmán Blanco, although its pacifist message is directed toward the armed factions who fought for power towards the end of the century. The first chapters describe in a *modernista* manner the patriarchal world of Felipe: the beautiful and wild nature, the abundant coffee harvest, the bucolic simplicity of country life, the domestic order under the care of Gertrudis (wife) and Encarnación (daughter), humble and hard-working women. Very much against his will, Felipe must abandon his small farm, for he has been drafted by Guzmán Blanco's army to crush the rebellion of a conservative strong man. Then suddenly, the situation changes, and with it the language of the novel, which takes on realist and naturalist features from that point forward. In Felipe's absence, his harmonious paradise is swept by a series of calamities: soldiers from both sides steal his sacks of coffee, cows, and breeding livestock; his house is destroyed by fire, and Gertrudis dies from burns; Encarnación is seduced by Don Jacinto, the owner of the local store, and becomes his public lover. After receiving a letter relating these unhappy events, Felipe, who is convalescing from a machete wound in the head, begs the general of the loyal forces to give him permission to visit his family. Granted leave, Felipe goes home. When he sees the scorched ruins of his house and his crops invaded by weeds, lizards, and snakes, he falls into despair. After killing Don Jacinto with a bullet, he commits suicide by throwing himself over a precipice.

The novel is dedicated "To the honorable and industrious people of Venezuela – true victim of our civil wars." His clear and direct pessimism denounces the violence generated by the political factions struggling for power. Picón Febres does not care, in the last analysis, about the modernization of Venezuela under the liberal project, nor does he care about the triumph of the conservative project. His novel places him outside both the Positivism of the one and the traditionalism of the other; he takes the side of the rural peasant, who has been and will continue to be the loser, regardless of which strong man emerges victorious.

In Colombia the civil wars between Liberals and Conservatives were even more frequent and bloody than in Venezuela. The points of conflict between the national projects of one party and the other were, basically, what type of political system the country ought to have, that is to say, the Centralist/Federalist confrontation and, in second place, what role the church should play within the Colombian state. In the third quarter of the century the liberal project (federalist and anticlerical) prevailed, while in the last two decades the conservative project was installed in power with the government of Rafael Núñez, who was to initiate the so-called Period of Regeneration. Nevertheless, the armed conflicts between Conservatives and Liberals were to continue for many years, and as the century came to a close, the bloody War of One Thousand Days (1899–1903) began, won by the Conservatives.

The principal novelist who emerged in this turbulent era was Tomás

Carrasquilla (1858–1940) one of the most important and least-read writers of Spanish American literature. Although his major works were written in the twentieth century, his first novel *Frutos de mi tierra*, corresponds to this period. In this novel Carrasquilla already exhibits the powerful and mature realist–naturalist language which was to characterize him as a twentieth-century writer. Nevertheless, beyond its contemporary language, *Frutos de mi tierra* follows the strategies of the Spanish American novel of the end of the century in criticizing the more or less modernized society of the period. Given Carrasquilla's conservative ideas, his criticism is orientated by the codes of the Catholic church, and in this he is not far from Lizardi. In *Frutos de mi tierra*, as in Periquillo, we see a picaresque character take advantage of those who place their trust in him. In effect, César, a youth of loose morals from Bogotá, seduces his Aunt Filomena, a rich spinster from Medellín. After marrying, with a dispensation from the bishop, César steals Filomena's entire fortune and disappears, provoking her death. This denouement, where the picaresque hero is not reformed and the crime goes unpunished, reflects the difference between Lizardi's optimistic didacticism and Carrasquilla's pessimistic version, which is invested with the irony and Naturalism typical of the novel of the end of the century.

By way of recapitulation, one should note that in the novels of this period the nations of Spanish America are a long way from representing the projects advocated by the writers of the post-Independence period. In reality, political reconciliation had not been achieved, and national order could be accomplished only under the strong hand of dictators and authoritarian governments; slaves had been liberated and the Indians relieved of their tribute, but both continued to be oppressed and discriminated against both for their race and for their culture; educational programs had not managed to "civilize" the rural peasant, and the hoped-for white immigration had not brought, in general, either Anglo-Saxons or Germanic peoples, but rather Asians, Jews, and rustic people from Galicia, the Canary Islands, Sicily, Calabria, and other peripheral areas of Europe; exports had grown, but along with them, so had foreign debts and investments; the large cities had been somewhat modernized, but only for the benefit of the upper and middle classes; the Catholic church had lost much of its iron power over the lives of the faithful, and customs had become much more tolerant, but a wave of immorality, lust for luxury, crime, and vice swept over the national territory from one end to the other. Certainly, from Lizardi's time until that of Carrasquilla, things had changed not only for the better but also for the worse. The national projects, without disappearing altogether, had been worn down by their compromises with the political, economic, social, and cultural realities of each nation; Positivism had aged along with Sarmiento and was represented, at the close of the century, by the decadent figure of Porfirio Díaz. Spanish America had not been united, as Bolívar had once hoped for, nor had the novel limited itself to recounting edifying themes, as Bello would have preferred. Even the patriotic novel – I am thinking here of *Juan de la Rosa* by the Bolivian Nataniel Aguirre (1843–1888), the series by Acevedo Díaz, and *Durante la reconquista* by Blest Gana – leaves the reader with the certainty that the nation was divided from its very beginnings by differences of all kinds. The hero of these novels is no longer the statuesque figure of *El Capitán de Patricios* by Juan María Gutiérrez, but a collective character with virtues and defects: the people. Thus in the nineteenth century the novel traveled a parabolic route in its dialogue with the nation. It began by singing of the nation's potential and ended by listing its faults. It proposed to gather the disperse elements of nationality via the romance, and ended by examining them up close and separately, as if they were sick organs of the social body. At this critical time the novel ceases to be in style as a major literary genre among Spanish American intellectuals; it has been vanquished by poetry. In effect, faced with the pompous exoticism and the metric and rhythmic fireworks of *modernista* poetry, the novel of Nationness folds up. Except for a few examples of foundational-style works which appear within the *modernista* artistic canons, the novel was not to reappear with vigor until the second decade of our century. When it does reappear, with more aesthetic experience and from other certainly no less illusory perspectives, it is basically in order to take up once again its paradoxical dialogue with progress and the land.

14

The brief narrative in Spanish America: 1835–1915
Enrique Pupo-Walker

The costumbrista sketch

By any account the history of nineteenth-century Spanish America appears as a relentless panorama of upheaval. After gaining independence from Spain, the former colonies endured a long process of ideological and territorial fragmentation. Frail republics emerged everywhere, soon to be split up by the vicious struggles caused by *caudillos* and local bosses. Quite suddenly this conglomeration of independent territories faced the need to view itself as a community of nations, linked by similar institutions and a common history. Yet in those initial days of turmoil they did not find it easy to think in terms of covenants and solidarity. Chile and Brazil managed to consolidate relatively stable political systems but such was not the case in Argentina, Colombia, Mexico, and other new republics. Cuba and Puerto Rico were still lagging behind as colonial possessions. The disruptions set in motion by independence were aggravated by the territorial ambitions of foreign powers. In 1833 England occupied the Malvinas Islands; in the 1840s the United States divested Mexico of half its territory and in the early 1860s France sought to control what was left of the impoverished Mexican republic.

Predictably, the widespread turbulence reigning in nineteenth-century Spanish America is reflected in the political discourse and literary output of that period. The early novels, and, above all, the massive flow of texts produced by the *costumbristas* offer striking descriptions of societies besieged by uncertainties and political violence. The *costumbristas* practiced "the sketch of customs and manners." They produced brief narratives of imprecise contours which we have come to know mainly as *cuadros de costumbres*. Because of their very diverse structures, it would be difficult to single out particular texts that could stand as emblems of the literary achievements of the *costumbristas* in the first half of the nineteenth century. Indeed, if one could think of such texts, "El matadero" (1837?) ["The Slaughterhouse"] by Esteban Echeverría (Argentina, 1805–1851) would be a valid choice. In spite of its brevity, "El matadero" offers a representative collage of prevailing narrative forms. It also anticipates works of greater complexity such as *Facundo* (1845) by Domingo F. Sarmiento (Argentina, 1811–1888).

In almost any reassessment of what has been written about Hispanic prose of the last century one will conclude that the most tentative of judgments are directed toward the *costumbrista* narrative. Many have made persistent efforts to discern the precursors of the *cuadro de costumbres*, while others insist on pigeonholing it by way of formal or historiographic definitions. In his prologue to the works of José María Pereda (1833–1906) Marcelino Menéndez y Pelayo concluded that the *costumbrista* sketch was not a narrative form "subservient to the novel" (p. 37). He alluded to the long history of the *cuadro de costumbres* and to the variety of its structural designs. Placing further emphasis on the ambiguities that have surrounded the *costumbrista* tale, José Montesinos warned us that not even Ramón Mesonero Romanos (1803–1882) – a leading Spanish *costumbrista* – was able to pinpoint its most distinctive features. Mesonero himself told readers of *Los españoles pintados por sí mismos*, II (1843): "Sometimes the *cuadro de costumbres* relates a story approaching the novel; in other instances it turns into a tale that nibbles at history" *Obras completas*, (p. 503). The definitions produced in Spanish America were equally vague. In his *Apuntes de ranchería* (1884), the Colombian José Caicedo Rojas (1816–1897), celebrated as the Mesonero of his country, chose to underline simple utilitarian notions. He argued that *costumbrista* sketches should be seen mainly as "indispensable complements to the historical narrative; they are particularly useful for appraising a society in all its contrastive aspects" (p. 7). If we consider the pragmatic bent of Caicedo's definition and the vague historiographic statements made by Menéndez y Pelayo and Mesonero, we can see the *cuadro de costumbres* as a text which tends to blend dissimilar rhetorical models. I believe that such a plurality of models explains, at least in part, why literary scholars have used so many labels to define the *costumbrista* tale.

In *El krausismo español* (1980) Juan López Morillas accurately characterized the *costumbristas* in these terms: "Their preoccupation with minute detail, local color, the picturesque, and their concern with matters of style is frequently no more than a subterfuge. Astonished by the contradictions they observed around them, incapable of clearly understanding the tumult of the modern world, these writers sought refuge in the particular, the trivial or the ephemeral" (p. 129). As a general characterization of the *cuadro de costumbres*, one would have to say that those texts tend to develop several lines of arguments linked to a slight anecdote. The *costumbristas* narrative also blends autobiographical information with satirical remarks, while incorporating quotations from journalistic sources, bits of poetry and traces of popular culture. But if these components of the *cuadro de costumbres* are not visible at times, it is because the presence of the storyteller often tends to overwhelm the story. Indirectly this kind of testimonial overkill illustrates the problematic relationship of the speaker with the main line of the tale. In other instances the *cuadro de costumbres* is a curious enactment of experiences, which masks its fictional status. In many instances, those narrative sketches come closer to the essay than to the well-structured story.

The *costumbristas* narrative generally exhibits a content so predictable that it turns writing into ritual. If we keep these features in mind, then we will understand why literary historiography has never known quite what to do with the *cuadro de costumbres*. A case in point is "El matadero," a landmark of *Costumbrismo* but which cannot be defined exclusively in relation to literary provenance. In fact, it is the eclectic make-up of that perplexing tale that makes it so distinctive. It alludes to concrete historical circumstances and prevailing ideologies, but on a more subtle level it describes an explosive situation which evolves in unforeseen ways. Echeverría's text thus demonstrates how alternate modes of narrative development are used in the *cuadro de costumbres*. Consequently, I would argue that any informed reading of narratives of this kind will have to recognize, first of all, their stubborn resistance to definitions. The disparities among *costumbrista* tales are even more noticeable when we examine the modalities they assumed in Spain and Spanish America.

Spanish *costumbristas* such as Mariano José de Larra (1809–1837), Mesonero Romanos, and Serafín Estebánez Calderón (1799–1867) achieved wide dissemination in Spanish America. It is a bit surprising that writers who often resented the institutional legacies of Spain were quick to confess their admiration for these peninsular authors. The well-known Argentinian Juan Bautista Alberdi (1810–1884) adopted the pseudonym "Figarillo" – an implicit tribute to Larra, who was known as "Fígaro." Sarmiento also called himself "Fígaro" in a letter he sent on January 10, 1876 to the Chilean writer and political leader José Victorino Lastarria (1817–1888), (Del Piño, *Correspondencia entre Sarmiento y Lastarria*, 94). The impact of the Spanish *costumbristas* on Spanish Americans is undeniable, but seem particularly odd when we remember the tide of nationalistic feelings prevailing in Spanish America during the nineteenth century. New nations had to be consolidated and this urgent agenda eventually pressed literary discourse into service as a means to strengthen national identity. No genre played a larger role in that effort than the *costumbrista* narrative. Indeed, their broad nationalistic statements conferred on many *cuadros de costumbres* the role of founding texts. Every regional feature or custom had to be registered in minute detail, and this task made literary activity accessible to almost everyone; unfortunately, writing was thus often reduced to a shallow descriptive performance. Moreover, the abundant references to minor events and personalities dated the scant imaginary content of the *cuadro de costumbres*.

Limitations of this kind did not, however, seem to inhibit the massive proliferation of the *costumbrista* narrative. The number of magazines, weeklies, and supplements devoted to the satirical depiction of customs and manners multiplied all over Spanish America. *Las Hojas de aviso* (1861–1862) or *La semana* (1865–1871) published by the Guatemalan José Milla (1822–1882), the Mexican magazines *Miscelánea* (1829–1832), *Minerva* (1834) or *El Museo Popular* (1840–1842) were quite receptive to all forms of the *costumbrista* sketch. Today, few realize how large is the *corpus* of narratives produced by the *costumbristas*. In his *Letras colombianas* Baldomero Sanín Cano (1861–1957) alludes more than once to the "tyranny" (p. 94) imposed on Colombian literary circles by the *costumbristas*. The overwhelming vogue of this particular narrative modality has been documented in great detail by Frank M. Duffey (*The Early Cuadro de Costumbres in Colombia*) and by Salvador Bueno in his *Temas y personajes de la literatura cubana*. The impact of *Costumbrismo* is recorded even more vividly in seminal publications such as: *Los cubanos pintados por sí mismos* (1852) and *Los mexicanos pintados por sí mismos* (1855). These and similar volumes appeared everywhere in Spanish America; they were regional variations of well-known precedents, namely *Los españoles pintados por sí mismos* (1843) and the *Enciclopedia de tipos vulgares y costumbres de Barcelona* (1844). Both of these Spanish encyclopedic undertakings were inspired by *Les français par eux-mêmes* (1840–1842). Though such models were acknowledged, the Spanish American *costumbristas* felt the need to establish a literary genealogy of their own, as they could no longer recognize themselves in the cultural and literary paradigms of a decadent Spain.

With no better options at hand, Spanish American authors gradually adopted some of the earliest historical depictions of the New World as cornerstones of their literary lineage. This change of perspective began to manifest itself in the twilight of the colonial period and is particularly evident in *Los infortunios de Alonso Ramírez* (1680) and in other works by the Mexican savant Carlos de Sigüenza y Góngora (1645–1700). Political independence led inevitably to a broad reassessment of the cultural heritage of Spanish America. The desire to identify texts that could stand as the matrix of a distinct literary tradition is particularly evident in "Modos de escribir la historia", a crucial article published by the Venezuelan Andrés Bello (1781–1865) in 1848. In it Bello underscored the need to establish the American narrative traditions which he wished to base on pre-Columbian traditions, and on the earliest historical accounts. Others advocated the same idea. In an ironic vein, Echeverría reminded us, at the beginning of "El matadero," that "The early Spanish historians of the New World ought to be our models" (p. 3). An even more complex elaboration of this notion also appeared in Echeverría's famous essay "Situación y porvenir de la literatura hispanoamericana" (1846), in which he responded to an article by the conservative Spanish writer Antonio Alcalá Galiano (1789–1865). Four decades later Bartolomé Mitre (1821–1906), a leading Argentine statesman and historian, exalted in *La Revista de Buenos Aires* (1881) the significance of *La historia verdadera de la conquista de la Nueva España* (1632) by Bernal Díaz del Castillo (1492–1581), a work which was still poorly known. Curiously enough modern echoes of these issues persist in Jorge Luis Borges's essay "Las alarmas del doctor Américo Castro" (1960).

If I give some prominence to this turn of events, it is simply to underscore a singular facet of Spanish American *Costumbrismo*, which has no equivalent in peninsular literary circles of that period. I refer here to the persistent links which exist between Spanish American *Costumbrismo* and the early historiography of the New World. Spawning a new historical consciousness appealed to the Romantics and particularly to Spanish American authors during the nineteenth century. That is partly why a wealth of anecdotes contained in chronicles of the colonial period repeatedly found their way into the *costumbrista* narrative. *Los comentarios reales del Perú* (1609–1617) by the Inca Garcilaso de la Vega (1540–1616), *El carnero* (1637) by Juan Rodríguez Freyle (1566–1640) and *El lazarillo de ciegos caminantes* (1773) by Alonso Carrió de la Vandera (1715–1783) are among the richest sources of anecdotes utilized mainly by South American *costumbristas*.

In fact, that imaginative reconstruction of Spanish American history is at the very root of Ricardo Palma's (Peru, 1833–1919) well-known *tradiciones* – a type of narrative structure which is a distinctive variant of the *cuadro de costumbres*. The *tradición* is usually a brief tale that thrives on rambling commentary and that is prone to ironic digressions. Palma blended these traits astutely, thus giving to his interpolations and asides an effective conversational flow that seemed awkward in the texts of his many imitators. The artful linking of subordinate clauses – which Palma learned from the colonial chroniclers he loved so well – gave his writing a certain archaic charm. "Amor de madre: crónica de la época del Virrey Brazo de Plata" (1880) and "Un cerro que tiene historia" (1875?) are certainly among his best *tradiciones*. His meandering tales appeared, almost without interruption, from 1872 to 1911.

Similar reconsiderations of past literary accomplishments are also evident in the articles of the prominent Chilean *costumbrista* José Joaquín

Vallejo (1811–1858), better known as "Jotabeche." Like many of his peers, Vallejo was a journalist and a political leader. That dual role as protagonist in and commentator on social and political events is even more visible in the cases of Echeverría, Alberdi, Sarmiento, Lastarria, and many other practitioners of the *costumbrista* sketch. The overt blending of political activity and literary creation helps to explain the strong ideological content of Spanish American *Costumbrismo*, a generalization which cannot be applied so freely to peninsular writers of the period. In some of the thirty-nine articles that "Jotabeche" published in *El Mercurio*, in the brief historical narratives he gathered in *El último jefe español en Araucho* (1845), and in *Francisco Montero; recuerdos del año 1820* (1847), the Chilean *Costumbrista* seems to follow Bello's advice. In his own limited fashion, Vallejo attempts to create a literature that will define the cultural profile of his new nation, and in a larger sense, of Spanish America.

Very similar concerns with a past that could sustain a new present surfaced in the articles, reviews, and sketches of other well-known *costumbristas*. The Colombians José Manuel Groot (1800–1878), Eugenio Díaz Castro (1804–1865), and José María Vergara y Vergara (1831–1872) cultivated a kind of *costumbrista* narrative which was loosely based on historical facts and regional legends. The bulk of their writings appeared in *El Mosaico* (1858–1872), a journal largely devoted to the miscellaneous agendas of *Costumbrismo*. Capricious weaving of fiction and factual data is what one often finds in the writings of the Venezuelan Juan Manuel Cagigal (1803–1856) and in the tales of the Peruvian Felipe Pardo Aliaga (1806–1868), although the latter was severely hampered by his reactionary outlook and by the nostalgic bent of his ruminations. For sharper reflections on the imaginative use of history, we must turn to the *Artículos satíricos y de costumbres* (1847) by José María de Cárdenas Rodríguez (Cuba, 1812–1882). That text and the astute prologue written by the Cuban novelist Cirilo Villaverde (1812–1894) once again reexamine the past and the avatars of literary creation, but with an outlook shaped by American conceptions of history. Their compatriot Francisco Baralt (?–1890) characterized in greater detail ways of life derived from a lengthy colonial past, although in his *Ensayos Literarios* (1846) he yields to the classifying urge that trivializes much of the writing produced by the *Costumbristas*. "For the depiction of customs," he wrote, "there is no better context or more fertile source than direct observation. The gravity of the English is found alongside the agreeable frivolity of the French, the noble pride and disdain of the Castilian next to the lazy voluptuousness of the Spanish fortune-hunter in America. And because Columbus's followers mixed with the Ciboney indians, their descendants now enjoy the sensual habits and gentleness of that vanished race" (p. 21).

Even when writing in a humorous manner, Baralt and his contemporaries anticipated the observations made many years later by the erudite Venezuelan Mariano Picón Salas (1901–1965) in the brief introduction to his *Satíricos y costumbristas venezolanos* (1956): "*costumbrista* writing is seen as the primary path, if not towards autochthonous themes, certainly toward the earliest conceptualizations of our own literary tradition" (p. 5). That effort to focus on the distinct cultural traits of a society can also be detected in *Tipos y costumbres de la isla de Cuba* (1881), a large anthology of *costumbrista* writers edited by Miguel de Villa. In it, Antonio Bachiller y Morales (1812–1889) evokes a rapid sequence of images as he describes the social and economic activity surrounding him: "A collection of Cuban types: Negroes rising at the crack of dawn, four-legged creatures moving to the sea ... and the muleteers who stand by and await the cannon shot of the Ave María ... [and] beyond the rich leisurely at gambling tables and around them many other social types" (p. 27). Like most of his peers, Bachiller y Morales was attempting a taxonomic effort which can be traced to many shorter but seminal articles published in *El Papel Periódico de la Habana* (1790). A kindred inclination to categorize appears as well in the graceful pages of *Colección de artículos* (1859) by Anselmo Suárez y Romero (Cuba, 1818–1878). And, much to our amazement, that narrative bent of mind, intent on ordering and typifying, endured in the numerous *Estampas* that Eladio Secades (Cuba, 1908–) published during the 1950s in the *Revista Bohemia*.

The remarkable durability of the *costumbrista* narratives is not surprising if we remember that in the political and economic backwardness of the Spanish American nations the *cuadro de costumbres* was also an outlet for dissent and social commentary, via satirical characterizations. The distortions created by absolute power, privilege and social and economic deprivation are at the core of much that the *Costumbristas* wrote. The keen sketches gathered by the Guatemalan José Milla in his *Cuadros de costumbres* (1865–1871) touch on a wide range of issues frequently disguised by amusing anecdotes, as in many of Ricardo Palma's *tradiciones*. Likewise, behind the frivolous remarks made by the Cuban Luis V. Betancourt (1843–1885) in his *Artículos de costumbres y poesías* (1867) he conveys the sense of resentment felt by a majority that had no voice in the affairs of a still colonial society: "Science is long, life is short," Betancourt wrote, "Our country, who cares about it? ... we are born today to die tomorrow ... I hope the fatherland will be rewarded some day ..." (p. 25). In a larger sense, texts of this sort also express a persistent sense of marginality with broader geographical and cultural connotations. Toward the end of the nineteenth century, Spanish America was still very much on the periphery of the western world. The industrial revolution was to most Spanish Americans a distant spectacle of wonder and mythical progress. Occasionally Spanish Americans participated in the new networks uniting journalism, sciences, art, and modern technology, but in most instances those instruments of progress reached only limited sectors of Buenos Aires, Mexico City, Havana, Bogotá, and Santiago. The dazzling achievements of modernity described so ably by Walter Benjamin in his essay "Paris, capital of the nineteenth century" (1934) were only hearsay to most Spanish Americans. The mode of literary expression that best measures the distance separating the Spanish-speaking world from the striking accomplishments of the modern age is probably the *costumbrista* narrative; those texts often confirm that the material progress generated by scientific inquiry and by the industrial revolution was perceived in Spanish America mainly as a rhetorical experience. "Manual de cuquería o fisiología del cuco" (1857) by the Spaniard Eugenio de Ochoa (1815–1872), "Los tontos" (1881) by José Milla or *Los frutos de mi tierra* (1896) by the Colombian Tomás Carrasquilla (1858–1940), are valid examples of the myriad of texts which mimic, at a distance, the accomplishments of advanced societies. More often than not, they do so by means of parody or by representing incoherent traces of the discourses of modernity. In *The Spanish American Regional Novel*, Carlos Alonso, with much persuasive evidence, corroborated that for most Spanish Americans the modern age was indeed a "discursive event" (p. 22) which has been reenacted again and again in the contemporary fiction of Spanish America.

To appraise the *cuadro de costumbres* it is useful to keep in mind that it emerged outside the boundaries of established literary genres. The obvious link of *Costumbrismo* with journalism immediately places those sketchy texts on the margins of *belles-lettres*. In fact, if there is a narrative form that illustrates the breakdown of literary genres brought about by the disruptive endeavors of Romanticism, that form is the *cuadro de costumbres*. Once again, Mesonero Romanos's zeal to classify the possible genealogy of the *costumbrista* sketch only served to confirm its ambiguities. In his *Panorama matritense* (1825) Mesonero stressed that the "fantastic dreams and allegories written in the manner of Quevedo, Espinel, Mateo Alemán and Diego de Torres were the obvious precursors of the *costumbrista* tale" (I, 12). If such a tracing can be taken seriously, the antecedents of the *cuadro de costumbres* are very obscure indeed. Neither Mesonero nor his many imitators modeled their works on allegories or dreams. If any precursors of the *costumbrista* sketch are to be found, we must look at the numerous collections of tales published in the sixteenth and seventeenth centuries. It is in those forgotten books where some vague resemblances to the *costumbrista* text can be detected, particularly with regard to episodic arrangement and narrative point of view. The *Historias peregrinas* (1623) by Gonzalo de Céspedes y Meneses (1555–1638) or the *Floresta española* (1524) by Melchor de Santa Cruz

(1529–1595) might be seen as primary schemes for narratives centered on the satirical observation of social norms. Yet the contextual framework and the narrative agenda of those texts stand in clear contrast to what the *costumbristas* hoped to achieve.

Much more immediate and relevant are the affinities between the narratives of the Hispanic *costumbristas* and *L'Hermite de la Chaussée d'Antin* (1825–1827) by the French journalist Victor Etienne Joy (1764–1846). No less important as distant models of the *cuadro de costumbres* were the satirical narratives collected by Joseph Addison (1672–1719) and Richard Steele (1672–1729) for the *Spectator* (1711–1712) and the *Tatler* (1709–1711). Mesonero, Milla, Alberdi and many other *costumbristas* more than once confessed their admiration for the kind of incisive, free-flowing, and splintered tales disseminated by Addison and Steele. I believe that link is significant because one of the salient features in the shifty armature of the *costumbrista* sketch is its affinity with precisely that kind of journalistic fragment mastered by Addison and Steele. In its sardonic way the *costumbrista* text tells what it hears told more often than not, it seems to replot, summarize, or instruct. Following English and French models the *costumbristas* found sheer wit much more desirable than memorable writing.

Once again, such priorities point to the close kinship which *Costumbrismo* shared with journalism in its modern forms. It is no coincidence that the Cuban poet Julián del Casal (1863–1893) subtitled some of his narrative sketches as "fragments." That makeshift form of telling is deliberately retained in Casal's "La prensa" (1886) and in most of his *Bocetos habaneros* (1890), as well as in other *cuadros de costumbres* written by Milla, "Jotabeche," and Manuel Payno (Mexico, 1810–1894). The arbitrary ordering of events we identify in the first pages of "El matadero," in "Rosa" (1848) by José V. Lastarria or in the many tales contained in *El espejo de mi tierra* (1869) by the Peruvian Felipe Pardo Aliaga are all symptomatic of a narrative structure that focuses on daily activities in ways that are reminiscent of genre painting. In the *Escenas cotidianas* (1838) by the Cuban Gaspar Betancourt Cisneros (1803–1866), in *Instantáneas metropolitanas* (1846) by the Argentinian José Alvarez (Fray Mocho) (1858–1903) or in "Lanchitas" (1878) by the Mexican José María Roa Bárcena (1827–1908), one finds the happenstance of journalistic prose, epistolary devices, flashes of autobiographical data, and a bit of political commentary. These narrative devices are nearly always blended into a convoluted sequence that runs adrift without resolving its discursive predicament. In "La polémica literaria" (1833) Larra acknowledged quite openly the erratic reception accorded to the *costumbrista* writer. "Many are the obstacles that the writer of customs meets in this society, particularly the one who bases his material on the observation of the various characters who inhabit our cities. If he does well [his readers] will say: it must be a translation. If he shrinks from offending anyone, his writing will be seen as pale, without humor or devoid of originality..." (*Artículos*, 742).

A similar feeling of uncertainty also prevails in "Siempre soy quien capitula" (1855) by the Peruvian Manuel Ascencio Segura (1805–1871) as well as in many of the texts contained in *Artículos de costumbres* (1892) by José Victoriano Betancourt (1813–1875). But rather than documenting the uneven receptions granted to the *cuadro de costumbres*, what one needs to understand is why readers and literary scholars have felt uneasy about this particular narrative form. If there is no consensus about the ways in which one ought to read or define the *costumbrista* tale, it is because its narrative impulse stems more from a desire to instruct than from a cogent vision of anecdotal materials. Moreover, the *costumbrista* narrative is all too often an act of narrative mediation in which other discourses – historical, political or scientific – are mixed and dissolved into the trappings of a particular story. Larra's famous tale "El castellano viejo" (1832) is much more than an amusing depiction of the awkward social predicaments experienced by the narrator. The tale represents the urban dislocations produced in the nineteenth century by the precipitous growth of cities in which many social classes began to mingle in unprecedented ways. Those dislocations became central issues in treatises written by Claude H. de Saint-Simon (1760–1825), Charles Fourier (1772–1837), Thomas Carlyle (1794–1881), Auguste Comte (1798–1857) and Pierre Proudhon (1809–1865), among other political theorists. Ripples of Fourier's and Saint-Simon's theories are visible in Esteban Echeverría's *El dogma socialista* (1846) and are fictionalized vividly in "El matadero". *La guerra de la tiranía* (1840) by "Jotabeche" also incorporates traces of political theory in less intense form, but in his texts those concerns are usually reflected by way of secondary sources. It was in the essays of Lastarria, Sarmiento, and other political commentators that many Chilean and Argentinian *costumbristas* became acquainted with new political theories. Yet the representation of social and political theories in the *cuadro de costumbres* at times appears as a vague reminiscence, partly because those ideas were transmitted in faulty translations or through fragments interspersed in journalistic accounts.

As one reconstructs the broad lines of nineteenth-century scientific development, it is important to bear in mind that the social sciences (sociology, economics, and political theory) emerged in that period, largely in treatises by Saint-Simon, Fourier, Proudhon, and above all, Comte. As we know, the first initiatives undertaken in those new fields were quite tentative and largely devoid of experimental content. In fact, sociological inquiry in the writings of Fourier, Proudhon, and Comte amounts to an indiscriminate mix of precepts derived from historiography, ethics, jurisprudence, and the natural sciences. The pseudoscientific conceptualizations applied to the analysis of social structures were not based on quantitative analysis and had little to offer in the way of statistical data. Charles Fourier, in particular, was known at the time as a pioneer of the social sciences. He wrote profusely and with great enthusiasm on the "pathology" and "physiology" of specific social contexts. I believe that it is precisely from these and similar inquiries the *costumbristas* eventually derived their pedestrian obsession with the physiology of practically everything. The Cuban José María de Cárdenas (1812–1882) wrote on the "Fisiología del administrador de un ingenio" (1847) and countless others engaged in similar lucubrations.

In his much-admired *Theory of the Four Movements* (1808), Fourier had managed to classify customs, economic habits, marital arrangements, many of the human passions, psychic configurations, and much more. In most instances the central task of those embryonic forms of social inquiry was to classify whatever was being observed. The roster of categories conceived by Fourier and his followers seems endless. Categorization became synonymous with scientific endeavor and even with modern learning in general. Illustrated magazines in Europe and in Spanish America proceeded to represent, graphically and otherwise, new social types or classes that had emerged as by-products of demographic displacements. The well-known *aleluyas* which appeared throughout the nineteenth century, such as the ones reproduced in Volume XXIII of *Summa artis* (Madrid, 1988), are graphic and satirical representations of professions, customs or historical events. Early forms of scientific research were popularized mostly by journalistic means, and it is in these secondary sources that the *cuadro de costumbres* detected the categories and classifications it was to repeat and refine. "Los oficios" (1890) by Julián del Casal, "El pescador" (1891) or "El carbonero" (1889) by Ramón Meza (Cuba, 1861–1911) or *Semblanzas de mi tiempo* (1890) by Francisco de Sales Pérez (Venezuela, 1836–1926) are some, among thousands, of similar classifactory efforts published in Spain and in Spanish America.

Of all the scientific modes of inquiry that reached Spanish America in the nineteenth century, Positivism met with the most enthusiastic reception. In Mexico, for example, the dictatorial regime (1876–1911) of Porfirio Díaz adopted main tenets of Positivism as the basis for economic policy. Countless treatises and reviews were written in Spanish America in praise of Positivism. The learned essays of Lastarria, Alberdi, and Manuel González Prada (Peru, 1848–1918) as well as those by Enrique José Varona (Cuba, 1849–1933) were discussed in intellectual and political circles and reviewed by the most influential dailies. Of all the efforts made to adapt Comte's ideas to Spanish American realities, none was as successful as Lastarria's *Lecciones de política positiva* (1875), but it is largely a crafty parody of Comte's famous texts. "Lo positivo" became an ambiguous notion that penetrated learned quarters and seeped into all realms of popular culture. In his greatly admired *Cours de philosophie positive* 1830–1842) and in the *Systéme de polítique positive* (1851–1854) Auguste Comte enunciated, with more eloquence than precision, the fundamental premises of his theories.

What Comte proposed was essentially the systematic study of values and norms which, once established, could be used to understand patterns of change within a given social context. Like many of Proudhon's ideas, Comte's theories were partly rooted in ethical and legal concepts. As in the case of his predecessors (Saint-Simon, Condorcet, and Fourier), Comte's thinking was little more than a scattered response to the drastic social and economic changes brought about by the industrial revolution. In a general sense, his program was centered on social reorganization and on the modernization of institutional structures. Yet, in the end, Comte's theories were perceived in Spanish America not as solutions to specific problems but as the means to elaborate a critique of our past and, more importantly, as a way to break with it. In *The Children of the Mire* (1974) Octavio Paz indicated persuasively that Positivism gave to Spanish American elites a tangential participation in the modern age. If nothing else, Comte's theories seemed the most effective way to formulate a critical evaluation of our traditional institutions. The lure that such a possibility held for Spanish America cannot be underestimated. But, in the end, the internal inconsistencies of Comte's premises did not produce the concrete achievements many had hoped for. The sophisticated analytical means desired by educated minorities began to emerge at the turn of the century in the impressive monographs of Emile Durkheim (1858–1917) and Max Weber (1881–1961), among others.

If one development surfaces in any overview of the social sciences in the nineteenth century, it is likely to be the sustained interaction between the emerging social sciences and literary creation. In his admirable book *A New Science*, Bruce Mazlish – a historian of the social sciences – admits quite freely that

> It is philosophy, prophecy, poetry and creative literature, in my view, which inspired sociology, as much as or more than the other way around ... Sociology takes deeply felt concerns and tries to objectify them and give to them scientific form. One does not necessarily reduce the "science" of sociology by seeking to understand the passional roots, which indeed compromise part of the social facts one is attempting to order and classify. (p. 163)

As a suggestive backdrop, Positivism in many ways reinforced the taxonomic gesturing of the *costumbristas*. To observe, demarcate, enclose and reorder became quite fashionable among writers of many nationalities who were active in the second half of the nineteenth century. "Los carnavales" (1855) by the Peruvian Asencio Segura, or "El médico pedante y las viejas curanderas" (1838) by José V. Betancourt or "Costumbres y fiestas de los indios" (1842) by the Mexican Guillermo Prieto (1818–1897) stand as obvious examples of the kind of taxonomic narrative fostered by positivistic notions. Indeed, that frequent connection between pseudoscientific endeavors and literary creation becomes even more visible in *Artículos de costumbres* by José V. Betancourt:

> It is certainly useful to observe popular customs, particularly when one wishes to improve the ethical standards of our people. But the truth is that not all customs will ultimately yield beneficial results. However, it is not my intention to enter into a full examination of the habits and manners of my native country. There are many customs one can think of, some belonging to foreigners and others to our natives. Some can be considered as the pale reflection of habits which were dominant in Europe many centuries ago, while others are manners recently imported from Paris. *I gladly leave an investigation of such depth to the celebrated* Comte and to others who, like him, can win everlasting fame with their immortal vigilance on behalf of human society.   (p. 13)

Betancourt's concern with ethical issues is a dominant feature of the text. Superficial comments focused on public morality were indeed common denominators of the *cuadro de costumbres*. When characterizing such tendencies among Hispanic *costumbristas*, José Montesinos noted that whereas in France the *roman de moeurs* dealt with broad ethical questions, the Hispanic *costumbristas* restricted themselves to incidental matters that are valued because of their picturesque connotations. The void of scientific and philosophic knowledge experienced by the Spanish-speaking nations in the nineteenth century explains the trivial polarizations toward the ethical issues lamented by Montesinos (p. 48).

It is fair to conclude that the *costumbrista* sketch, bloated by contradictions and posturing, was nonetheless the harbinger of intellectual developments of considerable significance. But in the *cuadro de costumbres* such developments were perceived and related in the casual gloss, the anecdote, or in parodies. Depending on the circumstances of their publication, these texts could be titled and thought of as *artículos*, *cuadros de costumbres*, *estampas*, or even *bocetos*. Within their limited means, these texts also represented successive fragmentations of knowledge which occurred repeatedly in the early phases of modernity. When we view them in that context, we understand more fully why the *cuadro de costumbres* has evaded all the narrow categories that literary scholarship had tediously designed for it. They continue to be indeterminate narrative modalities and byproducts of the secular discourses engendered by the modern age. The *costumbrista* sketch is perceived as a slippery subgenre partly because it often tended to mirror its own discursive make-up. Indeed, the *cuadro de costumbres* frequently represented influential discourses generated by scientific inquiry rather than external realities. In those instances, the narration appears to the reader as the duplicitous image created by facing mirrors. Such an image illustrates both the mediated nature of language and the opacity of narratives that sought to link a text to the events that generate it. To no one's surprise, those evasive contextual references are the ones that the romantic short story will explore in order to construct some of its most memorable fabulations.

The dawn of the short story in Spanish America

In a ground-breaking work (*The Short Story in English*), for which there is no equivalent in Spanish, Walter Allen traces the emergence of the modern short story in the English-speaking world. Among other things, Allen tells us that the short story appeared on the margin of romantic literary activity. He also demonstrates that in its inception the short story is linked to a peculiarly romantic view of creativity. Much the same can be said about the earliest forms of the short story in the Spanish-speaking world. The *cuento literario*, as we now refer to it, emerged mainly as a lyrical narrative that fed on radical notions of originality. In Spanish America, as elsewhere, the short story introduced a new form. Yet we know that it is linked to textual practices of the past; modalities such as the romantic legend, the *costumbrista* sketch of manners, and narratives in verse stand as some of the indirect precursors of the modern short story.

One of the short story's earliest guises was the interpolated tale; it often appeared lodged in more extensive narrative forms such as lyrical novels, profuse legends and turn-of-the-century literary journalism. One of the first romantic short stories written in Spanish America can be found in the novel *María* (1867) by Jorge Isaacs (Colombia, 1837–1895). In chapters 40–43 of that novel, one finds the tale of Nay and Sinar. It is an exotic episode that came into being as a direct reelaboration of the story of Nay and Atalá in *Atalá* (1801) by François R. Chateaubriand (1768–1848). Similar interpolated narratives recur in many novels of the nineteenth century; most notably, in *Amalia* (1851–1855) by the Argentinian José Mármol (1817–1871), and in *Cumandá* (1889) by Juan León Mera (Ecuador, 1832–1894). If the romantic short story frequently emerged as an interpolated narrative, it was in part because those stories sought to complement the larger format of the novel. Moreover, they often appear as the result of a sudden poetic intuition. In preceding sections of this chapter, I have drawn attention to the hybrid nature of early forms of the brief narrative. Esteban Echeverría's "El matadero" or Pardo Aliaga's "Los carnavales" (1855) are perhaps among their most persuasive examples of this uneven convergence of narrative patterns. But no less could be said of stories written by José V. Lastarria, Manuel Payno, Ricardo Palma, Cirilo Villaverde and others who wrote in the *costumbrista* mode.

The association of the romantic short story with other narrative typologies should not surprise us. Throughout the nineteenth century the periodicals showed a marked preference for the *costumbrista* sketch. Indeed, the predominance of a hybrid discursive form such as the *cuadro de costumbres* accounts for the uneven development of the short story in Spanish America. In his *Costumbrismo y novela*, José Montesinos repeatedly noted that for the romantics, the *cuento literario* was indeed an enigmatic form (p. 37). For some, the *cuento* was linked to the *chascarrillo*, a type of riddle associated with folkloric tales, while, for most, the *cuento* was synonymous with the fairy tale. Unlike English, Spanish does not have an established term for the modern short story. Predictably, Mesonero Romanos was not able to distinguish significant differences between "tales, episodes and *cuentos*" (*Obras Completas*, 59), in spite of the fact that some of his texts, "El recienvenido" (1838), for example, intermittently approached the syntactical cohesion that we associate with the modern short story.

The lyrical tales written in nineteenth-century Spain by Cecilia Bohl de Faber, better known as Fernán Caballero (1796–1877), which appeared in her *Relaciones* (1857), closely resemble the distinctive features of the *cuento literario*, but unfortunately, most of these texts went unnoticed by her contemporaries. The same fate was reserved for one of the finest romantic short stories written in Spain, namely "La tormenta," a delicately erotic story that appeared within the novel *La hija del mar* (1859) by Rosalía de Castro (1837–1885). Largely because of its tenuous make-up, the *cuento literario* was gradually isolated from the journalistic aims of the *costumbristas*. They tended to look askance at tales, of which de Castro's work is an example, because they considered them ephemeral, amusing or excessively subjective representations of insignificant events. In all fairness, it should be stressed that in Spanish the romantic short story does not exhibit the imaginative subtleties achieved by the French, German, or North American short fiction of the same period. To appreciate the differences, one has only to evoke the celebrated tale of "Councillor Krespel" (1816) by Ernest T. A. Hoffman (Germany, 1776–1822), or "My kinsman, Major Molineux" (1929) by Nathaniel Hawthorne (US, 1804–1864).

Once we are aware of the subtleties of these stories, it should not surprise us that the romantic short story met with erratic receptions in the Spanish-speaking world. Nevertheless, it is rather disconcerting that most readers in nineteenth-century Spanish America continued to praise the *costumbrista* sketch as the most appealing of all short narrative forms.

Such preference is odd in light of the fact that the *cuadro de costumbres* often trivializes social activity or seems obsessively intent on classifying all sorts of marginal events. In contrast, however, the *cuento literario* often concerned itself with the abstruse nature of human desire. The intimate and paradoxical nature of human endeavors was seldom a fundamental concern of the *costumbristas*. In fact, the keen introspection valued by romantic sensibility rarely appears in the works of the prevailing *costumbrista* mode.

As one traces the narrative practices of the period, one must remember that inner life is a major discovery of Romanticism. In fact, interior scenes of an intimate character were favored by most painters during the nineteenth century. The canvases of Gustave Courbet (France, 1819–1877), Mariano Fortuny (Spain, 1838–1879), James A. McNeill Whistler (US, 1838–1879), and Edouard Vuillard (France, 1868–1940) illustrate the intimate scenes that are frequently at the core of the romantic short story. Montesinos in his *Costumbrismo y novela* reflected upon this important shift in perspective (p. 61).

In that book he derides the tales of Serafín Estébanez Calderón and, in doing so, noted that most of the texts written by this Andalusian writer suffered "from a certain lack of focus, and from a general structural looseness" (pp. 28–9). Those shortcomings he attributed to Estébanez's emphasis on mere description rather than the inner life of his characters. Montesino's observations remind us indirectly of a letter written in 1824 by Washington Irving. The North American writer there tries to identify distinctive features of the short story. To Irving these innovative fictions are "expressively delineated [and always seem to bear a touch] of pathos and humor" (p. 212). Henry James (US, 1843–1906), when referring to his story. "The Figure in the carpet," reflected on the "strange mystifying uncomfortable delicacy" (*The Notebooks of Henry James*, 223) that often appear in short fictions. In the prologue of *The Ambassadors*, he also commented on "The grace of intensity," (p. 9) as a central characteristic of the short story. Most descriptive of the nuances of brief narratives, however, is the review by Edgar Allan Poe (US, 1809–1849) of *Twice-Told Tales* by Nathaniel Hawthorne (US, 1804–1864). In that famous essay Poe alludes to "the unity of effect or impression" (*The Works of Edgar Allan Poe*, II, 37) and further insists upon the "poetic sentiment" (p. 7) inherent in the short story. He also recognized that in the short story every word "*tells*" (p. 44). In many ways, these formulations are the beginnings of a body of criticism intent of representing the distinctive traits of this new literary form. Of those early theoretical statements, some are particularly insightful. Notably the essays by Anton Chekhov (Russia, 1860–1904), Brander Mathews (US, 1852–1929), and Sidel Camby (US, 1878–1961), collected in Eugene Current-García's *What is the Short Story* (1974), merit close scrutiny. In Spanish the Argentinians Jorge Luis Borges

(1899–1986) and Julio Cortázar (1914–1984) have written the best critical assessments of the short story.

The distinctions made by these authors and critics tend to assess the short story in the light of textual practices evident in modern fiction. At some point, however, one has to address the relationship between the short story and modern poetry. My intent is not to characterize the short story, once again, as poetry in prose form. If nothing else, generalizations of that sort are prone to overlook the specific textual strategies employed on the one hand by romantic poets and on the other hand by writers of short fiction. Nevertheless, it is clear that short narratives produced in the first half of the nineteenth century recall many of the lyrical qualities that one associates with romantic verse. The lyrical tension that abounds in romantic poetry often seeks to achieve idealized harmonies between anthropomorphic landscapes and the creative spirit; that particular imaginative bent is one that reoccurs in much of the romantic fiction produced in Latin America and elsewhere. In any event, the intricate convergence of modern poetry and the short story amounted to a radical break with the past. The short story exemplified a rejection of previous codified narrative forms such as the legend, the fable and the *cuadros de costumbres*. In its explicit rupture with previous models, the short story was guided by many of the radical aims of modern poetry. Much like romantic verse, the short story focused on the paradoxical flow of human events; it sought to create narrative structures which reflected its unconventional aims. Indeed, the short story at times dramatizes the intrinsic limits of language. What is often dramatized in the romantic short story is the inability of writing to contain the totality of experience. In the introduction by Gustavo Adolfo Bécquer (Spain, 1836–1870) to his *Leyendas* (1868), we are reminded of the writer's anxiety when faced with the frailties of language.

> Through the dark corners of my brain, curled tightly and naked, sleep the extravagant children of my fantasies, hoping in silence that art might acknowledge them through language ...   (p. 39)

> I would like to forge for all a fantastical quilting of exquisite phrases through which you may be wrapped in pride, like a blanket of indigo. I would like to possess the ability to shape the form that will contain us, just as one shapes the etched crystal vial that contains the perfume. But it is impossible ...   (p. 40)

In romantic poetry these notions concerning the shortcomings of language are dramatically articulated to the point of becoming a codified topic in western literary tradition. The concern with the limits of language can be detected in the works of prominent writers. William Wordsworth (England, 1770–1850), in his memorable "Expostulation and reply" (1798), warns us:

Sweet is the lore which Nature brings; / Our meddling intellect / Mis-shapes the beauteous forms of things:- / We murder to dissect ...
(*The Poetical Works of W. Wordsworth*, 82).

Similarly, in his poem "Vejeces" (1889), the Colombian José Asunción Silva (1865–1896) alludes to the limitations of the written word; his is a text constructed with a subtle narrative bent and in which the poet admits that even: "Faded, sad, old things / without voice and without color know secrets" (*Obras completas*, 30). He seems to be telling us that the illuminations and flow which the poet seeks to capture will always transcend the expressive capacity of the written word. This sense of incompatibility between the means used to represent and that which is represented can also be perceived visually.

Influential romantic painters constructed vast landscapes which often remind us of the fleeting presence of the human being and of our limited possibilities. It is as if the composition of the paintings was meant to illustrate the radical disparity that exists between the artist and the magnitude of the task facing him. The canvases and watercolors of the famous English painters J. M. W. Turner (1775–1851) and R. P. Bonnington (1802–1828) or those produced by the North American Frederick E. Church (1826–1900) illustrate these disparities. Church's impressive depictions of vast Latin American landscapes dramatize the contrasts indicated above. More than the spectacle or the mechanics of an anecdote, what romantic poetry and painting often expressed is the void between experience and its representation. The short story does something similar. It is assumed that verbal creation seldom encompasses the full range of our experiences. Bécquer himself, in the text above, points repeatedly to the impediments of verbal creation. He notes, "But, alas, that between the world, the idea and its formulation, there exists an abyss that only the world can fill..." (*Obras completas*, 39). [Yet] – Bécquer notes – "the timid and lazy word is the one which always undermines its own efforts" (p. 40). Indeed, these attempts to transcend the conventions of language as well as the limits imposed by literary genres in part account for the emergence of new and more flexible narrative forms. The short story is historically and rhetorically inscribed in this process of radical deviations. Consequently, with the passing of time, it adopted the loose format that links it to the lyrical narrative, the essay and to the many guises of literary journalism.

"El mendigo" (1843) by José Victoriano Lastarria (Chile, 1817–1888) published in his *Miscelánea literaria* (1855) illustrates the kind of writing in which one can corroborate many of the observations made above. Lastarria drew on almost all the discourses prevalent in the nineteenth century. For him, as for most of his contemporaries, the brief narrative was mainly a complementary form to other types of writing. In fact, this particular story exhibits the various narrative conventions of the romantic story in its seminal forms. In its general configuration, "El mendigo" reminds us of Ernest T. A. Hoffman's tales contained in his *Fantasy Pieces* (1815). Perhaps more identifiable links exist between "El mendigo" and two well-known romantic fictions: "The two drovers" (1827), by Sir Walter Scott (Scotland, 1771–1832), and "Mateo Falcone" (1832?) by Prosper Mérimée (France, 1803–1870).

Yet the comparison of "El mendigo" with prestigious texts belonging to other literary traditions might lead us to think that in Spanish America the short story was rapidly consolidating its new status. This was not the case. In fact, "El mendigo" appeared as a subsection of Lastarria's book devoted to "Preliminary forms of the historical novel." But curiously Lastarria's tale was far from being what this label suggests. The story itself, as is the case with so many others written during this period, begins by foregrounding a solitary and self-reflective narrator. While taking a stroll along the tree-lined avenue of Mapacho, the narrator seems to enjoy the "magnificent landscape" (*Miscelánea*, 55) before him. He appreciates the view as one would the generous affections of a mother, he rejoices in the comforting beauty of that moment. He recalls: "How often this same view has made me feel this sensation of genuine happiness" (p. 57). At this point, the narrator interrupts his reverie to describe the enigmatic character who suddenly appears at his side. This individual seems to be the personification of uncertainty. The narrator tells us that the man does not utter a word. Gradually the narrative confers on the stranger a startling and laconic presence. The "grave and melancholic aspect" (p. 58) of *el mendigo* is emphasized repeatedly. The narrator is quick to underscore once again that he is a mysterious person of whom nothing is known. He queries: "Do you know me good man? I am quite eager . . . to know something of your life" (p. 59).

This is how the narrator begins to construct the idealized biography of the beggar. The narrative process relies on exclamations and truncated phrases as it slowly unveils the identity of the stranger. He was an "old soldier of this land (Chile)" (p. 59). His name is Albaro Aguirre. When asked the beggar responds: "I was born in Serena." (p. 61). At this moment, the narrator lets us know that he fought in the wars of independence against Spain. These references to the beggar's past lead the narrator to evoke "a thousand mysterious possibilities" (p. 60). We soon realize that the present condition of this individual contrasts with a previous life of heroic feats. The fragmented account of the beggar's biography seems to place him in a void. Yet that initial absence of knowledge is filled by bits of information that seem to clarify the beggar's identity. But what we learn about the stranger is more suggestive than factual. As is frequently the case in romantic fiction, the sparse information we cull from the man often undermines and contradicts itself. As if he were passively awaiting his fate, the beggar's life has led him through a succession of enigmatic sequences, loves and misfortunes. It does not surprise us to find out that in his youth, he heard an omen of a "future filled with tears and blood" (p. 62). He related these and other portents "hiding his face" between sobs. His life has been one long series of curious accidents. Even the heroic image of the Chilean liberator Bernardo O'Higgins becomes part of the backdrop of the tale. He admits to the narrator how close he has been to the abyss of madness and vice. We know that the beggar's downfall was not determined by his gradual decline into mendicancy, but rather by a loss of a more intimate sort: the love denied to him by the evasive Lucía. In his anguish, he begs the narrator to leave him alone in his pain: "Leave me, dear sir, to cover my past in a shroud, because I cannot recount events of my past without falling again into madness" (p. 114). In the end, the figure of the beggar fades once more into the anonymity of crowded streets and alleyways. "Some time later, I saw him again," the narrator tells us, "But for a long time I have heard nothing of the poor old man; maybe he has died, and, by now, Lucía must be, through the wealth of her husband, one of the noble ladies of Spain" (p. 115).

If we remove the sentimental veil placed between the reader and this tale, we realize that this depressing story stands as an allegorical representation of the process of creation as it is often witnessed in the modern short story. It becomes clear that the plot is not centered on the factual content of the story, but rather on the story telling. What vindicates the tale is not the interest of the anecdote itself, but the imaginative content that emerges from dispersed fragments of information.

The complex narrative structure of "El mendigo" separates it from the rhetorical legacies of the *cuadros de costumbres*. It is clear that the mimetic intent of this text is broader and that it projects the story well beyond the scope of concrete data. The same could be said of the condition of the beggar Albaro Aguirre, for in many ways he is an embodiment of the creative impulse which impels the writing of the short story. Even the curious spelling of his name – normally spelled Alvaro – alludes indirectly to the unusual character of the beggar. The exaggerated manner in which his *persona* and actions are outlined implicitly leads to an almost superstitious veneration of his individuality. Indeed, he seems to stand for all that can be perceived as genuine or unique. The parallelism between the beggar and the short story itself reveals *el mendigo* as an unparalleled being, one devoid of antecedents. Aguirre tells us: "I was born in Serena, I said, and my birth caused the death of she who gave me life" (p. 61). Soon thereafter we find out that he has abandoned forever all contact with his family.

The content of this tale clearly implies that in the narrative act, as in human existence, one cannot be unequivocal, and usually any attempt to be so leads to falsification. In the life of *el mendigo*, as in the case of the short story, all precedents have been erased. The beggar exists as an indefinable presence, and if something illuminates him, it is not the precarious state of his present condition but rather the narrative, that is to say, the word, the tale that he incarnates. Language is what limits and determines his enigmatic individuality. More powerfully than the indiscriminate facts and regional sketches so favored by the *cuadros de costumbres*, Lastarria's short story depicts an unforeseen outcome which was gradually revealed to the reader by way of subtle allusions and gestures. Lastarria's writing demonstrates – with uneven effectiveness – how fleeting words and allusive language are used to produce a deeper sense of personal and historical meaning. Today as we look back to nineteenth-century writers, such as Poe, Chekhov, and Guy de Maupassant (1850–1893), we realize that the anecdotal content of the short story was always to transcend facts rather than corroborate them.

But if, in "El mendigo," Lastarria employs rhetorical strategies inherent to the short story, it is also true that in other texts included in his *Miscelánea literaria*, the narrative process is less successful. A much more limited vision is evident in, for example, "Rosa" (1847) or in "El manuscrito del diablo" (1849). In this latter story, we are inclined to imagine a suggestive tale of a diabolical or esoteric nature very much in the vein of romantic fiction, but we are misled by a false start that returns us instead to more traditional forms. The opening passage sounds familiar, "We were travelling from Santiago to Valparaíso: the night was cold and sinister..." (p. 275). The plot is typical of the horror stories of the period: after a carriage accident the travellers gather around the light of a fire, and there, an old man, the narrator, encounters a suitcase full of manuscripts abandoned on one of the carriage seats by a missing traveller. But the writings in question are far from being the "devil's manuscript." Unfortunately, what follows is an incoherent series of passages labelled with such titles as "Country" and "Society," thus digressing from what might have been a more coherent project into political ruminations. If I single out this particular story it is to demonstrate that during this period different stories by the same writer often exhibit an extraordinary heterogeneity that results, in part, from the varied sources used by the author. Within Lastarria's own body of work one can identify brief narratives of an elusive character. Referring to his collection of tales *Antaño y ogaño: novelas y cuentos de la vida hispanoamericana* (1855), Lastarria noted somewhat casually how these texts "are simply the result of one's artistic sensibility, they are the narrations concerned with characters and events" (p. 22). Lastarria's comments hardly describe the range of narrative forms which converge in his stories.

Without undermining the detailed representation valued by the *costumbrista* sketch of manners, the short story in Spanish America gradually forged a space for itself in the literary journalism of the period. Prestigious reviews such as *La Revista de Buenos Aires* (1863–1871), *El Mosaico Mexicano* (1836–1842), *La Revista Chilena* (1875–1880), and Puerto Rico's *El Almanaque Aguinaldo* (1859–1889) published and reprinted very dissimilar stories which anticipated the eventual dominance of the *cuento literario*. Specifically, in *La Revista de Buenos Aires*, Spanish American writers and journalists printed countless anonymous translations. The Chilean Guillermo Blest Gana (1829–1904) published translations of texts which had previously appeared in European literary journals. Examples of these stories appeared in 1842, in volume VII of *Revista de Buenos Aires*. "Carmen" and "El camino y el aldeano" are anonymous translations of texts published in Europe. In addition the Cuban poet José María de Heredia (1803–1839) occasionally translated brief narratives, such as his "Narraciones sueltas," which appeared as installments in *Miscelánea* (Mexico, 1829–1832). "El pobre" (1830) published in volume II of that review exemplifies the uneven construction and journalistic character that stand out in many early romantic stories.

Ultimately, it was in Mexico that the romantic short story gained a larger and established readership. The Mexican José María Roa Bárcena (1827–1908) demonstrated a particular affinity for the Nordic legends, a preference which was shared by many of his contemporaries, including leading *modernista* [modernist] poets. In his *Historia del cuento hispanoamericano* Luis Leal indicates, quite correctly, that some of the early literary journals I mention above introduced into Spanish America seminal European models of the romantic short story. Leal points out how those models were imitated and he underscores the powerful influence that Edgar Allen Poe had on Roa Bárcena and other Spanish American authors. This enthusiastic reception of Poe's fiction is partially documented in John Engelkirk's monograph *Edgar Allan Poe in Hispanic Literature* (1934).

Roa Bárcena's work, like that of Lastarria, interests us as an embryonic form of the short story in Spanish America. In Bárcena's tales, we identify variants of the *cuento literario* that would later reappear in the stories of other Mexican authors such as Ignacio M. Altamirano (1834–1893), Vicente Riva Palacio (1832–1896), and Justo Sierra (1849–1912). The insecure format of the romantic short story can also be seen in the prose works of the Ecuadorians Juan Montalvo (1832–1889) and Juan León Mera (1832–1894). But what distinguished Roa Bárcena from his contemporaries was his sustained commitment to the short story. His *Noches de raso* (1870) stands out as one of the first collections of short stories published in book form and in a carefully structured manner. Yet his best stories were written at a later date. In "Lanchitas" (1878), for example, one perceives a desire to capture the expressive possibilities of the inaudible. Other stories by Roa Bárcena, such as "El rey y el bufón" (1883) or "Combates en el aire" (1891) appear as ineffectual adaptations culled from various literary sources. Such practice, common in those days, is also evident in stories that many have attributed to the Cuban José María Heredia. "El hombre misterioso" (1834) published in the magazine *Minerva* is very much a case in point. In these early guises, the short story was permeated by tensions of narrative forms which were still in the process of defining their contours and possibilities.

The structural looseness that one detects in the brief fictions of Roa Bárcena, Heredia, or Montalvo, seems to blur the early history of the short story in Spanish America. But that perception is not entirely correct. Writers such as José Tomás Cuéllar (1830–1894) broke away from the overwhelming sentimentality exhibited in "Pepita" (1892?) by Manuel Payno (1810–1894) or in *Impresiones y recuerdos* (1882) by Pedro Costera (1846–1906). Roa Bárcena, Payno, and Riva Palacio, among others, continued to perfect stories clearly based on European models or ones that they adapted from local sources. In addition, the work of these men provides a significant example of the complex phenomenon of literary reception which took place in Spanish America toward the middle of the nineteenth century. The ways in which dissimilar narrative traditions travelled to and fro across the Atlantic is a process that we have only begun to explore.

In the last three decades of the nineteenth century, the short story emerged in Spanish America as a more refined literary form. It gradually assumed a larger role in the works of well-known Mexican authors such as Altamirano and Justo Sierra. It can be argued that as the short story became more clearly defined as narrative form, its readership grew proportionately. The publication of *Cuentos frágiles* (1883) by Manuel Gutiérrez Nájera (1859–1895) points to this growing acceptance of the short story. But the success of the Mexican Modernists undoubtedly owes much to their romantic predecessors. Justo Sierra's "Fiebre amarilla" (1893), published as part of his *Cuentos románticos* (1896), displays a sophisticated register of romantic narrative devices that will reappear in *Almas que pasan* (1906) by Amado Nervo (Mexico, 1870–1919), and also in *Cuentos fatales* (1926) by Leopoldo Lugones (Argentina, 1878–1938). In "Fiebre amarilla" the omniscient first-person narrator acts simultaneously as the story's protagonist. As already exemplified in Lastarria's story "El manuscrito del diablo", the plot of Sierra's narrative tells of travellers on a stagecoach to Veracruz. In its somewhat convoluted form the story reminds us of "Errantes" (1899) by Pío Baroja (Spain, 1872–1956), a story which also employs the conventional devices used in nineteenth-century fictions about travellers. In the New World, however, travel accounts, beginning as early as the eighteenth century, often set out to rediscover unique features of American realities. In a similar fashion, the large and elaborate canvases of the Mexican landscape painter José María Velasco (1840–1912) portrayed this imaginative exploration of sites that eventually came to be accepted as national emblems.

In Sierra's story the narrator evokes the legend of Starei, a mythic figure. She is the Muse of the Gulf of Mexico, framed in this instance by splendid tropical landscapes: "As in the background of a large portrait [...] [at the point where] the sea becomes deified, arose haughty groupings of clouds, above the blue-grey lines of the horizon ... [there] appeared a flock of seagulls that slowly folded their expansive wings" (*Cuentos románticos*, 28). Through the legend of Starei the narrator quickly brings to a close the sentimental and fatalistic development of the plot. Sierra's other tales which appear in the same collection, including "Playera" and "Sirena" also evoke legends which are rooted in the cultural, varied legacies present in the Gulf of Mexico. Typically, in several of these legends, the fable-like structure of the story becomes excessively digressive.

In the second half of the nineteenth century the Spanish American short story began to take on a more distinct image. But often, some of the most gifted writers of this period are better known for their political activities than for their accomplishments as story tellers. Such is the case of Esteban Echeverría, Juan Bautista Alberti, Juan Mantalvo, and the Cuban José Martí (1853–1895). No less can be said of Eugenio María de Hostos (Puerto Rico, 1839–1909), and the Peruvian Clorinda Matto de Turner, among many others. In their writings one detects at times, a growing tendency toward the politicization of fiction. Representative texts of that period can be found in Montalvo's first stories which appeared in his journal *El Cosmopolita* (1866–1869). Most of Hostos's tales were compiled in *Cuentos a mi hijo* (1878) and Martí's in *La edad de oro* (1889). The *Leyendas y recortes* (1893) and the *Tradiciones cuzqueñas* (1894) by Matto de Turner followed the more traditional narrative conventions employed by the *Costumbristas*. Indeed, in most Spanish American countries the short story emerged in a haphazard fashion and very often went unnoticed. In the 1870s few critics turned their attention to the short story. Alberto Blest Gana who was closely in tune with the literary activity of his time said very little about the short story. His two studies, "De los trabajos literarios en Chile" (1859) and "Discurso" (1861) barely mention the short story as innovative genre. But those omissions are not surprising if we bear in mind that Blest Gana's long story entitled "Un drama de campo" (1859) lacks the cohesion and audacious narrative turns that we identify with the short story. In most instances, the stories of Blest Gana, and those of the Mexican Manuel Payno follow the broader narrative techniques which they learned from the long novels of the nineteenth-century European Realists.

The Ecuadorian Juan León Mera, who was a painter as well as a novelist, was deeply influenced by Chateaubriand's *Atalá*. Mera's stories "Porque soy católico" (1873?), "Un matrimonio inconveniente" (1876) and "Las desgracias del Indio Pocho" (1874?) collected in *Novelitas ecuatorianas* (1909) are texts that he designated loosely as "*historietas*." In general, Mera and many of his contemporaries were more concerned with the narrative options offered by historical writing and lyrical novels than with the intricacies of the short story. Quite similar to Mera's is the famous *costumbrista* legend "La bellísima Floriana" (1874) by Nataniel Aguirre (Ecuador, 1843–1888). It is a tale inspired by *Historia de la Villa Imperial de Potosí* (1675) by Bartolomé Sanz de Ursúa (1676–1736) and one that is far removed from the impressive forms of condensation that we admire in the modern short story.

Themes linked to the search for cultural identity are at the forefront of much of the short fiction written in the last two decades of the nineteenth century. The first stories by the Honduran Juan Ramón Froilán Turcios (1878–1943), collected in *Renglones* (1899) and *Tierra maternal* (1911), are texts in which notions of origin and cultural singularity are of central importance. But on the whole they lack the imaginative content in the earliest stories of Mariano Latorre (Chile, 1886–1955) and Salvador Salazar Arrúe (El Salvador, 1899–1975). Occasionally the legacies of romantic fiction give to several of their stories a visionary quality that is slightly akin to twentieth-century Magical Realism.

Latorre's story "La desconocida" (1929), published in his *Catorce cuentos chilenos* (1932) is a vivid example of the kind of imaginative writing to which I have alluded. Like the Romantics, Latorre evokes at the outset vast landscapes which are set against the personal quest of a narrator–protagonist. A similar narrative perspective is evident in the story "Cómo se formaban los caudillos" (1901?) by Lucio V. Mansilla (Argentina, 1831–1907) and the numerous tales of the Costa Rican Manuel González Zeledón (1864–1934). Much like these authors, Latorre constructs an elaborate regional framework that serves as a nationalistic emblem of sorts. In "La desconocida" Latorre underscores the image of a covered wagon which winds its way through the colossal Andean landscape. The dialogue is, at best, laconic and gradually the reader's attention is brought down to the travellers as they stop along the way. The enigmatic presence of a woman and what actually happened between her and the young traveller sheltered in the covered wagon is left to our imagination. It is through the suggestive power of this incident that we come to perceive the poetic content of Latorre's story.

These references to particular texts demonstrate that the advent of the short story in Spanish America took place slowly amid the many hybrid forms employed by nineteenth-century writers of fiction. At that time, remnants of journalism as well as legal and scientific discourse struggle within the subtle framework of fiction. Thus, any history of the brief narratives produced in the last century is likely to misrepresent the unique features of such varied texts. In the specific case of late nineteenth-century Spanish American fiction, one does not detect the clear predominance of any particular narrative modality. The romantic short story was not necessarily undermined or supplanted by the lyrical tales of the *modernistas*, nor was it entirely superseded by the pseudo-scientific stories of the naturalists.

For many years, very different narratives, in the modalities mentioned above, existed in a loose pattern of permutations that eventually coalesced in the *criollista* short stories of the twentieth century. Thus, for example, "El fardo" (1888) by Rubén Darío contains a representative blend of all of the narrative forms which prevailed in the last century. Clearly the same could be said of Manuel Gutiérrez Nájera's "La mañana de San Juan" (1833), an exquisitely crafted tale centered on an episode in which death assumes the morbidity that often delighted the romantic imagination. Finally, we must see the consolidation of the Spanish American short story, the *cuento literario*, as a distinct creation of modern sensibility. In Spanish America and elsewhere, it is naive to explain the consolidation of the short story as a process determined by the emergence of a bourgeois readership. In a larger sense, the short story represents the merging of a radical narrative plurality that began to coalesce in the works of Poe, Hawthorne, and Chekhov, and that achieved a dazzling synthesis in the stories of William Faulkner (US, 1897–1962), Jorge Luis Borges, and Gabriel García Márquez, among others. In retrospect, it seems fair to add that romantic authors such as Echeverría, Lastarria, or Bárcena, never anticipated that their tentative stories would, in time, be seen as precursors of a genre that has immeasurably enriched the scope of Spanish American fiction.

The short story at the turn of the century: 1888–1915

Both politically and economically, the last three decades of the nineteenth century stand as a long cycle of successes and setbacks for Spanish America. It was a period marked by the accelerated integration of the American republics into the vast economies of the Western world. As a consequence, the use of steamships, railroads, refrigeration, and telegraphic communication spread rapidly through many regions. This, in turn, brought an almost overnight expansion in the export of raw materials and foodstuffs. Such commercial activity quickly fostered a prosperity that benefited, most notably, Argentina, Mexico, Uruguay, Chile, and Cuba. Not many, however, expected this accumulation of new wealth ultimately to change the extant social and demographic structures of emerging nations. Nevertheless, the last few years of the century saw the rise of labor unions and the parallel development of an increasingly influential middle class, especially in the Southern Cone republics. Additionally, total modernization became somewhat of an obsession, though it was, at times, more of a matter of appearance than substance. This was an era conditioned by the achievements of a modernity that was mostly known vicariously and which reached its height at the beginning of the First World War. In reference to these new turns of history, the Uruguayan José Enrique Rodó (1872–1917) noted that Modernism (as a literary expression of modernity) led to a compulsive desire for the unknown sensation and for the artificial in sentiment and form. He also speaks of the Modernists' "obsessive preoccupation with all that is new, even if it is so in a superficial manner" (*Escritos de la Revista Nacional de Literatura y Ciencias Sociales*, 240).

Indeed, the cultural dynamics of this period are corroborated – with rare unanimity – in celebrated texts by José Martí (1853–1895), Rubén Darío (1867–1916), and especially in Rodó's *Ariel* (1900). The ideological tensions, which become particularly intense at the turn of the century, are also represented in a genre that did not yet possess the visibility which it certainly acquired towards the beginning of the twentieth century: such was the case of the short story. In the condensed rhetoric of the *cuento literario*, we detect the many abrupt changes that Spanish American societies endured at the turn of the century and in it we perceive as well the growing links between Spanish American fiction and the narrative traditions of other continents.

As we appraise the brief narratives produced between 1888 and 1915, it would be erroneous to restrict that range of stories to mere categories. The sheer variety of these texts thwarts nearly every attempt at classification. Clearly, the dates suggested above may seem a bit arbitrary, but nevertheless I believe they can be justified if we relate them both to major historical events and to the publication of books in which the short story achieved degrees of sophistication without precedent in the Hispanic world.

If we think of historical events and major literary achievements as landmarks, we would agree that Rubén Darío's *Azul* (1888) signals the dawn of a major literary movement, and that the nineteenth century actually ended with the beginning of the First World War. Those are, in general, the chronological parameters of this section. In that context, it is equally evident that, in *Azul*, the short story reached unparalleled levels of refinement. Of course, one can always allude to the refined features contained in *Cuentos frágiles* (1883) by the Mexican Manuel Gutiérrez Nájera or to the delicate uses of plot shown in *Cuentos de colores* (1889) by the Venezuelan Manuel Díaz Rodríguez (1871–1927), but in fact neither of these important books displays the imaginative range or the gift for story-telling achieved by Darío in *Azul*. Naturally, the mere mention of texts written by Nájera, Darío and Díaz Rodríguez reminds us once again of the profuse links which exist between the short story and the poetry of the *Modernistas*. With a dazzling narrative style, they brought to prose fiction the poignancy and syntactical frugality inherent in lyric verse. Many years after *Azul*, that kind of verbal economy was still present in works which today we regard as landmarks of the short story at the turn of the century.

Cuentos de muerte y de sangre (1915), by the Argentinian Ricardo Güiraldes, is certainly one of those books. In this difficult and uneven collection of stories, one perceives the distinctive narrative strategies developed by Güiraldes and by the best *criollista* fiction of the period. The title and contents of this brief book – which Güiraldes completed around 1900 – seemed to anticipate the famed short stories of the Uruguayan Horacio Quiroga (1878–1937), which began appearing around 1906 in Argentinian newspapers and magazines. Though little known at the time, Quiroga's early stories eventually served as the foundation for his renowned *Cuentos de amor, de locura y de muerte* (1917), a book that has since been recognized as a milestone of Spanish American short fiction.

As one begins to review the consolidation of the Spanish American short story at the turn of the century, one may come away with the impression that texts written between 1888 and 1915 responded to either the poetic dictates of *Modernismo* or to the telluric vision extolled by *criollista* writers. However, dichotomies of this sort tend to be excessively limiting, if not absurd. In Spanish America, literary activity at the turn of the century was much more varied and complex than one might now suppose. Most of the modalities perfected in the short story during the last century reappeared indiscriminately in important literary magazines and dailies being published around 1900. Even a swift inspection of journals and weeklies will show that, embedded among the advertisements and headlines, there appeared *artículos de costumbres*, legends, fables, romantic and modernist short stories, as well as casual anecdotes that were complemented by elaborate graphic illustrations. Ironically, that erratic mix of brief narrative forms attracted a readership that devoted the thrust of its attention to the short story. But there are other factors that greatly affected the course of its development.

In the avant-garde sectors of the press, translations of stories by celebrated authors began to appear with increasing frequency, and some untranslated texts also circulated among the literary elites of the period. We know, for example, that original or translated stories of French, Russian, and English writers were known to Rubén Darío and the Bolivian Ricardo Jaimes Freyre (1868–1933), and that those texts were also discussed by Güiraldes and Leopoldo Lugones (Argentina, 1878–

1938). Horacio Quiroga and the Chileans Augusto D'Halmar (1882–1950) and Baldomero Lillo (1867–1923) avidly sought the short fictions of Kipling and Chekhov, among others. Near the turn of the century, masterly stories by Edgar A. Poe – mostly translated from the French – had already been published, as had some brief fictions by Alphonse Daudet (1840–1897), notably *Contes du lundi* (1873). Guy de Maupassant's (1850–1893) famous *Contes de la Bécasse* (1883) were read with special fascination, as were the partial translations made of *Les Soirées de Médan* (1880), the influential anthology sponsored by Emile Zola (1840–1902).

Near the turn of the century, the short story followed a path cleared mainly by French models. Conversely, the Spanish short story writers of the period drew much less attention. Some stories by Leopoldo Alas (Clarín, 1852–1901), and especially the *Cuentos escogidos* (1891) by Emilia Pardo Bazán (1852–1921), were known mainly in conservative literary circles. In the Southern Cone, one of the most celebrated writers was the Englishman Rudyard Kipling (1865–1936), a writer who learned much from the skilful fictions of Maupassant and Gustave Flaubert (1821–1880).

Nonetheless, if we return to the numerous nineteenth-century journals published in Spanish America, other relevant but little known facts pertaining to the short story immediately come to light. We will verify, for instance, the unexpected impact of several Russian authors on important story-tellers of this period. Largely in French translation, short stories by Fyodor Dostoyevsky (1821–1881), Ivan Turgenev (1818–1883), and a few by Anton Chekhov (1860–1904) were being read at the time, yet it seems that little was known about the memorable stories of Nikolai Gogol (1809–1852) or of Aleksandr Pushkin (1799–1837). The Chileans Baldomero Lillo and Augusto D'Halmar, the Uruguayan Javier de Viana (1868–1926), and the Argentinian Juana Manuela Gorriti (1818–1892) all became aficionados of Russian letters. It is quite evident in any case that, by 1900, the modern short story could display a *corpus* of texts that were seen internationally as models of a genre and that also represented the spirit and agenda of modernity.

The aforementioned stories by Poe, Maupassant, Turgenev, and Kipling captured the arrhythmic and fragmented tempo which prevailed mainly in the urban cultures of the period. By 1900, the short story was no longer a casual or sporadic presence in periodicals. The increasing number of anthologies and volumes of short stories published at the turn of the century confirms the presence of a growing readership. Important collections mentioned above by Güiraldes, Quiroga, Roberto Payró (Argentina, 1867–1928), and Javier de Viana began to reach readers in countries well beyond the Southern Cone.

Between 1890 and 1920, the *naturalista* [naturalist] short story became the prevalent mode in most regions of Spanish America. The loose nexus implicit between that kind of fiction and scientific discourse lent a certain prestige to narratives associated with the hypotheses of *naturalismo* [Naturalism]. The unadorned representations of contextual realities adopted by the Naturalists often evolved into slight parodies of pseudo scientific discourses. Texts of that sort, however flimsy, were viewed by many as appropriate expressions of modernity.

In the stories of Maupassant, Flaubert, Kipling, and, above all, Zola, a narrative took shape that had its closest antecedent in the meticulous style developed in the realistic fiction of Balzac, Dickens, Pérez Galdos, and Eça de Queiroz. At times, the techniques employed by these writers and those utilized by the *Naturalists* were so similar, that for years, both trends were discussed as parallel forms of nineteenth-century fiction. Detailed allusions to those similarities can be found, for example, in the famous monograph by Ferdinand Brunetiére (1849–1906), entitled *Le Roman naturaliste* (1883). It could be argued, in any event, that both trends favored a type a narrative focused on the crude facets of daily life. Clearly, at its roots this kind of literature rejected the transcendentalist idealism that emerged from the artistic and philosophical tenets of Romanticism.

Perhaps what distinguishes the *naturalista* short story most visibly is its affected use of medical terminology, particularly in reference to pathological syndromes. If, at times, the findings of nineteenth-century science can be detected in the prose of the *costumbristas*, it is fair to say the Naturalist drew from scientific notions to excess. Ultimately the intent of the Naturalists was a very old one: to enhance the verisimilitude of the story. With unprecedented freedom, the Naturalists blended discourses that were traditionally considered extraneous or tangential to literary creation. In doing so, the writer hoped to transfer the aura of novelty that surrounded scientific discoveries to the literary text. In most instances pseudoscientific terminology lent exceptional precision to *naturalista* fiction. That terminology, to be sure, also served to conceal the imaginative content inherent in fiction.

With the aura of his fame, Emile Zola became the most eloquent proponent of a scientific fiction that he saw as the wave of the future. In *Une Campagne* (1880–1881) he claimed, for instance, that metaphysical man had been replaced by physiological man. It is precisely this concept of literature that clearly emerges in *La Bête humaine* (1890) [*The Human Animal*]. Few literary trends have had the benefit of a spokesman as persuasive as Zola was for *Naturalismo*. His influence was felt worldwide. In a monograph devoted to the works of Roberto Payró, Germán García noted that Zola created a furor in Argentina and that his books crept into the bedrooms of many a reader. García underscores the overwhelming impact Zola's writings had amongst the novelists of the day "among them Podestá, Sicardi, Cambacérès" (*Roberto Payró*, 28). Zola's concern with scientific methodologies and his interest in the sciences are almost legendary. On the whole, his notions concerning evolutionary determinism are rooted in the famous essays and treatises of Hippolyte Taine (1828–1893) and on the spectacular investigations that Charles Darwin summarized in *The Descent of Man* (1871).

It is not surprising then that the stories written by the *Naturalistas* are often marked by references to race, hereditary features, or to pathological conditions. As we shall see, beneath the scientific façade of these stories there is a light phenomenological bent that repeatedly calls for meticulous observation, experimental activity, or narrow classifications. But, by and large, the legacies of the scientific discourses produced in the nineteenth century remained as distant echoes for most Spanish American writers at the turn of the century.

In the lethargy of neo-colonial Spanish American societies the content of naturalist theories was often reduced to mere sketches produced for journalistic accounts. The most evident traces of that theoretical *corpus* can be perceived, for example, in stories that highlighted ethical concerns, forms of exploitation, or the fatalistic views put in vogue by European fiction at the turn of the century. Representations of sordid relationships or congenital abnormalities prevail in the gory scenes that Horacio Quiroga developed in "La gallina degollada" (1909) and in "El almohadón de plumas" (1912). No less can be said of Javier de Viana's "Los amores de Bento Segrera" (1896) and "La alpargata" (1910). In many ways these texts are optimal examples of a fiction that obsessively explored degraded aspects of human behavior.

Greed and the effects of incurable illness are often at the core of Viana's stories. Among them one could single out "La tísica" (1909), a brief text originally published in *Macachines* (1910). The story is almost an elliptical account and one that could be taken as a narrative that exemplifies the devices used by storytellers of the River Plate region at the turn of the century. "La tísica" blends anthropomorphic visions derived from River Plate folklore with diagnostic hints provided by a narrator. This improbable equation became, in due time, a syncretic formula used by many storytellers who subscribed to naturalist theories. The narrator, a physician, evokes *la tísica* in these terms: "She had a small face, small and pointed like that of a small dog"; or, "She coughed in the clammy early-morning hours. It was the consumption that wandered within her sickly lungs" (p. 5). Cast aside because of her presumed illness and by the fears of superstitious peons, the young woman becomes increasingly shrouded in mystery. Some see her as "a chameleon [which] is the smallest and most dangerous of animals" (p. 5). Several months later, the reader is informed by a newspaper article that, "On the X hacienda, many have perished as a result of pastries poisoned with arsenic, including Don Z . . ., his wife and daughter, the overseer, and all of the servants, with the exception of one peon known only by her nickname, *la tísica*" (p. 7).

Although much of what the narrator reveals to us comes as no surprise, the reader is gratified nonetheless by the swift progression of the story and particularly by the concealed balance achieved between its elements. Yet the understated virtuosity of this text is not the norm in Viana's short stories. Like Quiroga, Viana wrote under the pressures of deadlines imposed on him by magazines and newspapers. For many years, he felt besieged by the lack of stability in his life. Yet in spite of endless difficulties, his interest in the short story became almost an obsession. Viana began to write brief tales when he was seventeen years old and, by the time his life ended, he had surpassed the output of nearly all of his contemporaries. He wrote novels with little success. Above all, he is remembered as a writer of short stories, the best of which are contained in *Campo* (1896), *Gurí y otras novelas* (1901), *Macachines* (1910), *Leña seca* (1911), and *Yuyos* (1912). The Argentinian critic Enrique Anderson Imbert (1910–) was correct in saying that Javier de Viana "had the power of synthesis that we sense in gifted storytellers (Anderson Imbert and E. Florit *Literatura hispanoamericana*, 5). Indeed, he was capable of weaving a highly condensed tale. As in "La tísica," he could reveal an expanding knowledge that is contained at every turn. But the distilled elaboration that he so admired in the stories of Daudet, Turgenev, and Maupassant were often the result of lengthy periods of rewriting that Viana could not afford.

When reading Viana, one is prone to recall the many similarities that exist between his best stories and those of his compatriot Eduardo Acevedo Díaz (1851–1921). Díaz is remembered for stories such as "El combate de la trapera" (1892) and "Soledad" (1894); these and many others were collected in 1931, but none of his refined fabulations has received the critical attention they deserve. "El combate de la trapera," in particular, is one of the best examples of gaucho narrative produced in the River Plate area. Historically, the story is set in the hellish battle of Catalan that took place in the eastern sector of Uruguay on January 4, 1817. But if we look beyond the brutal scenes, we notice how skillfully Acevedo Díaz balances conventional features of romantic fiction with the crude descriptive rhetoric of the Naturalist.

That subtle blend of narrative perspectives is less fortunate in the short stories of Luis Orrego Luco (Chile, 1866–1948); although now forgotten, many of his stories were well-received both in Chile and abroad. But for Orrego Luco, literary success faded rather quickly. All too often his stories remained flawed by their internal inconsistencies, and by their reliance on caricature or on the superficial characterizations that many Chilean writers learned from the *Costumbristas*. "Un pobre diablo" (1915) ranks among his best-known stories. When compared to many of the texts produced by his contemporaries, his stories are less burdened by the abundance of contextual references that today seem pointless and dated. His most perceptive depictions and keen anecdotes are compiled in *Páginas americanas* (1897) and in *La vida pasa* (1918).

The light and evocative anecdotes we may single out in Orrego Luco's books were developed, with greater success, by the Argentinian Roberto Payró. He is remembered most of all for the short stories collected in *Pago chico* (1908) and *Violines y toneles* (1908). The critical acceptance these works enjoyed is surprising, particularly when one notices their structural weakness. Most of Payró's texts are closer to the métier of the *Costumbristas* than to the tight weaving of the short story.

While much of his fiction seems dated to the contemporary reader, it is fair to say that some of his stories are energized by piercing intuitions. "Metamorfosis" (1907), in *Pago chico*, is exemplary in that regard. The story focuses, quite successfully, on a very old theme: vulnerable aspects of the human condition. We witness in it the vanity of a man who is prepared to endure a sequence of elaborate deceptions in order to keep up appearances. There is a picaresque bent in this story that often emerges in Payró's fiction and that is also present in the short stories of his compatriot Benito Lynch (1880–1951). In *La evasión* (1922) and *De los campos porteños* (1931), Lynch mainly evokes rural life in Argentina. Like Payró, Lynch was deeply affected by the pseudoscientific rhetoric employed by the Naturalists. But he is much closer than Payró to the telluric visions and the rural folklore preferred by the *Criollistas* who wrote mainly in the 1920s and 1930s. Both demonstrated a marked preference for the gauchoesque fiction that flourished for many years in the River Plate area.

Many of the stories written by the Chilean Federico Gana (1867–1926) are also linked to the idealized cultural syncretism evident in Payró's and Lynch's fiction. Repeatedly, Gana's stories depict the vicissitudes of peasant life in Chile. However, the affectations contained in dialogues and descriptive passages often show the hand of a cosmopolitan writer. His cultivated adherence to the *naturalista* creed is hidden, more than once, behind the sentimental bent of his short stories. The many subtleties that he found in the pages of Flaubert and Turgenev impressed him far more than did the descriptive virulence of Zola. Gana also wrote in the modernist vein. That inclination is evident, at times, in his collection of short stories, *Días de campo* (1916). But his best pages are the ones that blend the harsh rhetoric of the Realists with sentimental anecdotes derived from romantic fiction. The story entitled "Un perro" (1894), also known as "Un carácter," deserves special attention. It morosely recounts the extreme circumstances of a dispossessed man who has committed murder in order to avenge the death of his dearest companion, a dog. In its parable-like fashion, the story dramatizes the harsh inequalities of a society in which justice often becomes a curious abstraction.

It is Gana's preference for lyric motifs and serene reflection that frequently distinguishes him from his compatriot Baldomero Lillo (1867–1923). In his two volumes of his stories, *Sub terra* (1904) and *Sub sole* (1907), Lillo subscribes openly to theories articulated by the Naturalists. His best stories are conditioned by a fatalistic view which is prone to caustic but gratuitous descriptions. That propensity to narrative hyperactivity stands out in "La compuerta número 12" (1902) – perhaps his best-known story – and in "El chiflón del diablo" (1903). Narrative overkill often reduces the broad outlines of these stories to mere caricature. In addition, the ideological content that many critics have underlined in Lillo's stories often tends to distort the merits of the text. Anecdotal peripetia aside, some of Lillo's stories show how a sharp intuition can yield a surprising range of descriptions. That imaginative bent, characteristic of his best works, is evident in his posthumous collection *El hallazgo y otros cuentos del mar* (1956), and also in the stories compiled by Raúl Silva Castro in Lillo's *Obras completas* (1960).

But even in his first two books one finds stories that transcend the urge to preach or the obsessive depiction of sordid events. In ways reminiscent of the stories of the North American Erskine Caldwell (1902–1987), Lillo sought to condemn the systematic exploitation suffered by the working classes; he focused particularly on Chilean miners. Yet Lillo is most effective when indigence or brutality assumes a secondary role in the narrative structure. As much is evident in "El pozo" (1902), a story included in *Sub terra*. What distinguishes this story at first glance is the delicate articulation of anecdotal material. The narrative recalls Dostoyevsky's careful use of meaningful details and indirect allusions. The references in "El pozo" to unpredictable forms of behavior resulting from obsessive frames of mind evoke some of Dostoyevsky's passages in *The Possessed* (1871–1872) and in *A Raw Youth* (1875). These similarities are not merely coincidental, given the unqualified admiration Lillo felt for the Russian novelist.

In "El pozo" a self-destructive youth serves as the focus of the narrative process. This violent story takes place in the Chilean countryside and depicts a sexual attraction fueled by insecurity and rejection. The tension that arises between the adolescent sensuality of Rosa and the almost sickly presence of Remigio, who desires her, is powerful, indeed. The effectiveness of this conflict stems from the skill with which Lillo maintains the conflictual rhythm of a short story that seems propelled by the violence it depicts. In the less accomplished portions of the story, however, the physiological echoes of *Naturalismo* suggest a latent pathological condition. Although Remigio suffers from strabismus and the paroxysms of cholera, his physical condition is all but superseded by the description of his psyche, a repository of subtle irrationality and rancor.

As a whole, the techniques of *naturalista* fiction are evident in Lillo's most celebrated texts. "Los inválidos" (1904), included in various anthologies, is less fortunate. In this story one perceives the oblique and ancient legacies of the fable. In its precise use of detail the story reminds us of the crude scenes in Vittorio de Sica's film *The Bicycle Thief* (1949) and in other neorealist films produced in Italy mainly in the late 1940s. There is also a notable affinity between Lillo's works and the vigorous paintings of his compatriot Pablo Burchard Eggiling (1875–1964), who, like Lillo, delighted in simplicity, the kind of minimal creation that seeks only what will suffice. I stress this comparison not to digress, but to highlight the process of condensation which enhances the mature fiction of Baldomero Lillo.

The power to synthesize is quite noticeable in the stories of the Cuban Jesús Castellanos (1879–1912), a writer who shared many of Lillo's best qualities. Like Orrego Luco, Castellanos was admired both at home and abroad, but regrettably he died just when his considerable talents were beginning to mature. He pursued his literary career in Mexico and Cuba. Castellanos also achieved some recognition as a skilled draughtsman and painter. At times it is clear that his thorough training in the graphic arts and his firm appreciation of line and color enriched many of his pages.

Like most writers of his time, Castellanos fully assimilated much of the best short fiction France could offer at the turn of the century. In Havana he met the great Portuguese writer Eça de Queiroz, with whom he shared a fondness for Nietzsche. Inevitably, the harsh tenets of French *Naturalismo* are present in his best stories. But Castellanos's subtle depictions of Cuban society are not always guided by the affected conventions preferred by the Naturalists. Among his works, published in Cuba and Spain, the masterful short story "La agonía de la garza" (1907) is of special interest. This text relates with admirable simplicity a brutal struggle for survival. It also stands as a significant example of an artistic iconography which is often associated with the Caribbean. In its broad depiction of landscapes and the hardships of the sea, Castellanos's story evokes the paintings of the North American master Winslow Homer (1836–1910), and particularly his famous oil *Gulf Stream* (1899). In it, an exhausted black sailor passively contemplates the sharks that circle his storm-worn schooner in the rough waters of the Caribbean. *The Old Man and the Sea* (1952) by Ernest Hemingway (1899–1961), set in the coastal regions of Cuba, is also linked to this artistic tradition that emerges from the Caribbean basin.

In "La agonía de la garza," as in the works mentioned above, the sequence of events is both slow, and swift. This story focuses on an enfeebled vessel surrounded by a ravenous school of sharks. The narrator patiently tells us: "Perhaps their hunger propelled them; one of the sharks, a whitish mass rising from the water, attacked the side of the boat. There arose a collective howl and a weaker child inadvertently slipped away from its mother as she shouted: "José! . . . darn child . . . where are you?" (*La agonía de la garza*, 66). In Castellanos's short story each wrenching incident is recounted in a language rich in colorful images. Describing the passengers in the frail boat, the narrator tells us how: "The little black ones displayed their teeth, white like coconut meat" and "at that moment, the fleeting shadow of a seagull stained the flow of light" (*La agonía*, 62).

The same descriptive flair stands out in "Naranjos en flor" (1906). In this text Castellanos comes quite close to the Parnassian sensuality of the Modernists. The plot opens with the architectural framework of a Byzantine arch that leads to a gate, from which one sees "the reddish blossoms of the acacias." "Naranjos en flor" is a luminous narrative, though imbued at times with an affected sentimentalism which clearly harks back to romantic fiction.

In Cuban literature, Castellanos's works helped free the brief narrative from the long-standing dictates of Peninsular *Costumbrismo*. By and large, his best stories are unencumbered by the descriptive formulae most writers learned from nineteenth-century realist fiction. But the innovative thrust of Castellanos's fiction was not perceived by many of his contemporaries. The graceful agility of his plots is rarely present in the stories of his compatriots Carlos Loveira (1882–1928) and Luis Rodríguez Embil (1880–1954). Yet Miguel de Carrión (Cuba, 1875–1929) at times displays a grasp of narrative techniques not unlike that of Castellanos. Indeed, Carrión's *Inocencia* stands as a seminal collection of stories for Cuba's short fiction at the turn of the century.

Once again the paradoxes inherent in literary historiography become evident when one notes that Castellanos's innovative fiction is akin to the works of much younger Cuban storytellers. Several fairly recent collections of stories are clearly akin to Castellanos's texts. One thinks of *Dos barcos* (1934), by Carlos Montenegro (1900–1967?); *La luna nona y otros cuentos* (1942) by Lino Novás Calvo (1905–1980); and *Carne de quimera* (1947) by Enrique Labrador Ruiz (1902–1990?).

Just as gifted as Castellanos was Augusto Jorge Goeminne Thompson (Chile, 1882–1950). Augusto D'Halmar was his fortunate pseudonym. Like Castellanos, D'Halmar is a largely forgotten writer and also a precursor of subtle fictions produced by several of his compatriots in the 1940s and 1950s. D'Halmar's shrewd references to suggestive details evoke the best texts of Manuel Rojas (1896–1972), María Luisa Bombal (1910–1980), José Donoso (1924–), and Jorge Edwards (1931–). He learned much from Russian and Scandinavian authors, Turgenev and Tolstoy were among his favorites. In fact, this fondness was so deeply felt that D'Halmar once attempted to organize a colony of writers which followed models proposed by Tolstoy. The delicate compositions of his short stories recalls, at times, Turgenev's famous collection of stories *A Sportsman's Sketches* (1852).

At first glance it seems logical to identify D'Halmar with the tenets of *Modernismo* [Modernism], yet that assertion is only partially correct. We might remember that, when D'Halmar published his first novel *Juan Lucero* (1902), he was very much under the spell of the French Naturalists. But shortly thereafter, he became intrigued by fictions of a very different kind. His diplomatic duties took him to the Far East, where his longstanding fascination with mystical thought became an overwhelming concern. Few writers of his time travelled as extensively as he did through the Far East, Europe, and Latin America. Inevitably the impact of knowledge acquired in foreign lands surfaces in much of his fiction. His first collection of short stories, *La lámpara en el molino*, contains surprising references to experiences connected with his travels. While this book was published in 1914, nearly all of the stories in it appeared between 1903 and 1910. Two more volumes were yet to come: *Capitanes sin barco* (1934) and *Amor, cara y cruz* (1935). The former collection of stories is marked by subtle traces of the short fictions of Joseph Conrad (1857–1924). Though evident, the complex links that exist between D'Halmar's fictions and texts of Conrad, Bertolt Brecht, and Herman Melville remain to be explored. The extraordinary length of his works is likely to discourage close readings of his texts. In their latest edition, D'Halmar's works encompass twenty-five volumes. In that voluminous output the short stories occupy a very limited sector, yet they are his most memorable achievements.

D'Halmar's short stories are also the focus of his best critical assessments. In a brief note published in 1948 in the prestigious Chilean journal *Atenea*, he admitted that his best works were gathered in *La lámpara en el molino*. Moreover, he added that nothing since then had surpassed the quality of those stories. He referred specifically to texts such as "Sebastopol," "Ternura," and "En provincias." Of the three stories, "En provincias" is the one that has appeared in many anthologies, and is quite clearly among the best short stories produced in Spanish America during this period.

It is thin and, at times, even colorless. Predictably, its episodic brevity and its indirect pattern of allusions enhances the poetic effect of the text. In the story, the repressed passion that the timid Borja feels for Clara is consummated in one powerful and fleeting moment, but the erotic intensity of that episode is gradually eroded by the sterility of guilt and their daily routine. Here the deliberate monotony of the narrative process evokes the famous passage from Dostoyevsky's *A Friend of the Family* (1859). Almost imperceptibly, the tension of the story seems to arise from the enumeration of humble objects which from day to day, assume a disproportionate importance in the life of this undistinguished employee. The growing vacuity of his existence is captured with amazing precision, in references to the flute, photographs, or the opening of a window which, paradoxically, inspires introspection. For the ageing Borja, these objects, and others like them, slowly create a suggestive narrative iconography that evokes skillful passages from such works as Flaubert's *A Simple Heart* (1877), Tolstoi's *Ana Karenina* (1876), and Jorge Luis Borges's "Una señora mayor" (1969).

Much of what is told in "En provincias" is greatly enhanced by the skillful reference to casual details. A similar yet delightful parsimony is evident in "Un mendigo" (1929) by Manuel Rojas; in "El preceptor" (1928) by José Santos González Vera (Chile, 1897–1970); and particularly in José Donoso's "Paseo" (1959). The links that exist between "En provincias" and these stories confirms, in many ways, the precocious character of D'Halmar's fictions. But his stories, like those by Lillo or Castellanos, have been forgotten by contemporary readers.

Even though we still have but scant knowledge of the fiction produced at the turn of the century, at least one can argue with a fair degree of certainty that, by then, the short story had claimed a space of its own among literate Latin American readers. An expanding range of authors were devoting their best efforts to the new, slender genre. A preference for the short story is evident even in the fiction of writers who had achieved limited recognition. The accomplished stories of Darío Herrera (Panama, 1883–1914) and Adolfo Montiel Ballesteros (Uruguay, 1888–) are a case in point.

In spite of its minority status, the short story gradually began to be perceived as an autonomous form which reflected the alienated condition of many literate sectors of Spanish American society. Though many praised the *cuento literario* as an innovative form, the truth is that in the daily press, the short story continued to appear next to a broad range of anecdotes, *costumbrista* pieces and graphic illustrations that often seemed to reduce the story to the status of a passing commentary.

Some of the disparities that can be detected in the short fiction that emerged with this century are apparent in the stories that the Dominican writer Fabio Fiallo (1865–1943) compiled in his *Cuentos frágiles* (1908). Nearly all of these stories were written in the guise of romantic fictions. They have a parodic bent that often brings to mind the fictions of Heinrich Heine (1797–1856), Larra, Gustavo Adolfo Bécquer, and Manuel Gutiérrez Nájera. Fiallo's stories, though evocative, tend to be fragmented by unfortunate digressions and also by a declamatory style of writing. Yet his story "El castigo," which appears in several well-known Spanish American anthologies, is one of Fiallo's most memorable creations. Its slender plot and poetic nuances largely account for its success.

Fiallo's stories and those of Payró and Herrera often appear as contrasting variants of the short story. It is fair to assume that arbitrary demands made by all sorts of magazines and periodicals tended to disfigure some of the short fiction published at the turn of the century. The contrasting of stories produced at that time became evident in the lengthy tales of Tomás Carrasquilla (Colombia, 1858–1940), a prolific writer who practiced many forms of the brief narrative. Between 1903 and 1936, he published three books of short stories: *Salve regina* (1903), *Dominicales* (1934), and *De tejas arriba* (1936); other volumes appeared posthumously. If we review Carrasquilla's best-known stories, such as "Blanca" (1897), "San Antoñito" (1899), "El rifle" (1915), and "Rogelio" (1926), it becomes evident that these stories are linked in a rather indiscriminate fashion to the romantic legend, the *tradición*, the *artículo de costumbres*, and the modern short story. In part, the regressive design of some of Carrasquilla's stories reflects the conservative orientation of Colombian literary circles before the 1940s. "San Antoñito," for instance, is a narrative that draws heavily from the slightly picaresque tone of the *tradición* and even more from the loose rhetorical devices used by the *costumbristas*.

The formal uncertainties characteristic of the brief narrative at the beginning of this century are not as visible in the works of other writers. Clemente Palma (Peru, 1872–1946) and, above all, Amado Nervo (Mexico, 1870–1919) understood better than most the possibilities and limitations of the short story. Both began writing during the final phases of *Modernismo*, and their affinity for the goals of the movement is obvious, for example, in a collection of Nervo's short stories compiled by Alfonso Méndez Plancarte in *Mañana del poeta* (1938). But soon after their initial attempts, both Palma and Nervo rejected the affected anecdotes favored by the Modernists.

In *Almas que pasan* (1906) and *Cuentos misteriosos* (1921), both written between 1895 and 1916, Nervo's short stories display considerable imaginative content. The careful weaving of these stories brings to mind *Las fuerzas extrañas* (1906) by Leopoldo Lugones, as well as some stories included in *El plano oblicuo* (1920) by Alfonso Reyes (1889–1959). Appropriately, Reyes more than once confessed his admiration for Nervo's talents as a storyteller. When reviewing Nervo's *Cuentos misteriosos* (1921), Reyes alluded specifically to "Un sueño," which is set in the Toledo of El Greco. In that story, Reyes noted that "the entire plot is interwoven in the veil of light which, at sunrise, slips through the gaps of the window frame" (*Obras completas*, 287).

In "El ángel caído," "Una esperanza," and "El diamante de la inquietud" Nervo demonstrates his growing fascination with mystical experiences and with the mental processes that approach hallucination or morbid states of mind. While much of his curiosity was polarized toward interests of that kind, his best stories focus mainly on the enigmatic nature of love and the imminence of death. But it is regrettable that so many of his best stories are marred by digression. Nervo's overwhelming fondness for H. G. Wells, Nietzsche, Victor Hugo. Kierkegaard, and for the manifestations of esoteric thought, often led him to the sort of interpolated reflection which the short story cannot tolerate. With few exceptions, much of what one can say about Nervo's texts applies to many stories written by Clemente Palma (1872–1946). The experiences emanating from dreams are at the core of Palma's most successful texts. Such is the case of "La granja blanca" (1903?). Miguel de Unamuno, among others, wrote fondly of Palma's short stories, which are compiled in three volumes: *Cuentos malévolos* (1904), *Mors ex vita* (1923), and *Historias malignas* (1925).

Palma began to experiment with the short story late in 1903. Critics and reviewers noticed, more than once, striking similarities between his texts and some of those written by Maxim Gorki (1868–1936), Chekhov, Huysmans, and Borges. His most acclaimed short story is, perhaps, "Los ojos de Lina," (1902) which appeared in *Cuentos malévolos*. Its unusual organization recalls the famed tales of Boccaccio and exhibits a subtle drift toward perceptions of asymmetry or disfigurement. Palma's tales often contained descriptions that led to unexpected conclusions. "La granja blanca" also reflects some of the imaginative turns we admire in *Sonatas* (1902–1905) by Ramón del Valle Inclán (1866–1936), and evokes the revealing conclusion of "Las ruinas circulares" (1941) by Jorge Luis Borges. But due, in part, to stylistic affectations and structural looseness, many of Palma's texts fall short of the goals that the reader presumes at the beginning of the text. In Nervo's and Palma's stories the plot often seems to exhaust its possibilities in the early stages of the narrative process. Perhaps this is because much of the writing is focused on impulses or initial intuitions that are not sustained by the development of a plot.

The same cannot be said of the twenty-two short stories collected in *La guerra gaucha* (1905) by Leopoldo Lugones. These first stories are imbued with cultural references and theoretical statements that eventually burden the narrative structure. Also, many of his stories are congested by the rhetorical devices that Lugones absorbed from the Naturalists and from the telluric discourse that had widely infiltrated Spanish American literature. Sly allusions to famous texts by Sarmiento and Alberdi appear in these short stories; with some ease, we recognize traces of *Facundo* and *Las memorias descriptivas de Tucumán* (1834), respectively. But occasionally these inopportune allusions tend to distort the narrative.

Reflecting on Lugones's works, Borges noted that "the stunning features present in this book [*La guerra gaucha*] such as the episode of the gaucho who keeps the arm of a Spanish soldier for his dog, may be based on fact, yet they are not convincing" (*Leopoldo Lugones*, 70–1). This objection seems reasonable, but not applicable to Lugones's more skillful representations of imaginary events. In those instances, the impact of Poe's fictions on Lugones's texts is rather obvious. But, fortunately, the disparities and descriptive excesses that stand out in Lugones's first book of stories will be less evident in *Las fuerzas extrañas* (1906).

In this second book, the so-called "real" or historical becomes a mere point of departure. In most of the stories paradox and the process of representation is the writer's central concern. The making of the story and its structural autonomy is recognized as the process through which meaning can be communicated. It is indeed that sophisticated concept of the narrative act that gives *Las fuerzas extrañas* a prominent role in River Plate fiction at the turn of the century. Most of the stories found in it dramatize the illusory convergence of verbal creation and the sciences, but almost always Lugones will do so with a sense of irony and humor that was largely unknown to the Naturalists. It is, indeed, that particular outlook that we have later come to admire in many of Borges's best stories. At the time of their publication, *Las fuerzas extrañas* represented the advent of a new kind of science fiction that endowed the physiological excesses of the Naturalists with a richer imaginative content that, in turn, was linked to the mysteries of esoteric thought. Some of the most successful examples of this type of fiction are found in "La lluvia de fuego," "Yzur," and "Los caballos de Abdera." "Yzur" is a narrative founded on rather weak nineteenth-century theories of verbal communication and on a very vague definition of the unconscious. As a contextual reference, it is useful to bear in mind that this kind of fiction coincided with the beginnings of experimental psychology. But to many scientific activities of that sort seemed then like a fable, perhaps not too different from "Yzur."

The pathetic denouement of this story occurs when an ape finally manages to speak to his trainer, only to die at once. This text is an intrepid piece of writing and its sophistication endures; partly this is so because the pseudoscience on which it relies does not trivialize the narrative process. It is surprising, however, that the stories Lugones compiled in *Cuentos fatales* (1924) do not go beyond the imaginative range achieved in *Las fuerzas extrañas*. On the whole, the innovations introduced by Lugones stand as landmarks of Argentinian fiction at the turn of the century. In his texts one foresees the artful weaving of Borges's *Historia universal de la infamia* (1935). And the same may be said of *Trama celeste* (1948) by Adolfo Bioy-Casares (1914–), *Final del juego* (1956) by Julio Cortázar, and *El grimorio* by Enrique Anderson-Imbert.

In a lesser vein, Alberto Edwards (Chile, 1878–1932) wrote several stories – mostly between 1913 and 1916 – that show his compulsive fascination with misfortune or with inscrutable experiences. The stories were eventually collected in *Cuentos fantásticos* (1921). Some of Edwards's best short fictions are reminiscent of Huysmans's *A Rebours* (1884) and of *Contes cruels* (1883) by Jean M. Villiers (1838–1889). By and large Edwards's short pieces are much closer to the stories of G. K. Chesterton (1874–1936) and Arthur Conan Doyle (1859–1930). He frequently wrote under the pseudonyms "J. B. C." and "Miguel Fuenzalida," and clearly wanted, above all, to transform the detective story into an artistic achievement. Yet his meticulous descriptions and experimental leanings often thwarted the cohesion of the plot. "El secuestro del candidato" (1913) possibly ranks as his best story of this kind. Regrettably, Edwards's texts have been read largely in unimaginative ways.

The works of the Peruvian dandy Abraham Valdelomar (1888–1919) are less accomplished than those of Edwards. If Valdelomar's works had a dominant theme, it would be the dramatization of existential conflicts, a concern visible in the turn-of-the-century literature that will persist well into the 1940s. However, those introspective inquiries often led to a disproportionate representation of the narrator and of his particular sense of crisis. When compared to Valdelomar's voluminous journalistic production, his short stories appear as a marginal sector of his output. His novels *La ciudad de los muertos* and *La ciudad de los tísicos*, both dated 1910, merited some attention; both novels are rooted in the last and most strident phases of *Naturalismo*.

More than to scientific theories, Valdelomar's fiction responded to the pressures of nationalist discourses that had plagued Spanish American literature since the beginning of its republican era. As in the case of many of his contemporaries, Valdelomar's texts were linked to the ideological and ethical concerns expressed in the *criollista* narrative that took root in Spanish America around 1915. But the discursive legacy of *Criollismo* is not always predominant in his best works. Among his short stories, "El Caballero Carmelo" (1915?) and "Hebaristo el sauce que murió de amor" (1918) come close to the subtle representations that one finds in the best stories of Jesús Castellanos and Augusto D'Halmar. Perhaps his best achievements are the perceptive representations of individuals whose existence gradually evolves into a stolid marginality.

Most of the texts described above illustrate the dissimilar stages of literary activity prevailing in Spanish America toward the end of the *belle époque*. At that juncture, the industrially advanced nations hurriedly began the rituals of a war that, eventually, would reinforce the almost chronic marginality of Spanish America. The profuse literary activity of that period took place in large metropolitan settings. The power and centrality of urban life was glorified by the crystal palaces, the technology and the art displayed in the spectacular world fairs of London (1851), Chicago (1893), and Paris (1899). These images were vividly captured by impressionist painters and by a multitude of graphic illustrations. In the industrialized countries, economic activity and political power fell into the hands of a class dominated by the commercial bourgeoisie. In Spanish America, Buenos Aires was, perhaps, the only city to approximate this dazzling sequence of events. Inevitably, the abrupt prosperity that followed the Great War also brought an unprecedented literary boom reflected in the output of new Argentinian, Mexican, Chilean, and Cuban publishing houses.

In the River Plate area, the works and the *persona* of Ricardo Güiraldes (1886–1927) represented quite accurately this growing context of prosperity and cultural refinement. His fiction and poetry convey the intellectual concerns that ran through the coterie of literati at the turn of the century. Though his stories depict rural settings, one immediately recognizes the craft and elegance of a cultivated writer. Among the literati who frequented Buenos Aires's refined "Café Richmond," the short story was considered to be a resplendent novelty. Güiraldes not only cultivated this new narrative genre, but also understood quite well many of its untested possibilities.

In Buenos Aires and in Europe, Güiraldes read the best short-story writers of the period, and was equally familiar with the insights some of them had developed regarding the nature of the modern short story. The theoretical alertness of Güiraldes is evident in the writing of *Cuentos de muerte y de sangre* and also in the correspondence that he kept up with his friends Valéry Larbaud and Guillermo de Torre, among others. These informal pieces are peppered with comments on the texts of Poe, Baudelaire, Flaubert, Kipling, Mallarmé, Conrad, and Ibsen. And at times his letters also show that he followed rather closely the emerging theories concerned with the modern short story.

In *Cuentos de muerte y de sangre*, "El pozo" and "El trenzador" clearly showed the care with which Güiraldes developed some of his short stories. His attention to meaningful detail reminds us of Chekhov's observations regarding the delicate articulation of the short story. In *Letters on the Short Story, the Drama and Other Literary Topics* (1924), the famous Russian writer had advised his nephew that "in description one ought to seize upon the little particulars" (p. 81). It is precisely this narrative approach that we come to admire in "El remanso" and other stories by Güiraldes. The passing references that eventually affect the narrative processes are particularly evident in "El pozo," a text which leaves both the reader and the protagonist under the cruel gaze of a superstitious gaucho. In this story, a man has accidentally fallen into a well while sleeping; momentarily the shock prevents him from returning to the world he had known, but gradually he climbs to the surface. But upon emerging from the well, he suddenly feels paralyzed by an access of terror and violence that causes his death.

That sort of stunning brevity was Güiraldes's goal. In a letter dated 1926 and addressed to Valéry Larbaud, he referred to his works in these terms: "I want my prose to be condensed, brief, powerful; indeed, what I like most about my hand is that it can become a fist" (*Obras completas*, 789). In another letter to Larbaud, he alludes to Whitman, D'Annunzio, and Poe, and then adds: "recently a new and pioneering rebel [has] joined the realms of the psychological short story and the novel; this time he is a Norman: Joyce" (p. 777). The letter was written as he read, for the first time, Joyce's *Dubliners* (1914).

But this fascinating corpus of letters does not merely indicate Güiraldes's awareness of European literature; his correspondence also contains astute comments on the short stories of Horacio Quiroga that were appearing in magazines such as *Fray Mocho* and *Caras y caretas*. In yet another letter, also dated 1926 and written to his friend Héctor Eandi, Güiraldes pauses to comment on the Uruguayan's texts:

> Quiroga sees America as an untamed and struggling continent frightened by man's possession, and affected by a dangerous climate, by its flora, fauna, and also by illnesses that lead to ill-fated mental conditions. Most of the time, Quiroga sees his dwellers [protagonists] as exiles in a hostile land. (*Obras completas*, 792)

And later on, he adds, "[in his texts] man struggles, woman vegetates, like a flower transplanted to a soil of unhappiness where she embraces unreal fantasies or torpid hallucinations" (p. 793). His acute observations concerning Quiroga's stories are reinforced in other remarks contained in the same letter: "More than the environment in Quiroga's short stories, internal conflicts are the true cause of the tragedies that he wants to relate" (p. 792).

Talented writers such as Alfonso Reyes and Lugones admired Güiraldes's short stories, but we know that *Cuentos de muerte y de sangre* was mostly read by the small vanguard circle of literati who prospered in the River Plate area. Nonetheless, Güiraldes's "El trenzador" figures among the finest short stories produced in Spanish America at the turn of the century. The text already contained most of the memorable qualities that we recognize in Quiroga's "A la deriva" (1912), Borges's "La intrusa" (1966), and "La prodigiosa tarde de Baltazar" (1961) by Gabriel García Márquez (1927–).

Toward the end of the First World War, the short story was clearly overcoming its marginal status. In practically all Latin American capitals, publishers issued new collections of short stories. Many of the books discussed in this essay corroborate the gradual emergence of a readership which became particularly attuned to this new genre. These developments are all the more remarkable when one realizes that large sectors of Spanish America were illiterate and that, for many others, books remained a luxury item. But these considerable obstacles did not hamper editorial productivity or the growing acceptance of the short story.

As an example, the many collections of short fictions produced by Venezuelan writers, such as *Cuentos de poeta* (1900) and *Cuentos americanos* (1903) by Rufino Blanco Fombona (1874–1944), *Los abuelos* (1909) by Luis Manuel Urbaneja Achepohl (1873–1937), and *Los aventureros* (1913) by Rómulo Gallegos (1884-1969) confirm the acceptance of the short story in Spanish America as an established genre of fictional discourse. The same can be said of *Dolorosa y desnuda realidad* (1944) by Ventura García Calderón (Peru, 1886-1969), and of *Los gauchos judíos* (1910), by Alberto Gerchunoff (Argentina, 1883–1950). With similar industry, Chilean publishing houses issued *Escenas de la vida campesina* (1909) by Rafael Maluenda (1885–1963) and *Cuentos del maule* (1912) by Mariano Latorre (1886-1955). Many sophisticated stories appeared in *Cuentos pasionales* (1907) by Alfonso Hernández Catá (Cuba, 1885–1940), and in *El hombre que parecía un caballo* (1915) by Rafael Arévalo Martínez (Guatemala, 1884–1975).

Even the most cursory review of the books mentioned above will frustrate almost any attempt at rigid classification. The stories written by Urbaneja, Blanco Fombona, Gallegos, García Calderón, and Latorre are contrasting variations of the naturalist fiction set in rural locations of Spanish America. The echoes of ancient Semitic legends appear in the works of Gerchunoff. And in stories written by Hernández Catá and Arévalo Martínez the subconscious and the world of dreams often leads us to powerful anthropomorphic images reminiscent of Franz Kafka. The dissimilar content of these books is but a part of the vast spectrum that emerges in Spanish American short fiction at the turn of the century. It is important to bear in mind that, after 1915, Mexican literature largely followed a course of its own; directly or otherwise, the Mexican Revolution dictated a new literary agenda for that country.

In Walter Benjamin's masterful essay, "The Storyteller" (1936), the German critic underlines the peculiar dilemma encountered by modern writers as they seek new forms of credibility that might validate their works. Distracted by the successive ruptures and displacements that have characterized modern societies, especially in urban contexts, the modern writer – according to Benjamin – has been progressively detached from the collective wisdom that traditionally existed in societies where a wide range of daily experiences was shared by all. Lost in the anonymity imposed by the great, modern cities, and without other alternatives, the writer has emphasized structural sophistication as a way to lend coherence to his texts. Undoubtedly this is why modern texts frequently show a reflexive bent, geared toward introspection or even to parody. More than contextual realities, these texts often represent forms of alienation, or of cultural marginality.

In Spanish America, many authors attempted to rewrite the texts of Daudet, Zola, and Maupassant. But American historical and cultural contexts differed considerably from those dramatized in European models. The disparity between historical reality and textual practice accounts, in large measure, for the contradictory and off-center quality of much Spanish American fiction at the turn of the century. The progress, excesses, and cultural shock produced by the industrial revolution fed into the discourse of the Naturalists. But for most Spanish Americans, those events, equated with the great achievements of modernity, were merely a narrative experience.

Given such circumstances, Spanish American fiction chose to legitimize writing in the only context that could lend validity to its enterprise: the rural setting. As modern fiction became increasingly tied to a cosmopolitan discourse, Spanish American fiction opted for a telluric iconography which propelled it away from literary currents in other Western nations. *Cuentos de muerte y de sangre* by Ricardo Güiraldes, *Guri* by Javier de Viana, or *Cuentos de amor de locura y de muerte* by Horacio Quiroga gradually unveil some of the best creations produced in that long and conflicting phase of literary activity. It was a period prone to experimentation. In the words of José Lezama Lima (Cuba, 1910–1976), Spanish American fiction at the turn of the century must have appeared to many a reader as a bewildering "showcase of paradoxes and enchantments" ("Verba criolla," 166).

15

The Spanish American theatre of the nineteenth century
Frank Dauster

Theatre in Spanish America in the nineteenth century was limited to a few larger cities. Neoclassicism was dominant until about 1810; thereafter the dominant aesthetic was essentially romantic, although often disguised by forms borrowed from other schools. While European Romanticism disappeared after mid century, the Spanish American version is more long lasting, and is closely related to two developments which span the late nineteenth and early twentieth centuries: *Costumbrismo*, the depiction of regional customs which is often a mask for growing nationalism, and a popularly based urban theatre. Traditional terms such as Neoclassicism, Romanticism, post-Romanticism, or Modernism are misleading, for these trends often coexist and are profoundly influenced by romantic attitudes. These complexities and the difficulties involved in treating jointly a number of national literatures make the historiography of Spanish American letters a complicated and often polemical undertaking on which there is no broad agreement. For purposes of convenience, the organization used here is that developed by José Juan Arrom, which follows a generational scheme based on a thirty-year pattern. This deals adequately with literary change and development overall if applied with flexibility allowing for the considerable variations within individual nations and each generation.

The Generation of 1804

Although it includes the movement for political independence, the Generation of 1804, born between 1774 and 1804, is a transitional movement, a tie to the past rather than a rupture with the status quo. There were no profound socio-economic changes, despite political chaos, and the period tends toward the retention of forms and ideas inherited from the preceding generation. The period of the wars of independence lacks any significant theatre, and where they existed such productions have left little trace. The general tendency was neoclassical and the repertoire almost exclusively foreign: Voltaire, Alfieri, Addison, Quintana, Moreto, the European dramatists of liberal inspiration and neoclassic aesthetics, although toward the end of the period we can see the beginnings of Romanticism. Meanwhile, the musical theatre continued to gain popularity; the triumph of Neoclassicism over the *zarzuela grande* is also the arrival of the opera. This is a theatre based in the few cities; the reduced population, chronic political instability, lack of a stable economy, low standards of living and education of the vast majority of the population and the firm opposition of many clerics made the theatre tenuous indeed. Almost unknown to the cultured public there existed a more modest theatre, popular in inspiration and expression and aimed at a primarily rural audience.

The greatest activity was in Argentina. By 1818 opera and *zarzuela* had arrived, with negative results for serious theatre. When other nations began to show greater activity, the Argentinian movement deteriorated into the repression of the Rosas regime. The majority of plays have been lost; there were provincial playwrights, some quite productive, whose entire output has disappeared. The primary note of *rioplatense* theatre of the period was oratorical patriotism; the texts are static with little dramatic action. In 1817, the revolutionary government, attempting to take advantage of propagandistic possibilities, established the Society of Good Taste. Although it sought to raise the level of popular taste by copying the rationalistic neoclassical French model, there were other ends in view: the theatre as political instrument. The Society lasted only a short time and produced few plays of lasting interest, but it aroused interest in the theatre amongst humbler social strata, which the dictator Rosas would use against his enemies.

This Argentinian movement is primarily of historical and sociological interest. Its most important dramatist, director, translator, and actor, also active in Chile after 1821, was the Peruvian Luis Ambrosio Morante (1775–1837), neoclassical defender of the theatre as vehicle for doctrinaire propaganda. It is impossible to determine which of the many plays attributed to Morante are his, but he is important for *Túpac Amarú* (1821), based on the 1780 uprising of the hereditary Inca ruler. It is a work of political outbursts, verbal excesses, and the deliberate Americanisms typical of the time, but there is a nucleus of real dramatic action seen in few plays of the period. More picturesque is the Chilean priest, doctor, and journalist Camilo Henríquez (1768–1825). His work is didactic and schematic, peopled by talking symbols rather than people. Typical of the period are *Didi* (1823) and *Argía* (1824) by Juan Cruz Varela (1794–1839). Never staged, schematic and slow, they maintain the unities, verisimilitude, the cult of reason and order and all the other neoclassical conventions, but there is a hint of romantic passion to come. Varela's real interest lies in a little-known *sainete* written before 1816 but only published in 1959. *A río revuelto, ganancia de pescadores* speaks of the rights of women and children in an urban setting, with different theatrical languages being used by different social classes for comic effect. There was also an early rural theatre: *El amor de la estanciera* (1792), *El detalle de la acción de Maipú* (1818), *Las bodas de Chivico y Pancha* (1823), *Un día de fiesta en Barracas* (1836). The first expresses its violent anti-Spanish message in crude popular language. *Bodas* is more dramatic; its careful linguistic differentiation between characters and classes anticipates the rural theatre. Despite their relative simplicity, these works are still fresh because of their distance from the static declamation of the official theatre.

The first known Chilean play is the anonymous *Hércules chileno* (1693) but there was little activity until well into the nineteenth century: opera, pallid imitative Neoclassicism, some poorly documented popular activity. Camilo Henríquez, before leaving for exile in 1817, fought for a theatre responsive to national needs and teaching civic virtues. In 1818 Bernardo O'Higgins ordered the organization of a theatre company, the first in Chilean history. The liberal anti-clerical tone of the European repertoire and the Senate's prohibition of the *autos sacramentales* in 1821 provoked controversy, but by the late 1820s this became muted, and the theatre more of a pastime.

In Mexico we find almost exclusively Spanish works. From 1805 to 1808 the newspapers *La Gazeta* and *El Diario* held three contests for Mexican playwrights, but only seven plays were entered. The earliest serious interest is a premiere in 1823 by an unknown Mexican, and in 1824 the first stable theatre company was founded. Again, *zarzuela* and opera rule; the few Mexican plays are almost all lost. José Joaquín Fernández de Lizardi (1776–1827), novelist and journalist, wrote a number of short plays expressing liberal political attitudes. Attributed to him is the satire of society as a madhouse *Todos contra el payo*, an intriguing prefiguring of contemporary forms. The barely documented rural popular theatre is seen in *El charro* (1797?) and *Los remendones* (1801), brief pieces by José Agustín de Castro (1730–1814) exposing the prevalent poverty.

An illustrious figure of Hispanic theatre is Manuel Eduardo de Gorostiza (1789–1851). While theatre was threatened by the passion for comic opera, he is impressive for the solidity of his compositions. Son of a Spanish official, Gorostiza lived in Spain and England from 1794 to 1833. His plays, most of which were first performed in Spain, are lacking in regional or national allusions, but he took Mexican citizenship in 1824, served as Minister Plenipotentiary in Britain and the United States, and fought against the American invaders in 1847. Even much of Gorostiza's considerable production has been lost. His plots are not original, but he developed them carefully and understood the theatre. His humor, didactic purpose and rejection of new ideas and morality imported from France, lie between the rigorous Neoclassicism of Leandro Fernández de Moratín and the gentler moralizing of Manuel Bretón de los Herreros. Best are *Indulgencia para todos* (1818), an amusing lesson in tolerance, *Don Dieguito* (1820), a satire on vanity and false adulation, and *Contigo pan y cebolla* (1833). The latter uses the author's favorite structural technique, the double plot, to poke fun at romantic daydreaming. Gorostiza's characters are sometimes more caricature than character and he used the same plot resources repeatedly, but his plays still delight.

Colombia too saw limited activity. Incipient Romanticism can be seen in the mixture of dream and fantasy of *La ilusión de un enamorado* (1813) by Mario Candil (1789–1841) or the *indigenista* [indigenist] themes of José Fernández Madrid (1789–1830) in *Atala* and *Guatemocín*, both from 1825. Luis Vargas Tejada (1802–1829) wrote static pseudoclassical tragedies on *indigenista* themes, but he is known for his *costumbrista* comedy *Las convulsiones* (1828), based on Capacelli's *Convulsioni* and still produced successfully. In the other new nations there were almost exclusively translations of French works. Plays are sometimes cited because their authors are illustrious in other fields, such as Andrés Bello, José Joaquín de Olmedo or José María Heredia, but the texts offer little of interest except for the growing importance of *Indigenismo* [Indigenism]. Many of these authors also wrote brief popularly based comedies that compare favorably with the more ambitious efforts at tragedy which motivated their other works. This popular theatre was rooted in the American reality, and authors like Francisco Covarrubias (Cuba, 1775–1850) nationalized Spanish popular forms and prepared the way for the popular comic theatre of the end of the century.

The Generation of 1834

Despite political uncertainty this period saw more productions and a profound Americanization of the work of its authors, born between 1804 and 1834. The earlier faint *Indigenismo* became a major thrust equivalent to European Romanticism's fascination with the medieval past. Romanticism had a profound impact; it continued as the dominant aesthetic long after it had all but disappeared in Europe. Spain exercised a powerful influence, while developing regional differences began to produce individual variations in theatre. The theatre passed from pseudoclassicism to romantic melodrama to critical *Costumbrismo* and finally to Naturalism, but all with a heavy romantic tinge.

By 1829 the musical theatre, followed by the romantic landslide of French sentimental comedies and Spanish melodramas, had left Argentinian theatre exhausted. Rosas's tyranny blighted the stage from 1840. His followers produced sensational propagandistic works, and opponents in exile were almost equally propagandistic, though there are surprises. *El gigante Amapolas* (1841), an attack on Rosas by Juan Bautista Alberdi (1810–1884), shows a lively sense of the absurd and an avoidance of romantic commonplaces. From Rosas's fall in 1852 until 1877, the repertoire copies Spanish late romantic models, often with a heavy political bias. The Uruguayan theatre was primarily a reflection of the Argentinian, and the same characteristics prevail.

While the Argentinian theatre decayed, the Chilean theatre flourished. The polemic of 1842, and debate between Chileans and Argentinian exiles over the existence of a Chilean theatre, ended the tepid neoclassical translations which dominated the stage. The confrontation between Andrés Bello and Domingo F. Sarmiento created an intense atmosphere of intellectual debate, although Bello was closer to Romanticism and the polemic itself less polarized than usually represented. The resulting rupture with the literary past overwhelmed Chilean theatre with the most truculent Romanticism, although the works are disappointing. Heroic sentimentalism does not mask the increasingly political thrust. The blending of Realism with Romanticism is visible in *El jefe de la familia*, written in 1858 by the novelist Alberto Blest Gana (1830–1920), but only produced in 1954 when it had considerable success. Its satire on demanding wives, weak husbands, rascally suitors, and marriages of convenience is familiar, but the controlled prose dialogue marks a step forward from the prevailing verse declamation, pointing to a shift toward a more controlled technique. In 1859 Daniel Barros Grez's *La beata* established *Costumbrismo* as the dominant school, a regionalist variant of Realism, although its emphasis on Chilean subjects and its efforts to stimulate a less Europeanized movement never lost its romantic base.

Civil unrest did not destroy Mexico's cultural continuity. Literary societies provided members of opposing artistic and political factions with a common ground, and the most diverse currents coexisted. The repertoire is Spanish, and Maximilian's empire brought with it the mania for the French musical theatre in the fashion of Offenbach. Nevertheless, Mexico boasts several important figures, notably Fernando Calderón (1809–1845) and Ignacio Rodríguez Galván (1816–1842). The latter is the archetypal Romantic; his life was a series of misfortunes, and his plays are allusions to the current political scene and paradigms of romantic aesthetics: energetic dialogue, exaggerated action, a fixation on individual honor, externalized emotion, abrupt reaction rather than rational response, all of them hallmarks of the Spanish romantic drama which was his model. His characters live in a permanent state of irritation and wear their emotions on their sleeve, but his work is interesting for its treatment of pathologies in *El privado del virrey* (1842) and *Muñoz, visitador de México* (1838). The latter is a truly Gothic figure presented as evil incarnate, but he becomes a fascinating case study. Calderón's plays are almost indistinguishable from those of Sir Walter Scott *et al*, combining neoclassical mythology with exaggerated romantic technique and Medievalism of theme. But *Ninguna de las tres* (1839?), written in response to Bretón de los Herreros's *Marcelo o ¿a cuál de las tres?*, pokes fun at the failure to educate women, at affectation and sentimental Romanticism. Although his works were produced very shortly after those of Gorostiza, there is a world of difference between them, except for *Ninguna de las tres*, which in many ways echoes Gorostiza's humor and common sense. It is typical of the fusion of Spanish American movements to find an orthodox romantic writing a *costumbrista* comedy with neoclassical echoes.

Like much theatre of the time, Mexican plays favored plots relating to the nation's history; Guillermo Prieto (1818–1897), whose poetry attempted to create a national literature based on local types, did the same with a theme from a colonial conspiracy in *Alonso de Avila* (1841). Between 1861 and 1864 Juan Mateos (1831–1913) had fifteen commercial successes, primarily *sainetes* and comedies written with the novelist Vicente Riva Palacio (1832–1896), but Mateos's potentially most interesting work has been lost, a problem endemic to nineteenth-century theatre. His *La muerte de Lincoln* (1867) was suppressed as subversive, and he developed the political sketch which presented stresses between social classes and brought contemporary political figures to the stage.

In Colombia the situation is familiar: neoclassical French plays followed by the Spanish Romantics. But in the satirical comedies of customs the Colombian theatre found the vein that would dominate for the remainder of the century and much of the early twentieth. Typical was José María Samper (1828–1888), who adopted a progressive stance in his presentation of the conflict between city and countryside, between change and conservative nostalgia. He satirized conservative regional governments and a repressive social system. The early Peruvian theatre is poorly documented, but Peru produced two major heirs of the colonial satirical tradition: Felipe Pardo y Aliaga (1806–1868) and Manuel Ascensio Segura (1805–1971). Both specialized in the *costumbrista* comedy, but they were diametrically opposed. Pardo y Aliaga was a conservative with a colonialist mentality, a Europeanizing, aristocratic Neoclassicist opposed to the democratic ideal. All his work is didactic satire. Despite its implacably reactionary nature, his theatre is often humorous, as in the first play staged in independent Peru, *Los frutos de la educación* (1829).

Segura, who stands out amid the orthodox Romanticism of his

contemporaries, was the antithesis of Pardo y Aliaga, a liberal whose plays are much more alive and less rooted in upper-class attitudes. His themes, language, and characters come from everyday life. *El sargento Canuto* (1839) is the Roman *miles gloriosus* mocking the plague of militarism; his best-known play is *Ña Catita* (1856), an acid portrait of a procuress in the Spanish medieval tradition. In spite of the neoclassical apparatus – comedy in verse, the three unities, and a moral – Segura's comedies are still alive because of their popular roots and their humor.

In Cuba, activity grew considerably starting about 1830, and 1838 saw the beginning of orthodox medievalizing Romanticism. Much of this masked attacks on Spain's rigid political control. Like most Spanish American romantic drama, it is grandiloquent and mannered, but certain peculiarities place it among the more interesting of its kind. José Jacinto Milanés (1814–1863), of humble birth, self-taught, and somewhat of a recluse, found refuge in escapist works like *Un poeta en la corte* (written in 1840) and *El conde Alarcos* (1838). The former was never produced, probably for political reasons, since it is critical of the government and the corruption of power; a formal request for publication languished in the censor's office for six years. *El conde Alarcos* is an example of the Romanticism in vogue at the time, and makes use of such stock figures as contrasting women, one angelic, one passionate. Milanés also wrote two short didactic pieces. He was primarily an ethical writer, championing liberal causes in conventional melodramatic fashion, but escapism was the only way to treat themes like patriotic conscience or opposing loyalties.

Like many of his time, José Lorenzo Luaces (1826–1867) wrote much, but little was performed or published during his lifetime, although he had a considerable impact on Cuban intellectual circles. *El becerro de oro*, written in 1859 but never produced until 1968, mocks pretension and the venal interests hidden behind the mask of culture by parodying the vogue of opera. The vernacular popular theatre created earlier by Francisco Covarrubias was continued by José Agustín Millán and José Crespo y Borbón, better known as Creto Gangá. Millán's *costumbrista* comedies are close in spirit to political sketches; Crespo y Borbón wrote *sainetes* whose satire was disguised by the barely comprehensible language of the slaves who were his favorite characters.

The others of this generation pale before one of the great figures of the drama in Spanish, Gertrudis Gómez de Avellaneda (1814–1873), whose theatre profiles her passionate life. Although all her plays were initially performed in Spain, she is Cuban by birth and formation and belongs to both literatures. Her plays, her poetry, and her life demonstrate her determination and free spirit; an admirer of George Sand, she created strong female characters committed to the right to decide their own fate.

Throughout her theatre there is a rebelliousness more understandable when we learn that despite her stature as an artist, she was denied entry to the Spanish Royal Academy because of her sex.

Gómez de Avellaneda's Romanticism is more eclectic, solidly constructed and psychologically penetrating. Its violence lies not in unmotivated action but in the passions which torment her characters. She created tragic figures who affirm freedom of spirit and integrity by violating the dogmas and rules of society. *Balthasar* (1858), a version of the biblical theme of Daniel and Nebuchadnezzar, studies a solitary melancholy protagonist who anticipates Camus's Caligula and the *mal du siècle*. *Alfonso Munio* (1844) appeared in 1869 in a revised version under the title *Munio Alfonso*. It deals with pride and responsibility, the freedom to choose one's own companions in life. Rather than the customary resolution of such problems of honor and the slaughter dear to romantic dramatists, Gómez de Avellaneda offered depth of understanding. Of her many plays from 1846 to 1858, the majority very successful, not all were devoted to such themes; she was also outstanding in a lighter vein, like *La hija de las flores o Todos están locos* (1852), a delightful comedy of intrigue reminiscent of Lope de Vega in its form.

The neighboring islands saw little activity. An early romantic play was *Don Pedro de Castilla* by a Dominican residing in Cuba, Francisco de Javier Foxá (1816–1865), and the first Dominican play with an indigenous subject is *Iguaniona* (1867) by Javier Angulo Guridi (1816–1864), although it is closer in spirit to Calderón than to an authentic Indian survival. In Puerto Rico censorship and commercial isolation made for sporadic activity until the middle of the century. Productions were primarily Spanish, with an abundance of opera in the first half of the century and *zarzuela* in the second. The earliest dramatist of importance is Alejandro Tapia y Rivera (1826–1882), whose escapist works of honor and frustrated love, were in reality disguised political attacks. Surprisingly modern is *La parte del león* (1880), a plea for the rights of women within marriage. More typical was *Roberto D'Evreux*, which provoked Tapia's exile and was only performed in a much altered form in 1856, eight years later, because of the prohibition against presenting sovereigns in terms which might humanize them. This seems incomprehensible, since the plot dealt with Elizabeth of England and the Earl of Essex, but it is, in fact, a bitter political commentary. All Tapia's historical dramas suffer from romantic clichés: monologues, long speeches, final curtain revelations. Most interesting of his plays is *La cuarterona* (pub. 1867, perf. 1878), an attack on racial prejudice burdened by complicated plot and excessive intrigue, but more agile, more moderate and more human than the majority of plays of the same school. As in Cuba, beside this cultivated and European-oriented drama existed a little-documented popular theatre. One of the few examples is *La juega de gallos o El negro bozal* by Ramón C. F. Caballero (b. 1820), published in 1852.

Bolivia, far more prosperous than it is today, boasted considerable activity in the second half of the century, but few texts have survived; in Venezuela, imports and comical, often satirical, *zarzuelas* dominated. Alongside them existed a popular tradition of brief plays, usually associated with religious feast days. In Paraguay, as in so many countries, a few figures wrote with, at best, only relative success. Paraguay does offer two curiosities: the persistence of the missionary theatre among the Indians, and the abundance in Asunción of professional companies stranded there by civil instability and a lack of paying audiences.

The Generation of 1864

Born between 1834 and 1864, this is the generation that saw the beginnings of *Modernismo* [Modernism], which ruled the Spanish American literary world during the last two decades of the century, but in the theatre Modernism made no significant contribution. It has been argued that the spirit of Modernism is seen in the drama's growing Americanism, corresponding to the exoticism of other genres. The stage is dominated by a late Romanticism under the influence of the Spanish playwright José Echegaray and the old *costumbrista* tradition. The political and economic situation, aggravated by the uneven distribution of material progress, is seen in tepid Realism and nascent Naturalism.

During the dictatorship of Rosas, the Argentinian theatre became a forum for attacks on his enemies. From his fall in 1852 until the appearance of the rural theatre more than three decades later, Argentinian dramatists were unrelievedly late-romantic. In the 1870s more Argentinian works were staged, and in a few short comic pieces there are touches of local color. In Uruguay there was considerable activity, but little work of distinction; the first Romantics wrote under the influence of the Argentinian enemies of Rosas, many of whom took refuge in Montevideo, while the next group devoted itself to historical dramas and urban *costumbrista* comedies. Francisco Fernández (1841–1922) is author of *Solané* (pub. 1881), never produced although widely known at the time, and soon forgotten in spite of the considerable importance of its theme. A case study in the new psychophysiological theories, it is based on the history of a gaucho, once a medical student, later a rural medicine-man, who was murdered by a mob. In Fernández's version he is a redeemer of the exploited and persecuted gauchos, sacrificed by corrupt justice. Better written than the more famous *Moreira* and more authentic than many later gaucho dramas, *Solané* is still somewhat rudimentary, excessively verbose and romantically idealized.

The gaucho theme led to the development of a native theatre that ruled the stage during a considerable period and is still viable in the work of contemporary dramatists. The extraordinary growth of Buenos Aires through massive immigration led also to a sudden Europeanization. The privileged lived in luxury; the majority of immigrants found themselves isolated and marginalized. Social progress did not extend either to them or to the rural semi-nomadic gauchos, who were harassed by a society which saw in them an obstacle to progress and who had to compete for land with those immigrants who left the cities. The theatre was the pastime of cultured society; the populace hungry for entertainment flocked to the circus. In spite of antecedents like *El amor de la estanciera* or *Solané* there was no theatre reflecting popular restlessness.

The birth of such a theatre is due to a series of fortuitous circumstances. The Carlos brothers, owners of a highly successful circus, decided to put on as a pantomime, a standard part of their functions, a version of *Juan Moreira*, a novel by Eduardo Gutiérrez (1853–1890) based on the life of a rebellious gaucho chieftain and criminal killed by the police. The pantomime version is primitive, composed of brief scenes, militantly pro-gaucho, and unsophisticated in its theatrical resources. The actors were acrobats and clowns. In the novel Gutiérrez had inverted the roles, transforming the criminal into a defender of the poor and a symbol of resistance to oppression. This violent figure focused the resentments of the marginal sectors of society. Two years after the resounding success of the 1884 première, the pantomime was presented with dialogue by Gutiérrez. The chasm between this new theatre and standard stage fare is seen in the fact that the première of *Moreira* took place in the same year that Sarah Bernhardt made her first appearance in Buenos Aires in a play by Sardou.

Impresarios soon realized the potential of these enormously popular schematic melodramas. Soon more talented writers began to treat this raw material in more sophisticated terms, and eventually produced works of lasting merit. This new theatre arrived when the audience was ready for it; it coincided with a social struggle between city and country and with the immigration which, on the one hand, displaced the gaucho and, on the other, created an alienated urban mass who saw in the militancy of *Moreira* an idealization of their own situation. In its individualism, its cult of valor, xenophobia, and hatred for the establishment, *Moreira*, no matter how rudimentary, spoke to an audience which felt equally marginal. One of the odd aspects of *Moreira* is that it made of an immigrant Italian one of the principal causes of the protagonist's sufferings; paradoxically, within a few years, Italian immigrants would find identification within an urban theatre descended in part from the gaucho melodramas which had attacked them. This development, including the growing influence of European Naturalism, belongs more to the next generation of 1894; one of the important forces which characterize the shift between generations is precisely the growing strength of this new drama.

Mexican theatre suffered the customary highs and lows; at times almost moribund, due largely to the mania for the cancan or the opera, at others flourishing. Despite the beginnings of Realism, the stage was still dominated by late-romantic values: complicated settings, sentimentalism, exalted passions, exaggerated actions, and declamatory dialogue, as seen in the fact that the new Theatre of the Authors was inaugurated in 1873 with Fernando Calderón's *El torneo*, an archetypal romantic melodrama. The 1870s saw the appearance of a serious social theatre, in response to political unrest. During this entire period there existed the same regional theatre which we have seen in earlier generations.

In 1875 President Lerdo de Tejada, although frequently attacked in plays, ordered subsidies for Mexican works, and in 1876 the astonishing total of forty-three Mexican plays were premiered. He also established censorship, and Alberto Bianchi was jailed for staging for a working-class audience his *Martirios del pueblo*, an attack on one of the favorite weapons of nineteenth-century tyrants, the military draft. Interesting, because they point toward the fusion of realistic and romantic elements, are Rafael Delgado (1853–1914), better known as a novelist, and Juan A. Mateos (1831–1913). Interest in the Indian past grew, and we find mixtures of social and historical drama or of romantic and realistic or even naturalistic elements within the same author.

The most important Mexican dramatist of this generation is José Peón y Contreras (1843–1907), conservative politician and physician specializing in mental illness, whose work tends toward pseudo-Realism in late-romantic garb. He avoided excess, concentrating on individual psychology. As a result his theatre tends toward the schematic; his characters are well developed but lacking in depth, and his historical dramas are superficial. Nevertheless, he was highly successful; in 1876 he staged ten new plays, almost a quarter of the total production in Mexico City that year. He could hardly maintain such a pace, but did continue to stage new plays until 1906. Much of his work echoes Spanish Golden Age comedies of intrigue, but in *La hija del rey* (1876) he created a clinical study of the romantic cliché of father and son in love with the same woman. The Romantic roots are visible in the resolution: father kills son and the woman goes mad, but this crashing finale does not hide the fact that this was a new modality for Mexico. In reality, Peón y Contreras is a playwright between two periods; his popular success was due to commercial effect, but there are clear signs of a more serious theatre.

This rebirth of the theatre about 1870 is also true of Chile, where the dominant tendency is *Costumbrismo*. Some of Daniel Barros Grez's

(1834–1904) works are still staged. His plays are broadly comic, his characters from the tradition of farce, his favorite theme the satirizing of the middle classes. Barros Grez also incorporated rural elements, including types hitherto ignored in the theatre. Due to official support and an unusual number of foreign companies, there was an unaccustomed degree of activity; the last quarter of the century saw some 200 Chilean plays performed. Little is of lasting interest, due perhaps to the political turbulence which occupied the time and talents of most writers and the dominance of realistic *Costumbrismo*, which tended to reward facility rather than seriousness. Román Vial (1833–1896) wrote far-fetched, melodramatic plots, but he created comic satires based on popular speech. He also dealt with more serious themes like the beginnings of European immigration (*Los extremos se tocan*, 1872) and the humiliating social situation of women (*La mujer hombre*, 1875). Other dramatists continued working within the traditions of Romanticism (Domingo Antonio Izquierdo, 1860–1886) or created Calderonian melodramas of love and honor (Daniel Caldera, 1851–1896), but more interesting today are popularly based works like *Chincol en sartén* (1876) of Antonio Espiñeira (1855–1907), or *Don Lucas Gómez* (1855) of Mateo Martínez Quevedo (1848–1923), whose success was due to the inclusion of regional types in a traditional plot, of city against country.

In Cuba, alongside moribund Romanticism, grew a social theatre based on national problems, but weakened by the political tensions which would culminate at the beginning of the following generation in the War of Independence. José de Armas y Cárdenas (1866–1919), influenced by French Naturalism, attacks the voracious hypocrisy of the upper classes in *Los triunfadores* (1895). The play is typical of the late work of this generation; it is a bitter portrait, but it suffers from the weakness of nineteenth-century social theatre: exaggerated characters and a forced melodramatic plot. The ethnic theme so important in Caribbean literature appears in *El mulato* by Alfredo Torroela (1845–1879). Like many other Cuban works of the last century censored by the authorities, *El mulato* was first staged in Mexico. A semi-realistic anti-slavery tract, it achieves a relatively moderate tone. José Martí (1853–1895), notable as poet, prose stylist, and leader of Cuba's struggle for independence, also cultivated the theatre. *Abdala* (1869), a youthful patriotic work, *Adúltera*, a symbolic morality play, and *Patria y libertad* (written in 1873), arguing for the redemption of the Indian, are all literary in tone, but *Amor con amor se paga*, without moral or political purpose, is a fresh and delightful minor piece.

One of the most important currents is the persistence of popular theatre. We have already seen the creation of a comic tradition based on the linguistic changes wrought in Spanish by the African slaves. Through the dialect of these Cubans of African origin the authors mocked the colonial government and attacked slavery. In 1868 a company appeared known as the Bufos Habaneros, inspired by the Arderíus *bufos* of Spain and through them by the *buffes* of Paris, with traces of cancan and daring operetta. Like the *sainete orillero*, the *bufo* adapted Spanish forms to popular theatre and to regional culture. Beginning in 1884, the *bufo* degenerated into semi-pornographic frivolity, while the River Plate version tended toward more serious forms. But beneath its comic surface based on picturesque popular types, the *bufo* reflected the feelings of the mass of Cubans. *Bufo* works favored independence and surviving texts show the censors' mutilations. The attacks must have been sharp, since in 1869 loyalist volunteers opened fire on the audience which applauded the insurrectionist tone of Juan Franciso Valerio's *Perro huevero aunque le quemen el hocico*. Such episodes led to a drastic reduction in *bufo* activities from 1869 to 1878.

The Cuban version reacts against the cultivated romantic theatre through characters like the Gallego immigrant, the ex-slave, or the peasant. These attitudes culminate in a mythology of the slum, another marked similarity to the Argentinian version. In their golden period, the latter always ended with the tango, the former with the conga; both were socially oriented, and music and dance came at times to outweigh dialogue. But in Cuba the democratic egalitarian tone led to special characteristics, above all the *choteo*, a comic verbal structure satirizing materialism and greed. There is a parodic tone and a rejection of order, a lack of respect for all authority.

The creator of the *bufo* as it appeared in 1868 was Francisco Fernández, with *Los negros catedráticos*, *Política de Guinea*, and others. Given the ephemeral nature and extraordinary number of plays performed, it is almost impossible to point out individual authors. Among the most important are Ignacio Sarachaga (1852–1900), whose *Mefistófeles* (1896) parodies Gounod's *Faust* in terms of Plautus and the *commedia dell'arte*, the brothers Robreño and Benjamín Sánchez Maldonado, whose *Las hijas de Talía* (1896) is pure metatheatre as the three levels of the work coalesce reality and fiction. There are obvious reasons why this tradition should be of such interest to Cuban playwrights of recent years, a phenomenon also true of Argentina. It is regrettable that the majority of *bufo* works remain unpublished, lost or savaged by the censor.

Probably influenced by Cuba, the *bufo*, the musical theatre, and often political satire are all important in Puerto Rico. This is the period of the beginning of the *jíbaro* or peasant theatre in the farces of Ramón Méndez Quiñones (1847–1889). With *Un jíbaro como hay pocos* (1878) a popular audience began to frequent these performances with their comic vision of peasant virtues. This moralizing *costumbrista* Regionalism is typical of the time, but its careful use of peasant language created vivid portraits which would set a pattern for later dramatists. By 1880 there was a flourishing rural theatre; even the most sophisticated dramatists wrote for the vernacular stage since their more serious plays stood little chance of being staged. Salvador Brau (1837–1912) is best known for verse historical dramas within the conventions of Romanticism, but almost all have a sociopolitical projection: *La vuelta al hogar* (1877), the adventures of a famous local corsair; *Héroe y mártir* (1871), class struggle in the *comunero* revolts in Castille; *Los horrores del triunfo* (1887), the thirteenth-century Sicilian rebellion against an invader king.

In Colombia and Venezuela activity was almost exclusively and routinely romantic, alternating with standard *Costumbrismo* and the Spanish short lyric theatre, the *género chico*. Peru offers little more. Clorinda Matto de Turner and Ricardo Palma, famous for their work in other genres, achieved little distinction in the theatre. In most countries almost the only plays capable of being staged today are comic works in the popular vein. Sporadic government aid did little to alter the steady diet of routine commercialism, where that existed. Bolivia saw one of the most productive periods of its theatre history, but the majority of plays are impossible to locate.

The Generation of 1894

This is a period of transition. Modernism contributed only a few seldom-produced works usually of greater interest for their relationships to the author's other work. *Costumbrismo* is important until well into the twentieth century and still current commercial fare. Romanticism's final decades, corresponding to the flourishing of *Costumbrismo* and the beginning of Realism and Naturalism, degenerate into routine sentimentality. This generation also saw the beginning of a more modern theatre, but it made no significant impact until about 1910. In this sense the generation of 1894 is cut off; halfway through it visibly becomes something quite different, neither romantic nor nineteenth-century. The real end of the nineteenth century is the symbolic year of transition, 1910.

An intriguing aspect of this period is the importance in Buenos Aires of the *sainete orillero*, derived from the rural theatre, the Spanish *género chico*, and traditional popular theatre. The *género chico*, born about 1867, is a shorter version of the *zarzuela*. Because of its brevity and popularity, it was soon presented several times each day. It is a mixture of social criticism, *zarzuela*, regional Realism, and caricature where the urban masses saw themselves reflected; their problems appeared with humor and a festive spirit. This new genre was an immediate success in America, especially in the River Plate, where there was a preexisting tradition of similar popular works dating from the eighteenth century. There were also, from the time of Rosas at the latest, rudimentary *sainetes* performed in the circus ring, in addition to the pantomime tradition that culminated in *Moreira*. All these had in common a series of formal and thematic characteristics which most closely resemble those of the *género chico*. In contrast, the serious theatre of the period offered little to compete with such popular theatre for the mass audience. By 1890, for example, almost no Argentinian plays were being performed. At the same time, the difficult political and economic situation provoked a number of satirical sketches. Because of the local tradition rooted in rural problems and the lack of a serious theatre adapted to the Argentinian situation, the panorama was ripe for the appearance of a popular-based theatre.

About 1890 plays began to appear whose urban characters are as much variants of the rural figures of the traditional *sainete* as they are copies of the Madrid types. From this it was but a step to the true *sainete orillero*, whose founder is Nemesio Trejo (1862–1916), author of more than fifty works, usually satirical and often filled with allusions which are now impenetrable. He produced the definitive fusion that would become the classic form. Justo López de Gómara, a Spaniard settled in Buenos Aires since 1880, had already worked toward adapting local material in *Gauchos y gringos* (1884), and *De paseo por Buenos Aires* (1890), influenced by the classic of the *género chico*, *La gran vía* (1886), helped establish the form. Important as director, promoter, and author was Ezequiel Soria (1873–1936); in his *Justicia criolla* (1897) the definitive scene of the action became the *conventillo*, the old colonial mansions that had become urban slums. In the same way his later *sainetes* fixed the role of the tango. The *sainete* soon contended with the serious theatre for control of the stage and had a decisive influence on drama. Soon the *sainete* became more complex, due in large part to the innovations of dramatists like Florencio Sánchez, while at the same time one can perceive a movement toward the deformation which would become the twentieth century *grotesco criollo*. About 1910 the rot set in; originality lost out to box office success. Although they lie outside the bounds of our study, the culmination of these various strands are the works by Alberto Vacarezza (1896–1959), the most successful author of *sainetes*, Armando Discépolo (1887–1971), who after 1910 evolved toward the Grotesque, and Francisco Defilippis Novoa (1891–1930), who developed a dramatic *sainete* of religious dimensions.

The *sainete orillero* is more theatrical than literary; the text is of little importance and there is a strong element of social satire whose meaning is often lost today. The archetypal *sainete* is built on a series of shocks rather than a systematic dramatic conflict. The violent action takes place in the *conventillo*, an urban slum dwelling; the resolution is almost always more dramatic than comic. The characters tend toward types and speak urban slang; at times they achieve a certain individual dimension, and even the comic characters have a dignity which underlines the genre's plebeian origins. More dramatic and more melodramatic than the Spanish version, of a greater psychological complexity that often verges on the tragic, it is a portrait of the urban slum, a product in large measure of the new industrial system. It is an often uncomplicated theatre which offers a Romantic and truculent vision, in part the heritage of Romanticism and in part due to the material itself. It is obviously a formulaic theatre. Seen with the perspective of time, the *sainete orillero* is very much of its moment, but some, even without the humor of the staging for which it was created, are still of interest. It gave a special flavor to the *rioplatense* theatre, and at the time brought with it a much-needed life and vigor. Many dramatists, actors, and musicians developed their skills in the *sainete* before moving on to other types of theatre. Just as the great comic "Cantinflas", Mario Moreno, came from the street theatre of Mexico City, the inimitable Carlos Gardel arose from the music hall.

The growing rural–gaucho theatre slowly edged out the foreign repertoire. The first step was *Calandria* (1896) of Martiniano Leguizamón (1858–1935), who followed the episodic structure of his model *Moreira* but eliminated much of the superficial effect. Calandria is the alienated and persecuted gaucho, but rather than dying at the hands of the pursuing police he is pardoned and becomes a useful member of society. The second step was *La piedra de escándalo* (1902) of Martín Coronado (1850–1919), whose earlier works are romantic excesses in an outmoded style. With *La piedra de escándalo* he began a series of sentimental socialist works, clearly influenced by the *Moreira* tradition. He applied a series of mechanical effects learned from European Romanticism to rural subject matter. In the same year Nicolás Granada (1840–1915) produced *Al campo*, the old conflict between urban social-climbing and rural freedom, and a year later *La gaviota* (1903), on a related theme. All these authors demonstrate the continuing domestication both of the gaucho and of the gaucho theatre.

The cultural unity of the River Plate soon led to the incorporation of Uruguayan dramatists. The authors of the first rural wave were born toward the end of the previous generation, and their works lie between two extremes, not yet having abandoned Romanticism but pointing toward a different theatre. Their rural plays are largely expressions of social protest related to the new Naturalism. It is the authors born after 1870 who finally leave behind the limited repertoire of xenophobia, the cult of bravery, and hatred for the establishment. The giant of all is the Uruguayan Florencio Sánchez (1875–1910). Disillusioned by the revolution of 1897, he abandoned traditional politics for anarchism. Often presented as a subversive, he began to write for political reasons. Sánchez is said to have created plays rapidly and carelessly, but his work is anything but improvised; he was a serious artist aware of artistic necessity. His fame was guaranteed by *M'hijo el dotor* (1903), which ran for thirty-eight performances, the most ever recorded by a serious play in Buenos Aires at the time. He died at thirty-five of tuberculosis.

Sánchez's theatre was the most restless and the most unconventional of the period; it treats country and city, the middle classes and the slums. His themes are often common to other dramatists, but he cleansed them of the echoes of their rudimentary origins. The progress is remarkable if we recall that he wrote only a year or two after such far less sophisticated works as *La piedra de escándalo* and *Al campo*. His masterpiece, from the rural trilogy which also includes *M'hijo el dotor* and *La gringa* (1904), is *Barranca abajo* (1905), the tragedy of an ageing gaucho unable to adapt to a changing society. His work is notably difficult to classify, due to its fundamental unity. It is a didactic, socially committed theatre, exposing the sufferings of the marginal members of society and attacking the abuses of power and privilege. Committed theatre is dangerous without human commitment, but Sánchez possessed the latter as well. His works are compassionate and understanding. Sánchez was a moralist, which occasionally led him into psychological simplification, but his characters are real human beings.

Around 1910, several other members of this same generation began to produce important works. Ernesto Herrera (Uruguay, 1889–1917) created rhetorical naturalistic analyses of social problems. *El león ciego* (1911) is a powerful portrait of an ageing political chieftain unable to comprehend the failure of a system based on civil wars and partisan obscurantism. Like his Naturalism, Herrera's insistence on the tension between the need to recognize the virtues of the past and the need to abandon barbarism points to the end of a period. Like Herrera, Julio Sánchez Gardel's (1879–1937) best plays appear after 1910; they portray rural customs and folklore. The linguistic and thematic excesses are the result on the one hand of the declamatory heritage of the nineteenth century and on the other, of the new Italian symbolist theatre which applied such techniques to a rural setting. The other principal dramatist of this generation is Gregorio de Laferrère (1867–1913), political leader and member of the elite, who found commercial success with satirical comedies about the superstitions and foibles of the urban middle class. He was one of the best craftsmen of the period and his plays show careful control of technical resources as well as a moralizing humor. Some critics have seen the prejudices of the privileged classes in Laferrère's theatre, but it can equally well be seen as being rooted in the best *costumbrista* tradition.

Favoring moral observation and influenced by the European vanguard was Roberto J. Payró (1867–1928), a cultured militant Socialist and author of eight plays connecting the still immature rural theatre with the professional. Enrique García Velloso (1880–1938) is best known for *sainetes* and rural melodramas with religious implications, like *Caín* and *Jesús Nazareno* (1902). Víctor Pérez Petit (Uruguay, 1871–1947) published eight volumes of plays; although the majority belong to a later period, he was active during the late nineteenth and early twentieth centuries in the rural and *sainete* veins. Both in his work and chronologically Pérez Petit marks a moment when the theatre was evolving from the romantic survival toward a new and radically different form.

Mexico at the end of the century was limited almost entirely to foreign companies and to the musical theatre; the Revolution of 1910 and the First World War caused a serious relapse. Although the *género chico* never had the same impact in Mexico as in Buenos Aires, by 1890 there were *zarzuelas* by Mexican authors and with Mexican themes or settings. Best known of these is José P. Elizondo (1880–1943), author with Rafael Medina and Luis Jordá of the *zarzuela* entitled *Chin-Chun-Chan* (1904), the first Mexican play to achieve 1,000 performances. During the last years of the century the political review grew in importance, and there was a progressive identification of the *zarzuela* and *sainete* with popular and folkloric forms, especially under the pressure of the difficult political situation. Rubén M. Campos wrote in 1903 *La sargenta* of the soldiers' women; *La hacienda* (1907) by Federico Carlos Kegel treated the problem of the exploited rural workers. This kind of political review culminated in works like *El tenorio maderista* (1912) by Luis Andrade and Leandro Blanco, or a whole series of successes by Elizondo, among them *El país de la metralla* (1913) and *Tenorio Sam*. This type of review, in more rudimentary form, remained important in the metropolitan zone during much of the twentieth century; the comic peasant became the *payo*, the slum rascal perfected by Cantinflas.

The rhetorical Romanticism of Echegaray set the model for the so-called serious theatre, with traces of Ibsen and Catalan Naturalism. The two most important figures are Federico Gamboa (1864–1939) and Marcelino Dávalos (1871–1923). The former used the same Naturalism in his plays that he employed in his novels of the same period. The emphatic dialogue and daring subject matter reveal their roots in late Romanticism. *La venganza de la gleba* (1905) treats the exploitation of the peasant and an incestuous love affair between half-brother and half-sister; melodramatic and sensational, the play is perhaps the first serious denunciation in the Mexican theatre of the sufferings of the rural poor. Dávalos developed from Romanticism to Realism; *Así pasan* uses three key moments in the life of an actress to create a work of solid psychological insight. It is interesting to speculate what its author might have accomplished had he not been imprisoned in 1916 and later exiled for political reasons.

As political calm returned to the nation there were attempts to revive the theatre, but they belong to the history of the twentieth century. A few playwrights had already established themselves within an older tradition but adapted to the new currents. José Joaquín Gamboa (1878–1931) wrote a *zarzuela* and youthful work influenced by Naturalism; after living in Europe from 1908 to 1923 he was a prime figure in the renewal. A similar case is Carlos Díaz Dufoo (1861–1941), a consummate modernist who, in 1885, staged two inconsequential comic works, to return to the theatre as a member of the *Vanguardia* [Vanguard] over forty years later. Meanwhile, about 1907, a regional theatre in Mayan took hold in Yucatán, perhaps stimulated by the memory of nineteenth-century theatre in Merida, and certainly as a result of the popular tradition. There had been theatre in Mayan, with pre-Hispanic roots, about 1850, and José García Montero wrote in Mayan in the second half of the century. The plays were usually short and comic, with music and dance, and a hybrid language. Although the flourishing of this movement came later, its appearance meant the revindication of the Indian and of the *mestizo* as protagonist and as author. This theatre even influenced known playwrights, such as Antonio Médiz Bolio (1884–1957), who wrote youthful works in the vein of Echegaray, but in later years plays displayed the unusual double influence of Benavente and the indigenous Mayan theatre.

Cuba offers the usual panorama of Spanish touring companies with a commercial romantic repertoire. The popular theatre was dominated by the *bufo* and the frivolous musical theatre, and most authors wrote at least in part for these. Most productive was Federico Villoch, author of hundreds of stereotyped works, from *sainetes* to expensive reviews. The most important playwright is José Antonio Ramos (1885–1946), exiled for his political ideas. Ramos's major works, characterized by their adaptation of new European currents, began to appear about 1911. With him, the new Cuban theatre begins.

In Chile the last quarter of the century saw the standard mix of outdated Romanticism, unsophisticated theatre on rural themes, sentimental high comedy based on French models, and the authentic *Costumbrismo* of Barros Grez. The year 1900 saw the fever of the *zarzuela*, but in 1910 began an important surge of realistic examination of the national reality leading to the social theatre of importance amongst workers after 1912. At the same time, the commercial theatre began to study the middle classes, which led to the dominance of the sentimental comedy influenced by the many visits by foreign companies after 1910, the same key date which throughout Spanish America indicates a fundamental change of direction in the theatre. Playwrights typical of the moment are Manuel Magallanes Moure (1878–1942), for his efforts to create a musical theatre, and Victor Domínguez Silva (1882–1960), author of a number of works on radical political themes.

In Peru, Romanticism and *Costumbrismo*, the staples of late nine-teenth-century theatre, decayed rapidly, and there began a long sterile period relieved only by imitations of the Echegaray and Marquina or by a superficial frivolous theatre. Leónidas Yeroví (1881–1917) modified the Argentinian *sainete orillero* to the Peruvian situation. *La de cuatro mil* (1903) shows his compassion and his disdain for hypocrisy. His later works, after 1914, prove that Yeroví's early death deprived us of a dramatist of real promise. Venezuela presents the same general situation of *Costumbrismo*; Simón Barceló (1873–1938) was successful with the *sainete*, but the general panorama offers little.

In Puerto Rico, works by national authors except for those of the previous generation are virtually nonexistent. In Central America, the limited potential audience, lack of technical facilities, and public instabi-lity reduce the movement to the almost unknown efforts of a few people. Typical is El Salvador, where Francisco Gavidia (1863–1955) combined echoes of Victor Hugo, Modernism, and some *costumbrista* touches; Salvadoran theatre of the period consists almost entirely of sporadic performances of Gavidia's works. Nicaragua possessed a vigorous popu-lar theatre, but the professional theatre was reduced to occasional visits by foreign companies, and the Costa Rican drama consisted of *Costum-brismo*, which would culminate in a satirical popular-based theatre several decades later. Ecuador offers the same panorama of irregular publication rather than production. The vigorous although barely known Bolivian movement decayed rapidly; soon there were only Ricardo Jaimes Freyre, Franz Tamayo, and M. P. Roca, who wrote of national and pre-Hispanic history, but were fascinated more by the exotic than by any real American interest. And with this the nineteenth century and the romantic period come to an end. If they expire somewhat ingloriously, in almost every country the stage was being set for the new theatre which would, within a relatively short time, come to fruition.

16

The essay in Spanish South America: 1800 to *Modernismo*
Nicolas Shumway

Of all the literary forms, the essay is the least defined and can include texts as diverse as letters, biographies, speeches, newspaper articles, political decrees, and philosophical treatises. While this chapter does not pretend to define the essay as a literary form, the texts discussed do reflect the many forms essays assume. More vexing than the question of genre is the question of organization. As the principal medium of published thought, the essay is intimately linked to developments in intellectual history generally. Consequently, it is very tempting to categorize Latin American thinkers using terms like Liberalism, Utilitarianism, and Positivism that have emerged in European thought. Applying European labels to Spanish American thought, however, assumes a near-perfect transmission of ideas from Europe to Spanish America since, without such transmission, European categories merely substitute preexisting concepts for real understanding. As it turns out, tracing the penetration of European thought into Spanish America is a complex and largely unresolvable problem. We have only sketchy ideas of what texts nineteenth-century South American essayists read, and we know even less about how well or completely they read. Moreover, even when influence seems undeniable, it is seldom definitive. Indeed, what distinguished Spanish America's most creative nineteenth-century thinkers, Sarmiento for example, is their ability to modify and even deform European thought as they mix it with insights applicable to their special circumstances. In view of the above, I have organized this article around old-fashioned notions of time, place, and generation.

While it is dangerous to connect Spanish American essayists to European movements, other concerns such as the war against Spain, civil wars between local elites, and attempts to form new nations do link Spanish American thinkers to each other. Most nineteenth-century essays emerge against this background of war, domestic tensions, and uncertain identities. Only a very few writers enjoyed the luxury of abstract speculation or purely imaginative literature. Although these are duly noted, they constitute a small minority.

The Andean countries
Simón Bolívar (1783–1830)

Spanish America's best known military leader is one of its most interesting essayists. Born in Caracas to a wealthy family, Simón Bolívar lived richly off the inheritance left by his father, who died when young Bolívar was only six years old. Between the ages of sixteen and nineteen, he studied in Spain, viewing at first hand the decadence of the government of Charles IV. In 1804, he travelled to Paris, where he witnessed Napoleon's coronation, an act that both attracted and repelled him. Also in Paris he renewed contact with a former tutor, Simón Rodríguez, who introduced him to the work of European Rationalists like Locke, Voltaire, Montesquieu, and Rousseau. He also became aware of criticisms of the French Revolution, as developed by men like Edmund Burke, which contributed to Bolívar's lifelong distrust of universal suffrage. After Napoleon's invasion of Spain, Bolívar joined conspirators in Venezuela who on April 19, 1810 formed a junta which expelled the Spanish governor. Sent by the Junta, Bolívar travelled to London seeking British support for the Revolution. Although the British government paid little attention to the young Venezuelan, he found England's political institutions apt models for much of his theory of government. Back in Venezuela, Bolívar became enmeshed in the political and military struggles that would characterize the rest of his life. After local rule of less than two years, in 1812 Spain regained control of Venezuela. Bolívar sought refuge in Cartagena, New Granada, now Colombia, where in that same year he published his first great political statement: *El Manifiesto de Cartagena*.

Despite its title, the *Manifiesto* is less a declaration of intent than an explanation of why Venezuela's first independence movement had failed. Bolívar's major point is that the rebels lost to the Spanish because of an excessive concern for abstract moral principles, "the fatal adoption of a tolerant system" toward the enemy. The codes of conduct followed by the failed revolutionaries, Bolívar tells us, were not based on any "practical knowledge of government" but on ideas formed by "well-intentioned visionaries" who tried to reach "political perfection, based on the premise that the human race was perfectible. As a result we had philosophers for leaders; philanthrophy for legislation; dialectics for tactics, and sophists for soldiers" (Bolívar, *Escritos políticos*, 48) Particularly damaging in Bolívar's view were "the exaggerated maxims of the rights of man" (p. 51), a phrase by which he tellingly distances himself from the idealism of the French Revolution. Bolívar's contempt for notions of human perfectibility also places him in odd ways alongside the most articulate and reactionary critic of the Revolution: Joseph de Maistre. While Bolívar's anti-clericalism would never permit him to speak of original sin, his concept of a flawed humanity ever needful of a strong guiding hand unites him to some degree with de Maistre's authoritarian Catholicism.

The visible result of "the fatal adoption" of tolerance and the "exaggerated" concern for the rights of man was what Bolívar calls "federalism", by which he means representative government if not of equal citizens, at least of equal regions. Federalism, he tells us, "is the most opposed to the interests of our fledgling states", partly because it engenders a cumbersome bureaucracy, often paid with unbacked paper currency, of "office chiefs, secretaries, judge magistrates, [and] provincial and federal legislators" (pp. 50–1). Obviously, government under one man would cost less. Bolívar concedes that Federalism might work where all citizens "are prosperous and serene." If, however, the people are "calamitous and turbulent, [the government] should respond with terror" ["mostrarse terrible"], and arm itself with a firmness appropriate to the danger, without worrying about laws or constitutions until peace and happiness are reestablished." Not surprisingly, Bolívar also condemns popular elections for giving voice to "country-dwelling rubes and city-dwelling schemers" (p. 52). What emerges from all this, of course, is Bolívar's fatal flaw: his fascination with personal authority and particularly his own. Federalism meant sharing power and, as Bolívar would show time and time again, however much he talked of liberty and freedom, he wanted to govern. Indeed, his fondness for one-man rule (his own) eventually created such enmity against him, even when he was old and sick, none of the countries he liberated from Spain wanted him as a citizen. Bolívar ends the *Manifiesto* with a ringing call to all Colombians to make war on the Spanish in Venezuela: "be not insensitive to the lament of your brothers. Go quickly to avenge the dead, give life to the dying, freedom to the oppressed and liberty to all" (p. 57). In view of Bolívar's reservations about self-rule, it is not clear what he means by all this. He is obviously calling for freedom from Spain. What comes after such freedom is won, however, is not obvious at all.

Following the *Manifiesto*'s rousing call to arms. Colombians followed him to Venezuela, where he again routed the Spanish. This time, however, the Spanish returned with a cavalry of *llaneros*, semi-barbarous plainsmen, under the leadership of José Tomás Boves, who forced Bolívar to flee for his life. Spain's alliance with this rural militia only reinforced Bolívar's suspicion of the popular classes. After another failed attempt to oust the Spanish, Bolívar escaped to Jamaica, and there, unfettered by military obligations, he wrote his most thoughtful essay, commonly called *La carta de Jamaica*. Dated September 6, 1815, the *Carta* responds to an inquiry from an unnamed gentleman about the Revolution and its future. Although the letter from the *caballero* has been lost, Bolívar quotes enough of it to give some idea of its content.

What makes the *Carta de Jamaica* unusual among Bolívar's writings is its contemplative tone. Not needing to respond to immediate political situations or military needs, Bolívar speculates about the past and the future. And here, Bolívar shows himself a remarkably informed reader of Spanish American history as well as a political observer of no mean prophetic gifts. Acutely aware that the novice nations to emerge from the creole rebellion would have no ready-made mythology of national identity, Bolívar tries to create a history justifying rebellion against Spain. To this end, he suggests that the real America, the foundational America, was that of the Indians. He cites admiringly the "philanthropic bishop of Chiapas" Bartolomé de las Casas, who in the mid-1500s wrote damning accounts of Spain's mistreatment of native Americans (*Escritos políticos*, 63) and also alludes to other chroniclers of the Conquest from throughout the continent (p. 68), thus revealing a familiarity with early colonial history which sets him quite apart from most of his contemporaries. What Bolívar wants, of course, is to forge a link between his struggle and the Indian resistance of nearly three centuries earlier. In this fashion, he can refer to "America" as a preexisting entity whose history the Spanish interrupted. In Bolívar's scheme the Spanish are "conquerors, invaders and usurpers" (p. 73), and the creole rebellion becomes not just a new stage in history but a restoration of a lost independence. Unfortunately, Bolívar, like virtually all other nineteenth-century Spanish American liberals, never addressed in any practical way the problems of real Indians. Native Americans were a useful symbol, but little else.

Spain, on the other hand, is blamed for all of Spanish America's problems. He argues that Spanish mercantilism consigned the American colonies to producing only for the metropolis and even forbade "the construction of factories that even Spain did not possess" (p. 71). He holds that Spain's refusal to appoint creole leaders left Americans in a state of "permanent infancy," unprepared for self-rule. "Americans," he writes, "rose to power suddenly, without previous knowledge" (p. 72). "We are dominated by the vices brought on by ... Spain, which has distinguished herself only in savagery, ambition, vengefulness and greed" (p. 75). Aside from the exaggerations, one cannot but note the patricidal effect of all this. Bolívar's blanket condemnation of Spain, Spanish America's immediate parent, and his attempts to glorify an idealized Indian past, which figured not at all in the basically land-owning, urban society Bolívar wanted to liberate, left him doubly orphaned.

More interesting than Bolívar's questionable (albeit strategically useful) reconstruction of the past are his observations on the future.

Following a detailed account of revolutionary activity throughout Spanish America, Bolívar expresses his desire to see a single nation emerge in Spanish America, but he quickly concedes that such will not occur. Rather he predicts that six large countries might emerge: Mexico, Central America, Colombia (consisting of Venezuela, Ecuador, and present-day Colombia), Peru, Chile, and the River Plate. Of these, he rightly predicted that Mexico, because of its greater spiritual cohesion, would maintain its territorial integrity (pp. 82–3). (He did not foresee the Unites States landgrab of 1848, but who could have in 1815?) He correctly saw that Peru would fall in the hands a most reactionary elite (pp. 80–1), that a Buenos Aires-based oligarchy, with the help of a powerful military, would dominate the River Plate, and that Chile would produce the first stable republic, which indeed occurred with the initial "Portalian" government of 1830. He was wrong about his own area, Nueva Granada, now Venezuela, Colombia, and Ecuador. Nor did he foresee the fragmentation of civil war that would produce countries like Bolivia, Paraguay, Uruguay, and the seven countries of Central America. Bolívar did not foresee this fragmentation, but he feared it enough to make two controversial recommendations for South American governments: a life-long but nonhereditary presidency and a legislature consisting partly of a nonelected senate whose seats would be hereditary.

These ideas emerge full bloom in later writings, the most significant being his *Discurso de Angostura* of 1819 and again in his *Discurso ante el Congreso Constituyente de Bolivia* of 1825. In both cases Bolívar recommends emulating the British system. Instead of a monarch, he wants a life-long president. Instead of a House of Lords he wants a senate of "principal citizens" who would be the first appointed by congress and thereafter bequeath their seats to deserving heirs. Only the lower house would be regularly and freely elected (*Escritos políticos*, 93–140). In 1826, Bolívar also drafted the constitution of his namesake, Bolivia, which encodes in law ideas he had previously espoused only in theory: a powerful and life-long executive, a limited legislature and judiciary, and a severely restricted suffrage. Unfortunately, many of Bolívar's contemporaries feared, perhaps with reason, that the Liberator merely wanted to make himself a dictator with constitutional justification. As a result, although in 1826 he was president of lands stretching from Bolivia to Venezuela, when he died in 1830, he was a man without a country, and civil war was already breaking his great country apart. Viewing the civil strife around him from his deathbed, a disheartened Bolívar reportedly lamented, "We have ploughed the sea."

One last of Bolívar's ideas deserves comment: his Pan-Americanism. Although, as we saw in the *Carta de Jamaica*, Bolívar pragmatically recognized that a single Spanish American country was not practical, he never gave up on notions of regional cooperation. In 1822, long before all Spanish troops were expelled, Bolívar contacted regional leaders in the hope of forging economic and military alliances. By 1824, such treaties had been ratified by Mexico, Central America, Colombia, Peru, and the United Provinces of the River Plate. Also in 1824, he issued an invitation to the "plenipotentiaries" of each of those countries to send representatives to a continental congress in Panama. Such a congress, he writes, "will find the plan for our first alliances which in turn will outline the path of our relations with the universe" (*Carta a los Gobiernos de las Repúblicas de Colombia, México, Río de la Plata, Chile y Guatemala, Escritos Políticos,* 146). Although representatives from only four countries (Mexico, Central America, Colombia, and Peru) actually arrived at the meeting held in Panama in 1826, its existence and Bolívar's hand in organizing it show that the Organization of American States as well as the United Nations must recognize Bolívar as one of their progenitors.

Juan Montalvo (1832–1889)

Perhaps more than any other essayist in nineteenth-century Spanish America, Ecuador's Juan Montalvo, a man of many passions, also knew the passion of literature and language. While his writings contain frequent political commentary, they also include graceful essays on literature, musings on the nature of beauty and art, and an artful imitation of Cervantes's *Don Quixote*. Of largely Indian descent, he was born in 1832 in Ambato, a small town near Quito. He was conscious of his non-European appearance and once noted that "my face is not the kind one wants to show in New York" (cited by Benjamín Carrión in *El pensamiento vivo de Montalvo*, 41). His prose, on the other hand, attracted wide attention, so much so that in 1883 several of Spain's best writers – including Juan Valera, Emilia Pardo Bazán, and Ramón de Campoamor – proposed him for membership in the Spanish Royal Academy of the Language (which did not admit him).

After completing a degree in philosophy at the Seminario de San Luis in Quito, Montalvo served in Ecuador's diplomatic corps for four years, first in Italy and later in Paris. In 1866, back in Ecuador, he founded *El Cosmopolitano*, the first of several magazines he would edit. His writing soon found disfavor with the dictator Gabriel García Moreno, who exiled Montalvo to Ipiales, a desolate, small town on the Colombian border. While in exile he would write his most famous essays: *Siete tratados* (1882–1883), *Capítulos que se le olvidaron a Cervantes*, and *Geometría moral*. Of these only *Siete tratados* was published during Montalvo's lifetime. In 1875 García Moreno was assassinated, to which Montalvo claimed, improbably, "My pen killed him." But no sooner had García Moreno died than another dictator, Ignacio de Veintimilla, took his place.

Montalvo responded with yet another literary magazine, *El Regenerador*, and in the meantime, in Panama, published *Las catilinarias*, a violent political satire modeled on Cicero. Exiled again, Montalvo eventually found his way to Paris, where he died. But before dying he dressed in black and spent his little remaining money on flowers, believing that no one should die without appropriate props.

Montalvo's prose anticipates the kind of expression that today might be called neo-baroque. His style is difficult, his ideas frequently unclear, and he often seems more interested in turning a phrase than making a point. Indeed, in his book on Montalvo's prose, Anderson Imbert insists that style alone justifies Montalvo today. This seems unfair. Admittedly, Montalvo loved linguistic experimentation, but his is not a prose without ideas. His posthumous *Geometría moral*, for example, is a vindication of America over Europe in which the American man is not only more resourceful, but more energetic by virtue of his youth and more varied cultural heritage. What strikes us, however, is not the message but Montalvo's medium. The figure he chooses to demonstrate cultural differences and America's superiority is Don Juan as he might have appeared in different cultural and historical contexts, including ancient Rome and the Spain of Amadís de Gaula. As a result, although Montalvo concludes that America is somehow superior to all that preceded it, he also uses the many personae of Don Juan to comment on human love, feminine beauty, and whatever else happened to cross his mind. Moreover, he ties the several manifestations of Don Juan to different geometric figures in which a parabola represents Goethe and an ellipse delineates Chateaubriand and Lamartine. The American Don Juan surpasses all these figures while also blending them into one. What all this means for sure is anybody's guess. It is, however, highly suggestive prose that clearly separates Montalvo from his more literal-minded contemporaries.

Similar in its uncertain purpose is Montalvo's posthumous *Capítulos que se le olvidaron a Cervantes (Ensayo de imitación de un libro inimitable)*. The book begins as a satire in which Montalvo portrays his own enemies as enemies of Don Quijote. But this initial emphasis soon gives way to short commentaries Montalvo places in Don Quijote's mouth which speculate on everything from Roman virtue to the importance of madness in poetic inspiration to admiration for different fruits and vegetables. Again, what saves the book is Montalvo's voluptuous prose in which linguistic dexterity overshadows any specific message. It has been suggested that Montalvo may have inspired Unamuno and Ortega y Gasset in their famous parodic studies of the *Quixote*.

Montalvo's best-known work is the only one published during his lifetime, the *Siete tratados*. His choice of "tratado" (treatise) for the title suggests a solemnity not at all characteristic of his work. Rather, the themes in the *tratados* recall the short essays of Bacon and Montaigne, in both their subject and conception. Montalvo's *tratados*, however, are not short. Rather, they ramble far and wide, seemingly driven more by language than by concepts. The titles give only a sampling of their themes: *De la nobleza, De la belleza en el género humano, Réplica a un sofista seudocatólico, Del genio, Los héroes de la emancipación americana de la raza hispanoamericana, Los banquetes de los filósofos-preliminares,* and *El buscapié.* While each essay starts off in a particular direction, Montalvo cannot resist adding anecdotes, asides, and digressions of various sorts that often show little relation to any central argument. Perhaps the most honest title in the *tratados* is the enigmatic *El buscapié.* Difficult to translate, *buscapié* can suggest a hint, a rumor, or even a conversational feeler to determine someone's real attitude on a particular subject. Such a term describes Montalvo's prose remarkably well. He hints, suggests, and palpates, all the while bidding his readers to join him in the same process. But this process often becomes his most visible goal. Someone wanting clear, unadorned, well-supported ideas should look elsewhere.

Montalvo's fame is as variegated as his prose. Some accuse him of self-serving obtuseness while others praise him as one of the great virtuosos of Spanish prose. People who have admired him included Juan Valera, Rubén Darío, Miguel de Unamuno, and José Enrique Rodó. His essays stand in some sense as mountains to be conquered, heights to be mastered. While his political ideas often seem bound to past times and events, his prose anticipates the most daring experiments of writers like José Lezama Lima and Severo Sarduy. Not without reason Montalvo continues to delight and exasperate.

Other essayists of note

Not all Andean writers reflected the basically liberal orientation of Bolívar and Montalvo. For example, debates in Colombia throughout the last century reveal an interesting dichotomy between liberal and traditional values, much analyzed in the political life of that country but less in its intellectual life. Most noteworthy for their difference are Colombia's intellectual traditionalists. In 1873 Ricardo de la Palma (1815–1873) published *Cartas de filosofía moral,* an early attempt to refute Bentham's Utilitarianism. Later, José Eusebio Caro (1817–1853) reasserted that point of view in attacks on Colombia's Liberal party. Without doubt, however, the most significant Colombian philosopher of the nineteenth century is José Eusebio's son, Miguel Antonio Caro (1843–1909), whose attacks on Positivism still resonate in Colombian debate. The younger Caro found his views reinforced by the encyclicals of Pope Leo XIII, *Aeterni Patris* and *Rerum Novarum,* which reaffirmed Catholic authority while asserting a new role for the church in social justice.

Chile

Andrés Bello (1781–1865)

Chile's most admired essayist was actually born in Venezuela, lived for many years in London, and did not become a Chilean citizen until after his fiftieth year. Nonetheless, because his work in Chile dwarfs his earlier accomplishments, and his intellectual life is so tied to Chilean history, it only makes sense to consider him here. It must also be pointed out, however, that the most significant scholarly work on Bello has been carried out by Venezuelans, who still claim Bello as a native son.

Andrés Bello was arguably the most formidable intellectual of all Spanish America in the last century. His knowledge of history, science, classical and modern languages, literature, jurisprudence, philosophy, philology, and almost any other branch of knowledge would place him among the best in any society of his time. Yet, despite his enormous output, Bello is little read today. In some sense, he performed his most lasting service as a stimulus for others and a supreme example of the scholarly life.

Born in Caracas in 1781 to a family of modest but comfortable means, Bello distinguished himself early on as an exceptional student. Studying almost exclusively with priests, he received as good an education as Venezuela could offer, with a heavy dose of Latin and classic rhetoric. Good-looking, sincere, and well-mannered, Bello made friends quickly and moved easily among Venezuela's elite. On receiving his university degree in philosophy and letters, he worked as a minor functionary in the colonial government. To deal with the English-speaking islands off Venezuela's coast, Bello taught himself English, following the unusual method of translating into Spanish John Locke's *Essay Concerning Human Understanding*. After the rebellion of 1810, he accompanied Simón Bolívar to England in an unsuccessful attempt to gain British support for the revolutionary cause. The mission failed, Bolívar returned to Caracas, and Bello, who had little stomach for armed rebellion, remained in London for the next nineteen years.

Bello could not have used his time in England better. With the help of close friend José María Blanco White, descendant of prominent families in both Spain and England, Bello met several of England's best intellectuals. He worked with James Mill as a translator, and tutored the children of William Richard Hamilton, Undersecretary of International Relations and a collector of Greek and Egyptian art for the British Museum, to which Bello was a frequent visitor. Bello later became associated with Jeremy Bentham whose Utilitarianism made a lasting imprint on Bello's own legal thought. Around Bello there formed an important community of Spanish and Spanish American exiles which included Francisco de

Miranda, who placed his London library at Bello's disposal, the Mexican revolutionary priest Servando Teresa de Mier, Argentinian independence fighters, Carlos de Alvear, José de San Martín, and Manuel de Sarratea, and José Joaquín de Olmedo, the Ecuadorian poet. Unlike most of his contemporaries, Bello showed pride in Spain's intellectual accomplishments and struck up a lasting friendship with Bartolomé José Gallardo, an eminent bibliophile who consulted with Bello on numerous philological questions. Bello also wrote for and in some cases edited several Spanish-language magazines for the Hispanic community in London, including *El Español* from 1810 to 1814, *Biblioteca Americana* of 1823 and *Repertorio Americano* of 1826–1827. Published widely, Bello's articles informed Hispanic readers on both continents about developments in philosophy, literature, history, theatre, and virtually every other humanistic subject.

In 1829, Bello accepted a position in the Ministry of Foreign Relations in Santiago de Chile. Scarcely a year later, Diego Portales's landowning *estanqueros* (also known as *pelucones* or bigwigs) won national elections, beginning over forty years of conservative but often enlightened rule. Bello fitted in well with the conservative regime. Although an intellectual's intellectual, his devotion to high culture, devout Catholicism, and fear of disorder made him a willing partner in the regime's cultural endeavors. In 1830 he began collaborating in Portales's newspaper, *El Popular* and later became the cultural editor of the government's newspaper, *El Araucano*, a position he held until 1853. In 1842, the government directed that the Universidad de San Felipe become the Universdad de Chile, and Bello was named its first rector. As editor of several publications and head of the university, Bello created a cultural atmosphere in which ideas could be freely debated. Although a conservative himself, he opened his pages and the university halls to younger thinkers like José Victorino Lastarria and Francisco Bilbao who often attacked him. Also touched by Bello's love of debate and ideas were Argentina's two most famous nineteenth-century essayists, Domingo Faustino Sarmiento and Juan Bautista Alberdi, both of whom lived in Chile for extended periods between 1840 and 1853.

While Bello's articles and public lectures at some time or other address virtually every humanistic and scientific subject, two themes stand out: linguistics and jurisprudence. In 1835 Bello published his first major essay on language entitled *Principios de la ortología y métrica de la lengua castellana* in which, among other things, he suggests ways of modernizing Spanish spelling. Many of his suggestions became standard in Chilean publishing, and have disappeared in that country only in the last few decades. In 1841 he published the first of his major linguistic studies, *Análisis ideológico de los tiempos de la conjugación castellana*, a profound consideration of tense relationships in Spanish grammar. What separates Bello from other grammarians is his devotion to language as he heard and read it. Discarding the Latin underlay that defined and deformed virtually all Spanish grammar before him, Bello discovered the remarkable logic of the Spanish tense system, displaying its elegance for the first time on its own terms. Four years later, in 1847, Bello published what in my view is his masterpiece: *Gramática de la lengua castellana, destinada al uso de los americanos.* While the title suggests a textbook, the book is in fact a remarkable reflection on the nature of language as well as a study of Spanish grammar, so elegant and so complete that attempts by contemporary linguists to modernize it usually do more harm than good. Bello often advocated greater knowledge of Spain's Golden Age writers as a way of unifying American expression; moreover, he was a superb Latinist who frequently defended a conservative education in which old-style scholasticism mixed with modern science. Yet, what emerges in his *Gramática* is a work of striking modernity. Like modern linguists, Bello approached language as a natural phenomenon whose laws, like those of nature, should be discovered rather than prescribed; then, on the basis of this "natural" grammar, he sought to regularize Spanish usage among contemporary speakers. Bello's grammar thus becomes both descriptive and prescriptive. It also placed beyond debate any questions about the validity of American Spanish. Although the Royal Academy of the Language in Madrid recognized Bello's contribution in 1851 by making him an honorary member, in some sense Bello's grammar marked the end of the Academy's preeminence.

The second area where Bello's thought remains influential is in jurisprudence. Bello draws his theory of law from disparate sources. A devout Catholic, he never loses sight of the worth of the individual as a divine creation with inherent rights. At the same time, he greatly admires the institutions and civil codes of Roman law, as he shows in his book *Instituciones de derecho romano,* published in 1843. He was also much influenced by Jeremy Bentham's Utilitarianism, particularly in his sense that individual security formed the only practical basis for law. Bello's greatest study on legal theory was first published in 1832 under the title *Principios de derecho de gentes,* later to appear in expanded versions in 1844 and 1864 under the title *Principios de derecho internacional.* Of interest nowadays primarily to legal scholars, Bello's work nonetheless contributed ideas popularized throughout much of Spanish America such as the doctrine of non-intervention, sealed in his most famous aphorism: "If non-intervention is a duty, counter-intervention is a right." Elected national senator in 1837, Bello along with Senator Juan Egaña was asked in 1840 to write Chile's civil code. Egaña died in 1846, leaving this enormous task entirely to Bello. In 1853, Bello completed the Civil Code, bequeathing to Chile what was at the time the most modern code of any

Western country, later to be imitated throughout Latin America. Although much modified, Bello's code still resonates in Chile's jurisprudence.

José Victorino Lastarria (1817–1888)

Bello's most famous student (and detractor) was José Victorino Lastarria, an impassioned liberal who spent his life opposing conservative governments. Lastarria produced writings now collected in fourteen volumes. Born in 1817 in Ranacagua to a family of modest means and minimal social station, Lastarria left home at the age of ten to study at a Catholic school in Santiago known for its pious curriculum and frequent floggings. Two years later in 1829, sponsored by President Francisco Pinto's liberal government, Lastarria enrolled in the Liceo de Chile where he studied under José Joaquín de Mora, a Spanish liberal forced into exile by the repressive Ferdinand VII. Mora imbued the eager adolescent with a passion for enlightened ideas, romantic Nationalism, and a thorough disdain for Spanish absolutism in religion and politics. An irony: Lastarria's contempt for Spain was largely inspired by a Spanish exile.

These pleasant schooldays ended in 1830 when General Joaquín Prieto with the collaboration of wealthy businessman Diego Portales overthrew Pinto and initiated nearly forty years of conservative, oligarchical rule. One of Prieto's first moves was to close the Liceo and exile Mora, whose Liberalism, as revealed in a public debate with Bello, struck the new government as too radical. Although Bello would later help Lastarria gain prominence in Chilean intellectual life, Lastarria remained loyal to Mora's memory and was a frequent critic of Bello's cozy relationship with the successive conservative regimes.

Following completion of his law degree in 1836, Lastarria made a modest living as a teacher, journalist, newspaper editor, and sometime lawyer. In 1842 he was invited to head a newly founded Literary Society, members of which included Francisco Bilbao (studied below) and Juan Bello, Andrés's son. Members of the society are usually referred to as the Generation of 1842. In his inaugural address to the Society, Lastarria enunciated ideas that recur throughout his subsequent work. Chile, he tells us, triumphed heroically over the Spanish oppressors only to fall into an oppression even more insidious, that of a single-minded obsession with prosperity and economic progress, an obsession that supported oligarchy and limited individual freedom (*Recuerdos literarios*, 95–6). His target, of course, was the conservative government which, following the lead of Diego Portales, cultivated commercial, agricultural, and mineral development while neglecting universal education and enlightenment. In fact, as Spanish American governments went in the mid 1800s, Chile's was probably the most tolerant. But Lastarria wanted a real democracy, and that meant the education and participation of all Chileans, including those of Lastarria's own humble background. In his view, literature was the most effective instrument for national regeneration because only literature "reveals in the most explicit manner the moral and intellectual needs of the nations." He further argues that literature comprehends all knowledge, including "the most elevated concepts of the philosopher and jurists, the irrevocable truths of the mathematician and historian . . . and the rapture and delicious ecstasy of the poet" (p. 97). While respectful of erudition, Lastarria cautions against undue reliance on European models. "We must be original," he argues. "We have in our society all the necessary elements to attain that goal, to convert our literature into the most authentic expression of our national nature." But he warns that truly national expression cannot be "the exclusive patrimony of the privileged classes." Rather, it should also reflect "the likes of the multitudes, who, after all is said and done, are the best judge" (pp. 104–5). Lastarria's literary populism must be read as a deliberate counterpoint to Bello, who, although supportive of a national literature, showed little interest in the artistic achievements of the lower classes.

However much Lastarria criticized Bello, Bello disagreed only as a gentleman and continued to provide ways for his sometime student to lecture and publish. Indeed, Lastarria's next memorable foray into Chilean intellectual life came in 1844 when Bello, now rector of the University of Chile, invited him to give the inaugural address of what would become a long-lived lecture series on Chilean history. Following historiographical premises popularized by Guizot and Cousin, Lastarria argued that history should not concern itself only with facts but also with the systems and ideas that produced those facts. He further maintains that historians should write with an eye to the present and future, to explain wrongs and correct them for future generations. While he recognizes that history evolves in somewhat systematic ways, he also insists that evil men can frustrate historical progress just as men of good will can restore history to its proper path of progress for all. What this meant in Chile's case, he continues, is that the Spanish Conquest and colonization of America were retrograde events that must be undone for Chile to be restored to the kind of progress that was her historical destiny. Consequently, Chile's first task was to *desespañolizarse*, to cleanse itself of Spain (*Miscelánea histórica y literaria*, 19–20). Only after that necessary historical corrective could the country begin the task of modern nation-building.

Lastarria's speech met considerable opposition, most specifically from Bello, who persuasively argued that judging the Spanish Conquest with the ethical eyes of the nineteenth century was history based on ideology rather than fact. He further argued that Spain's work in America involved many positive aspects, including much of the thought behind the independence movement Lastarria admired. He particularly deplores reducing history to simple-minded notions of "correct" historical movement, and counsels Lastarria to avoid the excesses of "philosophical history" and to return to the "narrative history" of demonstrated fact and concrete evidence. Forty-four years later in his *Recuerdos literarios*, Lastarria confesses that Bello's refutation devastated him and his young coreligionists, but he further argues that historians and philosophers like Henry Thomas Buckle and Johann Herder had essentially vindicated his youthful efforts (*Recuerdos literarios*, 210–13).

Despite Bello's able refutation of "philosophical history," Lastarria continued writing history, always with the implicit intention of judging the past and informing the future. His most representative work in this regard is a pamphlet titled *Juicio histórico sobre don Diego Portales* of 1861 in which he condemns Portales's obsession with material progress and his disdain for the popular classes. At the same time he laments the conservative bent of every government since that of Portales which, although more sophisticated, continued governing for the privileged few while neglecting the nation's spiritual potential. Also of note is his collection *Miscelánea histórica y literaria*, first published in 1855 and again in expanded form in 1868, which includes essays, speeches, sketches, literary musings, and some of his historical novels.

In 1874, Lastarria published the first edition of his most influential book, a series of lectures under the title *Lecciones de política positiva*. As Lastarria admits in his *Recuerdos literarios*, he was first attracted to Comte's Positivism since the Frenchman's notions of historical evolution seemed to vindicate Lastarria in his debate with Bello of three decades past (p. 229). The *Lecciones* is, however, much more than a restatement of Comte's ideas. In the first two of the book's three sections, Lastarria studies Comte's notions of historical development and sociology, and manages to restate many of his own ideas using a positivist framework. The last section, however, departs significantly from Comte's proposal of a religion of humanity and advocates what Lastarria calls a *política positiva* which ends up being not much more than a restatement of the old liberal agenda of Pinto's *pipiolos* of five decades earlier: reform of institutions, greater participatory democracy (which meant less power for the church and the wealthy), and more autonomy for the provinces. For this not so new idea, Lastarria proposes a new term: a *semecracia*, or "self-government" (from the Latin *semet* for "self", and the Greek *kratos* for government) and thereby converts Comte's slogan of "order and progress" to "liberty and progress." His model for reform is the United States, which in his view had reached the highest degree of self-government in history. Lastarria's positivism then is a peculiar hybrid that accepts in the main Comte's history and sociology but remains firmly committed to liberal practice. The book was widely read in Latin America, perhaps because it successfully mixes European trendiness with a familiar liberal agenda.

Lastarria's most read book today and his last major effort was his monumental *Recuerdos literarios* of 1878. Much more than a personal memoir, the book offers a fascinating portrait of Chilean intellectual life during the mid 1800s; even Argentinian exiles like Sarmiento and Alberdi are vividly portrayed in Lastarria's memoires. The book also includes lengthy quotations and occasionally complete texts, so much so that at times it feels almost like an anthology. Although Lastarria makes no attempt to hide his opinions, he deals with his intellectual enemies with a remarkable even-handedness, and is particularly interesting in his portrayal of Bello. For the rich and the materialistic, however, Lastarria shows little mercy. To the end, he remains loyal to the country urchin from Rancangua who by dint of his superb intellect was allowed a place at the margin of Chilean society only to become that country's most noteworthy native-born intellectual of the last century.

Francisco Bilbao (1823–1865)

In his short life, Francisco Bilbao opposed every government of his native Chile, was involved in several armed rebellions, repeatedly attacked Catholicism as a betrayal of true Christianity, spent much of his life in exile, and suffered two excommunications. The son of a militant liberal, Bilbao had a good background in the encyclopedists, Rousseau, and Vico. But he also had an almost Protestant interest in the Bible and was greatly influenced by Robert de Lamenais, whose attempts to excise the Vatican from Christianity earned him the enmity of the church and the unfailing devotion of young Bilbao.

Bilbao's first important essay, *Sociabilidad chilena*, was published in 1844 when Bilbao was only twenty-one years old. The essay's attack on the Chilean oligarchy and the church earned the young writer exile and a fine for blasphemy and public disorder. Like Lastarria, he attributes Chile's ills to its Spanish heritage, but he goes much further in singling out the church as the repository of "Spanish barbarism." Catholicism, he tells us, amounts to little more than "eastern myths dressed up as revelation" (*Obras completas*, II, 5). The church is particularly culpable in America, he argues, for legitimizing the Spanish Conquest, supporting the Chilean plutocracy, and hypnotizing the downtrodden with pomp and empty promises. In a strikingly modern turn, Bilbao argues that the family constitutes the basic instrument of the church's oppression. Through the family, class lines are maintained, new ideas proscribed, and the young kept in "misanthropic isolation." In his view, the most visible victims of familial oppression are young women whose "passion must be contained [since] exalted passion is the instrument of instinctive revolution" (p. 13). He further argues that, just as the family controls its young through brute force, oligarchical governments dominate the poor by threat of violence. Bilbao was thus one of the first in Spanish America to link women and poor people in their struggle against a common enemy: the traditional family and the oligarchical state.

Bilbao goes on in *Sociabilidad chilena* to argue that the God of Reason as manifested in the intelligence of new prophets like Luther, Descartes, Voltaire, and Rousseau had unseated the God of Faith. The attempts of these reformers to better society were motivated by Infinite Love, which in Bilbao's scheme is the true god, the god hidden by the machinations of Catholicism and its wealthy allies (pp. 17–20). The true god's plan is based on principles of liberty, equality, and brotherhood. Consequently, any deviation from these principles is heretical (pp. 23–7). Liberty for Bilbao, however, also means "the liberty of all to [own] land. By removing the support of land ownership from those who support the old order, we also destroy their authority" (p. 27). Industry and commerce should also be open to all, "exalting Nationalism over European perfection" (p. 31). That is to say, even if European manufacturers surpass local goods in quality, local products should have preference in order to raise the economic level of all. Similarly, all Chileans should have access to quality education, without social distinctions or special privileges. In moral matters, Bilbao draws in both concept and language from the Hebrew and Christian scriptures and concludes with Jesus' injunction to love God and neighbor. And who is God? "We have to define his essence ... and decide if he is a thought and its extension or a personal being. The sublime spontaneity that assaults us says that he is a personal being. The creation of liberty for me is the proof of a divine liberty. Divine liberty is the individualization of the creator." Similarly, love of neighbor, of the "other I, who is the depository of the same spirituality that is mine," is the "unconquerable foundation of democracy" (p. 39).

Later essays by Bilbao reflect similar concerns but with even more religious emphasis. In *Prefacio a los evangelios*, written in Paris in 1846, Bilbao presents the Christian gospel as a revolutionary text that inveighs against materialism and social distinctions (pp. 76–9). Jesus in these pages becomes a revolutionary ideologue whose true message of material and spiritual redemption for the poor has been repressed by the church and its plutocratic allies. In *La ley de la historia*, unpublished until after his death, Bilbao identifies the struggle for justice and equality, particularly in America, as the force behind historical progress and the true expression of the divine presence on earth (pp. 137–67). Such arguments anticipate currents in today's liberation theology which borrows heavily from

Marxist notions of historical development. Bilbao's enthusiasm for an American Christianity emerges again in *Los araucanos* of 1847 in which he sees the hand of God in the anti-Spanish resistance of Chile's first inhabitants (pp. 305–50). Particularly surprising in this regard is his lengthy essay of 1861 on St Rose of Lima, the Peruvian mystic and most Catholic of saints, whom he sees as a forerunner of his gospel of spiritual and economic liberation for America's poor (*Estudios sobre la vida de Santa Rosa de Lima*, 351–443).

In view of these precedents, it is not surprising that his longest, last, and most famous essay is entitled *El evangelio americano*. Published in 1864, a year before Bilbao's death from consumption in 1865, this American gospel begins with an invocation to the true god, the god whose names are truth, light, love, eternal, the Supreme Power (*El evangelio americano*, 69–70). What emerges in Bilbao's thought is an uneasy identification of faith and reason. Bilbao repeatedly refers to God, yet, at the crucial moment of proclaiming the link between his thought and God, Bilbao claims that reason is the true channel of revelation, that only through reason can the true meaning of words like faith, justice, and grace be ascertained. This is not, however, reason apart from God, but reason as God's revelatory instrument. For that instrument to function properly, individuals must live under a true "self-government," a term he takes from English (p. 72). Any system that negates the sovereignty of free individuals, whether religious, metaphysical, political, or economic, defies Bilbao's sense of the divine order.

While *El evangelio americano* claims that all humans can reason and therefore gain access to the divine mind, Bilbao sees himself as a special witness of some sort, equal perhaps to others but charged to proclaim in America "the fraternity of the species, the unity of rights, and the glory of duty" (p. 70). "Fraternity" and "unity of rights," of course, merely restate slogans of the French Revolution; what is new in Bilbao's formulation is his concern for duty. Reason, in his view, must lead to social action which in turn must liberate people from oppression and give them the material means to live better. The enemy of duty is selfishness, the selfishness that Europe "practices in her institutions, doctrines, customs and [in the doctrines] of force, of national selfishness over supreme law, of centralization, of administrative despotism..." (p. 85).

Much of *El evangelio americano* fleshes out these ideas, sometimes with historical examples, sometimes in abstract musings about the nature of true equality and justice, and sometimes as concrete proposals for enfranchising the poor and redistributing wealth. Not surprisingly the revolutionary left in Spanish American considers Bilbao one of their precursors. It must be noted, however, that no coherent message comes from his work. He argues for reason but is not given to reasoned argument. Rather, he proclaims, often in terms more reminiscent of Isaiah than Rousseau or even Lamenais. These proclamations still warm us with their heat and passion, if not their intellectual rigor. They also show Bilbao to be a forerunner of Chile's greatest reformers.

The River Plate

Mariano Moreno (1778–1811)

Raised in a strict Catholic home where not even cardplaying was allowed, Argentina's Mariano Moreno studied at the best schools colonial Buenos Aires could offer and later at the University of Chuquisaca, now Sucre, Bolivia. Although Moreno trained in law, progressive priests enriched his studies with ideas from the Spanish *iluministas* as well as from the more radical French thinkers, Montesquieu, Raynal, Voltaire, and Moreno's favorite, Rousseau. In 1805, Moreno returned from Upper Peru to Buenos Aires, became involved in politics, and participated in Buenos Aires's successful resistance of the British invasions of 1806 and 1807. In 1808, he sided with the Spanish representative of the Cadiz government against Santiago de Liniers, a hero of the anti-British struggle. Only a few months later, Moreno turned on his Spanish friends and wrote a lengthy critique of the Spanish government's economic policies, which is discussed below. On May 25, 1810, he supported the *movimiento de mayo*, now simply known as "Mayo," in which the Buenos Aires *cabildo*, or city council, declared independence from Spain – in the name of Ferdinand VII. Moreno became secretary of the Primera Junta, as the first revolutionary government is known, but fell out with the Junta president, Cornelio Saavedra, mostly out of frustration over Saavedra's popularity with the popular classes. In early 1811 Moreno embarked for England, hoping to garner support against Saavedra from Argentina's former enemies. He died *en route* of a mysterious fever. On hearing of Moreno's burial at sea, Saavedra reportedly remarked, "They needed that much water to put out that much fire."

Despite his short life, Moreno wrote voluminously. His production includes legal briefs, speeches, newspaper articles, and a frightening plan of operations. Most of his shorter pieces appeared in *La Gazeta de Buenos Aires*, the Junta newspaper Moreno founded. These articles, never republished in their entirety, address many topics in a variety of ways, often to the point of contradiction. At times, for example, he is a strict centralist; on other occasions, he seems to support a federalist government structure which would allow the provinces considerable autonomy. Although he is claimed by Argentinian liberals, Moreno's prose reveals at least two Morenos. The first is an heir to the Enlightenment who defends freedom of expression, free trade, common sense, *vox populi*, and the usual ideological fare of the moment. The second Moreno is a frightening authoritarian figure who recalls both the Grand Inquisitor and the French Jacobins.

A representative example of Moreno's contradictions is found in an early essay, "Sobre la libertad de escribir," which appeared in the *Gazeta* on June 21, 1810. Predictably, Moreno praises public opinion as a reliable path to the truth and argues that evil is best repelled "by giving space and liberty to public writers so they can attack it vigorously and without pity." Then, in a marvellously contradictory line he affirms that "the people will languish in the most shameful stupor unless they are given the right and liberty to talk about all subjects as long as they do not oppose in any way the holy truths of our august religion and the dictates of the government" (Moreno, *Escritos*, 237). In short, anything can be discussed as long as it supports the church and the government. Not even Rousseau, Moreno's intellectual idol, is spared Moreno's authoritarianism. In the foreword of his translation of large portions of the *Social Contract*, Moreno predicts that Rousseau "will be the marvel of all ages" and that his translation "is a necessary part of educating the people" (*Escritos*, 379). But no sooner has he praised Rousseau than he announces that "since [Rousseau] had the misfortune to wax delirious on religious matters, I am suppressing the chapter and main passages where he addresses such matters" (p. 377). In sum, Moreno introduces into Argentinian political discourse all the vocabulary of the Enlightenment, but such vocabulary does not keep him from censoring to protect the "truth."

In addition to these short articles, Moreno wrote two lengthy essays, each quite different from the other. The first is a legal brief, written in 1808 under the unbrief title of *Representación a nombre del apoderado de los hacendados de las campañas del Río de la Plata dirigida al excelentísimo Señor Virrey Don Baltasar Hidalgo de Cisneros en el expediente promovido sobre proporcionar ingresos al erario por medio de un franco comercio con la nación inglesa*. Viceroy Cisneros, who represented the Cadiz government, had expressed reservations regarding British attempts to increase trade with the River Plate. Cisneros argued that increased trade with the British would tie River Plate economic development to a foreign power and thereby compromise Argentinian sovereignty. He also maintained that making available cheap manufactured goods from England would devastate local industry which had made Argentina largely self-sufficient in small manufactures like clothing, leather goods, and furniture.

Moreno's response in the *Representación* anticipates contemporary positions on free trade and shows the extraordinary degree to which Spanish American elites were in tune with European economic theory. Moreno argues that taxes on trade with England would nourish the public purse, stimulate growth in Argentina's cattle industry, and give Argentinians access to inexpensive, high-quality British goods. Indeed, he argues that

> A country just beginning to prosper cannot be deprived of [goods] which flatter good taste and increase consumption. If our artists knew how to make them as well they should be preferred ... Is it fair to deprive one of ... a good piece of furniture just because our artisans haven't committed themselves to make one as good? (*Escritos*, 217)

Two points stand out in this remarkable statement. First the consuming classes of Buenos Aires "deserve" the best, which in this case means British goods. And second, native artisans make inferior goods because they lack commitment. Advertisers and union busters could not have said it better.

The *Representación* can be read in two quite different ways. In one sense, it merely retells the economic wisdom of the times with clear echoes of Smith, Quesnay, and of course, Gaspar Melchor de Jovellanos, whom Moreno quotes with delight since he was at the time president of the governing board in Cadiz and thereby Cisneros's superior. In another sense, however, the *Representación* marks Argentina's tragic flaw: Buenos Aires turning towards Europe and her virtual indifference to the economic needs of the interior and the working classes.

Moreno's other large essay is a mysterious document of uncertain date. Entitled *Plan de las operaciones que el gobierno provisional de las Provincias Unidas del Río de la Plata debe poner en práctica para consolidar la grande obra de nuestra libertad e independencia*, the document came to light when a handwritten copy, accompanied by an affidavit affirming that Moreno wrote the original, was discovered in the Archivo General de las Indias in Seville. Norberto Piñero published the Plan in his 1895 anthology of Moreno's works, the one used here. Since the Plan presents a view of Moreno radically at variance with that of Official History, Moreno-admiring liberals like Paul Groussac and Ricardo Levene immediately questioned the document's authenticity. The most thorough investigation of the Plan's origins is nationalist historian Enrique Ruiz-Guiñazú's *Epifanía de la libertad: documentos secretos de la Revolución de Mayo*. While conceding that some corruption exists, Ruiz-Guiñazú shows that the plan coheres point by point with other writings where Moreno's authorship is unquestionable. He also shows that many of Moreno's contemporaries as well as later historians, including Bartolomé Mitre, knew of the Plan's existence.

Pro-Moreno Liberals' nervousness about the Plan is understandable. Moreno begins by advocating ruthless suppression of dissent: "Moderation at an inappropriate time is neither sanity nor truth ... never in times of revolution has a government followed moderation or tolerance; a man's slightest thought that opposes the new system is a crime because of the influence and obstacles such a thought might cause by its example, and its punishment is unavoidable" (*Escritos*, 458). He later affirms that suppression of dissent should use any means necessary: "No one should be scandalized by the intention of my words, to cut off heads, spill blood, and sacrifice at all costs, even when they [my words] resemble the customs of cannibals and savages . . . No decrepit state or province can regenerate itself nor cut out its corruption without spilling rivers of blood" (p. 467). To identify enemies, Moreno recommends establishing a secret police force: "In the capital and in all towns, the government should retain spies, to be recruited not according to talent or circumstance, but by their manifest devotion to the cause" (p. 473). He also recommends, in clear contradiction to his previous stand on the freedom of the press, that the government be "silent and reserved with the public, even the healthy part of the people, so that our enemies will not understand anything about our operations" (p. 470).

The Plan also addresses economic development, but in terms decidedly different from those of *Representación*. He advocates an aggressive redistribution of wealth and property, from rich to poor, with the first targets being the property of the wealthy "enemies." "Let five or six thousand grow unhappy," he tells us, "so that the advantages [of prosperity] can fall on eighty or a hundred thousand inhabitants" (p. 512). He further advocates the creation of state commissions to supervise all sales, prevent the concentration of wealth, stop the export of goods needed at home, and control all imports, especially those products that "like a corrupting vice, represent excessive and sterile luxury" (p. 523). As for foreign policy, Moreno produces a far-fetched scheme through which Buenos Aires would destabilize other areas of South America, and then enter an agreement with Britain by which Britain and Buenos Aires would divide up the conquered territories (pp. 535–40).

Moreno's exact place in Argentinian intellectual history remains in dispute. Liberals, Nationalists, Centralists, interventionists, rightists, leftists, militarists – all can find something in Moreno to quote. Whatever else he did, Moreno introduced into Argentinian discourse concepts of universal equality, freedom of expression and dissent, individual liberty, representative government, and institutional rule under law. And even though Moreno sometimes betrayed those goals, the vocabulary he introduced into Argentinian thought became the framework within which all governments would be judged, the necessary point of departure for every attempt to reform and improve the *Patria*.

José Gervasio Artigas (1764–1850)

Now proclaimed as the hero of Uruguayan independence, Artigas in fact had little to do with Uruguay's nationhood. Indeed, he spent his best years trying to make a place for Uruguay in a federation associated with but not dominated by Buenos Aires. While not an author of formal essays, he left thousands of documents still being collected in the *Archivo Artigas* which since 1950 has published twenty volumes and still remains incomplete. Since Artigas' writings consist mainly of letters, speeches, position papers, and decrees, he might not be an essayist in most traditional senses of the term. His work, however, offers an indispensable view of what might be called pro-provincial, federalist, or even populist thought. As such it occupies an important place in this overview.

Artigas was forty-seven years old when Buenos Aires declared Independence from Napoleonic Spain in May of 1810. Previously a national police officer charged with protecting Uruguay's western flank from incursions of Indians and Portuguese soldiers, Artigas visited Buenos Aires in 1811 and offered his services to the Junta. Appointed lieutenant colonel in the Patriot army, he returned to Uruguay and quickly mobilized a peasant army that triumphed in several key battles against the Spanish Royalists. Buenos Aires, however, soon became suspicious of Artigas's popularity, fearing that his army of mixed-blood gauchos, Indians, and country folk constituted a form of "popular arbitrariness" that threatened Buenos Aires's aspirations for central control. From that point onward, relations between Artigas and the successive governments of Buenos Aires grew more distrustful, so much so that in 1815 Artigas organized a parallel government that included most of Uruguay and the Argentinian provinces of Entre Ríos, Corrientes, and Santa Fe. During the next four years, Artigas produced his most significant writings.

More frequently dictated than written, Artigas's decrees and letters address four main issues: protectionism versus free trade, economic as well as civic egalitarianism, inclusion of all Americans regardless of race or social class, and a kind of Nativism that assumed an underlying American identity waiting to be uncovered once the colonial power was repelled.

Unlike contemporaries educated in the economic theories of François Quesnay's *laissez-faire* physiocrats and Adam Smith's invisible hand, Artigas suspected that free trade would only benefit the already wealthy. He therefore argued in 1815 that the British should be allowed into Uruguayan ports only at the discretion of the Uruguayan government and only on the condition that they respect local law and "never try to interfere in local affairs" (*Documentos*, 147). In the same year, he banned the importation of products that would compete with local manufacturers, indicating a desire to develop local industry and resist becoming merely a supplier of raw materials (see, for example, "Reglamento Provisional" of 1815 in *Documentos*, 148–9). Later, recognizing that the British could be both useful and dangerous, he limited their role in Uruguay's economy to international shipping only (see "Tratado de Comercio" of 1817 in *Documentos*, 151–2).

Artigas also sought to implement internal reforms that even today seem progressive. Recognizing that democracy would work best among economic equals, he tried to redistribute large haciendas to "the most worthy beneficiaries of this grace, with the premise that the most unfortunate will be the most privileged" ("Reglamento Provisorio," *Documentos*, 159–60). Yet, fearing that such land once distributed might return to the already wealthy, as happened repeatedly in later homesteading schemes, Artigas further decreed that "the beneficiaries cannot transfer ownership nor sell these kinds of *estancias* [ranches], nor contract against said properties any kind of debt." He further mandated that cattle, equipment, and seed be made available to the new landowners (pp. 160–2). And from where would such land and cattle come? From the "Europeans and bad Americans" who did not support the revolution. Artigas's disdain for the landowning elites no doubt contributed to his downfall as well as to a kind of black legend among conservative historians who see him more as a populist zealot than as a national hero.

Particularly remarkable in Artigas's sense of democracy are his attempts to include all races and castes. In arguing for equitable land ownership, Artigas explicitly says that "free Negros, *zambos* [Indian-African mix] of this class, Indians, and poor Creoles, all shall be graced with some kind of *estancia*, if with their labor and manliness they work toward their happiness and that of their province" ("Reglamento provisorio," 160). In a similar vein he wrote:

> My desire is that Indians in their communities govern themselves, so they can tend to their interests as we tend to ours. Thus they will experience a practical happiness and escape from that state of annihilation to which misfortune has subjected them. Let us remember that they have the principal right and that it would be a shameful degradation for us to keep them in the shameful exclusion that until now they have suffered because they were Indians.   ("Reglamento provisorio," 164)

Artigas's concern for Indians and mixed bloods sounds a noteworthy counterpoint to the prevailing attitudes of the time. However abusive colonial laws were, they did allow the native populations certain rights, including the right to community ownership of land. Such rights came under assault as the Bourbon kings applied physiocratic notions of private ownership of property as the sure road to material prosperity. With the fall of colonial government, these rights disappeared altogether, so much so that the indigenous populations and their mixed-blood cousins experienced increasing poverty and marginalization as new governments embraced economic and social theories that favored the already rich. Against this backdrop, Artigas's inclusiveness seems particularly praiseworthy.

Artigas's place in Spanish American history was assured when Uruguayans made him their founding father, although Artigas himself never sought more for Uruguay than the status of equal province in the United Provinces of the River Plate. Artigas's egalitarianism has also made him a *cause célèbre* of modern Spanish American leftists ever anxious to claim American roots. Whatever history's changing view of him might be, however, one thing seems clear: no one at so early a time in Spanish American intellectual history articulated provincial and lower-class concerns more clearly than he.

Esteban Echeverría (1805–1851)

Esteban Echeverría was a founding member and chief mentor of what has become known as the Generation of 1837. The Generation of 1837 takes its name from a Buenos Aires literary salon founded in that year under the twin rubrics of *La asociación de la joven generación argentina* and *La asociación de mayo*, this last being a reference to the 1810 revolution of which they considered themselves the intellectual heirs. What first defined the generation was its love of ideas and its common opposition to the dictatorship of Juan Manuel de Rosas, governor of the Province of Buenos Aires and virtual dictator of the entire country from 1835 to 1852. When Rosas fell, ideological differences split the generation forever.

Considered Argentina's first great poet, Echeverría had lived in France and was greatly influenced by the social theories of Saint-Simon and Victor Cousin as well as the romantic poetry of Schiller, Goethe, and Byron. He also hoped to recreate in *La asociación de la joven argentina* something of the spirit motivating Giuseppe Mazzini's *Giovine Italia* founded in 1831 and widely imitated throughout Europe.

Aside from occasional writings, Echeverría is credited with two important essays. The title of the first, *Dogma socialista*, written in 1837, reveals his sympathy for Saint-Simon's sense of Socialism as a scientific and wholly rational approach to understanding and governing society, this being a forerunner of Comte's sociological ideas. It also includes speeches given at meetings of the *Asociación* and provides a good idea of the group's central concerns. Echeverría's second essay, written in 1845, is titled *Ojeada retrospectiva sobre el movimiento intelectual en el Plata desde el año 1837*. Written after Echeverría was in exile in Uruguay, the second essay differs from the first in perspective but not in ideas.

Two key ideas emerge in Echeverría's work. First, he sought to bridge the gap between Argentina's competing political parties, "to unitarize the Federalists and federalize the Unitarians" (*Ojeada*, 86–7). Critical of both parties, he condemned the "exclusivist and supremacist attitudes" of the Unitarians (*Ojeada*, 83), while attacking the federalist party, as a "system supported by the popular masses and the genuine expression of their semi-barbarous instincts" (*Dogma*, 83). Second, Echeverría felt that governing power should be left to "the natural hierarchy of intelligence, virtue, capacity and proven merit" (*Dogma*, 201) – a position that ties him much more to the elitist Unitarians than to the Federalists. He further argues that:

> The sovereignty of the people can only reside in the reason of the people, and the most sensible and rational portion of the social community is called to the exercise of reason. The ignorant portion remains under the tutelage and guardianship of laws formulated according to the uniform consensus of the rational people. Democracy, then, is not the absolute despotism of the masses, nor of the majority; it is the rule of reason.   (*Dogma*, 201)

In sum, for all their pious words about reconciliation, Echeverría and his entire generation advocated an exclusivist democracy which would include lesser mortals only when "the people become a people" (*Ojeada*, 106).

Juan Bautista Alberdi (1810–1884)

Founding member of *La asociación de mayo*, lawyer, writer, and intellectual father of the Constitution of 1853 (which until late 1994 continued to rule Argentina), Juan Bautista Alberdi despite such activity lived a lonely life. Except for a brief stint as Ambassador at Large for Justo José de Urquiza's Confederation during the mid-1850s, he participated little in the affairs of his country and spent most of his life in exile, first in Uruguay and later in Chile and France. Argentina, however, was always his passion, and although more than a century separates us from him, his ideas continue to astound us with their prescience and clarity.

Alberdi's first important essay, *Fragmento preliminar al estudio del derecho*, was published in 1837 when the author was only twenty-seven years old. Despite the modesty of its title – both fragmentary and preliminary – the *Fragmento* shows unusual independence in explaining Rosas's rule and the *caudillo* phenomenon in general. Favored by Alejandro Heredia, *caudillo* of Alberdi's native province of Tucumán, and supported in his studies by Facundo Quiroga, *caudillo* of La Rioja, Alberdi came by his sympathy for the *caudillos* naturally, and it is this sympathy that most stands out in the *Fragmento*. With considerable influence from Friedrich Karl von Savigny's theories on the *Volkgeist*, Alberdi argues that a country can develop only when its written laws (*leyes*) are based on its organic law (*derecho*) "which lives in lively harmony with the social organism" (Alberdi, *Obras completas* [OC], I, 105). From this premise, he develops an astonishing apology for Rosas, whom he sees as "the great and powerful person who ... possesses a sturdy intuition of [the American spirit] as witnessed by his profound, instinctive antipathy to exotic theories." He then calls on young Argentinian intellectuals to follow "what the great magistrate has tried to practice in politics" by studying "all elements of our American existence, without plagiarism, without imitation, and only in the intimate and profound study of our people and our things" (*OC*, I, 116–7). Unfortunately, Rosas remained unmoved by Alberdi's enthusiasm, and scarcely a year later, Alberdi fled for his life to Uruguay, thus beginning a long life in exile.

Alberdi's next important essay is his best-known and in odd ways his least representative: *Bases y puntos de partida para la organización política de la República Argentina*. Published in Chile in 1852, *Bases* exercised decisive influence on Argentina's 1853 constitution. After discussing why several Spanish American constitutions failed, Alberdi concludes that in South America only a powerful executive can produce a stable government. "Give to the executive all the power possible," he writes, "but give it to him by means of a constitution" (*Bases*, 352). He approvingly quotes Simón Bolívar: "The new states of formerly Spanish America need kings under the name of presidents" (*Bases*, 229). *Bases* also addresses Argentina's economic needs, a subject largely neglected by other writers of the Generation. First in Alberdi's prescription for economic health is immigration, a concern that produced his most famous aphorism, *gobernar es poblar*, "to govern is to populate." He writes:

> Each European who comes to our shores brings more civilization in his habits, which will later be passed on to our inhabitants, than many books of philosophy ... Do we want to sow and cultivate in America English liberty, French culture, and the diligence of men from Europe and the United States? Let us bring living pieces of these qualities ... and let us plant them here.   (*Bases*, 250)

As well as immigrants, Alberdi seeks foreign capital. He recommends abolishing all protective tariffs and opening the country up to foreign investments, loans, and business partnerships in order to build railroads, develop lands, and establish new industries. "Is our capital insufficient for [building railroads]?" he asks. "Then let foreign capital do it" (pp. 264–5). With foreign capital and foreign immigrants everything is possible. "Open your doors wide," he advises his fellow citizens, "to the majestic entrance of the world" (p. 272).

Rosas's fall in 1852 and Argentina's subsequent division between Bartolomé Mitre's Buenos Aires and Justo José de Urquiza's Confederation headquartered in Paraná set Alberdi on a very different ideological course from that of the *Bases*, and in ways reminiscent of the *Fragmento*. Although living in Chile at the time, Alberdi allied himself with Urquiza against *porteño* [pertaining to the port of Buenos Aires] hegemony and in the process had to reevaluate his attitudes toward the Argentinian masses and their natural leaders, the provincial *caudillos*. The forum for this reevaluation was a debate sustained with a former ally against Rosas, Domingo Faustino Sarmiento, subject of the next section. Irritated at Urquiza's failure to offer him a significant post in either the struggle against Rosas or the Confederation government, Sarmiento returned to Chile and launched a no-holds-barred campaign against the Confederation and Urquiza, whom he called "the new Rosas." Alberdi responded to Sarmiento's attacks in four famous essays called the *Cartas quillotanas* (1853), named after the town of Quillota, Alberdi's temporary home. In the *Cartas*, Alberdi identifies Argentina's chief enemy: Argentinian Liberalism as reflected in old-time Unitarianism whose attempts to impose order amounted to "wars of extermination against the nature (*modo de ser*) of our pastoral classes and their natural representatives [the caudillos]" (*OC*, IV, 12). He sees "the journalism of combat" of Sarmiento and Mitre as another dimension of Buenos Aires's war against the interior and against the proper organization of the republic; he is particularly incensed at Buenos Aires's refusal to participate in Urquiza's constitutional convention:

> We should establish as a theorem: any delay in writing the Constitution is a crime against the *Patria*, a betrayal of the republic. With caudillos, with Unitarians, with Federalists, with every kind of person who shapes and lives in our sad Republic, we should proceed to its organization, excluding not even the bad people, because they also form part of the family. If you exclude them, you exclude everyone, including yourselves ... Remember that imperfect liberty is the only kind available in view of the possibilities of the country ... [I]f you want to build the *Patria* you have, and not the one you wish you had, you must accept the principle of imperfect liberty ... The day you believe it proper to destroy and suppress the gaucho because he doesn't think as you do, you write your own death sentence and revive the system of Rosas.
>
> (*OC*, IV [*Cartas*] 16–17)

Not only a call to pluralism, the passage clearly places Alberdi at odds with the immigrationist pro-European Alberdi who wrote *Bases*. It also recalls the Alberdi who wrote the *Fragmento* and signals ideas that would dominate his writing for the rest of his life.

After Urquiza's mysterious surrender to Mitre in 1861, Alberdi took up permanent residence in Paris, a man without a country who could write about nothing but his country. An acerbic critic of the presidencies of both

Mitre and Sarmiento, Alberdi mercilessly attacked Argentina's involvement in the War of the Triple Alliance (1865–1870), in which Brazil,
Argentina, and their puppet government in Uruguay ganged up on
Paraguay. Alberdi viewed the war as yet another example of *porteño*
hegemony and liberalism's irrational fear of the *caudillos* (see for example
El Imperio del Brasil ante la democracia de América of 1869 in OC, VI,
267–308). He also criticized Mitre's landmark biographies on Belgrano
and San Martín as distorted attempts to exalt Buenos Aires over the
interior. Alberdi's well-honed attacks on Mitre's scholarship published
mostly during the 1860s are available in a useful anthology of Alberdi's
later work, *Grandes y pequeños hombres del Plata*, published in Paris in
1912.

Alberdi's criticism of Mitre's histories also introduces one of the most
seductive and durable images of modern Argentina's historical revisionism: the notion of Argentina actually being two countries with two
different histories whose fate holds them in the same geographical space.
In Alberdi's view, the failure of Buenos Aires to live according to the ideals
of the May revolution "has created two countries, different and separate,
behind the appearance of one: the metropolis state, Buenos Aires, and her
servant state, the Republic. One governs, the other obeys; one enjoys the
national income, the other produces it; one is fortunate, the other
miserable" (*Grandes y pequeños hombres*, 107). What Alberdi suggests
here is an alternative to the official history developed and promoted by
Mitre and other pro-*porteño* historians. Alberdi's ideas still resonate in
virtually all discussions Argentinians have about their nation. Liberals
and economic traditionalists quote *Bases* at length, while his defense of
the *caudillos*, his vindication of the rural lower classes, and his attacks on
porteño pretense echo in nationalistic writing of both the right and the
left.

In 1878 Alberdi returned to Argentina, an exhausted and sometimes
confused old man. Although the reconciliatory government of Nicolás
Avellaneda, president after Sarmiento, tried to make him welcome, he
soon tired of public attention, and returned to Paris in 1881, where he died
alone in 1884.

Domingo Faustino Sarmiento (1811–1888)
Although associated with the Generation of 1837, Domingo Faustino
Sarmiento met most of its members long after the *Asociación* had
disbanded. Born and raised in the isolated Province of San Juan, child of a
ne'er-do-well father and an ambitious mother, and only son in a family of
daughters, Domingo Faustino Sarmiento served as President of the
Republic, governor and later senator of his native province, Ambassador
to the United States, and Minister of Education. Throughout his life he

tirelessly promoted public education, founding schools wherever he landed and staffing them with teachers from normal schools, which he also founded. In addition to these achievements, he also wrote, constantly, on subjects ranging from history to social theory, biography to philosophy. His books, articles, education manuals, and correspondence fill fifty-two volumes, all marked by a prose style remarkable for its fluidity, expressive richness, and impeccable timing. Yet, despite his accomplishments and renown, Sarmiento was controversial during his lifetime and still inspires as much criticism as praise. In fairness, it must be noted that the Argentinians who criticize him probably learn to do so in schools he founded.

Feeling called to greatness, Sarmiento was always drawn to politics. Virtually all his writings in one way or another support his political ambitions by passing judgment, prescribing remedies, and drawing attention to his erudition and knowledge of other cultures. Not without cause his contemporaries nicknamed him *Don yo*, Mr I. When only seventeen, Sarmiento joined Unitarian forces in a rebellion against a local *caudillo*, and at nineteen he was exiled to Chile, where he taught school, read everything available, learned to read English and French, and began writing newspaper articles. Later, in 1840, after a short stint back in San Juan, Sarmiento returned to Chile and made himself a prominent figure in Chilean intellectual life, largely through frequent contributions to local newspapers and disagreements with just about everyone, notably Andrés Bello. Also in Chile, between 1840 and 1852, he published his most memorable book-length essays.

The first of these was *Civilización y barbarie: vida de Juan Facundo Quiroga*, commonly called the *Facundo*, published in Chile in 1845 and arguably the most important Spanish American essay of the last century. Sarmiento originally planned to write a biography of Quiroga, the man who first exiled him from Argentina, but quickly grew impatient and began writing with few sources other than hearsay and his enormous imagination. Not without cause he often said, "Las cosas hay que hacerlas. Salgan bien o salgan mal, hay que hacerlas." ["Things have to be done. Whether they come out well or not, they have to be done."] But no sooner had he begun writing than the Argentinian government, offended by Sarmiento's attacks on Rosas, demanded his extradition. Chilean president, Manuel Bulnes, refused to comply, but urged Sarmiento to soften his criticism. Not given to softening anything, Sarmiento refocused his biography of Facundo, converting it into a compelling indictment of Rosas in particular and *caudillismo* in general.

Given these motives, Sarmiento produced an unusually complex text, part biography, part history, part sociology, part political commentary, and yet somehow more than all these. In large terms, one might say that the *Facundo* has two main purposes. First, it is an explanation of national failure as the result of barbarism, Second, the *Facundo* prescribes remedies for that failure which in due time would make Argentina a civilized nation. Civilization versus Barbarism are the options Sarmiento gives us, and he allows no middle ground.

Sarmiento attributes Argentina's failure to three main causes: the land, the area's Spanish/Catholic tradition, and the race of most of its inhabitants. In an argument influenced by Montesquieu's *De l'Esprit des lois*, he holds that "the evil that afflicts the Argentinian Republic is its vast emptiness" (*Facundo*, 19). That emptiness, particularly as found in the pampas (which Sarmiento had never seen), produced a collective personality that however picturesque, was for Sarmiento singularly inappropriate for modern civilization. Buenos Aires, he tells us, would already be a civilized European city, had not "the Spirit of the Pampa . . . breathed on her" (p. 22). The *caudillos* in Sarmiento's view are the incarnation of "the Spirit of the Pampa" and Rosas a barbarian birthed "from the deep womb of the Argentinian earth" (p. 10). He describes at length gaucho customs and how they match those of nomad populations in similar "topographies and climates in Africa and North America. Such similarities are proof of the gaucho's barbarism which in turn explains why they fall easily into the thrall of *caudillo* leaders. Sarmiento's condemnation of the gauchos, however, is not without ambivalence. Sarmiento the romantic writer, finds the gaucho attractive, as indicated by his beautiful portrayals of gaucho types, customs, songs and poetry (pp. 21–34). In contrast, Sarmiento the liberal progressive sees no place for gauchos in a modern Argentinian state. And in fact, in his public life he constantly sought to eradicate gaucho and Indian life, by extermination if necessary, and force survivors into his vision of civilization: a modern, Europeanized Argentina.

A second source of barbarism for Sarmiento is the Spanish/Catholic tradition of Argentina's colonial forebears. He repeatedly laments that Argentina was colonized by "the backward daughter of Europe," a country characterized by "the Inquisition and Spanish absolutism," and he attributes to Spain "the Spanish American peoples' lack of ability in political and industrial matters which keeps them in constant turmoil, like a ship churning in the ocean, with no port or rest in sight" (p. 2). Spain in his view was the cradle of barbarism, a parent to be cast off and replaced.

Finally, the *Facundo* attributes Argentina's failure to the inadequacy of the area's "races," a term Sarmiento uses to connote culture as well as bloodlines. Particularly unfortunate in his view are the mixed bloods which after 300 years of miscegenation included virtually all of Argentina's lower classes. Following received racialist theories of the time, Sarmiento writes:

A homogenous whole has resulted from the fusion of the [Spanish, African, and Indian] races. It is typified by love of idleness and incapacity for industry, except when education and the demands of a social position succeed in spurring it out of its customary crawl. To a great extent, this unfortunate outcome results from the incorporation of the native tribes through the process of colonization. The American aborigines live in idleness, and show themselves incapable, even under compulsion, of hard and prolonged labor. From this came the idea of introducing Negroes into America which has produced such fatal results. But the Spanish race has not shown itself more energetic than the aborigines, when it has been left to its own instincts in the wilds of America.   (p. 15)

Sarmiento explicitly links Rosas's political success to the support of mixed-blood *lomos negros* or "black backs" (p. 130) and argues that Rosas maintained power through a "zealous spy network" of black servants from "a savage race" placed "in the breast of every Buenos Aires family" (p. 141).

Having thus described the sources of barbarism. Sarmiento can now attack its principal manifestations: *caudillismo*, Quiroga, and Rosas. The *caudillo*, he writes, is "the mirror which reflects in colossal proportions the beliefs, the necessities, the concerns and customs of a nation of a given moment in history" (p. 6). A predetermined enemy of progress, he is the natural man sprung from the savage American soil and also heir to the medieval Spanish tradition (p. 18). His rise to power is "destined, inevitable, natural, and logical" (p. 14). Sarmiento postulates a mystical bond between the masses and their leader by which the *caudillo* articulates and performs the inchoate will of the masses (p. 130). Sarmiento's crucial point, however, is that progress will come, not by suppressing the *caudillos* themselves, but by changing the circumstances from which they emerge.

To change the land, Sarmiento argues for economic development in terms substantially similar to, but less detailed than, Alberdi's: build railroads and telegraph lines, establish river navigation, and construct fences. To change the race, bring immigrants to Argentinian shores, give them land (wrested from the gauchos and Indians who could be exterminated if necessary), and a place for their own kind of worship. To replace Hispanic culture, bring even more immigrants and build schools everywhere to educate locals in the ways of Europe. All this Sarmiento and his generation did with remarkable energy and success. But as we shall see below, Sarmiento died thinking he had failed, perhaps because the task he laid for himself was simply too big.

The *Facundo* was by no means Sarmiento's last essay, but it anticipates virtually every theme in Sarmiento's later production. Other significant essays include his delightful, three-volumed work: *Viajes por Europa, Africa y América*. Published in 1849 after a three-year trip through Spain, France, Italy, Germany, Switzerland, Northern Africa, and the United States, Sarmiento's *Viajes* expand on themes seen previously. As anticipated in the *Facundo*, he criticizes the Mediterranean countries, finding Spain barbaric and primitive, Italy impoverished and money-grubbing, France disorganized and dirty. Germany and Switzerland, in contrast, seemed worthy of emulation, and he explored ways of attracting immigrants to South America from those countries. Most fascinating for him was the United States, where he spent time in virtually every region east of the Mississippi. While far from uncritical of North America, he nonetheless left feeling that the United States offered the best model for Argentina to emulate.

Also fruit of his journeys was a report, also of 1849, to the Chilean government entitled *Educación popular* in which he details observations on educational systems in the countries he visited, and makes recommendations for establishing a public school system in Chile. Many of these ideas – the need for independent financing of public schools, kindergartens, class size, nature of buildings, training of teachers, and the like – show the influence of Horace Mann and appear in later essays, specifically *Memoria sobre educación común* of 1856 and *Las escuelas – base de la prosperidad y de la república en los Estados Unidos* of 1866.

Not long after returning to Chile, Sarmiento received news of Urquiza's rebellion against Rosas. Elated, Sarmiento quickly penned a long essay titled *Argirópolis*, published in 1850 and dedicated to Urquiza. A lengthy treatise on how to organize Argentina, *Argirópolis* repeats ideas already found in *Facundo*, but on a plane so abstract as to make one wonder how well Sarmiento actually knew the country he would govern. Particularly amusing to critics was his intention to locate the national capital in the centrally located but wholly inappropriate bug-infested islet of Martín García. In sum, the book is conceived wholly in the abstract and shows how impractical Sarmiento could be even when sounding very good.

Urquiza took little notice of *Argirópolis*, and when Sarmiento joined Urquiza's troops in the campaign against Rosas, he received only a minor position as editor of daily *boletines*, a post Sarmiento much resented. Appalled at Urquiza's refusal to abandon federalist colors, Sarmiento left Buenos Aires shortly after Urquiza's triumph and eventually ended up in Chile, where he wrote an open letter to Urquiza, the *Carta de Yungay*, dated October 13, 1852, in which he denounces Urquiza as "the new Rosas" whose behavior would "require the indulgence of history" (OC, xv, 25–34) In the same year, he also wrote *Campaña en el ejército grande*, an entertaining, albeit libelous, account of Urquiza's triumph over Rosas and an attack on the Paraná constitutional convention. Alberdi rose to

Urquiza's defense in the *Cartas quillotanas* mentioned above. Sarmiento's public letters of rejoinder are found in *Las ciento y una* of 1852 whose intellectual vacuity is matched only by Sarmiento's superb epithets. He calls the *Cartas quillotanas* "a hodgepodge ... flavored with a dialectic sauce of arsenic" and refers to Alberdi as "a stupid fool who can't even lie well, who doesn't suspect that he makes people vomit (OC, xv, 147) "[who] has the voice of a woman and the valor of a rabbit" (xv, 181). In 1855, Sarmiento joined Mitre's government in Buenos Aires and immediately saw his political fortunes improve. After serving as Mitre's ambassador to the United States, he was elected to a six-year term as president beginning in 1868. While continuing to write throughout this period, he published no significant essays until he left office. Then, in 1883, five years before his death, he published the first two volumes of his last famous essay, *Conflictos y armonías de las razas en América*.

Described by Sarmiento himself as a *"Facundo* grown old," *Conflictos y armonías* is a sad work. Like the *Facundo*, *Conflictos* is an explanation of failure; unlike the *Facundo*, however, it offers no plan for redemption. Although the Argentina of the 1880s was booming, Sarmiento saw fraud everywhere, and the immigrants he had worked to attract were Latin instead of Germanic and alarmingly resistant to assimilation. Moreover, in the presidency of Julio Argentino Roca, which began in 1880, Sarmiento saw a new kind of *caudillismo* based on personalism, fraud, and patronage that frustrated institutional rule just as surely as Rosas and his gaucho militia had a half-century earlier.

To explain the new barbarism, Sarmiento resurrected one of his pet theories from the *Facundo*: failure because of race. He surveys the national history of every American country and notes that only in the United States had a real democracy taken root in which immigrants assimilated and became new Yankees. Then, with some reference to European eugenics, he argues that the only difference between the countries of South and North America is race. He then notes that of all Christian peoples only "the Latin races in America have been unable for more than seventy years to organize a lasting, effective, government" (OC, xxxvIII, 273). Argentina, he feels, is better off than other Spanish American countries because it has more white people. In contrast, a country like Ecuador "has a million inhabitants, of whom only 100,000 are white. Result: three military strongmen make up nearly all of her history" (xxxvIII, 282–3). Perhaps *Conflictos* is the only possible ending for *Facundo* because Sarmiento defined success in such unattainable terms. Land, cultural heritage, and race were simply too indelible to be eliminated.

Other essayists

Other essayists of note in the River Plate include Olegario Andrade (1839–1882). Primarily known as a poet, Andrade wrote one significant essay, *Las dos políticas*, probably of 1866, in which he denounces Buenos Aires hegemony over the provinces and argues that the political dispute between *porteño* Unitarians and Federalists was essentially a family squabble that masked the real dichotomy of Buenos Aires against the provinces. Also important is José Henández (1834–1886), best known for his famous poem, *El gaucho Martín Fierro*. Hernández's best essays are found in the articles he wrote for the newspaper *El Río de la Plata* (1869) in which he presents a careful defense of provincial interests against the centralist policies of President Sarmiento. Both Hernández and Andrade were also acerbic critics of the Paraguayan War. Finally, some mention should be made of Carlos Guido y Spano (1827–1918). Son of Tomás Guido, who represented Rosas in Brazil, Guido y Spano spent much of his life trying to escape his father's reputation. He also wrote some lovely poetry and two volumes of essays collected in *Ráfagas* (1879). While politics occupies much of Guido y Spano's attention, particularly in his powerful critiques of Mitre, Sarmiento, and the Paraguayan War, he also left graceful essays on literature characterized by gorgeous prose and loving references to classical literature.

17

The essay of nineteenth-century Mexico, Central America, and the Caribbean

Martin S. Stabb

Given the fact that in the early decades of the nineteenth century northern Spanish America, except for Cuba and Puerto Rico, had only just proclaimed its independence it is not surprising that the many issues raised by nationhood (achieved or hoped for) should be of primary concern among the region's essayists. Thus the essay tends to be a "serious" genre, one in constant contact with the realities of the times, with what Spanish Americans often refer to as *la problemática nacional*. While more literary essays were produced – texts in which the author gives free rein to imagination, to speculation on eternal questions, to writing in which stylistic elegance, word play, or humor take precedence over content – the works that are remembered were those that reflected the pressing issues of the period. Although some of the essayists sought original, or at least "American," formulations of these problems, more often than not they were guided by existing European social and political thought. Thus, during the first half of the century the thinking of the Enlightenment was very much in evidence, while during the latter half various versions of Positivism and social organicism held sway.

Our survey begins with Mexico and the work of José Joaquín Fernández de Lizardi (1776–1827). Best known as the author of the long, rambling picaresque novel *El Periquillo Sarniento* (Mexico, 1816) [*The Itching Parrot*], along with other works of didactic fiction, Lizardi was also a prolific journalist and pamphleteer: his major efforts in this area were *El pensador mexicano* (Mexico, 1812–1814), the *Alacena de frioleras* (Mexico, 1815), the *Conductor eléctrico* (Mexico, 1820), the *Conversaciones del payo y el sacristán* (Mexico, 1824–1825), the *Correo semanario* (Mexico, 1826–1827), and a host of uncollected tracts and pamphlets. Like his North American counterpart Benjamin Franklin, he even published several almanac-calendars. There is no single definitive essay or book of essays in this vast production. Moreover, many of his expository texts defy generic classification: for example, he frequently uses "dialogs" as vehicles for his ideas. On other occasions he casts his "essays" in the form of barely fictionalized allegories wherein "Truth" or "Experience" appear to the author in a dream and proceed to guide him through the city or universe. Though he reveals vast reading and encyclopedic breadth in his subject matter, one notes a constant attempt to reach an audience of only modest intellectuality. His frequent and historically important use of slang, Mexicanisms, and the like is further evidence of this. Despite the fact that Lizardi was seldom an essayist in the classical sense of the term, this substantial *corpus* of nonfictional, generically mixed prose falls under the broad rubric of *ensayismo* by virtue of the author's overriding desire to convince and to mold the opinions of his readers.

Few commentators would say that Lizardi was an original thinker or even very rigorous in adapting the ideas of others in his own writing. In general terms he reflects the eighteenth-century Enlightenment, though he typically shies away from the more radical or revolutionary implications of the century's thought. His political thinking during the struggle for independence is characterized by doubts, ambiguities, and compromise. While he could attack certain aspects of the Spanish colonial regime like the Inquisition (*Obras*, III, 172–88) he nonetheless considered Hidalgo and the early insurgents as troublemakers, guilty of a "reprehensible lack of tact" (*Obras*, III, 247). However, after suffering censorship despite the promises of the liberal Spanish Constitution, and after his disenchantment with the ill-conceived Iturbide movement, Lizardi emerges as a supporter of genuine independence. The establishment of the nation's first autonomous government and the adoption of the Constitution of 1824 led him to write some of his most interesting political essays. Two of these, "Pragmática de la libertad" and the "Constitución política de una república imaginaria" appeared in his rather charming, folksy periodical, *Conversaciones del payo y el sacristán.*

The "Constitución política" is a wonderful example of Lizardi's strengths and weaknesses as a thinker and writer. Like so many of his texts it is framed as a dialog rather than in conventional essay form. The interlocutors, the *payo* (rustic, bumpkin) and the somewhat more cultured sexton are quite a pair to discuss political theory, economics, penology and the like. One suspects that Lizardi – always the educator – hoped that the ordinary Mexican of the day could identify with these types and so become more involved in public affairs. Thus, when the more humble *payo* suggests that ordinary citizens might not possess the education or background to write laws and reform the nation, the ebullient sexton informs him that patriotism and good intentions can make up for any such lack: "I've seen ranchers that seem to be men of letters and men of letters that appear to be ranchers; so heck! Let's get going and fix up our republic just the way we want to!" (*Obras*, V, 16).

The 116 "articles" of the "Constitución" reveal a curious *mélange* of serious fundamental political notions along with many trivial, perhaps facetious details. In a serious section on land tenure and reform, Lizardi calls for limiting holdings to a mere "four square leagues." He notes that in Mexico there are many rich people who have "ten, twelve or more properties...some of which take four days to traverse, while there are millions of individuals who don't own a handsbreadth of their own land" (*Obras*, v, 435). The sections on government organization, crime and punishment, economics, freedom of expression, and the role of the military are especially rich. As for government, we find Lizardi to be a strong proponent of the separation of powers and a militant monitor of legislative propriety: ecclesiastics, while they could be elected as deputies, would have to abstain on votes involving church interests. The foregoing provides only a small sample of Lizardi's vast essayistic production. Scattered through the pages of *El pensador*, the *Alacena*, the *Conversaciones* and his many other works one finds evidence of an amazing range of interests: reforming (not abolishing) bullfighting, critical notes on gambling, attacks on merchants who overcharge, the reform of the military, comments on the tyranny of fashion, darts aimed at doctors and pharmacists, the benefits of free trade, discussions on elementary education, and a host of other topics. While he could produce some of the most stultifying prose to be found in Spanish, he could also write pages exceedingly rich in folksy humor. At times he reveals an upper- or middle-class disdain for ordinary people, yet he apparently relished depicting the everyday speech, foibles, and idiosyncrasies of the *payos* and *pícaros* that people his pages.

As the writings of Lizardi suggest, Mexico's break from Spain was, except on the strictly political level, rather superficial. The colonial legacy of a conservative, economically well-entrenched church, of a self-serving ambitious military and of a corrupt, inefficient administrative bureaucracy remained to plague the nation during the early decades of independence. In the work of historians, *pensadores* and essayists, certain key terms soon come to reflect the desire to improve the young republic: thus the words *Liberalismo* and *reforma* dominate the work of many intellectuals. The late 1850s saw the institutionalization of these concepts in the Reform Laws, the adoption of which Mexicans view as a watershed event in the history of the nation. There are a number of writers who reflect the *reforma* and the genesis of the Mexican Liberal party: José María Mora (1794–1850), Manuel C. Rejón (1799–1849), and Miguel Ramos Arizpe (1775–1843). During the same period Lucas Alamán (1792–1853) raised a strong voice as a defender of traditionalism. But with the possible exception of Mora, these writers were essentially historians rather than essayists. By contrast, Ignacio Ramírez (1818–1879), nicknamed "El

Nigromante" ["The Sorcerer"], not only represents the reformist–liberal tradition in full flower, but is also a man of letters of considerable merit.

Somewhat like Lizardi, Ramírez was a polygraph: it would be difficult to find any single essay that sums up the essence of his thought. Unlike the *Pensador mexicano*, Ramírez did not identify linguistically or psychologically with the lower classes, though he appreciated the intellectual potential of the ordinary Mexican, especially the Indian. His literary style is correct, clear-cut, and perhaps more formal than that of his predecessor. As a member of Juárez's cabinet, he became deeply involved in politics and many of his journalistic articles, speeches, and letters reflect political concerns. Like Lizardi he was also intensely interested in education. But what Ramírez is best remembered for is his unremitting attack on religion, more specifically on that version of Catholicism brought to the New World by Spain. Indeed, it is often difficult to determine whether his primary target is the church as a religious institution or as an expression of Spanish values. There is certainly no doubt regarding Ramírez's basic attitude toward *la madre patria*: "One should have no illusions; the last nation in the world that other countries would wish to resemble are the Spaniards....Just one drop of Spanish blood, when it has coursed through the veins of an American, has produced...the Santa Annas, has engendered traitors" (*Obras*, I, 319).

What seems to anger Ramírez most about Spain's role in Mexico is that Iberian institutions, values, and attitudes represented an all-embracing alien culture imposed upon the native and emerging *mestizo* society. In one of his most significant texts, the Mazatlán speech of September 16, 1863, he makes this point very clear: "Mexico was the new Spain; Andalusian dances, the idolatrous festivals of Castile's villages, the ridiculous court dress, Góngora's literature dominating the pulpit and the forum...and saints, taking charge of our pleasures, our sorrows...our dining tables and our beds; everything was Spanish: to go to Heaven, one had to go by way of Spain" (*Obras*, I, 152). In other contexts Ramírez berates the church on the question of divorce, on the celibacy of the clergy, and on other issues. As one of the principal authors of the *Reforma* he insisted that the church should only exist within and subordinate to the secular government: he would withhold citizenship from clerics who might seek economic or political privilege by virtue of their special status. Finally, Ramírez even objected to the use of the phrase "In the name of God" at the beginning of Mexico's new constitution of 1857. He explains his position by noting that this invocation suggests that the document, and the government which it was to establish, existed by virtue of divine right.

Ramírez's basic ideas on the form of Mexico's new government and its relation to society are closely linked to his reaction against the Spanish colonial heritage. Thus it is not surprising that he should support freedom of religion and of the press. But Ramírez went considerably beyond these rather typical liberal positions in pressing for children's rights, for legal protection of illegitimates and especially for women's rights. His attitudes, while not advanced by contemporary standards, represent fairly open views for the mid nineteenth century: "Everywhere people have tried to base the inferior social position of women on the inferiority of their makeup; to make this inferiority even greater they have confused ...certain transient defects; and from this true or exaggerated inferiority they have deduced a lessening of rights which would not be applied to men except in the case of a scientific or judicial declaration of incompetence" (*Obras*, II, 234). And in his extensive writings on education he vigorously refutes those who hold women to be inferior when he declares, with only minor reservations, that "the education of women should be the same as that of men" (*Obras*, II, 186).

On more technical matters of governmental form and function Ramírez pressed for the direct election of officials (he feared the politicking of intermediate electoral bodies) and for the establishment of active, independent local governments. Problems, he held, are best solved at the "grass roots" level; he also believed that neither utopian regimes of the future nor existing central governments work very efficiently. In some of these texts one can almost sense an anarchistic tone. For example, in a short piece of 1868, "Principios sociales y principios adminstrativos," he goes so far as to state that "It is difficult to prove the goodness and need for governments, but it cannot be hidden from anyone that this system of handing over communal affairs to...agents breeds corruption and tyranny" (*Obras*, II, 7). In short, while he agrees that man cannot live in isolation, that "natural" productive associations are necessary, he believes that government, and especially central government, will always be at odds with these less formal but more genuine groupings.

It would be erroneous, however, to emphasize this seemingly anarchistic trend in Ramírez's thinking. Typical of nineteenth-century Liberalism, his critique of government administration derives more from his faith in the progressive, "positive" role of untrammeled economic activity – *laissez-faire* – than from any dedication to genuine anarchism. Perhaps his most extreme statement of this position, and one that reveals the growing Positivism of the period, appears in the same essay: "From now on the world will not study itself in kings or congresses, but in banks, in companies, in entrepreneurial organizations where even the very poor can become powerful, where the general welfare is not translated into royal celebrations nor in showy monuments...but rather in railroads, in scientific enlightenment, in asylums for the unfortunate, in educational institutions for our youth and in the amassing of capital" (*Obras*, II, 89).

Unlike some of the social Darwinists of the late nineteenth century,

Ramírez believed the native American to be fully educable. He felt, moreover, that the melioration of the Mexican Indian, whose lot had not improved under independence, was clearly a major responsibility of the nation. While he appears to be genuinely interested in preserving the indigenous cultural and linguistic heritage, he would not wish the Indian to pursue a life of picturesque isolation: "They should participate with their intelligence...in industry, in agriculture, in commerce, in politics, and in the theatre of civilization and progress" (*Obras*, II, 183). To accomplish all this he advises that they not be taught catechism, metaphysics, or classical history. Rather, the Indians – women as well as men – should have a modern education centered on science, law, civics, etc. Finally, in a note that prefigures the basic outlook of twentieth-century *indigenista* thinking, Ramírez suggests that "the Indians must know themselves" (*Obras*, II, 184).

During the two decades from the *Reforma* of 1857 to Ramírez's death in 1879 Mexico underwent an important transition. The complex details of the period cannot be discussed here: it is sufficient to note that by the end of the 1870s Porfirio Díaz's authoritarian regime, based upon a loosely defined but pervasive sociopolitical philosophy, Positivism, became firmly entrenched under the leadership of Porfirio Díaz and his advisors, the *científicos*. A concise, objective assessment of the *Porfiriato* is rather difficult to make. Justo Sierra (1848–1912), a major essayist who held important positions within the regime and was yet one of its more articulate critics, is probably the best spokesman for the period. He was, in addition, a contributor to or director of several of the most important periodicals of the period, a member of the national Chamber of Deputies, a Supreme Court Justice, Undersecretary and then Minister of Public Education, and finally, one of the founders – if not the guiding spirit – of the National University. In addition to all these activities, he found time to produce some fifteen volumes of expository prose. Today he is perhaps best known for his interpretive history, *México: su evolución social* [*The Political Evolution of the Mexican People*] and his historical biography, *Juárez, su obra y tiempo* (Mexico, 1905). Sierra was not a literary stylist comparable to his South American contemporary, José Enrique Rodó, or to his twentieth-century compatriot Alfonso Reyes: yet his historical writings, his speeches, and especially his journalistic pieces reveal qualities typical of the best essayistic writing, especially the ability to see specifics in a broad context.

At first glance Sierra seems to be a typical proponent of that distinctive blend of Positivism and social Darwinism that came to dominate much of Spanish American thought during the latter decades of the nineteenth century. Citations from his texts would appear to support this point strongly; note for example: "the word *social organization* is not a metaphor; it is the expression of a biological fact: society is an organism in the real sense of the word" (*Obras*, V, 213). On closer examination, however, it becomes clear that Sierra viewed mankind and society in much broader terms than those associated with a narrowly conceived scientism. His polemics with certain hard-core Positivists – Gabino Barreda, for example – bear this out. In a well-wrought essay of 1874 dealing with the question of including philosophy in the National Preparatory School's curriculum, he accepts Positivism as a method, but not as an all-embracing world-view: "We believe in the existence of the spirit....For, to put it succinctly, there is something spontaneous and original in man, there exists that *quid propium* of which the eminent Claude Bernard speaks....that which doesn't pertain to chemistry, nor to physics...something that enters into the realm of ideas...these things are in the province of spirit" (*Obras*, VIII, 23). It is significant that the foregoing was written when Sierra was only in his mid twenties; his distrust of orthodoxy, whether philosophic or scientific, was evident throughout his career. Some thirty-five years later his magnificent "Discurso en el teatro Arbeu" (Mexico City, 1908), often referred to as the "dudemos" ["Let us doubt"] speech, illustrates the persistence and development of this basic attitude. In it he expresses some remarkably modern ideas regarding the limitations of science, the need for "perpetual discussion" and the revision of scientific concepts.

Sierra's intellectual honesty and basic open-mindedness are especially evident in his analysis of Mexico's educational needs. This subject, moreover, can be seen as the key to his thought, since in a very real sense "El Maestro," as he was called, saw the entire nation as a vast classroom: his political thinking, his ideas on society and his view of future Mexican culture were all inextricably linked to this basic vision. Underlying his many essays, articles, and speeches on education is a simple idea: people, virtually all people, are educable. It should be noted that this apparently innocent notion could be, and was, disputed in nineteenth-century Mexico. Closely related to this belief was his conviction that education should be obligatory in any viable democratic society. Recalling Mexican experience during the early years of independence, Sierra notes that where formal democracy exists without effective, free, obligatory education, it quickly degenerates and the people fall into the hands of corruption and tyranny. Education was central to Sierra's thinking in another very fundamental way: as one who accepted social organicism – with reservations – he held that for the selective process to function properly a broad-based primary educational system must be provided, along with its secondary and higher components.

The United States often served as Sierra's model for development and modernity. His admiration, however, was not unqualified and he clearly saw Mexican identity as something which must be protected and nurtured. Here again, the role of education was decisive. In a pithy essay, "Americanismo" (Mexico, 1884), he discusses a plan by the government of Coahuila, a border state, to invite a North American Baptist group to establish a teacher training institution in the city of Saltillo. While he frequently endorsed freedom of religion and the right of all religious groups to offer instruction, he foresees a possibly divisive effect in having Yankee Protestants take on a responsibility that he felt belonged to a Mexican state. Aside from the legal questions involved, Sierra was deeply concerned because this act would violate the "much more sacred law of patriotism." His sense of *mexicanidad* was offended by the image of young Mexicans standing in awe before the foreigners: "No, we will not permit the money of Mexicans to be spent...in training teachers who might learn to kneel before American greatness and to disdain their homeland....We desire, by contrast, that they be taught not to take as their ideal the unfamiliar prosperity of the United States; this would be fatal and would result in producing hopelessness and desperation" (*Obras*, VIII, 139).

In his copious writings on education Sierra was very much aware that the presence of Indians, often culturally and linguistically isolated from the rest of the nation, posed special problems for a developing country. He was convinced that this group could not be ignored or relegated to second-class status. Most importantly, his adherence to social Darwinism did not lead him to accept the then widely held, fundamentally racist, view that the native American was "inferior" and hence condemned by nature to live beneath the heel of "superior" or "more fit" groups. In opposition to this notion, he considered the Indian to be fully educable and the *mestizo* to be "the dynamic factor in our history" (*Obras*, IX, 131). Perhaps Sierra's most eloquent defense of his racial views surfaced in his 1883 polemic with Francisco G. Cosmes (1850–1907), a journalist and *Positivista* of conservative learnings who attacked the view that obligatory education was practical in the context of Mexico's social and ethnic complexity. In refuting Cosmes, Sierra reveals his firm conviction that the "inferiority" of any group is not an innate characteristic but simply a matter of inferior education: "given equality of circumstances, of two individuals or two groups of people, the one that is less educated is inferior" (*Obras*, VIII, 110). Sierra, in explaining his views that the Indian is educable and that society may be thus modified and shaped by human effort, demonstrates a remarkably critical attitude toward the doctrinaire social evolutionists, many of whom held essentially racist views.

On balance Sierra demonstrates an intellectual breadth and vision that clearly transcend the limitations of his times. His intelligent rather than blindly mechanistic understanding of evolution, his preoccupation with the total development of the Mexican nation, his recognition of the Indian's worth and his appreciation of the country's *mestizo* culture all prefigure a twentieth-century outlook.

As in the case of their northern neighbor, the agenda for Central American essayists during much of the nineteenth century was set by the pressing issues facing these emerging nations. The problems of Central American identity were, moreover, compounded by the area's proximity to Mexico (which early in the century threatened to absorb the entire area within Iturbide's imperial scheme) and by uncertainties regarding the possibility of forming a single nation encompassing the entire region. At any rate, for a brief period during the 1820s a United Provinces of Central America did exist: among its supporters was the journalist, educator, and writer, José Cecilio del Valle (1780–1834).

Although born in Honduras, Valle spent as much of his life in Guatemala as he did in his native country. In addition to his many political activities he taught economics for a number of years at Guatemala's San Carlos University and upon his death he was mourned as a citizen of both nations. Among his more important essayistic projects were the quaintly titled *Soñaba el Abad de San Pedro y yo también sé soñar* (Guatemala, 1822) in which he proposes an Hispanic American federation; a journal, *El amigo de la patria* (Guatemala, 1820) which in some respects parallels Lizard's *El pensador mexicano*; and a number of speeches, miscellaneous essays and political tracts.

Valle was typical of that important generation of early Spanish American activist writers – men like Argentina's Manuel Moreno, Venezuela's Simón Bolívar and Mexico's Fernández de Lizardi – who combined the rationalistic spirit of the Enlightenment with elements of romantic idealism. Like these more famous contemporaries, Valle also shows in his work an interesting blend of "Europeanism" along with strong Americanist sympathies. Several specific texts illustrate these diverse currents, but his essay of 1821, "América", offers perhaps the best summation of his thought. The opening paragraph is remarkable in that Valle presents pre-Columbian America as a viable entity, not merely as the object of European conquest and colonization. Despite the vast geographic separation between the Old World and the New, "Those of one hemisphere, like those of the other, were free, equal and masters of the property they possessed. The Americans knew nothing of the existence of Europe, Europeans were ignorant of that of America, and this ignorance by one and the other part of the globe insured the liberty of both" (*Pensamiento*, 107). He goes on to note that the "copper-hued" Indian had the full right to protect himself against the European invader, that "Color is no title of superiority...Copper-skinned, swarthy or white you are a man...and the essence of man gives you inviolable rights...the hand of arbitrary authority has no right to oppress you" (p.107).

At this point Valle shifts his emphasis to the future. In his optimistic view, Americans, once having fully affirmed their independence, will go on to exceed the achievements of the Europeans. He devotes the remainder of the essay to spelling out how this will come about: Spanish Americans should, he says, work hard to amass enough capital to develop the new nations, "But they will not crawl into the caverns of the earth to extract from its entrails precious metals to be sent to the other continent" (*Pensamiento*, 117) Rather, as free citizens, the people of the New World will be able to trade profitably with all nations: "Flags of all colors will brighten its ports" (p.117). In short, classical free trade will, he holds, solve most of the problems of the emerging countries. Among the accompanying benefits will be the expansion of agriculture, the growth of population both internally and through immigration. In Valle's optimistic view foreigners will be attracted by the promise, freedom and fertility of the Americas, and "they will bring skills and tools. . .European industry will flourish in the factories of America, and native sons, developing their own genius will at first imitate and later create" (*Pensamiento*, 119). Thus Americans – including the downtrodden Indians – will, he feels, "rise to the level of Europeans." He sees that eventually Spanish America will become a veritable utopia where the dictum of Valle's most admired mentor Jeremy Bentham, "the greatest good for the greatest number," would hold sway.

A half-century later Central America had yet to fulfill Valle's rosy vision: lack of economic progress and the endemic problem of dictatorship still obtained. As in Díaz's Mexico and elsewhere a frequently recommended remedy to improve government and society was the application of positivist thought to social, political, and economic problems. The foremost Central American representative of this trend was the Honduran Ramón Rosa (1848–1893); a poet, statesman, and essayist. Although he wrote a great deal on such issues as education, politics, and literature, his best-known work is the essay "The Social Constitution of Honduras" (Tegucigalpa, 1880).

In social organicist fashion Rosa begins his text with an epigraph from a biologist, Linnaeus, and with the remark that societies "live, grow and perfect themselves under the influence of ideas" (*Escritos selectos*, 9). His main point, however, is that in the case of Honduras, guiding ideas have been absent, that sheer political ambition has been the determinant of the national trajectory. He rejects the programs of both the conservative and liberal parties as signifying nothing more than "fifty years of turmoil, trivialities, and nonsense" (*Escritos*, 12). His own program, that of the Progressive party, is however quite similar to those of classical nineteenth-century Liberalism: *laissez-faire* economics and a minimum of state intervention in society. Yet he cannot recommend these policies for Central America given the region's backward state: "The application of these ideas needs firmly-rooted habits of work and order which depend on moral, intellectual and social education" (*Escritos*, 13). Since he felt these habits were lacking in Honduras, he calls for gradualism in the sense of limiting suffrage, and of maintaining a strong central government until education could bring about the desired changes in society.

Two other essays of Rosa merit at least a brief mention. The first, "Importancia de la instrucción pública" (Tegucigalpa, 1874), parallels some of the specifics incorporated into the "Social Constitution": he again calls for a system of basic popular education which would be free, secular and under state, rather than private, control. Further, he recommends the establishment of a normal school not only for the professional training of pedagogues but also for the creation of greater civic and social morality. In short, like many positivists from Comte onward, he viewed education as the great transformer of society. Finally, his brief essay "La intolerancia" (Tegucigalpa, 1892), reveals Rosa as a man of impressive intellectual probity. In it Rosa, himself a freethinker, rebukes strident "liberals" for their vehement hatred of Catholicism and for their obvious desire to suppress freedom of expression: "You liberals criticize. . .Catholics as being intolerant and yet you are even more intolerant!" (*Escritos selectos*, 338). He even speaks of "the fanatical sectarians of positivistic religions" giving futher evidence of his ability to transcend ideological orthodoxy.

There were, of course, essayists in the other nations of Central America, but few are remembered today. In Costa Rica, for example, substantial progress was being made in developing a modern educational system and other progressive institutions which would later set that nation apart from its less stable neighbors. However, there were few essayists who bore witness to these activities: what activity there was is documented by Luis Acosta Ferrero in his *Ensayistas costarricences*. Clearly there were no essayists in the nineteenth century comparable to writers such as Roberto Brenes Mesén or Joaquín García Monge who, in the early twentieth century, would establish Costa Rica's importance in the genre.

The essayists of the Hispanic Caribbean faced a somewhat different situation than did their Mexican and Central American counterparts. While the general ideological framework of the nineteenth century – the persistent influence of the Enlightenment, followed by romantic Liberalism and then by Positivism – were essentially the same throughout the region, intellectuals of Cuba and Puerto Rico had to deal with the fact that independence was a desideratum rather than a fact. Even the Dominican Republic gained its independence rather late (1844) and was subject to serious Spanish attempts to retake the former colony. Despite the political situation, the Spanish Caribbean nonetheless maintained vigorous literary activity and, in the case of the essay, produced at least two figures of continental stature: the Puerto Rican patriot and educator, Eugenio María Hostos y Bonilla (1839–1903), and one of the geniuine masters of nineteenth-century Spanish American letters, Cuba's José Martí (1853–1895).

Before discussing the work of the *apóstol*, as Martí is frequently called by his compatriots, some remarks regarding the Cuban essay of the early part of the century are in order. Three writers, all of whom were in effect philosophical essayists (or, as Spanish Americans often call such figures, *pensadores*) rather than strictly literary men, and all of whom were involved in the early separatist movement, may be noted. The first of these was Father Félix Varela y Morales (1787–1853) who, despite his religious vocation championed the study of science, rationalistic philosophy, and independence from Spain. Closely associated with Varela was José Antonio Saco (1797–1879), another defender of progressive ideas such as educational reform and the abolition of slavery. The third was the pedagogue and philosopher José de la Luz y Caballero (1810–1862), who argued for independence and, in passing, formulated an impressive refutation of the then dominant Hegelian notions of historical determinism.

While Varela, Saco, or Luz y Caballero are known chiefly to specialists in Cuban literature, the life and works of Martí have been studied, discussed, and revered by Spanish Americans of virtually all nations and of all degrees of sophistication. A magnificent poet as well as prose writer, his collected works fill some seventy volumes in one edition. His commitment to the cause of freedom, his deep humanitarianism transcending political boundaries, his dramatic life (and death), and finally the sheer literary excellence of his work are all factors that have made him a uniquely powerful presence in Spanish American letters. Martí's essayistic writing is prolific, multiform, and quite difficult to categorize. As a political exile in the United States and elsewhere he earned his living as a journalist: thus many of his finest essays first appeared in newspapers as feature articles or foreign reportage. Other essayistic texts were originally speeches devoted to the cause of Cuban independence; some were cast as literary studies; and others were primarily political pamphlets. A wide range of themes are found in this unwieldy *corpus* of writings: the Cuban question, the broad issue of Hispanic American identity, foreign cultures (especially his rich comment on the United States), and a host of social, economic, and philosophical concerns. Yet Martí wrote no extensive integrated essay as did his South American counterparts Domingo Faustino Sarmiento (1811–1888) or José Enrique Rodó (1871–1917).

Martí's position as a thinker and sociopolitical observer presents interesting problems. Though he wrote at a time when Positivism and social organicism were dominant forces in Latin America, he demonstrated remarkable independence of thought in the face of these powerful trends. Recent polemics surrounding his ideological kinship to the ideas and ideals of the Cuban Revolution of 1959 have raised additional questions. For intellectuals supporting the Castro regime Martí was clearly a precursor of the Revolution. Others, however, view him as much less radical than the *castristas* would have us believe, and in support they point to his espousal of the ideas of Simón Bolívar, Henry George, and Herbert Spencer – hardly leftists by any count. They also point to his basic affection for North America, despite his frequent censure of Yankee society. The truth may well lie somewhere between these two contrasting views. What must be remembered is that Martí was not an ideologue; rather, he was a perceptive observer whose occasional critical darts were characteristically tempered by a remarkable spirit of generosity. In short, he could point out the evil in people or the injustice in institutions while still seeking the good: he seemed incapable of hatred.

One of the clearest examples of how Martí thought may be seen in his essays on the question of race, an issue that figured prominently among Spanish Americans of the period. Martí's ideas are presented in texts such as "Mi raza" (New York, 1893), "Nuestra América" (Mexico, 1891) and in several pieces dealing with race in the United States. In all of these writings he emerges as a writer remarkably free of the virulent racism typical among the pseudo-scientific Positivists of his day: "There is no race hatred because there are no races. Sickly thinkers, thinkers who work by dim lamplight piece together and warm over bookish races that the fair observer cannot find in Nature, where the universal identity of mankind stands out. The same, eternal soul emanates forth from all, regardless of form and color" (*Obras completas* (1946), II, 112). In his most celebrated essay on this question, "Mi raza" he is even more eloquent: "Man is more than white, more than mulatto, more than black...On the field of battle all died for Cuba and the souls of whites and blacks ascended to heaven together" (*Obras*, I, 487). In the same text he states simply that "whatever divides men, everything that separates, specifies or groups them is a sin against humanity" (p.487). Martí's criticism of North American racial attitudes and policies are consistent with these views. In impassioned articles such as "El problema del negro" (Buenos Aires, 1889) ["The Negro problem"] or his "Los indios en los Estados Unidos" (Buenos Aires, 1885) ["The Indians in the United States"] he restates his remarkably modern, open views. Thus in the latter essay he points out the American Indian's apparent indolence and alcoholism are not inherent but result from a longstanding system of abuse.

Although specific concern for Cuba underlies much of Martí's thinking, the foregoing illustrates that his vision extended well beyond the limits of his native island. The single text that best reveals his fervent Spanish Americanism is unquestionably "Nuestra América" ["Our America"], a relatively short essay that may be compared with the longer and better known *Ariel* (1900) of the Uruguayan, José Enrique Rodó. Like the latter work (which it antedates by almost a decade), Martí's essay is presented as an idealistic call to Hispanic Americans to assert their own identity and to be wary of the growing material and spiritual power of the United States. Stylistically the two texts also bear some resemblance: Martí's long rolling sentences replete with parenthetical phrases and colorful imagery prefigure the *arielista* prose of the turn of the century. Yet the similarity with Rodó should not be pushed too far. One of Martí's key points is that Hispanic America should develop in harmony with its own indigenous realities, that foreign models were to be distrusted. Thus he calls for reorientation in the educational system, for youth to stop looking at the world through "French or Yankee" spectacles and for the establishment of an "American University" where the history of the Incas might be studied, even at the expense of eliminating some classical learning. As he succinctly put it, "Our Greece is preferable to the Greece which is not ours" (*Obras*, II, 108).

Throughout "Nuestra América" and elsewhere Martí speaks of Hispanic America as "*mestizo* America," underscoring its indigenous, non-European elements. He also emphasizes the decisive role of ordinary folk, those whom he calls *los hombres naturales* as opposed to "the artificially lettered." This is an interesting point and is one that distinguishes him from another near contemporary, the celebrated Argentinian essayist, Domingo Faustino Sarmiento. In a direct reference to the latter he states, "There is no conflict between civilization and barbarism, but rather between false erudition and nature" (*Obras*, II, 107). He goes on to note that uncultured "natural" people can and should govern, especially when the educated classes have not learned well the lessons of proper rule. Not surprisingly, these views have been enthusiastically received by the Castro regime in Cuba and its supporters.

Martí's references to the United States occupy an important place in his conclusion to "Nuestra América." He warns that in addition to internal dangers (the love of luxury, for example) an external threat menaces the area in the form of "an enterprising and aggressive people who are ignorant of us and disdain us." This "virile," ambitious, "pure-blooded" nation – North America – will, he fears, take advantage of Spanish America's disunity. Therefore it is incumbent upon these nations to demonstrate that they are "united in spirit and intent" (*Obras*, II, 111). Similarly, it is imperative that the United States' disdain be mitigated by a deeper knowledge of the Latin world and its people. Martí apparently believed that contact, familiarity and understanding between nations could, in fact, resolve conflict. This view distinguishes his anti-Yankeeism from that of many of his contemporaries; it is further corroborated by his eloquent and oft-quoted statement toward the end of "Nuestra América": "One must have faith in the best of man and distrust the worst of him" (*Obras*, II, 112).

The foregoing gives a rather incomplete view of Martí's essayistic writing since little has been noted of his more informal pieces. Many of these highly colored descriptions of notable events, people, and places have been anthologized. Two excellent examples of this aspect of his work would be the North American impressions "El terremoto de Charleston" (Buenos Aires, 1886) and his wonderful picture of the great blizzard of 1888, "Nueva York bajo la nieve" (Buenos Aires, 1881) ["New York under the snow"]. While these might be considered vignettes or journalistic sketches rather than essays in the strict sense, they show Martí to be a very creative, highly skilled prose writer whose manipulation of authorial viewpoint, adjectivization, and sense of structure were truly remarkable for his day and are impressive by any standard. In short, Martí, by virtue of the content, originality, and technical quality of his essays must be considered one of Spanish America's greatest cultivators of the genre.

The Cuban Enrique José Varona (1849–1933) was actually born before Martí, but his long life and the fact that many of his major works were published after Martí's death place him as writer who bridges the nineteenth and twentieth centuries. Varona's ideological trajectory begins with his adherence to a rather strong deterministic, positivist orientation. As his thought develops he gives more weight to freedom of choice, or at least to his idea that man "believes himself to be free". This notion, expressed in various forms in his *Conferencias filosóficas* (Havana, 1880–1888) suggests a kind of middle ground between outright affirmation of freedom and narrowly restrictive determinism. A number of other works show Varona's serious philosophical concerns: perhaps the best known of these is *Artículos y discursos. Literatura, política, sociología* (Havana, 1891).

Like many of his contemporaries Varona was deeply concerned about Cuba's vulnerable position with respect to the United States. In his Havana University lecture of 1905, "El imperialismo a la luz de la sociología," for example, he first addresses the general question of imperialist expansion in terms of world history and then with regard to Cuba's specific situation. As in most of his other political writings his frame of reference is clearly that of social organicism: "In the growth of any human group, we do not see laws different from those that obtain in the growth of the individual organism" (*Textos escogidos*, 22). If neighboring organisms are weak, or suffer from "defective organization" that inhibits development, then, Varona claims, they may become absorbed by the stronger, more robust entity. It is not difficult to see the direction in which his argument is moving: imperial Rome, nineteenth-century Britain, and now the United States represent powerful socio-political "organisms." Cuba, then, must take deliberate measures to ensure the new nation's development and identity. The steps by which this might be accomplished include encouraging the Cuban birthrate, diversifying the economy, and strengthening the educational system. While some aspects of this program seems to be based on positivistic thinking, Varona also appeals to more spiritual values: thus here, as in a related essay, "Los cubanos en Cuba" (Havana, 1888), he stresses the decisive role that commonly held ideals, passions and beliefs can play in shaping the national destiny.

Before leaving Varona a few remarks are in order regarding his most light-hearted essayistic work – the short, frequently humorous, mini-essays, and sketches found in his well-known collections *Desde mi belvedere* (Havana, 1907) and *Violetas y ortigas* (Madrid, 1917). The delightful vignette "No Smoking" [*sic*] is, for example, a half-serious tribute to the Cuban's inordinate fondness for tobacco as opposed to the less tolerant attitudes of Anglo-Saxon society; "Mi tarjeta," in much the same tone, examines the ritual of exchanging calling cards; "El hombre del perro" describes the symbiotic relationship of man and dog, but in this case the focus is on an oversized animal that reverses the usual rules and takes his master for a walk; and "Renan and Emerson" renders homage to those authors. In sum, these informal texts provide a very human perspective on a writer often considered to be one of the most intellectual Cubans of his era.

Puerto Rico, like Cuba, remained under Spanish domination until the very end of the nineteenth century. Not surprisingly the island's writers reflect similar concerns regarding questions of political and cultural autonomy. The life and works of Puerto Rico's leading essayist, Eugenio María Hostos (1839–1903), illustrate this situation very well. Comparable to Varona in his eclectic positivist–idealist position and somewhat like Martí in his life-long devotion to the cause of independence, events forced Hostos to become a genuine citizen of the hemisphere. Long periods of residence and pedagogic contributions to Chile and the Dominican Republic led both these countries to claim him as an honorary citizen. He was a fervent supporter of Cuban independence and, were it not for a shipwreck, would have gone to the island to take an active role in the struggle against Spain.

Though he pursued several careers, it was as a teacher and organizer of educational institutions that Hostos made his mark. A great deal of his writing reflects, and suffers from, this devotion to pedagogy. For example, his best-known work, the *Moral social*, was actually intended to be a text: its format and style are heavily didactic and reveal a mania for symmetry common among educators of the period. Throughout this work and elsewhere, Hostos frequently employs the vocabulary and catch-phrases of the social organicists. However, like Varona, just below this positivistic veneer he reveals a deep-seated idealism. This is seen in his frequent appeals to his readers' sense of *deber*, of moral commitment. In general, his manipulation of positivistic ideas in the *Moral social* and in other works leads to positions hardly typical of hard-core Darwinism. In his discussion of race, for example, he attempts to show that the apparent "inferiority" of Blacks or Indians is not the result of a genuine biological struggle but is a product of cultural forces, of what he calls *la torpeza sociológica* ["sociological stupidity"]. Throughout the essay he stresses the idea that morality, sense of duty, and the human consciousness have, like organisms, gone through developmental stages and are now clearly superior to what they were in the past. Again, despite the superficial use of positivistic notions, his stress on these ethical or "moral" values distinguishes him from orthodox social organicists.

Hostos approaches the central issue of the *Moral social* by first considering the individual, then the immediate community, followed by the national state and finally imperial states. His analysis demonstrates how his devotion to Antillean independence could modify certain positions typical of the Darwinists. While the latter might justify imperial states as the political embodiment of the "survival of the fittest," Hostos held that any strongly centralized state or empire is corrupt by its very nature in that it "absorbs the initiative of provincial and municipal organisms" (*Obras completas*, XVI, 215). In other instances he speaks of revolution as a "moral duty," though he makes only a few frontal attacks on Spain's control of Puerto Rico and Cuba.

Toward the end of the *Moral social*, Hostos examines a number of institutions, professions, and miscellaneous "activities of life." This section of the essay contains several curious items: a diatribe against the modern novel as a "necessarily unwholesome" genre; a discussion of religion that reveals his appreciation of Protestantism (and, by extension, of Anglo-Saxon culture); and a rather critical analysis of journalism. In sum, Hostos's well-meaning essay was designed to instruct, uplift and provide moral guidance for its readers: while one can respect his intentions, as an example of consistent or original thought it misses the mark. However, in fairness to Hostos, it should be noted that this was only one of his many essayistic works. In fact, some of his lesser-known texts may indeed provide better examples of his expository prose. In this regard critics have praised his speeches, certain literary essays – his study of *Hamlet*, for example – and many brief informal sketches describing famous people and places.

In retrospect the nineteenth-century essayists of northern Spanish America were so deeply and actively involved in the affairs of their new nations – or nations to be – that their literary activities might appear secondary. Yet in a few cases, for example those of Martí or perhaps Sierra, the quality of their writing would have given them a place among the major essayists of Spanish America regardless of their contributions in the non-literary sphere.

18

The gaucho genre
Josefina Ludmer

Introduction

The gaucho genre[1] or gaucho poetry originates in the Río de la Plata region at the beginning of the nineteenth century. Its constitutive elements include: the traditional Spanish songs and ballads that were disseminated by the Spanish explorers and conquerors from as early as the sixteenth century, the poetry of the *payadores* (illiterate peasants who, accompanied by their guitars, roamed the country singing ballads and often competing against each other in *payadas* or *contrapuntos*), the dramatic essays that brought to the stage the dialogues in rustic language of the colonial peasantry, and, finally, contemporary "cultivated" poetry. From the traditional sources, the genre adopts its octosyllabic meter and strophic forms; from the poetry of the *payadores*, it appropriates the character of the gaucho-singer, together with many tones and themes of his song; the dialogue, meanwhile, is inherited from the primitive theatre. But the gaucho genre was written, in its entirety, by literate, urban poets, many of whom also wrote neoclassical and romantic poetry. These poets, who were sometimes involved in either the military or in politics, utilized the rustic language of the gauchos and politicized it, on the basis of the wars of independence, which can be designated as the beginning of the genre. Some critics look for the genre's origins in the last years of the eighteenth century, during which colonial Argentina battled with Portugal and, more specifically, in an anonymous one-act farce entitled "El amor de la estanciera," which was staged in the last decade of the century and made reference to the Argentinian–Portuguese war. This short play

---

[1] *Translator's note*: The word "género" in Spanish means both literary genre and sexually marked gender. The double meaning is not translatable into English as a single word, but is probably best rendered by an orthographic play that remits to both semantic possibilities: something along the lines of gen(d)re. Ludmer's reading of the "género gauchesco" subversively lends itself to both semantic fields and can be interpreted as a way to think not only about a literary category, but also about sexual difference. When the term "genre" appears in the English text, therefore, both meanings should be considered.

marked the emergence of patriotic dialogues in a rustic language. The poems of Pantaleón Rivarola, against the 1806 British invasion of Buenos Aires, can also be considered antecedents to the gaucho genre. But it is not until the appearance of Bartolomé Hidalgo's *cielitos* and patriotic dialogues that the genre is truly constituted as such. Hidalgo's works underscore, moreover, one of the genre's central operations: the transformation of lyric and romantic themes into political and military ones. The most important writers of the genre were, in addition to Hidalgo, Hilario Ascasubi, Luis Pérez, Estanislao del Campo, Antonio Lussich, and José Hernández.

The distinctive trait of the genre is the appropriation, in verse, of the gaucho's oral register. The question of the gaucho's identity has been the source of numerous studies and polemics. Polemics, aside, however, the gauchos can be defined as illiterate peasants (often the sons – or descendants – of an Indian mother and a *conquistador* father), who were landless, and sometimes vagrant, and who comprised a significant military and political (as well as labor) force in the years between the wars of independence (1810–1821) and the definitive constitution of the Argentinian state (1880). These dates mark the opening and the closure of the genre. The gauchesque poets wrote as if it were a gaucho speaking or singing in his own words, style, and tone, to transmit his ideas to his troops or party. But it is not merely a question of political propaganda. The gaucho genre is one of the fundamental mediators between "civilization" and "barbarism" as well as one of the seminal discourses of nation (and of nationalism) in the Río de la Plata. The genre's culmination is found in José Hernández's *Martín Fierro* (1872), the classic text of Argentinian literature and culture.

Limits of the genre

Two intertwined functional chains can serve to mark the boundaries of the gaucho genre.

Laws

The first generic boundary is popular illegality. On one hand, the so-called "rural delinquency" (the wandering gaucho, landless, without a stable job or address, the well-known equation: dispossessed = delinquent) and, on the other, as an objective correlative, the existence of a dual system of justice that differentiates urban and rural: the law of vagrants and its corollary, the laws of *levas*[2] or conscription, ruled over everything in the backlands. This distinction is in turn bound to the existence of a

---

[2] *Translator's note*: Recruitment for compulsory military service, specifically the enforced recruitment of vagrants, who were sent off to fight wars.

central, written law that in a provincial setting is confronted by an oral, traditional, consuetudinary code – the juridical ordering of rules and presciptions upon which the rural community is founded. The gaucho's delinquency is nothing but a byproduct of the difference between these two juridical codes and between the differential application of one over the other; it responds, furthermore, to a practical necessity: to provide laborers for the landowners and soldiers for the army.

Wars

The second boundary of the gaucho genre is constituted by the Revolution and the wars of independence (1810–1818), which inaugurate the military initiation of the gaucho and his demarginalization. Together, the laws and the wars establish a functional chain which effectively unifies and gives meaning to the genre:

(a) utilization of the "delinquent" gaucho at the service of the patriotic army;

(b) utilization of the gaucho's oral register (his voice) at the service of a written culture: the gaucho genre; and furthermore,

(c) utilization of the genre to integrate the gaucho into a "civilized" (read liberal and governmental) lawfulness.

The chain, almost circular in composition, opens with the texts of the Uruguayan Bartolomé Hidalgo (written between 1818 and 1821) and closes with *La vuelta de Martín Fierro* (1879) by the Argentinian José Hernández.

Voice and legality modulate from war and army to national statehood. It is this transition and this modulation that constitute the history of the genre's form.

The chain not only marks the time of the genre and gives it meaning, it also narrates the passage between "delinquency" and "civilization" and positions the genre as one of the producers of that transition. It postulates, moreover, at its center, a definitive parallelism between the use of the gaucho's body by the army and the use of his voice by the literate culture. It is through this very use of the body, that literally takes the gaucho from one field (the pampas) to another (the battlefield), that the voice is born: the first fictitious speaker in gaucho literature is the gaucho who is both singer and patriot. The voice, the register, appears in written form, hypercodified, and subject to a series of formal, metric, and rhythmic conventions; it passes, moreover, through the disciplinary institution of written poetry, in much the same way that the gaucho passes through the army, and is transformed into a literary sign. The two institutions, army and poetry, embrace and complement one another. In verse, the gaucho can "sing" or "speak" for all precisely because he fights in the country's army: his right to a voice rests on his right to bear arms in the defense of his country. Because he has weapons, he needs a voice, or rather, because he has weapons, he assumes another voice. What arises therefrom is the position that defines the gaucho genre from the outset: language as weapon. Voice as law and voice as weapon intertwine in the chains of the genre.

The word "gaucho" in the gaucho's own words[3]

The militarization of the rural sector during the Wars of Independence in the Río de la Plata region and the consequent emergence[4] of a new social sign, the patriot gaucho, can serve as the bases of the genre inasmuch as they provide the gaucho's verbal register with access to the statute of literary language, its only written representation. War provides not only the foundations of the gaucho genre, but also its subject matter and its logic. Furthermore, it may be said that the semantic transformation of the word "gaucho" at once inaugurates and constitutes the genre. The new locutions – "brave," "patriotic" – give rise to a scandal (the same one produced by the Revolution): they are added to the definition of the term "gaucho," merging with its former meaning of "delinquent," without altogether erasing it. The meaning remains in oscillation; the semantic indefiniteness coincides with the gaucho's own vacillation between accepting discipline or deserting. The genre intervenes and dramatizes this indefiniteness. It seeks to make the oscillation/vacillation indifferent by means of definitions; not only does it assume the voice of the patriot to define the gaucho, but also to define the delinquent/that of the delinquent. The word "gaucho" is thus defined/spoken in the gaucho's own voice, in his own words. Because there are two meanings inscribed in the term "gaucho," a new one and a pre-existent one which continues to resound, because there is a differential and dislocated system of laws and of military and economic worlds that applies to the gaucho, and finally, because he can choose either discipline or desertion, there is use of the differential *voice* of the gaucho.

The second functional chain is thereby inserted into the center of the first, somewhere between the use of the gaucho's body by the army and that of his voice by a culture, and has/possesses the written word. This second chain is the chain of the term and its meanings:

---

[3] *Translator's note*: The Spanish text here (and throughout this section) reads "La voz gaucho en la voz del gaucho." Like "género" (see note 1, above) the word "voz" is imbued with two meanings (one of which is necessarily sacrificed in the English translation), that are at play thoughout Ludmer's text: "voz" means voice but also word, locution.

[4] *Translator's note*: Here, again, the Spanish "emergencia" incorporates a double meaning that is lost in translation: "emergencia" is translatable as both "emergence" and "emergency." Ludmer's use of the word exploits the semantic duplicity that colors the originary moment (emergence) with a sense of urgent necessity (emergency).

(a) the army's use of the gaucho adds a different meaning to the word "gaucho";

(b) the meanings of the word "gaucho" are defined in the use of the differential voice of the gaucho: the gaucho genre; and furthermore,

(c) the genre defines the meaning (the sense) of the differential uses of the gaucho.

The use of the gaucho's voice implies a specific mode of construction of that voice. The genre explores the meaning of the word "gaucho" by submitting it to precise rules: frames, limits, interlocutions, distortions, and silences. Moreover, the genre, like the army and the law, serves to define the word "gaucho"; it can substitute the law (which defines him as "patriot"), inasmuch as it defines/determines the conditions of one and the other, and their meanings, in the very construction of the gaucho's voice. Genre defines the possible uses of the term and with it, of the body; it specifies what a gaucho is, how a gaucho can be divided into legal and illegal, "good" and "evil," what he is good for, and what his place is/his function and his place; all this in the gaucho's own voice. If the gaucho is good for anything, the word has meaning and a possible use in literature; if he is unusable, withdrawn, the word "gaucho" takes on a negative meaning. The genre explores the meaning of the word "gaucho" in the gaucho's own words; the use of the gaucho's words becomes identical with the use of the gaucho. The genre is a treatise on the differential uses of the voices and the words that define the meanings – the senses – of the uses of the body.

The outlining of the genre's boundaries by the two chains separate the world of the gaucho genre (that which uses the gaucho's voice) from the world inhabited by all other literature, that of the written word. On the one side, Sarmiento's *Facundo* (1845), Echeverría's *El matadero* (1838), [*The Slaughterhouse*], Pedro de Angelis's *Biografía de Rosas* (1829), Alberdi's *Bases* (1852), Mansilla's *Excursión a los indios ranqueles* (1870). On the other side, the genre. The frontier zone that mediates between the two camps is occupied by the links of the two chains, which form rings or alliances between the uses of the gaucho's voice and the written word.

Distribution of voices

In its emergence, the genre demonstrates the operation that defines it: the linking of two verbal zones: the oral and the written. In and among those zones it distributes tones, pronouncements, names; it assigns functions and hierarchies. The first operation consists of constructing the gaucho's word as "spoken voice": the verse register and the context of its emission belongs to an oral culture. Bartolomé Hidalgo (1788–1822) founded the genre by tracing out the first written distribution of the gaucho's voice. In his second dialogue, the written word pronounces and defines that voice from outside the text, in the title ("Nuevo diálogo patriótico," 1821) and subtitle ("Entre Ramón Contreras, gaucho de la Guardia del Monte y Chano, capataz de una estancia en las islas del Tordillo"). The title and subtitle function as the first frame of the texts. The second, internal frame is found at the opening of the poems in the textualization of the oral context wherein the song, or in this case, the dialogue, takes place. The texts incorporate and represent the situation of singing a *cielito* or of the meeting and dialogue between two friends: the hearer is made present in the song or dialogue of an idle moment (with greetings and the offering of drinks). The transition from the oral scene to the written text effects a "production of reality." In other words, there is a literate writer who, from the outside, writes, "represents," or "quotes" that which the "oral authors" "sing" or "say". The first rule of the genre is the fiction inherent in the written reproduction of the spoken word of the other *as* the word of the other and not of the writing subject. The second rule is the construction of an oral space, the frame of the "spoken voice," in the text's interior. The two voices are distinctly separated. The written frame of the title/subtitle can be broadened and becomes autonomous, to the point of constituting the "Carta a Zoilo Miguens" in the first part of *Martín Fierro*, or the "Cuatro palabras de conversación con los lectores" in the second. The written word "gives" voice to the oral "speaker," who is constituted as an interior fold relative to the written text: effect of the subject. The fictional relation creates the alliance that defines the genre between the written word and the spoken voice. The two frames (the title and the scene of oral representation) contain the text itself, that which the gaucho "sings" or "speaks." And what he sings or speaks is nothing but the convergence or alliance between the two words: the narration or celebration of political and military incidents or of the revolutionary process (until *Fausto*). In the oral scene, rapidly transformed into convention (and thus a possible object of parody), the gaucho's voice speaks of the political, of the official realm, of the public life of the country. The intonation of the gaucho's voice and the military and political enunciation are thus wed, and this pairing is in turn reflected in the marriage of a traditional context of oral diffusion with modern journalism. The genre appeared at the outset as a form of popular journalism; it circulated precisely in this manner, through leaflets and handbills. It also circulated, through its dialogues, as a form of popular theatre, giving rise to the two subgenres which divided the gaucho genre from the beginning: texts in song form [*cielitos*] and texts in dialogue form. One of the characteristics of a literature for the people, and for a new audience, is that it represents, in its interior, the manner of its circulation or reproduction: a song, a dialogue between two countrymen, or one who reads aloud for another.

The two "characters" or voices that speak in Hidalgo's text are that of the gaucho Contreras, the illiterate singer of *cielitos* and that of Jacinto Chano, the "capataz" [foreman] who can read and write. The popular zone dramatizes the warring dialogue with the enemy and accommodates the genre's polemological register into the zone of the song: it is the basic attitude of the *cielitos*, language-as-weapon: Contreras's position. The zone of the written word is propagandistic and didactic; it is directed at the gauchos, identified as allies, and constitutes the basic attitude of the dialogues, language-as-law: Chano's position. The alliance between the two positions is at once a poetic and political affiliation between a new, revolutionary culture and a traditional one. The writing of this alliance, postulated on reality and realized in literature, constitutes the logic of the gaucho genre as well as the agent of its historic transformation. According to the function of the written voices and the allegiances of war, the distribution of the different parts of the verbal pact (which is political, military, juridical, and economic) modulates until the genre's closure in *La vuelta de Martín Fierro*.

The different allegiances brought about by the genre produced a result that was unique in the culture of Río de la Plata: the popularization and "oralization" of the political (as well as of the written, the "literary"), and, conversely, the politicization and textualization (that is, the writing) of that which belonged to a popular, oral culture. The gaucho genre constituted a political literary language; it politicized popular culture, leaving an indelible, founding mark upon it. The genre also popularized, oralized, and politicized the writings of European culture; there is not a single text in the gaucho genre that does not somehow contain these writings – from Hidalgo's paraphrase of the *Social Contract* to the narration of the opera *Fausto*. European literature can manifest itself in the genre as a literary tendency (especially in those writers of gaucho literature who also wrote more "civilized" poetry like the "neoclassical" Hidalgo or the "romantic" del Campo), or as a "civilizing" political program translated to the gaucho orality (such as Hilario Ascasubi's annotated commentaries to the newspaper *El Comercio del Plata*), or, even, as a series of anti-European intimations (as in the texts of Luis Pérez). There is no text in the genre that omits the European word and the European culture of its writer. Not even *El gaucho Martín Fierro* (*La ida*), a text that seems alien to anything European, can escape the tendency; it may be posited that its publication together with "El camino transandino," a proposal for modernization written in a very literary language, serves, precisely, to reestablish the genre's constitutive duality, although doing so only through the physical contiguity of two otherwise autonomous texts.

Tones of voices

The fundamental tones of the gaucho genre are the challenge and the lament, both borrowed from the voice of the *payadores*. Bartolomé Hidalgo, gaucho founder, distributed both tones and voices in his first *cielito*[5] and in his first dialogue. In "Cielito que compuso un gaucho para cantar la canción de Maipú" (1818), the first gaucho text inasmuch as it is the first that identifies the voice of the singer as that of a gaucho, the challenge to the Spanish enemy can distinctly be read:

> Cielito, cielo que sí,
> le dijo el sapo a la rana,
> canta esta noche a tu gusto
> y nos veremos mañana.
>
> [Oh, Heavens, my heavens, yes,
> said the toad to the frog,
> sing all you want tonight,
> because tomorrow you'll meet me.]

and

> Cielito, digo que no,
> no embrome amigo Fernando
> si la patria ha de ser libre,
> para qué anda reculando.
>
> [Oh, Heavens, I say, no way,
> no tricks, my pal King Fernando, [of Spain]
> if the country is to be independent,
> why would you now move backwards.]

The song's popular, "oral" voice is directly addressed to the enemy as a dare; it constitutes language-as-weapon, both military and political. It is accompanied by a "high," solemn, written voice which gives meaning and direction to the oral voice:

> Viva nuestra libertad
> y el general San Martín,
> y publíquelo la fama
> con su sonoro clarín.
>
> Cielito, cielo que sí,
> de Maipú la competencia
> consolidó para siempre
> nuestra augusta independencia.

[5] *Translator's note*: The *cielito* was a popular form of song and dance that began with a refrain in which the word appeared. In the refrain the word may mean "Heavens," or could be a term of endearment. It is also used for the poem to address itself. The *cielito* became politicized during the wars of independence.

[Long live our liberty,
and General San Martín,
and let fame's loud clarion
proclaim it far and wide.

Oh Heavens, heavens, oh, yes,
in the Maipú battlefield
was forever and ever sealed
our most solemn independence.]

The genre constituted the message of war through its defiant tone and its
verbal duel; it created direction, objectives, and a space for the words of
the popular rebellion, linking them at every step with a universal code of
fame, liberty, independence, and the hero who leads the battle. The code
of universal reason gives meaning to the violence and legitimates it; it
represents the literate zone of the alliance. It is the two new protagonists,
the revolutionary ideologist and the wartime soldier, who join their words
in the emergence of the genre. The tones of voices are simultaneously
verbal actions, positions, and functions in and of the alliance.

The lamenting tone appears in Hidalgo's first dialogue, "Diálogo
patriótico interesante" (1821) in the voice of the literate Chano:

> Pues bajo de ese entender
> empriestemé su atención
> y le diré cuanto siente
> este pobre corazón;
> que, como tórtola amante
> que a su consorte perdió
> y que anda de rama en rama
> publicando su dolor,
> ansí yo, de rancho en rancho
> y de tapera en galpón
> ando triste y sin reposo
> cantando, con ronca voz
> de mi patria los trabajos,
> de mi destino el rigor.
>
> (lines 69–82)

[And so, with this understanding,
please, pay attention to me,
and I will let you know how
this broken heart suffers so,
and how, like a lovesick turtledove
who has lost her mate, goes
from twig to branch,
making public its despair,
I go from ranch to ranch,
and from shed to stall,

sad and without a break,
singing in a hoarse voice
the trials of my motherland
and harshness of my destiny.]

If the defiant tone constitutes the position of language-as-weapon, then the lamenting tone introduces language-as-law: Chano, literate and lamenting, inaugurates the figure of "the knowledgeable gaucho" and the characteristic sequence of the didactic dialogues. This sequence, reiterated throughout the genre, develops in the following manner: recognition of the knowledgeable gaucho's knowing by the individual to whom the lesson is addressed; lament over difference before the law (rich and poor, gauchos and non-gauchos); enunciation of the written law (above all, definition of theft and its punishment); and the division of the gauchos as either legal or illegal. Propagation of the category of "crime" among the gauchos (whose own code did not include the principle of private property) is, precisely, one of the goals of the lamenting lesson during a peaceful juncture.

The modulation of challenges and laments traces the history of the genre. Challenges are directed at the political enemy or the rival:

> Allá va Cielito y más Cielo
> Cielito de la Ensenada
> Al que ande sin la divisa
> Arrimale una topada.
> (Luis Pérez, "Cielito Federal" in *Torito de los Muchachos*, no. 17,
> October 14, 1830)

> [Here you go, *Cielito*,[6] and more *Cielito*,
> *Cielito* from Ensenada,
> if a man has no insignia,
> run him over with your horse.]

> Mira, gaucho salvajón,
> que no pierdo la esperanza
> y no es chanza,
> de hacerte probar qué cosa
> es Tin tin y Refalosa.
> (Hilario Ascasubi, "La Refalosa" in *Paulino Lucero o Los Gauchos del Río
> de la Plata, cantando y combatiendo contra los tiranos de las Repúblicas
> Argentina y Oriental del Uruguay [1839–1851]*)

> [Look out, you brutal gaucho,
> 'cause I haven't lost hope,
> no joke,

---

[6] *Translator's note*: *Cielito* is kept here because this appears to be a case where it is the poem itself that is being addressed.

to let you find out what are
the Tin Tin[7] and Refalosa.]

Yo soy toro en mi rodeo
y torazo en rodeo ajeno;
siempre me tuve por güeno
y si me quieren probar
salgan otros a cantar
y veremos quién es menos.
(José Hernández, *El gaucho
Martín Fierro*, lines 61–6)

[In my own ring I'm a bull,
and a bigger bull elsewhere.
I always thought I was good,
but if you want to test me
have others come here and sing
to see who's really the lesser.]

Al ver llegar la morena
que no hacía caso de naides,
le dije con la mamúa:
'Va...ca...yendo gente al baile.
(*Ibid*, lines 1151–64)

[When I spied the dark-haired girl
disdaining everyone's attentions,
I told her, drunk as I was,
My, cow many people are coming!]

While the challenge constitutes the dominant position of the dominated, the lament represents the dominated position of the dominated, expressing a criticism of injustice:

¡Ay! en la presente ocasión...
suelto al viento mis pesares,
yo también vengo infeliz
dende allá de Güenos Aires –
dende allá de Güenos Aires;
yo era mozo acomodao,
pero ahora por el tirano
me miro tan desgraciao.
(Hilario Ascasubi, "Los
payadores" in *Paulino Lucero*)

---

[7] *Translator's note*: "Tin Tin" was a kind of music played with the violin, in which the player's gesture with the bow is reminiscent of the movement made with a knife when cutting somebody's throat. "Refalosa," that is "resbalosa," or "slippery one," is a dance in which the slipperiness is created by the blood of someone whose throat has been cut.

[Ay, I'll take this opportunity
to air out all my sorrows,
for I too came here unhappy
from way back in Güenos Aires,
from way back in Güenos Aires;
I used to be a well-heeled lad,
but now thanks to the tyrant
I find myself in great calamity.]

Aquí me pongo a cantar
al compás de la vigüela,
que el hombre que lo desvela
una pena estraordinaria,
como el ave solitaria
con el cantar se consuela.
(José Hernández, *El gaucho
Martín Fierro*, lines 1–6)

[I sit me here to sing my song
to the beat of my guitar,
for the man who's lost his sleep
over an extraordinary sorrow,
like the solitary bird,
singing his song can find comfort.]

The tones of spoken voices that the genre adopted from the *payadores* in order to constitute itself established the foundations for the construction of a series of representations that became identified with Argentinian nationality. The tradition of the genre worked and debated the oral material while a musical tradition fixed it in certain movements; from that moment on, these representations offered themselves up to any symbolic work that postulated itself as Argentinian. Challenge and lament are postures, verbal actions, and they are accompanied by stories. They constituted, moreover, a system of sociocultural integrations/inclusions and exclusions. They provided the rhythmic base of the tango, which laments the rupture of the pact with a woman or a friend, as well as of the milonga, which inscribes in music the challenge between rival men or rival sexes. The theatrical–grotesque combined and alternated challenge and lament in an effort to represent another contradictory pact, this time with a newly arrived "other": the immigrant. They were politicized, depoliticized, and aestheticized. The lament constituted itself as a popular representation of the Argentinian people, reappearing in the suffering aesthetic of social Realism, while the challenge was read as an antipopular representation. In Borges, defiance over the name and violence against the lettered representative of European culture positioned themselves as founding fictional centers.

Also present were various strains of Nationalism, each directed against different manifestations of "otherness," from a certain linguistic Nationalism, against other tones and against the threat of linguistic corruption by the new immigrants, to political Nationalism that constituted the community's central nuclei against foreigners, to popular Nationalism, against an oligarchy that was affiliated with foreign interests, to a racist Nationalism, against Indians, Blacks, and immigrants. And upon the base of universal values that were merged with the tones of voices, there emerged an essentialist Nationalism, wherein the voice of the gaucho embodies the essence of the Argentinian in his battle for liberty and justice.

The genre with its tones provided the space in which the nucleus of Nationalism could be thought about: by the alliance that constituted it, by the governmental function it served, by the system of inclusions and exclusions it propagated, and by the fusion of the poetic and the political it effected.

Junctures and variables

The total time-span of the genre is history, which is that of the nation's process of political and legal unification following Independence, becomes minuscule and textual at the junctures, as a function of the moments of crisis, radicalization of conflicts, war, conciliation, and pacification experienced by those sectors battling over hegemony until 1800.

The political junctures form part of the genre inasmuch as it defines itself as political and junctural. Texts up until *Fausto* are punctual/to the point and journalistic: they register battles, celebrations, peace treaties, and the issuing of decrees, functioning, largely, as chronicles. The junctural specificity of the genre is shared, albeit with diverse regimens, by all of Argentinian literature before 1880. The difference resides in the action of and at the juncture, on the one hand, and its textual representation on the other. This presentation is what evolves throughout the genre and leads to the first mutation: *Fausto* marks the date and the genre appears as "literature."

The political juncture, which allows for the typification of the genre's polemic system (wherein texts debate with each other, with their antecedents, and with the predecessors that will rewrite them) is a way of joining the war of definitions of the gaucho's voice with the war of political definitions between Independence and 1880. The junctures determine the terms of the debate over the uses of the gaucho's body and over his integration into civilization, while defining the changing space/position of the writer. Only the junctural differences can account for the differences between *La ida* and *La vuelta de Martín Fierro* (1872 and 1879), between the two versions of *Los tres gauchos orientales* by Antonio Lussich (1872 and 1877), between Hilario Ascasubi's *Paulino Lucero* (written between 1839 and 1851) and *Santos Vega* (published in 1872). What could seem like an ideological change on the part of a writer, is, from a genre perspective, actually due to a change at the junctures: different positions, so that each time there is a variation in the combination of tones and voices that form alliances. The theoretical fiction that considers the juncture an exterior–interior element (the genre is a whole filled with holes), represents, in the text, the variable in the positions of speech and action, and the relations between them. The junctures affect situations, interlocutionary circles, hierarchies, degrees of antagonism, story and character types: they incorporate a multiplicity of facts into the complex system of genre.

The interplay among and between junctures can be outlined/traced according to the confronting sectors' experiencing times of war or peace (extreme cases) and according to the degree of power or opposition that marks the sector to whom the writer lends his voice. In each of these circumstances, two positions are possible.

At the juncture of war, the writer's voice imbues violence with meaning and direction. Texts become weapons (the classic example is Ascabusi's *Paulino Lucero*); they denounce the gaucho's enemies and exalt his military leaders. An attempt is made at political and military unification against the enemy, through the use of the gaucho's body–voice. At the juncture of peace, the voice that issues forth is that of work and the law, of the lesson and of political criticism; the attempt here is juridical unification against the delinquent, the "bad gaucho."

The debate of the genre establishes itself then in the interior of each juncture. At the juncture of war, crisis, and mobilization, what is at stake is the use of the gaucho's body and of his space: soldier or worker. This debate houses another within it, one that orders and directs the gauchos. The agrarian sector, burdened by the indiscriminate *levas*,[8] reacts against the exclusive use of the gaucho as soldier: the voice turns against military power and texts assume the *payadoresque* form of life story, colored by anarchism, especially when the discourse is spoken from the opposition. Gauchos seem to "sing" or "speak" throughout the entire field: the paradigmatic texts are "Cielito del blandengue retirado" (anonymous, between 1821 and 1823), Luis Pérez's "Biografía de Rosas" (1830), and *The gaucho Martín Fierro* (or *La ida*, 1872). From the other side, the side of those sectors that claim an apolitical–military or an exclusively military alliance, as in Ascasubi's texts during the siege of Montevideo (between 1839 and 1851), the gaucho turns the war into a festival and exalts his

[8] *Translator's note*: See Note 2, above.

heroes and leaders (and it is the gaucho of the opposing army who laments oppression and coercion).

Anarchism or militarism: the difference can be read in the relations between speech and action. In the first case, the voice who sings has participated in battles and army life and tells of horrors and losses; in the second, the voice narrates battles and victories and journalistic distancing, while exalting the leaders. The construction of alliances and the network of tones of each case are radically at odds.

At junctures of pacification or agreement among the sectors, writers assume a fundamental function. The debate revolves around the education and civilization of the gauchos and around the separation between legality and illegality. Writers no longer lend their voices to various political sectors, but rather speak for themselves, serving specific functions: law, education, language, poetry. At issue is the figure of the gaucho who knows or educates, and the legitimacy of his knowledge. Texts of peaceful junctures distance themselves from events in order to approach the lettered literature of the times (theatre in the case of Hidalgo's dialogues, the romantic *feuilleton* in Ascasubi's *Santos Vega*, the picaresque novel in *La vuelta de Martín Fierro*). The opposing discourses are those of the Christian moralist, who neatly divides gauchos into good and bad by nature, and the reformist who takes up the gaucho's protest against the unjust application of law and proposes institutional reform. There is an effort made to impress upon the gauchos a civilized and state law. *Santos Vega* reproduces the voice of an absent priest who sends his Christian message to the gauchos, while in Hidalgo's first dialogue and in *La vuelta de Martín Fierro* the individual with knowledge is present in the text, reciting the law and proclaiming his reformist program. Both cases involve the gaucho's abandoning of his oral, consuetudinary code and changing, in the process, his category of crime.

Parody in/of the genre

In order to establish periodization according to the genre's own internal history, a first division can be drawn in 1866, the year of publication of the parody *Fausto. Impresiones del gaucho Anastasio el Pollo en la representación de esta ópera* by Estanislao del Campo (1834–1880). It is the first text of the genre that neatly separates literature and politics. It defines the former by the exclusion of the latter and introduces a typically modern sequence that may be expressed as follows: autonomization of the literary, questioning of the genre's representative constructions, and the opening of a new debate among writers.

The process can be synthesized as a break and a change in position; the break is the leap produced by the progressive depoliticization of one of the genre's lines, the dialogues concerning the gaucho's visit to the city on the occasion of a political celebration. The change in position is, in reality, a displacement of the newspaper section that frames the written story: the chronicle of the festivity is no longer civic and political, but is now purely cultural, a play at the Colón Theatre. From Hidalgo's "Relación de las fiestas mayas" (1822) to "Diálogo que tuvo lugar entre el Señor Chuche Gestos y Antuco Gramajo, con motivo de las fiestas en celebridad del ascenso al mando del ilustre Restaurador de las leyes Brigadier General D. Juan Manuel de Rosas, dedicado por su autor a S.E." (1835) by Manuel de Araucho (1803–1842) to the first dialogue in Uruguay by Ascasubi (1807–1875), "Jacinto Amores, gaucho oriental, haciéndole a su paisano Simón Peñalva, en la costa de Quequay, una completa relación de las fiestas cívicas, que para celebrar el aniversario de la jura de la Constitución oriental, se hicieron en Montevideo en el mes de julio de 1833," through *Fausto*, it is possible to read a story the center of which is constituted by the political and economic pacts between the city and the country. As the significance of the political sphere decreases, the economic one gains in importance and autonomy. *Fausto* is witness to a generalized depoliticization, which preserves the autonomy of the commercial and the cultural spheres, embodied by the dialogues' two protagonists: Laguna and his selling of wool and Pollo and his eventful visit to the theatre where he, in turn, is witness to another pact: the selling of the soul.

Fausto effectively marks the closure of stories about the gaucho's visit to the city. Pollo recounts the opera to his compatriot Laguna; the dialogue between two cultures, between the gaucho genre and "civilized" poetry, delineates the axis of the text. The two cultures parody one another; the act of reading invites laughter by bringing two apparently incompatible social models into contact and interaction. The parody of *Fausto* inscribes itself in a conception of literature as an autonomous system, and plays in the interior of that conception by reading one sector (genre, text, convention, register) from another that is opposite and alternative to it, and that appears as its complement within the system. The parody thus represents a purely cultural conflict; instead of opposing two political, economic, or military sectors, as in the earlier genre, *Fausto* effects a confrontation of two literary spaces, one cultured, the other popular. By parodying the gaucho genre, by reading it from within "civilized" poetry and with its laws, *Fausto* effectively grants it status as a literary genre. The genre becomes literaturized or aestheticized, but also fictionalized by means of the parodic inversion of some of its *topoi* and the parodic exaggeration of others.

What the gaucho Pollo witnesses in the theatre and recounts to the gaucho Laguna is how Doctor Fausto, taking advantage of the absence of Margarita's brother, who is serving in the military fighting the war, forms an alliance with the Devil in order to trick her. While the figures invested with knowledge and command (represented by the voice of writers of the genre) visit the country to propose diverse alliances to the gauchos, the gaucho in the city contemplates the performance of their battle with each other. And in the midst of that dispute, the writer, who with del Campo deliberates about the construction of credible representations and about the Argentinization of European culture, ends up distancing himself, like the gaucho, positioning himself in a no-man's land, between two cultures and two literary languages.

The center of the text is constituted by the exclusion of a juridical code in the character of the "lawyer" Fausto and in his perverse pact with the Devil that is at once legal and illegal. From this moment on, *Fausto* plays the game of the plurality of laws confronted by the Law. There can now appear, for the first time in the genre, a popular code of consuetudinary justice, in direct opposition to the written law:

> Cuando a ust' un hombre lo ofiende,
> ye, sin mirar para atrás,
> pela el flamenco y ¡sas! ¡tras!
> dos puñaladas le priende.
> Y cuando la autoridá
> la partida le ha soltao,
> usté en su overo rosao
> bebiendo los vientos va,
> naides de usté se despega,
> porque se haiga desgraciao,
> y es muy bien agasajao
> en cualquier rancho a que Uega.
>
> (lines 921–32)

> [When you are offended by a man
> and without turning you pull
> your blade and swish, plunk,
> with two stabs you lay him low;
> and when the police
> sends after you the posse
> while on your pink steed
> you fly drinking up the winds,
> no one shies away from you
> because you're a fugitive
> and all take you in
> at whatever ranch you reach.]

The elements of popular culture that were not integrated into alliances, and that served no purpose for the written culture, establish another view, another legality, and another consensus all of which detail the dominant legality. And then, in a way that is characteristic of parody, ambiguous and doubled, the two cultures confront one another in the form of two eccentricities or specificities, and no longer as center versus periphery. *Fausto*, with its parody, with its alternate legality, with the gaucho's voice spoken and heard as the voice of man, becomes a founding condition for *Martín Fierro*.

The Argentinian classic

La ida

Voice and tones

The first song of the first part of *Martín Fierro* already establishes the identity between the voice of the singer, his word, and the voice of the gaucho. The presentation of the singer, first step of the *payada* ritual, reveals this identity; the singer will reproduce the code of oral culture at the same time that he introduces himself as an illiterate, courageous, and sought-after gaucho. The chain of reasoning over identity that takes place in the prelude concludes with the mutual implication of tones, challenges, and laments.

Everything is in the song, the singer claims from the outset, and this assertion must be taken literally, since it serves as grounding for *La ida*. The song contains the entire life of the singer, because song and life are interrelated; both allies (God and the saints) and rivals (other singers) are established. The game, the pastoral economy of the rodeo, and the use of the body are made present. The song is the oral code, at once the cultural expression and the cultural cohesion of the gaucho community, and inscribing within it the community's literature, as well as its religious, social, juridic, economic, and sexual system. In the prelude song, José Hernández (1834–1886) wrote a fiction about a full, undivided culture that existed without the state, and, at the same time, about its fracture and division. For the first time in the genre, there emerged a voice that does not seem to form allegiances with written culture, a voice that fuses with a reasoning and a law that are radically opposed to Hidalgo's illuminist universals.

The genre can be read in its entirety from *La ida*. Therein resides its emergence and its closure, inasmuch as there is a disclosure of the genre's logic, which is the logic of the singer and of the uses of the voice of the other. The prelude text claims that the uses of the voice, of the body, and of reason coincide. And it does so through a text that is exemplary for its double meaning, double usage, and double interpretation. The voices of Martín Fierro and of Cruz, the two gauchos (the only alliance in the text) reveal that words mean different things according to who uses them and for what reason, and that the very word "gaucho" is defined in opposite ways as a function of the register and the code that defines it:

> Soy gaucho y entiendaló
> como mi lengua lo esplica:
> para mí la tierra es chica
> y pudiera ser mayor;
> ni la víbora me pica
> ni quema mi frente el sol.
>
> (lines 79–84)

> [I'm a gaucho, know it well,
> just as my tongue here proclaims:
> to me even the whole earth is cramped
> and I would not mind were it bigger;
> the snakes don't dare sting me
> and the sun can't burn my brow.]

The meaning of "gaucho" is free and without properties; not servant, not useful. The tone of the lament is established immediately thereafter, as a result of the distance between two different meanings of "gaucho," one determined by the gaucho's own language and reason, and the other by those of the differential written code.

> Y atiendan la relación
> que hace un gaucho perseguido,
> que padre y madre ha sido
> empeñoso y diligente,
> y sin embargo la gente
> lo tiene per un bandido.
>
> (lines 109–14)

> [Listen to the story
> of a persecuted gaucho,
> who to his child has been
> devoted father and mother,
> but the people want to see
> as a lawless renegade.]

Hernández went so far as to carry the tone of lament that is born of the difference between the two juridical orderings to the extreme of the non-voice: the logic of the pursued singer concludes with the explosion of the guitar, of silence, and of exile to yet another language and reason, namely the Indians'.

The texts about double meaning and the confrontation of two codes are also texts about metamorphosis and silence. *La ida* appears as a field of transformation, a place of passage between each thing and its opposite. And at the center of these transformations is the gaucho hero himself, condemned saint, illegally legal, traitor–hero of justice.

The biography

The focal point of *La ida* is the oral biography. The biographical story, told to a rural bandit, deserter, or wanderer, was sung in geographical regions where large landholding (*latifundium*) existed and which were in the process of modernization: the south of Italy, Andalucía, Brazil; its manifestation in Argentinian folklore is the *relación* or *argumento*. The *relación* or *argumento* narrates the series of actions whereby a gaucho is accused of a crime and confronted by the representatives of the law. The crime is always one that either he did not commit or that does not constitute a crime according to his own code of oral justice. The oral autobiography is a juridical narration, entirely constituted by the inter-play between different codes of law; its subject is guilty before a modern, written, hegemonic legal code, but innocent before another one, his own. The biography is, moreover, a collective one: the fiction of a divided society, in existence before the state's political and juridical unification, but also after it, when the opposing codes have still not ceased to stir consciences. But what made the oral biography an exemplary narrative in Argentinian literature (and culture) is that its meaning changes as a function of how it is written (and sung): as biography or autobiography. The voice can come from without (and above) the subject or from below and within him. The writing of the life anecdote was divided into two functions: Sarmiento's biographical use (in *Facundo*) and Lucio V. Mansilla's (*Excursión a los indios ranqueles*, 1870) and José Hernández's autobiographical use. The biographical function served to attack the subject and proffer him as an example of criminal barbarism while the autobiographical function was used to defend the writing subject and attack his political enemies.

In *La ida*, the autobiographies of Fierro and Cruz are violently anti-juridical narratives (against the conscription law of *levas y vagos*, which belied the concept of equality before the law and reduced the labor force available to the plantation owner) and violently anti-military (it is his passage through the army which despoils Martín Fierro and transforms him into a "bad gaucho"; it is the army commander who robs Cruz of his woman, ushering in his chain of crimes). In both cases, the judge makes arbitrary – and opposing – rulings: he applies the law of *levas* to Fierro, allegedly because he failed to vote (although this was not a crime before the law) and destines Cruz (a delinquent who was fleeing justice) to confront those who confronted the very same law of *levas*. Cruz says that the judge said (and he does this without using the judge's language, in an indirect style):

> Y me largó una proclama
> tratándome de valiente,
> que yo era un hombre decente,
> y que dende aquel momento
> me nombraba de sargento
> pa que mandara la gente.
>
> (lines 2053–8)

> [And he issued a proclamation
> declaring me a brave man,
> saying too that I was decent
> and that from that moment on
> I was being named a sergeant
> for the people to command.]

Bravery, the supreme value of the oral code (indeed, its law, in order to survive in an implacable world), can be construed as "decency" or "delinquency" according to whom it serves. It has, like the gaucho and his biography, two uses. This is the reason why Cruz and Fierro, at the most critical moment of *La ida*, the moment of confrontation, represent both codes, one from either side; Fierro is "delinquent" before the written law but courageous according to his own system of justice and his own code of literary language; Cruz's courageousness is deemed as "decency" within the judge's legal code. When Cruz recognizes Fierro's bravery and becomes a deserter in order to join forces with him, he inverts the category of crime:

> Cruz no consiente
> que se cometa el delito
> de matar ansí un valiente.
>
> (lines 1625–6)

> [Cruz will never allow the crime
> that such a courageous man
> be slain just like that.]

Hernández wrote the most radical text of oral autobiography and hurled it to his political enemies; its radicalness resides, in part, in its proving the existence of two separate juridical orders and demonstrating how one of the two, applied in a differential mode, can place the other outside the law.

The text was read as a paternalist and liberal-democratic defense of the gaucho and also as a defense of landholders' interests, who sought to protect the available labor force from indiscriminate conscription: the serf/peon versus the soldier. Both of these readings are framed in the text. But the reading that oralized and folklorized the poem (and endeavored to forget its construction as a written transcription) centers on the juncture at which the text turns upon itself, in the meeting of the two gauchos. One tells the other his life story, and both lives are the same. The autobiographical narratives not only serve for the transmission of memory, but accord the space for the elaboration and reproduction of a way of life and a collective identity.

La vuelta

La vuelta de Martín Fierro (1879) is the primary national and didactic text of Argentinian literature: a space of diverse forms of knowing and teaching, of instruction and advice (how to treat the Indians, how to cross the desert, how to cheat at games, or how to spend the night beneath the stars). Even God is a teacher:

> En las sagradas alturas
> está el maestro principal
> que enseña a cada animal
> a procurarse el sustento
> y le brinda el alimento
> a todo ser racional.
>
> > (lines 463–8)
>
> [In the holy heavens dwells
> he who's the principal master,
> who teaches each animal
> to find its sustenance,
> and gives each rational being
> enough to nourish himself.]

But the text is also a space of conversion and reform: all those who speak have passed through some sort of disciplinary apparatus (exile, jail, army) and all narrate their past as a final promise of mending their ways. These scenes and spaces are constructed on a foundation of basic binary opposition: "good" advice versus "bad," "good" and "bad" parents and aunts.

The culmination of knowing may be found in the *payada* between Martín Fierro and El Moreno: the knife duel of *La ida* is transformed into a verbal duel in *La vuelta*. The linguistic confrontation constitutes a true test, a necessary condition for the final advice that will be imparted to the next generation. The winner will be legitimated in his knowing and will then be able to teach. Fierro defeats El Moreno because El Moreno knows nothing of the labors of the land; he does not possess a knowledge that is specific to the gauchos. Fierro, in contrast, is the popular hero of *La ida* who is now old; he knows because he has suffered; his role as teacher is also biologically justified, as he is the father of his students. The pluralization towards class in *La ida*, the fact that in order to constitute a principle of association Fierro joins with Cruz, his equal, is replaced in *La vuelta* by a familiar pluralism: the two generations represent the natural relation of transference of lived experience.

El Moreno is defeated in the *payada* because his teacher was a friar:

> Cuanto sé lo he aprendido/porque me lo enseño un flaíre
>
> (1.4005)

> ['cause everything I know/I was taught by a friar]

Here, at the very core of the *payada* debate, *La vuelta* remits to one of the central debates of the genre: who should educate the gaucho. The *payada* between Fierro and El Moreno not only defines the duel that empowers Fierro as teacher, but also contains, in the words of the black man, a criticism of inequality in the application of the law:

> La ley se hace para todos,
> mas sólo al pobre le rige
> (lines 4333–4)

> [The law is made for all
> but only applies to the poor]

> La ley es como cuchillo:
> no ofiende a quien lo maneja
> (lines 4245–6)

> [Like a knife, the law
> won't hurt he who wields it]

In both Hidalgo and Hernández, at the two extremes of the genre, the lament over inequality is immediately followed by the educational scene, narrated in the voice of the knowing educator. Fierro's advice reaffirms the law through the prohibition against stealing, killing, and drinking and the assertion of a work ethic that includes prudency and moderation. Fierro neatly differentiates crime and establishes the definitive division between the legal and the illegal gaucho. The solution proposed by the genre for the eradication of both rural delinquency and of inequality in the application of the legal code is to educate the gaucho in the written, "civilized" law at the expense of his traditional code that does not prohibit stealing or killing to defend his honor. The true criminals of *La vuelta* are defined as criminals in both codes: the Indians and Vizcacha who kill women and children. In this sense, *La vuelta* is textual complement to *La ida*, with which it forms a sequence: the censure of injustice in the application of the law of *levas* to the gauchos is followed by *La vuelta*, the didactic text that vocalizes the written law and advocates the abandonment of a popular legal code as a way to eliminate injustice. Only from this type of reading can the texts be considered complementary, pronounced at different political junctures.

The folklorization of *Martín Fierro* and its incorporation into Argentinian language and culture corrected the text of the state law in the genre. The old Vizcacha represented the evil father whose advice constituted the Old Testament of the rustler, a code to be rejected and sacrificed as it failed to make use of the body for work. At the other extreme is Fierro's capacity for advice, the New Testament of a work ethic. But the textual references, repetitions and transmissions mixed what had been separated, effectively incorporating what had been excluded: a montage was born of the low zone of Vizcacha's *voseo* and the high zone of Fierro's almost literary language. There emerged a new alliance that went beyond alliance, wherein "hacete amigo del juez" ["become a friend of the judge"] (Vizcacha) was joined, for example, with "los hermanos sean unidos" ["brothers should be united"] (Fierro), or "el que nace barrigón es el ñudo que lo fagen" ["he who's born with a big belly, there's no belt will make him thin"] (Vizcacha) with "debe trabajar el hombre para ganarse su pan" ["man should work to earn his bread"] (Fierro). Here the voice of the writer is erased, making audible the voice of readers and listeners. What resounds is the voice of history, the voice of readers and listeners, the voice that through its chain of uses and following the same law of alliance that founded the genre, appropriated what it needed, and did so in (and on) its own terms.

Index

New Spain (*cont.*)
Botanical Garden 331; convents 133;
Enlightenment learning 327–8;
Humboldt's expedition 330; Jesuit
colleges 327; missionaries 306, 327;
printing 316; theatre 318; viceroyalty
287; *see also* Mexico
newspapers 382, 427, 434; *see also*
individual titles and journals
Newton, Isaac 327, 328, 333, 365
Nicaragua: theatre 265, 276, 555
Nieto, Juan José 432, 456–7, 465
Nietzsche, Friedrich Wilhelm 524, 529
nineteenth century xv, 4; 1870s as period
of change 430–1; *see also* essays;
Modernismo; modernity; Positivism;
and under lyric poetry; novel; theatre
Nobel Prizes xi, 30–1
Noble Savage 432, 444, 452
"Noche Triste" 72, 76, 183, 236, 238
non-intervention 566
Novás Calvo, Lino 525
novel 417–89; allegory 428, 444–5, 480–1;
autochthonous themes 424–5, 452;
Bello and 4, 417–20, 454, 474, 489;
Boom of the Latin American 29,
30–1; brief 441–2, 463; *campesino*
theme 443; censorship 107, 419, 434,
437; changes of 1870s and 430–1; of
chivalry 118, 244, 250; contexts
425–35; *Costumbrismo* 437, 480–1;
18th-century rise 426–8; epistolary
347–8; European models 429, 430,
434, 477; extraterritorial legitimation
429; foundation 480, 482–3, 489;
gaucho 432, 443, 452, 453, 465, 522;
historical 448–9, 456–7, 464; and
historiography 141; Hostos on
unwholesomeness of modern 606;
Indian themes 430, 432–3, 445–6, 448,
452, 464, 465, 478–9, 485;
international currency 30–1; irony 79,
84, 132, 190; in journals 434, 436,
437, 453, 479; local themes 430, 448,
452, 455; melodrama 434, 437; and
modernity 420–5; neoclassical
429–30, 437, 441, 452, 454, 458, 469,
480; origins 426–8; pastoral 233, 250,
278; patriotic 489; picaresque 132–3,
184–5, 189–90, 622; as pre-eminent
literary genre 419; regional 433;
science fiction 468; short story
originates as interpolated tale in 503,
504; on social marginality 434, 437;

testimonial 478–9; *de la tierra* 23,
376; urban themes 430, 433; *see also*
under didacticism; nationalism;
Naturalism; Realism; Romanticism
Nueva Andalucía (Venezuela) 312, 324
Nueva Galicia 192
Núñez, Rafael 487
Núñez Bela, Blasco 244
Núñez Cabeza de Vaca, Alvar; criticism of
Spanish conquest 89, 90, 93; and
heroic stance 88, 91, 93; on Indians
91–2, 99; *Naufragios* 1, 87–93, 171,
176; *relación* genre 61, 90–1, 92–3
nuns, *see* convents (writing)

Ocaña, Diego de 278
Ocantos, Carlos María 470
Ochoa, Anastasio de 384–5
Ochoa, Eugenio de 497
octava real 191, 210, 232, 241, 246
Odriozola, Manuel de 217
O'Gorman, Edmundo 2, 59, 127, 128
O'Higgins, Bernardo 509, 538
Olavide y Jáuregui, Pablo de 346–8
Ollantay (anon. Quechua drama) 55, 262,
406–7
Olmec civilization 139
Olmedo, José Joaquín de 565; plays 539;
poetry 20, 21, 385–7, 388, 396
Olmos, Fray Andrés de 47, 197, 269, 308,
313
Oña, Pedro de 202, 238–9, 246, 252;
Arauco domado 15, 16–17, 171, 236,
238–9
Oña, Fray Pedro de 239
Oñate, Juan de 245
Onís, Federico de 21
opera 537, 538, 543, 546
oral tradition, indigenous 39, 40–1, 47–8;
Acosta's use 128–9; Garcilaso El Inca
and 137, 139; gaucho genre and
610–11, 612–14, 625; journals and
381–2; loss in translation 136;
manuscript from Huarochirí 38, 42,
54–5; metrical form 41, 48; Pané's
incomprehension 69; *payadores* 608,
625, 629–30; and Romanticism 380;
Suárez de Peralta's use 129, 130;
títulos 49; *see also* indigenous peoples
(written tradition)
Orbea, Fernando de 281
Ordás, Diego de 237
Ore, Luis Jerónimo 313
Orellana, Francisco de 119